D0204914

Contemporary
African American
Novelists

CONTEMPORARY AFRICAN AMERICAN NOVELISTS

A Bio-Bibliographical Critical Sourcebook

Edited by
EMMANUEL S. NELSON

Greenwood Press
Westport, Connecticut • London

Library of Congress Cataloging-in-Publication Data

Contemporary African American novelists : a bio-bibliographical
   critical sourcebook / edited by Emmanuel S. Nelson.
      p.   cm.
   Includes bibliographical references and index.
   ISBN 0–313–30501–3 (alk. paper)
   1. American fiction—Afro-American authors—Bio-bibliography—
Dictionaries.   2. American fiction—20th century—Bio-bibliography—
Dictionaries.   3. Novelists, American—20th century—Biography—
Dictionaries.   4. American fiction—Afro-American authors—
Dictionaries.   5. Afro-American novelists—Biography—Dictionaries.
6. American fiction—20th century—Dictionaries.   7. Afro-Americans
in literature—Dictionaries.   I. Nelson, Emmanuel S. (Emmanuel
Sampath), 1954–   .
   PS374.N4C658   1999
   813'.5409896073—dc21   98–26438

British Library Cataloguing in Publication Data is available.

Library of Congress Catalog Card Number: 98–26438
ISBN: 0–313–30501–3

First published in 1999

Greenwood Press, 88 Post Road West, Westport, CT 06881
An imprint of Greenwood Publishing Group, Inc.

Printed in the United States of America

The paper used in this book complies with the
Permanent Paper Standard issued by the National
Information Standards Organization (Z39.48–1984).

10 9 8 7 6 5 4 3 2 1

FOR ANTON, *with affection*

CONTENTS

PREFACE

A most significant development that has taken place on the global literary scene during the last two decades or so is the dramatic emergence of African American voices as a distinct and dominant force. This force has been gathering momentum since the 1950s, when James Baldwin published some of his most compelling works, and Ralph Ellison stunned the literary establishment with his dazzling *Invisible Man* (1952). Empowered by the Civil Rights movement and revitalized by the Black Arts movement of the 1960s, this force became more potent and pervasive during that momentous decade. And the publication of Toni Morrison's *The Bluest Eye* in 1970 marked a nodal point in the literary history of the United States: with a voice as original as America itself, she began to conquer the English language and redefine the international literary landscape. Along with Toni Morrison scores of African American fiction writers, poets, playwrights, autobiographers, and essayists have mapped bold new territories; they have firmly entrenched themselves in the forefront of contemporary American literature. This reference volume is designed as a joyous celebration of this exciting new phenomenon and as a scholarly guide to the lives, works, and achievements of many of those artists.

The focus of this volume is exclusively on contemporary African American novelists. A total of seventy-nine writers receive close and careful attention here. All major novelists—James Baldwin, Ralph Ellison, Toni Morrison, Alice Walker, and Gloria Naylor—figure prominently. But I have made a conscious effort to include many lesser known writers—Tina McElroy Ansa, Bebe Moore Campbell, Randall Kenan, Reginald McKnight, Marita Golden, and Arthur Flowers—whose works I believe deserve greater attention. This volume strives to be inclusive: forty-one of the seventy-nine writers who receive consideration are women;

a dozen or so of the authors included here are self-identified as gay, lesbian, or bisexual.

Whereas once the overarching theme in African American writing was racism and its devastating implications, these contemporary writers thematize a wide range of issues and concerns. Some are popular writers (Terry McMillan, Frank Garvin Yerby) with mass appeal; others write science fiction (Samuel Delany, Octavia E. Butler) or detective novels (Walter Mosley, Chester B. Himes). Some are distinguished poets (Gwendolyn Brooks, Michelle Cliff) or talented playwrights (Ed Bullins, Ntozake Shange) but have also published one or more significant novels that earn them a place here. Though my objective is not necessarily to define a canon, I am acutely conscious of the fact that a reference volume such as this is, indeed, likely to be implicated in canon formation. My primary objective rather is to provide the reader with a nearly comprehensive introduction to the contemporary African American novel.

This sourcebook offers reliable, thorough, and up-to-date biographical, critical, and bibliographic information on the seventy-nine writers who are included. Advanced scholars will find this volume a useful research tool; its user-friendly style, format, and level of complexity, however, should make it accessible to a wider audience that includes undergraduate students and even general readers. Each entry begins with relevant biographical information on the novelist, offers a critical commentary on his or her works, provides an overview of the critical reception accorded, and concludes with a selected bibliography that lists, separately, the primary works and the secondary sources. To facilitate cross-referencing, whenever a writer who is also the subject of a chapter in this volume is first mentioned, an asterisk appears next to his or her name. The critical commentary by Deborah G. Plant that follows my prefatory remarks offers a lively and concise introduction to contemporary African American fiction.

Let me take this opportunity to thank all of the contributors to this volume; without their effort this volume would not exist. I would also like to thank Dr. George Butler, Associate Editor at Greenwood Press, for his enthusiastic support for this as well as many other projects. In addition, I would like to acknowledge my gratitude to Professor Plant for writing the introductory essay.

INTRODUCTION

Deborah G. Plant

As freedom was one of the predominant themes of the African American literary tradition in its incipient formation, what constitutes freedom and how that freedom is to be realized and expressed are predominant themes in the literature of African American writers of the latter twentieth century. The shackles of physical and spiritual bondage decried in the narratives of enslaved Africans have not so much been removed as they have been transformed and replaced. The malignant force of European imperialism, of which African enslavement in the Americas is one consequence, has an intrinsic transmutative capacity. So many of the malevolent social, political, and economic forces with which African Americans, indeed, African peoples around the world, have been faced are refigurations of European politics of domination initiated in the fifteenth century. For example, the stereotypes of black inferiority, depravity, and bestiality created in the scientific, medical, philosophical, and religious treatises of eighteenth- and nineteenth-century Europe and America have been duplicated in the mass media and reformulated in works like Murray and Herrnstein's *The Bell Curve* (1995). The "slave castles," which became an integral part of the landscape of Africa's west coast and the holding pens of the east coasts of the Americas and the Caribbean have been reconstructed as "inner-city" housing projects and modern-day "correctional facilities," built in accordance with the U.S. government's scheme for its Jail-Industrial Complex. Jim Crow masquerades as de facto socio-economic stratification. White paternalism and plantation socialization are reinscribed in government dependency programs. The economics of the share-cropping system is refigured in the high debt, minimum wage, and zero-benefits packages of late capitalism.

The insistent and persistent agenda of the politics of Euro-American industrial capitalism has compelled black writers to reexamine the dynamics of oppression and to reconceptualize the experiences of black peoples in face of Euro-American economic and cultural domination. In exploring the historical phenomena that have contributed to the inferior social, political, and economic status of African peoples in the global community, black writers see more clearly and profoundly the ties that bind one group of African peoples to another in terms of their political circumstances and their resistance to domination. The Pan-Africanist vision of the Garvey era has reemerged and is revitalized in the politics and aesthetics of an African diasporic consciousness. In the struggle for cultural, political, and economic autonomy, black artists are engaged in what Toni Cade Bambara describes as the "diasporic hookup": connections forged among people of African descent as part of a "global agenda of cultural defense." In the United States, the diasporic aesthetic is exemplified in the films of Julie Dash, the drawings of Tom Feelings, the plays of August Wilson, the poems of Audre Lorde and Dolores Kendrick, the essays of June Jordan, and the novels of Toni Morrison, Paule Marshall, Charles Johnson, and Michelle Cliff, among others.

African American writers, like their brother and sister writers in the diaspora, have had to continually redefine what freedom means and to rethink strategies for obtaining it. African American literature is, in part, a documentation of the insidious, metamorphic nature of oppression. The obstacles blacks have had to negotiate in American society have been multifaceted, each manifestation requiring particular responses as blacks pursued personhood and self-determination. Narratives such as those of Frederick Douglass, William and Ellen Craft, Olaudah Equiano, and Harriet Jacobs tell of the horror of physical bondage and the psychological and spiritual anguish blacks experienced as objectified Others. Flight, literacy, and defiance were prevalent themes in the literature that bespoke the strategies blacks used to escape the horrid conditions into which they had been forced. Narratives of enslaved Africans and novels like William Wells Brown's *Clotel; or The President's Daughter* (1853), the first novel in African American literature; Harriet Wilson's *Our Nig; or Sketches from the Life of a Free Black in a Two-Story White House, North* (1859), the first novel written by an African American woman; and Frances Ellen Watkins Harper's *Iola Leroy* (1892) were as much declarations of the humanity of African peoples as they were indictments of America's peculiar institution. Given that the enslavement and maltreatment of blacks, enslaved or "free," were rationalized by the supposed subhuman status of African peoples, the assertion of the humanity of black people was a recurring leitmotif in the literature of the period of enslavement and that of the Civil War and Reconstruction eras. The 1863 Emancipation Proclamation brought little change in the social status of African Americans. Post–Civil War America was hostile terrain for newly freed blacks thrown in desperate competition with poor whites for remunerative work. In spite of the violence perpetrated against blacks, the black writer was expected to conform to the dictates of European literary models and social conventions that declared white society as just and benign. As narratives of enslaved blacks could only hint at the nefarious treatment dealt them at the hands of enslavers and their agents, postbellum novelists like Charles

Chesnutt were constrained by the plantation politics of the white publishing industry. Chesnutt, nonetheless, managed to express his discontent with American society and its white supremacist underpinnings in the The House Behind the Cedars (1900), The Marrow of Tradition (1901), and The Colonel's Dream (1905). In Contending Forces; A Romance of Negro Life North and South (1900), Pauline Hopkins, like Chesnutt, addressed the political and social issues of the day. A less restrained voice is heard in the novels of Sutton Griggs. In Imperium in Imperio (1899), Overshadowed (1901), Unfettered (1902), The Hindered Hand; or, The Reign of the Repressionist (1905), and Pointing the Way (1908), Griggs espoused black nationalist views that recalled earlier radical voices and presaged the militancy of later writers.

Accommodation, whether in literature or politics, was another strategy utilized by blacks in dealing with a society bent on their subjugation. As the accommodationist politics of Booker T. Washington was challenged by W. E. B. Du Bois, so the image of the "Old Negro," servile, docile, and puerile, was set in stark contrast to the "New Negro" in African American literature. Intelligent, proud, militant, urbane, and independent, the "New Negro" symbolized the zeitgeist of the Harlem Renaissance movement of the 1920s and 1930s. A time of reclamation of African heritage and celebration of the folk roots of African American culture, the Harlem Renaissance movement incited a virtual burgeoning of black cultural expression. The many voices, themes, and issues conveyed in the literature of the Harlem Renaissance period underscored the complexities of black life, rightly deconstructing the idea of black people as monolithic. Underlying the often contradictory concerns and efforts of the writers remained the cultural imperative of Freedom: Freedom from the limitations imposed by white society; Freedom from the humiliation of Jim Crow practices in the workplace, in the armed forces, in government, and in society at large; Freedom from the stereotypes that mocked any notion of merit.

Just as black writers sought freedom of literary expression vis-à-vis the white literary establishment, many also demanded a loosening of the constraints imposed by the black intelligentsia. Writers like Zora Neale Hurston chafed under the mandates of the black literati. In discussing her first novel, Jonah's Gourd Vine (1934), Hurston commented that she felt pressured to write about the "Race Problem" and that she was afraid to tell a story the way she wanted to or the way the story told itself to her. Ever vigilant over the image of "the Negro," members of the black intelligentsia were highly censorious of works they believed detracted from the proper New Negro profile of their own figuration. In Langston Hughes' "The Negro Artist and the Racial Mountain" (1926), Hughes and other members of "the younger generation of Negro artists" declared their artistic autonomy. In style, theme, and form, they would write to suit themselves.

The Great Depression ended the boon enjoyed by black artists as it ushered in despair and misery for America in general. The economic bleakness of the era and its impact on blacks were subject matter for modernist writers like Richard Wright and Ann Petry. The bitterness engendered by economic deprivation and social alienation and the pain of existing in a world that would deny one's existence are explored in the works of Ralph Ellison and James Baldwin. The writers of the 1940s and 1950s also gave expression to the rage welling in the souls of America's native sons and daughters. Characters like Bigger Thomas in Richard Wright's *Native Son* (1940), Lutie Johnson in Ann Petry's *The Street* (1946), and the antihero of Ralph Ellison's *Invisible Man* (1952) speak to the consequences and ramifications of dreams deferred.

The Civil Rights movement, the Black Power movement, and the Black Arts movement of the 1960s sought to address the imbalance of power on all levels of American society. Though poetry and drama were the primary modes of literary expression of that period, prose works, such as John Williams' *The Man Who Cried I Am* (1967), also reflected African Americans' quest for equality. The movement forward, the struggle for the freedom to fully participate in American society, was often fraught with fear. The experience of fear has been less fully explored than the experiences of anger and rage. Ernest Gaines examines this theme in *In My Father's House* (1978), a novel that captures the dynamics of the Civil Rights movement, and more thoroughly in his 1983 publication of *A Gathering of Old Men*.

Calvin Hernton points out in *The Sexual Mountain and Black Women Writers* (1987) that the narrative form in black literature has been the primary literary vehicle in exposing white oppression and articulating the struggle of blacks, collectively, in their bid for freedom. This mode of expression, he states, has also been dominated by men. With *The Color Purple* (1982), Hernton declares that Alice Walker advanced the tradition of the black narrative form by extending it to include the particular struggles of black women. The struggle Ms. Celie wages in Walker's novel is not against white oppression but against black male domination. Her story is one of survival (from incest) and emancipation (from spousal abuse). The freedom she seeks is the freedom from violation and exploitation and the freedom to be and to love.

The angry responses to Walker's work parallel the negative reception of the works of Zora Neale Hurston. The role of the writer, the proper subject of the writer, and the form and style of expression a writer employs were again a matter of debate. Walker's work, nevertheless, chartered new narrative territory. As she "appropriated" the black narrative form in the liberation of black womanhood, she also treated themes considered taboo in "literary" texts. Walker and other women writers of the 1970s addressed in their works issues of gender, sexism, black womanhood and black female identity, mother–daughter relations, sisterhood, sexual orientation, black heterosexism, family, community and culture, domestic violence, and AIDS. Toni Morrison's *Sula* (1974) treats friendship and sisterhood, as *Song of Solomon* (1977) examines the themes of identity, community, and cultural heritage. Sexual orientation and lesbianism are explored in Ann Allen Shockley's *Loving Her* (1974), as black homophobia is challenged in her later work *Say Jesus and Come to Me* (1982). The themes introduced in the

1970s continued to be sounded by writers, male and female alike, in the 1980s and 1990s. April Sinclair's bildungsroman, *Coffee Will Make You Black* (1994), offers a reexamination of the mother–daughter relationship, friendship, and black female sexual identity. Shay Youngblood's debut novel *Soul Kiss* (1997) continues these themes as it also addresses the subject of rape and focuses attention on the relatively less sounded theme of father–daughter relationships. The discussion surrounding the individual and the community and the politics of difference and marginality are compellingly revisited in Audre Lorde's *Zami: A New Spelling of My Name* (1984), Randall Kenan's *A Visitation of Spirits* (1989), Melvin Dixon's *Vanishing Rooms* (1991), and Steven Corbin's *Fragments That Remain* (1993).

There is perhaps no treatment of sexual violation more poignant than that found in Sapphire's *Push* (1996). Sexually abused by both parents, twice impregnated by her father, functionally illiterate, and HIV positive, Precious Jones, the novel's protagonist, is shackled. This novel recalls the narrative tradition of enslaved Africans in that the protagonist's struggle to free herself from an inimical environment pivots on her ability to read and write. Literacy, or, more specifically, mastery of the language of the establishment, also proves to be a significant issue in A. J. Verdelle's *The Good Negress* (1995). Homelessness, "street life," drug culture, and AIDS are matters addressed in *Push* and in *A Hundred Days from Now* (1994).

As African American novelists analyze patterns of oppression and their refigurations, they necessarily call attention to the capitalist economy of American society and the entrapments of materialism. The pursuit of money in a system designed to ensure that the masses have none is a deleterious act that is potentially enthralling. Corporate America, a synecdoche for global capitalism and a refiguration of European imperialism, is, for African Americans, a metaphor for slavery. Jill Nelson's autobiographical *Volunteer Slavery* (1993) testifies to that reality. Philip Lewis' novel *Life of Death* (1993) and Barry Beckham's *You Have a Friend: The Rise and Fall and Rise of the Chase Manhattan Bank* (forthcoming 1999) give insight into the phenomenon of economic enslavement.

The works of writers of the 1970s, 1980s, and 1990s are indicative of a shift from intergroup dynamics to intragroup dynamics. As earlier novelists documented, critiqued, and responded to external forces harmful to the black community, particularly white supremacy, later novelists, in the tradition of Hurston and Hughes, began to focus on the black community itself. This look inward is significant in that it charts black people's movement from the margins to the center of their own lives and the consequent debunking of white authority and its decentering in the black literary imagination. The dilemma presented by the Du Boisian double consciousness is less prominent and problematic as novelists of the latter half of the twentieth century create in their works characters who strive to achieve a fully integrated self. This self is rooted in an African-centered cultural paradigm. In essence, contemporary novelists have achieved what Michael Cooke describes as intimacy:

a condition in which the Afro-American protagonist . . . is depicted as realistically en-joying a sound and clear orientation toward the self and the world. . . . More than this, it suggests at once a thorough involvement with the world and along with that a degree of immunity from and superiority to sociopolitical shibboleths, as a result of what Alice Walker has called "a wider recognition of the universe." (*Afro-American Literature in the Twentieth Century*, New Haven: Yale University Press, 1984, p. x)

Certainly, as African American novelists reclaim their historical legacies, they create narrative ritual space wherein healing and wholeness are possible. A clear orientation toward self and world requires a re-membering of the past. For African Americans, it also requires an understanding of the multifaceted, shape-shifting nature of oppressive forces or, in jazz idiom, the ability to recognize the changing same. This ability is what allows one to be dispassionately involved with the world, transcend the sociopolitical shibboleths, embrace a wider universe, and, in the words of Carter G. Woodson, "live life more abundantly."

As they repair to the past, novelists repair centuries-old wounds that allow their characters to achieve healing selfhood and collective identity. The contem-porary black novel that looks toward the new millennium is at once historical and temporal, it is visionary, mythic, and prophetic, and it manifests an African diasporic consciousness. Black novelists no longer seek recognition for their hu-manity; they assume it and explore all that has historically constituted their humanity: spirituality, ancestor reverence, oneness with nature, balance, community, and memory. Toni Morrison's *Beloved* (1987), Paule Marshall's *Praisesong for the Widow* (1983), Toni Cade Bambara's *Salteaters*, Michelle Cliff's *No Telephone to Heaven* (1987) and *Free Enterprise* (1993), Gloria Naylor's *Mama Day* (1988), Charles Johnson's *Middle Passage* (1990), and Sandra Jackson-Opoku's *The River Where Blood Is Born* (1997) are sterling examples of the con-temporary black novel. Winners of national and international awards, African American novelists are no longer viewed as narrow and provincial but have commanded attention on the global stage. They have done so by continually seeking freedom and having found it within.

Among the writers in this volume are preeminent literary figures whose voices are blended with more recently emergent voices like Jewell Parker Rhodes (*Voo-doo Dreams: A Novel of Marie Laveau* 1993 and *Magic City* 1997), Randall Kenan (*A Visitation of Spirits* 1989), Tina McElroy Ansa (*Baby of the Family* 1989, *Ugly Ways* 1993, and *The Hand I Fan With* 1996), and Michelle Cliff (*Abeng* 1984, *No Telephone to Heaven* 1987, *Free Enterprise* 1993). A particular strength of *Black Novelists* is that it also treats lesser-known writers, lesser-known works of high-profile authors, subgenres of the novel, and works that have been classified as nonliterary. Novels written for children and young adults are represented as biographers look at authors Sharon Bell Mathis, Joyce Carol Thomas, and Jacque-line Woodson. This collection of seventy-nine writers is an excellent introduc-tion to the lives and works of African American novelists and to the voices that will resound in the approaching millennium.

Contemporary
African American
Novelists

TINA McELROY ANSA
(1949–   )

Joyce L. Cherry

BIOGRAPHY

Tina McElroy Ansa was born and grew up in the middle-Georgia city of Macon. For a time, her family lived in the "Pleasant Hill" section of that midsize city, a cozy community typical of many African American enclaves in the South. She carves out of her memory of this community and its lifestyle, personalities, and rhythms a mythical small town named Mulberry, which is the setting of her three major novels, *Baby of the Family* (1989), *Ugly Ways* (1993), and *The Hand I Fan With* (1996). Her novels present a southern community that is the environment experienced by middle- and upper-middle-class African Americans during the decades immediately before and after the desegregation that comes after the Civil Rights movement of the 1960s. Influence, power, position, and the status of the individual are primarily centered in, and defined by, the community itself. In presenting this mythical cosmos, Ansa's achievement is the opening of a private world to public view. That world is the common experience of African Americans in the South, the environment that enfolds its people within a value system that includes pride in family, culture, professional achievement, and an appreciation for spirituality and individual differences.

Ansa's vision emanates from her personal experience. The daughter of working-class people, Ansa's world was filled with a wide variety of interesting characters—from gamblers to educators. Her father, Walter James McElroy, was a self-made businessman who, for many years, ran a café and liquor store; her mother, in later years, became a teacher's assistant. While her parents were not college-educated, they were voracious readers who gained much sophistication through the pages of books and magazines that they devoured. Her father often reminded her that he had gone to school with novelist John Oliver Killens, also a native of Macon, Georgia. She was impressed and enraptured by the power of the word through the stories told by her grandfather. As a student at Spelman College in Atlanta, Georgia, Ansa was introduced to the work of Zora Neale Hurston, through whom she became aware that writing about African Americans from a posture of love and acceptance of their unique culture and its rhythms could be considered art.

Before beginning her career as a fiction writer, Ansa worked as a journalist with the *Atlanta Constitution* and the *Charlotte Observer*. Currently, she lives on Saint Simons Island, Georgia, with her husband, cinematographer Joneé Ansa, a graduate of the American Film Institute in Hollywood.

MAJOR WORKS AND THEMES

Baby of the Family, Ansa's first novel, introduces the setting of Mulberry and a panorama of its people. At its center is Lena McPherson, whose birth with a caul over her face provides the rich complication for a coming-of-age theme. Being born with a caul over one's face signifies that a person is special, endowed with sensibilities and a level of spirituality that marks the person as extraordinary. The little girl Lena was "chosen by God as a special person on this earth" (264), being touched by God to do something great in life. Entrusted to this special community, Lena is nurtured and shaped, buffeted and protected by its influences.

Ansa's skill at telling a good story is evident in this first novel. From birth until her readiness to face a wider world is achieved, Lena's growth is chronicled in compelling fashion, with wit, humor, and dramatic foreshadowing. Lena's initiation to sex, her understanding of loss through broken friendships, rejection, and death, her abiding sense of alienation are all told with great skill. Lena's experience of the real world is artfully juxtaposed with her traumatic and inescapable adventures with the spiritual world. Within the small community of Pleasant Hill in Mulberry, her daily activities range from the sophisticated, stable home environment created and nurtured by her mother, Nellie, with the stabilizing influences of her grandmother and the hired man, Frank Peterson, to the earthy atmosphere of the Place, a bar, grill, and liquor store run by her father, Jonah McPherson. But her innermost life is influenced by her special spirituality, with intimations, urgings, and specters from the other side. From these depths comes the impetus for Lena's awakening to wider vistas. The appearance of Rachel, the ancient slave apparition, on the beach where her family was vacationing propels Lena to an understanding of her inescapable destiny. But the return of her grandmother from the spirit world helps Lena to gain her balance.

This infusion of the spirit world in the plot of *Baby of the Family* links Ansa to such earlier contemporary writers as Gloria Naylor, Paule Marshall, and Toni Morrison, in whose stories the spiritual dimension is a conduit to an illusive African American past. Like them, Ansa treats spirituality and ritual as a vital part of the African American belief system. In *Ugly Ways*, her second novel, she develops this theme through the return of a mother after death to goad and cajole her three daughters into a fuller understanding of her right to be the person that she had been in life by not giving up her place in their lives. In the story of Esther Lovejoy, known as Mudear, and her three daughters—Betty, Emily, and Annie Ruth—Ansa develops the theme of mother–daughter relationships through the interweaving of narrative voices from all of the characters, including the already deceased Mudear. Reacting to an unfulfilling, though relatively stable, marriage, Mudear had undergone a "change of life." Withdrawing from her responsibilities as wife and mother, she began to live seemingly only for herself. In so doing, she forces her young daughters to resort to their own resources for nurture and development, even as she chided, chastised, and criticized. Ironically, they become self-sufficient, though they never fully understand the pride that Mudear finds in this achievement, for which she, characteristically, takes credit.

Also set in Mulberry, *Ugly Ways* is the exploration of an unconventional element in African American communal life. Although the story is primarily told from the perspective of the three daughters, the novel is unified through Mudear, who is its thematic center. According to Ansa, Esther Lovejoy challenges the accepted line on what "mother" is and means in African American culture. Her negative approach to child raising contrasts sharply with that of Nellie McPherson of *Baby of the Family*, but significantly, her standards are just as high. She rejects before she is rejected, alienates herself before others alienate her, and approaches life from the negatives to achieve positive effects. In her final reflections, she thinks with pride, "Nobody can't say I didn't teach my girls how to dress. And how to carry themselves. Ain't got to say one time to any of 'em to pull up their chins and look to the stars today" (175). In her convoluted way, she, too, represents and reflects Mulberry's values and standards and enriches the community through her strange way of nurturing three daughters to self-sufficiency and maturity.

Ansa's skillful use of details to create scenes that come alive with sound, color, and textural details is evident in her third novel, *The Hand I Fan With*, which is again set in Mulberry. In this work, she returns also to Lena McPherson, now a mature woman who has distinguished herself in business. At age forty-five, Lena has amassed a small fortune. She is the hand that fans to meet everyone's needs in this still close-knit community. But if it is out of her material resources that she supplies everyone else's needs, it is out of her spiritual resources that she must supply her own. She does this by conjuring up Herman, a 100-year-old ghost, whose incarnate visit allows her to fulfill her life. Herman is funny, sensual, sensitive, and intelligent. He is, like Zora Neale Hurston's Teacake, wholly satisfying, but, unlike Teacake, he is not real. To be with him, Lena must withdraw significantly from real life into a lifestyle of sheer hedonism. In the final analysis, the novel resonates with the notion of the impossibility for women like Lena to sustain a fulfilling life without resorting to the fantastic. The power of mystical ritual out of the African American experience to sustain a rational existence is a challenge that awaits a future Ansa novel.

CRITICAL RECEPTION

Ansa's novels, all published within the last nine years, have met with popular and critical acclaim. Each is an award winner. Both *Baby of the Family* and *The Hand I Fan With* were winners of the Georgia Authors Series Award for 1989 and 1996, respectively. *Baby of the Family* was also named a "Notable Book of the Year" in 1989, the year of its publication, by the *New York Times* and was on the African-American Best Sellers List for Paperback Fiction. In 1990 the American Library Association named it "A Best Book for Young Adults." Her second novel, *Ugly Ways*, earned the title of "Best Fiction" by the African American Blackboard List in 1994.

While in-depth critical appraisal of her works is yet to come, reviews of these first three novels have been generally favorable. The works are consistently cited for a strong sense of place, a narrative style that is witty and compelling, and a panorama of characters within the African American community that are strongly individualized and engaging. Her positive vision of African American life and culture in the segregated South is the enduring quality that she presents in this body of work to date.

BIBLIOGRAPHY

Works by Tina McElroy Ansa

Baby of the Family. New York: Harcourt Brace Jovanovich, 1989.
Ugly Ways. New York: Harcourt Brace Jovanovich, 1993.
The Hand I Fan With. New York: Doubleday, 1996.

Studies of Tina McElroy Ansa

Ball, Cheryl Gray. "Mom Put Freedom above All." Review of *Ugly Ways*. *Richmond (Virginia) Times-Dispatch* (Nov. 28, 1993):A13.
Barrett, Nina. "In This Novel, Mama Doesn't Always Know Best." Review of *Ugly Ways*. *Chicago Sun Times* (July 18, 1993): A14.
Burns, Ann, and Bibi Thompson. "First Novelists." Review of *Baby of the Family*. *Library Journal* 114:16 (Oct. 1, 1989):52–58.
———. "Review of *The Hand I Fan With* by Tina McElroy Ansa." *Library Journal* 121:18 (Nov 1, 1996):82.
Davis, Thulani. "Don't Worry, Be Buppie." *Village Voice* 39:19 (May 8, 1990): S26-S29.
Farrell, Beth. "Review of *The Hand I Fan With* by Tina McElroy Ansa." *Library Journal* 122:6 (Apr. 1, 1997):144–45.
Farrington, Carol Cain. "Books in Brief: *The Hand I Fan With* by Tina McElroy Ansa." *New York Times Book Review* (Nov. 24, 1996):18.
Grooms, Anthony. "Big Bad Mudear—*Ugly Ways* by Tina McElroy Ansa." *Callaloo* 17:2 (Summer 1994):653–55.

Harris, Andrea. "*Ugly Ways* Has a Light Way with Ugly Subject." Review of *Ugly Ways*. *Houston (Texas) Chronicle* (Oct. 31, 1993):C5.

Irven, Krystal K. "Fiction—*Baby of the Family* by Tina McElroy Ansa." *School Library Journal* 36:6 (June 1990):144–46.

Jordan, Shirley M. "Putting the Magic on Words." Review of *Baby of the Family*. *American Visions* 5:5 (Oct. 1990):38–39.

Kane, Eugene. "Ansa's Drama Shows Time Doesn't Always Heal Scars of Childhood." Review of *Ugly Ways*. *Milwaukee (Wisconsin) Journal* (Nov. 14, 1993):A14.

Kridler, Chris. "Late Mother Smothers Daughters in Some Powerfully *Ugly Ways*." Review of *Ugly Ways*. *Baltimore Sun* (Oct. 24, 1993):C4.

Martin, Gale. "Ansa's *Baby of the Family* Stands Tall as First Novel." *Charlotte (North Carolina) Observer* (Dec. 17, 1989): C4.

Peterson, V. R. "Tina McElroy Ansa: A Real Mother's Tale." *Essence* 24 (Dec. 1993):54.

Robertson, Deb. Review of *Baby of the Family*. *Booklist* (Nov. 1, 1989):524.

Sayers, Valerie. "The Girl Who Walked with Ghosts." Review of *Baby of the Family*. *New York Times Book Review* 6:1 (Nov. 26, 1989):7.

Scherer, Catherine. "Review of *Baby of the Family* by Tina McElroy Ansa." *Chicago Review* 37:2–3 (1991):166–71.

Seaman, Donna. Review of *Ugly Ways*. *Booklist* 89:21 (July 1993):1942.

Steinberg, Sybil. "Fiction: *Baby of the Family* by Tina McElroy Ansa." *Publishers Weekly* 236:10 (Sept. 8, 1989):56.

———. "Fiction: *Ugly Ways* by Tina McElroy Ansa." *Publishers Weekly* 240:21 (May 24, 1993):67–68.

———. "Review of *The Hand I Fan With* by Tina McElroy Ansa." *Publishers Weekly* 243: 32 (Aug. 5, 1996):428.

Whittaker, Lynn Page. "Mudear Dearest—*Ugly Ways* by Tina McElroy Ansa." *Belles Lettres: A Review of Books by Women* 10:2 (Spring 1995):93.

Woods, Paula L. "Tina McElroy Ansa's Spirited, Southern Style." *Emerge* 8:1 (Oct. 1996): 75.

DORIS JEAN AUSTIN
(c. 1949–1994)

Evora Jones

BIOGRAPHY

Doris Jean Austin was born in Mobile, Alabama, where she lived until she was six years old. She grew up, after this time, on Belmont Avenue in Jersey City, New Jersey, and attended School 12 and Lincoln High School in Jersey City, where she found inspiration from her high school English teacher, Reverend Ercell F. Webb, to write. Reverend Webb performed the ceremony for Austin's first marriage.

Austin's family tradition of church attendance, church loyalty, and morality was passed on to her through her mother, Tommie Letitia Austin, and her grandmother, Rebecca Stallworth. Salient personal experiences, such as those in the Monumental Baptist Church and in her Jersey City neighborhood, gave Austin insights and motivation for her first novel, *After the Garden* (1987).

Austin was a journalistic critic, a novelist, a newscaster for NBC radio, a writer for the *Amsterdam News*, *Essence* magazine, and *The New York Times Book Review*. She distinguished herself as a MacDowell Colony fellow and as the recipient of the DeWitt Wallace/Reader's Digest Award for Literary Excellence. During the last five years of her life, she conducted fiction workshops at Columbia University's School of Writing; Austin was cofounder and executive director of the New Renaissance Writers' Guild and member of the Harlem Writers' Guild. Near the end of her life, she had begun a novel about Rosalie Tompkins, the grandmother in her first novel.

Austin died in 1994 of liver cancer.

MAJOR WORKS AND THEMES

Austin's first novel, *After the Garden*, set in the period between the 1940s and the 1960s in Jersey City, New Jersey, captures the experiences of two multigenerational families as they struggle to support the coming-of-age of young Elzina Tompkins, a sheltered, cultured high school freshman living on Astor Place, and the independence of Jesse James, a free-spirited high school senior living on Kearney Avenue, who share a mutual romantic attraction, in spite of the class boundary line drawn between the families by Elzina's grandmother and guardian, Rosalie Tompkins, and by Jesse's mother, Truselle James. This struggle—the plot—becomes intriguing when, at age fourteen, Elzina becomes pregnant by Jesse and marries him, aware of the differences between the moral and social traditions of her family and those of Jesse's. While Elzina continues to live with her grandmother, and Jessie continues to live with his family, the two try to minimize the apparently strained relationship resulting from the inability, in some instances, and the unwillingness, in others, of Elzina and Jesse to merge the lifestyles of the two households—backgrounds—and build a family The novel's setting, characters, and plot render it a study in metaphorical and intraracial divides—the "weeds" and the "garden"—in America's urban and suburban communities.

Intraracial divides are funneled through Austin's setting as well as through her characters. Elzina's grandmother dresses her in clothes too large to reveal her feminine shape, hoping that boys will not be attracted to her. Grandmother, Rosalie Tompkins, has, after all, been caretaker of Elzina since Elzina's father and mother were killed together in an automobile accident when the child was four years old. Anxious to see her granddaughter thrive in a cultured environment, like that found in Rosalie's comfortable, ordered, religious household, Rosalie frowns upon Elzina's attraction to the star football player, Jesse James, at the local high school. Characteristically, the grandmother's feelings about Jesse's mother, Truselle, are based largely on Truselle's seemingly unordered lifestyle—several children with different fathers—and in the social indulgences of the family—drinking, card playing, and other similar activities—reserved for families whose moral and social allegiances vacillate between churchgoing rituals and fun-loving parties.

Kearney Avenue is off-limits for Elzina, so it is not surprising that when Jesse and Elzina marry, Elzina is torn between remaining with her grandmother, who would otherwise be left alone, and moving to Kearney Avenue, an already overcrowded residence. Elzina's love for Jesse, nonetheless, is indisputable, but the cultural divide between Jesse and Elzina, apparent throughout the novel, is obviously acerbic. Austin's metaphorical rendering of these two cultures—the "weeds," the James household, and the "garden," the Tompkins household—is the frame for understanding the significance of the novelist's craft. Austin's treatment of the cultural divide begins with the opening church scene, where Elzina's reserved posture and behavior are contrasted with Truselle's spontaneous sleeping and snoring in church. Rosalie's impatience with, and disdain for, Truselle are unmistakable when Austin projects Truselle as a "sinful" character. Austin writes, "Of all the world's poor sinners whom Rosalie disapproved—and there were many—Truselle James had a place of her own" (5).

Austin's setting provides insight into cultural divides. Rosalie's carefully kept yard and home are contrasts to Truselle's frequently used yard and home. After church on Sundays, Elzina would go home and enjoy the comfort of the swing under the grape arbor in her backyard. "The swing was like a little house of its own, with two green wooden benches facing each other and a floor and a lattice-work ceiling with curling tendrils full of grapes" (7). Jesse, on the other hand, would return to his home "with five sagging steps leading to a faded, once yellow, two-story wood-frame building with four storm windows looking out on the splintered porch" and where even from the porch the music was "overpowering" (2).

Austin's skill with metaphor is especially strong as she gives Rosalie voice: when Rosalie tries to convince Elzina that she is making an unwise choice in selecting Jesse as a life-mate, she says:

'Aint no good can come outta them no account Jameses. They scandalous, wild folks. I can see Jesse the best a the lot. But they's weeds. All of 'em. Ever' last one of 'em. And just 'cause Jesse the best weed sure don't mean you qualified to handle no weed, baby girl. . . . You been raised in a garden, child. You don't know nothing 'bout no weeds.' (40)

The home at 1035 Astor Place, Elzina's residence, was very different from Kearney Avenue, Jesse's residence. Cissy, Truselle's ten-year-old daughter, gives her feelings on the troublesome divide on one occasion when Elzina is visiting on Kearney Avenue. Cissy tells Elzina:

Your grandma think y'all better than anybody 'cept God, huh? . . . People like your grandma—they read the Bible and dress up in all that outside Christianity, even though they mean as hell inside. . . .

'Ya see,' . . . 'they just *acting*. But ma mama,' . . . 'my mama a *real* saint—inside.' . . . 'Where it counts.' (31–32)

This view of intraracial conflict is not simply a two-family crisis in Jersey City; it is also a national crisis in many cities.

Meanwhile, Elzina's maturation, paradoxically, continues in spite of the death of her grandmother and her husband. Her mental and physical health deteriorates later in the course of the novel, a condition that forces her to live with the Jameses, a needed development in reconciling the weeds and the garden. Jesse's independence, on the other hand, becomes elusive and hampered amid the charges leveled against him for his role in a robbery and the time he spent in jail for his role in the theft.

Jesse and Elzina, by this time, have had a son, Charles, who develops into a responsible young man but who also, accidentally, shoots his father while hunting. Austin's rendering of this accident colors the remaining pages of the novel. She writes:

Charles stumbled over the twisted root of a tree and his gun flew forward, aimed straight at Jesse's back. Charles tried to catch it, but in doing so he pulled the trigger. It fired and caught Jesse close range on an upward slant through his neck, erupting through the right side of his head. The shot echoed in the stillness. Jesse felt the impact to his brain like the sudden explosion of a brilliant but forbidden insight. L. D., his face stern with unspoken rebuke, rushed forward in time to see Jesse sink to his knees. (262–263)

Elzina's health deteriorates, and in her miserable state she imagines the presence of Jesse in Charles. This detachment from reality leads Elzina to an intimate encounter with Charles for which Charles suffers guilt. The burden of guilt for his father's death, added to the burden of guilt over the encounter with his mother, keeps Charles in a state of unawareness that he is "Not Guilty." Slowly, with the help of Jesse's illegitimate daughter, Elzina gropes her way back to mental soundness, isolating herself in Truselle's attic in a fog of rememberings—real and unreal.

This novel mirrors the moral, social, and religious dilemmas inherent in cultural traditions that may harm yet eventually heal and help those with character and insight sufficient for valuing, choosing, and growing.

Austin's *Streetlights* is a collection of forty-nine short stories coedited with Martin Simmons in which Austin's "Room 1023" appears as the lead story, and Martin Simmons' "Excerpt from *Blood at the Root*" appears as the forty-third story. "Room 1023" is a gripping, first-person account of Lelah Vanessa Frederick's psychological and financial struggle to regain dignity and independence after a divorce that leaves her waiting for that monthly "check in the mail" to pay rent for her "five-by-twelve room with a bath" (3) in a women's residential hotel in New York. Narrowly, yet suggestively, Austin probes the circumstances leading to Lelah's plight—depressed, dependent, unemployed, single, and anxious about her future. The narrator's self-esteem has dwindled to the point where she must tell herself that she is loved.

Austin's stream-of-consciousness mode of narration deliberately and skillfully develops a character who simultaneously mirrors the darkness of several national dilemmas facing women in urban communities—indignity, loneliness, poverty, divorce, homelessness, unemployment. The feeling of worthlessness accompanying the plight of the homeless heightens the serious and potentially damaging effects of lingering social ills, specifically as Lelah acknowledges her own anxieties and sighs, "There is indignity in my cotton mouth, in my paper dry hands as I ring for the elevator in a state that bears for me the earmarks of a high-wire act at the World Trade Center. No net" (14). The loneliness accompanying the feeling of worthlessness is reflected in the tone of Lelah's self-pitying remarks when she assesses her individual plight and says: "I walk into the narrow corridor of my single room. I note that it has never felt so much like home, but now I feel totally earthbound, alone in the pit of my room. I haven't locked the door. Few of us do" (12). The generosity of a lady who feels Lelah's plight and responds by giving her twenty dollars in a note to help her live until her check comes, through its compassionate tone, brings to Lelah hope amid despair, a belief necessary for survival.

Austin's combination of metaphor and subtle humor shapes a gripping story about America's homeless. Lelah outsmarts the hotel manager by remaining—hiding—in the room under the bed for a few days beyond the planned date of her eviction. This action, however, forces a self-questioning for the narrator that could lead to her healing and survival. She questions, "I can't just hide under the bed, can I?" (16). This questioning alone portends the depth of one of inner cities' tragic social ills—homelessness.

Austin's "The Act behind the Word," included among the stories in Marita Golden's *Wild Women Don't Wear No Blues*, is a retelling of Austin's personal crisis as a rape victim on a Saturday evening in Jersey City when she was twelve years old and its devastating effects. This personal story of healing and survival recounts how she "forgot" the incident until she was forced to tell a therapist whose services she sought after her second divorce. The writing of this story was part of Austin's catharsis. Austin's "The 30-Year Rape" is a reprint of this story.

"An Almost Perfect Romance" is Austin's personal story of disappointment in what she had hoped to be a long-term relationship with Billy Thomas, the fictional name for a real person. She explores and relives her life with Billy through his deceptions, his drug addiction, and her slow route to recovery after their separation.

"Looking for Home" is drafted from *After the Garden* but does, indeed, single out a moment of awareness and growth for Jesse, who is returning "home" to Kearney Avenue after his incarceration. This short story is the spiritual coming-of-age of Jesse James as Austin narrates how "[e]ach step he took was a thundering miracle that brought Jesse closer to the God of his childhood" (Austin, "Looking . . ." 32).

"Holistic Healing" brings together four major traumatic experiences in Austin's life over a brief period: the finality of her second divorce, the death of her mother, the diagnosis of her illness—cancer—and an awareness that she needed help with her alcohol dependency. She tells of how she learned to manage her despair, rather than attempt to run away from it.

"The Men in My life" is a self-analysis of how and why Austin responded to different men in her past and how she grew to accept her "one constant lover": herself.

CRITICAL RECEPTION

Critics have labeled *After the Garden* "startlingly autobiographical" (Sheehy) and "not strictly autobiographical" (Guy-Sheftall). Sheehy presents a noteworthy, but brief, biography of Austin.

Steinberg sees Austin's fiction as "having many virtues, not the least of which is the exuberant life pervading it" (72).

The Kirkus Review positively appraises Austin's work as "energetic but fairly standard first novel" (739).

Robert G. O'Meally praises *After the Garden* for its presentation of "the tragicomic education of Elzina Tompkins, sheltered flower on black Jersey's snooty

Astor Place" (20). O'Meally also sees strength in Austin's metaphorical use of the "garden" and the "weeds" to draw the distinction between the perceived classes within one culture in Jersey City.

BIBLIOGRAPHY

Works by Doris Jean Austin

After the Garden. New York: New American Library, 1987.
"Looking for Home." *Breaking Ice.* Ed. Terry McMillan. New York: Penguin Books, 1990. 21–32.
"The 30-Year Rape." *Essence,* January 1991: 21, 59, 88–90.
"An Almost Perfect Romance." *Essence,* February 1991: 56–57, 103–106.
"Holistic Healing." *Essence,* May 1992a: 106–107.
"The Men in My Life." *Essence,* November 1992b: 44.
"The Act behind the Word." *Wild Women Don't Wear No Blues.* Ed. Marita Golden. New York: Doubleday, 1993.
"Room 1023." *Streetlights.* Ed. Doris Jean Austin and Martin Simmons. New York: Penguin Books, 1996a.
Streetlights. Ed. Doris Jean Austin and Martin Simmons. New York: Penguin Books, 1996b. 1–19.

Studies of Doris Jean Austin

Andrews, William L., Frances S. Foster, and Trudier Harris, eds. *The Oxford Companion to African American Literature.* New York: Oxford University Press, 1997: 33.
Guy-Sheftall, Beverly. "Word Star." *Essence,* October 1987: 28.
King, Christine. Review of *After the Garden. The Library Journal,* July 1987: 91.
Nathan, Paul. "Rebel, Sleuth, and Slaves." Review of *After the Garden. Publishers Weekly,* 13 May 1988: 246.
O'Meally, Robert G. "Naughty Kearney Avenue." Review of *After the Garden. New York Times Book Review,* 16 August 1987: 20.
Review of *After the Garden. Kirkus Reviews,* 15 May 1987: 739.
Sheehy, Maura. "Spiritual Evolvement of Family Related in *After the Garden.*" *The Jersey Journal,* 1 December 1987: 23.
Steinberg, Sybill. Review of *After the Garden. Publishers Weekly,* 12 June 1987: 72.
———. Review of *After the Garden. Publishers Weekly,* 22 April 1988: 80.
Wilkerson, Isabel. "On Top of the World." *Essence,* June 1996: 51–52, 123.
Williams, John A. Introduction. *Streetlights.* Ed. Doris Jean Austin and Martin Simmons. New York: Penguin Books, 1996.

JAMES BALDWIN
(1924–1987)

Emmanuel S. Nelson

BIOGRAPHY

The circumstances of James Baldwin's birth were unremarkable. He was born on 2 August 1924 at Harlem Hospital in New York City to a poor, unmarried, twenty-year-old woman named Emma Berdis Jones. But his death sixty-three years later on 1 December 1987 at his home in southern France was an event reported on the front pages of newspapers around the world. Indeed, his journey from a difficult childhood in Harlem to his eventual status as a celebrity-artist with a large and loyal international audience constitutes one of the most compelling life stories of the twentieth century.

Baldwin's early years were deeply troubled. Three years after his birth his mother married David Baldwin, many years her senior, who was a laborer and a fundamentalist Baptist minister. With him she had eight children. Her husband, meanwhile, grew increasingly angry, abusive, and violent; soon he began to terrorize his wife and children. James, presumably because he was a stepchild, became a favorite target for the elder Baldwin's violent outbursts. This problematic relationship with his stepfather would haunt Baldwin for many years to come.

At age fourteen Baldwin underwent an experience of spiritual conversion—an experience vividly recreated in his first and explicitly autobiographical novel, *Go Tell It on the Mountain*, and for the next three years he was a teenage minister who preached in evangelical churches in and around Harlem. He left the church at age seventeen, but the three years in the ministry were crucial to his personal and artistic development. Though he formally abandoned the pulpit when he was seventeen, he remained very much a preacher for the rest of his life. The language of the church—the biblical imagery and cadences, the grand rhetorical strategies of the African American pulpit oratory—left its unmistakable imprint on his distinct prose style. The social and theoretical imperatives of African American Protestantism fundamentally shaped his vision and granted urgency and authority to his message.

Soon after graduation from De Witt Clinton High School in Brooklyn in 1942, Baldwin became a laborer at a railroad construction site across the Hudson River in New Jersey. Although he had been subjected to racial taunts and occasional racial violence in New York City, he was totally unprepared for the brutally racist hostility that greeted him in New Jersey. A long series of encounters with petty apartheid culminated in a spectacular incident at a diner that Baldwin later recounted in his classic essay "Notes of a Native Son." Soon he relocated to Greenwich Village, supported himself by doing a variety of odd jobs—he was at times a busboy, a waiter, and an elevator operator—and started to write. His book reviews and essays began to appear in some of the most prestigious journals in the eastern intellectual establishment. He was gaining attention. But everyday encounters with racism, coupled with his growing awareness of the personal and political implications of his homosexuality, left him deeply unsettled. In a frantic attempt to escape what he felt was impending madness, Baldwin, with the money he had received as part of a Rosenwald Fellowship, purchased a one-way ticket to Paris. He was twenty-four, spoke no French, and had forty dollars in his pocket when he landed in Paris on 11 November 1948. Thus began his transatlantic exile, which would continue, on and off, for the rest of his life.

Given the many dilemmas generated by Baldwin's profound sense of racial, sexual, and artistic exclusion from his homeland, expatriation for him was not only a desirable option but a compelling necessity. In Baldwin's own words, he left the United States "to survive the fury of the color problem" (*Nobody Knows My Name* 17). He wanted to be a writer, and the United States did not seem to him to be a congenial place to become one. But it is important to acknowledge the sexual dimension of his exile as well. When he left for France in 1948, he was fleeing not only the racial lunacy of his country but also the personal troubles of his sexuality. Indeed, his flight to France was a flight away from American sexual codes. In France he met and fell in love with Lucien Happersberger, with whom he forged one of the enduring relationships of his life. France, then, became a liberatory space where Baldwin could jettison American scripts of masculinity, a place where he could begin charting the troublesome geography of his homosexual longing.

Race and sexuality—two of Baldwin's primary preoccupations—became the subject of his first major works: *Go Tell It on the Mountain* (1953), *Notes of a Native Son* (1955), and *Giovanni's Room* (1956). In 1957, seeking personal involvement in the burgeoning Civil Rights movement, he returned to the United States. During the 1960s, perhaps the finest decade in Baldwin's career, Baldwin emerged as a most eloquent civil rights activist. Though an angry prophet, he advocated not a program of violence but a path of reconciliation, forgiveness, and love. With such a message, often articulated in precise and elegant prose, he soon drew a very large American and international audience. Works such as

Nobody Knows My Name, Another Country, Blues for Mister Charlie, and *Tell Me How Long the Train's Been Gone*, all published during the 1960s, made him one of the preeminent artists of his generation.

During the 1970s, though still quite prolific, Baldwin began to show signs of exhaustion. The Civil Rights movement largely over, the reception of Baldwin's message began to grow less enthusiastic. The emergence of African American women writers such as Alice Walker* and Toni Morrison* during the late 1970s and 1980s meant that he no longer held the center stage of the literary scene. His failing health, coupled with heavy drinking, began to compromise the quality of his writing. Too, he clearly became disillusioned with the emergence of the New Right in American politics, the election and landslide reelection of Ronald Reagan to the White House, and the escalation of racial animosities—though he continued to insist, even during the reactionary 1980s, on his vision of an America free of its racial pathologies and sexual hypocrisies.

Baldwin chose to die in France. In December 1987, after an emotional funeral service at St. John the Divine Cathedral in New York City, attended by thousands of friends and admirers, the casket carrying his frail body was driven through the streets of Harlem—the streets of his troubled childhood. Baldwin's journey ended at Ferncliff Cemetery, a few miles outside the city.

MAJOR WORKS AND THEMES

Go Tell It on the Mountain, a modern classic and perhaps Baldwin's magnum opus, was published in 1953. Given the abundant evidence of autobiographical material present in the narrative, *Go Tell* is arguably a record of the author's attempt to come to terms with the given of his complex inheritance. But *Go Tell* is much more than an autobiographical tale. Imbued with an epic sense of history and resonant with elaborate biblical imagery, it is a universal story of initiation, of coming-of-age, of a young man's struggle to forge an autonomous identity in opposition to surrounding authority figures.

Go Tell is divided into three parts. Book I focuses on the consciousness of the adolescent protagonist, John Grimes. Part II, the longest of the three, follows a historical-generational pattern: subdivided unto "Florence's Prayer," "Gabriel's Prayer," and "Elizabeth's Prayer," it familiarizes the reader with the personal histories of the three characters through flashbacks. Although John is unaware of the personal struggles of Florence, his aunt, Gabriel, his raging father, and Elizabeth, his mother, the reader is given a telescopically expanding vision of the protagonist's familial and racial histories that have shaped his identity. The three "Prayers" provide a broad framework for the novel's central situation, John's search for self; they also collectively reveal the historical essence of African American experience. As we understand the protagonist's history, we grasp the various forces that inform his inheritance, the interconnectedness of the past and the present, the link between history and self. Book III culminates in John's spiritual conversion, his acceptance of the Holy Spirit, before the altar of the Temple of the Fire Baptized.

Because critics in general have privileged the novel's racial content, many have failed to acknowledge fully the sexual aspect of John's struggle for self-definition. *Go Tell*, in fact, offers one of the most sensitive portrayals of the developing adolescent consciousness in American fiction. The first suggestion of John's homosexual leanings becomes evident when he keeps staring at Elisha, as the seventeen-year-old Sunday school teacher explains a biblical lesson. John finds himself "admiring the timbre of Elisha's voice, much deeper and manlier than his own, admiring the leanness and grace, the strength, the darkness of Elisha in his Sunday suit" (13). When Elisha dances in a state of religious frenzy, the adolescent protagonist is fascinated by the "muscles leaping and swelling in his long, dark neck" and his thighs, which move "terribly against the cloth of his suit" (16). John and Elisha's playful wrestling on the church floor, too, has obvious sexual overtones. After the wrestling, the protagonist stares "in a dull paralysis of terror at the body of Elisha" and looks at the older boy's face with "questions he would never ask" (54). Toward the end of the novel, after John's spiritual conversion, he touches Elisha's arm and finds himself "trembling" (220). He looks at his Sunday school teacher and struggles "to tell him something . . . all that could never be said" (220). When Elisha places a "holy kiss" on John's forehead, the new convert views it as a "seal ineffaceable forever" (221), thereby suggesting a new awareness on his part. Thus, Baldwin hints at the doubts, anxieties, and moments of dim excitement that accompany John's sexual awakening.

This theme of sexual identity dominates Baldwin's second novel, *Giovanni's Room* (1956). Prior to the publication of this work, Baldwin had already established himself as an eloquent essayist and gifted novelist. Readers and critics had come to recognize him as an insightful interpreter of the African American experience. Therefore, *Giovanni's Room*, with its all-white cast and its focus on the issue of sexual identity, disappointed and disturbed many. But publishing such a novel in the mid-1950s was a singular act of courage and defiance on the part of Baldwin, because by doing so he risked his career and the possibility of alienating a substantial segment of his audience. Yet now, more than four decades after its publication, *Giovanni's Room* remains a classic piece of American gay fiction.

As much a Jamesian tale of expatriation and its discontents as a lyrical novel of remembrance and atonement, *Giovanni's Room* begins with David, the narrator, standing at the window of a great house in the south of France as the night falls "and dreading the most terrible morning" (7) of his life. An American in his late twenties, he has fled to France to escape the haunting memories of his dead mother, an irresponsible father, and an adolescent homosexual encounter. In Paris, after a brief affair with Hella, an American drifter who soon leaves for Spain, he reluctantly falls in love with Giovanni, a handsome young Italian. But

David remains sexually confused: he is simultaneously attracted to, and repelled by, his lover; sometimes he goes out alone to "find a girl, any girl at all" (126) to reassure himself that he is, indeed, capable of functioning heterosexually. When Hella returns to Paris from Spain, David leaves Giovanni to resume his difficult relationship with her. Abandoned by his only close friend, Giovanni resorts to prostitution to pay for his room and food. In a rather sensational turn of events, Giovanni murders Guillaume, an employer who humiliates and exploits him. Soon Giovanni is caught, tried, found guilty, and sentenced to death. On the eve of his execution the narrative begins; in an extended flashback David reconstructs his relationship with Giovanni and his own role in pushing Giovanni to his present plight.

Its despair and violent conclusion notwithstanding, *Giovanni's Room* is a bittersweet remembrance of a gay romance. In it Baldwin reveals one of the primary dilemmas of the American gay male: on one hand, he is faced with rigid social definitions of masculinity and cultural expectations of heterosexual conduct; on the other hand, he has to deal with his sexual feelings for other men, feelings that militate against all the belief systems that he has, for the most part, internalized. The crisis resulting from such a conflict provides the central drama of Baldwin's second novel.

This inability to love authentically resurfaces as a dominant theme in *Another Country* (1962), Baldwin's best-selling third major work of fiction. Here Baldwin, for the first time, explicitly combines racial and sexual protest. Though an angry work, it nevertheless embodies Baldwin's vision of "another country"—a new Jerusalem, an imaginary America—free of repressive racial boundaries and sexual categories.

Another Country is a complex narrative, structured to reveal Baldwin's outrage with maximum force. It has a multiethnic cast of eight major characters: Rufus is a black jazz musician; Leona is a poor white from the South; Ida, Rufus' sister, is an angry and ambitious blues singer; Vivaldo, an aspiring writer of Irish and Italian background, is a friend of Rufus and a lover of Ida; Richard, a Polish American of working-class origins, is a friend of Vivaldo and a fairly successful novelist; his wife, Cass, is a WASP from a wealthy New England family; Eric, a southern white male, is an actor; and Yves, a former Parisian prostitute, is Eric's lover. All the women are exclusively heterosexual. Among the male characters, Rufus and Vivaldo are bisexual, although they generally prefer women; Eric and Yves are also bisexual, but their primary attraction is to men; and Richard, the least likable character, is the novel's one exclusively heterosexual male. These regionally, economically, ethnically, and sexually diverse characters constitute a microcosmic America; Baldwin's exploration of the conflicts among them, then, is a commentary on the larger tensions in American society.

In *Another Country* Baldwin argues, on one hand, that labels and categories warp human relationships, that racial histories inform individual encounters, that the politics of color shapes even the most casual of cross-racial connections. Yet, on the other hand, Baldwin insists that labels and categories are merely artificial constructions, that history can, indeed, be transcended, that color has no intrinsic validity in any genuinely human terms. "Another country," then, is a territory without barriers, a place where individuals can connect with one another unhindered by any imposed labels. But that country is not merely a geographical place but also symbolic space within ourselves—a space where we may imaginatively transcend national, racial, and sexual categories.

For a pre-Stonewall novel, the treatment of homosexuality in *Another Country* is remarkably sophisticated. Refreshingly absent is the ubiquitous Freudian pattern of ineffectual fathers, overprotective mothers, and homosexually inclined sons that recurs insistently in many "gay" American novels published before the 1970s. Here homosexuality is hardly an occasion for panic or reason for guilt. True, it causes suffering, as it does in the case of Eric, but in Baldwin's theology suffering can lead to redemptive self-knowledge, to a more humane understanding of the self and the other. Gayness, therefore, has redemptive potential. Significantly, *Another Country* is one of the very few pre-Stonewall novels in which gay romance does not terminate in murder or suicide; on the contrary, the relationship between Eric and Yves at the end of the narrative reveals at least tentative signs of wholeness and durability.

That homosexuality may contain redemptive possibilities is developed even more vigorously in Baldwin's fourth novel, *Tell Me How Long the Train's Been Gone* (1968). It is the story of Leo Proudhammer, a bisexual, thirty-nine-year-old, highly successful black actor. While recuperating in a San Francisco hospital from a massive heart attack, Leo looks back on his eventful life—from his bleak childhood in a rat-infested Harlem tenement house to his present status as a phenomenally successful actor. He recalls his romantic involvement with Barbara, a white actress, and the disapproval of a racist society that destroyed that romance. He elaborately remembers his relationship with black Christopher, a young militant committed to radical change. The story is narrated entirely through Leo's flashbacks, with shorter flashbacks embedded within larger ones. Leo examines his life, seeking a pattern that would grant at least a semblance of order to the accumulated anarchy of his experience. He wants to invest his suffering "with a coherence and authority" (99). This larger quest unifies his extended and sometimes disjointed recollections.

Many of Baldwin's thematic concerns—such as the failure of love, the loneliness of the artist, the maiming impact of racism on individuals and on relationships—resurface in *Tell Me*. Once again, Baldwin casts the gay character in a redemptive role. Black Christopher's name itself, for example, suggests his role as a racial savior; his absolute commitment to revolutionary politics shows that he is part of the transforming process that is challenging and changing America. But Christopher is also comfortably and confidently gay. By combining black militancy and gay sexuality in Christopher's character, Baldwin suggests that there is no fundamental conflict between the two. One is tempted, of course, to speculate whether Baldwin, in creating Christopher's character, is defensively responding to the hostile criticism that the gay content of *Giovanni's Room* and *Another Country* elicited from homophobic black militants such as Eldridge Cleaver and Amiri Baraka.

Baldwin's fifth novel, *If Beale Street Could Talk*, was published in 1974. A poignant love story, it is a relatively short novel that centers around an unborn baby, its unwed mother and unjustly jailed father, and the families of the parents. The story is told in the first person by the mother of the baby, Clementine "Tish" Rivers, a nineteen-year-old who lives with her parents and sister in Harlem. The father of the baby she is carrying is Alonzo "Fonny" Hunt, a self-taught sculptor.

Through Tish's recollections we are familiarized with the action antecedent to the novel's beginning: Tish and Fonny fall in love and plan to get married, but their hopes are shattered when Victoria, an emotionally disturbed Puerto Rican woman, falsely accuses Fonny of raping her. Despite flimsy evidence Fonny is imprisoned without bail. The novel begins with Tish's visit to the Tombs, the jail where Fonny is held, to inform him of her pregnancy; it ends just prior to the birth of the baby. The events of the intervening months constitute the bulk of the narrative.

Structured as a blues lament, *If Beale Street Could Talk* focuses on the unsuccessful attempt by Tish and her family members to gain Fonny's release from jail. The plot allows Baldwin to explore the complex links between racism and sexuality, the insidiously racist nature of the American judicial system, the moral bankruptcy of institutionalized religion, and the redemptive potential of unconditional love. Conspicuously absent in this novel, however, is one of Baldwin's major preoccupations: the theme of homosexual desire.

Just Above My Head (1979), Baldwin's sixth and final novel, centers around the life of Arthur Montana, a black gay gospel singer, as seen through the eyes of his surviving brother, Hall Montana, a forty-eight-year-old advertising executive. Arthur, at age thirty-nine, was found dead of a heart attack in a men's room of a London pub. Hall's thoughts about Arthur's life and death are triggered by his fifteen-year-old son's question of why his friends at school refer to his musically renowned uncle Arthur as a "faggot." Troubled by his son's query, Hall begins to reconstruct the past—his brother's and his own—in an attempt to understand their particular fates so that he may face "both love and death" (407).

Hall's elaborate recollections offer vivid pictures of Arthur's troubled life as well as the narrator's own evolving attitude toward the content and meaning of his deceased sibling's life. At the core of the narrative is Arthur's anguished search for love; central to the novel, therefore, is the subject of homosexuality. What is noteworthy here is Baldwin's treatment of that subject. Unlike some of his earlier novels, *Just Above My Head* reveals a relaxed and more sophisticated attitude toward gay sexuality: Baldwin treats it less self-consciously, less polemically, and less stridently. The gay theme, in fact, is more smoothly woven into the narrative; and it is presented as an essentially unsensational, though problematic, element in Arthur's search for identity and meaning.

CRITICAL RECEPTION

Though there is consensus that James Baldwin is one of the most gifted essayists of the twentieth century, his reputation as a novelist remains contested. Many
fans of Baldwin are wildly enthusiastic about Baldwin's fiction and shy away from
identifying his artistic lapses or interrogating the ideological assumptions that
inform his narratives. But many critics are openly hostile to Baldwin: often their
criticism is tinged with racism or homophobia or both. Only a few critics appear
to make a conscious effort to be balanced in their perspectives and fair in their
assessments of Baldwin's achievement as a novelist. Perhaps the fact that Baldwin
continues to provoke a broad spectrum of intellectual and emotional responses
in itself is a measure of his provocative relevance and value as an artist.

Go Tell It on the Mountain, Baldwin's first novel, continues to be his most
celebrated work. It has spawned more scholarship than any of his other works.
Critics are nearly unanimous in acknowledging its nearly epic vision, complex
narrative design, hauntingly eloquent prose, and sharp psychological insights.
Giovanni's Room, however, disappointed many reviewers: the absence of African
American characters baffled some; the focus on homosexual relationships an-
noyed others. For example, James Ivy, commenting on Giovanni's Room in the
respected and often politically progressive black periodical The Crisis, begins his
review—sarcastically titled "The Faerie Queenes"—by announcing that in this
novel Baldwin "tackles the scabrous subject of homosexual love" and concludes
by asserting that it is a "pity that so much brilliant writing should be lavished
on a relationship that by its very nature is bound to be sterile and debasing"
(123). Another Country, which generated several favorable reviews, also elicited
considerable hostility: critics such as Robert Root and Roderick Nordell were
repulsed by the graphic depictions of interracial and homosexual lovemaking.
Such hostility reaches its nearly hysterical proportions in Eldrige Cleaver's infamous essay titled "Notes on a Native Son," in which he prefaces his vicious
attack on Baldwin with the following declaration: "Homosexuality is a sickness,
just as baby-rape and wanting to be the head of the General Motors" (110).
However, Addison Gayle, Jr., promptly came to Baldwin's defense: in an essay
aptly titled "A Defense of James Baldwin," he offers a convincing retort to the
irresponsible criticism leveled against Baldwin by Eldridge Cleaver, Robert Bone,
and others.

The receptions accorded the other three novels by Baldwin were similar. While
some reviewers were enthusiastic, others were condescending or downright hostile. Such trends continue in more recent scholarship as well. Trudier Harris, in
her Black Women in the Fiction of James Baldwin, sees him as a spokesperson for
African American patriarchy. However, several gay male critics praise him for
his brilliant and progressive deconstructions of the conventional views of human
sexuality. It is safe, then, to state that the mixed reception accorded Baldwin's
fiction points to the need for a thorough reevaluation and judicious reassessment

of the meaning of Baldwin's work and his significance as a twentieth-century cultural phenomenon.

BIBLIOGRAPHY

Works by James Baldwin

Fiction

Go Tell It on the Mountain. New York: Dell, 1953.
Giovanni's Room. New York: Dell, 1956.
Another Country. New York: Dell, 1962.
Going to Meet the Man. New York: Dell, 1965.
Tell Me How Long the Train's Been Gone. New York: Dell, 1968.
If Beale Street Could Talk. New York: Dial Press, 1974.
Just above My Head. New York: Dell, 1979.

Nonfiction Prose

Notes of a Native Son. Boston: Beacon Press, 1955.
Nobody Knows My Name. New York: Dial Press, 1961.
The Fire Next Time. New York: Dial Press, 1963.
No Name in the Street. New York: Dial Press, 1972.
The Devil Finds Work. New York: Dial Press, 1976.
Evidence of Things Not Seen. New York: St. Martin's Press/Marek, 1985a.
The Price of the Ticket: Collected Non-Fiction, 1948–1985. New York: St. Martin's Press/
    Marek, 1985b.

Drama

Blues for Mister Charlie. New York: Dial Press, 1964.
The Amen Corner. New York: Dial Press, 1968.

Poetry

Jimmy's Blues. New York: St. Martin's Press/Marek, 1985.

Studies of James Baldwin

Adams, Stephen. *The Homosexual as Hero in Contemporary Fiction.* London: Vision Press,
    1980.
Bergman, David. *Gaiety Transfigured: Gay Self-Representation in American Literature.* Mad-
    ison: University of Wisconsin Press, 1991.
Bloom, Harold, ed. *James Baldwin.* New York: Chelsea House, 1996.
Cederstrom, Lorelei. "Love, Race and Sex in the Novels of James Baldwin." *Mosaic* 17.2
    (1986): 175–88.
Cleaver, Eldridge. "Notes on a Native Son." In *Soul on Ice,* 77–111. New York: Dell,
    1968.
Foster, David. " 'Cause My House Fell Down: The Theme of the Fall in Baldwin's Novels."
    Critique: Studies in Modern Fiction 13 (1971): 50–62.

Gayle, Addison, Jr. "A Defense of James Baldwin." *College Language Association Journal* 10 (March 1967): 201–8.

Harris, Trudier. *Black Women in the Fiction of James Baldwin.* Knoxville: University of Tennessee Press, 1985.

Ivy, James. "The Faerie Queenes." *The Crisis* 64 (February 1957): 123.

Kinnamon, Keneth, ed. *James Baldwin: A Collection of Critical Essays.* Englewood Cliffs, NJ: Prentice-Hall, 1974.

Macebuh, Stanley. *James Baldwin: A Critical Study.* New York: Third World Press, 1973.

Mengay, Donald. "*Giovanni's Room* and the (Re)Contextualization of Difference." *Genders* 17 (Fall 1993): 59–70.

Nelson, Emmanuel. "Continents of Desire: James Baldwin and the Pleasures of Exile." *James White Review* (Fall 1996): 8, 16.

———. "Critical Deviance: Homophobia and the Reception of James Baldwin's Fiction." *Journal of American Culture* 14.3 (Fall 1991): 91–96.

———. "James Baldwin's Vision of Otherness and Community." *MELUS* 10.2 (1983): 27–31.

Nordell, Roderick. "Old and New Novels on Racial Themes." *Christian Science Monitor* 19 July 1962: 11.

O'Daniel, Therman, ed. *James Baldwin: A Critical Evaluation.* Washington, DC: Howard University Press, 1977.

Porter, Horace. *Stealing the Fire: The Art and Protest of James Baldwin.* Middletown, CT: Wesleyan University Press, 1989.

Pratt, Lewis. *James Baldwin.* Boston: Twayne, 1978.

Root, Robert. Rev. of *Another Country* by James Baldwin. *Christian Century* 7 (1962): 1354–55.

Rowdan, Terry. "A Play of Abstractions: Race, Sexuality, and Community in James Baldwin's *Another Country.*" *Southern Review* 19.1 (Winter 1993): 41–50.

Spurlin, William. "Rhetorical Hermeneutics and Gay Identity Politics: Rethinking American Cultural Studies." In *Reconceptualizing American Literary/Cultural Studies,* 169–83. New York: Garland, 1996.

Standley, Fred, and Nancy Burt. *Critical Essays on James Baldwin.* Boston: G. K. Hall, 1988.

Standley, Fred, and Louis Pratt. *Conversations with James Baldwin.* Jackson: University Press of Mississippi, 1989.

Trope, Quincy, ed. *James Baldwin: The Legacy.* New York: Simon and Schuster, 1989.

Washington, Bryan. *The Politics of Exile: Ideology in Henry James, F. Scott Fitzgerald, and James Baldwin.* Boston: Northeastern University Press, 1995.

TONI CADE BAMBARA
(1939–1995)

Nanette Morton

BIOGRAPHY

Activist, writer, and filmmaker Toni Cade Bambara was born Miltona Mirkin Cade in New York City on March 25, 1939. Named for her father's employer, she insisted on using "Toni" in grade school. In 1970 she added "Bambara," a name she found written in her grandmother's sketchbook. This decision to re-name herself, to stress her autonomy and honor African American matrilineal heritage instead of the Euro-American status quo, is consistent with the themes of her work.

Bambara's interests, both in writing and in African American communal her-itage and self-determination, were sparked early. Although she never fulfilled her journalistic ambitions, Bambara's mother, Helen Brent Henderson Cade, nur-tured the artistic talents of Toni and her brother Walter. "[H]er thing was to give us access. To give us access to materials, to museums, to libraries, to parks" (Bambara, *Deep Sightings* 213). Material also included permission to daydream and an uncrushed spirit: Bambara's mother regularly forced teachers to publicly apologize for racist remarks (220).

A child curious about her surroundings, Bambara immersed herself in the cul-turally rich world of Harlem, Bedford-Stuyvesant, and the other New York bor-oughs where the family lived, eavesdropping on conversations anywhere people gathered to talk and adopting a series of "grandmothers" and "relatives." At Harlem's Speaker's Corner she heard trade unionists, Muslims, Garveyites, Pan-Africanists, and others, an exercise that taught her to "raise critical questions, to be concerned about what's happening locally and internationally" (215).

In 1959 Bambara graduated from Queen's College with a B.A. in theatre arts and English and the John Golden Award for fiction. That same year she published her first story, "Sweet Town," in *Vendome* magazine. Bambara worked as a social worker at the Harlem Welfare Centre between 1959 and 1960 while pursuing graduate studies in modern American fiction at the City College of New York. In 1961 Bambara studied at the Commedia del'Arte in Milan while working as a freelance writer. Between 1962 and 1965 she completed her master's degree while serving as program director at Colony House, Brooklyn, and as the director or coordinator of various programs.

Between 1965 and 1969 she began teaching at City College of New York while serving as adviser for various publications sponsored by the college's SEEK program. Between 1969 and 1974 Bambara taught at Livingston College in New Jersey. Moving to Atlanta in 1974 with her daughter Karma, Bambara became writer in residence at Spelman College between 1974 and 1977 while helping to found several cultural groups, including the Southern Collective of African American Writers. Bambara's activism extended abroad with trips to Cuba (1973) and trips to meet with the Federation of Cuban Women and Vietnam (1975) and the Women's Union. Increasingly interested in film, Bambara produced several scripts for television and film, writing the script for *The Bombing of Osage Avenue* in 1986. Bambara continued her activism until her premature death in Philadelphia in December 1995.

MAJOR WORKS AND THEMES

After editing and contributing to two anthologies (*The Black Woman*, 1970 and *Tales and Stories for Black Folks*, 1971) Bambara published her first collection of stories, *Gorilla, My Love*, in 1972. Although Bambara noted in a humorous, vernacular note she called "A Sort of Preface" that she decided to "deal in straight up fiction . . . cause I value my family and friends," the stories were undoubtedly informed by Bambara's own activism and her experiences in New York neighborhoods. "I am about the empowerment and development of our sisters and of our community. That sense of caring and celebration is certainly reflected in the body of my work" Bambara told Claudia Tate (15). Indeed, as critic Ruth Elizabeth Burks notes, Bambara's works chronicle the progress of the Civil Rights movement (Burks 48). The balance of the stories are remarkable for Bambara's agile use of everyday African American speech, rhythmic and nonlinear as jazz and bebop and rich with cultural and geographical allusions. In at least three of the stories the narrator, whether a young girl (as in "Gorilla, My Love" and "Raymond's Run") or a middle-aged woman (as in "My Man Bovanne"), is named Hazel, a name that embodied particularly positive, powerful qualities for the author. All three voices are articulate, earthy, and forthright, possessing, demanding, or realizing what Bambara has called "the truth about human nature, about the human potential." Truth for Bambara is not only honesty: it is social responsibility and the "unrelenting pursuit of knowledge and wisdom" (Tate 17). In "Raymond's Run," for example, the narrator insists on being a sprinter, not a ladylike Maypole dancer. Absorbed in beating a fellow competitor at a track meet, she becomes transfixed by the sight of her mentally handicapped brother's agility and speed. Deciding to foster her brother's potential, Hazel then shares with Gertrude, her former enemy, "this big smile of respect" and the unspoken insight that this respect is earned by being "honest and worthy of respect . . . you know . . . like being people" (Bambara, *Gorilla, My Love* 32).

Bambara's second collection of short stories, *The Sea Birds Are Still Alive*, was published in 1977. Geographically wide-ranging, they reflect the writer's increased interest in international activism. The title story frequently shifts point of view to depict the feelings of a group of evacuees on a boat off the coast of Vietnam. Some of the passengers bear the scars, internal and external, of a corrupt dictatorship and Western colonization and oppression. In spite of this they remain spiritually unbroken: an exile "straightened, back stiff with the conviction that he . . . was totally unavailable for servitude" (Bambara, *Sea Birds* 77). Underscoring this resistance is the boat pilot's recollection of an old village woman's continued efforts to defy successive waves of invaders and colonizers. In contrast the Westerners on board the boat, including an American official, attempt to catalog an official picture of events, denying individuality while reproducing Eurocentric "knowledge" about them.

In *The Seabirds Are Still Alive* Bambara turns to standard English, producing didactic and more explicit accounts of activism and oppression. In "The Organizer's Wife" Virginia, a quiet, rural woman who once desired to escape her community, marries an organizer who works to save that same community from being swallowed up by developers. Virginia fights the desire to leave—symbolized by her neglected garden—and goes to tell her jailed husband that his bail has been paid; "her strength was back, and she sure as hell was going to keep up the garden. How else to feed the people?" (23).

Bambara's only novel, *The Salt Eaters*, tells, with many shifts in point of view, time, and space, of the healing of Velma Henry, a spiritually bereft activist who has attempted to commit suicide. Bambara said the book came out of a "problem-solving impulse": "our activists or warriors and our adepts or medicine people don't even talk to each other. Those two camps have yet to learn . . . to appreciate each other's visions, each other's potential" (Tate 16). It is clear that Velma's sickness is part of a greater, community malaise, a lack of community cohesion, symbolized by both the fragmentary nature of the narrative and the divisions within the Academy of the Seven Arts, which Velma and her husband founded, and the apathetic alienation of bus driver Fred Hoyt. The scientific ministrations of Dr. Meadows, himself isolated from the community, have failed to help Velma. Only Minnie Ransom, a medium, can help Velma achieve "wholeness": "To be *whole*—psychically, spiritually, culturally, intellectually, aesthetically, physically, and economically whole—is of profound significance. . . . There is a responsibility to self and to history that is developed once you are 'whole' " (Chandler 348). The restoration of Velma's health at the end of the novel—just as the town's festival, with its celebration of the past, is about to begin—suggests empowerment potentially regenerated and renewed.

Deep Sightings and Rescue Missions: Fiction, Essays and Conversations was edited posthumously by Bambara's friend and editor Toni Morrison.* The book contains an extensive interview and some perceptive essays on African American films, including an in-depth examination of Spike Lee's *School Daze*. One story may have been personally inspired: a woman, knowing that she has cancer, urges her spiritually gifted daughter not to waste those gifts and, as importantly, to let the mother continue her own spiritual journey.

CRITICAL RECEPTION

Since the mid-1980s a number of critical essays on Bambara's work have appeared. Because she has so consistently dealt with issues of community activism and feminism, critics such as Elliot Butler-Evans and Susan Willis have chosen to examine her work as a whole. Willis focuses on the developing relationship between self and community. In *Gorilla, My Love* "individual characters are sharply defined, but the notion of the individual is not problematized" (141). Indeed, young Hazel's defiance of authority, demands for honesty, and the foreshadowed alliance with Grechen in an effort to realize Raymond's potential make Hazel "[prefigure] the explicitly revolutionary characters" found in *The Sea Birds Are Still Alive*. *Sea Birds* "develop[s] the integral relationship between the revolutionary leader and the community" (149). The extended family of *Gorilla, My Love* is replaced by an expanded community. Parenting is redefined, becoming the responsibility of the community and designed to develop "a strong and positive sense of race and culture" in children (150). Willis argues that *The Salt Eaters*, unlike Bambara's other two books, problematizes the relationship between the activist and her community. Velma's suicide attempt is a "renunciation of any connection with society, it is the individual's ultimate statement of autonomy. The failure to commit suicide offers the group the opportunity to redefine itself, affirm its importance for the alienated individual, and bring her back into the collectivity" (153). To be revived, Velma must find a balance between autonomy and submersion, in a community unlike the male-dominated movement of the 1960s and 1970s. The redefined community, though not well developed in the novel, is suggested by the presence of the interracial Seven Sisters theater group, which is "lively, spontaneous, creative, and caring" (158).

Elliot Butler-Evans gives a more detailed feminist perspective of Bambara's works. He notes that Bambara fits Walter Benjamin's definition of a storyteller: " 'rooted in the people' " she "creates a narrative largely grounded in the oral tradition of . . . her culture" (Butler-Evans 91). Nevertheless, Bambara disrupts the African American nationalist ideology her stories espouse: "Bambara's insertion of themes related to the desires of Black women and girls disrupts and often preempts the stories' primary focus on classic realism and nationalism" (92). Hazel's refusal to participate in the traditionally feminine Maypole dance in "Raymond's Run" serves to question traditional female roles. Other stories "focus on women's need to establish protective bonds with young girls . . . [and] . . . the necessity of examining and questioning traditional male–female relationships" (101). *The Sea Birds Are Still Alive* contains "the tensions, ambivalences, and irresolution endemic to the attempt to synthesize Black nationalist and feminist ideologies" (108). Characters like Virginia of "The Organizer's Wife" and Lacy in "Broken Field Running" "respond ambivalently to their roles within the social and political structure created by the totalizing enterprise of Black cultural nationalism" (109). Nonetheless, they exemplify "the total submerging of one's personal identity and needs" demanded by that ideology. This ideology is subverted in *The Salt Eaters*: "Velma's attempted suicide can be read as an act of rebellion against the injustices experienced by her and other women, an act that allows her to reexamine and reconstruct her life" (181). Although the book does not reject male participation outright, Butler-Evans, like Willis, sees the Seven Sisters as representative of "a possible future community" (183), although that community is "fragmentary" and "yet to be realized" (182).

Although Butler-Evans criticizes Gloria Hull and Elinore Traylor for deemphasizing Bambara's feminism, their examinations of *The Salt Eaters* offer illuminating insights into what many readers consider a difficult text. Traylor likens *The Salt Eaters* to jazz, which "is a revision of the past history of a tune, or of its presentation by other masters, ensuring what is lasting and valuable and useful in the tune's present moment and discarding what is not" (59). Hull writes that, in this fragmented narrative, "[p]ast, present, and future are convenient, this-plane designations which can, in fact, take place simultaneously" (222). In " 'What It Is I Think She's Doing Anyhow' " Hull notes that the novel "radiates outward in ever-widening circles" from Velma and Minnie Ransom to the twelve healers supporting Minnie and out into the town of Claybourne itself. "[U]ndergirding this emphasis on spiritual unification is Bambara's belief (shared by geniuses and mystics) that all knowledge systems are really one system and that 'everything is everything,' that the traditional divisions are artificial and merely provide the means for alienating schisms" (226).

In *The Salt Eaters* "all systems were the same at base—voodoo, thermodynamics, I Ching, astrology, numerology, alchemy, metaphysics . . . myths" (*Salt Eaters* 210). This reference prompts Margot Kelley to use thermodynamics to explain concepts of time and space in the novel, making the text accessible to students used to regarding science as "truth" and unfamiliar with African American culture. This approach is problematic, for it risks reinscribing the hegemony of Western science, which Bambara, with her validation of the healing powers of Minnie Ransom, so explicitly rejects. Nonetheless, this approach does point out the complexities of Bambara's only novel.

BIBLIOGRAPHY

Works by Toni Cade Bambara

The Black Woman: An Anthology. Ed. Toni Cade. New York: Signet, 1970.
Tales and Stories for Black Folks. Ed. Toni Cade Bambara. Garden City, NY: Zenith, 1971.

Gorilla, My Love. New York: Random House, 1972.

The Sea Birds Are Still Alive. New York: Random House, 1977.

The Salt Eaters. New York: Random House, 1980a.

"What It Is I Think I'm Doing Anyhow." *The Writer on Her Work*. Ed. Janet Sternberg. New York: W. W. Norton, 1980b.

Deep Sightings and Rescue Missions: Fiction, Essays and Conversations. New York: Random House, 1996.

Studies of Toni Cade Bambara

Alwes, Derek. "The Burden of Liberty: Choice in Toni Morrison's *Jazz* and Toni Cade Bambara's *The Salt Eaters*." *African American Review* 30 (1996): 353–378.

Burks, Ruth E. "From Baptism to Resurrection: Toni Cade Bambara and the Incongruity of Language." *Black Women Writers (1950–1980): A Critical Evaluation*. Ed. and Preface Mari Evans and introd. Stephen E. Henderson. Garden City, NY: Anchor-Doubleday, 1984. 48–57.

Butler-Evans, Elliot. *Race, Gender, and Desire: Narrative Strategies in the Fiction of Toni Cade Bambara, Toni Morrison, and Alice Walker*. Philadelphia: Temple University Press, 1989.

Byerman, Keith E. "Healing Arts: Folklore and the Female Self in Toni Cade Bambara's *The Salt Eaters*." *Postscript* 5 (1988): 37–43.

Chandler, Zala. "Voices beyond the Veil: An Interview with Toni Cade Bambara and Sonia Sanchez." *Wild Women in the Whirlwind: Afra-American Culture and the Contemporary Literary Renaissance*. Ed. Joanne M. Braxton and Andree Nicola Mc-Laughlin. New Brunswick, NJ: Rutgers University Press, 1990. 342–362.

Deck, Alice. "Toni Cade Bambara." *Dictionary of Literary Biography: Afro American Prose Writers after 1955*. Detroit: Gale Research, 1985. 12–22.

Ensslen, Klaus. "Toni Cade Bambara: *Gorilla, My Love*." *The African American Short Story 1970 to 1990*. Ed. Wolfgang Karrer and Barbara Pushmann-Nalenz. Trier: Wissenschaftlicher, 1993. 41–56.

Hargrove, Nancy D. "The Comic Sense in the Short Stories of Toni Cade Bambara." *Revista Canaria de Estudios Ingleses* 11 (1985): 133–140.

———. "Toni Cade Bambara." *Contemporary Fiction Writers of the South: A Bio-Bibliographical Sourcebook*. Westport, CT: Greenwood Press, 1993. 32–45.

———. "Youth in Toni Cade Bambara's *Gorilla, My Love*." *Southern Quarterly* 22 (1983): 81–99. Reprinted in *Women Writers of the Contemporary South*. Ed. Peggy Whitman Prenshaw. Jackson: University Press of Mississippi, 1984.

Hull, Gloria. " 'What It Is I Think She's Doing Anyhow': A Reading of Toni Cade Bambara's *The Salt Eaters*." *Home Girls: A Black Feminist Anthology*. Ed. Barbara Smith. New York: Women of Color Press, 1983. 124–142. Reprinted in *Conjuring: Black Women, Fiction, and Literary Tradition*. Ed. Marjorie Pryse and Hortense J. Spillers. Bloomington: Indiana University Press, 1985. 216–232.

Kelley, Margot Anne. " 'Damballah Is the First Law of Thermodynamics': Modes of Access to Toni Cade Bambara's *The Salt Eaters*." *African American Review* 27 (1993): 479–493.

Korenman, Joan S. "African-American Women Writers, Black Nationalism, and the Matrilineal Heritage." *CLA Journal* 38 (1994): 143–161.

Lyles, Lois F. "Time, Motion, Sound and Fury in *The Sea Birds Are Still Alive*." *CLA Journal* 36 (1992): 134–144.

Morrison, Toni. "City Limits, Village Values: Concepts of the Neighbourhood in Black Fiction." *Literature and the Urban Experience.* Ed. Michael C. Jaye and Ann Chalmers Watts. New Brunswick, NJ: Rutgers University Press, 1981. 35–43.

Porter, Nancy. "Women's Interracial Friendships and Visions of Community in *Meridian, The Salt Eaters, Civil Wars,* and *Dessa Rose.*" *Tradition and the Talents of Women.* Urbana: University of Illinois Press, 1991.

Stanford, Ann Folwell. "He Speaks for Whom? Inscription and Reinscription of Women in *Invisible Man* and *The Salt Eaters.*" MELUS: *The Journal of the Society for the Study of the Multi-Ethnic Literature of the United States* 18 (1992): 17–31.

———. "Mechanisms of Disease: African American Women Writers, Social Pathologies, and the Limits of Medicine." *NWSA Journal* 6 (1994): 28–47.

Tate, Claudia, ed. "Toni Cade Bambara." *Black Women Writers at Work.* New York: Continuum, 1988.

Traylor, Elinore W. "*The Salt Eaters*: My Soul Looks Back in Wonder." *First World* 2 (1981): 44–47, 64. Reprinted in revised form as "Music as Theme: The Jazz Mode in the Works of Toni Cade Bambara." *Black Women Writers (1950–1980): A Critical Evaluation.* Ed. and Preface Mari Evans and introd. by Stephen E. Henderson. Garden City, NY: Anchor-Doubleday, 1984. 58–70.

Vertreace, Martha M. "Toni Cade Bambara: The Dance of Character and Community." *American Women Writing Fiction: Memory, Identity, Family, Space.* Ed. Mickey Pearlman. Lexington: University Press of Kentucky, 1989. 155–171.

Willis, Susan. "Problematizing the Individual: Toni Cade Bambara's Stories for the Revolution." *Specifying: Black Women Writing the American Experience.* Madison: University of Wisconsin Press, 1987. 129–158.

BARRY BECKHAM
(1944–   )

Loretta G. Woodard

BIOGRAPHY

Barry Beckham was born in Philadelphia on March 19, 1944, to Clarence and Mildred (William) Beckham. He moved with his mother, at age nine, to a black section of Atlantic City, New Jersey, which offered him a wealth of cultural exposure. He attended interracial public schools and graduated from Atlantic City High School. While there, he enjoyed the popularity of his peers and reading such writers as James Weldon Johnson, Richard Wright, and Chester Himes.* In 1962 he entered Brown University as one of only eight black members of the freshman class. Inspired by the craft of novelist John Hawkes, Beckham, in his senior year, began writing his first book, *My Main Mother*. He graduated in 1966 with a B.A. in English and married Betty Louise Hope.

Prior to his seventeen-year tenure at Brown, Beckham briefly attended law school at Columbia University on a scholarship. While in New York, he served as public relations consultant for Chase Manhattan Bank (1966–1967) and as urban affairs associate (1969–1970). In addition, he held positions as a public relations associate for Western Electric Company (1968–1969), including assistant editor of the *Chase Manhattan News*. At age twenty-five, he completed *My Main Mother* in 1969.

Beckham returned to his alma mater in 1970 as a visiting lecturer in Afro-American studies and English. In 1972, he published *Runner Mack*, his most acclaimed and accomplished work to date, nominated for the National Book Award and now among the first editions of the Howard University Press Library of Contemporary Literature. He also wrote the play *Garvey Lives!*, produced in 1973 by George Bass, director of the Rites and Reasons theater group, and began his portrait of the Chase Manhattan Bank. After a year of tape-recorded conversations, he began his third book, *Double Dunk*, a novelized biography of Harlem basketball legend Earl "the Goat" Manigault. In 1975 Beckham separated from his wife of almost ten years and was divorced two years later. Unable to write, he resigned from his position at Brown but was given a sabbatical leave to reclaim his niche. He married Geraldine Lynne Palmer in 1979 and served as director of the Graduate Writing Program at Brown a year later. In 1980 Holloway House released *Double Dunk*, a novel initially rejected by other publishers.

After experiencing difficulties with publishers, Beckham, with the assistance of students from Brown, compiled, edited, and published the first edition of *The Black Student's Guide to Colleges* in 1982. He divorced his second wife in 1983. Beckham joined the English Department at Hampton University in 1987. In 1989 he retired as writer in residence and founded Beckham House Publishers, a major black-oriented book company, in Maryland, initially formed while at Brown. He explains, "I decided to stop complaining about African Americans not having any power in book publishing and try to do something about it" (Morris). Putting his own work aside for nearly a decade, Beckham has provided more opportunities for black writers, and he now has a list of over sixteen titles. In 1997, Madison Books published the fourth editon of Beckham's *The Black Student's Guide to Colleges*, along with the companion volume, *Black Student's Guide to Scholarships*. For almost two decades, Beckham has devoted much of his time consulting with colleges and organizations about black student recruitment and retention throughout the country. In addition, he conducts workshops on the college selection process and publishes *The Black Student Advisor*, a bimonthly newsletter to assist guidance counselors and deans with much-needed information for black youth.

Scheduled for publication in 1999, Beckham's long-awaited fourth novel, *You Have a Friend: The Rise and Fall and Rise of the Chase Manhattan Bank*, which germinated in 1972, is the first serialized, full-length book on the Internet (telephone interview with Barry Beckham Aug. 6, 1997). Beckham plans to finish his autobiography begun in 1983, responding to his perceived "need for a description of a passionate black love relationship." He states, "I am committed to opening up doors to other black writers, . . . but I feel a tremendous need to get back to my own writing" (Morris). Beckham lives in Maryland.

MAJOR WORKS AND THEMES

In all of Beckham's works various forms of oppression and a struggle for identity exist. His first novel, *My Main Mother*, which is set in an abandoned, wooden station wagon, presents a psychological profile of a young man driven to matricide by his mother's avarice, promiscuity, betrayal, and abuse of his possessions. Through flashbacks, Mitchell Mibbs relives his experiences in rustic Maine, in Harlem, at an Ivy League college, and in Boston at his Uncle Melvin's funeral. Revealed throughout the novel is a lonely young man's quest for love, attention, and respect and the extent one will go to be recognized as a human entity. He is shunned by his mother, stepfather, and other relatives, but his uncle provides him with unconditional love and buys him two dearest possessions, a boxer dog and a pair of drumsticks.

The title is a triple allusion to his main "mother," who was Mitchell's uncle, their living in Maine, and an indictment of Mitchell's beautiful, self-centered mother, Pearl.

Beckham's highly acclaimed second novel, *Runner Mack*, is essentially Henry Adams' journey to self-discovery in a racist society. As an aspiring black baseball player, he encounters several forms of oppression, especially racial oppression. The novel highlights three crucial agents of oppression: big business, the military, and professional sports. Henry would not advance "to the top" at Home Manufacturing when his supervisor, Boye himself, has remained in his current position for thirty years. In the war in Alaska, the soldiers spend their time killing defenseless animals rather than defending themselves from the invisible enemy.

Of the three agents, baseball is Henry's forte. He is completely in control of his life and thinks it will give him a fair advantage to succeed. However, Henry's introduction to the fast-talking revolutionary Runner Mack indicates it is a false perception. His impact upon Henry is likened to the force of a Mack truck. Beckham suggests that Henry must be armed with much more than talent and ambition. Through this metaphor the reader watches Henry grow, and this transformation symbolizes the impact of black consciousness on millions of other blacks who seek to achieve personal fulfillment and identity in an oppressive society.

In *Double Dunk* Beckham uses the second person to chronicle the life of Earl Manigault, "the Goat," well-known inventor of the patented double dunk shot. Like Henry Adams in *Runner Mack*, Earl has much talent and ambition but lacks the self-control needed to fulfill his dream to become a national basketball star. He succumbs to heroin addiction and petty crimes for three years but makes a miraculous recovery while in jail. Once out, he forms his own summer Goat Tournament for youngsters. With discipline and determination, Beckham shows how a brother from the mean streets can survive, give back to the community, and live his dreams through others.

Beckham's masterful blend of the stream-of-consciousness technique and especially dialogue of the streets bridges Earl's experiences with the reader and makes them genuine and heartfelt. Earl's experiences serve as a constant reminder of numerous basketball stars who remain trapped on the streets with dreams unachieved.

You Have a Friend: The Rise and Fall and Rise of the Chase Manhattan Bank is Beckham's latest novel and the first serialized, full-length book on the Internet (1998). A compelling narrative combining historical events with the novelist's eye for detail, scene, setting, and dialogue, it details the drama of human interaction and a richly textured social history of corporate America. Beckham presents from firsthand experience as a Chase public relations writer a portrait that goes beyond mere institutional history and focuses on landmark characters and events. One of the dominant themes to surface throughout the novel is the inability of the Chase Manhattan Bank to define itself with authority during the 1960s and the 1970s, two of the most turbulent decades of the bank's existence.

CRITICAL RECEPTION

Since the 1969 publication of My Main Mother, Beckham has established himself quite rapidly as an excellent writer with a remarkable vision. However, with the exception of a few scholarly studies, critical assessments of his work have been confined to favorable reviews. A Booklist reviewer praises My Main Mother as "[a]n exemplary first novel of penetrating personal insight" (598). A contributor for Publishers Weekly describes the work as a "fine and sensitive story of Mitchell Mibbs" with "very real characterizations and situations" (41). Peter Rowley states, "It is to be hoped that My Main Mother is a forerunner of remarkable things to come" (65).

Of all Beckham's works, Runner Mack, nominated for the 1973 National Book Award, has garnered most of the critical attention. As a pioneer book, critics unanimously praise his craft, tone, and structure. Wiley Umphlett credits Runner Mack as "the first American novel by a black writer to draw an organized sports experience as a means of ordering fictional meaning and purpose" (73). Critics Joe Weixlmann, Hubert Babinski, and Mel Watkins agree that the novel is skillfully constructed. In the Introduction to the book, Watkins calls it "one of the most remarkably conceived and best-executed novels written by any of the young black writers who emerged in the . . . 1960s and 1970s" (vii). A contributor for Washington Post Book World notes the book is a "realistic, symbolic, serious, comic exploration of what it means to be a black American" (15). In more engaging studies, Phyllis Klotman places Runner Mack in the context of the African American literary tradition, growing out of the slave narrative, of the symbolic run toward freedom, and analyzes the novel as a satirical quest. Sanford Pinsker's interview with Beckham discusses the comic elements in his novel in more detail. He explains the influence of Ellison's Invisible Man and The Education of Henry Adams, the reasons he chose to use baseball as a subject and Alaska as a setting. He comments on the ambiguous ending as well. Watkins and Weixlmann favorably compare the novel with Invisible Man. Also, both Umphlett and Weixlmann effectively analyze the novel's structure and pay particular attention to the book's "pessimistic," "enigmatic" ending but seem to agree, as Umphlett writes, that "it implies that the plight of Henry Adams is representative of all Afro-Americans in their search for a positive socio-political identity" (82).

Although Double Dunk has received far less critical attention, reviews have been favorable. A contributor for Booklist observes that Beckham does not "romanticize his subject" and further praises his effective use of the stream-of-consciousness technique with streetwise dialogue, which he claims gives the book "a stylistic edge over the typically pedestrian sports biography" (1382). Ambassador Andrew Young assesses the book as "both a harsh look at the drug problem in the United States and an inspiring story of one man's ability to overcome the problem."

While some critics focused on the *Guide's* limitations and students' candid answers on questionnaires, Beckham's nonfiction book *The Black Student's Guide to Colleges*, was well received in the academy as "an extremely useful guide" (Quay). President Jon M. Nicholson finds the guide an important contribution to the field of minority student counseling and states that "it should be of considerable interest to any high school student searching for a college" (48). To *Black Enterprise* reviewer Elza Dinwiddie, Beckham discusses a major strength: "I think the biggest benefit . . . is to learn that in predominantly white schools you . . . have to face racism. . . . If we alert our students early on, . . . the disappointment, isolation, and alienation that they experience will be less of a shock" (23). Entertainer Bill Cosby has endorsed the recent fourth edition of the *Guidebook* and its companion volume, *Black Student's Guide to Scholarships*, and calls both of them "a must for every black family" (Morris).

Though all of Beckham's works have received critical acclaim, there are still too few scholarly studies to date. However, since the sixteen-year wait for *You Have a Friend: The Rise and Fall and Rise of the Chase Manhattan Bank* is over, and his autobiography is scheduled for release soon, Beckham will definitely receive more attention in the academy.

BIBLIOGRAPHY

Works by Barry Beckham

"Listen to the Black Graduate, You Might Learn Something." *Esquire* (September 1969a): 98, 196–199.

My Main Mother. New York: Walker, 1969b; London and New York: Wingate, 1970b; reissued as *Blues in the Night.* London: Universal-Tandem, 1974.

"Ladies and Gentlemen, No Salt-Water Taffy Today." *Brown Alumni Monthly* (March 1970a): 20–23.

Garvey Lives! Providence, RI: Churchill House, Brown University, November 1972a.

Runner Mack. New York: Morrow, 1972b; Washington, DC: Howard University Press, 1983.

"Why It Is Right to Write." *Brown Alumni Monthly* (May–June 1978): 23–25.

Double Dunk. Los Angeles: Holloway House, 1980.

The Black Student's Guide to Colleges. New York: Dutton, 1982; Lanham, MD: Madison Books, 1997a.

Black Student's Guide to Scholarships: 500+ Private Money Sources for Black and Minority Students. 4th ed. Lanham, MD: Madison Books, 1997b.

You Have a Friend: The Rise and Fall and Rise of the Chase Manhattan Bank (forthcoming 1999).

Studies of Barry Beckham

Babinski, Hubert. Review of *Runner Mack. Library Journal* (August 1972): 2639.

Coombs, Ordie. Review of *My Main Mother. Negro Digest* (February 1970): 77–79.

Dinwiddie, Elza. "Facts of Life for Blacks on Campus." Review of *The Black Student's Guide to Colleges. Black Enterprise* (February 1983): 23.

Donahugh, Robert. Review of *My Main Mother. Library Journal* 77 (December 1969): 4447.

Farrell, Charles. "Campus Ambiance for Blacks: A New Book Gives Low Grades to Some Prestigious Colleges." Review of *The Black Student's Guide to Colleges. Chronicle of Higher Education* (November 1982): 21–22.

Harris, Trudier. "The Barbershop in Black Literature." *Black American Literature Forum* 13 (1979): 112–118.

Klotman, Phyllis Rauch. "The Runner as Defector." In *Another Man Gone: The Black Runner in Contemporary Afro-American Literature.* Port Washington, NY: Kennikat, 1977. 127–148.

Loeb, Jeff. "Barry Beckham." *The Oxford Companion to African American Literature.* Ed. William L. Andrews, Frances Smith Foster, and Trudier Harris. New York: Oxford University Press, 1997. 55.

Morris, Glen. "Maryland Novelist Inspires HBO's Movie 'Rebound' Based on Earl the Goat Manigault." *The Black World Today* (27 May 1997): 9 pars. On-line. Internet. 26 June 1997. Available http://www.tbwt.com/views/feat/feat19.htm

Nicholson, Jon M. "A Guide to the College Guides: Or, How to Find a College, in 25 Easy Volumes." Review of *Black Student's Guide to Colleges. Change* (January/February 1983): 48.

O'Connell, Shaun. "American Fiction, 1972: The Void in the Mirror." *The Massachusetts Review* 14.1 (Winter 1973): 200.

Pinsker, Sanford. "About *Runner Mack*: An Interview with Barry Beckham." *Black Images* 3.3 (Autumn 1974): 35–41.

———. "A Conversation with Barry Beckham." *Studies in Black Literature* 5.3 (Winter 1974): 17–20.

Quay, Richard H. Review of *The Black Student's Guide to Colleges. Library Journal* (15 February 1983): 383.

Rettig, James. Review of *The Black Student's Guide to Colleges. Wilson Library Bulletin* (March 1983): 605.

Review of *The Black Student's Guide to Colleges. Booklist* 96 (June 1983): 1330.

Review of *Double Dunk. Booklist* 1 (July 1981): 1382.

Review of *My Main Mother. Publishers Weekly* 11 (August 1969): 41.

Review of *My Main Mother. Booklist* 15 (January 1970): 598

Review of *My Main Mother. Times Literary Supplement* 12 (February 1970): 173.

Review of *Runner Mack. The New York Times Book Review* 3 (December 1972): 78.

Review of *Runner Mack. Publishers Weekly* 17 (July 1972): 111–112.

Rowley, Peter. "The Rise and Fall of Mitchell Mibbs." Review of *My Main Mother. The New York Times Book Review* 30 (November 1969): 64–65.

Umphlett, Wiley Lee. "The Black Man as Fictional Athlete; 'Runner Mack,' the Sporting Myth, and the Failure of the American Dream." *Modern Fiction Studies* 33.1 (Spring 1987): 73–83.

Walker, Jim. Review of *Runner Mack. Black Creation* 4.2 (Winter 1973): 62–64.

Watkins, Mel. Review of *Runner Mack. The New York Times Book Review* 17 (September 1972): 3, 50.

———. Introduction to *Runner Mack.* New York: Morrow, 1972; Washington, DC: Howard University Press, 1983.

Weixlmann, Joe. "Barry Beckham: A Bibliography." *CLA Journal* (June 1981): 522–528.

———. "The Dream Turned 'Daymare': Barry Beckham's *Runner Mack.*" Melus 8.4 (Winter 1981): 93–103.

———. "Out-Of-Print No Longer: The Howard University Press Library of Contemporary Literature." *Black American Literature Forum* 18.4 (Winter 1984): 167–168.

———. "Barry Beckham." *Dictionary of Literary Biography: Afro-American Fiction Writers After 1955.* Vol. 33. Ed. Thadious M. Davis and Trudier Harris. Detroit: Gale Research, 1984. 17–20.

HAL BENNETT
(1930–   )

Adam Meyer

BIOGRAPHY

George Harold "Hal" Bennett was born April 21, 1930, in Buckingham, Virginia, although at an early age he relocated to Orange, New Jersey. Fictionalized as Burnside and Cousinville, respectively, these two cities provide the settings for most of his later writings. Attending public schools in New Jersey, Bennett published his first stories in the *AFRO-American Newspapers* at the age of thirteen. He edited his school's yearbook, won several writing awards, and worked part-time for the *Newark Herald News*. Rather than going to college after graduating from high school, however, Bennett joined the air force, where he continued his journalism career, including stints as writer for the Public Information Division, as editor of a base newspaper in Japan, and as combat correspondent in Korea during the war. Returning to America in 1952, he started a short-lived newspaper in Westbury, New York, subsequent to which he became an assistant editor at the *AFRO-American Newspapers*, headquartered in Baltimore. In 1956 he moved to Mexico, where he has lived ever since. After studying briefly at Mexico City College and being a fellow at the Centro Mexicano de Escritores, he began his fiction-writing career in earnest.

Following the small press publication of a collection of poems, *The Mexico City Poems*, and a play in verse, *House on Hay Street*, in 1961, Bennett's first novel, *A Wilderness of Vines*, appeared in 1966. Four more novels—*The Black Wine, Lord of Dark Places, Wait until the Evening*, and *Seventh Heaven*—were published in the following decade. During this same period Bennett published a number of short stories, one of which, "Dotson Gerber Resurrected," won him an award as the most promising new writer of 1970 from *Playboy* magazine, where it had first appeared. He also received a PEN/Faulkner Award in 1973. Fifteen of his stories were collected in the volume *Insanity Runs in Our Family* in 1977. Unfortunately, however, this is the last book that has been published under Bennett's name. Various sources in the 1980s described novels in progress titled *Dominions* and *The Bank Walkers*, but these have yet to appear. During this time Bennett did publish several works under pseudonyms—Harriet Janeway's plantation romance *This Passionate Land* and John D. Revere's five action-adventure novels in the Assassin Series, featuring Justin Perry—as well as a few additional stories under his own name. Bennett continues to live and write in Mexico, but it seems safe to say that his artistic legacy is contained in the six books he published between 1966 and 1977.

MAJOR WORKS AND THEMES

Each of Bennett's novels and many of his short stories can be seen as forming part of a larger saga, since they share locales, characters, and themes interchangeably. For this reason his works have been compared to the Yoknapatawpha cycle of William Faulkner, an acknowledged influence. Thematically, Bennett's primary concerns center around the self-loathing that he finds to be so prevalent in the African American community. In his fascinating autobiographical piece "The Visible Man" he recalls a turning point in his life: his mother's telling him, " 'One day, my dear son, you're going to find out that Negroes ain't worth a damn' " (79). Indeed, he asserts that African Americans have been taught in many ways "to harbor an intense dislike for themselves and for all things even vaguely resembling their hated color" ("Visible" 74). This feeling of the worthlessness of blackness, a legacy of slavery, guides the actions of his characters as they either succumb to it or fight against it. In his first novel, *A Wilderness of Vines*, for example, he shows how the town of Burnside has internalized racism to such a degree that all aspects of the community are guided by the question of skin color, with the light-skinned people at the top and the dark-skinned at the bottom. Although Bennett argues that the light-skinned—as embodied in Miss Ida Carlisle, the town's aristocratic leader—are lifeless and weak, while the dark-skinned are virile and strong, the events of the text demonstrate that both kinds of people are doomed by the racial madness that engulfs them. At the end of the novel, following Miss Ida's being sent to the home for the criminally insane after being judged guilty of the crime of thinking herself white, most of the residents of Burnside leave for New Jersey, hoping that they will escape the consequences of self-hatred in the North. However, as Bennett's second novel, *The Black Wine*, set largely in Cousinville, shows, this will not be the case; in their attempts to prove that they are somebody, the transplanted Virginians are again largely defeated, and the novel ends with a race riot from which no one emerges victorious.

One of the primary sources of black self-loathing, Bennett feels, is Christianity, the "hysterical" taking on of which, he asserts, "was probably the first important step in our long and painful pilgrimage towards immense self-hatred" ("Visible" 74). As he explained to Katharine Newman in his only published interview,

"Something happens to the mind who is using the Bible which has been put together by white people, which insists upon the basic Divine-mandated inferiority of the black man, and this same document is then used to show me how to achieve salvation" (366). Since all of Bennett's characters do desire to achieve salvation, the only way they can do this is by inverting Christian beliefs, a situation that is at the heart of his best-known and most controversial novel, *Lord of Dark Places*. Here Titus Market, the protagonist's father, starts a new religious sect on the premise that, " 'if no provision has been made for us to save our souls, we are perfectly free to seek salvation any way we can. My way has always been to be as *contrary* to everything as I can be. When the Bible says black, I say white. When it says good, I say evil. When it says, *Behold, Jehovah is a God of light*, I say *Behold, He is the lord of dark places; for his children gnash their teeth and cry unto Him and are not heard*' " (62). The protagonist himself, Joe Market, becomes the Christ figure in his father's theology; as the Naked Child and then the Naked Disciple, Joe exposes himself to his followers and even has sex with them as a way of ensuring their salvation through his own phallic powers. During the course of the novel Joe kills several people, including his own son and an older white woman, in order to save them, much as Reverend Winston Cobb, a character who appears in all five of Bennett's novels, had done to his wife in *Burnside* and his girlfriend in *Cousinville*. Joe's death in the electric chair at the book's conclusion, like Cobb's execution in *Wait until the Evening*, is seen as a kind of self-sacrifice analogous to Christ's Crucifixion. Black self-loathing clearly leads to madness here as the characters' attempts to assert their own power result in a turning against Western morality.

Sex and violence are pervasive in Bennett's works—including his final novel, *Seventh Heaven*, the title of which refers ironically to a New Jersey public housing complex—as these are two avenues through which African Americans, particularly African American men, can prove their value. As Bennett explained to Newman, "When you have an individual whose only freedom is the personal freedom of concentrating on his own being, he can make no free choice outside of his own being" (359); therefore, "I don't see any other way that a black man can save himself except through his penis" (367–368). Sex and death are also interconnected in Bennett's eschatology; in *Lord of Dark Places*, for example, no less than three of the female characters, including Joe's own mother, die during the act of intercourse. What Bennett does in this novel, in fact, is to take the cultural myth of the black stud to its logical conclusion, inverting and subverting white notions of black inferiority/superiority along the way. While some critics and readers have been offended by Bennett's "obsession with filth" (Newman 358)—and, indeed, there are scenes in each of his novels that are not for the fastidious—others have recognized Bennett's satirical intent, his method of extending the results of racism to such an extreme in order to demonstrate the madness inherent in contemporary American society; as he told Newman, "[T]here are times when we need to distort in order to see reality" (368). He has been compared to Wallace Thurman and George S. Schuyler among black satirists, for example, as well as to William S. Burroughs. Some of his most recent writings, such as the short stories "Chewing Gum" and "Wings of a Dove," are particularly biting in their ironic humor. At the same time, though, like all great satirists, Bennett is an intensely serious writer, trying to effect positive change in his community and in the world at large.

Taken as a whole, then, Bennett's fictional works present, as Ronald Walcott notes, "a history of the post–World War I black man as he makes the journey not only from South to North and from farm to city but also from one type of bondage and bewilderment to another" ("Hal" 21). Despite many attempts to overcome self-loathing, the African American remains consumed by it. Until African Americans can find a way to assert their own value without becoming crazy, Bennett demonstrates, America will continue to be unable to live up to its own lofty ideals; paraphrasing the title of his collection of short stories, insanity will continue to run in our collective family.

CRITICAL RECEPTION

Bennett's writings, like those of all too many black male writers of the mid-1960s and beyond, have received scant critical attention. The most valuable work to have appeared so far has been done by Ronald Walcott. Walcott seems a bit harsh in his view of A Wilderness of Vines here, calling it "a flawed, awkward, at times ineptly written, but insightful and provocative work" (37), and he goes a bit overboard in his praise of Lord of Dark Places, which he elsewhere describes as "an outstanding satirical novel, an experimental, assured, relentless, dazzling technical performance" ("Hal" 22), yet he does lay a solid foundation for Bennett scholarship, pointing out the central concerns that animate his work. Walcott followed up this early essay, which covered Bennett's first three novels only, with an entry in the Dictionary of Literary Biography that discusses his entire career; this remains the single most useful piece about Bennett to have appeared so far.

Among other critics, Bernard W. Bell has generally positive things to say about Bennett in his wide-ranging history of African American literature. Linking Bennett with Charles Stevenson Wright and Ishmael Reed* as writers of "fabulation and satire," Bell focuses his comments primarily on A Wilderness of Vines. He asserts that Bennett's "unique contribution to the tradition of the Afro-American novel is a highly eclectic, irreverent satirical style and scatological mythology of black American color prejudice, sexuality, and messianic hope" (329). Graham Clarke focuses on Bennett's use of language. He argues that Bennett's style "works against constricting structures[,] stretching the naturalistic fabric to its breaking point" (208); the language itself, he feels, "attempts to lead us to some kind of silent and renewed faith in the possibility of a human world" (219). H. Nigel Thomas, on the other hand, focuses on Bennett's preachers, pointing out that Titus Market and Reverend Cobb come "straight out of [African American] folklore" (53). Most recently, James A. Miller briefly discusses Bennett's "recurring stylistic and thematic concerns: his inversion of traditional Christian symbols and images; his preoccupation with sex, salvation, and insanity; [and] his perspective on the corrosive legacy of America's racial history" (58). He also mentions Bennett's use of Edenic imagery, as have several other critics, including Walcott and Bell.

Among reviewers of Bennett's books—and there weren't many—the consensus seemed to be that he was inconsistent. Irving Howe, for example, reviewing Bennett's first two novels, asserted that they were "wildly uneven and sometimes atrocious," that Bennett's "faults as a novelist are substantial," but that "at his best, Hal Bennett is very good" and that, "given hard work, discipline, and luck[,] he could become a first-rate writer" (133). Regarding A Wilderness of Vines, the reviewer in Choice noted that "a reader cannot help respecting Bennett's sensitivity and articulateness, but neither can he remain patient with the persistent thinness of the narrative, the repetitiveness, and the so-what ending." The reviewer of Lord of Dark Places for Publishers Weekly found most of it "artistically first rate" but then asserted that "it quickly goes downhill in the last 50 pages." David Haworth found the novel to be like the works of Jean Genet: "One can't look away, but [the] book is as agreeable as a blow in the face" (450). Dave Smith called Wait until the Evening "a raw, shocking, uneven novel," while Jonathan Yardley said that the novel "is, in several important regards, an impressive and provocative piece of work. It is also, in ways not much less important, frustrating and heavy-handed" (14). Reviewers of his short stories were generally more impressed, with Sandra Ruoff Watson's terming the collection "a compelling, thought-provoking work" and the Publishers Weekly reviewer calling Bennett "a master of plots, character and style." As Yardley concluded, and as many other reviewers agreed, "when Bennett is good he is very, very good" (15), a fact that makes his continued lack of public and critical recognition all the more disheartening.

BIBLIOGRAPHY

Works by Hal Bennett

Novels

A Wilderness of Vines. Garden City, NY: Doubleday, 1966.
The Black Wine. Garden City, NY: Doubleday, 1968.
Lord of Dark Places. New York: Norton, 1970.
Wait until the Evening. Garden City, NY: Doubleday, 1974.
Seventh Heaven. Garden City, NY: Doubleday, 1976.
(as Harriet Janeway). This Passionate Land. New York: NAL, 1979.
(as John D. Revere). The Assassin. Justin Perry Series No. 1. New York: Pinnacle, 1983a.
(as John D. Revere). Vatican Kill. The Assassin Series No. 2. New York: Pinnacle, 1983b.
(as John D. Revere). Born to Kill. The Assassin Series No. 3. New York: Pinnacle, 1984.
(as John D. Revere). Death's Running Mate. The Assassin Series No. 4. New York: Pinnacle, 1985a.
(as John D. Revere). Stud Service. The Assassin Series No. 5. New York: Pinnacle, 1985b.

Short Stories

Insanity Runs in Our Family. Garden City, NY: Doubleday, 1977.
"Virginia in the Window." *Virginia Quarterly Review* 59 (1983): 399–414.
"Chewing Gum." *Black American Literature Forum* 21 (1987a): 379–392.
"Miss Askew on Ice." *Callaloo* 10 (1987b): 1–12.
"Wings of a Dove." *Black American Literature Forum* 23 (1989): 223–230.

Poetry/Drama

The Mexico City Poems/House on Hay Street. Chicago: Obsidian, 1961.

Autobiography

"The Visible Man." *Contemporary Authors Autobiography Series.* Vol. 13. Ed. Joyce Nakamura. Detroit: Gale, 1991.

Studies of Hal Bennett

Bell, Bernard W. *The Afro-American Novel and Its Tradition.* Amherst: University of Mas-
sachusetts Press, 1987.
Clarke, Graham. "Beyond Realism: Recent Black Fiction and the Language of 'The Real
Thing.' " *Black Fiction: New Studies in the Afro-American Novel since 1945.* Ed. A.
Robert Lee. London: Vision, 1980. 204–221.
Haworth, David. "Hot Corridors." Rev. of *Lord of Dark Places. New Statesman* (Oct. 1,
1971): 449–450.
Howe, Irving. "New Black Writers." Rev. of *A Wilderness of Vines* and *The Black Wine.*
Harper's Magazine 239 (Dec. 1969): 130–136.
Miller, James A. "Bennett, Hal." *The Oxford Companion to African American Literature.*
Ed. William L. Andrews, Frances Smith Foster, and Trudier Harris. New York:
Oxford University Press, 1997. 57–58.
Newman, Katharine. "An Evening with Hal Bennett: An Interview." *Black American
Literature Forum* 21 (1987): 357–378.
Rev. of *Insanity Runs in Our Family. Publishers Weekly* (Mar. 21, 1977): 79.
Rev. of *Lord of Dark Places. Publishers Weekly* (Aug. 17, 1970): 48.
Rev. of *A Wilderness of Vines. Choice* 4 (July 1967): 529.
Smith, Dave. Rev. of *Wait until the Evening. Library Journal* 99 (1974): 2498.
Thomas, H. Nigel. *From Folklore to Fiction: A Study of Folk Heroes and Rituals in the Black
American Novel.* Westport, CT: Greenwood, 1988.
Walcott, Ronald. "Hal Bennett." *Dictionary of Literary Biography.* Vol. 33: *Afro-American
Fiction Writers after 1955.* Ed. Thadious M. Davis and Trudier Harris. Detroit: Gale,
1984. 20–28.
———. "The Novels of Hal Bennett, Part I: The Writer as Satirist." *Black World* 23.8
(June 1974): 36–48, 89–97.
———. "The Novels of Hal Bennett, Part II: The Writer as Magician/Priest." *Black World*
23.9 (July 1974): 78–96.
Watson, Sandra Ruoff. Rev. of *Insanity Runs in Our Family. Library Journal* 102 (1977):
1403.
Yardley, Jonathan. Rev. of *Wait Until the Evening. New York Times Book Review* (Sept. 22,
1974): 14–15.

DAVID HENRY BRADLEY, JR.
(1950–   )

Marilyn D. Button

BIOGRAPHY

Though claimed by many Philadelphians as a native author, David Bradley was born and raised in Bedford, Pennsylvania, a predominantly white, farming community in the soft-coal region in the western part of the state. The only son of the late Reverend David H. Bradley, Sr., and his wife, Harriette M. Jackson, Bradley acknowledges considerable family concern lest he adopt formal religion as a vocation. A love for books, however, inspired by his father's avocation as a church historian and journal editor, shifted his attention from the pulpit to the pen.

Bradley excelled as a student. He graduated from the Bedford Area High School in June 1968 with high honors and entered the University of Pennsylvania as Benjamin Franklin, National Achievement, Senatorial, and Presidential Scholar. His undergraduate years were crucial in laying the groundwork for two novels, *South Street* (1975) and his most important achievement, *The Chaneysville Incident* (1981), which won the 1982 PEN/Faulkner Award. Both works reflect his sensitivity and skill in depicting various facets of the black American experience. Upon receiving his B.A. in 1972 summa cum laude, he was awarded a Thouron British-American Exchange Scholarship for study abroad. He attended the Institute for United States Studies in London, where he affirmed his interest in nineteenth-century American history and received the M.A. from King's College, London, in 1974.

Bradley's career as a writer has been multifaceted. Although he is perhaps best known as a novelist, he has also been a prolific contributor of essays, stories, interviews, and reviews to magazines, newspapers, and scholarly periodicals. These include *Esquire, Callaloo, The New Yorker, New York Times Magazine, Time*

Magazine, Philadelphia Magazine, The Village Voice, New York Arts Journal, Southern Review, Los Angeles Times Book Review, New York Times Book Review, and *Washington Post Book World.* He has written three screenplays and is at work on a series of essays on race in America. In spite of having been labeled a "black writer," his artistic vision embraces, but extends beyond, racially defined issues to include such topics as religious faith, politics, and human relationships. Many of his best essays are autobiographical.

In addition to his writing, Bradley has held editorial positions with J. B. Lippincott, Charter Books, and Ace Science Fiction and has earned a reputation as a gifted teacher at such institutions as Massachusetts Institute of Technology (MIT), University of North Carolina, Mary Baldwin College in Staunton, Virginia, Colgate University, and Temple University, where he was professor of creative writing for twenty years. He is the recipient of numerous awards and honors, including a Guggenheim Fellowship in fiction (1989), an NEA Literature Fellowship for nonfiction (1991), a Hazelitt Award for Excellence in the Arts (Pennsylvania) (1982), and an American Academy and Institute of Arts and Letters Award for literature (1982). He currently lives and writes in La Jolla, California, and travels extensively as a guest lecturer.

MAJOR WORKS AND THEMES

Bradley's first published novel, *South Street* (1975), could be considered a tribute to the complex lives of Philadelphia's black ghetto dwellers. It was inspired by the author's frequent visits to a bar on South Street where he listened to, and learned from, its patrons.

The novel's structure accommodates a series of vignettes detailing the lives of men and women who frequent three popular locations: a bar, a church, and a hotel. Although Bradley uses multiple narrative perspectives, the experience of Adlai Stevenson Brown, a young black poet recently arrived in the ghetto to resume writing, provides the novel's narrative focus. By frequenting Lightnin' Ed's Bar and Grill, Brown participates in the loves and lives of some of South Street's regulars: Leroy Briggs, an abusive numbers runner; Rev. J. Peter Sloan, a lecherous preacher; Jake, Brown's benevolent drinking partner and confidant; and the prostitute 'Nessa, Leroy's former girlfriend and the source of Brown's renewed poetic inspiration. Bradley's success in creating vital, astereotypical characters in a depressed city milieu rests largely on his effective use of the vernacular, vivid physical descriptions, and the earthy, ironic humor by which his characters often rise above their circumstances. In spite of its strengths, however, *South Street* failed to sustain the popular and critical attention that it received when first published. Some critics have attempted to account for this phenomenon by noting an absence of thematic coherence among the vignettes in spite of the unifying features of character, plot, and setting.

Bradley's second novel, *The Chaneysville Incident*, was written over a period of eleven years and focuses on a different aspect of the black experience. It was inspired by his mother's discovery of thirteen unmarked graves in a Bedford County burial plot and the regional legend that describes the choice of thirteen escaping slaves to commit suicide rather than be recaptured. Bradley's interest in their fate led first to a short story and then to the four drafts that shaped his award-winning novel.

The novel's dual plot structure blends the story of thirteen escaping slaves with the personal search of John Washington, a black Philadelphia history professor, to come to terms with both his family history and the legacy of racism that informs his present. A telephone call summons him to the rural home of his father's dying friend, Old Jack Crowley, a raconteur in the black oral tradition. Here, he confronts many unanswered questions about both his father, Moses, and his ancestor C. K. Washington, both known in his childhood community for an ambiguous relationship to the white power structure. Researching family manuscripts enables the protagonist to understand both their complex motives and his father's suicide and thus to embrace the rich, but painful, heritage of his past. Washington's journey of historical and personal understanding is complemented by an evolving relationship with his white girlfriend Judith, whose profession as a psychologist emphasizes the many adjustments required when the conflicting demands of past and present, white and black, male and female converge.

CRITICAL RECEPTION

Because Bradley's first novel reflects the author's obvious mastery of narrative form and language, South Street received reviews that were generally positive. Critics alluded only summarily to the novel's lapses of thematic coherence and character credibility. Many recognized Bradley's potential.

Critical reception of The Chaneysville Incident, identified upon publication as a major text of African American fiction, was uniformly favorable. Bradley's achievement was described as brilliant and thoroughly original. His novel was favorably compared to the fiction of Ralph Ellison,* James Baldwin,* and Toni Morrison* and considered by some to be the most significant work by a black male author in two decades.

Critical studies of Bradley's fiction have examined a number of important artistic and thematic concerns. Callahan, for example, recognizes the importance of the oral tradition within which Bradley works. Several critics discuss Bradley's integration of fiction with history in documenting the African American experience. Other critics examine in The Chaneysville Incident the various narrative strategies used to reflect the protagonist's intellectual and emotional growth. Some have addressed the issue of symbolism in Bradley's work, most notably Martin Gliserman, who identifies metaphors of the body as central to the text.

Bradley himself has added generously to the critical debate about his work. In addition to affirming his particular interest in literary form and examining his unique contribution to the African American literary tradition, he identifies an "aesthetic of cost" as a standard of excellence for his work ("The Faith" 18). That cost for Bradley is a painful revelation of self that is demanded by each literary achievement. Critics and readers alike agree that he has amply paid the price of excellence.

BIBLIOGRAPHY

Works by David Henry Bradley, Jr.

Books

South Street. New York: Viking, 1975.
The Chaneysville Incident. New York: Harper and Row, 1981.

Short Stories and Essays

"The Faith." *In Praise of What Persists.* Ed. S. Berg. New York: Harper, 1983. 9–18.
"Christmas Eve." *While Someone Else Is Eating.* Ed. E. Shorris. New York: Doubleday, 1984. 175–98.
"Black and American." *Essays for the '80's.* Ed. W. Vesterman. New York: Random House, 1987a. 397–402.
"Foreword." *Eight Men: Stories by Richard Wright.* New York: Thunder's Mouth Press, 1987b.
"Bringing down the Fire." *Spiritual Quests: The Art and Craft of Religious Writing.* Ed. W. Zinser. Boston: Houghton Mifflin, 1988a.
"On Reading *Native Son.*" *Modern Critical Interpretations of Richard Wright's Native Son.* New York: Chelsea House, 1988b. 143–53.
"Harvest Home." *Family Portraits.* Ed. C. Anthony. Garden City, NY: Doubleday, 1989a. 49–66.
"Looking behind Cane." *The Southern Review* (July 1985). Reprinted in *Afro-American Writing Today.* Baton Rouge: Louisiana State University Press, 1989b.
"Foreword." *A Different Drummer: William Melvin Kelley.* New York: Anchor Books, 1990. xi–xxxii.
"Jim and the Dead Man." *New Yorker* (June 26–July 3, 1995): 126–33.
"Psalms and Gospels." *Communion.* Ed. D. Rosenberg. New York: Doubleday, 1996.

Studies of David Henry Bradley, Jr.

Blake, Susan L., and James A. Miller. "The Business of Writing: An Interview with David Bradley." *Callaloo* 7.2 (1984): 19–39.
Bonetti, Kay. "An Interview with David Bradley." *Missouri Review* 15 (1992): 69–88.
Brigham, Cathy. "Identity, Masculinity, and Desire in David Bradley's Fiction." *Contemporary Literature* 36.2 (Summer 1995): 289–316.
Callahan, John F. "Who We For? The Extended Call of African American Fiction." In *In the African American Grain: The Pursuit of Voice in Twentieth Century Black Fiction.* Urbana: University of Illinois Press, 1988.
Campbell, Jane. "Ancestral Quests." In *Mythic Black Fiction: The Transformation of History.* Knoxville: University of Tennessee Press, 1986. 137–53.

Cooke, Michael G. "After Intimacy: The Search for New Meaning in Recent Black Fiction." In *Afro-American Literature in the Twentieth Century: The Achievement of Intimacy*. New Haven, CT: Yale University Press, 1984.

Ensslen, Klaus. "Fictionalizing History: David Bradley's *The Chaneysville Incident*." *Callaloo* 11.2 (Spring 1988): 280–96.

Gliserman, Martin J. "David Bradley's *The Chaneysville Incident*: The Belly of the Text." *American Imago* 43.2 (Summer 1986): 97–120.

Hogue, Lawrence. "Problematizing History: David Bradley's *The Chaneysville Incident*." *College Language Association Journal* 38.4 (June 1985): 441–60.

Holt, Patricia. "David Bradley." *Publishers Weekly* 219.15 (10 April 1981): 12–14.

Smith, Valerie. "David Bradley." In *Dictionary of Literary Biography*. Detroit: Gale, 1984, vol. 33: *Afro-American Fiction Writers after 1955*. Ed. Thadious M. Davis and Trudier Harris. 1984.

Watkins, Mel. "Thirteen Runaway Slaves and David Bradley." *New York Times Book Review* (19 April 1981): 7, 20–21.

Wilson, Matthew. "The African American Historian: David Bradley's *The Chaneysville Incident*." *African American Review* 29.1 (Spring 1995): 97–107.

GWENDOLYN BROOKS
(1917–)

Suzanne Hotte Massa

BIOGRAPHY

Gwendolyn Brooks was born in Topeka, Kansas, on June 7, 1917, to Keziah Corinne Wims and David Anderson Brooks. Soon after Gwendolyn's birth, the family moved to Chicago, where her brother Raymond was born. They lived an orderly and structured life in a quiet neighborhood. As a young girl, Brooks kept to herself. So when she turned to writing poetry at the very young age of seven, her parents supported and encouraged her interest. Her mother was young Gwendolyn's first and most ardent fan, and her father provided inspiration for his daughter by reading to her a great deal from authors such as Paul Laurence Dunbar. Brooks graduated from Wilson Junior College in 1936 with an associate of literature and arts degree. In 1939 she married Henry L. Blakely, with whom she had two children, Henry and Nora.

In spite of the demands of motherhood and marriage, Brooks still devoted time to her illustrious professional career. She published her first book of poetry, *A Street in Bronzeville*, in 1945, followed by the publication of *Annie Allen* in 1949. Her only novella, *Maud Martha*, was published in 1953. Although she never again published fiction, she wrote and published numerous volumes of poetry. Central to her work are her personal preoccupations: racism, poverty, dignity, happiness, American family life, and the devastation of war. Brooks has spent her entire professional career as both a poet and a teacher, having taught at several universities. She currently holds the Gwendolyn Brooks Chair in black literature and creative writing at Chicago State University.

Brooks was awarded the Guggenheim Fellowship as well as the National Institute of Arts and Letters Award in 1946. *Mademoiselle* magazine named her Woman of the Year in 1947. Since 1968, Ms. Brooks has been Poet Laureate of

Illinois; in 1985 she was named Consultant in Poetry to the Library of Congress; and in 1988 she was inducted into the National Women's Hall of Fame. Additionally, she has been the recipient of numerous awards for her poetry. The most notable of the awards is the Pulitzer Prize for her collection *Annie Allen* in 1950, making Brooks the first African American to receive that honor.

WORKS AND THEMES

Gwendolyn Brooks, widely known as a Pulitzer Prize-winning poet, is also the author of the preeminent feminist novella *Maud Martha*. *Maud Martha* is the biography of a fictional woman. In the opening chapter, Maud is seven years old, and in the closing chapter she has just learned that she is pregnant with her second child. Although parallels can be drawn between Maud Martha and Gwendolyn Brooks, this novella is not Brooks' autobiography. Both Brooks and Maud have shared similar experiences, but so have innumerable other women. Maud is a typical young girl: she has dreams and questions, she is curious and loving, and at times she is insecure and envious. As she matures and gains life experience, she learns to cope with her youthful insecurities. Maud marries Paul Phillips and settles into a less than satisfactory marriage. Paul's wage-earning ability is limited; he does not share Maud's enthusiasm for the arts; and he is more interested in playing cards and drinking liquor with his buddies than developing a relationship with Maud. Instead of dwelling on her misfortune, Maud continues to be congenial and compassionate. She quietly ponders the irrational behavior of Paul as well as the other people in her neighborhood. Maud chooses to find her joy from within herself. It is exactly Maud's manner of coping that makes Brooks' *Maud Martha* an exceptional collection of poetic vignettes.

This novella is, arguably, the text that changed the face of contemporary African American women's literature, ensuring the acceptance and popularity of writers such as Toni Morrison* and Alice Walker.* Brooks, through Maud, speaks of the everyday life of an African American woman but deftly avoids stereotyping her. Brooks' exquisite impressionist poetry-prose story is set in Chicago. Maud Martha finds peace within herself and joy in her life despite the multiple layers of oppression that weigh upon her. Maud, like countless other typical women, seeks sparks of joy to brighten her life. Her voice is colored by her experience as a less than attractive African American woman, and Brooks' novella speaks of the manner in which oppression is specific to African American women. Maud is one of the early atypical African American females of contemporary fiction because she is not depicted as the mammy, mulatto, or exotic sex object. Maud is physically trapped in her oppressively small, bleak kitchenette apartment with her husband. She is additionally entrapped by society's dictum that forces women to forego displays of anger and instead requires that they be consistently *nice*. Maud silently (the voice society has appropriated to women) ponders the complex nature of her oppressions. In the process she reveals her spirit, which remains vital despite the inequities to which she is subjected.

Maud's appropriately subdued voice is a hallmark of Brooks' impressionistic style. However, Maud's subdued voice belies the feminist sensibilities that are the core of this text. When she and Paul first move into their kitchenette, Maud is consumed with optimism. She carefully scrutinizes every inch of the apartment, imagining how lovely it will be when she completes her decorating scheme, only to discover that the landlord does not allow the furniture to be rearranged. Shortly after learning about the obstacle that halts her redecorating plans, Maud sees her first cockroach, followed by the realization that sharing a bathroom with all of her neighbors is repulsive. Her early optimism was fading as she noted, "There was a whole lot of grayness here" (64). Maud's disappointment is clear; her dream of a cozy home in which to begin her marriage has been shattered by harsh reality.

Maud Martha, like most women, is a victim of the culture that assigns unreasonable standards of beauty to women. She does not fit into the stereotypical mold of beauty, which is characterized by light skin, European features, and silky hair. In an era when a woman is judged by the quality of the man she is able to attract, Maud's physical appearance leaves her few choices. Her husband, Paul, is as handsome as he is irresponsible. His oppressively meager income keeps her trapped in the disappointingly gray, tiny kitchenette rental. Yet, Maud carries with her the ability to find peace and joy in her everyday existence that she first recognized in herself as a young girl. She appreciates beauty in common, everyday objects and moments.

As a young girl she was enamored by the dandelions that speckled the lawn, calling them "[y]ellow jewels for everyday, studding the patched green dress of her back yard" (2). That optimism followed her into adulthood. Even in the *grayness* of her kitchenette life, Maud finds amusement and delight in observing the eccentricities of her neighbors. "Of the people in her building, Maud Martha was the most amused by Oberto . . . Oberto was a happy man" (108). When her mother comes to call for tea, Maud takes great care in preparing her table:

Maud Martha spread her little second-hand table—a wide tin band was wound beneath the top for strength—with her finest wedding gift, a really good white luncheon cloth. She brought out white coffee cups and saucers, sugar, milk, and a little pink pot of cocoa. She brought a plate of frosted gingerbread. Mother and daughter sat down to Tea. (166–167)

These are some of the sparks of joy that brighten Maud's life.

Maud is also subjected to racial oppression, which she tolerates in enraged silence. One day when Maud was treating herself in the beauty parlor, the stylist, Sonia, was interrupted by a white saleswoman. Maud overheard the saleswoman say, "People think this is a snap job. It ain't. I work like a nigger to make a few lousy pennies. A few lousy pennies" (138). To Maud's horror and chagrin, Sonia ignored the crass remark. After the saleswoman had gone away, Maud confronted Sonia, who nonchalantly replied, "What would be the point? Why make enemies? Why go getting all hot and bothered all the time?" (142). Although Maud could understand the resignation in Sonia's silence, Maud was infuriated at the white saleswoman for her brazen insensitivity.

Maud is further oppressed by virtue of her gender: female, the second-class citizen. Society dictates that women forgo their emotions in favor of catering to men, children, and anyone else who might benefit from the comforts of a *nice woman*. After her daughter, Paulette, was born, Maud longed for the revival of some of her family traditions that built the memories of her own childhood. Paul, however, was uncooperative. So Maud spent Christmas Day alternating between entertaining and resisting Paul and his friends. "She passed round Blatz, and inhaled the smoke of the guests' cigarettes, and watched the soaked tissue that had enfolded the corner Chicken Inn's burned barbecue drift listlessly to her rug. She removed from her waist the arm of Chuno Jones, Paul's best friend" (107). Instead of building pleasant family holiday traditions, Maud quietly seethed as she dutifully acquiesced to her husband's desires.

Maud found her most blissful moments on the verge of motherhood. She found a new power in herself, as well as a new camaraderie with some of her neighbors. After Paulette had been bathed and dressed, Maud lost herself in reverie: "She preferred to think, now, about how well she felt. Had she ever in her life felt so well?" (98). Because her labor had been so rapid, two women neighbors were the only people present at Paulette's birth. Maud felt warm gratitude. "People. Weren't they sweet. She had never said more than 'Hello, Mrs. Barksdale' and 'Hello, Mrs. Cray' to these women before. But as soon as something happened to her, in they trooped. People were sweet" (99). Maud was officially connected with the ultimate sense of sisterhood that motherhood engenders, linking her with mothers of every kind since the beginning of time. Her joy on this occasion is unequaled. She takes great pleasure in the pulse of life. Fertility and progeny connect women with the cycles of nature, whether it is the birth of a child or the simple, unrestrained beauty of a new blossom.

Brooks' novella speaks to feminist sensibilities in a specifically impressionistic style. Despite the unpleasantness of her life, Maud finds solace and even joy in the beauty of nature, the bringing forth of life, and her relationships with other women.

CRITICAL RECEPTION

Maud Martha was originally published in 1953, the same year that James Baldwin's* Go Tell It on the Mountain* was published and the year after Ralph Ellison's* classic *Invisible Man* exploded on the literary scene. Even though Brooks won the Pulitzer Prize for poetry in 1950, there was a noticeable void of criticism for *Maud Martha* because it was obscured in the shadows of novels written by African American men. Although the critics wrote favorable reviews, they only scratched the surface by focusing on the novella's similarity to Brooks' poetry. The criticism was a reflection of the era in which it was written. In the 1950s, when women's voices were more apt to be muted, the novella was dismissed as trivial, if exquisite.

Most reviewers agreed that Brooks' style was delightfully impressionistic and dismissed the vignettes as musings of no relevance. *The New Yorker*'s nameless reviewer comments on "[t]he author's impressionistic style—a hopeful piling up of small details" (153). The reviewer dismissed the work as sparse, but frivolous, vignettes. Hubert Creekmore in the *New York Times* wrote, "It is presented in flashes, almost gasps, of sensitive lightness—distillations of the significance of each incident—and reminds of Imagist poems" (4). *Maud Martha* was barely recognized and grossly misunderstood.

But in the 1980s, when women's voices became noticeably audible, contemporary critics revealed the feminist value of *Maud Martha*. Mary Helen Washington explains the heightened awareness of racial and gender inequities, which were more readily recognized twenty-five years after *Maud Martha* was first published:

In 1953 no one seemed prepared to call *Maud Martha* a novel about bitterness, rage, self-hatred and the silence that results from suppressed anger. No one recognized it as a novel dealing with the very sexism and racism that these reviews enshrined. What the reviewers saw as exquisite lyricism was actually the truncated stuttering of a woman whose rage makes her literally unable to speak. (453)

In 1984, Patricia H. Lattin and Vernon E. Lattin pointed out, "It is a very loose organization consisting of a series of short vignettes, and with lyrical language never far from poetry, this short novel has a deceptively light and simple exterior which belies the complexity of the interior" (181). Barbara Christian also writes favorably about *Maud Martha*, talking about Brooks, being a pioneer in African American fiction: "Brooks's contribution was a turning point in Afro-American fiction, for it presented for the first time a black woman not as a mammy, wench, mulatto or downtrodden heroine, but as an ordinary human being in all the wonder of her complexity" (239).

It seems that the climate of the 1970s and the 1980s was more conducive to an understanding and acceptance of Brooks' themes. Now Brooks' novella continues to receive the honest and thoughtful recognition it deserves.

BIBLIOGRAPHY

Works by Gwendolyn Brooks

A Street in Bronzeville. New York: Harper, 1945. (Poetry)
Annie Allen. New York: Harper, 1949. (Poetry)
Maud Martha. New York: Harper, 1953, Chicago: Third World Press, 1993. (Novella)
Bronzeville Boys and Girls. New York: Harper, 1956. (Poetry)
The Bean Eaters. New York: Harper, 1960. (Poetry)

Selected Poems. New York: Harper and Row, 1963. (Poetry)
In the Time of Detachment, in the Time of Cold. Chicago: Centennial Commission of Illinois, 1965. (Poetry)
For Illinois 1968: A Sesquicentennial Poem. New York: Harper, 1968a. (Poetry)
In the Mecca: Poems. New York: Harper and Row, 1968b. (Poetry)
Riot. Detroit: Broadside Press, 1969. (Poetry)
Family Pictures. Detroit: Broadside Press, 1970. (Poetry)
Aloneness. Detroit: Broadside Press, 1971a. (Poetry)
Jump Bad: A New Chicago Anthology. Detroit: Broadside Press, 1971b. (Poetry)
The World of Gwendolyn Brooks. New York: Harper and Row, 1971c. (Poetry)
Aurora. Detroit: Broadside Press, 1972. (Poetry)
The Tiger Who Wore White Gloves. Chicago: Third World Press, 1974. (Poetry)
Beckonings. Detroit: Broadside Press, 1975. (Poetry)
Primer for Blacks. Chicago: Black Position Press, 1980. (Poetry)
To Disembark. Chicago: Third World Press, 1981. (Poetry)
Black Love. Chicago: Brooks Press, 1982. (Poetry)
Mayor Harold Washington: Chicago, the I Will City. Chicago: Brooks Press, 1983. (Poetry)
The Near-Johannesburg Boy, and Other Poems. Chicago: David, 1987. (Poetry)
Gottschalk and the Grande Tarantelle. Chicago: David, 1988a. (Poetry)
Winnie. Chicago: Third World Press, 1988b. (Poetry)
Children Coming Home. Chicago: David, 1991. (Poetry)

Studies of Gwendolyn Brooks

Butcher, Fanny. Review of *Maud Martha. Chicago Sunday Tribune,* 4 Oct. 1953: 11.
Christian, Barbara. "Nuance and the Novella: A Study of Gwendolyn Brooks's *Maud Martha." A Life Distilled: Gwendolyn Brooks, Her Poetry and Fiction.* Ed. Maria K. Mootry and Gary Smith. Urbana: University of Illinois Press, 1987. 239–253.
Creekmore, Hubert. Review of *Maud Martha. New York Times,* 4 Oct. 1953: 4.
Israel, Charles. "Gwendolyn Brooks." *Dictionary of Literary Biography.* Vol. 5. 1980: 100–106.
Kent, George E. *A Life of Gwendolyn Brooks.* Lexington: University of Kentucky Press, 1990.
Lattin, Patricia H., and Vernon E. Lattin. "Dual Vision in Gwendolyn Brooks's *Maud Martha." Critique: Studies in Contemporary Fiction* 25.4 (1984): 180–188.
Monjo, Nicolas. Review of *Maud Martha. Saturday Review* (31 Oct. 1953): 41.
Review of *Maud Martha. New Yorker* (10 Oct. 1953): 153.
Rosenberger, Coleman. Review of *Maud Martha. Herald Tribune,* 18 Oct. 1953, Bk. R: 4.
Shaw, Harry B. *Gwendolyn Brooks.* Boston: Twayne, 1980.
Washington, Mary Helen. "Taming All That Anger Down: Rage and Silence in Gwendolyn Brooks's *Maud Martha." Massachusetts Review* 24.2 (1983): 453–466.
Winslow, Henry F. Review of *Maud Martha. The Crisis* (Feb. 1954): 114.
Wright, Stephen Caldwell, ed. *On Gwendolyn Brooks: Reliant Contemplation.* Ann Arbor: University of Michigan Press, 1996.

CECIL MORRIS BROWN
(1943-   )

Samuel B. Garren

BIOGRAPHY

Cecil Morris Brown was born in Bolton, North Carolina, the son of Dorothy and Culphert Brown. Until he was thirteen years old, Cecil was raised, along with his younger brother, by his aunt and uncle, Amanda and Lofton Freeman. During this period, Culphert Brown served a prison sentence. Although Dorothy Brown lived nearby, she took no role in her sons' early upbringing.

Growing up in rural southeastern North Carolina, Brown worked from an early age in the cotton and tobacco fields. His aunt and uncle provided love and security and encouraged his interest in school. Brown had a strong, positive bond with Uncle Lofton, calling him Daddy throughout his early years. When his father got out of prison, however, Cecil and his brother reluctantly moved in with Dorothy and Culphert. Brown shared the father's hard life as a sharecropper, plowing the fields after school, tending his own five-acre field, and enduring the father's often harsh discipline.

His horizons broadened by a summer spent in New York City, Brown became determined to avoid his father's fate. In 1961, he won a scholarship to North Carolina A & T State University in Greensboro. He transferred to Columbia University, graduating with a B.A. in English in 1966. He then earned an M.A. in English from the University of Chicago in 1967. After teaching at several institutions, Brown worked as a screenwriter for Warner Brothers and Universal Studios. In 1977 he coauthored the screenplay for the movie *Which Way Is Up?*, starring Richard Pryor. Returning to the University of California, Berkeley, to teach, Brown received his Ph.D. in folklore in 1993, writing his dissertation on the African American folk hero Stagolee.

MAJOR WORKS AND THEMES

The Life and Loves of Mr. Jiveass Nigger was a trailblazing novel, published in 1969. It presents the picaresque adventures of George Washington, "hustler, jiveass" (8). In the Prologue we learn that Washington, a man of many names, was born and grew up in North Carolina. Most of the novel is set in Copenhagen, and many of his adventures involve sexual encounters with white women. George's affair with the consul at the U.S. Embassy, Ruth Smith, helps him stay in Copenhagen despite a shortage of money. After successfully surviving for some time with his wits and sexual ability, George becomes disgusted with the kind of life he is leading. Ruth Smith commits suicide, and he helps another acquaintance to obtain money for an abortion. Ready now to return to the United States, George hopes to put into practice back home the truth he has realized: "If you're black you don't need to get at anything. You're already there. You can live right out of your insides" (203). The novel's Epilogue, however, questions the validity of any of George's pronouncements. Instead, all may be "jive" (212).

The novelty of the book is its skillful blending of different literary forms. It succeeds both as bildungsroman and picaresque. It incorporates the spirit of the African American folktale as well. (In his Preface to the 1991 edition, the author states that he intended the book's hero to be "the childlike, amoral trickster from African American folklore" [xxxi]). The book also has the sexual frankness associated with the 1960s and occasionally uses stream-of-consciousness technique to reveal Washington's mind. The author realized, in fact, that this technique "was a metaphor for black consciousness in a white world" (1991, xxxiii).

As Gerald Early has noted, one theme of the novel is fatherhood. The comic irony of George Washington's name is one indication. Named for the father of his country, George almost always lies. His relationship with his father is troubled. Early in life, George "began to hate his father who was buried deep inside of him" (7). His adventures in Copenhagen are an attempt to run away from this part of himself. He discovers himself, however, only when he tires of his life abroad and decides to return home. As Early notes, black–white relationships, abortion, and homosexuality are part of the novel's complex exploration of this theme of fatherhood. Early also finds as a theme the problem of communication, especially among black men. Despite the pleasure the black expatriates seem to find in verbal jousting, the novel shows how the use of jiving and insults "ultimately defeats intimacy and leads to destructive self-hatred" (xix). At the end, George wonders whether jiving is a vicious circle from which he cannot escape.

One strength of the novel is the portrait of the expatriate African American community in Copenhagen. The individuals are sharply realized and varied. Their special perspective sharpens the book's satirical look at the United States. As the novel progresses, the episodic nature of the plot becomes apparent and reveals a weakness in the overall structure. The richness of the language, the exuberant comic spirit, and the sexual openness, however, earn the book an important place in African American fiction.

Brown's second novel, *Days without Weather*, which draws upon the author's experience as a screenwriter, was published in 1983. Jonah Drinkwater, a black comedian from the South, struggles in Los Angeles until his uncle finds him a job in Hollywood. Jonah becomes friends with the author of a hard-hitting screenplay about Gabriel Prosser's slave revolt in 1800. The script is bought by the studio, and Jonah is made a coproducer. When the studio rewrites the script, softening its radical nature, the black actors and actresses revolt. Cynically, the head of the studio records the riot and incorporates it into the film, further cheapening the final product. The film is a hit, and Jonah's disillusionment with Hollywood is complete. His consolation is to lash out at the audience during a routine at a comedy club that ends in another riot. Although he considers returning to the South, surprisingly, at the end of the novel, Jonah stays in Los Angeles. He shakes his fist at Hollywood, saying to himself, "Corrupted as you are . . . , I will conquer you!" (250).

One strength of the novel is an inside view of the world of black comedians in Los Angeles. The scenes set at the hangout for these mostly unemployed comics are well done. Other aspects of the book, however, are not successful. The theme that Hollywood filmmakers care for profits, not truth, is hardly new. Jonah's willingness to enrich himself in the process lessens his stance as rebel against the system. Characters seemingly introduced as part of important subplots vanish for long stretches. Many persons never rise above the level of stereotype. In terms of structure, the novel seems split between the portraits of comedy and Hollywood. The system Jonah attacks as a comic rewards him at the same time for helping make movies. If Brown had restricted himself to the world of black comedians, he could have created an incisive, unique work. By submerging this subject in a typically anti-Hollywood novel, however, he lost the possibilities of a worthy theme. In 1984, Brown did receive the Before Columbus Foundation American Book Award for this novel.

Brown's most recent work is *Coming Up Down Home: A Memoir of a Southern Childhood*, published in 1993, an eloquent account of the author's life up until the time of his going to college. He describes growing up in rural North Carolina, a difficult way of life made even more so due to the imprisonment of Cecil's father and the absence of his mother for his first thirteen years. Tension in the book derives from the contrast between Uncle Lofton, who raises Cecil in a living, supportive manner, and the father, a harsh taskmaster who takes over Cecil's life in his teenaged years. One theme is Cecil's struggle to break away from a way of life he feels doomed to follow. The father at times actively discourages his son's efforts at school. By winning a scholarship to college, Cecil succeeds in establishing his own direction in life. In the book's Coda, thirty years later, Cecil returns home. In an emotional confrontation with his father, he finally learns why his father was imprisoned. In a drunken argument, the father murdered his wife's favorite cousin. With this knowledge, Cecil feels freed of a major burden of his past.

The portrait of southern life is outstanding. Individuals, customs, ways of speech, and folk survivals are affectionately rendered. We follow the author's playing pass the button in school, learning why the king snake is the worst to kill, and anticipating the new preacher's first sermon. He wins the hog-judging contest, masters magical tricks only to be denied performance on local television because of his race, and observes beatniks in Greenwich Village during a summer of his high school years. The son's view of the father as the archetypical "bad nigger" (58) is a theme to be found in both of Brown's novels. The author's decision at the end to become a writer places the book within the *Künstlerroman* tradition represented by James Joyce's *A Portrait of the Artist as a Young Man*.

CRITICAL RECEPTION

Brown's critical standing rests primarily upon his first novel. Its republication in 1991 with a Preface by the author and an Introduction by Gerald Early shows its central place in African American literature. The novel's sexual frankness and comic spirit opened the way for such later authors as Ishmael Reed* and Clarence Major.* At the same time, the hero's quest for self-identity and the celebration of African American speech recall such earlier authors as Ralph Ellison.* Brown's going beyond white stereotypes to reveal in the frankest language the true self of George Washington shows the influence of writers of the 1960s whom he admired: Amiri Baraka, Malcolm X, and Eldridge Cleaver. Early also points out the wide range of influences on Brown, including the satires of Swift and Twain, the travel novels of Melville, and Fielding's *Tom Jones*.

Initial reviews were both positive and negative, but the consensus was that a major talent had appeared. Several critics, however, wondered if a remark made in the novel reflected the author's attitude. George Washington says, " 'All the publishers are interested in selling books and if you say something about sex and being a nigger then you got a bestseller" (206). Most critics, though, believed Brown rose above such cynicism and had serious goals for the novel.

Brown's second novel, *Days without Weather*, received little critical attention, and most of it was negative. David Bradley was especially harsh, criticizing the book's plot structure, character development, dialogue, and description. The exploitation of African American culture by the film industry and the difficult task facing the black satirist in the United States were themes not artistically realized by the novel.

The response to *Coming Up Down Home* was uniformly positive. The writing was viewed as realistic, entertaining, and inspirational. Randall Kenan noted that Brown's relationship with Uncle Lofton "provides a rare glimpse of a nurturing, patient, loving relationship between black men and boys." Kenan also praises the "music" of the southern language and the book's "complexity of vision and purpose" (13).

BIBLIOGRAPHY

Works by Cecil Morris Brown

The Life and Loves of Mr. Jiveass Nigger. New York: Farrar, 1969.
Which Way Is Up? Screenplay. With Carl Gottlieb. Dir. Michael Schultz. Universal. 1977.
Days without Weather. New York: Farrar, 1983.
The Life and Loves of Mr. Jiveass Nigger. Dark Tower Ser. Introduction Gerald Early. Preface Cecil Brown. Hopewell, NJ: Ecco, 1991.
Coming Up Down Home: A Memoir of a Southern Childhood. Hopewell, NJ: Ecco, 1993.
"Stagolee: From Shack Bully to Culture Hero." Diss., University of California, Berkeley, 1993. *DAI* 55 (1995): 2827A.

Studies of Cecil Morris Brown

Bradley, David. "Going Hollywood." Review of *Days without Weather. New York Times Book Review* (17 Apr. 1983): 26.
Bright, Jean M. "Cecil Brown." *Dictionary of Literary Biography.* Vol. 33. *Afro-American Fiction Writers after 1955.* Ed. Thadious M. Davis and Trudier Harris. Detroit: Gale, 1984. 32–35.
Carson, Warren J. "Brown, Cecil." *The Oxford Companion to African American Literature.* Ed. William L. Andrews, Frances Smith Foster, and Trudier Harris. New York: Oxford University Press, 1997. 100–101.
Early, Gerald. Introduction. *The Life and Loves of Mr. Jiveass Nigger.* Dark Tower Ser. Hopewell, NJ: Ecco, 1991. xi–xxiii.
Elder, Lonne, III. Review of *The Life and Loves of Mr. Jiveass Nigger. Black World* (June 1970): 51–52.
"Is Blindness Best?" Review of *The Life and Loves of Mr. Jiveass Nigger. Time* (2 Feb. 1970): 72–73.
Kenan, Randall. "Life with Both Daddy and Father." Review of *Coming Up Down Home. New York Times Book Review* (22 Aug. 1993): 13.
Lehmann-Haupt, Christopher. "If You're Black, Get Back, and Jive to Survive." Review of *The Life and Loves of Mr. Jiveass Nigger. New York Times* (14 Jan. 1970): 45.
Rhodes, Richard. Review of *The Life and Loves of Mr. Jiveass Nigger. New York Times Book Review* (1 Feb. 1970): 4.
Schraufnagel, Noel. *From Apology to Protest: The Black American Novel.* Deland, FL: Everett/Edwards, 1973. 132–33.

FRANK LONDON BROWN
(1927–1962)

Charles Tita

BIOGRAPHY

The eldest of three children, Frank London Brown was born in Kansas City, Missouri, on October 7, 1927, to Myrtle and Frank London Brown, Sr. In 1939, the Brown family left the Jim Crow South and migrated to Illinois in search of a tolerable social climate and economic opportunity. They settled in the slums of the South Side of Chicago, where Frank Brown attended Colman Elementary School and DuSable High School. The growth and maturation of Brown as an artist took root in the very South Side streets that registered on his mind grim daily statistics about the desperate nature of the human condition. While pursuing formal education, he was receiving, also, informal lessons from around him—lessons he would later tap into as he battered his way into adulthood. Kathleen A. Hauke notes that "his perspective was formed during the hours he spent in Morrie's Record Shop under the elevated tracks of Fifty-eight Street, listening to such jazz and blues performers as Thelonious Monk, Joe Williams, and Muddy Waters" (25).

In 1945 (at age eighteen), Brown graduated from high school and went on to Wilberforce University in Ohio, where he spent only a few months. He then joined the army in January 1946, and while in the army he sang baritone (thanks to the informal street lessons of his childhood) in a band. On November 30, 1947, he married Evelyn Mari Jones, his high school sweetheart, and they had three daughters, as well as a son, who died soon after birth. Brown had an unrelenting thirst for knowledge, and he read and studied voraciously. He attended Roosevelt University on the GI Bill, and while studying for his undergraduate degree he held different jobs to support himself and his family. He worked as machinist, postal clerk, loan interviewer, and tavern owner. At this time Brown was also beginning to write short stories that pointed to his budding creative genius.

Brown earned his B.A. degree in 1951 and briefly attended Kent College of Law in Chicago, while supporting his family working as bartender, jazz singer, union organizer of textile workers, and associate editor of *Ebony* magazine. In 1959, Brown earned his master's degree and also began working on his Ph.D. in political science at the University of Chicago. With the publication of *Trumbull Park* (1959), Brown gained recognition as a writer and social activist. He became a fellow of the Committee on Social Thought at the University of Chicago under John U. Nef, as well as director of the university's Union Research Center. Brown was filled with vigor like a locomotive picking up speed, but tragically he discovered in the summer of 1961 that he had leukemia. Although he was growing weaker physically, he remained vibrant intellectually to the very end. He died at the University of Illinois Educational Research Hospital on March 12, 1962; he was only thirty-four.

MAJOR WORKS AND THEMES

In *Trumbull Park*, Brown weaves a rich tapestry of themes that capture human endurance in the light of debilitating environmental and social impediments that threaten the will and zeal to live. Racial violence is the eye of the storm that stirs the actions delineated in the novel. The novel draws its material from recent history. *Trumbull Park* is set in Chicago at the dawn of the national thrust toward racial integration. The characters and incidents depicted are fictionalized tropes denoting difficulties that sought to frustrate integration. *Trumbull Park* feeds grudgingly on racialized archetypes that mirror the prevailing social climate in which Brown lived and experienced firsthand despicable acts of race-related violence. Because Brown, his wife, and children were actually the tenth family to move into Trumbull Park, where they lived through the racial violence of the years 1954–1957, as described in the novel, the narrative has an autobiographical orientation.

An appeal for minority activism within the confines of law is a theme that resonates throughout the novel. Because Brown was involved personally in the events described in the novel, he constructs in the narrative of *Trumbull Park* an authentic air of historical truth. Race and racism are depicted with telling poignancy, a sort of "unvarnished atmosphere of immediacy that stems from the long established tradition begun by the early slave narratives. There, too, the writer was driven to tell what happened to him, to make the readers see and hear exactly how it was so that they would be aroused to act on behalf of all who remain oppressed" (Miller 625). Although young people now have no direct personal knowledge of the 1940s and 1950s, guises of similar racialized tensions persist in our world of today that constitute a metaphorical vehicle for our understanding of the tenor of the protracted tensions described in the novel. *Trumbull Park* pays special attention to the resilience of the oppressed as they stoically resist the walls of cynical equivocations wrapped around them by callous law enforcement officials.

The exercise of agency by blacks to counter debilitating race problems is another important theme that qualifies black acitivism in *Trumbull Park*. The novel is a narrative that constructs a clash of man with fellow man, and this theme of interhuman conflict is denoted by a metaphor of two buildings: the Gardener for oppressed blacks and Trumbull Park for racist whites. The Gardener—dilapidated, rat-infested, and treacherous—is described (by a central character, Helen) as a monster that kills: "Look, look at that big, ramshackle, firetrap. Look at it, look at what killed babydoll. Look at it, Buggy!" (9). The Gardener captures the monstrosity of white oppression; its "red brick was covered with smudgy streaks, and the gray mortar had oozed between the red bricks and dried" (9), and it is named after Mr. Gardener, "the owner. He didn't live there, but it seemed like he did, because the Gardener Building was old, like Mr. Gardener, and rotten. Rotten from the inside out" (1).

Helen and Buggy, the two main characters, understand that countering this racism needs to be a slow engagement, lest they are devoured by it. Their quest begins with an open rejection of the Gardener; in spite of a concerted effort by the whites at Trumbull Park to keep them out, Buggy and Helen take up residence there, as is their right under the law.

In *Trumbull Park*, the image of the strong black woman as leader is of thematic importance. Long before feminism was fashionable, the black woman had to garner strength to give stability to her family when the tides of the social environment were not in her favor. Her assertion of strength, a common topos in slave narratives as well, is not at all an effacement of the man's maleness; it is simply a sustaining pool from which the family and community draw. In *Trumbull Park*, the women (Helen and Mona) pursue and apply for accommodation at Trumbull Park, at a time when their husbands are too overwhelmed by the crushing weight of racism and prejudice. Even when Buggy feels that it is easier to remain in the rat-infested Gardener rather than face white resistance at Trumbull Park, his wife (Helen) actively seeks to counter his reluctance: "Yes, I know what is going on in Trumbull Park. But that stuff can't last long. It just can't" (14). After they have moved into Trumbull Park, Helen notes (in the midst of all the violence that white tenants are inflicting on the few black tenants) that "we got to take this foolishness of these white folks in stride. Live in spite of them" (45). Then when the small community of blacks at Trumbull Park begins to feel overpowered by the consistent attacks by white tenants, Helen again comes up with a plan aimed at victory; she suggests to the other black residents of Trumbull Park that they should start having a few meetings of their own to find ways of aggressively countering racism.

Throughout *Trumbull Park*, an active resistance overrides the sort of passive acquiescence that characterized blacks' social life in the years that preceded the Harlem Renaissance. The black characters in the novel are poised to challenge the view that whites' brutalization of African Americans is an accepted social behavior in racialized American society. However, this theme of resistance captures the complexity of American racism as we have all come to know it. Although blacks are protected under the law to pursue economic and social well-being, there is still a degree of hypocrisy in the ranks of law enforcement—there are those officials who are bedeviled by racist passions. Thus, racism in itself becomes a living monster that victimizes both whites (who are possessed by it and seek to inflict it) and blacks (who run from it but also seek to fight it), and the pervasiveness of this monstrosity in a society built on the creed of freedom and equality gives a naturalistic twist to *Trumbull Park*.

Brown's second novel, *The Myth Maker* (1969), published posthumously, was written in the years between the publication of *Trumbull Park* and his tragic death in 1962. Although *Trumbull Park* marked Brown as a writer of great talent and brought him immediate literary recognition, in *The Myth Maker* he reveals extraordinary powers of character analysis, showing himself to be a significant, powerful thinker. Set in the city, presumably Chicago, *The Myth Maker* evokes such major subjects as crime, child abuse, starvation, racism, and the suffering of the innocent.

In *The Myth Maker*, its protagonist, Ernest Day, sees his "blackness" as the basis of his entrapment in a racialized society. At the beginning of the novel, he appears on "Fifty Eight Street near the corner of Calumet" (13), and his hunger turns immediately into anger when a young black boy runs up to him begging for a nickel. Ernest walks away because he sees a sad reflection of himself in the image of the famished black boy: "Ernest walked away from the child, glancing at himself in the mirror of the storefront windows. The light of the sun upon his dark skin made him seem shiny, and he hated himself when he was shiny. He turned away from himself" (13). The novel depicts racism as a monster that has been thrown upon society, turning Ernest into a skeptic who meditates on the meaning of life: "Once he asked himself what it was all for—this walking and reading and looking at people and hating his darkness" (14).

The Myth Maker also explores self-hatred as a basis of mental degeneration and crime. Since Ernest is possessed by self-hatred, he seeks to destroy anything that serves as a mirror reflection of himself. In a state of self-rejection, Ernest "leaned on a girder underneath the "L" stand, swallowing the odor of frying hamburgers and watching the people go by" (15), and one of the people he sees is an old black man whose smile and batteredness remind him once more of himself: "A man, old, bent a bit, and smelling like dry gin and talcum powder, walked by. The man smiled at him, and the light from the hamburger stand seemed to hit the old man's even, yellow teeth" (15). Ernest's self-hatred drives him to go after the old man, and he strangles him, returning a random act of kindness with death. He rationalizes the killing by convincing himself that life was meaningless for the old black man in a racist environment.

Everywhere in *The Myth Maker* the tragic is heightened by the indifference of the universe. The novel alludes to Sophocles' *Oedipus Rex*, in which King Oedipus, after learning about his ill-fated identity, suddenly feels completely alone in an indifferent world. Similarly, Ernest realizes that he has, indeed, killed his own soul in the very chilling act of strangling an innocent old man. He realizes, also, that the universe is unsympathetic with him: "He looked about, looked up at the sky, and at the stars that seemed flawless and still, and at the moon smiling idiotically as it always has no matter what tragedy, what death, what particular birth, took place below" (18).

The Myth Maker, like Dostoyevsky's *Crime and Punishment*, traces the theme of crime and punishment. As Ernest struggles to elude the police for the crime he has committed, his friend, Willard, reminds him that it is conscience, not the police, that he would have to deal with: "You poor son of a bitch. You killed a man to be free, and now you are a slave. . . . Your conscience has put you in jail. You're worse off than you were before!" (163). The ending of the novel is an irony on Ernest's attempt to escape from himself and the law. He tries to momentarily escape the stings of his conscience by indulging in a sexual act with his girlfriend, Freda, but they are interrupted by two police officers who have come to arrest Ernest:

And he moved into her, inside her. And he held her close to him. And he tasted her kiss, and breathed in every breath she breathed out. He gave himself to her, and took her to himself, and she called his name just the way he'd always wanted someone to call his name (178), [but just then] someone knocked on the door. (179)

CRITICAL RECEPTION

Published in 1959, *Trumbull Park*, named after a Chicago housing development, is the novel that propelled Brown to literary recognition and raised him to the ranks of major black writers of the early Civil Rights movement. Because Frank Brown was a budding creative genius when he died in 1962, the turmoil of the Civil Rights movement denied him an opportunity to gain a sustained place in American letters. Most of the limited published criticism on Brown's work focused on *Trumbull Park*. *The New Yorker* noted that the novel is "vigorous and exciting" (43) based on its portraiture of blacks' strident confrontation with racial hostilities and their ability to demonstrate admirable tenacity. South African novelist Alan Paton noted that Brown enables the foreign reader to respect the inner strength of African Americans. In spite of the early, few judicious reviews of *Trumbull Park*, Brown still remains basically unknown in American letters. His value as an artist is yet to be discovered.

BIBLIOGRAPHY

Works by Frank London Brown

Books

Trumbull Park. Chicago: Regnery, 1959.
Short Stories by Frank London Brown. N.p., 1965.
The Myth Maker. Chicago: Path Press, 1969.

Periodical Publications

Short Stories

"Night March." *Chicago Review* 11 (Spring 1957): 57–61.
"A Cry Unheard." *Chicago Review* 13 (Autumn 1959a): 118–120.
"In the Shadow of a Dying Soldier." *Southwest Review* 14 (Autumn 1959b): 292–306.
"A Matter of Time." *Negro Digest* 11 (March 1962): 58–60.
"Singing Dinah's Song." *Soon One Morning: New Writing by American Negroes 1940–1962.*
  Ed. Herbert Hill. New York: Knopf, 1963. 349–354.
"The Ancient Book." *Negro Digest* 13 (March 1964): 53–61.
"McDougal." *Phoenix* (Fall 1969): 21–28.

Nonfiction

"More Man than Myth." *Down Beat* 45 (October 30, 1958): 13–16, 45–46.
"Mahalia the Great." *Ebony* 14 (March 1960): 69–76.
"Chicago's Great Lady of Poetry." *Negro Digest* 11 (December 1961): 53–57.
"An Unaccountable Happiness: For Kermit Eby." *New City Magazine* 1 (April 1962): 14–
  15.

Studies of Frank London Brown

"Backstage." *Ebony* 14 (March 1959): 20.
Beier, Ulli. "The Whole Truth." *Black Orpheus* (1964): 71–73.
Brooks, Gwendolyn. "Of Frank London Brown: A Tenant of the World." *Negro Digest* 18
  (September 1962): 44.
Brownley, Les. "Frank London Brown: Courageous Author." *Sepia* 8 (June 1960): 26–30.
"The Departed." *Negro Digest* 8 (September 1962): 50.
Fleming, Robert E. "Overshadowed by Richard Wright: Three Black Chicago Novelists."
  Negro American Literature Forum 7 (Fall 1973): 75.
Hauke, Kathleen A. "Frank London Brown." *Dictionary of Literary Biography.* Ed. Trudier
  Harris. Detroit: Gale Research, 1984.
Miller, Ruth, ed. *Black American Literature 1760–Present.* Beverly Hills, CA: Glencoe
  Press, 1971.
Paton, Alan. Rev. of *Trumbull Park. Chicago Sunday Tribune,* December 12, 1959: 14B.
Pinkney, Alphonso. *Black Americans.* New York: Prentice-Hall, 1969.
Rev. of *Trumbull Park. New Yorker,* November 10, 1959: 43.
Serebnick, J. "New Creative Writers." *Library Journal* 84 (February 1, 1959): 507.
Stuckey, Sterling. "Frank London Brown." *Black Voices* (Special issue). (1968): 669–676.
Travis, Dempsey J. *An Autobiography of Black Chicago.* Chicago: Urban Research Institute,
  1981.

ED BULLINS
(1935–   )

Peggy Stevenson Ratliff

BIOGRAPHY

Ed Bullins (who also has written under the pseudonym Kingsley B. Bass, Jr.) is considered one of the most talented and prolific playwrights of the late 1960s and 1970s. He was also a producer, novelist, essayist, and short story writer of the Black Arts movement. Bullins was born July 2, 1935, in Philadelphia, son of Bertha Marie Queen and Edward Bullins. Bullins, who was raised by his mother, spent his childhood in the ghettos of Philadelphia. His experience on the streets served as a source for many of his plays. In 1952, at the age of seventeen, he quit school and enlisted in the navy, where he won the Lightweight Boxing Championship. Because he was unsatisfied with the way his life was proceeding and felt underprepared for the world, he began reading extensively. In 1955, Bullins returned to the city of his birth, Philadelphia, enrolled in night school, and completed his secondary education.

A great deal about Bullins' life during this period is not known. But in his novel, *The Reluctant Rapist*, which is discussed later, he insinuates that he was living a street life. In 1958 his writing career literally began when he departed Philadelphia and moved to Los Angeles, leaving behind a failed marriage and several children. Los Angeles was a positive move for Bullins, because there he enrolled in Los Angeles City College. He continued to read widely and began to write poetry, short stories, and plays. He was briefly the editor of the *Citadel*, a magazine he started for campus writers.

In 1964, Bullins enrolled in a creative writing program and began writing plays, which became the primary genre of his illustrious career. In 1967, Robert Macbeth, after reading some of his plays, invited him to join the newly established New Lafayette Theatre, where he became the principal writer, creating a panorama of characters never before seen on the American stage.

Additionally, Bullins served as the playwright in residence at the American Place Theatre in New York in 1973, and until 1983, he was on the staff at the Public Theatre's New York Shakespeare Festival.

He is the recipient of many awards, including an honorary doctorate from Columbia College in Chicago, two Guggenheim Fellowships, three Rockefeller grants, and Obie awards for *In New England Winter* (January 1971), *The Fabulous Miss Marie* (March 1971), and *The Taking of Miss Janie* (May 1975). He is currently residing in the San Francisco area.

MAJOR WORKS AND THEMES

Although the majority of Bullins' work is drama, he did write one novel, *The Reluctant Rapist*, in 1973. In *The Reluctant Rapist*, Bullins alludes to the situation in which he was caught, what he describes as life in the jungle in the late 1950s. He writes that his leaving Philadelphia to go to Los Angeles helped save his life. In *The Reluctant Rapist*, he voices through Steve Benson, the protagonist, that he felt at home in Los Angeles, where he met many people who were intellectual, dedicated to the study of black history, culture, and politics. Feeling somewhat alienated in Philadelphia, he now felt at home. In Philadelphia he writes that many members of the black middle class whom he encountered were artificial, pretentious, and phony. Therefore, he rejected the black middle class in favor of the street people. However, the street people became suspicious of him when he displayed knowledge of various subjects that he learned from his reading and traveling. Although Bullins often warns against turning to his novel to find out facts of his life, he does not deny that his work is autobiographical. Steve Benson speaks with a voice uncharacteristic of street characters. However, Bullins continues to romanticize the street life in his fiction and identifies himself as "a street nigger." His writings on certain occasions seem to value "the concreteness of street life" (Brouccli 45).

Bullins' fiction reveals that he is a moralist. His fiction can be described as didactic, and he often writes about the culture-specific experiences of African Americans. Critics have written that his fiction is basically concerned with black people and their dreams and values. His work often interrogates clichés, stereotypes, and values that are the norm to examine what is of significance in them. His main themes deal with the violence and tragedy of drug abuse and the oppressive life of the ghetto. Bullins' material is presented in a naturalistic and realistic style. Bullins, a product of the 1960s and the 1970s Black Nationalist movement, uses his fiction to probe the ideas of a people, a community, family, kinship, neighborhood and street life.

Bullins' best works are concerned with street life, because in these works most of his basic questions are articulated. Bullins' works deal with questions such as these: Have the dreams of African Americans been voiced concretely, and how can accepted values be sustained in the face of economic hardship? Additionally, how can blacks as members of a community make the move into a more materialistic and comfortable way of life? As a writer, Bullins can be characterized as a cultural nationalist.

His work is characterized by a disdain for ineffective political rhetoric as a replacement for action, which most frequently tests the lives of black people in the inner-city ghettos. His work does not concentrate on upwardly mobile or middle-class blacks but on economically deprived African Americans. His characters are the powerless and the disfranchised.

CRITICAL RECEPTION

When Bullins first began to write, he was criticized for writing about street life, and his reply was: "The urban-black-ghetto thing is not a new and fascinating thing to me. I been on the streets most of my life. . . . I learned how to survive. I'm a street nigger" (Draper 321).

The general public as well as the critics have been slow to accept Bullins' works. In the beginning, his works received a cool reception because of the "obscene" language and his unconventional style. Although he was disappointed by the indifference to his work, he continued to write—especially after seeing dramas by Imamu Amiri Baraka, such as *The Dutchman* and *The Slave*. A small number of black critics objected to how blacks are portrayed in his works, and a large number of reviews by white critics were negative. Bullins dismissed those white critics and stated, "It doesn't matter whether they appreciate it. It's not for them. They believe that niggers come from the moon and don't have a message" (Draper 523). Before long, black critics rallied and defended Bullins as a writer and attacked white critics for using color (white) as a standard to evaluate black art. Jerry H. Bryant states that in *The Reluctant Rapist* "a different Bullins is at work, one who is strongly autobiographical and reminiscent, personal, quietly honest" (521). He further notes that the novel possesses the content and tone of the nineteenth-century bildungsroman, where the young hero (Steve Benson, in this case) "is educated from innocence to experience" (502). Richard G. Scharine examines the role of Steve Benson in *The Reluctant Rapist* and in dramas such as *It Has No Choice, In New England Winter, The Duplex,* and *The Fabulous Miss Marie*. Scharine suggests that Benson's development in these works is very similar to Bullins' own growth as a writer. He proposes that Bullins "is no longer a revolutionary writer." Scharine wonders if the artist can continue to write effectively (104). In rebuttal, Bullins writes in *The Black American Literature Forum* that "I believe my characters sometimes have multiple identities, as parts of a whole, an ever-changing, interchangeable universe, as the points in a vision which expands dream like. I do not write realistic plays, I was a conscious artist before I was a conscious revolutionary, which has been my salvation and disguise. I do not feel I am severed from my roots" (Bullins 109).

Today, Bullins is considered to be one of the most significant artists to emerge from the Black Arts movement of the 1960s. Overall, reviews of Bullins' works have been positive, with at least one critic recognizing Bullins as "the playwright of the Black experience" with "his hand on the jugular vein of people" (Draper 323). Robert Macbeth, New Lafayette Theatre director, states that "there's no better playwright in American Theatre today" (Draper 323). In the 1974 issue of the *Black World*, Geneva Smitherman noted that "Ed Bullins is one of the 'baddest' brothers in the New York Theater Movement" (7), and Genevieve Fabre wrote that "next to LeRoi Jones, Ed Bullins is probably the most important black dramatist of the last twenty years" (Draper 323).

Whether critics approve of Bullins' fiction or not, they often agree that his portraits of black life are effective and striking and that he has, indeed, made a significant contribution to literature.

BIBLIOGRAPHY

Works by Ed Bullins

Novel

The Reluctant Rapist. New York: Harper and Row, 1973.

Books

How Do You Do: A Nonsense Drama. Mill Valley, CA: Illuminations Press, 1967.
Five Plays. Indianapolis: Bobbs-Merrill, 1969: revised as *The Electronic Nigger and Other Plays*. London: Faber and Faber, 1970.
The Duplex: A Black Love Fable in Four Movements. New York: Morrow, 1971a.
The Hungered One: Early Writings. New York: Morrow, 1971b.
Four Dynamite Plays. New York: Morrow, 1972.
The Theme Is Blackness: The Corner and Other Plays. New York: Morrow, 1973.

Studies of Ed Bullins

Brouccli, Matthew, gen. ed. *Dictionary of Literary Biography*. Vol. 38: *Afro-American Writers after 1955*. Detroit: Gale Research Center, 1985a.
————. *Dictionary of Literary Biography*. Vol. 7: *Twentieth Century American Dramatists*. Detroit: Gale Research Center, 1985b.
Bryant, Jerry H. "The Outskirts of a New City." *The Nation* 317, no. 16 (November 12, 1973): 501–2.
Bullins, Ed. "Who Is He Now? Ed Bullins Replies." *Black American Literature Forum* 13, no. 3 (Fall 1979): 109.
Clark, Sebastian. "A Black Radical: The Art of Ed Bullins." *Plays and Players* 20 (March 1973): 62–63.
David, George. Review of *The Reluctant Rapist* by Ed Bullins. *The New York Times Book Review* (September 30, 1973): 24.
Draper, James, ed. *Black Literature Criticism*. Vol. 1. Detriot: Gale Research, 1992.
"Ed Bullins, in The Task of the Negro Writer as Artist: A Symposium." *Negro Digest* 14 (April 1965): 54–83.
Evans, Don. "Up against the Wall." *Black World* 23 (April 1974): 14–18.

Gates, Henry Louis, Jr., and Nellie Y. McGay, gen. eds. *The Norton Anthology of African American Literature*. New York: W. W. Norton, 1997.

Hay, Samuel A. "African American Drama 1950–1970." *Negro History Bulletin* 36 (January 1973): 5–8.

———. "Structural Elements in Ed Bullins' Plays." *Black World* 23 (April 1974): 20–26.

———. "Structural Elements in Ed Bullins' Plays." In *The Theater of Black Americans: A Collection of Critical Essays*, edited by Errol Hill, vol. 1, 185–91. Englewood Cliffs, NJ: Prentice-Hall, 1980.

Jackmon, Marvin X. "An Interview with Ed Bullins: Black Theater." *The Negro Digest* 18, no. 6 (April 1969): 9–16.

Jackson, Kennell, Jr. "Notes on the Works of Ed Bullins." *CLA Journal* 18, no. 2 (December 1974): 292–99.

Mabunda, Mpho L., ed. *Black America*. Vol. 4. Detroit: Gale Research, 1997.

Magill, Frank N., ed. *Masterpieces of African American Literature*. New York: HarperCollins, 1992.

Scharine, Richard G. "Ed Bullins Was Steve Benson (But Who Is He Now?)" *Black American Literature Forum* 13, no. 3 (Fall 1979): 103–6.

Smitherman, Geneva. "Everybody Wants to Know Why I Sing the Blues." *Black World* 23, no. 6 (April 1974): 4–13.

True, Warren R. "Ed Bullins, Anton Chekhov, and the 'Drama of Mood.' " *CLA Journal* 20, no. 4 (June 1977): 521–32.

"What Lies Ahead for Black Americans." *Negro Digest* 19 (November 1968): 8.

Interviews

Gussow, Mel. "Bullins, the Artist and the Activist, Speaks." *New York Times*, September 22, 1971, 54.

Jenner, Cynthia Lee. "Once a Panther, Now a Pussycat?" *Artsboard*, September 30, 1976, 9.

Munk, Erika. "Up from Politics—An Interview with Ed Bullins." *Performance* 2 (July/August 1972): 52–60.

O'Haire, Patricia. "Bullins—A Philadelphia Story." *New York Daily News*, June 7, 1975, 25.

Young, Charles M. "Is Rape a Symbol of Race Relations?" *New York Times*, May 18, 1975, II: 5.

OCTAVIA E. BUTLER
(1947–   )

AnnLouise Keating

BIOGRAPHY

Born and raised in southern California, Octavia E. Butler has been reading and writing science fiction since she was a child. She credits her persistence and drive, as well as her love of storytelling, to her mother, who did domestic work to support herself and her daughter after her husband died. Butler was painfully shy as a child and spent a great deal of time alone, reading and writing. By the age of thirteen, she had decided to become a professional writer and began sending out her stories. Although her family encouraged her writing, they insisted that writing was far too impractical to be a full-time, paying career—especially for a black woman. Despite these warnings and despite the lack of role models (as a child, she was exposed to no openly identified black writers), Butler persisted in her goal.

After graduating from Pasadena City College, Butler attended California State University in Los Angeles and supported herself and her writing with temporary jobs at offices, factories, and warehouses. She would wake at two or three in the morning and write until she had to go to work. During this time, she amassed a large collection of rejection slips. Butler credits her participation in two work-shops—the Open Door Program of the Screen Writers' Guild of America, West (1969–70) and the Clarion Science Fiction and Fantasy Writers' Workshop in Pennsylvania (1970)—as the turning point in her career. At Clarion, she sold her first two stories and established a mentoring relationship with Harlan Ellison. Although these small successes motivated her to continue writing, not until 1975 did Butler sell her first novel. Today, Butler is one of only a very few African American women writing science fiction. She has won numerous prizes, including science fiction's highest awards—a Hugo in 1985 for "Speech Sounds"; a 1985

Hugo and a 1984 Nebula for "Bloodchild"—and a 1995 MacArthur "Genius" grant. She currently resides in the Los Angeles area.

MAJOR WORKS AND THEMES

Butler's genre of choice—science fiction—represents an especially inhospitable field for a black woman writer. For many years, most science fiction was written by "white" men for "white" male adolescents. With very few exceptions, women of any color did not write science fiction, female characters were generally portrayed as sex objects, and men of color rarely wrote or appeared in science fiction novels or stories. Thus, Butler's entry into this genre represents a significant breakthrough. Her novels contain strong black female protagonists whose wisdom and actions make them agents of change. She deals with complex issues, such as the struggle for power and control; the ways these struggles are inflected by gender, ethnicity, and class; fear of, and confrontation with, differences; the politics of survival; and the creation of new communities where peoples of many colors and often different species interact. These hybrid communities are especially remarkable and illustrate Butler's radical perspective on "race": by marking color unobtrusively, she challenges preconceptions concerning miscegenation and racialized identities.

Butler's interest in exploring broad themes and social dynamics from multiple perspectives has led her to write interlocking novels. Her first collection, the Patternist Series, consists of five novels. Arranged according to the story's narrative rather than publication dates, they are *Wild Seed* (1980), *Mind of My Mind* (1978), *Clay's Ark* (1984), *Survivor* (1978), and *Patternmaster* (1976). This series moves backward and forward through time, tracing the human race's transformation into three distinct groups that vie for domination and survival: the Patternists, human beings with heightened telepathic powers bound by the Pattern, an indissoluble psychic chain controlled by the Patternmaster; the Clayark, disease-mutated people with superhuman physical abilities and sphinxlike bodies; and the "mutes," ordinary, nondiseased, nonpsychic humans enslaved by the Patternists. Butler explores this struggle from multiple perspectives: in *Wild Seed* she focuses on the Patternists' creators—Doro, a psychic vampire, born before the Egyptian pyramids were built, and Anyanwu, a 300-year-old Igbo healer and shape-shifter; in *Mind of My Mind* and *Patternmaster* she depicts the Patternists; in *Clay's Ark* she narrates the genesis of the Clayark; and in *Survivor* she tells the story of a group of mutes who escape both Patternists and Clayark.

Butler's earliest novels are, in many ways, her most conventional, employing fast-moving plots filled with physical and psychic power struggles. In *Patternmaster*, set in the distant future, Butler uses a linear narrative and single point of view to explore the conflict between two brothers, Rayal and Coransee, who vie to become Patternmaster. *Mind of My Mind* continues this exploration of physical and psychic battles as it depicts the birth of the Pattern and the struggle for control between Doro and Mary, one of Doro's many offspring. The successful outcome of thousands of years of Doro's breeding, Mary becomes the first Patternmaster but must learn to employ her tremendous power in positive ways. Like *Patternmaster*, this novel explores the seductiveness of power and the responsibility to use power in mutually beneficial, rather than parasitic, ways. Although Butler has disowned *Survivor* for professional reasons and will not allow it to be republished, this novel introduces two interconnected themes—confrontations with difference and the politics of survival—developed in her later works. Depicting a group of "Missionaries of Humanity" who fought the Clayark by developing a religion that deifies the human form, *Survivor* exposes the powerful role belief systems play in enhancing or impeding survival. To survive, the Missionaries—who traveled to another planet to escape the Clayark on earth—must interact with the Tehkohn and the Garkhon, two warring types of Kohn, an animal-like, but highly intelligent, species. Yet the Missionaries' beliefs concerning human superiority prevent them from recognizing that they have become enslaved. The protagonist, Alanna, provides important insights into Butler's politics of survival. Unlike the Missionaries, who adopted Alanna after her parents had been killed by Clayark, Alanna can accept the differences between herself and the Kohn. Employing what she describes as " '[s]urvival philosophy' " (117), Alanna combines an intense desire to live with the ability to adapt, view situations from multiple perspectives, and mediate. This ability to compromise without losing a sense of self is essential to Butler's politics of survival.

Butler further develops this politics of survival in *Wild Seed*. Doro and Anyanwu engage in a series of struggles spanning two continents and several hundred years as they each create new communities and new forms of human life. Captured by Doro and transplanted from her precolonial African village to the North American colonies, Anyanwu must learn to adapt. As in *Survivor*, the flexibility to redefine belief systems and accept differences among people plays a pivotal role in survival. In *Wild Seed* Butler expands this theme to explore how survival strategies shape communities. Doro survives for millennia by parasitically using human beings; consequently, the community he creates is based on intimidation, violence, and an intense disrespect for human life. Anyanwu takes a different approach: she survives by creating symbiotic relationships between herself and the people she lives with; consequently, the community she creates is based on nurturance, acceptance, and respect.

Clay's Ark introduces a new ethical dimension into Butler's politics of survival: what happens when the price of survival entails the possible loss of humanity? Eli, an astronaut who returns to earth with an extraterrestrial, highly infectious microorganism that bonds with, and transforms, genetic structures, faces this dilemma. The microorganism intensifies infected humans' desire to live, resist capture, and spread their disease, thus ensuring the survival of their offspring, the Clayark. Although Eli attempts to kill himself and thus preserve the human race from contamination, he cannot do it; he becomes controlled by the organism's incredible biological urges. The novel traces his attempts to create a community of infected humans and Clayark, which satisfies the organism's drive to spread without contaminating the entire human race.

Originally designed as part of the Patternist series, *Kindred* is Butler's only novel not classified as science fiction. Like *Clay's Ark*, *Kindred* explores ethical dimensions of survival: how does one maintain humanity in the face of dehumanizing conditions? Set simultaneously in 1976 California and pre–Civil War Maryland, the novel follows Dana Franklin and her husband, Kevin, as Dana is pulled back through time whenever the life of her ancestor, Rufus, is threatened. The "white" son of a slave owner, Rufus represents a shocking, previously hidden element of Dana's family history that she must learn to understand and accept. This provocative family tie allows Butler to critique contemporary "race" relations by exposing the interconnections between the supposedly distinct "black" and "white" people. Significantly, Butler neither condemns nor absolves Rufus' abusive power but, instead, uses his interactions with Dana to explore the seductiveness of power and the ways social environments misshape human beings. Kevin's presence further complicates this exploration; as a "white"-identified man drawn into the antebellum South, Kevin must acknowledge the ways his color and gender give him unwarranted privilege.

Drawing extensively on nineteenth-century slave narratives, Butler attains a remarkable level of realism in this novel. Her use of first-person narration compels readers—who share Dana's twentieth-century misperceptions of slavery—to share her growing comprehension of slavery's dehumanizing process. Preconceptions concerning "mammies," "house negroes," masters, and other components of slavery undergo significant changes as Dana learns to survive in the antebellum South.

Butler's second series, the Xenogenesis trilogy, extends and develops themes present in her earlier writings, especially conflicts with difference, the politics of survival, and the creation of hybridized peoples and communities. These novels occur after nuclear war has almost entirely destroyed the earth and depict the interactions between the Human survivors and their rescuers, the Oankali. This ancient, extremely alien-looking species has three genders: male, female, and ooloi. The Oankali are genetic engineers, compelled to interbreed with every "race" they encounter as they travel through space. For Humans, the price of survival is interbreeding with these aliens, an interbreeding that radically transforms both parties. Their offspring—the product of five parents (Human male and female, Oankali male, female, and ooloi)—are known as "constructs." This series takes conventional, historically based notions of miscegenation and hybridity to new levels and radically challenges binary systems of gender and sexuality.

Butler again employs multiple perspectives to provide readers with nuanced explorations of new ways to mediate and transform difference. *Dawn*, which depicts the first contact between the Oankali and Humans, focuses on Lilith Iyapu, selected by the Oankali to serve as their spokesperson. Like Butler's earlier protagonists, Lilith is a mediator whose ability to accept the differences between herself and others leads to conflicting loyalties. Although she understands her fellow Humans' resistance to the Oankali, she also sees their humanity and the beneficial implications of alliance. Narrated from the perspective of Akin, one of Lilith's many "construct" children, *Adulthood Rites* explores the multifaceted conflict between Humans who have joined forces with the Oankali and the "resistors"—Humans who reject all alliances with the Oankali and attempt to re-create prenuclear earth. Captured by the resistors while an infant, Akin learns to understand and appreciate their perspective and becomes a mediator between resistor Humans and Oankali. *Imago* complicates this mediation process even further by focusing on Jodahs, the first of a new, potentially deadly species. Another of Lilith's many construct children, Jodahs represents a form of difference that even the Oankali fear.

Central to this series is "the human contradiction"—the genetic combination of intelligence and hierarchical behavior that compels Humans to use their intelligence to evaluate, rank, dominate, and control others. According to the Oankali, this lethal genetic contradiction leads to slavery, wars, and other violent actions that will doom human beings to extinction. Presenting the various ways Humans and Oankali respond to this contradiction, Butler compels readers to reexamine contemporary power struggles and debates concerning biological essentialism and genetic engineering.

Parable of the Sower marks the beginning of Butler's third series. Set in the not-too-distant future (the 2020s), *Parable* follows Lauren Olamina as she attempts to survive and create a new community in a radically altered United States, where most people live in total poverty, the government is almost entirely useless, and violence, murder, slavery, and crime are the norm. This novel critiques Afrocentrism, religious movements, capitalism, racism, colonialism, and other contemporary issues. Unlike Butler's previous protagonists—strong women who are often *forced* to handle power in order to survive and who experience great ambivalence in the creation of new communities—Lauren actively seeks power and attempts to create a community based on her beliefs concerning the acceptance of change. This quest combines two previous themes: the "human contradiction" and the role belief systems play in enhancing or impeding survival.

Bloodchild and Other Stories contains reprints of Butler's most successful short stories and personal narratives. The title novella, which Butler calls her "pregnant man story" (30), takes place on another world and explores the symbiotic relationship between human beings—people who fled earth in order to avoid slavery or death—and the Tlic, the native, highly intelligent, but extremely nonhuman, species that had been on the verge of extinction before the Humans arrived. The Humans have been allowed to remain on the planet, but they are restricted to "Preservations"; each family must temporarily donate one of their offspring to a Tlic female, who implants her eggs in the Human. The story follows Gan, a Human male adolescent, as he decides whether to allow Gatoi, the Tlic who chose him at birth, to plant her eggs in his body.

CRITICAL RECEPTION

Because science fiction has been classified as nonliterary, Butler's work has not received the attention it deserves. Early scholarship focused on Butler's strong female protagonists. Thelma Shinn, for example, examines women's "survival power" in *Patternmaster, Mind of My Mind, Survivor,* and *Kindred.* Dorothy Allison praises the remarkable independence and strength in Butler's female protagonists yet questions their "assumption that children and family always come first" (471), subtly pointing out the conservative functions this maternal emphasis serves. Missy Kubitschek celebrates *Kindred* as one of the earliest novels by a twentieth-century black U.S. woman to explore the interconnections between slavery and contemporary society.

Recent articles indicate an important shift in Butler scholarship as critics employ poststructuralist theory to examine Butler's contributions to contemporary thought. Roger Luckhurst, for example, argues that Butler's depictions of miscegenation historicize recent debates concerning hybridity and antiessentialism. Similarly, Amanda Boulter demonstrates that Butler reinterprets African American historical narratives and provides "a potentially homeopathic reworking that imbibes the violent structures of the past to create something new" (181). Cathy Peppers argues that Xenogenesis rewrites biblical, sociological, paleoanthropological, and African American origin stories, thus enabling readers to "imagine the origins of identity in powerful new ways" (162).

BIBLIOGRAPHY

Works by Octavia E. Butler

Mind of My Mind. 1977. New York: Avon, 1978a.
Survivor. Garden City, NY: Doubleday, 1978b.
Adulthood Rites. New York: Warner, 1988a.
Kindred. 1979. Boston: Beacon, 1988b.
Wild Seed. 1980. New York: Warner, 1988c.
Imago. New York: Warner, 1989.
Parable of the Sower. New York: Four Walls Eight Windows, 1993.
Patternmaster. 1976. New York: Warner, 1995.
Bloodchild and Other Stories. New York: Seven Stories, 1996a.
Clay's Ark. 1984. New York: Warner, 1996b.

Studies of Octavia E. Butler

Allison, Dorothy. "The Future of Female: Octavia Butler's Mother Lode." *Reading Black, Reading Feminist: A Critical Anthology.* Ed. Henry Louis Gates, Jr. New York: Plume, 1990. 471–78.
Boulter, Amanda. "Polymorphous Futures: Octavia E. Butler's *Xenogenesis* Trilogy." *Amer-*

ican Bodies: Cultural Histories of the Physique. Ed. Tim Armstrong. New York: New York University Press, 1996. 170–85.

Kubitschek, Missy Dehn. *Claiming the Heritage: African-American Women Novelists and History.* Jackson: University Press of Mississippi, 1991.

Luckhurst, Roger. " 'Horror and Beauty in Rare Combination': The Miscegenate Fictions of Octavia Butler." *Women: A Cultural Review* 7 (1996): 28–38.

Peppers, Cathy. "Dialogic Origins and Alien Identities in Butler's Xenogenesis." *Science-Fiction Studies* 22 (1995): 47–62.

Shinn, J. Thelma. "The Wise Witches: Black Women Mentors in the Fiction of Octavia E. Butler." *Conjuring: Black Women, Fiction, and Literary Tradition.* Ed. Marjorie Pryse and Hortense J. Spillers. Bloomington: Indiana University Press, 1985. 203–15.

BEBE MOORE CAMPBELL
(1950–   )

Joyce Russell-Robinson

BIOGRAPHY

Bebe Moore Campbell was born in Philadelphia, where, in the custody of her mother, she spent the fall, winter, and spring of each year. Her summers were spent in Pasquotank County, North Carolina, with her father, George Moore, the victim of an automobile accident and a paraplegic whose confinement to a wheelchair did not impair his ability to assume a meaningful role in the upbringing of his and Doris Moore's only child. Born in 1950, just four years before the Supreme Court's ruling in the landmark *Brown* case, Moore Campbell grew up during the time when the laws of American apartheid were being challenged across the nation, and when America held the promise of social and economic equality for Americans of African descent. Because she lived in two different parts of the country, young Bebe Moore came to understand that the laws of segregation in the urban North and in the rural South—believed by some to be more benign in the North—were essentially the same: all were mean-spirited and designed to equip black youngsters with the belief that everything they "wanna be colored people can't be" (*Sweet Summer: Growing Up with and without My Dad* 64). Some of those early memories of segregation would later have a strong influence upon the author's work as a social journalist, a memoirist, and a writer of fiction.

In 1957, while in North Carolina, seven-year-old Bebe Moore discovered that the public library in her county was off-limits to African Americans. Also around that time she realized that no black teenagers were appearing on the nationally known television dance show *American Bandstand*, which was broadcast from her own native city of Philadelphia. But perhaps the young girl's most alarming discovery that year was that in 1955 two white men had murdered a fourteen-year-old black boy (Emmett Till) while he was spending the summer in the South. Both men were acquitted, although one of them, in fact, confessed his guilt in the killing. Till's death and the white men's acquittal provided the seed for Moore Campbell's first novel, *Your Blues Ain't like Mine*, a work with settings in fictional Hopewell, Mississippi, and Chicago—the actual home of the slain youth.

In 1964, Moore Campbell enrolled in the Philadelphia High School for Girls, one of the city's two academic high schools; the other was Central High, which was attended by boys. Upon graduation in 1968 she entered the University of Pittsburgh and in 1972 received a bachelor's degree in elementary education. This degree qualified her to teach both elementary and middle school, and she did teach for approximately five years. But teaching became less exciting and fulfilling in 1976, when Moore Campbell enrolled in a writing class taught by the noted African American writer Toni Cade Bambara.* Soon after enrolling in the class, she began submitting her articles to different newspapers and magazines and eventually left teaching altogether. Since 1976, her articles and stories have appeared in many periodicals, with *Essence, Ebony,* the *New York Times,* the *Washington Post, Seventeen,* and *Black Enterprise* being among the first to publish her work.

Bebe Moore Campbell's mother and grandmothers were quite influential in her early life, though, in her memoir *Sweet Summer,* she recalls often feeling smothered by the "bosoms." Doris Moore, a Philadelphia social worker, held three college degrees: a bachelor's, a master's in sociology, and a master's in social work. When she obtained her master's in social work, she received a promotion in Philadelphia's Department of Welfare, an advancement that enabled her to purchase a new home in a multiethnic neighborhood. Living among Italian, Chinese, and Jewish Americans was eye-opening for Bebe and for Michael, a brother-cousin who, along with Ms. Moore's mother, was a part of the household. The two youngsters saw many of their white neighbors selling their homes and fleeing the West Oak Lane community, all because African Americans were buying property in the once all-white neighborhood.

To the left and right . . . down the street and around the block, whites were reducing the prices of their homes and leaving amid a colorful profusion of "Sold" signs. The neighborhood synagogues were sold and transformed into Baptist churches. The kosher foods in the market were replaced with chitterlings and fatback. (*Sweet Summer* 230)

"West Oak Lane," Moore Campbell recalls sardonically, "did not offer exemplary race relations" (231).

Segregation, often insidious and covert in the North, was more overt in the South, where "white" and "colored" signs were boldly posted on the doors of restaurants, movie houses, and water fountains. Such signs, however, held no significant power in the lives of the Moores, as noted in *Sweet Summer.* Bebe's paternal grandmother, for example, told her that "white" water was hot and nasty, a statement that was supported by Bebe's college-educated father, a county farm agent until an automobile accident left him paralyzed when his daughter was only ten months old.

George Moore died in 1977 as a result of another automobile accident while Moore Campbell was living in the Washington, D.C., area with her daughter and first husband, from whom she was later divorced. She and her daughter now live in Los Angeles with the author's second husband, Ellis Gordon, Jr., a banker and the father of a son, with whom Moore Campbell enjoys a close relationship. Her awards are numerous and include the following: a National Association of Negro Business and Professional Women's Literature Award, the 1994 NAACP [National Association for the Advancement of Colored People] Image Award, a National Endowment for the Arts Literature Grant, and the University of Pittsburgh's Distinguished Black Alumna Award.

MAJOR WORKS AND THEMES

At the core of Bebe Moore Campbell's body of writing is a preoccupation with relationships and the complexities of interpersonal alliances. By having her characters subject themselves and each other to tests that determine just how strong their relationships are, the author explores the lives of parents and children, wives and husbands, black women and white women, and sometimes dating couples. Her interest in relationships emerged in some of her first articles and stories and was solidified in her first two books, both of which were nonfiction.

Successful Women, Angry Men: Backlash in the Two-Career Marriage is a now out-of-print evaluation of the conflicts that often affect relationships when women and their partners are attempting to build their careers. Drawing from her own experiences and from those of more than 100 couples whom she interviewed, Moore Campbell makes the point that conflicts tend to arise when the involved partners disagree on what it takes to become successful in their respective careers.

In her second book, *Sweet Summer*, the author set out primarily to elegize her father; the memoir did, indeed, accomplish that objective, but it also accomplished much more. Sensitive and insightful on a number of issues like divorce, solo parenting, and grandparenting, *Sweet Summer* clearly has at its center personal relationships and what is required to sustain them. It also combats the negative attention that African American men, especially fathers, began receiving in the 1980s. Many responsible, drug-free, viably employed men appear in *Sweet Summer*, men who maintained good relationships with their own children and also with other children who lived in their communities.

Bebe Moore Campbell's most critically acclaimed and best-known work is *Your Blues Ain't like Mine*, a novel that appeared on the *Washington Post* and *Blackboard African American* best-seller lists. Recognized by the *New York Times* as one of the most notable books of 1992, *Your Blues* earned for Moore Campbell an

NAACP Image Award in the category of fiction. The plot centers upon two families: the family of fifteen-year-old Armstrong Todd (black), murdered because of the innocuous French words he utters to a white woman; and the family of Floyd Cox (white), acquitted in the murder by a jury comprising twelve white men. Consistent with other works by Moore Campbell, the novel explores intimate personal relationships. While some of those relationships would be considered good—those in the Todd family, for instance—others—like those of the Coxes, where neglect and physical abuse are prevalent—could only be considered bad; and while most are intraracial, some are interracial, as in the case of Marguerite (black) and Clayton (white). Clayton, whose relationship with his wealthy father is strained, is the longtime lover of Marguerite. Their relationship, clandestine but resembling a marriage, is subjected to many tests, including several accidental pregnancies, all of which, Clayton decides, must be terminated. When at last he proposes to Marguerite and drives out of Mississippi with her, their car is stopped by the police. An officer warns Clayton: "I'd slow down if you and your maid want to make it wherever you're going" (244). Because Clayton does not (perhaps cannot) correct the officer by telling him that Marguerite is his fiancée, the young woman is offended and concludes that Clayton has doubts about becoming her husband. This final test is too much for the relationship. The two go their separate ways.

To say that Bebe Moore Campbell makes sexual relationships her main theme would be a mistake. Attempts have been made, however, to compare her with African American writers like Terry McMillan* (female) and E. Lynn Harris* (male), both of whom tend to create characters who are unfulfilled and who are interested in filling their emotional voids primarily through sexual activity. For Moore Campbell, emotional voids and frustrations and traumas are nursed and healed when her characters subject themselves to rigid, probing self-analysis. In short, they work it out for themselves, without the temporary quick fix of sex. Rigid self-analysis, however, does, at times, exact a toll on the characters, causing some of them to teeter on the edge of insanity, as in the case of Wydell Todd in *Your Blues*. The death of his son lands him in a mental hospital for a short time. But Wydell survives, and he, as a result of his mental suffering (really a healing crisis), is able to become a better father to his younger son W. T.

Zeroing in on relationships in Los Angeles, Bebe Moore Campbell's second novel, *Brothers and Sisters*, is concerned with the social and economic lives of middle- and upper-class urbanites. The Rodney King beating, riots, and a smoldering Los Angeles are antecedent action for this story of greed and ambition and—consistent with the author's style—introspective characters who take stock of themselves often, in order to move their lives forward more effectively.

Esther Jackson, an African American operations manager in a branch of Angel City Bank, is a character who is prone to much self-analysis. A take-charge woman who is serious about her job, she is ambitious but methodical and analytical when it comes to getting promoted. What must she do in order to move to the more prestigious lending department? How should she deal with sexual harassment? How strong is her relationship with her white female colleague Mallory?

It is important to note that, although race provides a backdrop for Moore Campbell's fiction, it is not always the central theme in her work. Race becomes central only in those instances where it has a bearing upon a particular *relationship*, as in the case of Esther and Mallory in *Brothers and Sisters* and Lily (white) and Ida (black) in *Your Blues*. In both cases the "friends" are unable to sustain real closeness because race and cultural differences seem to intrude. In those rare moments when the characters forget about race, however, they become true friends and realize that their humanity and their ability to feel each other's pain unite them. Lily, for example, tells Ida of having been molested as a child. Ida feels her pain:

"He used to touch me, when I wasn't nothing but a little-bitty girl. He'd sit me on his lap and feel me and afterwards he'd give me candy. He made me promise not to tell. . . . " Ida quickly brushed away the tears that had begun falling from her own eyes and patted her friend's shoulder. (*Your Blues* 33–34)

Bebe Moore Campbell's ability to delve into the complexities of relationships of all kinds and her ability to demonstrate that more unites us than separates us give her distinction as a literary artist. As a novelist, she might be compared to the early Alice Walker*; as a memoirist, to Clifton Taulbert, whose *Once upon a Time When We Were Colored* brought him wide acclaim from the literary world, both here and abroad.

CRITICAL RECEPTION

Although Bebe Moore Campbell's work has not yet been the subject of scholarly inquiry, reviewers tend to agree that her two novels are deserving of much praise. Designated by *Publishers Weekly* as a book of unusual interest and merit, *Your Blues Ain't like Mine*, according to the reviewer, bears similarities to the fiction of Flannery O'Connor and Harper Lee. However, the sheer scope of the novel seems to impress the reviewer the most: "Moving quickly and believably from the eve of integration in rural Mississippi to the present-day street gangs in Chicago's housing projects, [*Your Blues*] captures the gulf between pre- and post-civil rights America" (44). Faye A. Chadwell comments on Moore Campbell's ability to "ably reveal the complex relationships among townspeople in this multilayered southern community," meaning Hopewell, Mississippi, where much of the action occurs (120).

Shirley Hilliard Tucker is generous with her praise of *Brothers and Sisters*. She admires Moore Campbell's decision not to make racism the overriding factor in this novel "about the black middle class" and "African Americans in corporate America" (224). Another plus, says the reviewer, is that Moore Campbell creates dialogue that is natural and situations that are not staged. She maintains that the situations really depict what "happens in the corridors of America's most prestigious workplaces" (224). Linda Villarosa believes that a central theme of the novel is relationships. The characters, she notes, "struggle to find love and friendship against the volatile backdrop of post-riot Los Angeles" (92).

BIBLIOGRAPHY

Works by Bebe Moore Campbell

Fiction

Your Blues Ain't like Mine. New York: Putnam, 1992.
Brothers and Sisters. New York: Putnam, 1994.

Nonfiction

Successful Women, Angry Men: Backlash in the Two-Career Marriage. New York: Random House, 1987.
Sweet Summer: Growing Up with and without My Dad. New York: Putnam, 1989.

Studies of Bebe Moore Campbell

Chadwell, Faye A. Rev. of *Your Blues Ain't like Mine. Library Journal,* July 1992: 120.
Johnson, Anne Janette. "Bebe Moore Campbell. *Contemporary Black Biography.* Ed. Barbara Carlise Bigelow. Vol. 6. Detroit: Gale Research, 1994. 57–59.
Jones, Malcolm, Jr. "Successful Sisters: Faux Terry Is Better than No Terry." *Newsweek,* 29 April 1996: 79.
Rev. of *Your Blues Ain't like Mine. Publishers Weekly,* 22 June 1992: 44.
Tucker, Shirley Hilliard. "Wheelin' and Dealin' in Corporate America." *Black Enterprise,* 7 February 1995: 224.
Villarosa, Linda. "A Talk with Bebe Moore Campbell." *Essence,* September 1994: 92.

BARBARA CHASE-RIBOUD
(1939–)

Sarah McKee

BIOGRAPHY

Barbara Chase-Riboud, an internationally acclaimed poet, novelist, and sculptor, was born in Philadelphia on 26 June 1939. The earliest recognition of her artistic talent occurred while Chase-Riboud was still in high school, when the Museum of Modern Art purchased several of her prints. Following this promising beginning, Chase-Riboud continued to develop her talent, receiving the B.F.A. from Temple University in 1957, as well as an honorary doctorate in 1981, and the M.F.A. from Yale University in 1960. In 1961 she married Marc Eugene Riboud, with whom she had two sons, David and Alexis, but the marriage ended in divorce. In 1981, she married art historian Sergio Tosi, with whom she currently lives in Paris, France.

Revealing to *Essence* magazine that she is "much less neurotic when I'm sculpting than when I'm writing" (Cain 60), Chase-Riboud remains an active and renowned sculptor. Focusing primarily on her sculpture during the early years of her career, she exhibited work internationally during the 1960s and 1970s. Awards and honors include the John Hay Whitney Foundation fellowship for 1957–58, a National Endowment of the Arts fellowship in 1973, and the title of Academic of Italy in 1978 for sculpture and drawing. Most recently, the Studio Museum in Harlem showcased her bronze work in its 1996 exhibition, *Explorations in the City of Light: African-American Artists in Paris, 1945–1965.*

Chase-Riboud explores, through her sculpture, many of the interests and tensions present in her writing, namely, race relations in the United States. As the artist herself explained to journalist Susan McHenry about race relations, "There are differences, but there is no escape from the influence of one to the other, from their interrelation and interlocking" (qtd. in "Chase-Riboud, Barbara" 98).

For example, one famous sculpture, *All That Rises Must Converge*, is named for the Flannery O'Connor short story dealing with a charged encounter between a black woman and a white one. As John D'Addario points out, the sculpture consists of bronze "used in a fluid, liquid way," with silk cords "placed at the bottom of the piece as though supporting it." The juxtaposition of the materials, then, "alludes to a common theme of alternating tension and unity amongst opposing forces" in both the story and the sculpture (31). Similarly, Chase-Riboud focuses much literary attention on the contradictory tension and unity existing between the African American and white communities as a result of their shared slave legacy. The very institution of slavery, in fact, as it exists in various contexts, comes under investigation throughout her work as a destructive union for both slave and master.

MAJOR WORKS AND THEMES

Chase-Riboud's first publication, a volume of poetry entitled *From Memphis and Peking*, appeared in 1974. As the title itself suggests, the volume covers a vast terrain of themes. However, the significance of time itself does provide some unity to this diverse array of poems, particularly dealing with the incursion of the past into the reality of the present. For example, "Anna" explores the poet's own connections with the past through her musings about three generations of maternal ancestors (Anna, Agnes, and Vivian, to whom Chase-Riboud dedicates the volume), while "Smiling Mao" investigates the ramifications of Mao Tse-Tung's reign on Chinese culture.

The controversial historical novel *Sally Hemings*, published in 1979, brought instant attention and acclaim to Chase-Riboud, who won the 1979 Janet Heidenger Kafka Prize for the work. Here, Chase-Riboud's interest in the legacy of slavery in the United States as *shared* legacy takes shape with her exploration of the infamous Sally Hemings, mistress to President Thomas Jefferson. Although little is known about this woman, Chase-Riboud creates a narrative that attempts to explain and explore the contours of a fruitful (producing seven children) and long-term relationship between Hemings and Jefferson. Using this particularly high-profile and ironic couple (the author of the *Declaration of Independence* and a slave woman), Chase-Riboud effectively challenges the taboo of miscegenation in the United States as a futile attempt to prevent a mixing that not only permeates but, in fact, defines much of American culture. The annihilation and denial of such relationships (demonstrated by the 1830 census of Albemarle County, Virginia, which lists Sally as white in order to protect Jefferson's reputation) only fictionalize the conceptions we hold of our own history and continue to heighten the tension of the present.

Valide: A Novel of the Harem (1986) continues to investigate the ambivalent nature of power relations in a slave society. Although the novel is set in Istanbul, Turkey, in 1781, the protagonist is an American Creole woman captured by pirates and sold as a slave into the harem of Sultan Abdulhamid I. This woman,

Naksh-i-dil, one of hundreds of harem occupants, eventually rises to power within the harem itself as the mother of the succeeding sultan. Again, the problems of human affection (if not love) complicate the reading of the master–slave relationship, so that the slave herself (as the fictionalized account of Hemings also posits) assumes some measure of power within the very system that holds her in bondage. The politics of the harem, however, only mimics the power relations of the "free" world, as the novel's enormous cast of powerful characters demonstrates. Navigating between the narratives of Naksh-i-dil, Catherine the Great, and Napoleon and Josephine Bonaparte, as well as the numerous characters who interact with them, the novel expands the definition of slavery by identifying various manifestations of it in often surprising contexts.

A second volume of poetry, *Portrait of a Nude Woman as Cleopatra*, was published in 1987. Inspired by a Rembrandt sketch of a nude woman entitled *Study of a Nude Woman as Cleopatra*, Chase-Riboud again undertakes the difficult task of humanizing a historical enigma. Interspersed with passages from Plutarch's account of the affair between Marc Antony and Cleopatra, Chase-Riboud creates a poetic dialogue between the lovers beginning in 41 B.C. Following their tragic story until Cleopatra's suicide in 30 B.C., Chase-Riboud's erotic and emotional lyrics provide a poignant counterpoint to the brutal politics that informed and ultimately destroyed that relationship. Again, love is frequently imaged as a political relationship by its very nature, creating masters and slaves of those involved. The destructive capability of love, then, emerges as an integral, though ironic, component within slavery, which depends on the acquiescence of the slave and the master to each other in order to exist.

Echo of Lions, published in 1989, is perhaps Chase-Riboud's most tightly focused novel. Dealing with the story of Joseph Cinque, an African captive who led a successful mutiny on board the slave ship *Amistad*, *Echo of Lions* examines the inherent contradictions of slavery in the United States. Cinque was captured in Africa and transported to America in 1839, after the supposed abolition of the slave trade, though well before the Emancipation Proclamation. Finally discovered off the coast of Connecticut, Cinque and his men were arrested and jailed while debate raged over their status as either cargo (purchased by a southerner) or Africans illegally transported from their homeland. With the help of an abolitionist family, the Braithwaites, a free African interpreter, James Covey, and aging former president John Quincy Adams, Cinque and his men are finally returned to Africa. The novel reveals the absurdity of the American justice system's attempting to deal simultaneously with its commitment to "inalienable rights" while bartering with human beings as a material investment. Here, Chase-Riboud demonstrates again her dedication to speaking the often unspoken narrative of slavery that informs American racial (un)consciousness to this day.

Unfortunately, however, Chase-Riboud's drive not only to speak but also to claim this story has recently created some controversy. During an attempt to sue Steven Spielberg's Dreamworks company for plagiarizing elements of *Echo of Lions* in the screenplay for its 1997 release *Amistad*, Chase-Riboud herself faced plagiarism charges. Apparently, parts of *Echo of Lions* are similar to William Owens' 1953 study of the *Amistad* affair entitled *Black Mutiny*, which is an acknowledged source for Spielberg's film. According to Dr. Clifton Johnson, an *Amistad* expert at Tulane University,

There is no fictional—as distinguished from history-based—element in *Echo of Lions* that appears in the film. . . . A number of things that Ms. Chase-Riboud claims as her original creation came, in fact, from actual history and/or were depicted in *Black Mutiny*. (Weinraub E6)

Chase-Riboud ultimately dropped the charges against Dreamworks the day before the film was nominated for six Academy Awards.

Chase-Riboud's last literary work to date is the 1994 historical novel *The President's Daughter*. A sequel to *Sally Hemings*, *The President's Daughter* chronicles the life of Harriet Hemings, the daughter of Hemings and Jefferson. Leaving Monticello at twenty-one to pass for white, Harriet determines to seek life in the white community, despite the enormous sacrifice of leaving behind family and heritage. Her life, though successful in many ways, is also a sad negation of her true identity. Losing her fingerprints, literally, in an accident with acid, Harriet struggles with the dishonesty of the erased identity that she assumes and passes along to her children. Harriet's identity as "the president's daughter" and the prestige usually associated with that position are irretrivably lost when combined with her legal status as runaway slave, which prevents her honest integration into free society. As a result, the tragic loss of Harriet's personal history is also the loss of American history and demonstrates clearly Chase-Riboud's recurrent theme of American culture's destructive denial and willful ignorance of a shared racial heritage. The final, devastating lack of communication between Harriet and both her black and white descendants at the end of her life highlights the ultimate consequences of the silence and lies necessary to maintain the illusion of racial separation.

CRITICAL RECEPTION

With the exception of Ashraf Rushdy's analysis of *Sally Hemings*, critical reception of Chase-Riboud's work consists mainly of reviews. Although many reviewers of the novels mention a certain hyperbole and sentimentalism in the writing style, most also note the important issues explored in the works. The Hemings–Jefferson narrative chronicled in *Sally Hemings* and *The President's Daughter* has garnered the most attention, due primarily to its controversial subject matter. As Rushdy points out, Chase-Riboud attempts to rewrite history by filling in the gaps created by the exclusion of previously silenced African American voices. Comparing Chase-Riboud's project to those of Walker, Williams, and Morrison, Rushdy notes that *Sally Hemings* "makes the relationship between supplemental memory and written historical records an issue involving the play between orality and literacy" (106).

Critics generally praise Chase-Riboud's attempt to give Sally voice, although reservations about the success of the project surface as well. Larry McMurtry, for example, describes *Sally Hemings* as "a gallant undertaking to intuit the life of a dead woman," while also claiming that "one feels too often that a cause is being pleaded" (66). However, an interest in the accuracy of Chase-Riboud's claims about Jefferson surfaces among critics of *The President's Daughter*. For example, *Virginia Quarterly Review* remarks that "serious scholars deny that there is any merit to her contention" (60), while Edmund Newton chronicles the debate generated by both novels in historical circles. Though many historians deny the affair, their vehement reactions to the novel's assertions perhaps validate Chase-Riboud's contention that many prefer to believe "that Thomas Jefferson could never have done anything so ignoble as to fall in love with a black woman" (Newton E1).

BIBLIOGRAPHY

Works by Barbara Chase-Riboud

From Memphis and Peking. New York: Random House, 1974.
Sally Hemings. New York: Viking Press, 1979.
Valide: A Novel of the Harem. New York: William Morrow, 1986.
Portrait of a Nude Woman as Cleopatra. New York: William Morrow, 1987.
"Why Paris?" *Essence* (October 1987): 65–66.
Echo of Lions. New York: William Morrow, 1989.
The President's Daughter. New York: Random House, 1994.

Studies of Barbara Chase-Riboud

Brooks, Valerie. Review of *Sally Hemings*. *The New Republic* (1 July 1979): 38–39.
Cain, Joy Duckett. "The Source of Our Magic." *Essence* (May 1995): 60.
"Chase-Riboud, Barbara." *Black Writers: A Selection of Sketches from Contemporary Authors*. Detroit: Gale Research, 1985. 97–98.
Crandall, Norma Rand. Review of *Sally Hemings*. *America* (3 November 1979): 267–268.
D' Addario, John. "Barbara Chase-Riboud: Speaking to the African-American Historical Experience." *School Arts* 95.6 (1996): 31.
Gardner, Paul. "When France Was Home to African-American Artists." *Smithsonian* (March 1996): 106–113.
Giddings, Paula. "Word Star." *Essence* (February 1989): 30.
Gillespie, Marcia. "The Seraglio, the Plantation—Intrigue and Survival." Review of *Valide*. *Ms.* (September 1986): 20–21.
Johnson, George. Review of *Valide*. *New York Times Book Review* (17 April 1989): 41.
Kimmelman, Michael. "Black Artists at Home in Postwar Paris." *New York Times*, 18 February 1996, sec. 2:39.
Larson, Charles R. "An American Love Story." Review of *Sally Hemings*. *Chronicle of Higher Education* (9 July 1979): R8.

Levin, Martin. "Jefferson, Cannibals and Others." Review of *Sally Hemings*. *New York Times Book Review* (28 October 1979): 14.

McMurtry, Larry. Review of *Sally Hemings*. *New York* (30 July 1979): 66.

Nash, Gary B. "Justice Sails on the Amistad Slave Ship." Review of *Echo of Lions*. *Los Angeles Times Book Review* (18 June 1989): 12.

Newton, Edmund. "A New Spin on Nation's Treasured History." Review of *The President's Daughter*. *Los Angeles Times*, 30 August 1994, E1+.

Olson, Kiki. Review of *The President's Daughter*. *New York Times Book Review* (6 November 1994): 24.

Review of *Echo of Lions*, by Barbara Chase-Riboud. *Kirkus Reviews* (15 December 1988): 1756–1757.

Review of *From Memphis and Peking*. *Choice* (January 1975): 1627.

Review of *From Memphis and Peking*. *Kirkus Reviews* (15 March 1974): 337.

Review of *Portrait of a Nude Woman as Cleopatra*. *Booklist* (July 1987): 1644.

Review of *Portrait of a Nude Woman as Cleopatra*. *Publishers Weekly* (8 May 1987): 66.

Review of *Portrait of a Nude Woman as Cleopatra*. *Virginia Quarterly Review* 71.2 (1995): 60.

Review of *Sally Hemings*. *Kirkus Reviews* (1 May 1979): 539.

Review of *Valide*. *Kirkus Reviews* (15 May 1986): 733.

Rushdy, Ashraf H. " 'I Write in Tongues': The Supplement of Voice in Barbara Chase-Riboud's *Sally Hemings*." *Contemporary Literature* 35.1 (1994): 100–135.

Smith, Wendy. Review of *Valide*. *New York Times Book Review* (10 August 1986): 22.

Weinraub, Bernard. "Filmmakers of *Amistad* Rebut Claim by Novelist." *New York Times*, 4 December 1997, E1+.

Wilson, Judith. "Barbara Chase-Riboud: Sculpting Our History." *Essence* (December 1979): 12–13.

ALICE CHILDRESS
(1916–1994)

Terry Novak

BIOGRAPHY

Playwright and novelist Alice Childress was born on 12 October 1916 in Charleston, South Carolina. Her year of birth is sometimes listed as 1920, a detail Childress, presumably in the name of privacy, never bothered to correct during her lifetime. In 1925, upon the separation of her parents, Childress moved with her mother to Harlem, where they resided with maternal grandmother Eliza Campbell White. Childress' grandmother exposed her to the arts and cultural affairs. Her grandmother also took her regularly to services at Salem Church, where the young Childress heard firsthand accounts of the troubles of the poor, accounts that she later would weave into the themes of her literary works. Childress was also an avid reader from her early days, visiting the public library often and reading at least two books a day. Despite this, she left high school after completing only three years of study.

In 1935 Childress gave birth to her daughter and only child, Jean R. Childress. Jean's father and Childress' first husband was the actor Alvin Childress. Marriage and divorce dates were kept strictly private by Childress.

Childress began an acting career in 1943 with the original American Negro Theater in Harlem. For this theater company she wrote her first play, the one-act *Florence*, in 1949. At the same time that Childress was performing and writing drama, she was also working a variety of jobs, including domestic service, in order to support herself and her daughter. The experience she gained in such jobs became an intricate part of much her creative work, such as the 1956 collection *Like One of the Family . . . Conversations from a Domestic's Life*.

In 1957 Childress married the musician Nathan Woodard. She continued her work in theater and participated in many honorary events in the 1960s. In June

1965 Childress was a resident at the MacDowell Colony. Also in 1965 she participated in a panel discussion on "The Negro in American Theater" for the BBC. Other panelists included James Baldwin,* Leroi Jones, and Langston Hughes. From 1966 to 1968 Childress served as playwright-scholar in residence at Cambridge.

Childress' first adolescent novel, A Hero Ain't Nothin' but a Sandwich, appeared in 1973. In 1974 the work won the Jane Addams Honor Award for young adult novels. The 1970s also saw Childress making visits to the USSR, China, and Ghana, West Africa, and writing her first novel for adults, A Short Walk, published in 1979. Childress continued to produce work in the 1980s and in the last years of her life worked on the story of her maternal great-grandmother, Ani Campbell, who was abandoned in Charleston, South Carolina, at the age of twelve after the "Juneteenth" liberation of American slaves and adopted by the white Anna Campbell.

Alice Childress died of cancer on 14 August 1994 in Queens, New York. She was preceded in death by her daughter, who died on Mother's Day 1990, also of cancer.

MAJOR WORKS AND THEMES

Childress' first play, Florence, was written overnight after Sydney Poitier and other actors at the American Negro Theater insisted that a good play could not be written in one night. Childress met this challenge with a one-act work that set the stage for her continuing interest in racial, gender, and socioeconomic issues. The title character of Florence is never met; instead, Florence's mother takes the predominant role in the play. Mama is on her way to New York to bring Florence back home to the South. Mama is convinced that it is time for her widowed daughter to give up her thus far unsuccessful acting dreams and come home to care for her son. While seated in the train station waiting room, Mama engages in a conversation with the white Mrs. Carter, an actress who is seated opposite Mama, on the white side of the color barrier. Mrs. Carter tells Mama of her acting life, and Mama, in turn, tells Mrs. Carter about Florence and her struggles. Mrs. Carter espouses liberal social views, but when Mama seeks help for theater contacts for Florence, Mrs. Carter thinks immediately of an opening for a maid at the home of a director. Mama makes the threateningly aggressive move of grabbing Mrs. Carter's wrist tightly in response to the white woman's absurd response, at which point Mrs. Carter makes an abrupt exit. This scene with the white woman gives Mama the courage to decide against retrieving her daughter; instead, Mama sends Florence the trip money along with a note urging her to "keep trying."

Childress continues the theme of racism and the theater in her play Trouble in Mind, first produced in 1955 but not published until 1971. Trouble in Mind centers around the rehearsal of a fictitious play titled Chaos in Belleville. Chaos is the product of a white playwright and deals with the lynching of a black man in the South whose "crime" was the act of daring to exercise his right to vote. The white director of this play is pleased with the "realistic" depiction of blacks, but the black actors become increasingly incensed with the stereotypical character-izations. The veteran actor Wiletta Mayer is particularly portrayed as a black member of the cast who has had enough of fantasy roles. Wiletta goes through a transformation during the play. At the beginning she is seen counseling the young black actor John Nevins to ingratiate himself to the white power figures, as she has successfully done for years. This is, she believes, the only way to succeed in one's acting career. By the end of the play Wiletta realizes that she and the other black actors are selling themselves and their race short by accepting absurd portrayals of blacks and refuses to continue the farce.

A year after *Trouble in Mind* appeared, Childress published the nondramatic *Like One of the Family . . . Conversations from a Domestic's Life*. Using her own work experiences and those of other people to whom she was exposed throughout her life, Childress presents in this work a series of vignettes revolving around the thoughts and concerns of a black domestic worker named Mildred. The work evolved into a column for the *Baltimore Afro-American* titled "Here's Mildred." In both the book and the columns, Childress uses Mildred as a sassy, lighthearted answer to the serious problems of black domestic workers (and presumably any black worker in a less than satisfactory job situation). Mildred points out the absurdities in the white employer–black employee situation and also strives to maintain her innate sense of dignity. In one instance she relates the following to her friend Marge (who is the audience for each of the vignettes) about a particular work situation:

The first day I was there she come into the kitchen and says, "Mildred, Mrs. James would like you to clean the pantry." Well, I looked 'round to see if she meant her mother-in-law or somebody and then she adds, "If anyone calls, Mrs. James is out shopping." And with that she sashays out the door.

Now she keeps on talking that way all the time, the whole time I'm there. The woman wouldn't say "I" or "me" for nothing in the world. (60)

Ten years after *Life*, in 1966, Childress' play *Wedding Band* was performed at the University of Michigan. With *Wedding Band* Childress moves to the arena of interracial relationships and the special racial strife that emerges from them. The drama tells the love story of Herman, who is white, and Julia, who is black. Herman and Julia have a long love affair that can never legally be transformed into marriage in their state of South Carolina. Despite the lack of a marriage certificate, the couple acts like family, even to the point of Julia's caring for Herman's ungrateful and prejudiced mother when she is ill. Herman is the owner of a bakery, and Julia works as a seamstress; they proceed through life as any legally married couple would, except for the societal pressures that are uniquely thrown upon interracial couples. After ten years of being together, Herman presents Julia with a wedding band. The play does not end happily. Herman dies of influenza, and Julia is left a widow with no legal rights or respect.

In 1973 Childress moved into the genre of the novel, writing her first adolescent novel, *A Hero Ain't Nothin' but a Sandwich*. This highly acclaimed novel is set in Harlem in the early 1970s and tells the tale of thirteen-year-old Benjie Johnson's struggle with heroin addiction as well as with his resentment of his mother, Rose's, love for Craig Butler. Benjie resents Butler's "stepfather" attitude and is keenly aware that Butler is not his "real" father. Benjie also struggles with giving up his own previous role as "man of the house." Benjie's rebelliousness eventually forces Butler out of the house for a time, but it never forces him out of Benjie's life. Butler sticks with Benjie as a strong, committed parental figure, even to the point of saving Benjie from falling off a roof. Benjie begins to realize on a certain level that Butler is a father figure to him, but the reader is left uncertain of Benjie's future at the end of the novel.

Childress followed *A Hero* with a second adolescent novel, *Rainbow Jordan*, in 1981. The fourteen-year-old heroine of this novel, Rainbow, shares with Benjie the lack of a biological father at home. Unlike Benjie, however, Rainbow also has to deal with periodic abandonment by her mother. Whereas Benjie has a stepfather to turn to, Rainbow has a foster mother. In both novels Childress portrays the mothers as weak and largely ineffectual. The teenagers must turn to parental surrogates in order to survive and be saved from the treacheries of life. To Childress' credit, however, she balances these surrogate parents by using a male figure in the one novel and a female figure in the other.

Childress left two other novels as part of her canon: *Those Other People* (1989), an adolescent novel, and *A Short Walk* (1979), her only adult novel. *A Short Walk* is significant not only because of its intended audience but also because it furthers the interracial themes of *Wedding Band* as well as the real-life themes with which her maternal grandmother and great-grandmother were faced. *A Short Walk* is the story of Cora, a biracial child whose black mother dies shortly after childbirth and who is given to adoptive parents, who move her from South Carolina to Harlem. The novel depicts many historical events of the first half of the twentieth century and also delves into the harsh realities faced by biracial children.

CRITICAL RECEPTION

While popular reviews of Childress' work have not always been positive, this can mostly be attributed to the social climate of the time in which the works made their first appearances. *Wedding Band*, for instance, though written in 1966, had no major production until 1972, when Joseph Papp "introduced" it at the New York Shakespeare Festival. Even then the play offended the sensibilities of some Americans. *A Hero Ain't Nothin' but a Sandwich*, though it won the Jane Addams Honor Award, was made into a film, and was acclaimed by many school and library journals, still was banned in school libraries in Savannah, Georgia, and in Long Island, New York. Serious literary critics, on the other hand, have overwhelmingly praised the work of Childress, touting her as an important figure in American literature at large and in African American literature very specifically.

Speaking of *Wedding Band*, critic Rosemary Curb gives extremely high praise to the play and its portrayal of interracial relationships and subsequent social strife as subject matter. Curb asserts that the play "deserves comparison with the most celebrated American tragedies" (91).

Trudier Harris praises Childress' writing style and her ability to remove herself from her work, allowing the characters to take over, especially in *Like One of the Family* (100). La Vinia Delois Jennings further expounds on the writing quality of this work: "Drawing from the black oral tradition of signification, especially the creation of a mythical, heroic self, Mildred uses indignation and a take-charge approach against the indignities that assail her during the execution of her work" (7). Here Jennings not only proves Harris' assertion by speaking of Mildred rather than of Childress but also grants the writing style a very particular place in the history of African American language and literature.

Jennings finds Childress' play *Florence* especially significant to African American culture as well. Jennings links Florence's journey north to the historical northern journeys of runaway slaves and newly emancipated slaves in the nineteenth century. Jennings asserts that "[Florence's] movement from the South to the North represents a quest for physical liberation as well as a conscious emergence of her own psychological autonomy" (24).

Writing in *Masterpieces of African-American Literature*, Childress scholar Elizabeth Brown-Guillory points out that *Trouble in Mind* assured Childress' place in theater and that Childress holds the distinction of being "the only woman playwright in the United States whose plays have been written, produced, and published consistently since 1950" (580). Brown-Guillory continues on to grace Childress with the following praise: "Alice Childress' intense and microscopic examination of life matches such great dramatists as Anton Chekhov, August Strindberg, Jean Anouilh, Sholom Aleichem, Sean O'Casey, Noel Coward, Tennessee Williams, and the Nobel Prize-winning African dramatist Wole Soyinka" (580).

Childress' adolescent novels have also gained high praise from critics. It may be that even the efforts to ban the books from some school libraries serve as a positive statement, pointing out very deliberately the realistic issues Childress sets forth to her readers. *A Hero Ain't Nothin' but a Sandwich* has earned especially high marks from readers and moviegoers alike. While critics find Childress' themes of drug addiction, racism, sexism, poverty, and even ageism moving and important, they are also interested in Childress' portrayal of a positive black male figure in the novel. Brown-Guillory, again in *Masterpieces of African-American Literature*, writes that "unlike many of her contemporaries, Childress creates a loving, sensitive, generous black man, Craig Butler, taking responsibility for his family" (196). Jennings agrees, stating that Childress "reverse[s] the portraits of emasculated and 'no count' black men that appear all too frequently in the literature of black women" (97).

BIBLIOGRAPHY

Works by Alice Childress

Young Adult Novels

A Hero Ain't Nothin' but a Sandwich. New York: Coward, McCann, and Geoghegan, 1973.
Rainbow Jordan. New York: Coward, McCann, and Geoghegan, 1981.
Those Other People. New York: G. P. Putnam's Sons, 1989.

Adult Novel

A Short Walk. New York: Coward, McCann, and Geoghegan, 1979.

Short Fiction Collection

Like One of the Family . . . Conversations from a Domestic's Life. Brooklyn: Independence, 1956; Boston: Beacon Press, 1986.

Published Plays

Florence: A One Act Drama. Masses and Mainstream 3 (October 1950): 34–47.
String. New York: Dramatists Play Service, 1969.
The World on a Hill. In *Plays to Remember*. Ed. Henry B. Maloney. Toronto: Macmillan, 1970. 103–25.
The African Garden. In *Black Scenes*. Ed. Alice Childress. Garden City, NY: Doubleday, 1971a. 137–45.
Mojo: A Black Love Story. Black World 20 (April 1971b): 54–82.
Trouble in Mind: A Comedy-Drama in Two Acts. In *Black Theatre: A Twentieth-Century Collection of the Work of Its Best Playwrights*. Ed. Lindsay Patterson. New York: Dodd, Mead, 1971c. 135–74.
Wedding Band: A Love/Hate Story in Black and White. New York: Samuel French, 1973.
Wine in the Wilderness: A Comedy-Drama. In *Plays by and about Women*. Ed. Victoria Sullivan and James Hatch. New York: Vintage, 1973. 379–421.
When the Rattlesnake Sounds. New York: Coward, McCann, and Geoghegan, 1975.
Let's Hear It for the Queen. New York: Coward, McCann, and Geoghegan, 1976.
Moms: A Praise Play for a Black Comedienne. New York: Flora Roberts, 1993.

Nonfiction

"For a Negro Theatre." *Masses and Mainstream* 4 (February 1951): 61–64.
"The Negro Woman in American Literature." *Freedomways* 6 (Winter 1966): 14–19.
"The Black Experience: Why Talk about That?" *Negro Digest* 16 (April 1967): 17–21.
"Black Writers' Views on Literary Lions and Values." *Negro Digest* 17 (January 1968): 36, 85–87.
" 'But I Do My Thing.' Can Black and White Artists Still Work Together?" *New York Times*, 2 February 1969.
"The Soul Man." *Essence* (May 1971a): 68–69, 94.

"Tribute—to Paul Robeson." *Freedomways* 2 (1st quarter 1971b): 14–15.

"Knowing the Human Condition." In *Black Literature and Humanism*. Ed. R. Baxter Miller. Louisville: University Press of Kentucky, 1981. 8–10.

"A Candle in Gale Wind." In *Black Women Writers (1950–1980): A Critical Evaluation*. Ed. Mari Evans. New York: Doubleday, 1984. 111–16.

"Alice Childress." *Speaking for Ourselves: Autobiographical Sketches by Notable Authors of Books for Young Adults*. Ed. Donald R. Gallo. Urbana: NCTE, 1990. 39–40.

Studies of Alice Childress

Brown-Guillory, Elizabeth. "Alice Childress." In *The Oxford Companion to African-American Literature*. Ed. William L. Andrews, Frances Smith Foster, and Trudier Harris. New York: Oxford University Press, 1997.

———. "A Hero Ain't Nothin' but a Sandwich." In *Masterpieces of African-American Literature*. Ed. Frank N. Magill. New York: HarperCollins, 1992. 193–96.

———. *Their Place on Stage: Black Women Playwrights in America*. New York: Greenwood Press, 1988.

———. "Trouble in Mind." In *Masterpieces of African-American Literature*. Ed. Frank N. Magill. New York: HarperCollins, 1992. 577–80.

Buck, Claire, ed. *The Bloomsbury Guide to Women's Literature*. New York: Prentice-Hall, 1992.

Curb, Rosemary. "Alice Childress." *Contemporary Literary Criticism* 96 (1993): 86–124.

Harris, Trudier. "Alice Childress." In *Dictionary of Literary Biography*. Vol. 38: *Afro-American Writers after 1955: Dramatists and Prose Writers*. Ed. Thadious M. Davis and Trudier Harris. Detroit: Gale, 1985. 66–79.

———. "Alice Childress." *Contemporary Literary Criticism* 96 (1993): 86–124.

Hay, Samuel A. "Alice Childress's Dramatic Structure." In *Black Women Writers (1950–1980): A Critical Evaluation*. Ed. Mari Evans. New York: Doubleday, 1984. 117–28.

Jennings, La Vinia Delois. *Alice Childress*. New York: Twayne, 1995.

Killens, John O. "The Literary Genius of Alice Childress." In *Black Women Writers (1950–1980): A Critical Evaluation*. Ed. Mari Evans. New York: Doubleday, 1984. 129–33.

Smith, Karen Patricia. *African-American Voices in Young Adult Literature*. Metuchen, NJ: Scarecrow Press, 1994.

MICHELLE CLIFF
(1946–)

Cora Agatucci

BIOGRAPHY

Michelle Cliff was born in Kingston, Jamaica, on 2 November 1946. Three years later, her family moved to New York. The light-skinned Cliffs could "pass" for white but were never truly assimilated in the United States. In 1956, her parents returned to Jamaica, where Cliff received a colonialist education at St. Andrews private girls' school. Her family again moved to New York in 1960. During college, Cliff became a civil rights activist (Raiskin 68) and was also drawn to the women's movement through her reading (Adisa 4). She earned her A.B. in European history from Wagner College in 1969.

Afterward, Cliff worked at W. W. Norton publishing house in New York until 1971, when she left the United States to study at the Warburg Institute of the University of London. In 1974, she earned the M.Phil., focusing on languages and comparative history of the Italian Renaissance. "I started out as a historian," Cliff explains; "I've always been struck by the misrepresentation of history," and later her fiction would undertake "to correct received versions of history, especially the history of resistance" (Adisa 6). She returned to New York and Norton in 1974, working as a copy editor, then as manuscript and production editor specializing in history, women's studies, and politics, until 1979. Cliff also taught at the New York School for Social Research (1974–76).

Cliff has not returned to Jamaica since 1975, believing that there she might not have been able to write (Schwartz 612). Years earlier, like *Abeng*'s adolescent protagonist Clare Savage, Cliff was moved by Anne Frank's diary to begin her own. But her parents' humiliating exposure of her diary stopped young Cliff from personal and creative writing for many years. This silence was finally broken in 1978, when she wrote "Notes on Speechlessness" for a New York women's writing group (Adisa 2). Frank "gave me permission to write, and to use writing as a way of survival," Cliff states (Raiskin 68). Moreover, she credits feminism for supporting her choice to become a writer—"not at all encouraged in the world in which I grew up"—and to foreground women's lives and their resistance to intersecting oppressions of class, race, gender, and sexual orientation (Adisa 4).

In 1978, Cliff published "Notes on Speechlessness" in *Sinister Wisdom*, a feminist journal of lesbian culture. In the same year, she edited *The Winner Names the Age: A Collection of Writings by Lillian Smith*, a white, southern social reformer and writer whose issues parallel Cliff's own—the power of language, the political responsibility of the creative person, the symbol-making possibilities of the mythic mind, and necessity of diversity (Cliff, *The Winner* 105). Her first collection of prose poetry, *Claiming an Identity They Taught Me to Despise* (1980), asserts her title claim "to be a whole person" and "not deny any piece of who I am" (Adisa 3). In 1980–81, Cliff took teaching positions at Hampshire College and the University of Massachusetts at Amherst; from 1980 to 1989, she served on the editorial board of *Signs: A Journal of Women in Culture and Society*; and from 1981 to 1983, she edited and copublished *Sinister Wisdom* with Adrienne Rich. The opportunity to spend six weeks of uninterrupted writing came with a Mac-Dowell fellowship in 1982, and at the MacDowell Colony, Cliff produced much of her first novel, *Abeng* (Raiskin 71).

Cliff then taught for the adult degree program of Norwich University's Vermont campus (1983–84), and was Massachusetts Artists Foundation fellow and Eli Kanto fellow at Yaddo in 1984. In the same year, *Abeng* was published, and Cliff moved to the West Coast, where she taught at Vista College in Berkeley and developed an experimental creative writing program for young black writers with the Martin Luther King, Jr., Public Library in Oakland. Her next book, *The Land of Look Behind* (1985), is a collection of poetry and prose that includes "Journey into Speech" and "If I Could Write This in Fire, I Would Write This in Fire." In San Francisco, long "intrigued by the black woman's role in revolution" (Adisa 5), Cliff sought out tangible traces of Mary Ellen Pleasant, an African American who helped finance John Brown's raid at Harper's Ferry and later became a central character in *Free Enterprise*.

Cliff also taught at the University of California at Santa Cruz and San Jose State and was visiting lecturer at Stanford University from 1987 to 1991. Interviews with Cliff suggest that her teaching, like her writing, is informed by a strong sense of social responsibility to educate others in the deep roots and damaging effects of racism and other oppressions. She teaches against the "official" versions of history to underscore "that there was resistance" (Raiskin 67) and tries to evoke "compassion for other human beings" (Schwartz 610). Her second novel, *No Telephone to Heaven* (1987), continues *Abeng's* story of Clare Savage. Cliff was awarded a Fulbright Fellowship in 1988 and a National Endowment for the Arts Fellowship in fiction in 1989. The title story of Cliff's next book, *Bodies of Water* (1990), fictionalizes Cliff's traumatic diary incident (Schwartz 603–604).

Toni Morrison's* *Beloved* (1988) influenced Cliff's most recent novel, *Free*

Enterprise (1993). Morrison "opened up my imagination with regard to the re-writing of history, revising the history we've all been taught." *Free Enterprise* might not have been possible, Cliff believes, "without Morrison's having taken on the whole idea of bondage and resistance" (Adisa 6). Cliff lectures widely, and her work has appeared in *Critical Fictions, Caribbean Women Writers, Between Women, Heresies, Village Voice Literary Supplement, Sojourner, Ms., American Voice,* and *Frontiers.* She is currently Allan K. Smith Professor of English Language and Literature at Trinity College, Connecticut, and lives in Santa Cruz, California.

MAJOR WORKS AND THEMES

The life and work of Michelle Cliff resist categorization—by nation, race, gender, class, or genre. Like the autobiographical character Clare Savage of her first two novels, Cliff is positioned at the "crossroads" ("Clare Savage as a Cross-roads Character"). Growing up Jamaican meant growing up colonized in a "wild," yet damagingly repressed, location, full of lost personal and collective histories, enforced silences, and deliberate erasures. From this location come the major themes of her fiction and poetry. At once privileged and oppressed, Cliff was born light-skinned ("red people" by Jamaican color hierarchies); resisted indoc-trination as a "collaborator" by a father descended of slave owners and a colo-nialist education; sought to recover her alienated African-Arawak-Carib maternal ancestry; and struggled to assert her lesbianism and writing aspirations. The themes and experimental techniques of "Notes on Speechlessness," *Claiming an Identity They Taught Me to Despise,* and *The Land of Look Behind* trace the process of rejecting speechlessness and inventing her "own peculiar speech" to claim all her identities ("Caliban's Daughter" 40).

This process, worked out in migration and exile, is also enacted through Clare Savage of *Abeng* and *No Telephone to Heaven.* In *Abeng,* Cliff exposes the erasures of "official" family and colonized history by tracing out submerged histories em-bedded in Jamaican Creole language and oral tradition. Alinear narratives layer the story of adolescent Clare's coming to politicized consciousness. In her search for reconnection to her mother and her African Amerindian identities, Clare revitalizes fabled Jamaican foremothers like Nanny, woman warrior of maroon resistance. The polyphony of narrative forms and voices consciously departs from literary realism. As Cliff observes of other African American women writers, one must "write beyond reality to describe reality" ("Women Warriors" 22).

No Telephone to Heaven continues Clare's quest to the United States, then England, and back to Jamaica. While autobiographical, Cliff's fiction relentlessly interrogates the multiple identities of a cross-section of characters for collective as well as personal ends. Cliff writes the erased story of the gardener Christopher, namesake of Jamaica's legacies of colonization and revolution, to explain mur-derous sociopolitical realities that official versions deny. Harry/Harriet, male and female, black and white, is another "crossroads" character coming to terms with conflicted identities and intersecting oppressions. He names his own rape and gender oppression as his mother's, chooses the revolutionary path, and moves Clare closer to a coming home to self. She, too, is on the truck, symbolically inscribed "No Telephone to Heaven," carrying Jamaican insurgents to a tragic act of resistance. Colonized to mutual distrust and betrayal, they forge a momentary, yet potentially transformative, unity.

As she has said of Harriet Tubman, Cliff's work aims "first to liberate the self and then to liberate the group" ("Women Warriors" 22). That project has widened the scope of her fiction, enabling her to speak to and for the many groups through her own experiences. Cliff moves the setting of her most recent novel, *Free Enterprise*, to slave-era and turn-of-the-century America. Appropriating history's characters and events, Cliff again challenges official versions by re-envisioning alternative histories of resistance for Mary Ellen Pleasant, Jamaican Annie Christmas, and other characters in a compelling fusion of genres and cultures. Caribbeanness is a confusion of cultural influences, without center and boundary, Cliff states, such "that you really have to create yourself" (Raiskin 63). Self-described as at once "outsider" to all groups and "connected to the peoples of the world" (Raiskin 57), Cliff exemplifies the creative conflicts, responsibilities, and possibilities of living and writing at the crossroads.

CRITICAL RECEPTION

If Michelle Cliff's work was "a country only recently discovered and still mostly unexplored" by academic literary critics in 1993 (Pollock 138), that situation is changing. *Free Enterprise* has been fairly widely and favorably reviewed in the United States, and her books appear frequently on course reading lists in the United States. (Internet searches also yield at least two Web sites devoted to Cliff.) The ambivalent Caribbean reception of her work may explain why critics have been slow to recognize Cliff's achievement. However, several influential Afrodiasporic feminist scholars have opened the way for reassessment. Postcolonial critics of resistance literature are increasingly drawn to *No Telephone to Heaven*, pivotal in crossing boundaries of culture, nation, and genre. However, Cliff's depths have not yet been plumbed. Furthermore, the intersecting lesbian themes and models of identity of her work deserve more critical attention.

Francoise Lionnet and Belinda Edmondson have addressed Cliff's problematic reception among Caribbean critics. Some place Cliff's work outside the Caribbean cultural mainstream because of her expatriate status, her U.S. acceptance as an African American writer, and her Western-influenced feminism. However, Carole Boyce Davies argues that migration and exile define New World experience (113) and recommends black feminist readings that "present a . . . trans-cultural/trans-local awareness of Black women's writing communities" (128). Within this framework, Davies commends *Claiming an Identity They Taught Me to Despise* and "If I Could Write This in Fire, I Would Write This in Fire" for "confront[ing] questions of subjectivity in a discursively lyrical manner" and "accept[ing] all facets of experience, history, and personhood in the definition of self" (122).

Other critics suspect fair-skinned Cliff's choice to claim her African heritage and to write predominantly in standard English presumably for non-Jamaican audiences in *Claiming an Identity They Taught Me to Despise* and *Abeng*. For example, Pamela Mordicai and Betty Wilson included Cliff in *Her True-True Name: An Anthology of Women's Writing from the Caribbean* (1989), while identifying her as "white" and "alienated" along with Jean Rhys and criticizing the "compromised authenticity" of Cliff's rendering of Creole (xvii). Lionnet challenges such attempts to apply rigid demarcations or "a false ideal of purity" to ever-changing syncretic Caribbean languages (328). Language and its role in (de)colonization and identity (re)formation are central to any discussion of Caribbean writing, and Lionnet judges *Abeng*'s technique of "linguistic archeology" (340) effective in "liberating the word," as well as the world (327). Cliff "dig[s] underneath the colonial process of subject formation" and its "cultural discontinuities" to "rewrite a different collective and personal history for the protagonist" (Lionnet 323).

Edmondson values Cliff for taking on issues of race and class embedded in her ambivalent "white Creole" status. In the "geo-political space of memory" arising from Clare Savage's "conflicting and multiple identities," "the white Creole history of privilege and collaboration" is integrated with "the unwritten black and Amerindian histories of suffering and resistance" (185), in a "restless tension" of mixed narrative techniques (187). Edmondson views *No Telephone to Heaven* as more successful than *Abeng* in moving beyond binary representation of race-gender power relations and relocating the "focal point of conflict in language itself, wherein gender and geo-political categories are both created and fixed in memory" (190). Not only is hegemonic "official" history thus undone, but an alternative reality is created in the narrative structure—and with it a new space for resistance and identity formation.

Critics praise Cliff's experimental narrative techniques, mixing linguistic and genre codes and appropriating Western traditions of autobiography and bildungsroman for communal, rather than solely individualistic, ends. Fiona Barnes identifies *No Telephone to Heaven* as resistance literature—particularly in "expos[ing] the newest and subtlest form of neo-colonialism in the Caribbean: cultural cannibalism" (23). Maria Helena Lima credits Cliff's second novel for "expos[ing] the complexity of the contradictions within generic conventions" and pursuing "the possibility of revolutionary social transformation" (35). *No Telephone to Heaven* is a "collective novel" (Glissant's term), "like many other postcolonial novels," because it parallels "the formation of the young self to that of the developing nation" (Lima 35). Cliff is "intent on the destruction of boundaries and inventive in new ways of seeing" (Lima 53).

Lima is less enthusiastic about the message of the novel ("the tragic impossibility" of social transformation) and Cliff's presumed audience. Lima assumes primacy is given "educated," class-privileged non-Jamaican readers (37). Thomas

Cartelli joins Lionnet in more positive appraisals. Cliff has "master[ed] the impulse to write back to the center" more successfully than many other postcolonial writers (5) in the "thoroughly creolized and womanized" *No Telephone to Heaven,* Cartelli argues (7). Moreover, Cliff's use of "Jamaican patois" "challenges the Western reader's confidence in his or her ability to map West Indian experience" (Cartelli 8). Clare Savage, reconfigured as a "new, New World Miranda," rejects the role of collaborator and "replaces both Prospero and Caliban as an agent of self-determination and cultural change" (Cartelli 7). More recently, Sethuraman reads the ways *No Telephone to Heaven* unmasks the "colonial gaze" and "the deleterious effects of visual politics" (250, 254). For example, the massacre of Paul H.'s family is presented from split perspectives to reveal Christopher's "evidence-cum-witness" to "history as trauma" (264). In aiming her Jamaican revolutionaries' attack at a Hollywood film crew, Cliff "strikes at the heart of the violence of visual culture" (276).

BIBLIOGRAPHY

Works by Michelle Cliff

Fiction

Claiming an Identity They Taught Me to Despise. Watertown, MA: Persephone Press, 1980.
Abeng. Trumansburg, NY: Crossing, 1984.
The Land of Look Behind. Ithaca, NY: Firebrand Books, 1985.
No Telephone to Heaven. New York: Dutton, 1987.
Bodies of Water (short stories). New York: Pantheon, 1990.
Free Enterprise. New York: Dutton, 1993.

Other Works

Ed. *The Winner Names the Age: A Collection of Writings by Lillian Smith.* New York: Norton, 1978a.
"Notes on Speechlessness." *Sinister Wisdom* 5 (Winter 1978b): 5–9.
"Clare Savage as a Crossroads Character." *Caribbean Women Writers: Essays from the First International Conference.* Ed. Selwyn R. Cudjoe. Wellesley, MA: Calaloux, 1990a. 263–268.
"Women Warriors: Black Writers Load the Canon." *Village Voice Literary Supplement* (May 1990b): 20–22.
"Caliban's Daughter: The Tempest and the Teapot." *Frontiers: A Journal of Women's Studies* 12.2 (1991): 36–51.
"History as Fiction, Fiction as History." *Ploughshares* 20.2 (Fall 1994): 196–202. Rpt. *InfoTrac 2000* Expanded Academic Index, Article A15759520, http://sbweb3.med.iacnet.com/infotrac/ (July 1997).

Studies of Michelle Cliff

Adisa, Opal Palmer. "Journey into Speech—A Writer between Two Worlds: An Interview with Michelle Cliff." *African American Review* 28.2 (Summer 1994): 273–

281. Rpt. *InfoTrac 2000* Expanded Academic Index Article A15787241, http://
sbweb3.med.iacnet.com/infotrac/ (July 1997).

Barnes, Fiona R. "Resisting Cultural Cannibalism: Oppositional Narratives in Michelle
Cliff's *No Telephone to Heaven.*" *Journal of the Midwest Modern Language Association*
25.1 (Spring 1992): 23–31.

Berrian, Brenda F. "Claiming an Identity: Caribbean Women Writers in English." *Journal
of Black Studies* 25.2 (Dec. 1994): 200–216.

Cartelli, Thomas. "After *The Tempest*: Shakespeare, Postcoloniality, and Michelle Cliff's
New, New World Miranda." *Contemporary Literature* 36.1 (Spring 1995): 82–102.
Rpt. *InfoTrac 2000* Expanded Academic Index Article A16791799, http://
sbweb3.med.iacnet.com/infotrac/ (July 1997).

Davies, Carole Boyce. "Writing Home: Gender, Heritage, and Identity in Afro-Caribbean
Women's Writing in the U.S." *Black Women, Writing and Identity: Migrations of
the Subject.* London: Routledge, 1994. 113–129.

Edmondson, Belinda. "Race, Privilege, and the Politics of (Re)Writing History: An
Analysis of the Novels of Michelle Cliff." *Callaloo* 16.1 (Winter 1993): 180–191.

Lima, Maria Helena. "Revolutionary Developments: Michelle Cliff's 'No Telephone to
Heaven' and Merle Collins's 'Angel.' " *ARIEL: A Review of International English
Literature* 24.1 (Jan. 1993): 35–56.

Lionnet, Francoise. "Of Mangoes and Maroons: Language, History and the Multicultural
Subject of Michelle Cliff's *Abeng.*" *De/Colonizing the Subject: The Politics of Gender
in Women's Autobiography.* Ed. Sidonie Smith and Julia Watson. Minneapolis:
University of Minnesota Press, 1992. 321–345.

Mordicai, Pamela, and Betty Wilson, eds. *Her True-True Name: An Anthology of Women's
Writing from the Caribbean.* Portsmouth, NH: Heinemann, 1989.

Nunez-Harrell, Elizabeth. "The Paradoxes of Belonging: The White West Indian in Fiction." *Modern Fiction Studies* 31.2 (Summer 1985): 281–293.

Pollock, Mary S. "Michelle Cliff (1946–)." *Contemporary Lesbian Writers of the United
States: A Bio-Bibliographical Critical Sourcebook.* Ed. Sandra Pollack and Denise D.
Knight. Westport, CT: Greenwood, 1993. 135–140.

Raiskin, Judith. "The Art of History: An Interview with Michelle Cliff." *The Kenyon
Review* 15.1 (Winter 1993): 57–71.

Schwartz, Meryl F. "An Interview with Michelle Cliff." *Contemporary Literature* 34.4
(1993): 595–619.

Sethuraman, Ramchandran. "Evidence-cum-Witness: Subaltern History, Violence, and
the (De)formation of Nation in Michelle Cliff's *No Telephone to Heaven.*" *Modern
Fiction Studies* 43.1 (1997): 249–287. Rpt. http://direct.press.jhu.edu/journals/
modern__fiction__studies/v043/43.1.sethurman.html (13 July 1997).

Shea, Renee Hausmann. "Michelle Cliff." *Belles Lettres: A Review of Books by Women* 9.3
(Spring 1994): 32–34. Rpt. *InfoTrac 2000* Expanded Academic Index Article
A16009736, http://sbweb3.med.iacnet.com/infotrac/ (July 1997).

CYRUS COLTER
(1910–)

Leela Kapai

BIOGRAPHY

Cyrus Colter was born on January 8, 1910, in Noblesville, Indiana. The families of both his parents, originally from North Carolina, had moved in the 1830s to this rural area in search of a safe place for free blacks. Colter's solid, middle-class upbringing had a decided effect on his writing. Though not college-educated, his father was an avid reader and an effective orator. He was active in the National Association for the Advancement of Colored People. After the death of their mother in 1916, Colter and his younger sister were brought up by their maternal grandparents. Colter had a happy childhood and never experienced any antiblack feelings in the early years of his life.

Colter received his high school education at Rayen Academy, a private school in Youngstown, Ohio, and later attended Ohio State University. In a literature course he was first introduced to the Russian authors who were to influence his own writing. He moved to Chicago in 1936 to attend the Kent Law School of Illinois Institute of Technology and supported himself by working at the local black Young Men's Christian Association (YMCA) at night. He set up his law practice in the South Side of Chicago in 1940 and was later appointed deputy collector of internal revenue. These years gave him an opportunity to observe people closely and later provided models for characters in his stories.

Colter enlisted in the army in 1942 and married Mary Imogene Mackay, a Northwestern University graduate and an educator by profession. He became a field artillery captain in the Fifth Army under General Mark Clark and took part in the liberation of north Italy. He resumed his law practice after the war and continued until 1950, when he was appointed commerce commissioner for the state of Illinois by Governor Adlai Stevenson. It was a position held by only one other black before him. His tenure on the commission lasted for over twenty-three years. Meanwhile, his interest in literature led him to try his hand at writing fiction; his success led to his appointment as the Chester D. Tripp Professor of Humanities at Northwestern University in 1973. He retired in 1978 in order to devote more time to travel, research, writing, and music and has published two more novels since then.

MAJOR WORKS AND THEMES

Though Colter had always been interested in literature, he did not start writing fiction until he was almost fifty. His rereading of the Russians—Pushkin, Gogol, Turgenev, Dostoevsky, and Tolstoy—left him in awe of these writers' wide canvas portraying people of all classes. He felt that the black experience, especially of the upper class, had been sadly neglected in contemporary literature. He took up writing fiction to fill this need.

In an array of interviews spanning a period of over twenty years, Colter has explained how he set out to accomplish his objective. He read Melville, Joyce, and Faulkner, authors he admired tremendously. Emulating Joyce, Colter attempted to portray the South Side Chicago black community in the short stories he wrote. Repeated rejections from national magazines did not faze him, and eventually "A Chance Meeting" was published by *Threshold*, an Irish magazine. His literary career began in earnest when *The Beach Umbrella* won the first Iowa School of Letters Award for Short Fiction in 1970. The book also won fiction awards of the Chicago Friends of Literature and of the Society of Midland Authors. Inspired by Faulkner's dictum that a great writer always deals with the "human heart in conflict with itself" (Bender 428), Colter presented a wide range of characters in varied situations in the fourteen stories.

Colter's subsequent fiction reflects some of the themes glimpsed in *The Beach Umbrella*. A major theme that emerges in the stories and recurs persistently in his later fiction is the inability of individuals to transcend their environment. His reading of Sartre and Camus clearly affected his worldview, for most of his characters suffer from a sense of alienation. They all seem trapped in the maze of their existence and eventually accept the emptiness of their lives. Another theme concerns the issue of blackness. In his novels, many characters ponder the question of their identity. What does it mean to be black? How does the African American historical past influence the present? In dealing with the quest for identity, Colter presents no clear-cut views. It is as if the characters have to find answers suitable for their own personalities. Though the relationship between the races invariably forms the backdrop of his fiction, Colter does not advocate either separatism or assimilation. He has never considered himself to be a black writer but simply a writer who happens to be black (Cross et al. 862).

Colter's first novel, *The Rivers of Eros*, came out in 1972. An omniscient narrator recounts the tragedy of Clotilda Pilgrim, a widow, who is taking care of her two grandchildren, Addie and Lester, by taking in boarders and working as a seamstress. Her precariously balanced world is shattered when she is unable to stop sixteen-year-old Addie's affair with an unemployed, married man. Clotilda takes this failure as a punishment for her extramarital affair years ago. Her only daughter, a child of this union, was brutally murdered by her own husband, who suspected her of infidelity. Her boarders, Ambrose Hammer and Letitia Dorsey, cannot save her or Addie despite their best intentions. Her own guilt topples Clotilda over the wall of sanity; she murders Addie and is committed to an asylum. Ambrose Hammer's fate also reinforces Colter's idea that human beings have little control over their destinies. Hammer's book *History of the Negro Race* seems unlikely to be finished as he marries Letitia and takes the responsibility of Lester.

Inability to take control of one's own destiny is seen again in *The Hippodrome*, Colter's second novel published in 1973. Jackson Yaegar, like several other protagonists of Colter's, is an aspiring intellectual who writes on religious topics. Against his better judgment, he marries a woman much younger than himself. The opening scene presents a disheveled Yaegar on the run with the severed head of his wife in a brown bag; he had killed her and her white lover in a fit of rage. What follows strains one's credulity. He is sheltered by Bea, the manager of the Hippodrome, a mobster-owned, pornographic theater. She plans to employ Yaegar for her shows. Yaegar's failure to act—to escape or even to end his life, as he had contemplated—shows his lack of courage to face the situation. He is a man engulfed by his own sexual inadequacy, his past failures, and his guilt. The novel fails to engage the reader despite vivid descriptions of the setting, for the characters do not come alive.

Night Studies, Colter's longest novel, came out in 1979. It is a panoramic work that spans the continents and historical events over centuries and moves between three subplots. It is essentially the tale of John Calvin Knight, the leader of Black People's Congress, and his search for an understanding of the black experience. The novel is structured in four books: "Convergence," "Chronicle," "Canticle," and "Crucible." "Convergence" introduces the characters who will touch Knight's life directly or indirectly. In San Francisco, Griselda, an unhappy white young woman, is attracted to Knight. In Paris, we meet Mary Dee Adkins, daughter of a Chicago surgeon and a talented young black artist, in love with an architecture student from a wealthy white Philadelphia family. Knight moves his main office to Chicago, where all the characters "converge." The first book ends with the attempted assassination of Knight. "Chronicle" recounts the history of black enslavement, the horrors of the Middle Passage, and slave revolts. The historically accurate and well-researched details of the section are conveyed through the consciousness of Knight, who lies sedated in the hospital. He had learned of his ancestral history from his father. The third book traces the journeys of various characters. Knight himself faces the opposition of his colleagues, who disapprove of his relationship with a white woman. Mary Dee is pressured by circumstances and her own sense of moral responsibility to accept Knight's proposal of marriage. In the final section, each character undergoes the test in the crucible: Griselda commits suicide, Mary Dee escapes to Paris, and Knight, forced to relinquish his leadership, goes to Georgia and continues his "night studies." The Epilogue brings a closure to the book by recounting the fate of all characters.

The research involved in the writing of *Night Studies* is, indeed, impressive. Colter succeeds in conveying a clear sense of place in his descriptions of Paris, San Francisco, and Chicago. However, the plot gets entangled in numerous characters—their variety a strength to some extent, but an annoyance mostly, since most of them become mere mouthpieces for particular viewpoints. The weighty issue of race relationships is never fully explored. The militants demand an exclusion of whites from the Black People's Congress; John Calvin Knight does not believe in separatism, yet he yields to appease the movement. How are these issues to be settled? Many questions of import are raised but remain suspended. The novel, in fact, suffers from a surfeit of information.

In *A Chocolate Soldier* (1988), Colter experiments with a different narrative technique. The novel is to be about Cager, the soldier in the title, but it is equally about the narrator, Mesach, who is now the pastor of a church in White Plains, New York, and remains obsessed by the memory of events thirty-five years ago when he and Cager were students at Gladstone College in Tennessee. The reliability of the narrator becomes questionable when we learn of his dishonesty, betrayal, and immorality. Mesach describes Cager as an earnest student, slated for success. His life undergoes a change when he discovers his sexual inadequacy. Instead of becoming an embittered sociopath, he turns his attention to more serious matters and decides that only black militia can get them rights. A likable character at the outset, he gradually seems to lose touch with reality. Perhaps the most impressive accomplishment is Colter's portrayal of old Mary Elizabeth Fitzhugh Dabney, a racist to the core. She is presented with all the contradictions in her character: her unswerving belief in the inferiority of the black race, her sense of noblesse oblige, and a commitment to those under her protection. Again, the tragic destiny is inescapable. Cager murders the wealthy woman and is himself burned alive before any trial can take place. The reader's ambivalent reaction to the chain of events attests to the complexity of issues raised in the novel.

Colter's last novel, *City of Light*, was published in 1993. Paul Kessey, a young, well-educated African American, comes to Paris after the death of his mother. The novel presents a fascinating study of a victim of the oedipal complex. Supported by his wealthy father, Paul is ostensibly busy researching "the long-neglected culture and mores of the African people" (23); in reality, when he is not entertaining the members of the "Coterie," a group of expatriates who come more for lunch than discussions of race issues, or having trysts with Cecile, an attractive Parisian doctor nine years his senior, he spends most of his time writing long letters to his dead mother. Through these confessional letters we learn of the personal history of Paul and what ails his psyche. Colter introduces many other characters who are described in details, but all are pedantic to the point of becoming boring. Somehow, sharing long, interminable, guilt-ridden confessions of Cecile as she prays one early morning, bringing her eight- and twelve-year-old daughters to the church, is not enthralling. Tosca Zimsu, a widow, who is incessantly scheming to find a father for her young son, fares no better. The backdrop of rising French nationalism provides the setting for the ensuing tragedies. Paul and his paramour are shot by the wronged husband: Cecile dies on the spot; Paul lingers for a while, necessitating his father's trip to Paris. Quo Vadis, another expatriate, is found brutally murdered after attending a nationalist gathering in disguise. Only Madame Zimsu succeeds in her goal. She and her son accompany Paul's body as it is transported to the United States. One can only breathe a sigh of relief as the nightmare of tragic events comes to an end.

CRITICAL RECEPTION

Colter's stories collected in *The Beach Umbrella* and *The Amoralists and Other Tales* received warm reviews unequaled by those for the later works. The careful crafting and deft characterizations in these stories were seen as a unique feature of his art (Bender 94–95; Hendin 55). His novels, on the other hand, received mixed reviews at best. Gibbons found *The Hippodrome* "an extraordinary creation" (899), but others agree with Bender that its "surreal cast of nightmare" makes this "experimental" work lose effect (Bender 97).

Night Studies was generally well reviewed. Seen as "an old-fashioned slice of life novel," it was considered "an uneven work" (Kennedy 46). Grosch noted the melodrama in character and plot but found the work admirable for its nobility (400). Morton admired Colter's narrative technique in *A Chocolate Soldier* and found the "self-mocking magniloquence of the narrator" a challenge to the readers (29).

In addition to several interviews that shed light on Colter's art and influences, three articles discuss his works. O'Brien brings out the deterministic features in the stories in *The Beach Umbrella* and in *The Rivers of Eros*. Bender comments on the Chekhovian quality of the stories and analyzes the first three novels. Gibbons, admittedly "a partisan of Colter's works," presents an exhaustive analysis of the themes, structure, and style of his novels. He admires the "unresolvable contradictions" in characters (899) and the philosophical underpinnings in his novels (900).

BIBLIOGRAPHY

Works by Cyrus Colter

The Beach Umbrella. Chicago: Swallow Press, 1970.
The Rivers of Eros. 1972. Urbana: University of Illinois Press, 1990.
The Hippodrome. Chicago: Swallow Press, 1973.
Night Studies. Chicago: Swallow Press, 1979.
The Amoralists and Other Tales. New York: Thunder's Mouth Press, 1988a.

A Chocolate Soldier. New York: Thunder's Mouth Press, 1988b.
City of Light. New York: Thunder's Mouth Press, 1993.

Studies of Cyrus Colter

Bender, Robert M. "The Fiction of Cyrus Colter." *New Letters* 48.1 (Fall 1981): 93–103.

Cross, Milton G., et al. "Fought for It and Paid Taxes Too: Four Interviews with Cyrus Colter." *Callaloo* 14.4 (1991): 855–897.

Fogarty, Robert S. "Work: Beginning to Write at Fifty: A Conversation with Cyrus Colter." *The Antioch Review* 36 (1978): 422–436.

Gibbons, Reginald. "Colter's Novelistic Contradictions." *Callaloo* 14.4 (1992): 898–905.

Grosch, Anthony R. "*Night Studies*: A Novel." *The Old Northwest* 6.4 (1980–1981): 398–400.

Hendin, Josephine. Review of *The Beach Umbrella*. *Saturday Review* 53 (August 22 1970): 55.

Kennedy, Eileen. Review of *Night Studies*. *Best Sellers* 40.2 (1980): 46.

Morton, Kathryn. Review of *A Chocolate Soldier*. *New York Times Book Review* 93 (August 28, 1980): 29.

O'Brien, John O. "Forms of Determinism in the Fiction of Cyrus Colter." *Studies in Black Literature* 4.2 (1973): 24–28.

STEVEN CORBIN
(1953–1995)

Terrence J. McGovern

BIOGRAPHY

Steven Corbin, son of Warren Leroy Corbin and Yvonne O'Hare, was born in Jersey City, New Jersey, on 3 October 1953. After high school he attended Essex County College for two years. He then studied at the University of Southern California's film school from 1975 to 1977 but never completed the degree. After leaving film school, Corbin supported himself by working as a secretary and also as a taxi driver while at the same time immersing himself in reading fiction, especially black fiction. Corbin began to aspire to be a novelist by reading the works of black writers such as Toni Morrison,* Alice Walker,* and Richard Wright. Reading the works of James Baldwin* convinced him that he should write about being gay and black. Corbin's interest in the Harlem Renaissance found artistic expression in his first novel, *No Easy Place to Be* (1989). His subsequent novels, *Fragments That Remain* (1993) and *A Hundred Days from Now* (1994), explore aspects of family, homosexuality, and race in contemporary American society. In addition to his writing, Corbin became involved in ACT-UP in order to help combat the high level of racial segregation that he noted in the Los Angeles gay community (Duplechan, 12). He also taught fiction writing at the University of California, Los Angeles. Corbin died in New York City of AIDS on 31 August 1995.

MAJOR WORKS AND THEMES

No Easy Place to Be is the story of three sisters—Velma, Miriam, Louise—who are coming of age during the 1920s. Raised in Harlem by their widowed mother, each sister seeks her place in society but is faced with racism not only in the society at large but in the black community, where "high yellow" or passing for white is prized, and dark complexion is devalued. The festive mood of the parade honoring the all-black 369th Infantry that begins the narrative is in counterpoint to Miriam's cynical observation that "what makes them [blacks] think they'll be treated any better than before?" (10). The rest of the novel, in many ways, answers that question. Velma, the principal protagonist, wants to become part of the Harlem Renaissance literary scene. As she attempts to get published, she quickly discovers that being a black writer and a woman is "no easy place to be." When she attends a Harlem Writers Workshop, she receives a very cool welcome from the all-male group but is befriended by a member of the group, Zachary Rudolph, known to his friends as Rudy. Velma falls in love with Rudy, only to find out later that he is gay. At a party given by Carl Van Vechten, one of the many actual personages of the era whom Corbin weaves into the narrative, Velma meets black novelist G. Virgil Scott. She, Scott, and Rudy form a friendship that proves to be a mixed blessing for all three. Scott knows wealthy whites who will support black writers and introduces Rudy and Velma to Mrs. Vanderpool, who is willing to support both of them financially on certain conditions. While Velma is pursuing a literary career, her sister Miriam, a nurse, has become an advocate of black solidarity and the back-to-Africa movement preached by Marcus Garvey. When the leaders suspect that Miriam is a lesbian, they ask her to quit the Universal Negro Improvement Association, despite her many efforts on its be-half. She discovers that homophobia can be found among her own people. Louise, who can pass for white, is turned down for a job when she admits to living in Harlem, and the prospective employer then realizes she is "colored." She becomes a dancer at the Cotton Club, where she meets Vittorio, a wealthy Italian playboy. Their relationship blossoms into love and marriage, since she has convinced him that she is Italian. When his parents arrive for the wedding, his mother senses that Louise, who has changed her name to Luisa, is not Italian and becomes hostile. When Louise becomes pregnant, she is fearful her ruse will be discovered. As the baby grows darker, her fears are realized. Suspicious, Vittorio confronts her. Her deception so angers him that he throws her out of the house. The story ends with a rather interesting triangle of love and friendship. Velma is still in love with Rudy, who is in love with Scott, the latter still struggling with his ambivalent feelings about his sexuality but intending to continue his liaison with Velma and his friendship with Rudy.

Fragments That Remain is centered around a dysfunctional black family, iron-ically named Whyte. It is a story of spousal and child abuse, drug addiction, self-loathing, and interracial love. Howard is a light-skinned black whose family is unhappy with Althea, his choice for a bride. She is the daughter of minimally educated, southern black parents, lives in Harlem, and initially is intimidated by her middle-class in-laws. As the story progresses, Althea sees her marriage slowly deteriorate to the point that when Howard is in the hospital dying, she voices her feelings in telling her son Skylar that his father would be "better off dead" (18). Skylar, who has become a successful actor, remembers the humiliations suffered at the hands of his father and thus, like his mother, feels very little, if any, real love for his progenitor. In contrast to the successful Skylar is Kendall, his younger brother, the father's favorite, who has become a drug addict. Skylar has a white lover named Evan Cabot, who has left him after the two had a major quarrel. The principal action of the story is Skylar's attempts to deal with that separation as well as reconciling with his father. Interwoven into the story is Sklyar's mother's own struggles with her husband and her ultimate success as an educated businesswoman.

A Hundred Days from Now tells the tale of two gay lovers, Dexter Baldwin and Sergio Gutierrez, both of whom are HIV-positive. Dexter is a famous black screenwriter and openly gay. Sergio is a wealthy Mexican of mixed parentage (his mother is American) and closeted. As Sergio's health begins to decline, Dexter has to deal with his lover's verbal abuse and internalized homophobia. Added to this burden, Dexter must also cope with the reaction of Sergio's parents to the announcement that their son has AIDS, is gay, and has a black lover. Sergio undergoes an experimental operation that may reverse the effects of the AIDS virus. However, it will be 100 days before the results of the operation will be known. During that time, Dexter and Sergio must confront the reality of AIDS and its effects on their relationship and on Sergio's conservative Catholic family.

No Easy Place to Be, the title of Corbin's first novel, sums up the major themes of his three novels: racism, homophobia, AIDS, and the family. Being black, gay, and HIV+ is no easy place to be. These themes are informed by Corbin's own experience as a gay black male who acknowledged in an interview that much of the material in his novels is autobiographical (Duplechan, 17).

For Corbin, racism permeates American society, and the anger he feels "both as a black and queer man" (Duplechan, 16) becomes more evident with each subsequent novel. The hope initially expressed in No Easy Place to Be that blacks, having served with distinction in World War I, "would not go unrewarded . . . they'd be full-fledged American citizens" (9) becomes a cruel deception that extends to the present day. Corbin's characters find out that education does not give an automatic entrée into white society. Velma, in spite of her degree from Barnard, initially can find a job only as a maid, where she is viewed by her white employer as an "uppity darkie" (No Easy Place, 19). Although Louise has the necessary skills and education to do office work, she does not get hired as a secretary once the interviewer finds out that she is black. In Fragments That Remain, Sklyar, now a successful actor, nonetheless has lost many acting parts because of his race. Good looks, intelligence, talent, Ivy League education were not enough (104). Besides overt prejudice, there is the subtle racism, which in No Easy Place to Be is personified in the wealthy Mrs. Vanderpool, who gives financial support to aspiring black writers but limits their writing to white society's stereotypical views of blacks as primitive and exotic, with a talent for music and dance (116). Even Evan, who endured taunts from family and friends for his willingness to befriend (and later to date) blacks occasionally behaves in a racist manner, albeit less overtly. In anger, he calls Skylar a "nigger" (Fragments, 17) and makes a pejorative reference to Skylar's upbringing in Harlem. Racism takes an interesting turn in *A Hundred Day from Now*. During an argument between Dexter and Sergio as to who has experienced more racial prejudice, Sergio states he knows as much about racism as Dexter since he has been victimized by whites for being Mexican and physically assaulted by blacks who thought he was white. Dexter counters with the fact "that to be black and male in this country is the lowest level on the totem pole" (68).

More insidious, however, than white prejudice is the racism of blacks directed against blacks. This variation on the theme of contraracial prejudice is particularly prominent in both *No Easy Place to Be* and *Fragments*. Light skin, not black, is deemed beautiful. Light-skinned Louise is considered "white and pretty," while her darker sister Miriam is taunted by Harlem neighborhood children as "black and ugly like an African" (*No Easy Place*, 27). In *Fragments*, Althea's light-skinned husband and his family consider themselves superior to her and treat her accordingly. Her husband refers to her family as "nothing more than lowlife niggers" (53).

Although the theme of homophobia is present to some extent in *No Easy Place to Be*, it permeates *Fragments* and *A Hundred Days*. Corbin also makes the point that homophobia is present among blacks as well as among whites, something both racial groups have in common. In fact, being gay and black in America, whether in the 1920s or now, is to swallow a double dose of hate and prejudice. In *No Easy Place to Be*, Velma has to confront her own homophobia when she finds out that Rudy is gay. He has to explain to her that being gay is not a choice and that she cannot change him (85). In *Fragments*, Skylar is taunted for being gay not only by classmates but more insidiously by his father, who throws him out of the house. Aubrey, Skylar's gay maternal uncle, is also a victim of Skylar's father's taunts and hatred and dies in a fire deliberately set by the father. In addition to her rejection by the Universal Negro Improvement Association because of her sexual orientation, Miriam has to struggle with her own internal homophobia. Internalized homophobia is spotlighted in *A Hundred Days*. Sergio, the wealthy Latino, is deeply closeted, determined to be straight-acting and very uncomfortable with Dexter's being openly gay. Before Sergio's parents arrive from Mexico for a visit, he asks Dexter not to wear an earring and to "act masculine" (77) for fear that they will think that Dexter is gay and by implication, that their son is, too.

AIDS and its effects on relationships are the dominant theme in *A Hundred Days from Now*. Both Sergio and Dexter are HIV-positive. Very early in the relationship both men acknowledge that they are infected. Such honesty is definitely viewed by Corbin as both praiseworthy and courageous, which, however, does not preclude a dread of the disease and its negative impact on relationships. AIDS for Dexter is a "nasty four letter acronym" that frightens him more than anything else (26). For Sergio, AIDS forces him to openly acknowledge both his sexual orientation and his disease to his twin brother, who is his business partner (36). Fear of the disease and the resultant emotional and/or physical isolation further complicate Sergio's life. When he is in the hospital dying, his parents keep their distance from him even after his assurances that they cannot catch the disease (149). AIDS makes Dexter reexamine his relationship with Sergio (171). He tries to decide whether Sergio's verbal abuse is the result of the disease or an intrinsic aspect of Sergio's personality. In *Fragments*, AIDS is linked to racism. In one of their many arguments, Evan wants to know Skylar's response to the theory that AIDS came from Africa. If that theory is true, then Evan states, "I could possibly catch AIDS from a black person" (17).

In all three novels, Corbin underscores the importance of family in the formation of values both negative and positive. Love, hate, acceptance, intolerance are learned in the home. They form lasting influences on the children even if they in later years attempt to reject the negative values. In a humble Harlem apartment three sisters learn love, tolerance, self-acceptance from their mother, Elvira. She tells her children that "colored folks come in all colors, like the rainbow. That's why we so beautiful" (*No Easy Place*, 27). This affirming attitude is in sharp contrast to Althea's mother-in law, who has taught her son to denigrate members of their race who are black. Despite her husband's attitudes, Althea tries to instill positive values in her two sons, including respect for their father. Evan has learned only intolerance from his parents: blacks are inferior, and God has planned it that way (*Fragments*, 47). Although he has prided himself as being above his parents' racism, Evan years later reverts to their bigotry when he refers to his lover as a "crazy nigger" (*Fragments*, 17) and echoes his father's apodictic statement: "[T]hose goddamn niggers, I'll tell you. Violent as the day is long" (*Fragments*, 45). Dysfunctional families are the norm in Corbin's fiction. Although Althea (*Fragments*) and the three sisters (*No Easy Place*) have grown up in a positive home environment, they find themselves caught up in troubled relationships, some of them suffering verbal and physical abuse. To a large degree, the successes and/or failures of Corbin's characters are the results of a dysfunctional home environment.

CRITICAL RECEPTION

Criticism of Corbin's novels consists only of book reviews, which range from very positive to extremely negative. Reviews of *No Easy Place to Be* are generally quite negative. Buckley's review is the most negative. She opines that Corbin has reduced this "fascinating time and place . . . to the level of absurdity" (8). Other reviewers echo her assessment, referring to Corbin's "valiant stab at a period re-creation" (*Kirkus Reviews*, 1626) or to his "interesting but flawed treatment of a period of great social flux" (Steinberg, 136). Steinberg considers his style as "often . . . stilted and woefully cliched" (136). Another reviewer finds "his prose occasionally cloying, mannered and just plain clumsy" (*Kirkus Reviews*, 1626). As for his characters, they lack "depth" (*Kirkus Reviews*, 1626), and the black male characters are "lamentable in the extreme" (Buckley, 8). The negative reviews are best summed up by Johnson's wry observation that "Harlem in the period between 1919 and 1929 is no easy place for Mr. Corbin to make his debut" (12). In contrast to these views are those of Giddings, who considers the novel "a joy to read," a "sparkling narrative" (20). For her, the Harlem Renaissance comes "alive while effortlessly educating the reader about the political and cultural events of the period" (20). Giddings considers Corbin a "masterful storyteller" (20) whose characters' personalities "emerge forcefully yet subtly through . . . skillful use of dialogue" (20). Robertson considers the novel "immensely readable" (835).

Fragments That Remain received largely positive critical reception in both the gay and straight press. It is a "blistering novel" with "stinging poignancy" (*Publishers Weekly*, 295). According to Seymour, Corbin's use of multiple voices in the narrative creates a "rich texture" (31). Corbin demonstrates "considerable writing abilities" (Harmon, 1782) in the development of plot, characters, and themes. However, one critic thought that the novel "skews closer to the political than to the aesthetic" (Lassell, 75).

A Hundred Days from Now received mixed reviews but generally more positive than negative. Corbin can "explicate and portray his characters with sympathy and care" (Bronski, 21). The novel is a "fierce exploration of love, race and sexuality," "easy to read" (*Kirkus Reviews*, 414). Lutes notes that the novel takes an "undeniably fresh look at relationships from an African American and Hispanic perspective" (156). However, one reviewer thinks that novel has "stylistic lapses" and "cliches" as well as dialogue that is "often forced and artificial" (*Publishers Weekly*, 79). The positive note sounded in the *Times Literary Supplement* that "American culture will be all the richer" (25) by the future literary output of novelists like Corbin has been silenced by his untimely death. Anyone who is seeking to understand better the gay black experience in American society would do well to read Corbin's novels and short stories.

BIBLIOGRAPHY

Works by Steven Corbin

Novels

No Easy Place to Be. New York: Simon and Schuster, 1989.
Fragments That Remain. Boston: Alyson, 1993.
A Hundred Days from Now. Boston: Alyson, 1994.

Short Stories

"Upward Bound." *Breaking Ice: An Anthology of Contemporary African-American Fiction*. Ed. Terry McMillan. New York: Viking, 1990. 164–177.
"Coming Full Circle." *More Like Minds*. Ed. Ben Goldstein. London: GMP, 1991. 179–197.
"Jazz." *Sundays at Seven: Choice Words from a Different Light's Gay Writers Series*. Ed. Rondo Mieczkowski. San Francisco: Alamo Square Press, 1996. 118–124.

Review

"Singularly Hemphillesque: A 'Gadfly Perched on the Ass of America' Breaks Through."
Rev. of *Ceremonies* by Essex Hemphill. *Lambda Book Report*, 5 July 1982: 18.

Studies of Steven Corbin

Blandell, Janet Boyarin. Rev. of *No Easy Place to Be*. *Library Journal*, 1989: 100.

Bronski, Michael. "No Easy Answers." Rev. of *A Hundred Days from Now*. *Lambda Book Report*, July–Aug. 1994: 20–21.

Buckley, Gail Lumet. "The Real Harlem Gets Mugged." Rev. of *No Easy Place to Be*. *Los Angeles Times*, 21 May 1989:8.

Duplechan, Larry. "Steven Corbin." *BLK* 1992:11–23.

Giddings, Paula. Rev. of *No Easy Place to Be*. *Essence*, July 1989:20.

Harmon, Charles. Rev. of *Fragments That Remain*. *Booklist*, 1 June 1993: 1782.

Johnson, Julie. Rev. of *No Easy Place to Be*. *New York Times Book Review*, 2 July 1989: 12.

Lassell, Michael. "The Dark Side." Rev. of *Fragments That Remain*. *The Advocate*, 4 May 1993: 75.

Lewis, Taisha. Rev. of *Fragments That Remain*. *Essence*, 3 July 1993: 46.

Libman, Gary. "Author Seeks a Renaissance for a Lost Era." *Los Angeles Times*, 26 Feb. 1989: VII.

Lutes, Michael A. Rev. of *A Hundred Days from Now*. *Library Journal*, 1 June 1994: 156.

Oliver, Myrna. "Steven Corbin; Novelist and AIDS Activist." *Los Angeles Times*, 3 Sept. 1995: A26.

Rev. of *Fragments That Remain*. *Publishers Weekly*, 3 May 1993: 295.

Rev. of *Fragments That Remain*. *Times Literary Supplement*, 18 June 1993: 24–25.

Rev. of *A Hundred Days from Now*. *Kirkus Reviews*, 1 April 1994: 414.

Rev. of *A Hundred Days from Now*. *Publishers Weekly*, 23 May 1994: 79.

Rev. of *No Easy Place to Be*. *Kirkus Reviews*, 15 Nov. 1988: 1626.

Robertson, Deborah G. Rev. of *No Easy Place to Be*. *Booklist*, 15 Jan. 1989: 835.

Seymour, Craig Allan. "History Embedded like Shrapnel." Rev. of *Fragments That Remain*. *Lambda Book Report*, July–Aug. 1993:31.

Steinberg, Sybil. Rev. of *No Easy Place to Be*. *Publishers Weekly*, 20 Jan. 1989: 136.

SAMUEL DELANY
(1942–)

Grace Sikorski

BIOGRAPHY

Samuel Ray ("Chip") Delany, Jr., one of this century's most prolific and pioneering writers of science fiction and one of the first "out" gay black writers of that genre, is perhaps best known for his novel *Dhalgren* (1975), his *Neveryon* series, and his memoir, *The Motion of Light in Water* (1988). Delany has published nearly two dozen volumes of fiction as well as nine volumes of nonfiction, including critical studies of literature. His innovative and radical ideas about identity, language, race, gender, and sexuality, represented both in his fiction and in his nonfiction, have attracted a great deal of popular and scholarly interest during the past thirty years. Since his first novel was published in 1962, when he was only twenty years old, Delany has been given four Nebula Awards by the Science Fiction Writers of America, two Hugo Awards, and the William Whitehead Memorial Award for Lifetime Contribution to Lesbian and Gay Writing.

Delany was born on April 1, 1942, into a middle-class family in Harlem. Despite his dyslexia, he received an accelerated education when he attended the Dalton Elementary School and the prestigious Bronx High School of Science. His undergraduate curriculum at the City College of New York, where he was editor of the literary journal *Prometheus*, was interrupted when his father, a funeral house proprietor, died of lung cancer in 1960.

In 1961, Delany married his high school friend, poet Marilyn Hacker, in Detroit's City Hall, because she became pregnant with his child. Although Hacker miscarried this first child, years later Delany and Hacker did have a daughter, Iva. They coedited *Quark*, a science fiction journal, and remained married until 1980, when they amicably divorced. Delany's memoirs describe his father's death, his interracial relationship with Hacker, and his bisexual adventures in New

York's Lower East Side. Hacker remains a constant influence in Delany's life and work.

Aside from brief periods in Italy, Greece, France, and Turkey, where he worked at various jobs, Delany has lived in New York City and lectured at universities in the United States. In 1975 he was professor of English at the State University of New York at Buffalo, in 1977 he became a fellow at the Center for Twentieth Century Studies at the University of Wisconsin at Milwaukee, and in 1987 he became a fellow in the Society for the Humanities at Cornell University. Since 1988, Delany has been professor of comparative literature at the University of Massachusetts at Amherst, where he served as acting head of the department for a brief time.

In response to a renewed interest in his older works, Wesleyan University Press has reissued some of Delany's novels. Meanwhile, Delany continues to write and publish both fiction and nonfiction, and his work continues to be read and appreciated by both popular and scholarly readers.

MAJOR WORKS AND THEMES

Delany's early science fiction novels, *The Jewels of Aptor* (1962) and *The Fall of the Towers* trilogy (1963–1965), establish character types, narrative structures, and themes to which Delany returns in later works such as *Nova* (1968) and *Dhalgren* (1975). Clearly influenced by mythology, Delany borrows the circular structure of the quest, as well as archetypal patterns and characters, in order to explore how myths and archetypes are formed and to reveal complications within systems of communication, both linguistic and cultural. Early in his career, Delany won recognition from many science fiction fans.

In *Babel-17* (1966), Delany demonstrates a sophistication some claim is lacking in the earlier works. This Nebula Award-winning novel is centered around its heroine, a female poet named Rydra Wong, who struggles to decode an alien language that could potentially be used as a weapon against earth culture. In Delany's next Nebula Award-winning novel, *The Einstein Intersection* (1967), earth's inhabitants are taken over by aliens who try to make sense of human artifacts, traditions, and language. Its hero is a black musician. Delany uses Jungian archetypes and the concept of the collective unconscious to explore the possibility for creating illusions of pleasure as a substitute for the reality of pleasure. The power of linguistics to structure reality, the role of the artist within society, and the complex process of interpreting signs are also themes very much at the heart of these two novels.

Dhalgren, Delany's longest science fiction novel, finds its hero, Kid, a dyslexic, bisexual artist, in the anarchic town of Belona. Reminiscent of *Finnegan's Wake*, the last sentence of this novel is completed by its first sentence. This thematization of complex characters and narratives that exceed binary thought and final closure is carried into *Triton* (1976). In this novel, an "ambiguous heterotopia," the heterosexual, macho protagonist Bron first can't seem to fit into a culture of perpetually shifting sexual identities, then becomes a woman, but is still spinning in a sea of variable lifestyles. Exemplified in these two novels, Delany's work raises a number of questions about the fixity of identity, the mechanisms of egocentrism, and the discrepancies between reality and representation.

Perhaps Delany's most often read works are those within the *Neveryon* series, including *Tales of Neveryon* (1979), *Neveryona* (1983), *Flight from Neveryon* (1985), and *The Bridge of Lost Desire* (1987), the second of which is a novel, while the others are collections of linked stories. In this sword-and-sorcery series, Delany explores the dynamics of sexual/erotic desire and fantasy, as he does elsewhere (in *The Tides of Lust* 1973, *The Mad Man* 1994, and *Hogg* 1995). Occasionally using graphic details and pornographic scenarios, Delany builds a complex cast of characters, a fantastic series of adventures, and a fabric of erotically charged symbols such as the slave collar, which takes on a different meaning for different characters in a variety of contexts. In this series, the quest for self-hood, freedom, self-worth, and control is brought to the foreground against a field occupied by the mechanisms of desire and power, identity and autonomy, and clear references to the AIDS epidemic.

Delany's nonfiction, *The Jewel-Hinged Jaw* (1977), *The American Shore* (1978), *Starboard Wine* (1984), *The Straits of Messina* (1989), *Silent Interviews* (1994), and *Longer Views* (1995), explicate some of his work as well as the work of other writers and shed light on his postmodernist attempt to define science fiction in terms of reader expectations, genre conventions, and semiotics. Influenced by the French theorists Foucault, Derrida, and Barthes, Delany explores the power of language to structure reality, the fluidity of identity, and the production of meaning through the act of interpretation. Some readers find Delany's nonfiction difficult for its poststructuralist jargon and theoretical complexity, but it is a valuable part of his corpus.

Throughout his career, Delany has returned to a cluster of major themes and subjects in his writing. Central to all of his work is an intense concern for the power and production of textual, artistic, cultural, and linguistic meaning. Specifically, the reification of certain cultural practices, ideologies, paradigms, roles, and myths and the marginalization and isolation of minority characters from certain cultures and communities fascinate Delany. His fiction is laced with metafictional commentary that remarks on the act of writing as well as the roles of art, religion, music, science, psychology, and philosophy in cultural production. In this way, Delany demonstrates a very deliberate self-consciousness as a writer.

Identity's production and performance are also a key concern in Delany's texts. In his autobiographical essay, "Coming/Out," Delany clarifies part of his philosophy on identity formation:

It's a philosophical paradox. Differences are what create individuals. Identities are what create groups and categories. Identities are thus conditions of comparative simplicity that complex individuals might move toward but (fortunately) never achieve—until society, tired of the complexity of so much individual difference, finally, one way or the other, imposes an identity on us.

Identities are thus, by their nature, reductive. (You don't need an identity to become yourself, you need an identity to become like someone else.) Without identities, yes, language would be impossible, (because categories would not be possible, and language requires categories). Still, in terms of persons, identity remains a highly problematic sort of reduction and cultural imposition. (19)

Inspired by the black, feminist, and gay liberation movements of the last three decades, Delany's thematization of social order, oppression, and variant identity politics is consistently accompanied by his indirect cultural commentary. He is always exploring the possibilities and potentialities of variant identity, desire, racial consciousness, and individual ego boundaries, as well as the role of the individual within community, the role of the deviant individual within a homogeneous collective, and the construction of personal reality amid conflicting and plural perspectives. His characters embark on quests for selfhood within a field of power differentials established by gender, sexuality, race, ability, political power, and economic power.

Delany's work has also expanded the boundaries of the genres of science fiction and fantasy. Autobiographical at times, Delany's fiction derives many of its details of people, place, and action from his native habitat of lower Manhattan. New York supplies Delany with a variety of character types, surreal landscapes, and uncommon plots. Throughout his career, he has pushed the boundaries of the science fiction or fantasy genre, challenging reader expectations and popular epistemologies by narrating scenarios of outlaw heros, kinky sex, alternative sexualities, sadomasochism, and pornography. Most striking, perhaps, in Delany's later fiction is his subtext toward tolerance, bending the boundaries of identity, which makes readers more deliberately conscious of their participation in a given text as arrangers or creators of meaning with specific reading habits and horizons of expectation.

CRITICAL RECEPTION

As Delany's writing has become increasingly complex and theoretically infused, the body of academic and scholarly responses has increased. Most recently, Peter Malekin's *The Self, the Referent, and the Real in Science Fiction and the Fantastic* (1994), Donald Hassler's *The Urban Pastoral and Labored Ease of Samuel R. Delany* (1995), and James Sallis's edited collection *Ash of Stars: On the Writing of Samuel R. Delany* (1996) reflect a continuing interest in this pioneering author. Although his pornographic fiction and his representations of sadomasochism and alternative sexualities have caused some readers to resist some of his work, the response to Delany's writing has been overwhelmingly positive.

Most readers have appreciated Delany's attention to marginal characters.

Women, people of color, homosexuals, and bisexuals tend to populate the land-scape of Delany's fiction. Sylvia Kelso argues that Delany's texts "gesture toward the postmodern attention to margins: endings, beginnings, the nature of borders, and the theoretical fields of feminism, queer theory, and post-colonialism, which deal with marginalized groups" (Kelso 290). Mary Kay Bray argues that "one of the definitive characteristics of Samuel R. Delany's fiction is its 'consciousness raising' function. The number of characters in his works who are marginal to their social contexts or outsiders to those contexts altogether calls attention to those social frameworks and what they offer or deny their inhabitants" (Sallis 17). Similarly, Robert Elliot Fox observes, "Speculative sexuality may be the final frontier for science-fiction writers, and Samuel R. Delany . . . has probably gone as far as anybody in penetrating it" (Sallis 43). Robert Reid-Pharr likewise writes that Delany's "goal is to demonstrate that the lines of demarcation between the Black community and the white, the gay and the straight, are themselves con-structions" (348) that he destabilizes "through a reversal of the value attached to each" (350).

Identity is not the only construct that is called into question in Delany's work. In fact, many critics have examined his treatment of linguistics, semiotics, and genre. Carl Malmgren observes that Delany's "view of language is Whorfian: he sees language as constitutive of reality, not as reflective of reality. We see what our language enables us to see; we think according to the ways that language makes available to us" (Sallis 7). If, as Delany says, "fiction makes models of reality" (*Jewel-Hinged Jaw* 151), then, in science fiction, "more than in any genre, one can legitimately undertake the search for new language models with which to construct or invent reality" (Sallis 14).

Sylvia Kelso more fully examines the ways in which Delany's works challenge reader expectations, specifically in their "outraging of generic conventions, and the demands it makes upon its readers" (300). In the same vein, Russell Blackford has observed that Delany is "using far-future sf tropes with a radicalism and ruthlessness that justifies the far-future sub-genre itself. If his work is uneven and not entirely satisfying, it is nonetheless pointing the way for the rest of sf in-cluding the works of less audacious but more conventionally perfect writers" (Sallis 42). David N. Samuelson points out that "Delany's critical writing always emphasizes interplay between reader and text" (Sallis 112) and that "Delany has done what other critics have not, by indicating and underscoring fundamental ways SF requires a unique kind of reading. In his efforts both to explain and to demonstrate this point, his best critical essays clearly shine with their own light" (Sallis 123).

Readers and critics generally value Delany's innovative treatment of science fiction, fantasy, and autobiographical and critical genres. His skill as a writer and as a critic is evident. Although he is less frequently discussed as a black author, his place within the canon of science fiction writers or gay writers is secure. As an author who has lived a unique life, who sees the world and imagines other worlds through a postmodern kaleidoscope, and who is a pioneer of science fiction fantasy, Samuel R. Delany will most assuredly fascinate readers with new fiction and nonfiction in the coming years.

BIBLIOGRAPHY

Works by Samuel Delany

Fiction

The Jewels of Aptor. New York: Ace, 1962.
The Ballad of Beta-2. New York: Ace, 1965.
Babel-17. New York: Ace, 1966a.
Empire Star. New York: Ace, 1966b.
The Einstein Intersection. New York: Ace, 1967.
Nova. New York: Doubleday, 1968.
The Fall of the Towers. New York: Ace, 1970. (Trilogy originally published 1963–1965)
Driftglass: Ten Tales of Speculative Fiction. New York: NAL, 1971.
The Tides of Lust. New York: Lancer, 1973.
Dhalgren. New York: Bantam, 1975.
Triton. New York: Bantam, 1976.
Tales of Neveryon. New York: Bantam, 1979.
Distant Stars. New York: Bantam, 1981.
Neveryona. New York: Bantam, 1983.
Stars in My Pocket like Grains of Sand. New York: Bantam, 1984.
Flight from Neveryon. New York: Bantam, 1985.
The Complete Nebula Award-Winning Fiction. New York: Bantam, 1986.
The Bridge of Lost Desire. New York: Arbor House, 1987.
We in Some Strange Power's Employ, Move on a Rigorous Line. New York: Tor, 1990.
They Fly at Ciron. Seattle: Incunabula, 1993.
The Mad Man. New York: Richard Kasak Books, 1994.
Atlantis: Three Tales. Hanover, NH, and London: Wesleyan University Press, 1995a.
Hogg. Boulder, CO, and Normal, CO: Fiction Collective Two/Black Ice Books, 1995b.

Nonfiction

The Jewel-Hinged Jaw: Notes on the Language of Science Fiction. Elizabethtown, NY: Dragon Press, 1977.
The American Shore: Meditations on a Tale of Science Fiction by Thomas M. Disch—"Angouleme." Elizabethtown, NY: Dragon Press, 1978.
Heavenly Breakfast: An Essay on the Winter of Love. New York: Bantam, 1979.
Starboard Wine: More Notes on the Language of Science Fiction. Elizabethtown, NY: Dragon Press, 1984.
The Motion of Light in Water: Sex and Science Fiction in the East Village, 1957–1965. New York: Arbor House, 1988a.
Wagner/Artaud: A Play of 19th and 20th Century Critical Fictions. New York: Anzatz Press, 1988b.
The Straits of Messina. Seattle: Serconia Press, 1989.
Silent Interviews: On Language, Race, Sex, Science Fiction, and Some Comics. Hanover, NH, and London: Wesleyan University Press, 1994.

Longer Views. Hanover, NH, and London: Wesleyan University Press, 1995.
"Coming/Out." *Boys like Us: Gay Writers Tell Their Coming Out Stories.* Ed. Patrick Merla.
New York: Avon, 1996. 1–26.

Studies of Samuel Delany

Barbour, Douglas. *Worlds Out of Words: The Science Fiction Novels of Samuel R. Delany.*
Frome, Somerset: Bran's Head Books, 1979.
Collings, Michael R. *Samuel R. Delany and John Wilkins: Artificial Languages. Science and
Science Fiction. Selected Essays from the 4th International Conference on the Fantastic
in Arts.* New York: Greenwood, 1986.
Cooper, Rebecca. "A Samuel R. Delany Checklist." *The Review of Contemporary Fiction*
16.3 (Fall 1996): 170–171.
Fox, Robert Elliot. *The Conscientious Sorcerers: The Black Postmodernist Fiction of LeRoi
Jones/Amiri Baraka, Ishmael Reed, and Samuel R. Delany.* New York: Greenwood
Press, 1987.
Gregory, Sinda. "Samuel R. Delany: The Semiology of Silence." *Science-Fiction Studies* 14
(1987): 134–164.
Hassler, Donald M. *The Urban Pastoral and Labored Ease of Samuel R. Delany.* Madison,
NJ: Fairleigh Dickinson University Press, 1995.
Johnson, Charles. "A Dialogue: Samuel R. Delany and Joanna Russ on Science Fiction."
Callaloo: A Journal of African-American and African Arts and Letters 22.3 (Fall
1984): 27–35.
Kelso, Sylvia. " 'Across Never': Postmodern Theory and Narrative Praxis in Samuel R.
Delany's *Neveryon* Cycle." *Science Fiction Studies* 24 (1997): 289–301.
Malekin, Peter. *The Self, the Referent, and the Real in Science Fiction and the Fantastic: Lem,
Pynchon, Kubin, and Delany.* New York: Greenwood, 1994.
McEvoy, Seth. *Samuel R. Delany.* New York: Frederick Ungar, 1984.
Moylan, Tom. "Beyond Negation: The Critical Utopias of Ursula K. LeGuin and Samuel
R. Delany." *Extrapolation* 21 (1980): 236–253.
Nilon, Charles. "The Science Fiction of Samuel R. Delany and the Limits of Technology."
Black American Literature Forum 18.2 (Summer 1984): 62–68.
Parrinder, Patrick. "Delany Inspects the Word Beast." *Science-Fiction Studies* 6 (1979):
337–341.
Peplow, Michael W., and Robert S. Bravard. *Samuel R. Delany: A Primary and Secondary
Bibliography, 1962–1979.* Boston: G. K. Hall, 1980.
Reid-Pharr, Robert F. "Disseminating Heterotopia." *African American Review* 28.3 (1994):
347–357.
Sallis, James, ed. *Ash of Stars: On the Writing of Samuel R. Delany.* Jackson: University
Press of Mississippi, 1996.
Samuelson, David N. "Necessary Constraints: Samuel R. Delany on Science Fiction." *The
Review of Contemporary Fiction* 16.3 (Fall 1996): 165–169.
Schuyler, William M. "Deconstructing Deconstruction: Chimeras of Form and Content
in Samuel R. Delany." *Journal of the Fantastic in the Arts* 1.4 (1988): 67–76.
Slusser, George Edgar. *The Delany Intersection.* San Bernardino, CA: Borgo Press, 1977.
Spencer, Kathleen L. "Deconstructing *Tales of Neveryon*: Delany, Derrida, and the 'Mod-
ular Calculus, Parts I–IV.' " *Essays in Art and Literature* 14 (May 1985): 59–89.
Weedman, Jane. *Samuel R. Delany.* Mercer Island, WA: Starmont House, 1982.

WILLIAM DEMBY
(1922–)

Peter G. Christensen

BIOGRAPHY

William Demby ranks as one of the most cosmopolitan of contemporary African American novelists. Born in Pittsburgh and raised in Clarksburg, West Virginia, his education at West Virginia State College was interrupted by World War II. He was stationed with the U.S. Army in Italy and North Africa, and, after attending Fisk University at the end of the war, he returned to Italy to study art at the University of Rome. He married and had a son there. For many years Demby worked consistently as a translator and screenwriter for the Italian film industry, while still managing to travel around the world and visit the United States frequently. In 1969, he joined the English Department faculty at the College of Staten Island, maintaining this position until retirement in 1989. He currently lives in Sag Harbor, New York, a community with a significant black history.

Demby's reputation rests on his three novels, all of which are rooted in personal experience. The first, *Beetlecreek*, a study of race relations in an emotionally dead small town, was written in Italy, and the small, eponymous town of the title is, in part, based on Clarksburg. The second and most important, *The Catacombs*, deals with a black novelist named William Demby, living in Rome between 1962 and 1964, who is attempting both to write a novel and to decide whether to return to the United States during the period of the Civil Rights movement. Because of its metafictional construction and plot ambiguity it is extremely difficult to summarize. The third, *Love Story Black*, tells of the adventures of a middle-aged New York City college English teacher who looks for true love with several women in the course of the months that he is interviewing a very old, black, female entertainer for a feature story for a lowbrow magazine.

Demby has not received the critical or popular attention that he deserves for several reasons. The number of years separating the appearance of his novels is considerable. The last one, published by a small press, received almost no reviews. Demby has given only one major interview and has not had attention-getting periodical publications. All of his novels are written in a different style, and he has eluded easy classification. His novels are relatively short and easy to read. However, his major novel, *The Catacombs*, requires several readings because of its complexity.

MAJOR WORKS AND THEMES

The major resource for understanding Demby's themes is his interview with John O'Brien conducted in November 1971. Yet in the interview Demby gives no authorial interpretations of his novels, just a general sense of what issues are important to him. Among black writers who may have influenced him, he mentions only Ralph Ellison* and claims, "I have a strong feeling that the novels of Richard Wright didn't influence me very much" (37).

Beetlecreek recalls, to some extent, Carson McCullers' novels of loneliness and alienation. There are five key characters to this story about lonely individuals in an emotionally catatonic, washed-up old mining town. Here any attempt at a human gesture is so threatening to the community that it is interpreted as dangerous or evil. Race relations are very bad and based on segregation, suspicion, and hate on both sides. In *Beetlecreek* an elderly loner, Bill Trapp, finally emerges from fifteen years of solitude to befriend a fourteen-year-old black boy, Johnny Johnson, and to give a party at his shack for both black and white children. However, the black community interprets the party as an attempt at child molestation and tries to ruin his life. Johnny, as part of his initiation ceremony for joining a gang of juvenile delinquents, burns down Bill Trapp's house and then hits him with a shovel, perhaps killing him. Meanwhile, Johnny's uncle, the artistic David Diggs, trapped in a loveless marriage with the small-minded Mary, runs off for Detroit with Edith, an old flame, who has come back from the city with great bitterness for the funeral of her mother, from whom she was estranged. The last scene shows David and Edith on the bus together, as they pass Trapp's burning house. David has probably exchanged one trap for another, but there is some possibility that he may be able to at least get a new perspective on the mess of his life.

Some critics have considered *Beetlecreek* "existential." Important but confusing are Demby's comments on existentialism, a term he uses extremely broadly. He says that he may have been indirectly influenced by Kierkegaard; admits the Dostoyevskian character of the lives of people like Malcolm X, Eldridge Cleaver, and Rap Brown; mentions Sartre's presence at a meeting he attended of the European Community of Writers; and recalls having written a review of Camus' *The Stranger* while at Fisk. Of these four authors, Demby seems to be closer to the Christian existentialism of Kierkegaard and Dostoyevsky than to the atheistic brand of Sartre and Camus. In *Beetlecreek* organized religion only keeps the villagers from accepting the burden of real freedom, and so we have here an echo of the parable of the Grand Inquisitor from *The Brothers Karamazov*. In *The Catacombs*, the author's wavering between his treatment of Doris as literary character and as lover calls to mind the contrast between the aesthetic and ethical modes of existence in Kierkegaard's *Either/Or*.

Demby does not promote revolutionary change, although he is not one to live in an ivory tower divorced from current politics. He states that, like the protagonist of *The Catacombs*, he went back to the United States for the March on Washington in 1963 and was still in the States when President Kennedy was assassinated. He returned to Italy and used these events in writing the rest of the novel. He does not think of himself as having been an expatriate, because he kept up strong connections with the United States. However, if he had not gone to Italy, he might have been tempted to write naturalistic novels. Yet he does not consider *Beetlecreek* naturalistic.

At the time of the interview Demby was working on a novel called *The Journal of a Black Revolutionary in Exile*, but he eventually abandoned it. Demby's non-revolutionary politics stems, in part, from his belief that our universe is intrinsically moral and ordered. Demby maintains that the writer cannot be totally involved in politics; politicians are the ones who are totally involved in politics. He feels that when people today talk about revolution, they fail to realize that it has already happened "and [that] we are speeding to try and catch up with it or at least to explain it to ourselves" (47). Revolutionary movements are "just expended energy" (47). According to Demby, during the two years covered in *The Catacombs*, there is no change, only the illusion of change. This is a strong statement to make, considering that the novel covers the Second Vatican Council, the Algerian War, and the Cuban missile crisis.

Demby's work in *The Catacombs* can be seen as a development of Sartre's ideas for the development of the *nouveau roman*. In the second novel, *The Reprieve* [*Le Sursis*], of the incomplete *The Roads to Freedom*, Sartre includes the use of news details from around the world and juxtaposes his characters to them. In some of the essays of *Situations I*, Sartre indicates that the novel must try to create characters who are free in their decision making. One must avoid the authorial control over a character's freedom. *The Catacombs* follows in this line of the *nouveau roman* in that it offers an open-ended conclusion that has not narrowed the possibilities of choice for his protagonist.

The Catacombs is a highly allusive novel, drawing from many areas of elite and popular culture. Because of these references it has been at times wrongly considered irrelevant to black American audiences. Yet the accusation that the novel bypasses black American experience of the 1960s is not justified, since most of these figures are recalled only in passing, and the author's reaction to the Civil Rights movement and black American culture is crucial. James Baldwin, Malcolm X, Martin Luther King, Louis Armstrong, Katherine Dunham, Muhammed Ali, Sonny Liston, and Floyd Patterson all receive attention. When Demby wrote

The Catacombs, there had not been much avant-garde modernism in African American fiction, so Demby's novel was not seen as part of the mainstream of black American literature.

The relationship of *The Catacombs* to the Italian film industry demands attention it has not received. The novel appeared at a time when, after over a decade, neorealism was finally dissipating and being replaced by more heterogeneous movements. The ending of Federico Fellini's *La Dolce Vita*, with its grotesque sea creature washed up on shore, is alluded to twice. In *La Dolce Vita*, Guido is faced with remaining true to his half-buried artistic nature or else selling out totally and becoming a cheap journalist. He resists, in the last scene, the beckoning girl. In *The Catacombs*, the author, who never gets very much done, although not as corrupted as Guido, also resists a beckoning female—Doris.

Demby's attention to the vulgarization of the supernatural is reminiscent of Fellini, who opened *La Dolce Vita* with the aerial shot of a huge crucifix being moved through the air over the city. Later, a sequence is devoted to the publicity event surrounding the report of children who claim to have seen the Virgin Mary. Demby, combing the newspapers for *faits divers*, finds in the spotting of a flying saucer (34) an event parallel to the report of the two children. Both events leave us with an Eliadean sense of the sacred trying to break through the profane but failing. In the spiritually dead Rome of *La Dolce Vita*, suicide is a major issue, and Guido is shocked when his mentor ends his own life. In *The Catacombs*, Marilyn Monroe's suicide is also unanticipated.

Other elements in *The Catacombs* also recall Fellini. The plot of an author undergoing a creative crisis while having marital difficulties is at the heart of his next film, *8 1/2*. Very early in the novel, Demby writes, "I feel not like God, but rather like some benevolently mad theatrical impresario who eagerly, paternally, leafs through the press clippings of countless actors and actresses, dispersed monads, who like nomads are wandering over the theatrical caravan routes of the world" (4). The passage evokes the image of Fellini's trying to find the appropriate cast for *8 1/2*. In that film the line between illusion and reality is blurred through the use of mise-en-scène, which makes certain settings impossible to accept except as projections of the protagonist's mind.

The Catacombs also has some of the ambience of Michelangelo Antonioni's films of the early 1960s, *L'Avventura* and the trilogy of *La Notte*, *L'Eclisse*, and *Il Deserto Rosso*. Doris' unanticipated disappearance in the Catacombs is no less striking than the sudden disappearance of the young woman in the middle of *L'Avventura*. The stagnation of the upper classes in economically revived Italy, analyzed in Antonioni's trilogy, resurfaces in the portrait of the world-weary Count in Demby's novel.

Demby indirectly mentions Pier Paolo Pasolini's second feature when he talks of "P's new film, *La Mamma*" (32). Demby shares Pasolini's concern with spirituality, most developed in *The Gospel according to Saint Matthew*. Demby's conversations with Doris refer to Christ's Crucifixion. Marilyn Monroe is presented by Doris, a potential madonna figure herself, as another crucified Savior. Pasolini's *Mamma Roma* and his first feature, *Accatone*, also have Christ imagery associated with their (male) protagonists.

In a sense, *The Catacombs* manifests the crisis that led to the end of Italian neorealism—the sense that it was time to find ways to move beyond the surface of things and to pay less attention to documenting reality and more attention to probing mental states of characters and developing a more personal authorial style.

Love Story Black is also open-ended like *The Catacombs*: key events are never totally clarified. In the last scene, Prof. Edwards has intercourse with ninety-ish virgin Mona Parriss as she dies. She had been in love for fifty years with a former black Pullman car man who discovered her talent as a singer, but he apparently (it's not entirely clear) was castrated by the Ku Klux Klan in Cincinnati, and she has been true to his memory. This true love, although he denies it, is probably actually her alcoholic neighbor in her New York City tenement, Gus, who dies just before the novel ends. At this point, the divorced protagonist has endured a humiliating courtship of Hortense Schiller, an African-oriented black activist. On their trip to Africa together, he ended up in a hospital, and she found a new love. Nor did Edwards succeed in salvaging his on-again, off-again relationship with Gracie, the woman's magazine editor who gave him the assignment. Edward's confusions in love are matched by his problems in teaching black literature and Chaucer to students who consider his committedness to the black cause inadequate. Thus, on an unexpected note of joy the novel closes, although it is literally unrealistic, and the nature of Gus and Mona's relationship has never been entirely clear.

CRITICAL RECEPTION

Two dozen studies, including reviews, constitute all the significant Demby criticism. The best place to start for an overview is the compendium of criticism appearing in *Contemporary Literary Criticism* ("William Demby," 1989). Here can be found excerpts from the reviews and essays by Jones, Derleth, Caxton, Rennert, Buitenhuis, Bone (1965, 1969), Margolies, Bayliss, O'Brien, Schraufnagel, Connelly, Gayle, and Lee. However, nothing after 1980 is included.

Demby is briefly discussed in books and articles on African American literature, and we find no consensus among their relatively brief comments on the first two novels. Bone (1965) and Whitlow (1973) consider *Beetlecreek* existential, but Hill (1967) and Lee (1980) consider it naturalistic, Bayliss (1969) humanistic, and Schraufnagel (1973) deterministic.

Four critics are impressed with *The Catacombs* as a religious novel. Margolies states that Demby "expresses his concerns in philosophical terms akin to Christian existentialism" (174). In *The Catacombs* the narrator returns as a "fulfilled man" to the United States, in part because his "deeply religious outlook has discovered for him the role he plays in the cosmos." Although Margolies finds the novel an "almost Manichaean vision of being and nonbeing locked in timeless combat," he feels that through Christianity the hero has "recovered his identity as a black man" (188). Bone (1969) insists without much textual evidence that *The Catacombs* illustrates the thought of Pierre Teilhard de Chardin. For him, Doris is the redemptive "dark Madonna" who helps Demby and the Count to move toward spiritual rebirth (141). From the novel we should get the sense that "to refuse the evolutionary challenge is to deny the will of God" (135). Nancy Y. Hoffman's two articles (1971, 1972) accept Bone's Teilhard-inspired reading, and she claims that Demby is "anti-existential and apocalyptically optimistic" (1972: 8). She also finds the reconciliation of yin-yang principles in the novel. Jaskoski (1994) reads *The Catacombs* as a debate between flesh and spirit in which there is no judgment as to which has the more significant claim. Given that the ending is inconclusive, she writes, "Dialogue itself, the process of coming to terms with the Other, appears to be the core of the novel's moral vision"—which is also an "ecumenical" one (191). One can see that much work can still be done toward an analysis of *The Catacombs*, a work that demands rediscovery.

BIBLIOGRAPHY

Works by William Demby

Books

Beetlecreek. New York: Rinehart, 1950. Rpt. Chatham, NJ: Chatham Bookseller, 1972.
The Catacombs. New York: Pantheon, 1965.
Love Story Black. New York: Reed, Cannon, and Johnson, 1978.

Story

"Saint Joey." *Fisk Herald* 40.2 (Dec. 1946): 20–23, 27.

Essays

"The Geisha Girls of Ponto-cho." *Harper's* 209 (Dec. 1954): 41–47. [on Kyoto]
"They Surely Can't Stop Us Now." *Reporter* 14 (5 Apr. 1956): 18–21. [on black resistance
    to integration in the poor rural South]
"A Walk in Tuscany." *Holiday* 22 (Dec. 1957): 140, 142, 144–45. [on Etruscan ruins]
"Blueblood Cats of Rome." *Holiday* 27 (Apr. 1960): 203–6. [a humorous fantasy]

Studies of William Demby

Bayliss, John F. "*Beetlecreek*: Existential or Human Document?" *Negro Digest* 19.1 (Nov.
    1969): 70–74.
Berry, Jay R. "The Achievement of William Demby." *College Language Association Journal*
    26.4 (June 1983): 434–51.
Bone, Robert. *The Negro Novel in America*. Rev. ed. New Haven, CT: Yale University
    Press, 1965. 191–96.
———. "William Demby's Dance of Life." *TriQuarterly* 15 (Spring 1969): 127–41.

Buitenhuis, Peter. "Doris Is Always Getting Pushed Aside." *The New York Times Book Review* (11 July 1965): 4, 32.

Caxton, Horace. "Defeated Lives." *The New York Times Book Review* (26 Feb. 1950):4.

Connelly, Joseph F. "William Demby's Fiction: The Pursuit of Muse." *Negro American Literature Forum* 10 (Fall 1976): 100–103.

Derleth, August. "The Racial Novel Turns the Tables." *Chicago Tribune*, 12 Feb. 1950, 4.

Fuller, Edmund. "Hermitt with Blacks." *The Saturday Review of Literature* (4 Mar. 1950): 17.

Gayle, Addison. Rev. of *Love Story Black*. *American Book Review* 2.6 (Sept.–Oct. 1980): 10.

Hansen, Klaus P. "William Demby's *The Catacombs* (1965): A Latecomer to Modernism." *The Afro-American Novel since 1960*. Ed. Peter Bruck and Wolfgang Karrer. Amsterdam: Grüner, 1982. 123–44.

Hill, Herbert. "Afterword." *Beetlecreek*. New York: Avon, 1967. 183–90.

Hoffman, Nancy Y. "The Annunciation of William Demby." *Studies in Black Literature* 3 (Spring 1972): 9–13.

———. "Technique in Demby's *The Catacombs*." *Studies in Black Literature* 2 (Summer 1971): 10–13.

Jaskoski, Helen. "*The Catacombs* and the Debate between the Flesh and the Spirit." *Critique: Studies in Contemporary Fiction* 35.3 (Spring 1994): 181–92.

Jones, Ernest. Rev. of *Beetlecreek*. *The Nation* (11 Feb. 1950): 139.

Lee, A. Robert. "Making New: Styles of Innovation in the Contemporary Black American Novel." *Black Fiction: New Studies in the Afro-American Novel since 1945*. Ed. A. Robert Lee. London: Vision Press, 1980. 222–50 [see 233–36].

Margolies, Edward. "The Expatriate as Novelist: William Demby." *Native Sons: A Critical Study of Twentieth-Century Black American Authors*. Philadelphia: Lippincott, 1968. 173–89.

O'Brien, John, ed. *Interviews with Black Writers*. New York: Liveright, 1973. 34–52.

Perry, Margaret. "William Demby." *Dictionary of Literary Biography*. Vol. 33: *Afro-American Fiction Writers after 1955*. Ed. Thadious M. Davis and Trudier Harris. Detroit: Gale, 1984. 59–64.

Rennert, Maggie. "Write One, Splice Two." *New York Herald Tribune*, 27 June 1965, 22.

Schraufnagel, Noel. *From Apology to Protest: The Black American Novel*. New York: Everett/Edwards, 1973. 75–76, 128–29.

Scott, Nathan A., Jr. "Foreword to the 1991 Edition." *The Catacombs* by William Demby. Boston: Northeastern University Press, 1991. ix–xxi.

Whitlow, Roger. *Black American Literature: A Critical History*. Chicago: Nelson Hall, 1973. 122–25.

"William Demby." *Contemporary Literary Criticism* 53 (1989): 98–115.

MELVIN DIXON
(1950–1992)

André Hoyrd

BIOGRAPHY

A novelist, poet, scholar, and educator, Melvin Winfred Dixon was born on 29 May 1950 in Stamford, Connecticut. He was one of five children born to Handy and Jessie Dixon. His parents were from the Carolinas, and they were a part of the large migration of African Americans in the 1940s and 1950s who moved from the rural and segregated South and settled in the urban North. His father, who was once a sharecropper and who came from Pee Dee, North Carolina, was a contractor and house painter, and his mother, who was from Irmo, South Carolina, was a nurse. Growing up in a black and notably southern community— located on the west side of Stamford—was deeply influential to Dixon: " 'The way in which blacks in Stamford kept ties with the South gave me a strong sense of community, and through that, I discovered the importance of these places. My parents kept close contact and we had a clear sense of who we were as first generation northerners' " (Stephania Davis D6).

The black people that populated the world of Dixon's youth were also a vital source of cultural transmission and passed on a rich black vernacular tradition. His neighborhood barbershop was, for example, not only a place of work but also a type of cultural theater where the oral tradition held center stage: " 'I worked in the shop and swept up hair and listened to the vibrant folklore and stories that the people had brought with them from the South' " (Stephania Davis D6). The significance of black culture, the South, and family ties would figure prominently in *Trouble the Water* (1989), Dixon's first novel in which his father's hometown of Pee Dee provides the geographical focus.

Despite the numerous visits that his family made back to the Carolinas, Dixon has stated that he did not comprehend the racial climate and Jim Crow laws of the South until he was a teenager: " 'There was a contrast between segregation in the South and a looser racial relation in the North, but at 10, I really didn't understand what it all meant' " (Peterson 42). Only when he was in junior high school, and only after he had read the works of James Baldwin* was he able to understand America's racialized landscape. Baldwin would have a profound impact on his life and literary career and would help him to interpret not only the complex racial markers in America's North and South but also issues of identity and homosexuality. " 'Baldwin is crucial to me,' " Dixon commented in an interview. " 'If he had not written what he wrote, I don't think I would have been able to write what I write' " (Peterson 42).

When he was seventeen, Dixon published his first poem in the literary journal *Vanguard*, and, while a student at Wesleyan University, he published his first critical piece—"Black Theater: The Aesthetics"—in *Negro Digest*. At Wesleyan, he majored in English and theater and was the director of the university's Black Repertory Theater, which performed, under his own direction, two of his dramatic works—*Confrontation* (1969) and *Ritual: For Malcolm* (1970). After he earned his B.A. degree from Wesleyan in 1971, Dixon entered graduate school at Brown University, where he was accepted into its American civilization program. He earned both his M.A. (1973) and Ph.D. (1975) from Brown. Although he had his third play, *Kingdom, or the Last Promise* (1972), performed while at Brown, he found writing for the theater unsatisfying and returned to writing poetry.

While in graduate school, Dixon traveled to France, where he resided primarily in Paris. For two years, he researched and retraced the ex-patriot journey of America's black artistic community. As he was undertaking this intellectual, historical, and aesthetic odyssey, of particular interest to him was Richard Wright, who had made Paris his home from 1947 until his death in 1960. Like the other African American writers and artists who helped shape his aesthetic and literary enterprise—especially Baldwin, Robert Hayden, Ralph Ellison,* and Romare Bearden—Wright's influence was profound. He later would pay homage to Wright and to his literary legacy in his first collection of poems, *Change of Territory* (1983), a provocative work that explores Dixon's concerns with family, art, exile, and racial and sexual identity.

After Dixon graduated from Brown University, he was an assistant professor in Afro-American studies at Fordham University (1975–1976) in New York and an assistant professor of English at Williams College (1976–1980) in Massachusetts. At Williams College, he was also chair of its Afro-American studies program (1977–1979). During this period in his life, he made several trips back to Paris, traveled to Haiti for his scholarly research, and continued to write poetry. In 1980, he joined the faculty of Queens College, City University of New York (CUNY) as an associate professor. In 1986, he became professor of English at Queens College, and, in 1987, he accepted an appointment as full professor at the Graduate Center (CUNY). Until his death, he jointly held both positions at Queens College and at the Graduate Center.

In the same year in which he accepted the teaching position at the Graduate

Center, Dixon published his influential critical work *Ride Out the Wilderness: Geography and Identity in Afro-American Literature*, which examines the various ways in which African American writers use spatial motifs—the wilderness, the underground, and the mountaintop—to create alternative landscapes of culture and identity. Images of the wilderness, the underground, and the mountaintop surface in *Trouble the Water* and in his searing and powerfully written work *Vanishing Rooms* (1991), which tells the story of a black gay dancer whose white lover has been violently raped and murdered by a roving gang of white teenagers. Although a fictionalized narrative, *Vanishing Rooms* is loosely based on an actual incident of gay bashing in New York's Central Park in the late 1970s.

Like his contemporary Audre Lorde,* Dixon was outspoken in his denunciation of America's racism and homophobia, and he was particularly vocal about how white gay males in interracial relationships were not immune to racist ideologies and fantasies. In a 1991 interview in *Christopher Street*, which he also criticized for ignoring black writers and black people, he stated how a white gay male can have " 'a black boyfriend and still be a racist' " (Cole 27). Dixon refused to accommodate the racism found in the gay and lesbian community and the homophobia found in the black community, and *Vanishing Rooms* can be read as a vivid and sterling critique of America's racist and homophobic society.

Dixon was an exceptionally accomplished scholar and writer. Some of his many honors include a Richard Wright Award in Criticism (1974), a Ford Foundation Postdoctoral Fellowship (1983–1984), a Fulbright Senior Lectureship (1985–1986)—in which he taught at the University of Dakar in Senegal—a National Endowment for the Arts Creative Writing Fellowship (1984), and a National Endowment for the Humanities grant (1977). In addition, Dixon translated from the French literary criticism and poetry. He was, for example, the translator for Geneviève Fabre's *Drumbeats, Masks, and Metaphor: Contemporary Afro-American Theater* (1983), and his translation of the poetry of Léopold Sédar Senghor—*The Collected Poems of Léopold Sédar Senghor* (1991)—is considered definitive. The Senghor collection was the final project that Dixon finished before he died on 26 October 1992 of an AIDS-related illness, in his home in Stamford, Connecticut.

On 4 March 1994, Dixon's life and work were celebrated at a conference titled "Reading Melvin Dixon: A Memorial Conference," which was held at the Graduate Center at CUNY. One of the presenters at the memorial conference was the poet Elizabeth Alexander, who was a friend of Dixon's. In her elegaic introduction to Dixon's *Love's Instrument* (1995), a posthumously published collection of poems, Alexander writes that he was " 'a person of letters' whose religion was writing, whatever form it took" (6).

MAJOR WORKS AND THEMES

Trouble the Water, which received the 1989 Nilon Award for Excellence in Minority Fiction, announces itself as a novel with intricate themes. Written in a lyrical and highly metaphorical style, the thematic terrain of *Trouble the Water* texturizes Dixon's concerns with place and history, family and identity. Intertwined throughout the narrative are images of the wilderness and mountaintop, figures of place and identity, which are the critical focus of *Ride Out the Wilderness*. Dixon also deftly incorporates elements from ascension and immersion narratives, generic forms of the African American literary tradition that feature an "enslaved" figure who journeys to a symbolic North (ascension) or a figure who journeys to a symbolic South (immersion).

Set against the rural landscape of North Carolina, *Trouble the Water* tells the story of Jordan Henry, who, as a young child, escapes his small town of Pee Dee and hitchhikes north to Philadelphia, to freedom. His flight from hilltop home and family is triggered by his maternal grandmother, Mother Harriet, who blames Jordan's father, Jake, for the death of her only child, Chloe, who dies during childbirth. Mother Harriet charges Jordan as the instrument for her vengeance and wants him to kill his father. Twenty years later, Jordan, who is now a professor of American colonial history and who teaches at a small college in Massachusetts, receives a letter stating that Mother Harriet is dead and that he is summoned home for the funeral. With his wife, Phyllis, Jordan journeys to the South, where he confronts the haunted memories of his childhood. In a violent episode, he encounters his father, who has come to claim the farmland that Mother Harriet has left. Jordan later discovers that his summons home is part of an elaborate revenge scheme, orchestrated by Mother Harriet, who is not dead but alive.

In *Trouble the Water*, Dixon critiques discourses that are particular to the African American literary tradition, including the North as a symbolic geography of refuge from racism—depicted in *Trouble the Water* as a type of racial wilderness—and the figure of the sentimental and kindly black matriarch as an upholder of family or communal traditions. Because Dixon utilizes imagery and symbolism from the African American church, Jordan, who is named after the River Jordan, functions as a character of transformation, a symbolic figure of reconciliation with loved ones. Jordan's hilltop home—symbolizing the biblical mountaintop of salvation—becomes a site of wrathful passions as well as reconciliation with the past and the waters which Jordan troubles are those of history, family, and self. These waters flow forward and backward, guiding Jordan to face his past and future.

Vanishing Rooms is Dixon's most significant work, a haunting and psychologically complex novel that examines gay and racial themes. In a lucid prose style, Dixon traverses the terrain of interracial gay relationships and internalized homophobia, homosexual gang rape, and a gay murder. This elaborate intersection of racial and gender issues makes *Vanishing Rooms* a novel that defies easy classification. Indeed, Dixon cautioned readers from interpreting his narrative as work that explores either a gay or black milieu: " 'I hope that the readers will realize that this is not just a gay novel, not just a black novel' " (Cole 25–26). Nevertheless, one of the major achievements of Dixon's mostly nonlinear narrative is a rewriting of well-worn generic forms, and *Vanishing Rooms* can be read as a type of hybridization of genres, which includes the detective novel, the black protest novel, and the gay novel.

Divided into four parts, like the four walls of a room, *Vanishing Rooms* is set in the fall of 1975 in New York City. It is a world of red leaves, dance, subways, and rotting warehouses. It is the world of the sexual underground and the emotional wilderness. The story—which revolves around the gang murder of a white gay man named Metro—is told through the alternating narrative voices of Jesse, who is a black dancer and who was Metro's gay lover, Ruella, who is also a black dancer who is in love with Jesse, and Lonny, an Italian youth who participates in the gay bashing, rape, and murder of Metro. These three voices, a type of narrative triptych, are framed by the absent narrative voice of Metro. Erasing Metro's narrative voice, as Dixon comments, was intentional: " 'We've heard a lot about white gay experience. Even though Metro was an individual character with a specific experience, his absence, from a contributing narrator's perspective, is deliberate, because we have not heard from Jesse in our literature, we have not heard from Ruella, we have not heard from Lonny' " (Cole 25).

In telling his story, Dixon paints a world of shifting images. From Lonny's dreamlike psychotic episode and own violent prison rape, to Jesse's racialized and sadomasochistic encounter with Metro during lovemaking and his quixotic romp through the Paradise Baths (a parodic allusion to Dante's *Divine Comedy*), Dixon weaves a narrative tapestry of disturbing colors, sounds, and perceptions. Although critics have compared it to Baldwin's *Giovanni's Room*, *Vanishing Rooms* also can be read as a rewriting of elements from Wright's *Native Son*. The famous "Brrrrrriiiiiiiiiiiiiiiiiiinng," which introduces readers to the conditioned and trapped environment of Bigger Thomas in *Native Son* is, for example, boldly evoked in one of Lonny's prison scenes, and because he is an individual who has been conditioned by society to hate his identity, and because his actions reflect the explosive consequences of that conditioning, Lonny echoes Bigger. However, unlike Bigger, Lonny's societal conditioning—internalized homophobia—is not centered in concerns of race but in questions of sexual identity.

Dixon's innovative use of genres and his exploration of transgressive themes establish *Vanishing Rooms* as a novel that resounds with contemporary urgency and vision. It is a work of rich textural depth, and, most importantly, Dixon's narrative challenges readers to discover "where the balm lies in the New Jerusalem" (Kenan 48). As Wilfred R. Koponen observes, "In exploring interracial gay relationships and gay bashing, from the point of view of victim and basher, and in his fusion of poetic and novelistic elements, Dixon breaks new ground" (114).

CRITICAL RECEPTION

Since his death, the literary enterprise of Dixon has been mainly ignored by the critical community, with critical assessments of Dixon's works resting primarily on reviews. Despite the critical silence that his novels have endured, there has been, recently, a growing interest in Dixon's aesthetic project. His work—especially *Vanishing Rooms*—is being embraced and scrutinized by a new generation of scholars who are probing the complicated relationship between racial and sexual identity.

With very few exceptions, reviewers praised *Trouble the Water* as a significant novel. Calvin Forbes compares it to Jean Toomer's *Cane* and describes it as a novel that "borders on myth" (8). Observing Dixon's deft use of "dialect, fairy tale elements, dreams and old songs," *Kirkus Reviews* lauds the narrative as "an eloquent family saga—at times surreal and expressionistic, at times naturalistic" (1186). Henry Louis Gates, Jr., extols *Trouble the Water*, calling it "a poet's novel" that is "propelled by the lyricism of its language" (7). Thulani Davis, who also admired its poetic contours, calls it a "smartly crafted novel" (27). Some reviewers felt hampered, however, by the text's ornate language. For example, Constance Kennedy criticizes Dixon's prose as overindulgent: "[U]nfortunately Mr. Dixon's lyrical prose cloys" (48).

Despite what Kennedy feels as problematic, the majority of the critical sentiment on the novel parallels the views of Leonard Feather, who compares Dixon's writing to that of Toni Morrison* and Alice Walker*: "The dualities and contradictions inherent in African-American life, in its folkloric background and its contrasting cosmopolitan sophistication, are superbly captured" (2).

Like *Trouble the Water*, *Vanishing Rooms* generally was greeted with acclaim. Although one reviewer found Dixon's depiction of homosexuality as unsettling—calling it "a lurid manual of homosexual lovemaking" (Condini 32)—most commentators embraced its originality and narrative ingenuity. Randall Kenan gives, for example, high praise to its thematic material and sophisticated narrative design, calling it a "bold, bloody, [and] beautiful" novel that is "[s]ubtly allusive in its construction" (48). Commenting on its sparkling lyricism, John Preston hails *Vanishing Rooms* as "so perfect that any distinction between poetry and prose is beside the point" (64).

Several reviews acknowledge Dixon's characterizations of Jesse, Ruella, and Lonny as the novel's singular achievement. The *Library Journal* states, for instance, that each "character has a distinct voice" (147), and *Publishers Weekly* describes it as containing "convincing psychological characterizations" (43). V. R. Peterson lavishes similar praise, noting how Dixon adroitly blends the characterizations into "a compelling work" (42). Jim Marks states that "Dixon's greatest success is the skill with which he enters the consciousness of the characters" (27), and Darieck Scott sees in the text an unveiling and analyzing—especially through the characters of Jesse and Ruella—of "white pathology" (314). *Kirkus Reviews* is, however, less generous in its criticism, describing the characters of Lonny as "all cardboard" and Ruella as "rather bloodless" (66).

With its unflinching exploration of racial and sexual themes, *Vanishing Rooms* distinguishes itself as an inventive work. As Michael Bronski states: "Melvin Dixon attempted to push the boundaries of what is permissible in the traditions of African American and gay male fiction. By insisting that race and sexuality be dealt with . . . he enlarged the possibilities for all writers and readers" (135).

BIBLIOGRAPHY

Works by Melvin Dixon

Change of Territory (poems). Callaloo Poetry Series. Lexington: University of Kentucky, 1983a.

Translation. *Drumbeats, Masks, and Metaphor: Contemporary Afro-American Theater*. By Geneviève Fabre. Cambridge, MA: Harvard University Press, 1983b.

Ride Out the Wilderness: Geography and Identity in Afro-American Literature. Urbana.: University of Illinois Press, 1987.

Trouble the Water (novel). Boulder: University of Colorado and Fiction Collective Two, 1989.

Translation and Introduction. *The Collected Poems of Léopold Sédar Senghor*. Charlottesville: University of Virginia Press, 1991a.

Vanishing Rooms (novel). New York: Dutton, 1991b.

Love's Instrument (poems). Chicago: Tia Chucha Press, 1995.

Studies of Melvin Dixon

Bronski, Michael. "Melvin Dixon." *The Gay and Lesbian Literary Companion*. Ed. Sharon Malinowski and Christa Berlin. Detroit: Visible Ink Press, 1995.

Charles, Nick, and Angela Mitchell. "Book Bag: Lifting Every Voice: Books That Speak for Us." Rev. of *Trouble the Water*. *Emerge*, January 1990: 79.

Cole, Clarence Bard. Interview. "Other Voices, Other Rooms." *Christopher Street* 14, no. 1 (1991): 24–27.

Condini, Ned. "Three Lives Entwined in Macabre Dance." Rev. of *Vanishing Rooms*. *National Catholic Reporter*, 10 May 1991:32.

Davis, Stephania H. "Stamford Author Comes Back Home." *Stamford Advocate*, 25 February 1990: D1, 6.

Davis, Thulani. "Black Novelists Head for the Mainstream." Rev. of *Trouble the Water*. *Voice Literary Supplement*, May 1990: 26–28.

Feather, Leonard. "The Homecoming of a Black Preppie." Rev. of *Trouble the Water*. *Los Angeles Times*, 1 October 1989: 2.

Flanagan, Margaret. Rev. of *Trouble the Water*. *Booklist* 86 (15 October 1989): 426.

Forbes, Calvin. "Writing from the African Diaspora." Rev. of *Trouble the Water*. *Washington Post*, 4 March 1990: 1.

Gates, Henry Louis, Jr. "Eros and Thanatos Both." Rev. of *Trouble the Water*. *American Book Review*, July–August 1990: 7.

Grant, Darryl. Interview. "Memories of a Long and Angry Night." *Washington Blade*, 26 April 1991: 43, 52.

———. "With *Vanishing Rooms*, Melvin Dixon Makes Powerful Appearance." *Washington Blade*, 26 April 1991: 52.

Kenan, Randall. "Bookbag: Closed Doors Opened: Portrait of a Gay-Bashing." Rev. of *Vanishing Rooms. Emerge*, April 1991: 46–47.

Kennedy, Constance Decker. Rev. of *Trouble the Water. New York Times Book Review* 9, no. 4 (24 September 1989): 48.

Koponen, Wilfred. "Melvin Dixon." *Contemporary Gay American Novelists: A Bio-Bibliographical Critical Sourcebook.* Ed. Emmanuel S. Nelson. Westport, CT: Greenwood Press, 1993.

Marks, Jim. "Mean Streets and Shades of Baldwin." Rev. of *Vanishing Rooms. Lambda Book Report*, May/June 1991: 27–28.

Peterson, V. R. "Melvin Dixon: Wrestling with Baldwin." *Essence* 22, no. 4 (August 1991): 42.

Preston, John. "Victory Dance." Rev. of *Vanishing Rooms. Outweek*, 10 April 1991: 64.

Rev. of *Trouble the Water. Callaloo* 13 (Fall 1990): 913.

Rev. of *Trouble the Water. Kirkus Reviews* 57 (15 August 1989): 1186.

Rev. of *Vanishing Rooms. Kirkus Reviews* 59 (15 January 1991): 65.

Rev. of *Vanishing Rooms. Library Journal* 116 (January 1991): 147.

Rev. of *Vanishing Rooms. Publishers Weekly*, 18 January 1991: 43.

Satuloff, Bob. "Improvising Destiny." Rev. of *Vanishing Rooms. New York Native*, 29 April 1991: 30.

Scott, Darieck. "Jungle Fever?: Black Gay Identity Politics, White Dick, and the Utopian Bedroom." *GLQ: A Journal of Lesbian and Gay Studies* 1, no. 3 (1994): 299–321.

LARRY DUPLECHAN
(1956–)

Emmanuel S. Nelson

BIOGRAPHY

Larry Duplechan, in a 1987 interview with a fellow novelist, makes a candid admission: "I don't have a strong black identity. My gay identity is much more important to me. But much more than that, I am very much an assimilationist" (Davis 62). With equal candor he goes on to acknowledge his preference for well-built white male bodies and speaks of his "blond beefcake fantasies" (Davis 62). Some may find his declarations politically tasteless; some others might see his preoccupation with blond men as a sign of his colonized sexual imagination. Yet what is intriguing is that Duplechan's novels, despite the author's disclaimers, reveal a strong ethnic consciousness. Ethnic markers are ubiquitous in his narratives. Three of his four novels focus on young black, gay, male protagonists and thus simultaneously help inscribe a black presence in contemporary gay American fiction and a gay presence in contemporary African American literature. At times he beautifully evokes the texture of middle-class black family life, envisions the nuances of southern black rural communities, effortlessly captures the cadences of African American speech patterns, examines the impact of the black church on the formation of sexual attitudes, and poignantly re-creates memories of subtle and overt racial injury. Moreover, African American musical tradition—along with mainstream popular culture—is integral to his artistic vision. By his own admission James Baldwin,* the legendary black gay writer, is a major source of inspiration for him.

Larry Duplechan was born in suburban Los Angeles on December 30, 1956, to Lawrence Duplechan, Sr., and Margie Nell Duplechan. After attending schools in Los Angeles and Sacramento, he studied at the University of California at Los Angeles (UCLA) and graduated in 1978 with a degree in English. He worked as a jazz vocalist for seven years but failed to secure even a single recording contract, so he decided, with some encouragement from friends, to write fiction. Now an author of four novels, he lives in Los Angeles, works part-time as a legal secretary, and occasionally teaches creative writing in the UCLA Continuing Education Program.

MAJOR WORKS AND THEMES

Eight Days a Week (1985), Duplechan's first novel, focuses on an interracial gay romance. Johnnie Ray Rousseau—an African American musician—and Keith Keller—a muscular, blond banker—fall madly in love with each other. Keith's whiteness fascinates Johnnie Ray; Johnnie Ray's blackness thrills Keith. Each is drawn to the other because of the racial difference, yet they are men with vastly different tastes and temperaments. The mutual sexual attraction alone, despite its explosive intensity, proves inadequate to sustain their relationship. The romance fails, but the novel ends on a teasing note that there is perhaps a vague possibility that Johnnie Ray and Keith might be able to resuscitate their friendship.

Duplechan's debut novel is a campy, sexy, funny novel. It is one of the few gay American novels to depict candidly and elaborately an interracial romance. What is rather disappointing, however, is the novel's general superficiality. The theme of sexual desire across racial boundaries, for example, is treated in great detail, but Duplechan retreats from exploring the complexities and subtleties of such desire. Too, the novel so narrowly focuses on the relationship between the two men that it fails to position that relationship in any significantly larger social contexts. Johnnie Ray and Keith make love often, but how the politics of color informs sexual transactions remains largely unexamined. Nevertheless, Duplechan's first novel merits serious consideration, for it at least attempts a bold confrontation with a politically charged subject.

Blackbird (1986), Duplechan's entertaining second novel, maps Johnnie Ray's initiatory journey to young adulthood. A gay coming-of-age narrative, it has many of the stock characteristics of such works: disappointed parents who fail to accept or even understand their son's sexuality; the anxiety and sense of isolation that accompany gay adolescence; the liberating thrill of sexual discovery; and the gradual movement toward healing self-acceptance and at least quasi-public acknowledgment of one's sexual self. Like *Eight Days a Week*, Duplechan's second novel is narrated in the first person and appears to have considerable autobiographical content.

At the beginning of the novel Johnnie Ray is a high school student from a comfortable, middle-class, suburban Los Angeles family. His primary preoccupation, perhaps not so atypically, is sex. The objects of his affection are invariably young white males with bulging crotches. When Johnnie Ray goes to audition for an acting role, he meets Marshall, an aspiring young filmmaker, who becomes central to Johnnie Ray's sexual development. Marshall helps him realize his sexual fantasies for the first time, and Johnnie Ray proves to be an eager and competent learner. Though by the end of the novel Marshall has left Los Angeles in search of his own dreams, Johnnie Ray cherishes his memories of Marshall and a postcard without a return address that he receives from him. In the concluding pages of the novel we find that the protagonist has survived his adolescence: he is now a freshman at UCLA. Along the way he has lost a few friends, endured a failed romance, and lived through his parents' bizarre attempt to "deliver" him from his homosexual desires through a religiously inspired act of exorcism. We see him discovering a multicultural gay community on the university campus and exploring his own possibilities within that milieu.

In *Tangled Up in Blue*, published in 1989, Duplechan charts new territory. Abandoning the autobiographical-confessional, first-person narrative style of his earlier novels, here he opts to tell the story in the third person. Absent, too, is Johnnie Ray, Duplechan's alter ego; in fact, *Tangled Up in Blue* has no African American characters. The plot centers around three white characters: Daniel Sullivan, who considers himself straight but, in fact, is bisexual; Crockett Miller, Daniel's ex-lover and now a platonic friend; and Maggie Sullivan, Daniel's wife and Crockett's close friend. Maggie accidentally finds out that her husband has tested for AIDS antibody and, subsequently, discovers his bisexual past but also the fact that he and Crockett were once lovers. The ensuing crisis nearly destroys the Sullivans' marriage and their friendship with Crockett. Ultimately, however, love heals the ruptures.

The plot of *Tangled Up in Blue* is at times flimsy; it nevertheless is an important contribution to the genre of AIDS narratives. It remains one of the early novels in American literature to face the artistically and politically problematic task of fictionalizing an all-too-real epidemic that had, by the mid-1980s, begun to devastate gay communities. Unlike many other novels published in the 1980s, *Tangled Up in Blue* broadens the literary representation of AIDS by exploring the complex connections among gay, bisexual, and straight characters who are at risk.

Captain Swing, Duplechan's most recent novel, was published in 1993. Johnnie Ray Rousseau, the protagonist of Duplechan's first two works, resurfaces here, but now he is a widower: his lover, Keith, has died recently in an accident. The novel begins with Johnnie Ray's flight home to St. Charles, Louisiana, from Los Angeles to see his estranged father, who is now on his deathbed. It ends with Johnnie Ray's reluctantly preparing to board a plane that will take him back to California. In between the two scenes is a personal drama that is enveloped in a larger familial drama. During the days he spends with his family in Louisiana, Johnnie Ray and his second cousin, Nigel, fall passionately in love with each other. Soon a disapproving family discovers the relationship. Meanwhile, Johnnie Ray's father dies, still resolutely rejecting his gay son. Prior to his departure from the South, Johnnie Ray invites Nigel to come with him to California. Nigel, though professing his love, declines but asks hopefully, "Can I come visit on summer vacation?" (182). Johnnie walks to the plane alone—a plane that he feels has "no business attempting to leave the ground" (184).

Captain Swing is a significant departure for both Johnnie Ray and Duplechan. Here the focus is on an intraracial romance. Such a focus, however, proves problematic: Duplechan is unable to write convincingly about two black gay men in love with each other. Nigel's character is wooden; the romance between him and Johnnie Ray lacks emotional authenticity. But the novel is hardly a failure. Duplechan succeeds in imagining a southern rural black family and community and capturing the moments of affection and elements of tension among their various members. The rhythms of southern black dialect come alive in the pages of the novel. The scenes of lovemaking are as elaborate as they are exquisite. Duplechan, as always, succeeds in entertaining his readers.

CRITICAL RECEPTION

Among the post–James Baldwin generation of gay writers in the United States, Larry Duplechan is certainly an important figure. However, unlike E. Lynn Harris,* who has managed to attract a considerable straight audience for his novels, Duplechan remains essentially a novelist with a primarily gay and predominantly white readership. All of his novels have generally received favorable reviews in the white-oriented gay press. Among his enthusiastic fans are other gay writers, such as Michael Nava, Christopher Davis, and Steven Corbin.* For example, while commenting on *Blackbird*, Davis asserts that the novel made him "feel happy to be gay" (60). Charles I. Nero addresses one of the central features of Duplechan's work: interracial gay desire. About Johnnie Ray's compelling attraction to blond men in *Eight Days a Week*, Nero says that his "sexual attraction to white men . . . allows Duplechan a major moment of signifying in African-American literature: the sexual objectification of white men by a black man" (237). Duplechan's work is yet to receive significant academic attention, however. The only scholarly article devoted entirely to Duplechan's novel so far is John H. Pearson's chapter on Duplechan that appears in *Contemporary Gay American Novelists*. Pearson, who offers a favorable assessment of Duplechan's work, concludes that he is "warm, funny, poignant, self-assured, and utterly readable" (121).

BIBLIOGRAPHY

Works by Larry Duplechan

Eight Days a Week. Boston: Alyson, 1985.
Blackbird. New York: St. Martin's Press, 1986.
Tangled Up in Blue. New York: St. Martin's Press, 1989.
Captain Swing. New York: St. Martin's Press, 1993.

Studies of Larry Duplechan

Davis, Christopher. "CS Interview with Larry Duplechan." *Christopher Street* 10 (1987): 60–62.

Harmon, Charles. Rev. of *Captain Swing* by Larry Duplechan. *Booklist* (September 1, 1993): 33.

Nero, Charles. "Towards a Black Gay Aesthetic: Signifying in Contemporary Black Gay Literature." *Brother to Brother: New Writings by Black Gay Men*. Ed. Essex Hemphil. Boston: Alyson, 1991.

Pearson, John H. "Larry Duplechan." *Contemporary Gay American Novelists: A Bio-Bibliographical Critical Sourcebook*. Ed. Emmanuel S. Nelson. Westport, CT: Greenwood Press, 1993. 116–21.

Poulson-Bryant, Scott. Rev. of *Tangled Up in Blue* by Larry Duplechan. *Village Voice* 34 (July 18, 1989): 61.

Steinberg, Sybil. Rev of *Tangled Up in Blue* by Larry Duplechan. *Publishers Weekly* 235 (January 6, 1989): 91.

RALPH WALDO ELLISON
(1914–1994)

Harish Chander

BIOGRAPHY

Ralph Waldo Ellison was born to Lewis Alfred Ellison and Ida Millsap Ellison on 1 March 1914, in Oklahoma City, Oklahoma. His grandparents were slaves. A native of South Carolina, his father, Lewis Ellison, was a soldier in the U.S. Army before he married Ida Millsap of Georgia, and the couple moved to the frontier state of Oklahoma in search of greater freedom and job opportunities than those available to African Americans in the Southeast. On arrival in Oklahoma, Lewis Ellison worked as a construction foreman and later became a trader in ice and coal. As Ellison writes in the essay "Hidden Name and Complex Fate" in *Shadow and Act*, his father, believing in "the suggestive power of names" (153), named him after the Concord poet-philosopher Ralph Waldo Emerson. When Ellison was three, his father died, and the family fell on hard times. To support herself and her two children, Ida Ellison worked as a domestic in white homes and later as a stewardess in the Afro-Methodist Episcopal Church her family attended.

Ellison attended the Frederick Douglass School in Oklahoma City from 1920 to 1932. In his adolescence, Ellison faced racial barriers, but he hoped to overcome them through hard work. As Ellison indicates in his interview with Richard G. Stern, titled "That Same Pain, That Same Pleasure," reprinted in *Shadow and Act*, he was fascinated with the idea of the Renaissance Man and cherished the ambition of "mastering . . . everything in sight as though no such thing as racial discrimination existed" (26). Music was then his first love, literature the second. He took private lessons in music from the conductor of the Oklahoma City Orchestra in exchange for mowing his lawn. As he tells in "Hidden Name and Complex Fate," he read widely at the Paul Dunbar Library (158). Along with the major white authors, he read Langston Hughes, Countee Cullen, Claude McKay, and James Weldon Johnson, feeling proud "to know that there were Negro writers" (161). In the same essay, he reminisces about the rich oral tradition in the black community, where on rainy days at the drugstore "the older men would sit with their pipes and tell tall tales, hunting yarns and homely versions of the classics," mixing "truth and fantasy" in their narration (159). In his "Introduction" to *Shadow and Act*, he says that through reading he created his own world of heroes, making idols of diverse characters such as jazz men and scientists, black cowboys and soldiers, stuntmen and movie stars (xiii).

In 1933, Ellison won a scholarship from the state of Oklahoma to study music at the Tuskegee Institute (now Tuskegee University) in Alabama. As he describes in "An Extravagance of Laughter" in *Going to the Territory*, he hopped on a freight car, only to be "hustled off" by police in Decatur, Alabama (167). When he finally reached Tuskegee, he found a more repressive discrimination for blacks than he had experienced in Oklahoma City. Here, he encountered not only "claustrophobic provincialism" (160) but several racial taboos—the so-called thou-shalt-nots—concerning public conduct in Alabama (148). To save himself from disappointment, he sought shelter in the library. As he says in his 1969 West Point lecture titled "On Initiation Rites and Power" in *Going to the Territory*, he "lived in books as well as in the sound of music" (39). At Tuskegee Ellison first read T. S. Eliot's *The Wasteland*, "which moved me but which I couldn't reduce to a logical system" (39). Despite his academic interests, Ellison was forced to leave college at the end of his junior year when his financial aid was not renewed. Ellison decided to find a summer job in New York to make enough money for his senior year and for lessons in sculpture.

Ellison arrived in Harlem in July 1936. He worked as a waiter, a receptionist in a psychoanalyst's office, a freelance photographer, and once as a trumpeter but could not find a job where he could save enough to finish college. In his spare time he studied sculpture under the tutelage of Harlem artist Richmond Barthe but later gave it up in favor of the study of symphonic composition with Wallingford Rieger.

In "Hidden Name and Complex Fate," Ellison reveals that he wrote his first book review at Richard Wright's urging. Wright published "Creative and Cultural Lag," Ellison's review of E. Walters Turpin's *These Low Grounds*, and also wrote his first short story, "Hymie's Bull," for *New Challenge*, but the magazine folded without publishing this issue. In this story, a black youth named Hymie kills a white bully in self-defense on a freight car. In 1939, Ellison published his first story, "Slick Gonna Learn," about the color-blind camaraderie among the union men that saves a black man named Slick from police revenge for his assault on a policeman who called him a racial epithet.

In late 1937, Ellison left New York for Dayton, Ohio, to be with his ailing mother. Robert Penn Warren says that while living in Dayton that winter and while hunting birds to sell to General Motors officials Ellison began to consider seriously writing as a profession (325–26). Ellison tells in his interview for the

Paris Review reprinted in *Shadow and Act* that while living in Dayton, he studied James Joyce, Feodor Dostoyevsky, Gertrude Stein, and Ernest Hemingway at night. He read Hemingway not only to learn how to lead a bird in flight but "to learn his sentence structure and how to organize a story" (169–70). As John F. Callahan describes in the "Introduction" to *"Flying Home" and Other Stories*, his "mother's illness and unexpected death became a painful catalyst" for Ellison to write (xi–xii). Ellison wrote two of his early stories "A Hard Time Keeping Up" and "The Black Ball" during his stay in Dayton (xxiii).

Upon his return to New York in April 1938, he worked for the Federal Writers Project. As a Project writer, Ellison reported on famous New York trials, wrote profiles of prominent black New Yorkers, and collected folklore. At night, he wrote his own fiction, becoming a regular contributor to the left-wing periodical *New Masses* and to the *Negro Quarterly*. He reviewed both Langston Hughes' autobiography *The Big Sea* and Richard Wright's *Uncle Tom's Children* for *New Masses*. In his review of *The Big Sea*, titled "Stormy Weather," Ellison commends Hughes for emphasizing the importance of folklore in literature and paying scant attention to ideology. In his review of Wright's *Uncle Tom's Children* in "Recent Negro Fiction," Ellison praises the book for successfully delineating "the universals embodied in Negro experience" (41). In 1942, Ellison became the managing editor of the *Negro Quarterly*, but this periodical ceased publication after four issues.

Soon, Ellison broke away from Wright's social realism, which tended to look upon blacks, in Jerry Gafio Watts' phrase, "as reactive subjects to oppression" (45). In his 1944 review of Gunnar Myrdal's "An American Dilemma" in *Shadow and Act*, Ellison asks: "But can a people . . . live and develop for over three hundred years simply by *reacting?*" (301). He prefers a more affirmative approach, saying that the "full solution" to the "problem of the American Negro" "will lie in the creation of a democracy in which the Negro will be free to develop himself for what he is and, within the large framework of that democracy, for what he desires to be" (290–91). He criticizes both the New Deal administration for its "perpetuation of a Jim Crow Army" and the American Communist Party for its "shamefaced support" of segregation in the U.S. armed forces (296).

Desiring to contribute to the war effort against fascism but reluctant to join the segregated armed forces, Ellison joined the U.S. Merchant Marine in 1943, serving for three years as a cook on a ship taking supplies to U.S. troops in Europe. In his 1942 essay "The Way It Is," reprinted in *Shadow and Act*, Ellison notes the dilemma faced by black people in fighting "the big Hitler over yonder . . . with all the little Hitlers over here" (278). In 1944, Ellison wrote three of his most important stories, "Flying Home," "King of the Bingo Game," and "In a Strange Country," all of which share the common feature of a black protagonist who seeks to control his own destiny only to fail due to the limitations imposed by the white world.

In 1944, Ellison met Fanny McConnell, an Iowa University graduate, whom he married in 1946. This was Ellison's second marriage. In a 1969 interview with

James Alan McPherson reprinted in *Conversations with Ralph Ellison*, Ellison reveals that "one reason that my [first] marriage came to an end was that my inlaws were disgusted with me, thought I had no ambition, because I didn't want a job in the Post Office" (181).

In the summer of 1945, as he tells in his West Point lecture reprinted in *Going to the Territory*, while on sick leave from the Merchant Marine, staying at a friend's farmhouse in Vermont, he wrote the words: "I am an invisible man" (42). He did not then know "[w]hat type of man would make that type of statement" (42). Over the course of the next seven years, the novel titled *Invisible Man* gradually evolved out of Ellison's effort, as he describes it in the "Introduction" to the thirtieth-anniversary edition of the novel, to reveal "the human universals hidden within the plight of one who was both black and American" (xviii). Most of the novel was written in Harlem, "where it drew much of its substance from the voices, idioms, folklore, traditions and political concerns of those whose racial and cultural origins I share" (viii–ix). Ellison published *Invisible Man* in 1952, winning acclaim immediately.

After the publication of *Invisible Man*, Ellison spent the remainder of his life writing, teaching and lecturing. In 1955, he began to work on a second novel but died of pancreatic cancer on 16 April 1994 without completing it. Nine excerpts from this novel, which concerns African American religious experience and politics and, above all, identity, have already appeared as stories in various journals. In "A Completion of Personality," Ellison states that "the central situation" of his second novel is "that of an old man searching throughout the years for a little boy who ran away" (11). A substantial portion of the manuscript of this novel was destroyed in a fire in 1967. Ellison's literary executor, John F. Callahan, has, as reported in *The Chronicle of Higher Education* of 14 July 1995, undertaken the formidable task of finishing Ellison's second novel (A5).

From 1958 onward, Ellison held a series of teaching appointments at academic institutions. He was Albert Schweitzer Professor in the Humanities, New York University, 1970–1979, and professor emeritus thereafter till his death. Ellison received numerous honors, including the Medal of Freedom from President Lyndon B. Johnson, 1969; the Chevalier de l'Ordre des Artes et Lettres from André Malraux, French minister of cultural affairs, 1970; and the National Medal of Arts, 1985. *Invisible Man* has been translated into fourteen languages.

MAJOR THEMES AND WORKS

Ellison is an artist, not an ideologue. He believes that the world of art and the world of politics are separate and is opposed to using art to achieve political ends. In "An American Novelist Who Sometimes Teaches," Ellison exclaims: "I am a novelist, not an activist" (179). In his 1957 essay "Society, Morality, and the Novel" in *Going to the Territory*, he makes a distinction between a novel that is "a work of art" and one that is "a disguised piece of sociology" (273). He explains that a novel "seeks to communicate a vision of experience" (242). He appreciates that the issues of the day will necessarily influence fiction but prefers that they do so not in an overt, polemical way. As he writes in "Hidden Name and Complex Fate" in *Shadow and Act*, a writer "is involved with values which turn in their *own* way, and not in the ways of politics, upon the natural issues affecting his nation and time" (165). In "Society, Morality, and the Novel," Ellison states that the function of the novel is "that of seizing from . . . our daily lives those abiding patterns of experience which, through their repetition and consequence in our affairs, help to form our sense of reality and from which emerge our sense of humanity and our conception of human value" (244). Ellison thus sees in fiction the possibility of furthering enlightenment through universal themes.

Though many of Ellison's themes deal with the situation of the African American in postwar society, Ellison dwells on the universal aspects of the African American situation, so he may impel readers to "identify that which is basic in man beyond all differences of class, race, wealth, or formal education" (*Shadow and Act* 273). In his interview with Richard Stern titled "That Same Pain, That Same Pleasure," Ellison points out that "what I have tried to commemorate in fiction is that which I believe to be enduring and abiding in our situation, especially those human qualities which the American Negro has developed despite . . . the obstacles and meannesses imposed upon us" (39).

Invisible Man is a portrait of an African American artist as a young man. The unnamed protagonist must reject various false identities imposed on him by others, before he can, in an epiphany, find his own authentic identity as an artist. Embedded in the story is the saga of the African American experience. At the same time, the Protagonist is a representative of depersonalized, deprived, and dispossessed persons of all races. The novel ends with the Protagonist's rhetorical question: "Who knows but that, on the lower frequencies, I speak for you?"

Growing up in the agrarian South, the Protagonist finishes high school and goes to a black college as a scholarship student. Because he inadvertently brings Trustee Norton in contact with Jim Trueblood, who recounts his story of incest to the Trustee, and the psychotic black veterans at the Golden Day saloon, the Protagonist is expelled from the college and sent packing to the industrial North. Working first at a paint factory and later as a spokesperson for the Brotherhood, a protocommunist organization, he is systematically denied his individuality. Caught up in a race riot in Harlem engineered by the Brotherhood, he escapes to an abandoned coal cellar, where he discovers "[t]hat I am nobody but myself" (15). Knowing himself, though he may be invisible to others, he is now able to see others distinctly.

Most of the major themes in Ellison's works can be found in his magnum opus. Dominant themes of *Invisible Man* are the quest for identity, freedom, and inner reality, the black man's invisibility to the outside world resulting from stereotype, an ambivalent stance toward philosophies of life, world, and people, black folklore as a source of self-affirmation and strength, and humor and pathos.

The Protagonist's search for identity becomes an arduous struggle against the people and organizations that are trying to impose false identities on him. As he complains, "Everyone seemed to have some plan for me, and beneath that some more secret plan" (190). In John O'Brien's *Conversations with Ralph Ellison*, O'Brien comments that "the invisible man must find the identity that was always there but hidden from him," and Ellison responds that the Protagonist's identity "has to be created too" (231–32). Comparing himself with Stephen Dedalus of James Joyce's *A Portrait of the Artist as a Young Man*, the Protagonist realizes that his problem, unlike Stephen's, is "one of creating *the uncreated features of his face*" (346)—that is, to create his own individuality.

The black college the Protagonist attends is mainly concerned with producing black graduates who fit in a white-dominated society, not individuals free to express their identities. Trustee Norton looks upon the Black College as a factory turning out a line of product—such as teachers, mechanics, and farmers—and to him the success of the college depends on the number of goods produced. He confides to the Protagonist that "if you fail I have failed by one individual, one defective cog" (45).

The Protagonist receives a similar depersonalizing treatment in his northern ventures. At the Liberty Paint Factory, he becomes a pawn caught between the union members, who consider him a "fink" (217), and the antiunion Brockway, who considers him a mole planted by the union. At the factory hospital where he is treated after the explosion in the boiler room, the Protagonist is given electric shock therapy to erase his memory. Symbolically fitted with a new identity, he is told that he should take another job because he cannot cope with "the rigors of industry" (241). Hired by Brother Jack as a district speaker for the Brotherhood, the Protagonist is asked to disregard his past (301) and is given a "new identity" in the form of a new name (302). The Protagonist gradually realizes that the Brotherhood does not allow its members any independent voice and that in its book individuals "don't count" (284). Brother Jack tells the Protagonist that he was "not hired to think" but "to talk" (458–59). Having lost his faith in the Brotherhood but still needing the job, the Protagonist tries his grandfather's advice "to agree 'em [whites] to death and destruction" (16) and starts "YESSING them" (502). He soon realizes, however, that "[b]y pretending to agree, I *had* indeed agreed, had made myself responsible for that huddled form lighted by flame and gunfire in the street, and all the others whom now the night was making ripe for death" (541).

Chased by the black nationalist Ras' men, the Protagonist dons dark glasses and a wide-brimmed hat to disguise himself, only to find that he has become Rinehart, the con man, who takes on multiple identities. He gives up on the Rinehart protean guises, however, because they unleash chaos. Wizened, the Protagonist burns the false identities he has been carrying in his briefcase—his high school diploma, Clifton's Sambo doll, his Brotherhood name slip, and the anonymous letter he has received disapproving of his work among the Harlemites. Finally, living as an "underground" man, the Protagonist discovers his authentic identity as a writer, as he articulates his experiences in the form of his memoir titled *Invisible Man*.

The quest for identity goes hand in hand with the quest for freedom. The Protagonist's discovery of his true identity is his passport to freedom: "When I discover who I am, I'll be free" (237). Having gone through the full gamut of the African American experience, the Protagonist finds himself now free to write about it to the best of his ability. Shorn of illusions, he is freed from fear and can tell the truth about the Jacks, Emersons, Nortons, Rases, and Rineharts of the world. He seems to agree with the old woman in his dream who describes freedom as follows: "First I think it's one thing, then I think it's another . . . I guess now it ain't nothing but knowing how to say what I got up in my head" (14). Being free to say what he has gotten in his head, the Protagonist can now "denounce and defend," "condemn and affirm," "hate and love" (566–67), and in that courage, conviction, and competence lies his freedom.

Search for inner reality—one's obsessive-compulsive desires and fears—is another major theme of Invisible Man. Through dreams, the Protagonist is able to fathom his personal psyche and the collective psyche—the primordial images and racial memories he shares with other African Americans. In a dream described in the Prologue, the Protagonist sees a beautiful girl on the Auction Block, "pleading in a voice like my mother's" (9). He encounters both Ras and Rinehart—"unrecognized compulsions of my being"—and finds himself running away from them (13). In a dream indicative of his constant fear of losing his individuality, the Protagonist finds himself "the prisoner of a group consisting of Jack and old Emerson and Bledsoe and Norton and Ras and the school superintendent and a number of others whom I failed to recognize," who castrate him with a knife (556).

Invisible Man exposes the failure of whites, looking through the blinders of prejudice and stereotype, to see the real black person. The novel opens with the Protagonist's observation: "I am an invisible man" (3). He points out that people see "everything and anything except me," "as though I have been surrounded by mirrors of hard, distorting glass" (3). As Ellison observes in "Twentieth-Century Fiction" in Shadow and Act, "the Negro stereotype is really an image of the unorganized, irrational forces of the American life, forces through which, by projecting them in forms of images of an easily dominated minority, the white individual seeks to be at home in the vast unknown world of America" (57). He adds that "[p]erhaps the object of the stereotype is not so much to crush the Negro as to console the white man" (57–58). In Invisible Man, whites straitjacket black men into a few personality types and roles, such a "sulky and mean" (17), humble and hardworking, sexually promiscuous and incestuous, with roles such as shoeshines and comic Sambos, spiritual singers and dancers. Whereas black people are ashamed of Jim Trueblood's incest, whites respond by giving him work and money because he confirms one of their black stereotypes.

Many of the characters in Invisible Man, most notably the Protagonist, reveal an ambivalent stance to life. In "The World and the Jug," reprinted in Shadow and Act, Ellison points to the African American "complex double vision . . . [an] ambivalent response to men and events" (137). Illustrative of this ambivalent approach is the Prologue sermon on the "Blackness of Blackness," with the grand text: "Black is" and "Black ain't," "It do, Lawd," "an' it don't" (9–10). In the "Battle Royal" scene, the Protagonist manifests an ambivalent attitude toward the naked blond woman: "I wanted . . . to caress her and destroy her, to love her and murder her, to hide from her, and yet to stroke her" (19). The old woman in the Protagonist's dream confesses to her love-hate relationship to the white father of her sons. Thereupon, like the persona in Robert Frost's "Acquainted with the Night," the Protagonist confides in her: "I too have become acquainted with ambivalence. That's why I'm here" (10). The Protagonist experiences ambivalence as he stands before a statue of the College Founder, who is depicted with his hands outstretched, moving a veil over the face of a kneeling slave, leaving the Protagonist uncertain whether the veil is being lifted or put more securely in place (36).

Ellison finds in black folklore a means to discovery of identity, self-affirmation, and a source of strength. In "Change the Joke and Slip the Yoke" in *Shadow and Act*, Ellison refers to the "stability" of the African American traditional culture of songs, tales, proverbs, and riddles and its "adaptability" to real-life situations— "pressure points," to use Richard Dorson's phrase. In "The Art of Fiction" in *Shadow and Act*, Ellison writes that some "slave songs, blues, [and] folk ballads" "have named human situations so well that a whole corps of writers could not exhaust their universality" (173). Folklore comes to the aid of Jim Trueblood, the pushcart man, as well as the Protagonist, who has earlier tried to "shut out" his southern heritage (170). Through singing the blues, Jim Trueblood comes to terms with his incest and decides to go back to his family: "I ain't nobody but myself and ain't nothin' I can do but let whatever is gonna happen, happen" (66). The parting advice of the pushcart man to the Protagonist is: "All it takes to get along in this here man's town is a little shit, grit, and mother-wit" (172). Realizing how he has been cheated by Dr. Bledsoe, the Protagonist sees himself as the poor Robin of the popular African American song: "O well they picked poor Robin clean" (190). At Tod Clifton's funeral, the Protagonist, along with other participants in the funeral procession, sings the plaintive old slave song "There's a Many Thousand Gone" (441) to cope with Clifton's death.

Like Dickens, Ellison blends humor and pathos in *Invisible Man* to laugh at, and bemoan, irrational human behavior and absurd situations. Illustrative examples are the tipsy man with the ample paunch at the "Battle Royal" scene winding his belly in a "slow and obscene grind" like an "intoxicated panda," each time the blond dancer sways her hips (20); and the drunken man at the Communist Party headquarters, who sings lines from black work songs, "his arms held out from his body like a penguin's wings, glass in one hand, cigar in the other" (304–5).

CRITICAL RECEPTION

Since its publication in April 1952, *Invisible Man* has received tremendous critical attention, perhaps unprecedented for a novel written by an American minority writer. It was at once recognized as a novel with a difference, winning the National Book Award the year following publication. The novel has fared well almost a half century of criticism. A 1965 *Book Week* poll of 200 well-known critics, authors, and editors adjudged *Invisible Man* to be "the most distinguished single work" published in America in the last two decades since 1945. Perhaps the greatest testament to the favorable critical reception to *Invisible Man* is the fact that it has now become a part of America's literary canon.

Invisible Man won laudatory reviews from prominent mainstream critics such as Wright Morris and Anthony West and moderate black critics such as Alain Locke and Henry F. Winslow. To Wright Morris, the *New York Times* reviewer, "It is a resolutely honest, tormented, profoundly American book" (5). To Henry F. Winslow, *The Crisis* reviewer, "it argues [for] the recognition of the individual apart from sociological design and ethnocentric morality" (397). Alain Locke in *The Negro in American Culture* judges it to be "one of the best-integrated accounts of interaction between Negroes and whites that has yet been presented in American fiction" (143).

On the other hand, left-wing scholars such as Irving Howe and black scholars such as John Oliver Killens and Addison Gayle criticize *Invisible Man* negatively for its nonmilitant stance and for its not being a racial "plight and protest" novel. In his essay "Black Boys and Native Sons," Irving Howe attacks Ellison for not writing a protest novel like Wright's *Native Son* (163), pointing to Richard Wright as a model black novelist because of his "clenched militancy" (159). In "The World and the Jug" in *Shadow and Past*, Ellison defends himself against Howe's charges, pleading that his novel be judged by aesthetic standards, "as art . . . not because I did or did not fight some ideological battle" (142). John Oliver Killens faults *Invisible Man* for its presentation of "Negro characters as Uncle Toms, pimps, sex perverts, guilt-ridden traitors" and for its "vicious distortion of Negro life" (7). Addison Gayle bemoans that Ellison's hero "chooses the path of individualism instead of racial unity," adding that the Protagonist's novel "is to be attributable more to Ellison's political beliefs than to artistic deficiency" (257). Ellison himself explains in his introduction to the work that his goal of "revealing the human universals" helps the reader recognize "the reality of black and white fraternity" (xviii). Lloyd Brown, in a typical communist critique, writes that *Invisible Man* "is profoundly anti-Negro" and marred by anticommunist rhetoric; he says that Ellison shares with Richard Wright and Chester Himes* "their hatred and contempt of the Negro working masses, their renegades' malice and their servility to the masters" (63–64).

Other important critical studies on themes and style of *The Invisible Man* include those by Thorpe Butler, Marcus Klein, Barbara Christian, Houston A. Baker, Jr., and Robert G. O'Meally. Butler points out that Ellison's *Invisible Man* does not discourage readers from action, only warns them that "complete disillusionment seems to be a necessary prerequisite for authentic identity or action" (330). Klein states that *Invisible Man* is a series of initiations for the hero, which "confirm again and again that the hero doesn't exist" (146), and notes its circular structure, the Protagonist's ending "back in the underworld from which he had tried to emerge" (107). Christian observes that, like James Joyce's Stephen, who "has to confront his Irish, Catholic, and family traditions," Ellison's unnamed "hero has to penetrate the illusions built around the fact that he is black, not only in others, but more importantly in himself" (357). Baker argues that Trueblood represents the "quintessential trickster," who justifies his incest by blaming it on his dream, rather than on his own sinful nature, thus challenging "the Christian orthodoxy" (835); Trueblood has perfected the art of telling his incest story to sell it for "an ever-spiraling exchange value" (839). O'Meally in *The Craft of Ralph Ellison* states that Ellison's works "employ modernist techniques—surrealism, multiple perspectives, stream of consciousness—to reveal a world tempestuous and out of focus" but adds that "what makes these works distinctly Ellisonian is the influx of black American folklore" (2).

The use of folklore in *Invisible Man* has also become a matter of critical debate. George Kent points to Ellison's dexterous use of black folklore but expresses "unease" at Ellison's efforts to interconnect the black folklore with "Western symbols and mythology" (169). Susan Blake contends that Ellison, by ritualizing African American experience as part of a larger human experience, has denied its distinctiveness. The definition of black American life becomes "not black but white" (135), as black identity becomes indistinguishable from American identity or the human condition. Blake concludes: "Ellison's adaptation of black folklore, however involuntarily, exchanges the self-definition of the folk for the definition of the masters" (135).

Of the numerous studies comparing *Invisible Man* with other literary texts, those by Robert N. List and Alan Nadel stand out. List shows the influence on *Invisible Man* not only of Joyce's *A Portrait of the Artist as a Young Man* but also of *Ulysses* and *Finnegans Wake*. Nadel places *Invisible Man* in the American tradition, following Emerson, Twain, and Melville, but with a subtext that critiques the trio's canonical texts (147). Another commentator, writing for Gale Research's *Contemporary Authors on CD*, celebrates the literary and folkloric antecedents of *Invisible Man*: "The novel is a fugue of cultural fragments—echoes of Homer, Joyce, Eliot, and Hemingway join forces with the sounds of spirituals, blues, jazz, and nursery rhymes" (7).

BIBLIOGRAPHY

Works by Ralph Waldo Ellison

Novels

Invisible Man. New York: Vintage, 1952 (Random House 30th Anniversary Edition, 1982). *Published excerpts from the untitled second novel:*
"And Hickman Arrives." *Noble Savage* 1 (1960a): 5–49.
"The Roof, the Steeple and the People." *Quarterly Review of Literature* 10 (1960b): 115–28.
"It Always Breaks Out." *Partisan Review* (Spring 1963): 13–28.
"Juneteenth." *Quarterly Review of Literature* 14 (1965a): 262–76.

"Tell It Like It Is, Baby." *Nation* 201 (1965b): 129–36.
"Night Talk." *Quarterly Review of Literature* 16 (1969): 317–29.
"A Song of Innocence." *Iowa Review* 1 (Spring 1970): 30–40.
"Cadillac Flambe." *American Review* 16 (Feb. 1973): 249–69.
"Backwatering: A Plea to the Senators." *Massachusetts Review* 18 (Autumn 1977): 411–16.

Short Stories

"Slick Gonna Learn." *Direction* (Sept. 1939): 10–11+.
"The Birthmark." *New Masses* (2 July 1940): 16–17.
"Did You Ever Dream Lucky?" *New World Writing* 5 (Apr. 1954): 134–45.
"Out of the Hospital and Under the Bar." *Soon, One Morning: New Writing by American Negroes 1942–1962*. Ed. Herbert Hill. New York: Knopf, 1963. 242–90.
"Flying Home" and Other Stories. Ed. John F. Callahan. New York: Random House, 1996.

Essays and Reviews

Shadow and Act. New York: New American Library, 1966.
Going to the Territory. New York: Vintage-Random, 1987.
The Collected Essays of Ralph Ellison. Ed. John F. Callahan. New York: Modern Library, 1995.
"Creative and Cultural Lag." *New Challenge* 2 (Fall 1937): 90–91.
"Stormy Weather." *New Masses* 37 (1940): 20–21.
"Recent Negro Fiction." *New Masses* 40 (1941): 22–26.

Studies of Ralph Waldo Ellison

Baker, Houston A., Jr. "To Move without Moving: An Analysis of Creativity and Commerce in Ralph Ellison's Trueblood Episode." *PMLA* 98 (Oct. 1983): 828–45.
Blake, Susan L. "Ritual and Rationalization: Black Folklore in the Works of Ralph Ellison." *PMLA* 94 (1979): 121–36.
Brown, Lloyd. " 'The Deep Pit'—A Review of Ralph Ellison's *Invisible Man*." *Masses and Mainstream* 5 (June 1952): 62–64.
Butcher, Margaret Just. *The Negro in American Culture: Based on Materials Left by Alain Leroy Locke*. New York: New American Library, 1971.
Butler, Thorpe. "What Is to Be Done?—Illusion, Identity, and Action in Ralph Ellison's *Invisible Man*." *CLA Journal* 27 (Mar. 1984): 315–31.
Christian, Barbara. "Ralph Ellison: A Critical Study." *Black Expression*. Ed. Addison Gayle, Jr. New York: Weybright, 1969. 353–65.
Corry, John. "An American Novelist Who Sometimes Teaches." *New York Times Magazine* (20 Nov. 1966): 54–55, 179–87, 196.
Foley, Barbara. "The Rhetoric of Anticommunism in *Invisible Man*." *College English* 59 (Sept. 1997): 530–47.
Gale Research. *Contemporary Authors on CD*. CD-ROM. 1997.
Gayle, Addison. *The Way of the New World: The Black Novel in America*. Garden City, NY: Doubleday, 1976.
Graham, Maryemma, and Amritjit Singh, eds. *Conversations with Ralph Ellison*. Literary Conversations Series. Jackson: University Press of Mississippi, 1995.

Hersey, John, ed. "A Completion of Personality: A Talk with Ralph Ellison." *Ralph Ellison: A Collection of Critical Essays*. Englewood Cliffs, NJ: Prentice-Hall, 1974. 2–19.

Howe, Irving. "Black Boys and Native Sons." *A World More Attractive*. New York: Horizon, 1963. Rpt. in *A Casebook on Ralph Ellison's Invisible Man*. Ed. Joseph F. Trimmer. New York: Crowell, 1972. 150–69.

Kent, George E. "Ralph Ellison and Afro-American Folk and Cultural Tradition." *CLA Journal* 13 (1970): 265–76.

Killens, John Oliver. "Invisible Man." *Freedom* 2 (June 1952): 7.

Klein, Marcus. "Ralph Ellison." *After Alienation*. New York: World, 1964. 71–146.

List, Robert N. *Dedalus in Harlem: The Joyce-Ellison Connection*. Washington, DC: University Press of America, 1982.

Locke, Alain. *The Negro in American Culture*. New York: Alfred A. Knopf, 1956.

Monaghan, Peter. "Finishing Ralph Ellison's 2nd Novel." *The Chronicle of Higher Education* (14 July 1995): A5.

Morris, Wright. "The World Below." *The New York Times Book Review* (13 Apr. 1952): 5.

Nadel, Alan. *Invisible Criticism: Ralph Ellison and the American Canon*. Iowa City: University of Iowa Press, 1988.

O'Meally, Robert G. *The Craft of Ralph Ellison*. Cambridge: Harvard University Press, 1980.

Schor, Edith. *Visible Ellison: A Study of Ralph Ellison's Fiction*. Westport, CT: Greenwood, 1993.

Warren, Robert Penn. *Who Speaks for the Negro?* New York: Random-Vintage, 1966.

Watts, Jerry Gafio. *Heroism and the Black Intellectual: Ralph Ellison, Politics, and Afro-American Intellectual Life*. Chapel Hill: University of North Carolina Press, 1994.

West, Anthony. "Black Man's Burden." *The New Yorker* (31 May 1952): 93–96.

Winslow, Henry F. "Unending Trial." *The Crisis* (June–July 1952): 397–98.

ARTHUR R. FLOWERS
(1950–)

Ymitri Jayasundera

BIOGRAPHY

A native of Memphis, Tennessee, Flowers returns to the locale of his childhood in his novels, even though he has spent most of his adulthood in New York City, with a stint in Vietnam in the late 1960s to early 1970. He is greatly influenced by John Oliver Killens,* the novelist and legendary founder of the Harlem Writer's Guild. Flowers studied under him at Columbia University on and off for thirteen years, and he shares Killens' beliefs in his own writing that "art is a form of propaganda and that it can have decolonizing uses" (May 281), so that writing is a political act for "reconceptualizing African American identity" (May 282). He also cofounded with other writers and directed the New Renaissance Writer's Guild in New York City. In the mid-1980s Flowers founded a literary workshop in Memphis called the Griot Shop, reflecting his interests in hoodoo and shamanism, becoming in essence a "literate" storyteller.

Through his participation in the Black Memphis Writer's Workshop and the symposium held January 1989 at LeMoyne-Owen College in Memphis, Flowers contributes a chapter from his second novel in progress, *Another Good Loving Blues*, to the anthology *Homespun Images*. Flowers also sets his novels specifically in Memphis' Beale Street—a section of town known for its blues and jazz music and also for its prostitution and drugs. Intimately connected to this scene as a blues musician himself, Flowers romanticizes this area in *Another Good Loving Blues*, downplaying the seamier side, but in *De Mojo Blues* we see Beale Street as urban decay has swallowed it up in the early 1970s, with mostly boarded up and gone-out-of-business stores.

Flowers' first novel, *De Mojo Blues*, is probably his most autobiographical, as he, like the three young black men in the novel, returning from Vietnam, had to adjust to civilian life in the early 1970s. The novel reflects his interest in hoodoo as the main protagonist, Tucept HighJohn, drifting through life and haunted by the death of his buddy Jethro in Vietnam, decides to search for the "Lost Book of Hoodoo" that Jethro had mentioned and discover the significance of the mojo bag, containing hoodoo bones, given to him by Jethro the day before he died.

MAJOR WORKS AND THEMES

Flowers' novels celebrate the culture of African Americans through his use of blues, hoodoo, the oral tradition, and the male experience without losing sight of the racism that is an everyday part of their lives. In both novels, the male protagonists face major forms of racism that affect the rest of their lives. In *De Mojo Blues*, Tucept HighJohn and his two buddies are accused of collaborating on a murder during a raid in Vietnam because a witness saw "black men" at the scene. In *Another Good Loving Blues*, set in the early 1920s, Lucas Bodeen faces a lynching and a flood that is reminiscent of Zora Neale Hurston's major novel, *Their Eyes Were Watching God*. Flowers is at his most political activist in *De Mojo Blues*, in which Tucept HighJohn tries to personally empower himself to lead black people in the early 1970s through the discipline of hoodoo. This is contrasted by his two buddies, Willie D. and Mike, who, respectively, help black people to a better life either as a political activist in the Bronx and Harlem, reclaiming old and abandoned apartment houses for black families, or as a lawyer in Washington entering into the bourgeoisie. Flowers describes hoodoo as a mystical experience in which a person trains and disciplines the mind to see into the inner self of himself and of strangers, a type of x-ray vision into the soul. HighJohn is guided in this quest through a wise old man, a shaman, whom he meets in Beale Street.

In *Another Good Loving Blues*, set against the backdrop of the Great Migration to the North in the early 1920s, Flowers tells the tale of Lucas Bodeen, a piano-playing blues musician, and Melvira Dupree, a conjure woman intent on helping people with her hoodoo abilities. Theirs is a love story as they leave the Mississippi Delta to search for her missing mother. They are drawn to Beale Street, which we see from a historical perspective, as Flowers de-emphasizes the prostitution, drugs, and violence in favor of the creative energy of the music and the community. Rather than continuing the migration farther up north, as was the norm, to Harlem or Chicago, Lucas and Melvira return south to Mississippi, where they reconnect with the traditional oral culture of the South. Flowers uses black folk speech and Hurston's technique of the speakerly text in which the narrative voice "slips" from the first person to second and third, singular and plural (Jablon 77).

Unlike the chronological and conventional third-person narrative with frequent flashbacks in *De Mojo Blues*, Flowers' second novel, *Another Good Loving Blues*, is part fable, part tall tale and is narrated by a griot named Flowers. The novel shows Flowers' influences by the Harlem Renaissance writers, such as Langston Hughes and Zora Neale Hurston, who make a cameo appearance in the novel. Stylistically, both novels show, through the lyricism of their prose, the blues influence and the oral tradition with its emphasis on fantasy, magic, play on reality, hoodoo, and so on, but in *Another Good Loving Blues*, we see him gaining maturity as an artist and approaching his material in a more sophisticated and complex manner.

Flowers' children's novel, *Cleveland Lee's Beale Street Band*, recapitulates the novels thematically. Set in Memphis, an old blues musician mentors a young boy against the backdrop of the Beale Street music scene, showing him the commitment and discipline it takes to be a musician.

CRITICAL RECEPTION

Both novels are reviewed as short paragraphs in trade journals, some mainstream magazines, such as *Time* and *Essence*, and the *New York Times Book Review*. Although generally praised, they are not critically acclaimed or singled out as exceptional by any of the reviewers. Nevertheless, the novels are important for students interested in southern regionalist fiction because of their setting mostly in Memphis and their Beale Street locale of blues music and poetry that Flowers offers through his obvious interest, knowledge, and experience.

De Mojo Blues was well received critically, with Paula Giddings calling it an "insightful and often compelling look into the emotional world of committed Black men" (32) and *Publishers Weekly* calling it "a sincere and creative first novel by a very promising writer" (56). *Another Good Loving Blues* received similar reviews, with Ducato praising it for its "great authenticity of time and place" (877) and its prose, which captures the blues music, lyrics, and poetry, but Kilpatrick criticized the novel as a "pretty, if predictable tale bordering on fantasy" (164).

Apart from the book reviews at publication, there is only one critical work on Flowers. Madelyn Jablon in her book *Black Metafiction* argues for reading *Another Good Loving Blues* as a *künstlerroman* in which the main protagonist, Lucas Bodeen, metamorphoses from a novice to a master musician by learning the importance of reading music, just as Melvira takes her study of hoodoo to another level through her learning to read. Reading the novel for its metafiction techniques, Jablon focuses on the novel's complex rendering of the oral tradition, storytelling, and the transformation of blues music in the 1920s from a solitary and improvisational endeavor of traveling blues musicians to the great jazz bands.

Although not of the same stature as John Edgar Wideman* and Ernest J. Gaines,* Flowers is important for his contribution as part of the contemporary African American writers exploring their experiences.

BIBLIOGRAPHY

Works by Arthur R. Flowers

Novels

De Mojo Blues: De Quest of HighJohn de Conqueror. New York: E. P. Dutton, 1985.
Another Good Loving Blues. New York: Viking, 1993.
Cleveland Lee's Beale Street Band. Illus. Anna Rich. Mahwah, NJ: BridgeWater Books, 1995.

Excerpts in Anthologies

Homespun Images: An Anthology of Black Memphis Writers and Artists. Ed. Miriam DeCosta Willis and Fannie Mitchell Delk. Memphis, TN: LeMoyne-Owen, 1989. (From *Another Good Loving Blues*)
Black Southern Voices: An Anthology of Fiction, Poetry, Drama, Nonfiction, and Critical Essays. Ed. John Oliver Killens and Jerry W. Ward, Jr. New York: Meridian, 1992: 172–77. (From *De Mojo Blues*)

Studies of Arthur R. Flowers

Ducato, Theresa. Rev. of *Another Good Loving Blues. Booklist* 89.10 (January 15, 1993): 876–77.
Giddings, Paula. Rev. of *De Mojo Blues. Essence* (June 1986): 32.
Handman, Fran. Rev. of *Another Good Loving Blues. New York Times Book Review* (March 7, 1993): 23.
Haskins, Jim. Rev. of *De Mojo Blues. New York Times Book Review* (January 19, 1986): 20.
Jablon, Madelyn. *Black Metafiction: Self-Consciousness in African American Literature.* Iowa City: University of Iowa Press, 1997.
Kanfer, Stefan. Rev. of *De Mojo Blues. Time* 127.7 (February 17, 1986): 78.
Kilpatrick, Thomas L. Rev. of *Another Good Loving Blues. Library Journal* 118.1 (January 1993): 164.
Lewis, Taisha. Rev. of *Another Good Loving Blues. Essence* (July 1993): 46.
May, Vivian M. "Flowers, A. R." *The Oxford Companion to African American Literature.* Ed. William L. Andrews, Frances Smith Foster, and Trudier Harris. New York: Oxford University Press, 1997: 281–82.
Quinn, Mary Ellen. Rev. of *De Mojo Blues. Booklist* 82 (December 1, 1985): 531.
Rev. of *Another Good Loving Blues. Publishers Weekly* 239 (November 30, 1992): 35.
Rev. of *De Mojo Blues. Publishers Weekly* 228 (November 8, 1985): 56.

LEON FORREST
(1937–)

Dana A. Williams

BIOGRAPHY

Born January 8, 1937, Leon Forrest grew up on the South Side of Chicago. He attended Wendell Phillips Elementary School, and in 1951 he was one of the few African American students who attended Hyde Park High School. After completing high school in 1955, Forrest attended Wilson Junior College for a year, Roosevelt University for a year, and, finally, the University of Chicago. Forrest's interest in writing emerged during his grade school years, and his formal work as a journalist began in 1960, when he became a public information specialist while touring Germany in the U.S. Army. Upon his return to Chicago, from 1964 to 1968, he worked for the *Bulletin Booster* newspapers, community weeklies on Chicago's South Side. In 1969, Forrest became an associate editor for *Muhammed Speaks*, a position he held until the publication of his first novel.

In the early 1970s, Forrest met Ralph Ellison,* whose support of the young novelist is detailed in *Conversations with Ralph Ellison*. Forrest also met Toni Morrison,* who was, then, an editor at Random House in search of new African American writers. Under Morrison's editorship, Forrest published his first two novels and established himself as a prodigious novelist. In 1985–1994, he served as chair of African American studies at Northwestern, where he was also a professor of English. Currently, he is working on another novel structured as a series of novellas.

MAJOR WORKS AND THEMES

Forrest's works are best understood when read as his attempts to transform the expressive modes of presentation of African American life and history, from everyday occurrences to life-explaining and life-sustaining events and achievements. His success as a major novelist rests in his ability to reinvent narrative strategy by employing African American vernacular traditions such as spirituals, folk speech, the blues, sermonic texts that observe conventions of oral language, repetition, and orality. In each of his novels, cultural themes and themes of religion, of flight, and of family are foregrounded and presented with substantial genre modifications. The action of each novel is presented using multiple narrative conventions, including the eulogy, the folk sermon, epistles, poetic monologues, and stream-of-consciousness-relayed surreal episodes. Collectively used and in conjunction with the classical and mythical allusions that frequent his works, these intertextual narrative conventions require astute readings for full comprehension. Like Ellison and Morrison, both of whom draw heavily from folklore and myth, Forrest expects his readers to bring to his texts culturally specific knowledge of the past to recognize and to understand his reinvented and transformed allusions.

In his first novel, *There Is a Tree More Ancient than Eden* (1973), Forrest presents the life of Nathaniel Witherspoon, who reappears in his later novels *The Bloodworth Orphans* and *Two Wings to Veil My Face*. Experiencing the agony of a motherless child, Nathaniel is the editor of his life and his family's history. His attempts to process fragments of biographical, sociological, and emotional information about his relatives, his ancestors, historical figures, and, finally, himself in order to cope with his mother's death serve as the nonconventional plot of the novel. Because his mother's death also involves a break in his link to his ancestral history, he must find a way to establish his own link to his history and to the past. Highly symbolic of the rootlessness experienced by an enslaved people removed from their native land and culture, Nathan experiences a sense of loss that can be rectified only by recovering the past.

As he sits in the back of a Cadillac with Aunty Breedlove en route to his mother's funeral, Nathan, through the process of (re)memory, explores the inner conflicts that have denied his sense of wholeness. In "The Lives," he begins to sort out the list of characters who have some bearing on his life. These biographical sketches include his family members as well as historical figures such as Louis Armstrong, Frederick Douglass, Harriet Tubman, and Abraham Lincoln, each of whom is culturally and personally significant to Nathan. In "The Nightmare" and "The Dream," Forrest reinforces the themes introduced in the first section, especially the motherless child motif, as Nathan attempts to resolve his inner conflicts. The central action in "The Vision," a crucifixion/lynching/dismemberment ritual, revolves around Billie Holiday's "Strange Fruit," which details the lynching of black men. In "Wakefulness," Nathan has achieved some sense of wholeness as he is persuaded to emerge from underneath the bed where he has been hiding in the midst of his confusion. Though he appears to have achieved some sense of self-identity, his journey toward reconciliation of the past and the present and their effect on the future continues. In the 1988 edition of the text, Forrest appended a section entitled "Transformation" in the form of an

"Epistle of Sweetie Reed." It is a letter to President Lyndon B. Johnson, dated May 7, 1967 and intended to warn the president of the world evils to come, including the election of Nixon and the assassination of Martin Luther King, Jr. In relation to the original sections, "Transformation" contrasts Nathan's rootlessness to Sweetie Reed's wisdom. As the 100-year-old Sweetie Reed is still alive at the novel's close, Nathan has found his link to the past, in all her wisdom, and, in turn, his hope for a better future.

Forrest's second novel, *The Bloodworth Orphans* (1977), continues the saga of the Witherspoon family. The novel opens in the early 1970s, when Forest County (Forrest's fictional county) has begun an era of civil unrest that is filled with violence and rioting in its inner city. Nathaniel has reached the age of thirty-three and has moved away from his role of journeyman, as in *There is a Tree*, to the role of witness to the fate of a family that has been largely orphaned either by death or because of miscegenation at the hands of the white Bloodworth clan. *Bloodworth Orphans* is divided into two large sections, Chapters 1–7 and Chapters 8–12, and it centers primarily around two events—the suicidal death of Abraham Dolphin and the death of Rachel Flowers, who succumbs to cancer. Their deaths serve as catalysts to the Bloodworth curse, triggering catastrophic doom among the entire Bloodworth clan. The novel concludes with a series of deaths reminiscent of a Shakespearean apocalypse, and as John G. Cawelti observes, "In this final movement, themes of classical and Christian mythology converge with African themes and Orphean sacrifices of Regal [Pettibone] and [Abraham] Dolphin seem to make way for the Christian hope of rebirth" (48).

In *Two Wings to Veil My Face* (1984), Forrest's third novel, Nathaniel returns as Forest County's central character. As in *There Is a Tree*, where Nathan and his aunt Sweetie Reed first appear, the main action in *Two Wings* has already taken place, but it is told through the process of (re)memory. Fourteen years prior to the story's opening, Sweetie has promised to tell Nathan why she refused to go to her husband's and Nathan's grandfather's funeral. Her explanation reveals the difficulties she has encountered as a woman who has had to come to terms with dearth and bounty. As Nathan has realized, her story is her father's story, her husband's story, Nathan's story, and, in a more general sense, the African American story. His task is to process this information, discarding what is useless and maintaining possession of what is essential. After years of giving Nathan pieces of the story in no particular order, she finally tells him that it is time to move from "listening and half hearing to listening and recording in long hand." Following Sweetie's orders, Nathan begins to transcribe the griot's tale. Forrest writes:

He [Nathan] looked over at the thick layers of writing paper. . . . Snatches of her [Sweetie] recall of I.V. Reed's words coming back to him now, and Nathaniel Witherspoon thought, she's cleaning up his language here and there, through the process of re-creation, memory transformed. Editing wherever possible . . . making it her own. How will it look when I transform it . . . he wondered. Or should I say, transpose it. (*Two Wings* 78)

This passage summarily renders Forrest's objectives as a writer—to render his versions of sermons, tales, and African American experiences passed to him through oral and written traditions, making them his own. Transposing, transforming, and re-creating, Forrest captures the importance of reviewing the past in the present moment and examining its effects on the future.

Forrest's latest novel, *Divine Days* (1992), returns to the liminal space between chaos and re-creation developed in the latter stage of *The Bloodworth Orphans*. Forrest introduces a new protagonist, Joubert Antoine Jones, and, like Nathan, he experiences an epiphany that reveals the redemptive power of African American cultural heritage and the necessity to re-create this force in his own life. Notably, the 1,135-page comic epic is Forrest's first presentation of a narrative in the first person. Narrated as Joubert's journal entries during the week of his return to Forest County from armed services duty in Germany, *Divine Days* develops around the conflict between the hipster Sugar-Grove and the trickster W.A.D. Ford and Joubert's relationship to them. However, the novel involves far more episodes and themes than this. As a whole, the novel richly explores a wide range of African American experiences, including spirituality, myth, culture, and music. Central to each of these themes is the quest for transcendence and the subsequent realization that each aspect can and must coexist.

CRITICAL RECEPTION

In May 1993, *Callaloo* devoted a section of its spring issue to studies on Forrest and his works, which Cawelti edited and which includes his seminal essay on *Divine Days*. In 1997, Cawelti also edited *Leon Forrest: Introductions and Interpretations*, the first and only book-length study on Forrest's works.

As a whole, each of Forrest's novels has been well received by the few critics who have taken the initiative to comment critically on them. At best, Forrest's writing is difficult and obscure and is, thus, not very widely read. However, it is mainly for these same characteristics that critics admire his novels as works of art. Sven Birkerts, as quoted in Cawelti, writes: "*Divine Days* is that rare thing in our self-conscious and ironic age—a full-out serious work of art. . . . Here is a work that runs the octaves, carries us from street jive to the mysterious whisperings of the self in spiritual consultation" (262). Commenting on the role of history in Forrest's Witherspoon-Bloodworth trilogy, A. Robert Lee writes that the collective African American memories, "stretching from the earliest African diaspora through slavery-times and from abolition and the northward 'Great Migration' into the cities, declare themselves in abundance in Forrest's fiction. . . . History, as he [Forrest] seeks to render it, indeed operates as a storm against all the canons of order" (qtd. in Cawelti 101). Suggesting what sets Forrest apart from other novelists, Bruce Rosenburg writes: "Forrest's . . . inventiveness lies in his language usage, a usage which foregrounds the word. . . . he wants us to experience life with the realization that he is recreating what is actually impossible to duplicate" (qtd. in Cawelti 115). As these critics have discovered, Forrest's novels, when read as attempts to reinvent the past to assess its effect on the present and the future, reveal themselves as meaningful and fulfilling readings.

BIBLIOGRAPHY

Works by Leon Forrest

Novels

There Is a Tree More Ancient than Eden. New York: Random House, 1973.
The Bloodworth Orphans. New York: Random House, 1977.
Two Wings to Veil My Face. New York: Random House, 1984.
Divine Days. Chicago: Another Chicago Press, 1992.

Essays

"Faulkner/Reforestation: Faulkner and Yoknapatawpha." *Faulkner and Popular Culture.* Ed. Doreen Fowler and Ann J. Abadie. Jackson: University of Mississippi Press, 1990. 207–213.
"A Solo Long-Song: For Lady Day." *Callaloo* 16 (Spring 1993): 332–367. *The Furious Voice for Freedom: Essays on Life.* Mount Kisco, NY: M. Bell, 1992. Rpt. as *Relocations of the Spirit.* Wakefield, RI: Ashodel Press/Moyer Bell, 1994.
"A Conversation with Ellison." *Conversations with Ralph Ellison.* Ed. Maryemma Graham and Amritjit Singh. Jackson: University Press of Mississippi, 1995. 215–221.

Studies of Leon Forrest

Bethel, Kathleen E. "Leon Forrest: A Bibliography." *Callaloo* 16 (Spring 1993): 448–454.
Byerman, Keith E. "Orphans and Circuses: The Literary Experiments of Leon Forrest and Clarence Major." *Fingering the Jagged Grain: Tradition and Form in Recent Black Fiction.* Athens: University of Georgia Press, 1985. 238–274.
Cawelti, John G. "Earthly Thoughts on *Divine Days.*" *Callaloo* 16 (Spring 1993): 431–447.
———, ed. *Leon Forrest: Introductions and Interpretations.* Bowling Green, OH: Bowling Green State University Popular Press, 1997.
Grimes, Johnanna L. "Leon Forrest." *Dictionary of Literary Biography.* Vol. 33. Ed. Thadious Davis and Trudier Harris. Detroit: Gale Research, 1984. 77–83.
Rosenburg, Bruce A. "Forrest Spirits: Oral Echos in Leon Forrest's Prose." *Oral Tradition* 9 (Oct. 1994): 315–327.
Taylor-Guthrie, Danielle. "Sermons, Testifying, and Prayers: Looking beneath the Wings in Leon Forrest's *Two Wings to Veil My Face.*" *Callaloo* 16 (Spring 1993): 419–430.
Warren, Kenneth. "Thinking beyond Catastrophe: Leon Forrest's *There Is a Tree More Ancient than Eden.*" *Callaloo* 16 (Spring 1993): 409–418.

Interviews

Cawelti, John G., ed. "Leon Forrest at the University of Kentucky: Two Interviews." *Leon Forrest: Introductions and Interpretations.* Bowling Green, OH: Bowling Green State University Popular Press, 1997. 286–313.

McQuade, Molly. "The Yeast of Chaos: An Interview with Leon Forrest." *Chicago Review* 41 (1995): 43–51.

Mootry, Maria K. " 'If He Changed My Name': An Interview with Leon Forrest." *Chant of Saints: A Gathering of Afro-American Literature, Art, and Scholarship*. Ed. Michael S. Harper, Robert Stepto, and John Hope Franklin. Urbana: University of Illinois Press, 1979. 146–157.

Warren, Kenneth W. "The Mythic City: An Interview with Leon Forrest." *Callaloo* 16 (Spring 1993): 392–408.

ALBERT FRENCH
(1943–   )

Jeffrey T. Loeb

BIOGRAPHY

Though the blurbs of Albert French's three books reveal nothing about him other than the fact that "he is a writer who lives in Pittsburgh," the actualities of his writing life are nothing short of astounding. Born into modest circumstances in Pittsburgh during World War II, French was equally modest in his early aspirations and joined the Marine Corps soon after graduating from high school. As he reveals in his 1997 memoir *Patches of Fire*, this decision provided the two signal experiences of his life: his encounters with the realities of racism in America and the Vietnam War, in which he was seriously wounded. These subjects, the destructive effects of racism, especially in the pre–civil rights South, and the trauma of war form the basis, both direct and indirect, of French's two novels, *Billy* (1993) and *Holly* (1995), written successively in a single year.

The most notable aspects of French's career are its long gestation and his self-confessed lack of formal education. After his discharge from the Marine Corps in 1967, he tried college for a semester but quit and then held a series of entry-level jobs in the steel industry before being hired as an apprentice photographer by a Pittsburgh newspaper. According to his testimony in *Patches*, he wrote nothing but ad copy for the first forty-seven years of his life. Then, in 1991, consumed by despair over the loss of both his father and his business (a local magazine for which he was business manager, photographer, and co-owner) and suddenly stricken by posttraumatic stress syndrome from Vietnam, French, like many veterans, began writing literally as a way of saving his life. The result was the first version of *Patches*, which he subtitled *A Story of War and Redemption* because it examines its own genesis as an instrument of catharsis.

Though *Patches* was, by French's account, extremely rough in its first version, his cousin John Edgar Wideman* and Wideman's wife, Judy, read parts of it at a family gathering. Judy Wideman, in particular, was so taken by it that she sent it to Wideman's agent, who eventually placed it with a publisher. Though it required several years' worth of revisions, years during which French wrote and published both Billy and Holly, Patches was finally published in 1997 and has been acclaimed as being among the most significant works on the Vietnam War yet published by an African American veteran (Gussow C15). At this writing French continues to live and work in his old Pittsburgh neighborhood.

MAJOR WORKS AND THEMES

Billy is a harrowing descent into the twin hells of racism and personal trauma. The novel is set in 1937–38 in rural Mississippi, and the title character is a ten-year-old black boy who, along with a friend, innocently blunders onto the property of some poor white sharecroppers. When Billy is spotted poking around in the shallow water of a pond's edge, they are pursued and beaten by two teenaged white girls simply because, as one, Lori Pasko, states, "That's my pond and I don't want their nigger asses in it" (24).

In defending himself, however, Billy stabs Lori with a pocketknife, and the blade nicks her aorta, causing her to bleed to death before help can arrive. The family and the white community vow revenge, the result being Billy's electrocution by the state. The concluding pages, when Billy's execution is carried out, constitute one of the most wrenching episodes in contemporary fiction. His terror and lack of understanding of his circumstances ("Ah wants ta go homes. Take me wit ya, Mama. Ah won'ts stick nobodies agins"), as well as his mother's unbridled grief at her helplessness, pitch the story at an emotional level that is unremitting (195).

The level of intensity at which Billy is told makes it a scathing indictment of the southern racial environment, at the same time that its linear structure gives it, in Michael Dorris' estimation, a tragic sense of inevitability (7). French's sympathies are not, however, exclusively with the black characters. Rather, the strength of his writing stems, in large part, from the fact that he is able to probe the ways that whites are also entrapped by their own received racial attitudes. His representation of the traumatic grief suffered by Lori Pasko's mother, for instance, nearly matches that of Billy's mother. Ultimately, the novel's power derives from this fact—it indicts racism but not necessarily the whites, who are equally engulfed by it. As French says,

The racism in Billy, quite honestly, is a backdrop. It's been written that it lights up the face of American racism; Billy was not meant to be that. My feeling about writing Billy was to get at the feelings of Billy himself, Cinder, his mother, her feelings, Lori Pasko, Ginger Pasko, these people involved. . . . If I wanted to just attack racism I could probably have started out with Pittsburgh. (Vedder 65)

The other major theme that French touches upon in all his books is the debilitating effect of trauma. As he intimates in *Patches* and in interviews, his own trauma of being badly wounded in Vietnam motivates his representations of human suffering (Gerrard 18). Thus, when Lori Pasko is dying of her knife wounds or her mother is grieving over her sudden and senseless death, French is clearly exploring our common humanity in the face of an uncaring or even cruel universe.

This same naturalistic philosophy marks both the themes and the style of *Holly*. Also set in the South, in a small town outside Wilmington, North Carolina, in 1943, it explores the consequences of an interracial relationship. Holly Hill, a poor white woman of twenty (one reviewer describes her as Lori Pasko grown up), finds herself cut loose from the certainties of her bucolic upbringing by the death of her fiancé and the wounding of her brother in the Pacific (Martelle n.p.). She finds solace in an unexpected place—with a young black veteran, Elias Owens, who has lost his arm fighting in Europe. Reared in a middle-class environment, Elias is a graduate of Howard who has been, before his injury, an aspiring pianist. In an attempt to come to terms with his loss, he has taken up painting and is visiting his grandmother, who lives in the Back Land, the rural area African Americans are consigned to live in, located just across a creek from Holly's parents' home. Holly and Elias meet at this creek and are drawn together by their losses, both having to overcome the prejudices of their respective backgrounds. When Holly is forced to reveal the fact that she has become pregnant by Elias, her enraged father beats her badly and undertakes to kill him. Elias manages to help Holly escape by train to the safety of his parents in Washington, but he himself is caught and dies of a severe beating in jail a short time later.

CRITICAL RECEPTION

The critical response to French's works consists almost entirely of reviews that emphasize their intensity and style. Both novels are marked by a vernacular narration rendered in free, indirect discourse, allowing us to share in the thoughts of many characters simultaneously. Most reviews find it both effective and innovative, though both Rhoda Koenig (90) and Scott Martelle (2) feel that the narrational voice is inconsistent at times. Michael Dorris praises *Billy* as "mythic in the sense that instead of the surprise, the twists of plot we might discover in a more typical contemporary novel, here we are confirmed in our worst dreads as destiny immutably and shockingly unfolds" (7). Scott Martelle says of French's style in *Holly* that it is "terse and revealing, . . . wasting few words or scenes" (n.p.).

BIBLIOGRAPHY

Works by Albert French

Novels

Billy. New York: Viking, 1993.
Holly. New York: Viking, 1995.

Memoir

Patches of Fire: A Story of War and Redemption. New York: Anchor Books, 1997.

Studies of Albert French

"Albert French." *Contemporary Literary Criticism*. Vol. 86. New York: Gale, 1995. 61–67.

Dorris, Michael. "No Place for a Black Boy to Swim." Rev. of *Billy*. *New York Times Book Review* (19 Dec. 1993): 7.

Gerrard, Nicci. "Flowing Fast and True from Vietnam." Rev. of *Billy*. *The Observer* (6 Feb. 1994): 18.

Gussow, Mel. "For an Unlikely Author, Life Is War and Redemption." Rev. of *Patches of Fire: A Story of War and Redemption*. *New York Times*, 4 June 1997: C13–15.

Koenig, Rhoda. Rev. of *Billy*. *New York* (13 Dec. 1993): 90.

Martelle, Scott. Rev. of *Holly*. *Quarterly Black Review* (1995): n.p. Online. Internet. 21 Dec. 1997.

Rev. of *Billy*. *Publishers Weekly* (30 Aug. 1993): 73.

Seaman, Donna. Rev. of *Billy*. *Booklist* (1 Oct. 1993): 254.

Vedder, Polly. Interview with Albert French. *CLC Yearbook*. Vol. 86. New York: Gale, 1995. 65–67.

ERNEST J. GAINES
(1933–)

Eberhard Alsen

BIOGRAPHY

Although Ernest Gaines has lived in California since he was fifteen years old, all
of his published stories and novels take place in his native Louisiana. Ernest
James Gaines was born on 15 January 1933 on the River Lake Plantation in
Pointe Coupée Parish, near New Roads, Louisiana. He was the oldest of twelve
children, nine boys and three girls. While his parents worked in the fields, Ernest
and his siblings were cared for by their crippled aunt Augusteen Jefferson, who
became a major influence in Gaines' life. Although Aunt Augusteen could not
walk but had to crawl on the floor like an infant, she cooked the family's meals,
did the laundry and ironed, and also raised vegetables in a small garden. She
taught Gaines the importance of "standing," of asserting one's human dignity,
and she later became the prototype of the many "aunty" figures in Gaines' fiction.
Since Aunt Augusteen could not visit others, there were always people coming
to see her, sitting on the "gallery," or porch, and telling stories. Listening to Aunt
Augusteen and her friends telling stories about the old times on the plantation,
Gaines absorbed the contents, structures, and speech patterns of folk narrative
that give his fiction its special flavor.

Gaines received his first six years of schooling in a one-room schoolhouse that
also served as the black church. He later attended a Catholic middle school in
New Roads, Lousiana, the town called Bayonne in his fiction. When he was
fifteen, he joined his mother and stepfather in Vallejo, California. There, he
began to read voluminously in the public library and decided to become a writer.
After graduating from high school and attending Vallejo Junior College, he was
drafted into the army and served two years in Guam. When he returned stateside,
he enrolled at San Francisco State College as an English major. In 1956, he

published his first two stories in the school's literary journal, *Transfer*: "The Boy in the Double Breasted Suit" and "Turtles." Upon graduating from college in 1957, Gaines won the Wallace Stegner Award and was admitted into the Creative Writing Program at Stanford University.

These early years of promise were followed by a period of uncertainty and self-doubt. During this time Gaines wrote a draft of his first novel, *Catherine Carmier*, sent it to a publisher, received the package back unopened, and burned it. Having failed—or so he thought—in writing "a simple little novel about people at home," Gaines tried to write about "the bohemian life in San Francisco" ("Miss Jane" 18, 32), the life celebrated in Jack Kerouac's *The Dharma Bums* (1958). About these efforts, Gaines says: "Within a year and a half or two years, I had written three of the worst novels that have ever been written by a published writer" ("Miss Jane" 32). Gaines never even tried to publish these novels.

Having decided to return to writing about his native Louisiana, Gaines revisited his birthplace for the first time in 1963. He stayed for six months, looking up and interviewing old neighbors and friends, doing research into the history of the area, and taking photographs of the locations in which most of his fiction is set. He later published these pictures in a "photo essay" entitled "Home" (1978). The pictures include the double row of identical cabins that form the "quarters" of the plantation where Gaines' family "lived for five generations"; the one-room schoolhouse and church, where Gaines "studied for the first six years of [his] education"; the big house of "the man who owned the plantation"; and the nightclub where the black field workers "drank, danced, fought and died" (53). Since his 1963 visit, Gaines has returned to Louisiana annually; and since 1981, he has been teaching each fall term at the University of Southwestern Louisiana.

After his return to California in 1964, Gaines published a much revised version of his abortive first novel, *Catherine Carmier*, and three years later a second novel, *Of Love and Dust* (1967). The two novels were followed by a collection of short stories entitled *Bloodline* (1968). After completing these three books, Gaines came to this realization: "I was writing in a definite pattern. One, I was writing about a definite area; and, two, I was going farther and farther into the past. I was trying to go back, back, back into our experiences in this country to find some kind of meaning in our lives" ("Miss Jane" 34). Indeed, one of the distinctive traits of Gaines' fiction is his awareness of the history of the relations between the many different ethnic groups in Louisiana. These ethnic groups include African Americans of all shades, from the blue-black "Singalese" (Africans from Senegal) to the very light-skinned French and Spanish Creoles, as well as Caucasians of Anglo-Saxon, French, and Spanish background.

Gaines most fully explores the history of race relations in *The Autobiography of Miss Jane Pittman* (1971), for that novel spans a whole century, from the Civil War to the Civil Rights movement. *Miss Jane Pittman* not only drew rave reviews but was also made into an acclaimed television movie. Moreover, the excellence of the novel helped Gaines win a Guggenheim Fellowship for the year 1973–74.

His subsequent three novels, *In My Father's House* (1978), *A Gathering of Old Men* (1983) and *A Lesson before Dying* (1993), secured Ernest Gaines' twofold reputation as the foremost writer of the Louisiana region and as a major figure in contemporary African American fiction. Moreover, *A Gathering of Old Men* was made into a TV movie in 1987 by the respected German Director Volker Schlöndorff, and the rights for *A Lesson before Dying* were bought by a major Hollywood studio.

In 1993, Gaines eclipsed all his previous successes: He received the Book Critics' Circle Award for his novel *A Lesson before Dying*; he earned the so-called "Genius Award" of the MacArthur Foundation worth $355,000; and he married Diane Saulney, an assistant district attorney in Miami, Florida, who is also a native of Louisiana.

MAJOR WORKS AND THEMES

Gaines' first novel, *Catherine Carmier* (1964), takes place some time in the 1950s on a plantation near the fictional town of Bayonne, Louisiana, in Pointe Coupée Parish where Ernest Gaines grew up. The novel introduces several of the major concerns in Gaines' fiction, but the two most important ones are that of the conflict between Creoles and darker skinned African Americans and that of the old culture of the region dying out because the Cajuns are taking over the plantations and are replacing tenant farmers with machinery.

The novel begins when the protagonist Jackson Bradley, who has just graduated from college in California, returns to the plantation to visit Miss Charlotte, the great aunt who raised him. He soon clashes with Miss Charlotte because he plans to return to California rather than teach school in Louisiana as she expects him to. He further alienates his aunt because he falls in love with a light-skinned Creole, Catherine Carmier, whose father Raoul hates dark-skinned people as much as he hates whites.

Jackson and Catherine go out three nights in a row, and on the third night have sex in a rooming house. Eventually Jackson convinces Catherine to leave for California with him. However, Raoul finds out about their plans and confronts Jackson. In the ensuing fistfight, Jackson has to knock Raoul down three times before Raoul admits defeat and allows Jackson to leave with Catherine.

But Catherine feels she must take care of her father because he is badly hurt. She promises to join Jackson in California after Raoul is well again. The novel ends with a conversation between Jackson and Catherine's mother, Della, who convinces Jackson that Catherine will, indeed, follow him to California because after his defeat Raoul is too proud to let Catherine stay on the plantation.

In Gaines' second novel, *Of Love and Dust*, the setting is again a plantation in southern Louisiana. This time the major themes are manhood, in the sense of both virility and human dignity, and interracial love. The protagonist is the twenty-two-year-old Marcus, who has killed another black man and is bailed out of jail by the white plantation owner Marshall Hebert. In return Marcus will have to work on the plantation for five years.

Immediately after his arrival on the plantation, Marcus announces that he plans to skip out of his contract with Hebert. He also starts to antagonize the Cajun overseer, Bonbon, who, in turn, tries to break Marcus' spirit by over-working him. Each tries to show the other that he is the better man. Marcus tries to out-male Bonbon by seducing Bonbon's black mistress Pauline. When Pauline rejects him, Marcus goes after Bonbon's Cajun wife, Louise. The two fall in love and decide to run away together. In planning their escape, Marcus gets the unexpected help of the plantation owner. Marshall Hebert wants to get rid of Bonbon because Bonbon has been blackmailing him. Hebert therefore prom-ises Marcus to provide him and Louise with a car and money. However, Hebert double-crosses Marcus and sees to it that Bonbon kills Marcus. At the novel's end, a white judge rules the murder a justifiable homicide; Louise goes crazy and is committed to an insane asylum; and Bonbon and his black lover Pauline disappear, presumably to live together in the North.

Before embarking on his next novel, Ernest Gaines published a collection of five short stories entitled *Bloodline*. This collection is notable for two stories. "The Sky Is Gray" has been widely anthologized and was turned into a film for the PBS series *The American Short Story*. It is an initiation story in which a mother, rather than a father, teaches her eight-year-old son by her example what man-hood is all about. The other story, "Just like a Tree," contains the thematic germs for Gaines' best-known novel, *The Autobiography of Miss Jane Pittman*, because it deals with the ninety-nine-year-old Aunt Fe's reaction to her great-nephew's civil rights activism. Moreover, by employing ten different first-person narrators, the story also introduces a narrative technique that Gaines used again in two later novels, in *A Gathering of Old Men*, which uses fifteen narrators, and, in the next-to-last chapter of *A Lesson before Dying*, which uses six.

The character of Aunt Fe inspired Gaines to create the 110-year-old Miss Jane, the protagonist in *The Autobiography of Miss Jane Pittman*. That novel is a compendium of Gaines' typical themes, from the major theme of the history of race relations, to minor themes such as the generation conflict, religious doubt, manhood, and the gradual disappearance of the old plantation culture.

The novel purports to be an autobiography spoken on tape and transcribed by an "editor." The narrative covers about 100 years, beginning near the end of the Civil War as Union troops arrive at the plantation where the eleven-year-old protagonist, Ticey Bryant, is a slave. The Union soldiers set the slaves free, and Corporal Brown from Ohio gives Ticey her new name, Jane Brown. When Jane joins a group of former slaves who are marching north, she witnesses a massacre in which ex-Confederate soldiers and Klansmen kill everyone in the group except Jane and a five-year-old boy named Ned. Jane and Ned try in vain to reach Ohio and eventually turn back. They wind up working for wages on a Louisiana plan-tation run by a kind northerner who sees to it that all his black field hands receive an education. When the plantation is returned to its original owner during Reconstruction, Jane is about twenty-four and Ned about seventeen. Ned leaves the plantation when vigilantes come after him because he has been working for a committee that reports to Washington how blacks are being treated in the South. He winds up in Kansas, where he gets married and becomes a schoolteacher.

Meanwhile, Jane takes up with a black cowboy by the name of Joe Pittman and moves to western Louisiana with him, where he works on a horse ranch. They live happily for some ten years until Joe gets killed while trying to break a particularly ferocious horse. After Jane moves back to southern Louisiana, Ned and his family join her there. Ned plans to build a school for blacks and teach his students, whom he calls "warriors," to stand up to white injustice. Before the construction of the school is completed, Ned is killed by whites.

After Ned's death, Jane joins the church and moves to the Samson plantation near Bayonne, where she serves as the Samsons' cook for many years. The story of Ned's martyrdom repeats itself with Jimmy Aaron, a boy from the quarters of the Samson plantation who is killed by whites when he organizes the desegregation of the drinking fountain in the Bayonne courthouse. The novel ends with Miss Jane and other blacks from the Samson plantation on their way to Bayonne for a rally to protest the arrest of a black schoolgirl who had dared to drink from the for-whites-only fountain.

Thematically, Gaines' next novel, *In My Father's House*, is a new departure for two reasons: it uses urban, rather than rural, settings, and it develops as its central theme a concern that has been of only minor importance in Gaines' previous work: the relationship between black fathers and their sons.

The novel is set in the fictional town of St. Adrienne, Louisiana, during the 1970s. The protagonist is the civil rights leader the Reverend Philip Martin, who abandoned his illegitimate son, Etienne, some twenty years earlier. Etienne's mother, Johanna, still loves Martin and is unable to have a lasting relationship with anyone else as long as Martin is alive. Therefore, she sends Etienne to kill Martin. But Etienne is not able to kill his father, nor is Martin able to make Etienne forgive him. After Etienne is jailed for loitering, Martin cancels the boycott of a white department store in return for Etienne's release from jail. Because of this betrayal, Martin is voted out as president of the Civil Rights Committee. But Etienne still does not forgive his father. Instead, Etienne kills himself by jumping off a railroad bridge. Because of his son's suicide, Martin loses his faith in God and goes temporarily insane. He recovers when his wife, Alma, and three of his close friends forgive him for his betrayal of his community and assure him of their continued support.

With *A Gathering of Old Men*, Ernest Gaines returned to the rural settings of his best work. Once again, the major theme is manhood, in the sense of both virility and human dignity. The time is the late 1970s, and most of the action occurs in the quarters of the Marshall plantation. The story is told by fifteen different narrators, ten black and five white. The key event is the killing of the

Cajun Beau Boutan by his black employee Charlie Biggs. However, for two-thirds of the book we don't know who actually killed Boutan. This is because Charlie's eighty-year-old godfather, Mathu, and two of his friends claim to have killed Boutan. This ruse inspires Candy Marshall, the white niece of the plantation owner, to send word to all those who have been hurt by the Boutan family to come to the plantation and bring twelve-gauge shotguns with empty number 5 shells. Fifteen old men show up, all in their seventies and eighties.

When Sheriff Mapes arrives, first Candy and then each of the old black men claim to have killed Boutan. Near the end of their lives, the old men realize that this is their last chance to prove their manhood by standing up to white oppression. Although the sheriff slaps some of the old men around, they all stick to their stories. To explain why they had to kill Boutan, some of them launch into long catalogs of injustices they and their kin have suffered at the hands of the Boutan family. However, the sheriff decides that the only one of them capable of killing Boutan is Mathu. He calls Mathu "a better man than most I've met, black or white" (74) and tries to arrest him, but all the other old men raise their guns and show him that they have live shells in them. The standoff continues for some eight hours until a notorious Cajun thug by the name of Luke Will and two associates show up to avenge Beau Boutan's death.

Before the Cajuns arrive at the quarters, the real killer of Beau Boutan, Charlie Biggs, asserts his manhood by coming out of hiding and giving himself up. He says: "A nigger boy run and run and run. But a man come back. I'm a man" (187). Just as Sheriff Mapes and Charlie Biggs come out of Mathu's house, Luke Will and his two cronies drive up and demand that Mapes hand over Charlie. When Mapes refuses, Will shoots Mapes in the arm, and a firefight ensues between Charlie Biggs and the eighteen old men, on one side, and Luke Will and his two cronies, on the other. In this fight, Luke Will and Charlie Biggs are shot dead, and one of Luke's friends is wounded, but none of the eighteen old men is hurt. A week later, there is a three-day trial. The upshot is that the judge puts the eighteen old black men and the two Cajuns on probation for five years and takes away their privilege of carrying any kind of gun.

Gaines' most recent novel, A Lesson before Dying, again deals with the theme of manhood, this time narrowed down to the question of what makes a human being different from an animal. The time is 1949, and most of the action takes place in the jail of the town of Bayonne. The person struggling for manhood is an uneducated young field hand named Jefferson. After witnessing a holdup in which both the white store owner and his two black assailants are shot dead, he is arrested as an accessory to the crime. During the trial, the public defender tries to save Jefferson's life by portraying him as an animal incapable of thoughts or plans, saying, "I would just as soon put a hog in the electric chair as this" (8). But the jury finds Jefferson guilty and sentences him to death.

Jefferson's godmother, Miss Emma, asks the young schoolteacher Grant Wiggins to visit Jefferson in jail to teach him how to die with dignity and prove to the whites that he is not a hog. Miss Emma turns to Wiggins because Jefferson has been acting like the hog he is supposed to be, and the Reverend Ambrose has been unable to make him change his behavior. Wiggins accepts the challenge because, even though he believes in God, he feels contempt for Ambrose and organized religion. In his attempts to win Jefferson's trust, Wiggins is helped by a sympathetic white deputy named Paul, who is willing to bend the prison's rules for him. After making Jefferson a present of a radio, Wiggins succeeds in convincing Jefferson that he respects him and that his concern for him is genuine. Later, Wiggins gives Jefferson a notepad and pencil to record his thoughts. One whole chapter of the novel consists of what Jefferson has jotted down on that notepad. One comment reads, "mr wiggin an nobody aint never been that good to me an make me think im sombody" (232). The notepad shows that Jefferson has learned that he is a worthwhile human being. It also shows that he is ready to die with strength and dignity. Indeed, when he is about to be electrocuted, he turns out to be "the strongest man in that crowded room" (253).

After the execution, Paul, the white deputy, expresses his admiration for Wiggins and credits him with having brought about Jefferson's transformation. But Wiggins has also changed. The courage of the Reverend Ambrose, who volunteered to witness the execution, has made Wiggins change his mind about organized religion; and the friendship of the white deputy has made him change his plan to leave the South for the North.

CRITICAL RECEPTION

Ernest Gaines' reputation has grown slowly but steadily. His first novel, *Catherine Carmier*, was ignored by reviewers and critics, but his second novel, *Of Love and Dust*, was reviewed in several national publications. While the reviewer for the *Nation* called *Of Love and Dust* a "serious, powerful novel" and praised the "authenticity" of the characters (Blackburn 185), the *New York Times Book Review* concluded that "Mr. Gaines's second novel is still an 'undergraduate' work, in which the author trusts craft formula too much, himself too little" (Granat 83).

With the short story collection *Bloodline*, Gaines convinced the critics that his art had matured, for the reviewers were almost unanimous in their praise of the book. Writing in the *Saturday Review*, the eminent critic Granville Hicks expressed the opinion that "Gaines has trouble winding up some stories," but he called them "strong stories" all the same, and he speculated that Gaines might turn out to be one of the writers "who will help to form the American literature of the future" (Hicks 19).

Gaines' reputation reached its apex after he published *The Autobiography of Miss Jane Pittman*. Several reviewers compared the characterization of Miss Jane favorably to that of Dilsey in William Faulkner's *The Sound and the Fury*. But the most extravagant praise came from *Newsweek*, whose reviewer said that Gaines brings to mind "the *Odyssey* for the way his heroine's travels manage to summarize the American history of her race, and *Huckleberry Finn* for the clarity of her voice" (Wolfe 102).

Gaines next novel, *In My Father's House*, was not as well received as *Miss Jane Pittman*. The most severe criticism came from the reviewer for the *Library Journal*, who found the novel to be flawed by "a weak plot, stick figures, and flat redundant writing" (Burke 1195).

Gaines redeemed himself in the eyes of the reviewers with his sixth novel, *A Gathering of Old Men*. A representative opinion is that of the *New York Times Book Review*. Its reviewer gives Gaines credit for the difficult narrative technique he chose and noted that the fifteen different first-person narrators are "nicely distinguished from one another in rhythm and idiom, in the nature of what they see and report, especially in their specific laments for past passivity in the face of suffering" (Price 15).

Gaines' most recent novel, *A Lesson before Dying*, earned him reviews that were almost as positive as those for *Miss Jane Pittman*. The reviewer for *Time* magazine noted that few writers have Gaines' "dramatic instinct for conveying the malevolence of racism and injustice without the usual accompanying self-righteousness" (Sheppard 65). The *Christian Science Monitor* said that "Gaines' craftsmanship and conviction . . . transform what might have been a moralizing tale into a convincing moral drama" (Rubin 13).

Scholarly interest in the fiction of Ernest Gaines began when he published his collection of stories *Bloodline* in 1968. Since then, an increasing number of critical articles have appeared every year. However, the first books on Gaines and his work did not come out until the early 1990s. As of this writing there are three studies of his life and work (Babb, Simpson, and Beavers), two collections of interviews (Gaudet and Lowe), and one collection of critical essays (Estes).

The novelist Alice Walker* summed up what many scholars and critics consider to be the most distinctive traits of Ernest Gaines' fiction:

It is a credit to a writer like Ernest J. Gaines, a black writer who writes mainly about the people he grew up with in rural Louisiana, that he can write about whites and blacks exactly as he sees them and *knows* them, instead of writing of one group as a vast malignant lump and of the other as a conglomerate of perfect virtues. (19)

BIBLIOGRAPHY

Works by Ernest J. Gaines

The Autobiography of Miss Jane Pittman (1st ed. 1971). New York: Bantam, 1972.
Bloodline (1968). New York: Norton, 1976.
"Home: A Photo Essay." *Callaloo* 1,3 (May 1978a): 52–67.
"Miss Jane and I." *Callaloo* 1,3 (May 1978b): 23–38.
A Gathering of Old Men (1983). New York: Random House, 1984.
In My Father's House (1978). New York: Random House, 1992.

Catherine Carmier (1964). New York: Random House, 1993.
A Lesson before Dying (1993). New York: Random House, 1994a.
Of Love and Dust (1967). New York: Random House, 1994b.

Studies of Ernest J. Gaines

Babb, Valerie Melissa. *Ernest Gaines*. Boston: Twayne, 1991.

Beavers, Herman. *Wrestling Angels into Song: The Fictions of Ernest J. Gaines and James Alan McPherson*. Philadelphia: University of Pennsylvania Press, 1995.

Blackburn, Sara. "*Of Love and Dust* by Ernest Gaines." *Nation* (5 Feb. 1968): 185.

Burke, V. M. "Ernest Gaines, *In My Father's House*." *Library Journal* (1 June 1978): 1195.

Estes, David C., ed. *Critical Reflections on the Fiction of Ernest J. Gaines*. Athens: University of Georgia Press, 1994.

Gaudet, Marcia, ed. *Porch Talk with Ernest Gaines: Conversations on the Writer's Craft*. Baton Rouge: Louisiana State University Press, 1990.

Granat, Robert. "Loner on Olympus" [Rev. of *Of Love and Dust*]. *New York Times Book Review* (19 Nov. 1967): 83.

Hicks, Granville. "Sounds of Soul" [Rev. of *Bloodline*]. *Saturday Review of Literature* (17 Aug. 1968): 19.

Lowe, John, ed. *Conversations with Ernest Gaines*. Jackson: University Press of Mississippi, 1995.

Price, Reynolds. "A Louisiana Pageant of Calamity" [Rev. of *A Gathering of Old Men*]. *New York Times Book Review* (30 Oct. 1983): 15.

Rubin, Merle. "Convincing Moral Tale of Southern Injustice" [Rev. of *A Lesson before Dying*]. *Christian Science Monitor*, 13 Apr. 1993: 13.

Sheppard, R. Z. "A-Plus in Humanity" [Rev. of *A Lesson before Dying*]. *Time* (29 Mar. 1993): 67–68.

Simpson, Anne K. *A Gathering of Gaines: The Man and the Writer*. Lafayette: Center for Louisiana Studies, 1991.

Walker, Alice. "The Black Writer and the Southern Experience." In *In Search of Our Mothers' Gardens*. New York: Harcourt, Brace, 1983: 15–21.

Wolfe, Geoffrey. "Talking to Trees" [Rev. of *The Autobiography of Miss Jane Pittman*]. *Newsweek* (3 May 1971): 103–104.

MARITA GOLDEN
(1950–   )

Loretta G. Woodard

BIOGRAPHY

Marita Golden was born on 28 April 1950, in Washington, D.C., to Francis Sherman Golden and Beatrice Lee Reid Golden. The 1960s was a pivotal period in Golden's life. She was only a senior at Western High School when Dr. Martin Luther King, Jr., was assassinated. With her faith in America shaken, she became a civil rights activist the summer of 1968. Her activism was to play a major role in her early life and in her work.

Golden entered American University in 1968 as a Frederick Douglass Scholarship student. She received her B.A. in journalism in 1972 and interned at the *Baltimore Sun*. In 1973, Golden received her M.S. in journalism from Columbia University. The study of journalism opened the door to writing for Golden. She worked as an editorial assistant in a publishing company for a year, wrote articles for the *Amsterdam News* and *Essence*, and was associate producer of WNET-Channel 13 from 1974 to 1975.

For the next four years, Golden lived in Nigeria as the wife of Femi Ajayi, a Nigerian architect, whom she met when both were students in New York. She taught English at the Lagos Comprehensive Girls' School and later taught journalism and English at the University of Lagos. Golden wrote articles for the *Daily Times* and *Essence*. Unable to adjust to the vast cultural differences of her adopted country and due largely to "emotional incompatibility" (*Saving Our Sons* 34), Golden separated from her husband and returned to the States with her son in 1979.

Golden lived in Boston, where she taught English at Roxbury Community College from 1979 to 1981 and taught journalism at Emerson College from 1981 to 1983. After eight years in the academy, Golden resigned from her job and returned to her hometown, Washington, D.C., where she found her niche as a creative writer. Although Golden's mother gave her the charge to write, and her father schooled her in how to tell a story (*Saving Our Sons* 30), she credits Nikki Giovanni, June Jordan,* and Audre Lorde* for the confidence she has in herself and in her talent.

With the 1983 publication of *Migrations of the Heart: A Personal Odyssey* and her first novel, *A Woman's Place*, in 1986, Golden emerged as "a new and distinct voice among contemporary black women writers" (Fisher 169). During this fruitful period, *Long Distance Life* was published in 1989. In the same year, she divorced Femi and joined the faculty of the M.F.A. Graduate Writing Program at George Mason University in Fairfax, Virginia, until 1994. Golden started the Zora Neale Hurston/Richard Wright Foundation in 1990 and married Joe Murray, a high school educator, in 1991. A year later she published *And Do Remember Me*, and she edited the anthology *Wild Women Don't Wear No Blues: Black Women Writers on Love, Men, and Sex* (1993). With Susan Richards Shreve, she edited the anthology *Skin Deep: Black Women and White Women Write about Race* (1995), and she also published *Saving Our Sons: Raising Black Children in a Turbulent World* (1995). She has received grants from the District of Columbia Commission on the Arts and Humanities to support her writings. Golden has done writer residences at Wayne State, Brandeis, Spelman, and Antioch. In addition, she has conducted workshops and presented lectures at numerous schools and colleges and served as a panelist at the National Black Writers Conference.

Since 1994 Golden has been a senior writer in the M.F.A. Graduate Creative Writing Program at Virginia Commonwealth University in Richmond, Virginia. Her most recent novel is *The Edge of Heaven* (1998). Golden currently lives in Maryland.

MAJOR WORKS AND THEMES

Packed with characters, action, various settings, and different voices, Golden's autobiography, *Migrations of the Heart*, introduces many of the recurring themes in her work. However, as in other contemporary African American women's fiction, the heroine's quests for self-discovery and fulfillment are the dominant themes in Golden's work. Using traveling as a metaphor, these quests usually involve a spiritual journey that is often both painful and instructive.

Structured in three parts, *Migrations* is the personal odyssey of a young black woman's struggle, change, and growth in the 1960s and 1970s. "Beginnings" recounts the narrator's childhood and her discovery of black consciousness in Washington, D.C., in the late 1960s. Through a series of emotional experiences with her parents, the narrator rejects being the little "colored girl" her mother raised and keeps herself "natural" against her father's wishes. Her quest for her own identity moves her a step forward in her spiritual journey of self.

Traveling is key in the second and longest section of the book, appropriately titled "Journeys." The narrator moves to New York to attend graduate school and travels to Nigeria to become the wife of Femi Ajayi. When her marriage fails, she begins her long journey into self, and, after much self-searching, she separates from her husband and returns to the United States to build a new life for herself.

"Coming Home," the title of the last section of *Migrations*, alludes to more than just a destination. Golden's journey is symbolic; it is an internal one that leads her to a crucial discovery of self. At the end of the book she concludes: "For, after a season of fitful migration, I had come home. To rest against the bedrock inside myself. I had wandered. Will wander still . . . and will take home with me wherever I go" (246).

In her second work of prose and first novel, *A Woman's Place*, Golden closely examines the lives of three black women, from their friendship at an Ivy League college in Boston through adulthood. Realizing that an education can no longer fulfill their needs, each of the women embarks upon a separate odyssey, to define her own identity. Faith marries an older man, converts to Islam, and takes on a new identity (Aisha). Serena becomes a social activist and makes her life in Africa. Crystal, the writer, marries a white man and struggles to confront both black and white society.

To portray the characters' lives, Golden uses alternating narrators, including relatives and friends of the trio who talk about each other, events, and occasionally themselves. By the novel's end, Golden skillfully presents three alternative ways of living for black women in the turbulent 1960s. On a deeper level, Golden suggests that, despite the tremendous conflict and tension in the characters' lives and despite the paths they have taken, unconditional friendship sustains them over the years. In most of Golden's works, including *Migrations of the Heart*, Golden's characters find "strength" and "sustenance" in female relationships.

Long Distance Life, Golden's second and most ambitious novel, chronicles the life of eighty-year-old Naomi Reeves Johnson and her family living in Washington, D.C., from the 1920s to the present. Through flashbacks, Golden takes the reader on a long, sometimes painful journey that vividly captures the struggles, determination, and renewal of Naomi's family.

Golden structures the chapters entitled "Naomi" in the first person so that the reader may identify more closely with her. In the earlier chapters, Golden reveals the quest of a woman determined to have a better life. She escapes a sharecropper's farm in North Carolina and fights her way into D.C.'s black middle class in the 1920s and becomes a self-made woman. She then marries Rayford Johnson, but he dies early in the novel, leaving Naomi alone to raise their daughter, Esther.

Since much of Naomi's quest is fulfilled by the time her daughter becomes of age, considerable focus is on the overprotected Esther, who cannot find her center or define who she is. As her name suggests, she must grow into her name and find the peace she needs to sustain her. With none of the ambition of her mother, she drops out of Howard University, abandons her son and lover, and flees to the South to become a civil rights activist like Alice Walker's* Meridian. Golden indicates that the Civil Rights movement serves as a catalyst for her development, which keeps her sane and free from a boring past.

When Esther returns to Washington, D.C., she has only a Bible and a diary. The Bible represents the power of the word, and the diary acknowledges her self-discovery. When she says, "Mama, I'm home," it means, as Golden does in the final section of *Migrations of the Heart*, that she is in touch with her innermost feelings. She finds peace and happiness again in Randolph, who can now offer Esther and their son, Logan, a home. Esther becomes pregnant, and, just before their wedding day in May, Randolph dies suddenly of a heart attack. Though she is without Randolph, and though she has to raise Nathaniel without a father and later lose her son, who is murdered by a drug pusher, Golden suggests that "we each have a destiny" and that we need spirituality to survive, to keep us in touch with reality.

And Do Remember Me centers on Jessie Foster's plight as she flees from home to escape incest and her distant mother. She meets activist/writer Lincoln Sturgis and joins the "movement people" at the height of the marches, sit-ins, jailings, and dangerous confrontations of the civil rights revolution. She also meets and makes a friend for life with Macon, a college student and later a professor married to activist Courtland Hightower. As Jessie continues to rebuild her life in New York, she discovers her niche as a professional actress, changes her name to Pearl Moon, and lives with Lincoln. Jessie/Pearl feels alive and complete through acting, but neither acting nor alcohol can fully erase her pain and suffering.

Golden's characterization and images of Pearl are carefully drawn. By the novel's end, Pearl stops drinking, renews her friendship with Lincoln, stands by Macon during breast cancer, and returns home to Mississippi to attend her father's funeral. Though Jessie/Pearl left home to rebuild her life, Golden suggests that Jessie (the old Jessie) cannot fully re-create her life until she confronts her past and renews her relationship with her mother. Once accomplished, she can genuinely love and connect with others.

Saving Our Sons, Golden's most recent work, is a personal narrative about her son Michael's growing up in the "crime-ridden" streets of Washington, D.C. The book largely addresses the fear parents have of raising black children when violence is at an all-time high in the inner city. More importantly, based on the high death rate among young black men, the novel raises endless questions as to why the collective nurturing of family and community is unable to save our sons. Ultimately, as in *Long Distance Life*, Golden strongly suggests that all sons need both a mother and a father as role models.

Golden's most recent novel, *The Edge of Heaven* (1998), focuses on the theme of re-creating family in the aftermath of prison and centers on a mother–daughter relationship told in the voice of a twenty-year-old narrator. The novel opens on the first day the mother returns from prison (telephone interview with Marita Golden, 4 August 1997).

CRITICAL RECEPTION

With the exception of critics Michael Fischer, Edward Jackson, and Carole Davies, assessments of Golden's work have been confined generally to several brief, but favorable, reviews. While Diane McWhorter claims that Golden's autobiography, *Migrations*, is a "rather unripe and overwritten memoir" (16), Malcolm Boyd writes that the book is "exquisitely written" . . . "filled with brilliance and promise" (4). Michael Fischer's brilliant, in-depth study offers an analysis of the work from an anthropological, cultural perspective and shows how Golden's use of Africa reveals "a dialectical or two-dimensional journey examining the realities of both sides of cultural differences" (217). Edward Jackson's longer study examines the black female–African male relationship and the work as a journey toward liberation.

The critics' responses to Golden's second work of prose and her first novel, *A Woman's Place*, have been mixed, but the majority of them have been favorable. Ann Fisher criticizes Golden's characters for not being fully developed but, nevertheless, acknowledges that she is "clearly a promising new novelist" (169). Faith Pullin applauds how skillfully the black women's lives are presented in a period of unrest and chaos but claims Golden leaves the reader with no new information (623). Yet, when compared to Gloria Naylor's* *Mama Day*, Pullin notes the technique of Golden's novel "is in some respects a more disciplined piece of work" (623).

Judging from the positive critical reception of *Long Distance Life*, Golden's writing developed considerably. Critics consistently focused on the novel's artistic excellence, prose, character development, and structure. In their assessment of the book, both Jill Sidoti and Laura Shapiro observe how the characters are well developed. Nagueyalti Warren's thorough and engaging review notes the author's structure, family struggles, and crucial issues raised by the author, especially sex roles that cast women as nurturers only. Carole Davies' interesting study examines the main characters' "struggle with the dialectics of home and the migratory meanings of placement and identity" (148).

The critics seem to agree that Golden's fourth novel, *And Do Remember Me*, shows further "growth" and offers incredible "insight" into the lives of African American women portrayed in the work. Benilde Little praises her "talent and sensitivity" and for making contemporary history accessible (42). A contributor for *Publishers Weekly* observes Golden's skillful command of language and the portrait's authenticity (250).

What seems to have attracted the most attention of critics in *Wild Women Don't Wear No Blues* is its range of "powerful" and "fascinating" essays told by fifteen African American writers with "unflinching honesty." Jennifer James observes that the anthology "leaves virtually no aspect of womanist issues unturned" (19). A contributor for *Kirkus Review* concludes they are all "[w]omen on the cutting edge of sexuality, sexual ethics, and the exhilarating art of the personal essay" (766).

Golden's next anthology, *Skin Deep*, has been praised for its "powerful" and candid essays, which draw on both fiction and nonfiction to explore racial issues between black and white women. Veronica Chambers applauds how editors Golden and Shreve "move past politeness and easy blame to real moments of insight, clarity, and honesty" (76). She further applauds how "the writers avoid easy answers, and, . . . take us one step closer to understanding" (76).

Golden's most recent book, *Saving Our Sons*, was unanimously received as an important social commentary. A contributor for the *Harvard Educational Review* points out that Golden's book "offers a different look at violence and illustrates how it can touch the lives of everyone" (881). Veronica Chambers believes that "[i]n sharing their lives so honestly, Marita and Michael bring us closer to empowering both ourselves and our sons" (52).

Since 1983, Golden has undoubtedly secured a place among contemporary African American writers. Hopefully, with *The Edge of Heaven* readership will increase and yield more scholarly studies.

BIBLIOGRAPHY

Works by Marita Golden

Migrations of the Heart: A Personal Odyssey. New York: Anchor-Doubleday, 1983.
A Woman's Place. New York: Doubleday, 1986.
Long Distance Life. New York: Doubleday, 1989.
And Do Remember Me. New York: Doubleday, 1992.
Ed. *Wild Women Don't Wear No Blues: Black Women Writers on Love, Men and Sex*. New York: Doubleday, 1993.
Saving Our Sons: Raising Black Children in a Turbulent World. New York: Doubleday, 1995a.
Ed. with Susan Richards. *Skin Deep: Black Women and White Women Write about Race*. New York: Nan A. Talese-Doubleday, 1995b.
The Edge of Heaven. Garden City, NY: Doubleday, 1998.

Studies of Marita Golden

Beerman, Jill. Review of *Migrations of the Heart*. *The Antioch Review* 42 (Winter 1984): 117–118.
Bovoso, Carole. "Touchstones of Black Women's Experience." Review of *Migrations of the Heart*. *Ms.* (June 1983): 37–38.
Boyd, Malcolm. "A Woman's Own Movement: Personal." Review of *Migrations of the Heart*. *Los Angeles Times Book Review* (17 Apr. 1983): 4.
Browne, Phiefer L. "Marita Golden." *The Oxford Companion to African American Literature*. Ed. William L. Andrews, Frances Smith Foster, and Trudier Harris. New York: Oxford University Press, 1997. 321–322.
Carroll, Mary. Review of *Saving Our Sons: Raising Black Children in a Turbulent World*. *Booklist* (15 Dec. 1994): 720.

————. Review of *Skin Deep: Black Women and White Women Write about Race*. *Booklist* (July 1995): 1844.

Chambers, Veronica. "A Mother's Tale." Review of *Saving Our Sons: Raising Black Children in a Turbulent World*. *Essence* (Feb. 1995): 52.

————. "Black and White." Review of *Skin Deep*. *Ms.* (July–Aug. 1995): 76.

Cleage, Pearl. "Saving Sons." Review of *Saving Our Sons*. *Ms.* (Jan.–Feb. 1995): 70.

Coleman, Wanda. Review of *A Woman's Place*. *Los Angeles Times Book Review* (7 Sept. 1986): 4.

Davies, Carole B. "Long Distance and Moving through Homes." In *Black Women, Writing and Identity: Migrations of the Subject*. New York: Routledge, 1994. 147–148.

Davis, Thulani. "Don't Worry, Be Buppie: Black Novelists Head for the Mainstream." *Village Voice* (May 1990): 26–29.

Fischer, Michael M. J. "Ethnicity and the Post-Modern Arts of Memory." In *Writing Culture: The Poetics and Politics of Ethnography*. Ed. James Clifford and George E. Marcus. Berkeley: University of California Press, 1986. 215–218.

Fisher, Ann H. Review of *A Woman's Place*. *Library Journal* (Aug. 1986): 169.

Hill, Christine M. Review of *Migrations of the Heart*. *Library Journal* (1 Feb. 1983): 202.

Hubbard, Dolan, et al., comps. "Studies in African-American Literature: An Annual Annotated Bibliography, 1989." *Callaloo* 13 (1990): 910–954.

Hyman Bass, Elayne B. "A Child-Woman's Quest for Her Past and Future." Review of *Migrations of the Heart*. *Washington Post Book World* (4 June 1983): D4.

Jackson, Edward. "The African Male–Black American Female Relationship in Lorraine Hansberry's *A Raisin in the Sun* and Marita Golden's *Migrations of the Heart*." In *Images of Black Men in Black Women Writers 1950–1990*. Indiana: Wyndham Hall, 1992. 33–41.

James, Jennifer. "Something to Say—and the Means to Say It." Review of *Wild Women Don't Wear No Blues: Black Women Writers on Love, Men and Sex*. *Belles Lettres* 9 (Winter 1993/94): 19–22.

Jones, Marie F. Review of *And Do Remember Me*. *Library Journal* (1 May 1992): 116.

Little, Benilde. Review of *And Do Remember Me*. *Essence* (July 1992).

McWhorter, Diane. Review of *Migrations of the Heart*. *New York Times Book Review* (1 May 1983): 16–17.

Pullin, Faith. "Acts of Reclamation." Review of *A Woman's Place*. *Times Literary Supplement* (3–9 June 1988): 623.

Review of *And Do Remember Me*. *Publishers Weekly* (27 Apr. 1992): 249–250.

Review of *Saving Our Sons: Raising Black Children in a Turbulent World*. *Harvard Educational Review* 66.4 (Winter 1996): 879–881.

Review of *Wild Women Don't Wear No Blues: Black Women Writers on Love, Men and Sex*. *Kirkus Review* (15 June 1993): 765–766.

Review of *Wild Women Don't Wear No Blues*. *Publishers Weekly* (7 June 1993): 58.

Rochman, Hazel. Review of *Skin Deep: Black Women and White Women Write about Race*. *Booklist* (Aug. 1995): 1935.

Shapiro, Laura. "In the Other Washington." Review of *Long Distance Life*. *Newsweek* (20 Nov. 1989): 79.

Sidoti, Jill. Review of *Long Distance Life*. *Booklist* (15 Oct. 1989): 426.

Trescott, Jacqueline. "Golden's Moments of the Soul: One Young Writer's Personal 'Migrations.'" *Washington Post*, 22 May 1983: K1–2.

Tucker, Debbie. Review of *Long Distance Life*. *Library Journal* (1 Oct. 1989): 114.
Warren, Nagueyalti. Review of *Long Distance Life*. *Black American Literature Forum* 24.4 (Winter 1990): 803–808.
Wilson, Judith. Review of *A Woman's Place*. *New York Times Book Review* (14 Sept. 1986): 30.

SAM GREENLEE
(1930–   )

Adam Meyer

BIOGRAPHY

Known largely for his first novel, *The Spook Who Sat by the Door*, Sam Greenlee has had an interesting and diverse career. Born in Chicago on 13 July 1930, Greenlee was educated at the University of Wisconsin (B.S., political science, 1952) and the University of Chicago (1954–1957). He served in the military from 1952 to 1954, earning the rank of first lieutenant. Later he went to work for the U.S. Information Agency (USIA), serving in Iraq—where he witnessed a revolution and earned a Meritorious Service Award—Pakistan, Indonesia, and Greece, undertaking further study at the University of Thessaloniki (1963–1964). He left government service in 1965 to pursue his writing career, living in Greece for the next three years and producing a number of unpublished manuscripts.

Greenlee's first publications were short stories, four of which appeared in *Negro Digest* between 1965 and 1967. During this time he also completed the manuscript of *The Spook Who Sat by the Door*, a black nationalist thriller. Greenlee returned to the United States in 1968 but could not find any publisher willing to accept the novel due to its strong, pro-violence, revolutionary stance. Eventually published in 1969, the novel became a surprising success, garnering a fair share of positive reviews, even being named cowinner of the *London Sunday Times* Book of the Year Award; the novel's domestic release occurred a year later. Shortly thereafter Greenlee wrote a screenplay from the novel and attempted to find funding for a film version. Despite difficulties securing the necessary capital—part of which was earned through aggressive marketing of the novel—Greenlee, serving as coexecutive producer, with Ivan Dixon as director, did manage to get it made. The movie's release was met with a good deal of protest for what seemed to some an "irresponsible" attitude toward black violence, but it was well received by others.

In 1971 Greenlee published a collection of poems, *Blues for an African Princess*; a second volume, *Ammunition! Poetry and Other Raps* appeared in 1975. Greenlee continued to publish short stories also, with four appearing in *Negro Digest* and *Black World* between 1969 and 1973. His second novel, *Baghdad Blues*, scheduled for release in 1973, was pulled at that time and issued as a paperback original in 1976. After the publication of *Baghdad Blues*, however, which attracted very little notice, Greenlee disappeared from the literary scene. He continued to produce films and to teach, but he did not publish any new writings until 1995, when a collection of poetry entitled *"Be-Bop Man/Be-Bop Woman,"* spanning his entire career, from 1968 to 1993, appeared.

MAJOR WORKS AND THEMES

Greenlee's novels are both set in the world of American military intelligence, reflecting the author's experiences working for the USIA. *The Spook Who Sat by the Door* tells the story of Dan Freeman, the first African American to be employed by the Central Intelligence Agency (CIA) in a more than menial capacity. Freeman pretends to be an Uncle Tom while gathering substantial information about foreign insurrections and guerrilla warfare tactics. After quitting the CIA, Freeman returns to his native Chicago, ostensibly as a social worker; what he really does is recruit and train a band of black rebels that becomes capable of bringing the country to its knees. Freeman is killed at the novel's end, but Greenlee indicates that his followers are ready and able to see his plan put into full effect. The vision of racial violence embodied in the novel was shocking at the time and remains troubling today.

The key word in the novel's title, "spook," is obviously a pun, being both a derogatory epithet for African Americans and a slang term for a spy. The word also calls to mind Ralph Ellison's* *Invisible Man*, which opens with the lines: "I am an invisible man. No, I am not a spook like those who haunted Edgar Allan Poe." Greenlee even writes that Freeman "moved through Washington like an invisible man" (60). What he means by this, as did Ellison, is that people don't see Freeman for what he really is; instead, they see in him a personification of what they already expect. This natural disguise is particularly handy for Freeman in his career as a spy, as well as in his long-range plan. He is able to learn what he needs to know from the CIA while at the same time planning to use this knowledge against the government that the agency was created to protect. Like the invisible man's grandfather, he is "a spy in the enemy's country," playing the role of Uncle Tom in order to achieve the destruction of the very people who call forth and approve of such behavior. Unlike the older man, however, whose mask became so closely aligned with his "real" personality that he was able to remove it only on his deathbed, by which point it was too late for him to make practical use of the knowledge he had gained, Freeman never loses consciousness of the fact that he is wearing a mask, that he is not just the only black working for the CIA but that he is also one of the few blacks actively working against it. As Greenlee writes, "No one ever blew Freeman's cover. They accepted at face value what he appeared to be, because he became what they wanted him to be. Working for the agency, in the agency, Freeman was the best undercover man the CIA had" (48). The irony, of course, is that Freeman is undercover even to the CIA itself; they believe he is on their side when he is, in fact, busily plotting their undoing.

Such irony is a constant throughout the novel. It comes into play again at the novel's end, for example, when Freeman is killed, not by whitey, but by a black police officer, Sergeant Dawson, who had been a childhood friend but, from Freeman's perspective, had gone over to the enemy. As a police sergeant, Dawson represents not only the government military-industrial complex but also the black bourgeoisie, a primary target of Freeman's (and Greenlee's) disdain. Freeman makes his feelings for the Negro middle class clear from the start of the novel. Observing the other African Americans who have been selected to join the CIA training program talking to each other about what kinds of cars they drive and how big their houses are, he encourages them, silently and sarcastically, to "blow [their] bourgeois blues, [their] nigger soul sold for a mess of materialistic pottage" (14). This does not mean that he is completely above such temptations, however. After he begins his social work career in Chicago he adopts precisely this kind of cover, "the white-type, uptight Negro of 'rising aspirations' and desperate upward mobility" (81) and senses its attractiveness. "It would only take a little lying to myself to think I was really into something," he says (189). Even so, he never allows the mask to subsume his revolutionary personality completely. He knows that blacks who subscribe to this ethic are not really helping the race. Despite his understanding of the "crabs in a barrel" mentality so prevalent among the black middle classes, however, Freeman tips his hand to Dawson, hoping that he can recruit the policeman to the rebel cause. This leads to his own undoing, though, as Dawson attempts to stop the black revolution in order to maintain and even enhance his own standing in the white community.

Ultimately, though, Dawson has not necessarily won the battle by killing Freeman, for the rebel leader had successfully created an army in which no individual is indispensable. Unlike other black revolutionary groups in American history, the Freedom Fighters will not disappear once their leader has been killed. Thus, the novel ends on a positive note for the revolution; the death of Freeman portends merely the creation of more free men, men who are determined to wipe out all vestiges of white control, both physical and mental. Like Freeman after he has blown his cover, they are no longer willing to be invisible.

Baghdad Blues, a lesser sequel to *The Spook Who Sat by the Door*, actually reads as if were written first. The events take place in the mid- to late 1950s rather than the late 1960s, for example, and they adhere closely to Greenlee's personal experiences during the Baghdad revolution in 1958. The central character, Dave Burrell, an aspiring writer and foreign service officer, becomes torn between his allegiance to the American government and his sense that the Arabs are justified in staging a revolution against the American-backed regime. As his interactions with the Arabs increase, Burrell comes to feel that they are more welcoming of him as a black man than are his American compatriots; "I get along better here than in Chicago," he muses at one point (57). Later in the novel a CIA agent asks Dave to spy on one of his Arab friends, even telling him that it is his patriotic duty to do so, but Dave refuses; his "Arab friends became like brothers" (104) in a way that his white American coworkers never could.

When the revolution comes, Dave notes that "everybody was shaken up except me. I was digging it" (130). It is all he can do not to root openly for the rebels. As the novel winds down, therefore, after Dave has distinguished himself by protecting some of the embassy's workers at the risk of his own life, he refuses an offer to become a "spook" for the CIA. Instead, Dave leaves government service entirely in order to observe the Arab struggle more closely, hoping that he can learn from their insurgency how to achieve a comparable one for his own people in America. On the whole, though, *Baghdad Blues* is not nearly as effective as *The Spook Who Sat by the Door*, featuring neither that novel's radical revolutionary stance nor its artistic merits.

Greenlee's short stories demonstrate a wider range, both thematically and stylistically, than do his two novels. Here he presents athletes, soldiers, gang members, and Boy Scouts, among others, often in first person. "Sonny's Not Blue," for example, depicts a young boy who dreams about becoming a professional basketball player. His primary motivation, in addition to his love for the game, is to earn enough money to buy his mother a color television. The story, going along with its title, is upbeat and optimistic. "Blues for Little Prez," on the other hand, although excellently written, is a depressing story about the life and death of a small-time thief and junkie whose nickname refers to his admiration of the great jazz musician Lester Young. His inability to play the saxophone the way his idol did, however, leads him to a life of drugs and crime, ending with his death from an overdose. Here Greenlee writes in a fluid, stream-of-consciousness style, a departure from his usual mode.

Greenlee's poetry falls mainly into two categories: satirical, epigrammatic pieces of social criticism, which he calls "Graffiti," and moving blues poems about particular individuals. The first volume's opening piece, "Metamorphosis," is both a good example of the former and an interesting gloss on *The Spook Who Sat by the Door*. Other poems in this vein, such as "Sunset Blvd. at High Noon," "McLuhan Revolution," "Instant Virgins," and "Suburban Soul," poke fun at members of the black bourgeoisie and others who, Greenlee feels, are not advancing the black cause. His blues poems are dedicated to figures such as Nikki Giovanni, Stevie Wonder, Langston Hughes, and Carolyn Rodgers, as well as the titular "African Princess." Greenlee's poetry is interesting, full of amusing or startling observations, but, in general, it is not as successful as his fiction.

CRITICAL RECEPTION

The Spook Who Sat by the Door is the only piece of Greenlee's writing to have received any critical response whatsoever, and even that has been rather limited. Reviews of the novel at the time of its release were mixed. On the positive side, the reviewer in *Booklist* asserted that "Greenlee successfully portrays the authentic voice of the ghetto activist through his protagonist and will arouse sympathy and recognition in the concerned readers," while the reviewer in *Publishers Weekly* called the novel "engrossing" and "much more than a thriller." Several reviewers, most notably Robert A. Gross, wrote approvingly of the novel's "sharp satirical thrusts at the American scene" (98). On the negative side, Elizabeth M. Guiney wrote that "the book is characterized by stilted dialogue, stereotyped characterizations, and an immobile plot," while Kenneth Graham stated that he couldn't "see beyond the inhuman single-mindedness, the naive caricatures, [and] the reactionary love of destruction"; David Pryce-Jones, similarly, found the novel marred by "bitterness" and "extremism."

More detailed critical appraisals can be found in pieces by Charles D. Peavy, Michael Adams, and Wanda Macon. Peavy describes the novel as "a handbook on how to be a successful revolutionary by beating the system at its own game" (222) and asserts that it demonstrates "the growing conviction that a final confrontation between the races is unavoidable" (223). Adams argues that, "as an attack on racism, [the novel] emphasizes, for the most part, the subtler forms of prejudice practiced by whites who falsely consider themselves enlightened and tolerant" (1329), especially those in the government and social work fields. He also notes that Greenlee "balances his overt anger with a satirical portrait of the foolishness of whites" (1329) and that he "reserves ridicule as well for African Americans who strive for success by imitating whites" (1330). Macon discusses the use of the word "spook" in terms of "double consciousness," indicating that Greenlee's use of this term "establish[es] a connection between Freeman's character and the African American experience during the turbulent 1960's" (696). She also analyzes the novel in relation to other examples of masking in African American literature.

Passing mention is made of Greenlee's novel in several general histories of African American literature, often grouped with other texts under a heading such as "The Black Rebel" (Gayle 167–202), "Themes of Armageddon" (Whitlow 167), "Black Avengers" (Starke 225–247), or "Militant Protest" (Schraufnagel 173–196). Noel Schraufnagel provides the most in-depth view, asserting that the novel is an attempt to prove the adage that "violence in the face of oppression restores self-respect" (192). He also writes of Freeman's role-playing abilities and his invisibility. Ultimately, he concludes that the novel "is a relatively successful book on both a propagandistic and an artistic level, although with more emphasis on the former" (195). While the writing may be weak, in other words, the message is strong. It is unfortunate that Greenlee's works, even

The Spook Who Sat by the Door, have not undergone a more thorough critical appraisal.

BIBLIOGRAPHY

Works by Sam Greenlee

Novels

The Spook Who Sat by the Door. London: Allison and Busby, 1969.
Baghdad Blues. New York: Bantam, 1976.

Short Stories

"Yes, We Can Sing." *Negro Digest* 15.2 (December 1965): 65–69.
"The Sign." *Negro Digest* 15.4 (February 1966): 61–66.
"Summer Sunday." *Negro Digest* 15.11 (September 1966): 60–61.
"Autumn Leaves." *Negro Digest* 16.3 (January 1967): 69–73.
"The D.C. Blues." *Negro Digest* 18.8 (June 1969): 86–92.
"Sonny's Seasons." *Black World* 19.12 (October 1970): 58–63.
"Sonny's Not Blue." *Black Short Story Anthology*, ed. Woodie King. New York: Signet, 1972. 91–96.
"Blues for Little Prez." *Black World* 22.10 (August 1973): 54–62.

Poetry Collections

Blues for an African Princess. Chicago: Third World, 1971.
Ammunition! Poetry and Other Raps. London: Bogle-L'Ouverture, 1975.
"Be-Bop Man/Be-Bop Woman" 1968–1993: Poetry and Other Raps. Cambrea Heights, NY: Natiki, 1995.

Studies of Sam Greenlee

Adams, Michael. "The Spook Who Sat by the Door." *Masterplots II: African American Literature Series*. Vol. 3. Ed. Frank N. Magill. Pasadena, CA: Salem, 1994. 1326–1331.
Burrell, Walter. "An Interview: Rappin with Sam Greenlee." *Black World* 20.9 (July 1971): 42–47.
Gayle, Addison. *The Way of the New World: The Black Novel in America*. Garden City, NY: Anchor/Doubleday, 1975.
Gould, Mark. "Through the Front Door with Sam Greenlee." *Biography News* 1 (1974): 39.
Graham, Kenneth. "Dandies and the Deluge." Rev. of *The Spook Who Sat by the Door*. *Listener* (20 March 1969): 396.
Gross, Robert A. "The Black Novelists: 'Our Turn.' " Rev. of *The Spook Who Sat by the Door*. *Newsweek* (16 June 1969): 94–98.
Guiney, Elizabeth M. Rev. of *The Spook Who Sat by the Door*. *Library Journal* (1 January 1970): 83.
Macon, Wanda. "Greenlee, Sam." *The Oxford Companion to African American Literature*.

Ed. William L. Andrews, Frances Smith Foster, and Trudier Harris. New York: Oxford University Press, 1997a. 327–328.

———. "The Spook Who Sat by the Door." *The Oxford Companion to African American Literature*. Ed. William L. Andrews, Frances Smith Foster, and Trudier Harris. New York: Oxford University Press, 1997b. 696.

Peavy, Charles D. "Four Black Revolutionary Novels, 1899–1970." *Journal of Black Studies* 1 (1970): 219–223.

Pryce-Jones, David. "First Novels." Rev. of *The Spook Who Sat by the Door*. *Punch* (30 April 1969): 657.

Rev. of *The Spook Who Sat by the Door*. *Booklist* (15 December 1969): 494.

Rev. of *The Spook Who Sat by the Door*. *Publishers Weekly* (6 October 1969): 50.

Schraufnagel, Noel. *From Apology to Protest: The Black American Novel*. DeLand, FL: Everett/Edwards, 1973.

Starke, Catherine Juanita. *Black Portraiture in American Fiction*. New York: Basic Books, 1971.

Whitlow, Roger. *Black American Literature: A Critical History*. Chicago: Nelson Hall, 1973.

BILL GUNN
(1934–1989)

P. Jane Splawn

BIOGRAPHY

William Harrison Gunn (15 July 1934–5 April 1989) was born to William Harrison and Louise Alexander Gunn in Philadelphia, where he grew up in a comfortable, middle-class environment. The Gunns were one of a select few African American families in their neighborhood to own their own home. In *All the Rest Have Died*, a semiautobiographical novel that takes its title from a line of one of Emily Dickinson's poems, Gunn's protagonist, Barney Gifford, whose prototype is Gunn himself, reflects fondly on the security and comfort he experienced living in his home. Barney Gifford describes his second boyhood home thus:

The new house had sounds and smells and felt as solid as could be. I crawled into closets and under staircases, and had fantasies about the cellar where the goblins lived. I climbed on chairs and hid my most prized possessions in secret places, never to be found again. (23)

Gunn received a well-rounded education from school as well as from his parents during the 1930s and 1940s. He received a very good foundation from the Philadelphia public school system, attending what were then well-integrated schools. His parents themselves were artists: his father a songwriter ("Ball and Jack"), musician, comedian, and poet; his mother a former beauty contestant, an actress who would later form her own theater company, and a founder, with the Reverend Leon Sullivan of Opportunities Industrialization Centers of America (OICA), of a self-help community services organization.

Early on in his life Gunn decided upon a career as an actor, which brought him benefits as well as frustrations. He would first serve for a short time in the

U.S. Navy, later moving to New York's East Village, where he hoped to pursue a career in acting. Because roles for black actors were limited in number as well as in range and scope, many African American actors found pursuing acting careers difficult during the 1950s and 1960s, the period in which Gunn arrived on the New York scene. The scant opportunities for significant roles for black actors in the 1930s and 1940s, in which issue plays like *Native Son* offered a few substantive roles on the stage, began to dwindle in the next decade. By the 1950s, when Gunn began his career as an actor, mostly stereotypical roles as servants remained for black actors. In such a contested site in which compromising one's artistry for the sake of earning a living was at stake, Gunn is said to have worried about paying his bills and reportedly had nightmares about being turned out penniless back in Philadelphia and made into a drug addict. As Ilona Leki has noted, he reflects his frustration about practices in casting blacks in film and theater in this 1964 statement in *Variety*: "When a good part for a Negro actor does come along, they offer it to Sidney Poitier. If he turns it down, they rewrite it for a white actor" (Leki, 112).

Gunn, however, overcame the odds against the struggling black actor of the 1950s and 1960s. He secured recurring roles on popular television shows during the 1960s, achieving sufficient success from his earnings as an actor to purchase and furnish a historic home in New York as well as to fund a second career as a writer. By the time of his death in 1989, the theater and film world would lament the loss of this noteworthy actor, filmmaker, playwright, and novelist in *New York Times* eulogies, a series of special issues in film journals, and edited editions of screenplays.

Gunn's stage credits include *Member of the Wedding* (1950), *The Immoralist* (1954), *Take a Giant Step* (off-Broadway, 1954), *Sign of Winter* (1958), *Moon on a Rainbow Shawl* (1962), and *Anthony and Cleopatra* and *A Winter's Tale* (both produced by the New York Shakespeare Festival, 1963). He has appeared on television in *American Parade* (Sojourner episode), *Danger, The Fugitive, Dr. Kildare, The Interns, Outer Limits, Route 66, Stoney Burke, Tarzan*, and *The Cosby Show*; and in the films *The Sound and the Fury* (1959), *The Interns* (1962), *The Spy with My Face* (1966), and *Losing Ground* (1982). Gunn's film *Ganja and Hess* (1973) was selected one of ten Best American Films of the Decade at the Cannes Film Festival, 1973, and he received an Emmy for Best Television Play, *Johnnas* (1972); several AUDELCO Black Theatre Recognition Awards for Best Playwright and Best Play of the Year, *Black Picture Show* (1975); and a John Simon Guggenheim Memorial Foundation Fellowship Award in Film Making in 1980.

Over the years Gunn developed close friendships with other artists, writers, actors, and directors. With his friend actor/director Duane Jones, Gunn starred in, and collaborated on, his close friend Kathleen Collins Prettyman's independent film *Losing Ground* (1982), in which he played a freethinking artist husband married to a more serious philosophy professor. Ironically, the three close friends Gunn, Prettyman, and Jones died within twelve months of one another. Jones died on 22 July 1988, and Prettyman, 18 October 1988. Gunn died of encephalitis at the age of fifty-nine on 5 April 1989 in Nyack (New York) Hospital one day before his play *The Forbidden City* opened at the Public Theater.

MAJOR WORKS AND THEMES

Arguably, Gunn's special contribution to the tradition of African American art and literature lies in his complication of the representation of race in American society. While many of his characters are middle-class, Gunn shows black Americans' quest, as stated succinctly by W. E. B. Du Bois half a century before him, to be seen as more than the "mere hewers of wood and drawers of water" (*The Souls of Black Folk*, 46). Yet Gunn's protagonists defy reduction to mere racial identity alone. Never comfortable in settings in which they are pigeon-holed into categories based on racial affiliation, they often surround themselves with largely interracial and international friends. Speaking through his I-narrator Barney Gifford, who addresses the reader in this excerpt in *All the Rest Have Died*, Gunn writes,

I am not concerned with what I am racially. I am nothing and I am everything; I am a part and I am all. I am only concerned with what you think I am, and how it affects you and your approach to me. I do not trust labels, or names. I do not trust people who pass out titles and categories to keep racial order. I am racially disorganized, my blood has been invaded by blood that is also mine. There is no part of me that came first. I am the rapist and the raped. I am victimized and I am responsible. I bear it and will have nothing to do with any of it. It is you, remember. It is all yours, the guilt and the pity. I am only the excuse. (59)

All the Rest Have Died is an important work in which Gunn establishes many themes (such as the complexities involved in positioning African American artists in society and the alienation of the artist-hero) that resurface throughout his career as actor, filmmaker, playwright, and novelist. The novel is divided into three sections: "Taylor," "Maggie," and "Bernard," each of which represents instrumental figures in the protagonist Barney Gifford's development as an artist.

Barney Gifford, a sensitive artist, who is described, much as Gunn might have been, as a startled fawn, shocks a largely white, upper-middle-class group gathered at a party toward the end of the novel when he "yell[s], 'The bigot says the Negro is all bad, the liberal says he's all good, but not one of you will admit that you don't know what the hell he is because you refuse to grant him individuality! Individuality'" (157). Barney Gifford moves from a shy, insecure artist unaware of his full power and creativity to a confident craftsman molded by the many challenges with which he has been faced during the short period of his life covered in the novel: the death of his best friend, Taylor; his poverty and struggle to establish himself as an actor in New York; his failed relationships with women; and the suicide of his friend Bernard.

Ganja and Hess (1973) has been hailed as one of the more innovative, independent film masterpieces produced during the early 1970s. Once *Ganja and Hess* was sold to a distributor, it was recut, edited, and retitled as *Blood Couple* (sometimes issued as *Double Possession*). According to Phyllis Klotman, "The film was withdrawn . . . when Gunn went beyond the vampire genre and created an original work: a densely symbolic film whose non-linear narrative is told from three different points of view" (18).

As Klotman has pointed out, *Ganja and Hess* is rendered from the eye/I witness of three principal characters: George Meda, a neurotic assistant to Dr. Hess Green; his wife, Ganja Meda; and the minister/chauffeur. Dr. Hess Green has been studying the Cult of Myrtha, presided over by Helgda, the Fourth Queen of a black kingdom predating the Egyptians by a thousand years. Having herself contracted a blood disease, Queen Helgda had many of her slaves bled to death for her blood transfusions. A series of tableaux representing Hess' nightmares shows Hess bound and tortured by the Queen of Myrtha, fantasy and reality fusing as the sound of the laughter of the Queen's female entourage is heard on tape, as if by magic, after that of Hess' tape-recorded notes. Many themes recurrent in Gunn's work, such as the alienation of artists in society resulting in their suicide, the sexual/emotional tension present in relationships between men and women, and the foibles of the black middle class, also appear in this published screenplay and film.

In the play *Johnnas* (1972) Gunn revisits issues of race and the isolation and alienation of the black artist, this time with catastrophic results. Johnnas Gifford, a sensitive fourteen-year-old artist, is taunted by his peers as being too delicate, too sensitive, too "white" for an African American male adolescent. He writes beautiful poetry, an activity encouraged by his mother and his white English teacher, but is shunned by his peers on the basketball courts. In this Emmy Award-winning teleplay, previously published as a play in the special 1968 issue on black theater in *Drama Review*, Gunn seems to suggest that neither black society nor American society in general is ready for young black artists/heroes. Echoing the tragic vision of Langston Hughes in his 1930s poem "Genius Child," in which the speaker claims society would rather "*kill*" than claim the artist/hero, Gunn's hero jumps to his death from the ledge of a large downtown office building to the taunts and jeers of an insensitive throng of onlookers.

CRITICAL RECEPTION

Gunn's critical reception has been substantial, particularly in recent years by film historians who recognize his unique contribution to American film as well as his role in breaking new ground in the area of black independent film. As early as the Black Arts movement, Gunn's work was praised, as evidenced by its inclusion in the special black theater issue of *The Drama Review*, under the heading "Theatre of the Black Experience." Phyllis Klotman codedicates *Screenplays of the African American Experience* (1991) to Gunn and to his good friend Kathleen Collins (Prettyman). A special issue of *Black Film Review* was dedicated to him in which film historians John Williams and Pearl Bowser commemorate his many achievements as a filmmaker, actor, playwright, and novelist.

The reception of Gunn's novels at the time of publication, though notable and significant, has been less enthusiastic than that of his plays/screenplays. Noel Schraufnagel, for instance, finds Gunn's first novel, *All the Rest Have Died*, to be an example of the existentialist novels of the decade, "encumbered by a melodramatic plot" (123). Notwithstanding, he avers that Gunn's "heav[y use of] . . . a stream of consciousness technique . . . lessen[s] the melodrama of the incidents and give[s] them instead an intellectual significance" (124–125). Schraufnagel concludes his assessment by arguing that the novel "is very limited in scope; Gunn is content to explicate his philosophy, and the racial materials that he presents are mere comments on a social situation rather than an integral part of the book" (125).

Other critics as well have found weaknesses in the plots of Gunn's novels. Barbara Cady writes in a *Los Angeles Times Book Review* of *Rhinestone Sharecropping* that the work is "plot-poor"; the protagonist Sam Dodd's "abrasive elderly father emerg[es], ironically, as the most engaging character" (10). She queries whether Dodd and Gunn are one and the same: "Is Sam Dodd really author Bill Gunn? . . . One can only speculate" (10), noting how this "slim novel" "rings with angst over a black artist's racially tinged run-ins and run-arounds in Hollywood" (10). On the other hand, Cady finds Gunn's use of descriptive language, particularly of the 1919 Chicago race riots, to be powerful and effective, seeing this as the novel's greatest strength.

Bill Gunn's special contribution to black independent film and to the novel as well as his conceptualization of race in American society mark him as an innovator, well ahead of his time, to whose work scholars of cultural studies, race theory, as well as film are sure to return repeatedly in the future.

BIBLIOGRAPHY

Works by Bill Gunn

Novels

All the Rest Have Died. New York: Delacorte Press, 1964; London: Joseph, 1965.
Rhinestone Sharecropping. New York: I. Reed Books, 1981.

Play

Black Picture Show. Berkeley, CA: Reed, Cannon, and Johnson, 1975.

Play Productions

Marcus in the High Grass, Connecticut, Westport Theatre, 1958.
Johnnas, Brooklyn, NY, Chelsea Theatre, 1968.
Black Picture Show, New York, Vivian Beaumont Theatre, Lincoln Center, 6 January 1975.
Rhinestone Sharecropping (a play with music), New York, Richard Allen Centre, October 1982.
The Forbidden City, Public Theatre, New York Shakespeare Festival, 1989.

Screenplays

Friends, Universal Studios, 1968a.
Fame Game, Columbia Pictures, 1968b.
Stop, Warner Brothers, 1969 (never released).
Angel Levine, adapted by Gunn and Ronald Ribman from Bernard Malamud's story "The
    Angel Levine," United Artists, 1970a.
Don't the Moon Look Lonesome, Chuck Barris Productions, 1970b.
The Landlord, adapted from a Kristin Hunter novel, United Artists, 1970c.
Ganja and Hess. Kely-Jordan, 1973; reedited as *Blood Couple*, Heritage Enterprises, 1973.
    The Greatest, the Muhammad Ali Story, Columbia Pictures, 1976.
Men of Bronze, Tri-Star Pictures/Danny Arnold Productions, 1988.

Television

"Johnnas," NBC, Washington DC., 1972.
"The Alberta Hunter Story," Southern Pictures/BBC, London, 1982.

Periodical Publication

"Johnnas" *Drama Review* 12 (Summer 1968): 126–138.

Studies of Bill Gunn

Arata, Esther Spring. *More Black American Playwrights. A Bibliography*. Metuchen, NJ:
    Scarecrow Press, 1978.
Bowser, Pearl. "Possibilities That Might Have Been." *Black Film Review* 5.2 (Spring 1989):
    12, 17.
Cady, Barbara. Rev. of *Rhinestone Sharecropping*. *Los Angeles Times Book Review*, 21 May
    1981: 8c.
Klotman, Phyllis R. *Screenplays of the African American Experience*. Bloomington: Indiana
    University Press, 1991.
Klotman, Phyllis R., and Manthia Diawara. "Vampires, Sex and Addictions: *Ganja and
    Hess*." *Jump Cut* 35 (April 1990): 30–36.
Leki, Ilona. "Bill Gunn." *Dictionary of Literary Biography*. Vol. 38 *Afro-American Writers
    after 1955: Dramatists and Prose Writers*. Ed. Thadius M. Davis and Trudier Harris.
    Detroit: Gale Research, 1985, 109–114.
Monaco, James. *American Film Now*. New York: Oxford University Press, 1979, 205–207.
Peterson, Bernard, Jr. *Contemporary Black American Playwrights and Their Plays. A Bio-
    graphical Directory and Dramatic Index*. New York: Greenwood Press, 1988.
Peterson, Maurice. "Interview with Bill Gunn." *Essence* 4 (October 1973): 27, 96.
Schraufnagel, Noel. *From Apology to Protest: The Black American Novel*. DeLand, FL: Ev-
    erett/Edwards, 1973, 123–125.
Valade, Roger M., III, with Denise Kasinee. *The Schomburg Center Guide to Black Literature
    from the Eighteenth Century to the Present*. Detroit: Gale Research, 1996.

E. LYNN HARRIS
(1957–   )

Grace Sikorski

BIOGRAPHY

The work of E. Lynn Harris has earned a good deal of attention and praise in the last decade. His work has appeared in *American Visions, Men's Style, Essence,* and the anthologies *Go the Way Your Blood Beats: An Anthology of Lesbian and Gay Fiction by African-American Writers* and *Brotherman: The Odyssey of African-American Men in America.* His four novels, *Invisible Life* (1991), *Just As I Am* (1994), *And This Too Shall Pass* (1996), and *If This World Were Mine* (1997), have appeared on the *New York Times* and *Essence*'s best-seller lists. The first two of these were nominated for the Outstanding African-American Novel by the Booksellers Association African-American Blackboard List. Harris claims that his major influences as a writer have been Terry McMillan,* Tina McElroy, and Bebe Moore, and his most avid "fans" seem to be African American women. His work, perhaps best known for its treatment of gay and bisexual characters and their struggle for authenticity, truth, honesty, and happiness, is semiautobiographical in content.

Harris was born in Flint, Michigan, in 1957 and later raised in Little Rock, Arkansas, by his mother, Etta Harris, a factory worker, in a small, four-room house he shared with three younger sisters. He attended a predominantly white high school, then majored in journalism at the University of Arkansas at Fayetteville. As an undergraduate, Harris was active as editor of the yearbook, president of his fraternity, and school cheerleader. Although he had begun to question his sexuality in college, he reassured himself that his attraction to men would pass. He remained closeted while he worked for ten years as a computer sales executive for corporations such as IBM in Dallas and AT&T in New York and eventually began to suffer from depression.

He reached a turning point in his life in his mid-thirties. With incidental encouragement from Maya Angelou, Harris quit his job and wrote his first novel, *Invisible Life*. His manuscript was rejected by a variety of major publishing houses; but in 1992, after investing all of his savings to publish 5,000 copies of the book and marketing them at African American-owned beauty salons, bookstores, and women's groups, Harris signed a four-book contract with Doubleday. He is currently writing his memoirs.

MAJOR WORKS AND THEMES

Harris' first novel, *Invisible Life*, whose title echoes that of Ralph Ellison's* *Invisible Man*, is narrated by Raymond, a young aspiring African American, struggling to define not only his sexuality but also his masculinity. As an undergraduate student at a southern "lily white university" (4), he is torn between his love for his cheerleader girlfriend, Sela, and his football star boyfriend, Kelvin. Haunted by the stereotypes that tell him that he is a "sissy" (14), driven by a "sinful sexual longing" (16), Raymond is filled with fear, shame, and self-loathing because of his bisexuality.

After graduation, Raymond moves north to New York City to attend Columbia Law School and begin his career as a sports and entertainment lawyer. Repeating the pattern of the first part of the narrative, he falls in love with Nicole, an understudy for *Dreamgirls*, who is "a porcelain Barbie doll dipped in chocolate" (123), and Quinn, a rich stockbroker who is "a black Adonis" (199). Although he acknowledges his bisexuality at this later point in his life, Raymond still torments himself with his own need to choose between Nicole and Quinn, between a heterosexual identity and a homosexual identity.

The critical point of this narrative is Raymond's discovery that his college lover, Kelvin, has infected a young woman, Candance, with HIV. When she dies, Raymond is consumed with guilt for being bisexual like Kelvin, the alleged conduit for HIV between the straight and gay communities. Raymond reflects:

I was overcome with a tremendous amount of guilt regarding Candance's death. I was part of a secret society that was endangering black women like Candance to protect our secret desires. Would this have happened if society had allowed Kelvin and I to live a life free from ridicule? Was it our fault for hiding behind these women to protect out futures and reputations? . . . Many of us passed in and out of their worlds. (253–254)

Raymond regards his bisexuality as an unavoidably duplicitous state of being, torn between two discreet worlds, experiencing a sexual double-consciousness, and ultimately destructive in his deception and his ability to pass.

These themes are continued in *Just As I Am*, Harris' sequel to *Invisible Life*. Raymond opens the novel bemoaning his fate in an "imperfect world" (4), calling himself a "sexual mulatto" (4), invoking the literary figure of the "tragic" racial mulatto. But this time, Harris uses a second narrator: Nicole is a former beauty queen, resentful of her friend Candance's demise, self-conscious of her skin color, and distrustful of men. Nicole is tempted to marry Pierce, a white man who treats her like a possession, and to star in his production of a musical version of the Anita Hill controversy called *To Tell the Truth: A Musical*. She struggles to come to terms with her own self-image, as well as her racial, religious, and sexual identity. Together, Nicole and Raymond narrate their searches for love, success, and happiness, both admitting something about themselves they had been concealing for quite some time, their fear of telling the truth about who they are.

The turning point in this novel is when Nicole and Raymond's mutual friend, Kyle, admits that he is dying of AIDS. Kyle teaches Nicole and Raymond the importance of honesty and faith. The novel closes with all of the other main characters uniting to set up an AIDS foundation in Kyle's name, and the reader is reassured of the redemptive powers of family, friends, faith, and honesty.

Harris breaks from the story line of Raymond and Nicole in *And This Too Shall Pass*. The main plot of this third novel revolves around Zurich, a young professional quarterback with southern Baptist roots who fights to clear himself of rape charges and to come to terms with his attraction to men. The subplots explore the repercussions of false accusations, false rumors, misleading evidence, and incomplete or repressed memories.

Harris' most recent novel, *If This World Were Mine*, introduces another quartet of characters/narrators, Riley, Dwight, Yolanda, and Leland, four college friends reunited in these pages as a journal-writing club. Each of them is experiencing a turning point in life, struggling through troubled marriage, coming to terms with racism, searching for true love, and coming out.

Harris' novels are consistently concerned with universal quests for love, truth, and faith as well as the unique ways individuals struggle for racial identity and sexual identity. He reveals the contradictions between appearance and reality, the phenomenon of "passing," which race and sexuality both allow, and the phenomenon of invisibility.

Harris is one of a very few African American authors who writes about bisexual, gay, and lesbian characters. Through his narratives, he seems to be working on the assumptions that bisexuals, gays, and lesbians are not a threat to the integrity and health of the African American community but that racism, sexism, and homophobia are.

In addition to racism and homophobia, Harris foregrounds issues such as sexism, religion, AIDS, hate crimes, drug and alcohol addiction, rape, and prostitution. Ultimately his main concern is the danger of masking the truth, repressing memories or feelings, disguising real intentions, remaining in the closet, and living a lie. His characters consistently move toward recovery, healing, happy ending, and honesty through their discoveries of love, truth, and faith.

CRITICAL RECEPTION

Harris' technique in his earlier novels has occasionally been criticized. Sybil Steinberg's review of *Just As I Am*, for example, complains that "when a character is introduced, a demographic stereotype is quickly outlined to elicit the reader's mechanical response" (41). Eric Washington's review of *Just As I Am* is equally critical of Harris' narration, claiming that "the operative gimmick seems to be name-dropping. The Afro-Americana include Whitney Houston song titles, well known 'buppie' haunts, African-American gay festivals, and even African-American fraternities and sororities" (74). Furthermore, Washington contends, "Afforded similarly trivial attention are such loaded issues as AIDS, gay bashing, mixed marriage, light skin versus dark skin, rape, religion, and Anita Hill . . . all paraded by unceremoniously as if to assure us of the book's contemporary (in other words, hip) appeal" (74). Whitney Scott's review of *Just As I Am* delivers a negative review of Harris' use of "daytime-TV dialogue unbroken by any narrative or description of the speakers" (1060).

Scholars have approached Harris' work from a variety of directions. Traci Carroll's essay places Harris' work within a tradition of "passing" narratives, including Frances Ellen Watkins Harper's *Iola Leroy*, Pauline E. Hopkins' *Contending Forces*, and Charles Waddell Chestnutt's "The Wife of His Youth," explaining, "The concept of passing links African American and gay literary traditions through their common reliance upon the notion of a fundamental, unitary identity, a truth whose denial offers myriad social benefits at the cost of political compromise and constant fear of exposure" (181). Whereas Harriette Richard, however, suggests that "[*Invisible Life*] provides a poignant description that should be useful to clinicians attempting to understand the dynamics of coming to terms with one's own homosexuality, specifically in the African-American community" (208).

Although Harris' narration does seem, at times, preoccupied with the appearances of its characters, their skin color, their clothes, and their bodies (especially in his character exposition and the occasional sex scenes), and his characters do appear to be materialistic and perhaps too color-conscious, Harris' work has been widely circulated and very well received. He has been applauded for his characterizations of strong African American women and men and his treatment of bisexuality and homosexuality and a variety of other current issues. His work has an obvious mainstream appeal. The author has expressed confidence that his technique is evolving, that his style is maturing, and that a growing number of readers appreciate his lively style as well as his treatment of contemporary issues.

BIBLIOGRAPHY

Works by E. Lynn Harris

Novels

Invisible Life. New York: Doubleday, 1991.
Just As I Am. New York: Doubleday, 1994.
And This Too Shall Pass. New York: Doubleday, 1996.
If This World Were Mine. New York: Doubleday, 1997.

Short Story

"Who's the Man?" *Essence* 27.7 (Nov. 1996): 92, 194.

Studies of E. Lynn Harris

Carroll, Traci. "Invisible Sissy: The Politics of Masculinity in African American Bisexual Narrative." *RePresenting Bisexualities: Subjects and Cultures of Fluid Desire*. Ed. Donald E. Hall and Maria Pramaggiore. New York: New York University Press, 1996.

Green, Leonard. Rev. of *Invisible Life*. *Lambda Book Report* 3.5 (July1992): 39.

Gregory, Deborah. "Just As He Is." Rev. of *And This Too Shall Pass*. *Essence* 26.12 (Apr. 1996): 88, 134.

Harmon, Charles. Rev. of *And This Too Shall Pass*. *Booklist* (Feb. 1996): 998.

"Harris, E. Lynn." *Current Biography* 57.6 (June 1996): 17–20.

Kelm, Rebecca Sturm. Rev. of *And This Too Shall Pass*. *Library Journal* 121.2 (Feb. 1996): 98.

Kilpatrick, Thomas. Rev. of *Just As I Am*. *Library Journal* 119.2 (Feb. 1994): 111–112.

Parker, Canaan. "Sell the Fantasy." Rev. of *Just As I Am*. *Lambda Book Report* 4.3 (Mar. 1994): 20.

Rev. of *Invisible Life*. *Lambda Book Review* 3.4 (May 1992): 48.

Richard, Harriette W. Rev. of *Invisible Life*. *Journal of African-American Psychology* 21.2 (May 1995): 206–210.

Scott, Whitney. Rev. of *Just As I Am*. *Booklist* 90.12 (Feb. 1994): 1060.

Steinberg, Sybil S. Rev. of *Just As I Am*. *Publishers Weekly* 241.4 (Jan. 1994): 41.

———. Rev. of *And This Too Shall Pass*. *Publishers Weekly* 242 (Jan. 1996): 84.

Stratton, Stephen. "E. Lynn Harris." *Contemporary Black Biography: Profiles from the International Black Community*. Ed. Shirelle Phelps. Detroit; Gale, 1996. 82–84.

"Sweet Bi and Bi." *People Weekly* 43.19 (May 1995): 115.

Washington, Eric K. "Over the Top." Rev. of *Just As I Am*. *Advocate: The National Gay and Lesbian Newsmagazine* 650 (Mar. 1994): 73–74.

CHESTER B. HIMES
(1909–1984)

Bruce A. Glasrud and Laurie Champion

BIOGRAPHY

Chester B. Himes was born on July 29, 1909, in Jefferson City, Missouri, the youngest son of Joseph Sandy Himes, who taught blacksmithing at trades colleges, and Estelle (Bomar) Himes, who was a public school teacher. When Himes was thirteen, he and his brother Joseph devised a science experiment for a presentation. Because Himes' mother punished Chester by forbidding him to participate in the presentation, Joseph attempted to demonstrate the experiment alone. During the presentation, the chemicals exploded and blinded Joseph. The family moved to Saint Louis and then to Cleveland, where Joseph could receive adequate medical attention. While in Cleveland, Himes worked for a hotel, where he fell down an elevator shaft and was injured. His brother's and his own injury immensely impacted Himes because he felt responsible for Joseph's accident and because both he and his brother were denied treatment at hospital facilities that treated only whites.

Himes enrolled at Ohio State University in 1926 but was dismissed from the university for a prank; he then engaged in criminal activities that concluded with his conviction at age nineteen of armed robbery. He was committed to Ohio State Penitentiary, where he served seven and one-half years of a twenty-year sentence. During his incarceration, he began publishing short stories, many of which illustrate his prison experiences. His first stories appeared in magazines such as *Abbott's Monthly* and *Esquire* and in black newspapers such as the *Atlanta Daily World*. His novel *Cast the First Stone* (the first he wrote) is also based on his prison experiences, although in order to get it published he changed the title from *Black Sheep* and recast the characters from black to white.

One important characteristic of Himes was his restlessness, a condition reflected in various ways. Released from prison in 1936, he married Jean Johnson in 1937 and performed jobs such as bellhop, waiter, and research assistant for the Cleveland Public Library. In 1939, he worked in Cleveland as a journalist for the *Cleveland Daily News*, a project supported by the Ohio State Writers Project. He also worked on a farm near Pleasant Valley, Ohio. In 1940, he moved to California and worked in the Los Angeles and San Francisco shipyards. In California, he also held over forty other menial positions such as carpenter, plumber, and waiter. In 1944, he moved to New York City, returned to California in 1945, and back to New York City in 1946. From 1946 to 1953, Himes lived in the New York City area, where he was employed in various jobs such as dishwasher, bellhop, porter, and caretaker for several estates. In 1948, he attended the distinguished Yaddo Writers Colony in Saratoga Springs, New York.

In 1953, Himes relocated to France, where he hoped to gain acceptance as an artist as well as to escape American racism. Although his experiences in France and Spain did not reflect the racial tolerance he had expected, the move provided him with insights about American culture and greatly impacted his artistic endeavors. In 1955, the French publisher Marcel Duhamel convinced Himes to write detective novels. Although the detective novels Himes produced between 1957 and 1969 earned Himes international recognition, until recently his works have always been more highly regarded in Europe than in America. All but one of his later novels were first published in France years before they appeared in the United States. In 1958, Himes was awarded the Grand Prix de Litterature Policiére.

While in Benissa, Spain, on November 12, 1984, Chester Himes, at age seventy-five, died of Parkinson's disease.

MAJOR WORKS AND THEMES

Himes' early works are representative of the naturalistic tradition, a mode during the 1930s and 1940s that writers such as Richard Wright used to illustrate realistically ways that people are influenced by powerful social and natural forces. Himes' characters are doomed because of social ills such as racism, oppression, and poverty. The realistic portrayal of the plight of blacks in a racist society is evident in Himes' novels and in his short stories. Some of his stories are based on his prison experiences and were published in *Esquire* as "Sketches from Prisoner #59623." In "To What Red Hell" he describes the disastrous 1930 fire that occurred at the prison. "The Night's for Cryin' " portrays a black man on death row for stabbing a man. "Pork Chop Paradise" is about a convicted rapist who, upon release from prison, becomes an evangelist and exploits ghetto residents.

The need for social change is also apparent in Himes' stories. In "Lunching at the Ritzmore," two men bet whether an upscale restaurant will admit a black man. While the black man and the two who have bet walk to the restaurant people begin to follow, until finally a huge crowd awaits outside the Ritzmore to see if the black man is served. Similarly, "Heaven Has Changed" shows that even heaven is segregated, with the black section ruled by Old Jim Crow. These and Himes' other short stories have been published in *The Collected Stories of Chester Himes*.

While the need for social change, especially as it relates to racism, is a prominent theme in all of Himes' works, his first two novels, set in California during World War II, especially develop this idea from a naturalistic perspective. In the first of these California novels, *If He Hollers Let Him Go*, the protagonist Bob Jones leaves Cleveland and heads west only to become disillusioned when he discovers that racism also exists in the West. While employed at a Los Angeles shipyard, racial slurs from a white coworker motivate Jones to seek revenge through murder. Madge, a white woman who refuses to work with Jones, is both attracted to, and repelled by, Jones. Serving as a foil for Madge, Alice, Jones' black girlfriend, encourages him to adopt the values of whites. One conflict of the novel involves Jones' predicament of whether to accept Alice's philosophy and become part of American society that denies blacks empowerment. When Madge falsely accuses Jones of attempted rape, he joins the army to get the charges dropped.

In *Lonely Crusade*, the protagonist, Lee Gordon, struggles with feelings of inferiority and suspicion of whites. He abuses his black wife, Ruth, and has an affair with a white communist organizer. Gordon eventually transforms his fight for racial justice into one against corrupt social institutions to seek through union efforts to fight for both black and white working-class citizens. Both novels represent proletariat fiction in their depiction of the struggles of the working class and tensions between workers and employers. The working conditions of the California shipyard in *If He Hollers* reflect racism and exploitation of workers. In *Lonely Crusade*, Gordon attempts to unionize black aircraft workers and end racism and poor working conditions.

Himes' novels *Cast the First Stone* and *The Third Generation* are highly autobiographical accounts. Although, unlike Himes, the protagonist of *Cast the First Stone* is a white homosexual, Himes provides realistic portrayals of prison life. Through the experiences of his protagonist, Jim Monroe, Himes demonstrates the cruelty and inhumanity of the American justice system. *The Third Generation* offers a more autobiographical account of Himes' experiences with racism. The novel details the experiences of a particular black family, told from the point of view of the youngest son. Among other issues, the novel explores the psychological impact on the family of the mother's feelings of superiority because she has light skin. The novel also shows ways generations of oppression affect the current family's struggle with racism.

Sex is also a prominent subject throughout Himes' works. Considered his best novel by a few critics, *The End of the Primitive* explores interracial sex. Both the black Jesse and the white Kriss hold stereotypical views about interracial sex. Because of psychological frustrations neither's expectations are fulfilled, and Jesse kills Kriss. In the naturalistic tradition, Himes shows that both characters are victims of social circumstances. In *Pinktoes*, a highly innovative novel, Mamie

Mason establishes interracial sexual orgies as a way to conquer racism; ironically, the orgies only perpetuate racism because those who participate seek only to experience interracial sex and are not interested in politics. Sex obviously plays a role in A Case of Rape, Himes' most serious novel.

Himes' detective fiction constitutes a significant portion of his work and has gained him his greatest fame. His ten detective novels were originally published in French translation between 1958 and 1983 (the first seven as part of Gallimard's Série Noire)—For Love of Imabelle (1957), The Real Cool Killers (1959), The Crazy Kill (1959), The Big Gold Dream (1960), All Shot Up (1960), Cotton Comes to Harlem (1965), The Heat's On (1966), Run Man, Run (1966), Blind Man with a Pistol (1969), and Plan B (1966). Except for Run Man, Run, which takes place in downtown New York and does not include Coffin Ed and Grave Digger, the detective novels form a cycle. They are set in Harlem, where Coffin Ed Johnson and Grave Digger Jones are police partners who try to solve various crimes. The novels reflect extremes of criminal actions and physical violence, sometimes grotesque violence. Incidents that occurred in one novel are referred to in later novels, and thematic patterns are established throughout the series. They portray poverty-stricken conditions, police brutality, and racism. The police often break the law themselves and are violent against criminals. Their loyalty is to each other and the black community as a whole, concerns that supersede individual needs and protection. When the novels are read chronologically, they demonstrate important social changes that occurred during the time surrounding the height of the Civil Rights movement.

The plots of some of the detective novels entail con games that Coffin Ed and Grave Digger must solve. Because they are concerned with mass society, they are interested as much in compensating impoverished victims as they are in catching con artists. The first in the series, For Love of Imabelle (later published as A Rage in Harlem), concerns a swindle known as "the blow," where people are told that $10 bills can be transformed into $100 bills. In Himes' most popular novel, Cotton Comes to Harlem, Coffin Ed and Grave Digger seek to solve a crime involving a religious swindle where a preacher cons $87,000 from innocent people in a back-to-Africa scam.

The detective series ends with Plan B, a novel fragment in which Tomsson Black distributes rifles to people in Harlem. His motive is revenge, for his family genealogy shows oppression of generations of African Americans. Grave Digger and Coffin Ed appear only briefly in the novel, where, at the end, Grave Digger kills Coffin Ed, who is killed by another character.

In his detective fiction, Himes blends humor with the grotesque to present situations that can be defined as absurd. For example, in Real Cool Killers a bartender axes off the arm of a patron, who scrambles to search for his arm that still holds the knife he had planned to use against the bartender; in All Shot Up a sheet of steel slides from a truck and decapitates a man on a motorcycle, yet he continues to ride headless for a while; also in All Shot Up a gunman runs down the street while a knife sticks through his head; and in Blind Man with a Pistol, a

Mormon persuades his wives to pose as nuns and beg for money, while his naked children eat stew from troughs, in a piglike fashion. Even Coffin Ed is described grotesquely. Because of an incident wherein a hoodlum threw acid in his face, Coffin Ed's face is distorted, giving him an appearance for which he sometimes is referred to as Frankenstein. These grotesque and absurd illustrations reflect the alienation that Himes experienced due to the incongruity between democratic ideals and racist practices in U.S. society, a situation Himes referred to as absurd. Himes notes that "in the lives of black people, there are so many absurd situations, made that way by racism, that black life could sometimes be described as surrealistic" (Fabre and Skinner 140).

Many of the novels depict the chaotic and violent atmosphere of Harlem, which is a microcosm for racist American society. Himes demonstrates the impoverished conditions and the frustrations of people desperate for dignity and economic equality. Coffin Ed's and Grave Digger's use of what might be considered excessive force toward criminals, especially black criminals, seems contradictory to their goal of progress for African Americans. However, their use of violence reflects their overriding philosophy: "We got the highest crime rate on earth among the colored people in Harlem. And there ain't but three things to do about it: Make the criminals pay for it—you don't want to do that; pay the people enough to live decently—you ain't going to do that; so all that's left is let 'em eat one another up" (*Cotton* 20). In Himes' view, crime is not the result of individual circumstances but of unequal opportunity and racism, larger social problems.

In addition to his fiction, Himes also wrote two autobiographies, *The Quality of Hurt* and *My Life of Absurdity*. More than providing a personal account of his life, these works document problems African Americans experienced throughout most of the twentieth century. Himes very explicitly points out instances of racist actions that hindered him and other African Americans.

CRITICAL RECEPTION

Although he is a major American writer, until recently Himes' works have been neglected by American critics, at least partially because his black perspective dominates his writing. Reviewers and critics of Himes' early works frequently commented on the portrayal of violence and considered Himes a writer of protest fiction. Early critics reduced his detective novels to popular fiction and either ignored them or faulted Himes for forfeiting literary art for commercial success. A. Robert Lee discusses the critical reception of Himes' works through 1978. In addition to providing an overview of Himes' works, James Sallis refers to various stages of the critical reception of Himes' works. Two book-length studies entitled *Chester Himes*, one by James Lundquist, the other by Gilbert H. Muller, provide overviews of Himes' career and surveys of his works. A scholarly appraisal of Himes' literary career is Stephen F. Milliken's book. *Chester Himes: An Annotated Primary and Secondary Bibliography*, compiled by Michel Fabre, Robert E. Skinner, and Lester Sullivan, provides a comprehensive bibliography of primary and secondary sources and is essential for anyone researching Himes. Overviews of Himes' career can also be found in the essays, interviews, and reviews collected in the 1972 *Black World* special issue that commemorated the publication of *The Quality of Hurt* and in the valuable collection *Conversations with Chester Himes*.

Many critics comment on the extreme violence portrayed in Himes' works. Especially in his early works, the violence reflects Himes' attitude that "the only way the America Negro will ever be able to participate in the American way of life is by a series of acts of violence. It's tragic, but it's true" (Fabre and Skinner 21–22). Stephen B. Bennett and William W. Nichols evaluate Himes' use of violence in context with other twentieth-century African American writers. Wilfried Feuser discusses Himes' depiction of violence in terms of protest fiction.

Much of the critical assessment of Himes' work focuses on his contribution to the detective genre. Raymond Nelson argues that Himes' use of folk traditions and his exposure of corrupt social institutions illustrate African American culture and history. John M. Reilly classifies Himes' detective novels as tough-guy fiction that extends naturalism by depicting characters as victims of social conditions. Himes' use of tough-guy or hard-boiled fiction is also explored by Jay R. Berry, Jr. Berry compares Himes' detective fiction with that of Dashiell Hammett and Raymond Chandler and notes that Himes blends elements of the hard-boiled tradition with African American history. Robert Crooks demonstrates how Himes and Mosley extend the hard-boiled tradition by portraying political and social issues relevant to African Americans. Edward Margolies, in "The Thrillers of Chester Himes," discusses the violent Harlem used as the setting in Himes' detective fiction. Seeking to develop a new interest and fresh perspective on Himes' works, Skinner's *Two Guns from Harlem: The Detective Fiction of Chester Himes* provides a book-length study of Himes' detective fiction. Skinner views Grave Digger and Coffin Ed as hard-boiled heroes, discusses Harlem as setting, looks at Himes' portrayal of skin color, and surveys in individual chapters the detective novels.

Himes' depiction of absurd situations and his use of humor are other topics critics explore. In "Chester Himes's Black Comedy: The Genre Is the Message," Margolies provides an excellent examination of ways Himes blends detective fiction with absurd humor to convey political and social messages. Similarly, David Cochran explores Himes' use of absurd violence and chaos in terms of a departure from protest fiction.

In a recent, insightful study, Edward Margolies and Michel Fabre evaluate *The Several Lives of Chester Himes*. As noted, Himes had considerable difficulty getting published in the United States; the title of a recent doctoral dissertation by Melvin Troy Peters tellingly shows why—"Too Close to the Truth: The American Fiction of Chester Himes."

BIBLIOGRAPHY

Works by Chester B. Himes

Novels (first U.S. editions)

If He Hollers Let Him Go. Garden City, NY: Doubleday, Doran, 1945.
Lonely Crusade. New York: Alfred A. Knopf, 1947.
Cast the First Stone. New York: Coward-McCann, 1952.
The Third Generation. Cleveland: World, 1954.
The End of the Primitive. New York: New American Library, 1956.
For Love of Imabelle. Greenwich, CT: Fawcett, 1957; revised as *A Rage in Harlem.* New York: Avon, 1965.
The Crazy Kill. New York: Avon, 1959a.
The Real Cool Killers. New York: Avon, 1959b.
The Big Gold Dream. New York: Avon, 1960a.
All Shot Up. New York: Avon, 1960b.
Cotton Comes to Harlem. New York: G. P. Putnam, 1965a.
Pinktoes. New York: G. P. Putnam, 1965b.
The Heat's On. New York: G. P. Putnam, 1966a.
Run Man, Run. New York: G. P. Putnam, 1966b.
Blind Man with a Pistol. New York: William Morrow, 1969.
A Case of Rape. New York: Targ, 1980.
Plan B. New York: G. P. Putnam, 1966; Ed. Michel Fabre and Robert E. Skinner. Jackson: University Press of Mississippi, 1994.
Un Joli coup de lune [*The Lunatic Fringe*]. Trans. Hélène Devauz-Minié. Paris: Lieu Commun, 1988.

Short Stories

Black on Black: Baby Sister and Selected Writings. Garden City, NY: Doubleday, 1973.
The Collected Stories of Chester Himes. Foreword Calvin Hernton. New York: Thunder's Mouth Press, 1991.

Autobiographies

The Quality of Hurt. New York: Doubleday, 1972.
My Life of Absurdity: The Autobiography of Chester Himes. Garden City, NY: Doubleday, 1976.

Studies of Chester B. Himes

Bennett, Stephen B., and William W. Nichols. "Violence in Afro-American Fiction: An Hypothesis." *Modern Fiction Studies* 17 (1971): 221–28.
Berry, Jay R., Jr. "Chester Himes and the Hard-Boiled Tradition."*Armchair Detective* 15.1 (1982): 38–43.
Cochran, David. "So Much Nonsense Must Make Sense: The Black Vision of Chester Himes." *Midwest Quarterly* 38 (1996): 1–30.

Crooks, Robert. "From the Far Side of the Urban Frontier: The Detective Fiction of Chester Himes and Walter Mosley." *College Literature* 22 (1995): 68–90.

Evans, Veichal Jerome. "Chester Himes: Chronicler of the Black Experience." Diss., Oklahoma State University, 1980.

Fabre, Michel, and Robert E. Skinner, eds. *Conversations with Chester Himes.* Jackson: University Press of Mississippi, 1995.

Fabre, Michel, Robert E. Skinner, and Lester Sullivan, comps. *Chester Himes: An Annotated Primary and Secondary Bibliography.* Westport, CT: Greenwood, 1992.

Feuser, Wilfried. "Prophet of Violence: Chester Himes." *African Literature Today.* Ed. Eldred Durosimi Jones. New York: Africana, 1978. 59–76.

Lee, A. Robert. "Hurts, Absurdities and Violence: The Contrary Dimensions of Chester Himes." *Journal of American Studies* 12 (1978): 99–114.

Lundquist, James. *Chester Himes.* New York: Frederick Ungar, 1976.

Margolies, Edward. "Chester Himes's Black Comedy: The Genre Is the Message." *Which Way Did He Go? The Private Eye in Dashiell Hammett, Raymond Chandler, Chester Himes, and Ross Macdonald.* New York: Holmes and Meier, 1982. 53–70.

———. "Experiences of the Black Expatriate Writer: Chester Himes." *CLA Journal* 15 (1972): 421–27.

———. "The Thrillers of Chester Himes." *Studies in Black Literature* 1 (1970): 1–11.

Margolies, Edward, and Michel Fabre. *The Several Lives of Chester Himes.* Jackson: University Press of Mississippi, 1997.

Milliken, Stephen F. *Chester Himes: A Critical Appraisal.* Columbia: University of Missouri Press, 1976.

Muller, Gilbert H. *Chester Himes.* Boston: Twayne, 1989.

Nelson, Raymond. "Domestic Harlem: The Detective Fiction of Chester Himes." *Virginia Quarterly Review* 48 (1972): 260–72.

Peters, Melvin Troy. "Too Close to the Truth: The American Fiction of Chester Himes." Diss., Michigan State University, 1978.

Reed, Ishmael. "Chester Himes: Writer." *Black World* 21 (1972): 23–38, 83–86.

Reilly, John M. "Chester Himes' Harlem Tough Guys." *Journal of Popular Culture* 9 (1976): 935–47.

Sallis, James. "In America's Black Heartland: The Achievement of Chester Himes." *Western Humanities Review* 37.3 (1983): 191–206.

Saunders, Archie D. "The Image of the Negro in Five Major Novels by Chester Himes." Master's thesis, Howard University, 1965.

Skinner, Robert E. "The Black Man in the Literature of Labor: The Early Novels of Chester Himes." *Labor's Heritage* 1 (1989): 51–65.

———. "Streets of Fear: The Los Angeles Novels of Chester Himes." *Los Angeles in Fiction: A Collection of Essays.* Ed. David Fine. Albuquerque: University of New Mexico Press, 1995. 227–38.

———. *Two Guns from Harlem: The Detective Fiction of Chester Himes.* Bowling Green, OH: Popular Press, 1989.

Walters, Wendy W. "Limited Options: Strategic Maneuverings in Himes's Harlem." *African American Review* 28 (1994): 615–31.

Wilson, M. L. *Chester Himes.* New York: Chelsea House, 1988.

Wilson, Ruth Ann. "The Black Sheep: The Novels of Chester Himes." Master's thesis, Stephen F. Austin State University, 1972.

KRISTIN HUNTER
(1931–)

Rennie Simson

BIOGRAPHY

Kristin Hunter was born September 12, 1931, in Philadelphia. Her parents, G. L. and Mabel (Manigault) Eggleston, were both schoolteachers. They wanted her, their only child, to also be a teacher, but her teaching career lasted less than a full year. Upon graduation from the University of Pennsylvania in 1951, she briefly taught third grade.

Hunter's interest was in literature and writing; she stated in an interview with Claudia Tate that she always knew she wanted to be a writer. She learned to read at the age of four and contributed poetry to school publications. At the age of fourteen she commenced her professional career as a columnist and feature writer for the *Pittsburgh Courier*. When she quit her teaching job, she went to work as a copywriter in an ad agency.

Her first novel, *God Bless the Child*, was published in 1964, and numerous short stories and novels followed. Her best-selling novel, *The Soul Brothers and Sister Lou* (1968), a book written mainly for young adults, sold 1 million copies and was translated into several languages.

She has received numerous awards for her work, including awards presented by the Council of International Books for Children, the National Conference on Christians and Jews, and the *Chicago Tribune*.

Since 1968 Hunter has been teaching creative writing at the University of Pennsylvania. Her husband, John, is a photojournalist.

MAJOR WORKS AND THEMES

God Bless the Child, Hunter's first novel, is also her best-known work. The title is taken from Billie Holiday's famous song of the same name, and the life of the heroine, Rosie Fleming, is as tragic as the life of the famous blues singer.

Rosie, who is seven years old at the start of the novel, is raised by two women, her single mother and her grandmother. Her grandmother's (Lourinda Huggs) philosophy of life becomes the impetus for all of Rosie's dreams and actions. Granny Huggs has worked for four decades for a very wealthy white family for whom she does everything, from raising their children to ordering their food and furniture. "She'd had a part in choosing every thread of fabric and every splinter of furniture," and she felt that everything in the house "was as much hers as theirs" (5). She is the prototype of the stereotyped mammy.

Granny respected and admired everything about the white family she worked for, especially their wealth. She herself was a light-skinned woman, but her daughter and especially her granddaughter Rosie were dark-skinned, a characteristic that she despised. She explained Rosie's skin color to her as a terrible mistake for which her mother was responsible. Her mother, Regina, had run off and married a man as "black as coal tar . . . without thinkin' about improvin' the race . . . she had completely bought into the concept of white as right" (21).

Granny brought home for Rosie all kinds of treasures from "her white family"—cast-off clothes, toys, food, knickknacks, and, most of all, stories about great luxury and wealth that fired Rosie's imagination. She determined to live as the white people lived; she would be surrounded by life's "treasures" no matter how she accomplished this. To attain her goal, Rosie worked hard. She first worked as a saleswoman but soon realized that most of the avenues to great wealth were closed to black women. She then followed the path many ambitious young people in the ghetto have pursued: she became a hustler. Her success, for a young black woman, was phenomenal. Through sheer determination, constant work, and huge debts, she attained her goal—a beautiful home in a white neighborhood and all the luxuries she wanted. In the process, however, she ruined her physical and emotional health. She died of lung disease shortly after her twenty-first birthday, and throughout her brief life she was so focused on her goal that she was harsh and selfish toward all the people who cared for her.

Hunter succeeded in showing how the dream of living in a rich white world can destroy black people. The dream caused Granny Huggs to have a totally unrealistic outlook on the world in which *she* and *her* family lived. Granny's dream became Rosie's dream, and she found that becoming a part of the underworld was the only way she as a black woman could hope to fulfill that dream.

The novel begins with Rosie's killing roaches in her slum home and ends with Rosie's lying on her deathbed in her mansion looking at a roach and commenting, "You sure followed me a long way. . . . How come you like colored people so much anyway?" (304). The much despised roach represents the reality of Rosie's life and Hunter's view that the reality *must* be faced; it cannot be escaped, as Rosie learns too late.

The only other novel by Hunter to receive widespread critical acclaim is a book written for young adults, *The Soul Brothers and Sister Lou* (1968). In this story of teenage life in the ghetto Hunter shows how a group of young people, led by the lively, ambitious Lou Hawkins, make a career for themselves in the world of music, one of the few avenues to fame and wealth open to African Americans at that time. They overcome the usual obstacles of their poverty through determination and hard work. Hunter does a particularly good job of detailing their constant struggle with police brutality in the form of Officer Lafferty and the murder by police of one of the young boys in their group. White people are seen by them as "natural" enemies. Even the well-meaning white teacher Mr. Lucitaanno is portrayed as naive and insensitive. The sequel to *The Soul Brothers and Sister Lou*, *Lou in the Limelight* (1981), shows how the main characters, now stars, deal with racial discrimination, including exploitation by white gangsters in the music industry. Both novels portray Black ghetto life harshly and realistically and offer young readers an honest look at a world many of them know little about.

Hunter's other novels, *The Landlord* (1966), *The Survivors* (1975), and *The Lakestown Rebellion* (1978), all deal with life in the ghetto and the characters' struggles to deal with that life. Hunter's main strength is her ability to portray that life in its full, bleak reality yet at the same time to show her characters' ability to maintain dignity and, above all, humor in their struggles to survive. Her main weakness is that the plots bog down at times in too little action and too much repetition. Kristin Hunter is definitely a writer whose works deserve more attention than they have received in the past.

CRITICAL RECEPTION

Most reviewers of Hunter's work praise her keen ability to portray realistically the life of the ghetto—its sights, sounds, and smells. Her characters, in the words of the title of one of her novels, are "survivors." She portrays well not only the relations of blacks in the ghetto among themselves but also their intersection with whites. In *The Landlord* Hunter creates a white slum owner who, in the words of Darwin Turner, considers blacks beneath him but views himself as liberal because he has convinced himself he does not dislike them. Granny Huggs in *God Bless the Child* is so enamored of white wealth that she does not deal with the constant condescension shown to her. In the novels *The Soul Brothers and Sister Lou* and *Lou in the Limelight*, the black protagonists have to deal with white exploitation in the form of police brutality and crooked business managers.

A major reason her novels have not been more widely acclaimed is, as Brickmaster comments relative to *God Bless the Child*, that "the novel is too long, the pace too frantic" (7). Frankel states the difficulty with Rosie in *God Bless the Child* is that "Rosie is a case we follow with interest and sympathy. Empathy . . . is withheld possibly because of the nature of Rosie's personality and drives which keep the reader from being one with her" (16). These limitations apply, in some measure, to most of her works. In spite of any limitations we must agree with Saal's conclusion that "Hunter's pill is bitter and it is strong," and her novels shed keen insights on mid-twentieth-century life in the African American ghettos.

BIBLIOGRAPHY

Works by Kristin Hunter

For Adults

God Bless the Child. New York: Scribner, 1964.
The Landlord. New York: Scribner, 1966.
The Survivors. New York: Scribner, 1975.
The Lakestown Rebellion. New York: Scribner, 1978.

For Younger Readers

The Soul Brothers and Sister Lou. New York: Scribner, 1968.
Boss Cat. New York: Scribner, 1971.
Guests in the Promised Land. New York: Scribner, 1973.
Lou in the Limelight. New York: Scribner, 1981.

Studies of Kristin Hunter

Brickmaster, Henrietta. Rev. of God Bless the Child. The Christian Science Monitor, Sept. 10, 1964, 7.
Emanuel, James. Dark Symphony. New York: Collier MacMillan, 1968.
Frankel, Haskel. Rev. of God Bless the Child. Book Week (Sept. 13, 1964): 16.
Harris, Trudier. From Mammies to Militants. Philadelphia: Temple University Press, 1982.
Hines, Darlene Clark. Black Women in America. Brooklyn, NY: Carlson, 1993.
Kelley, Mary. Rev. of God Bless the Child. Library Journal (Sept. 15, 1964): 3336.
Markowski, Daniel. Contemporary Literary Criticism. Detroit: Gale Research, 1985.
Polak, Maralyn Lois. "Kristin Hunter: A Writer and a Fighter." Philadelphia Inquirer, Nov. 24, 1974, "Today" Section, 8.
Saal, Rollene. "A God for the Children." New York Times Book Review (Sept. 20, 1964): 36.
Shockley, Ann, and Sue Chandler. Living Black American Authors: A Biographical Directory. New York: R. R. Bowker, 1973.
Tate, Claudia. Black Women Writers at Work. New York: Continuum, 1984.

BLYDEN JACKSON
(1910–)

Gwendolyn S. Jones

BIOGRAPHY

Blyden Jackson, professor emeritus of English and pioneer for today's scholars in African American literature, ended a distinguished career in education when he retired from teaching and administration at University of North Carolina at Chapel Hill. He is a specialist in the teaching of African American literature, a literary critic, and a writer of scholarly books and essays. His career started with an eleven-year tenure at Madison Junior High School in Louisville, Kentucky. There he was involved in community activities and in school activities to the extent that he and other teachers considered themselves in loco parentis. His next teaching position was at Fisk University in Nashville, Tennessee, where he taught for nine years. Although he began writing about African American literature in the early 1940's, at Fisk he became particularly interested in the African American writer. Following his appointment at Fisk, he spent fifteen years at Southern University in Baton Rouge, Louisiana. At Southern, he served as head of the Department of English and as the dean of graduate studies. He went from there to the University of North Carolina at Chapel Hill, where he remained until his retirement. At the University of North Carolina, Jackson was one of the first African Americans appointed to the rank of full professor. He also served as associate dean of the Graduate School and as special assistant to the dean of the Graduate School. In those two positions, his duties were primarily to promote the recruitment and retention of minority graduate students and to assist in securing scholarships and fellowships for them. The university's library houses Jackson's papers, which primarily concern his career as a professor of English.

Jackson, born in Paducah, Kentucky, in 1910, considers Louisville his hometown, where he spent his childhood, youth, and early adult years. He attended college at Wilberforce University and earned the bachelor of arts degree. He attended Columbia University several months of the 1931–32 academic year but did not graduate. He recalls that this "was still the Harlem of the Harlem Renaissance, although . . . the Renaissance in its most storied days was over" (*The Waiting Years* 12). Jackson earned the master of arts degree from the University of Michigan by attending summer sessions while a faculty member at Madison Junior High School, then later earned the doctor of philosophy degree.

Professional memberships and honors are numerous. He is a member of the National Council of Teachers of English and has served as Distinguished Lecturer. He has served as president of the College Language Association and is currently on the editorial board of *CLA Journal*. Jackson holds charter membership in the Fellowship of Southern Writers. Among the aims of the fellowship are "to recognize and encourage literature in the South and to encourage young writers." The Philological Association of the Carolinas honored him for important contributions to the field. He is also an advisory editor of the *Langston Hughes Review*.

Jackson's lectures and essays appear in such scholarly and professional journals as *CLA Journal*, *Journal of Negro History*, *Phylon*, *PMLA*, and *College English*. His essays treat such writers as William Faulkner, Langston Hughes, Claude McKay, Jean Toomer, and Richard Wright. He has written new forewords for inclusion in reprints of references; his works also include introductions for novels and reviews of reference works. Books include *Black Poetry in America: Two Essays in Historical Interpretation* (1974); *The Waiting Years: Essays on American Negro Literature* (1976); and *A History of Afro-American Literature: The Long Beginning, 1746–1895* (1989).

MAJOR WORKS AND THEMES

Operation Burning Candle is the code name for the single act that Aaron Rogers conceived, planned, and implemented in order to "break down the wall" so that all blacks could have a chance at success. A psychology major in undergraduate and graduate school, while a graduate student he develops the idea that what is needed is a single traumatic experience that will provide a "source of strength and pride" (93) in blacks that they are lacking because of their subjection to slavery and to segregation. At the same time, this single traumatic experience should "shatter [the white man's] own self concepts and . . . the concepts of black people as passive, accepting and afraid" (93).

Operation Burning Candle, set in Harlem during the Vietnam War years, is a tale of black militancy. Aaron Rogers, a former captain in the Special Forces and trained in guerrilla warfare, recruits and organizes a group of veterans trained in combat, electronics, and communications to carry out this single, traumatic event along with its attendant acts of conspiracy, sabotage, and murder. This tightly knit group of veterans successfully robs banks, stalls subway trains, ties up the city with false fire alarms, and commits murders as needed. They commandeer a local radio station for an announcement that claims responsibility for the various acts of sabotage in the city and promises that a more catastrophic event will follow.

The plan is to gun down twelve U.S. senators during the Democratic National Convention in Madison Square Garden. These southern senators were the ones who Rogers thought were responsible for maintaining ideals of slavery, segregation, and degradation. He blamed them for not doing what they could in the Senate to aid blacks.

In his essay "The Ghetto of the Negro Novel: A Theme with Variations" (published in *The Waiting Years*), Blyden Jackson writes, "The ghetto of the Negro novel . . . speaks of how very much Negroes resent the indignities America has forced upon them. . . . Always it calls for the end of one era of American life and the beginning of a genuine new day" (183). Throughout *Operation Burning Candle*, there are numerous references to these indignities. Aaron Rogers hoped for a "genuine new day" and thought it was his responsibility to make it happen. Rogers devises the elaborate plot designed as "a collective symbolic act of uprising against those who persecute us" (174). He believes that whites have one image of blacks as a group; his goal is to change the image of the group through collective psychological therapy. At the same time, the blacks would change their image of themselves. Aaron Rogers sees Operation Burning Candle through to its violent end.

Totem: A Novel is the second of Jackson's novels. The Totem of the Tribes, the Kabilaote, was made hundreds of years ago by tribal chiefs and medicine men and holds the spirit of all African people. It is bronze, carved with signs and faces of the many tribes, with secret instructions stored inside. Medicine men of each tribe imbued it with powers. With the unity of the African people that the Totem would restore, the African world would regain its power and independence.

Two groups are fighting to find the Totem of the Tribes, the Kabilaote. One group is composed of people in Africa and in America with strong sentiments for a unified Africa; they have no regard for tribal or national boundaries; they want the Totem returned for the good it will bring to all blacks in Africa. These people want unity and want to restore Africa to its former greatness. Mallery Brookson, president of the largest chain of black banks in America and based in New York City, wants to spearhead this hunt. He finances a search and is willing to pay thousands for it. He hires Billy Boy Harris to head a team to travel to Africa, find the Totem, and bring it to him so that he can return it to the African people. Billy Boy is an ex-paratrooper and ex-policeman; he is described as bright, strong, cool, sophisticated, quick-tempered, tough, and handsome. Billy Boy recruits a friend, Marty Williams, a computer programmer; he is good at locks, burglar alarms, security systems, and motor vehicles. The third member of the team is Abu Akman, a karate expert; he has strong religious beliefs and is a believer in Allah; he has extensive knowledge of African history. In Nigeria, a fourth person, Angie, persuades Billy Boy to let her join the team. Originally from Harlem, she has traveled in the United States, the Caribbean, Europe, and Africa. Her contribution would be translating for the Americans and the Africans who are helping them.

The opposition includes those who want the Totem to remain lost; they fear the legend; they are afraid of the power to be wielded by blacks if they unite (apartheid is in place). Nor do the police in South Africa, where apartheid is in place, want blacks in the United States to lobby for African blacks. The opposition also includes the Central Intelligence Agency (CIA), under the leadership of a chief of Africa section and a consultant professor of anthropology who is a specialist in African affairs. Others include officials in some republics that remain under the control of Europeans.

The search for the Totem takes the team to several countries in Africa, including Nigeria, Zaire, South Africa, and Ghana. They travel to towns and villages seeking details of the legend and the possible location of the statue.

A transcribed tale from the Ghana Coast says that the Totem was entrusted to a young slave girl who was brought to the United States. The Totem was traced to South Carolina, then to Harlem, with the CIA always one step ahead of the team.

CRITICAL RECEPTION

Operation Burning Candle was well received. The plot is well written and well organized; main characters are well developed; point of view is effective; actions are believable. Mel Watkins praises the novel for its precise plot, its plausibility, and the cinematic technique used. This technique enables "fast-paced development" and "provide[s] depth beyond the central plot" (31). By using the objective/dramatic third-person point of view, Jackson can shift from episode to episode, character to character, locale to locale, not necessarily in chronological order but without sacrificing the sequence of events. McKenna, however, describes the plot as a "little untidy," no doubt the result of the point of view used, allowing the narrator to treat first one scene or person or event, then another. He also describes *Operation Burning Candle* as "a highly revolutionary and inflammatory thriller and is clamping from the first word to the last." He describes the plot as "exciting" (3285).

Jerry H. Bryant sees that the novel is readable and well organized; the information doled out in snatches adds to the mystery. The semidocumentary style is bound by literary formulas and political stereotypes and in this aspect is different from those novels created from an author's imagination. The subject matter in *Operation Burning Candle* relies on current events that attracted the public's attention. Bryant also notes that *Operation Burning Candle* follows a spy-thriller formula. Nevertheless, this formula allows for clever planning, close escapes, and a strong, intelligent protagonist. Further, Bryant sees in this novel oversimplified thinking and a pedestrian style. Bryant also observes that other writers have repeated this theme in other novels and movies.

BIBLIOGRAPHY

Works by Blyden Jackson

Operation Burning Candle: A Novel. New York: Third Press/Joseph Okpaku, 1973.

Totem: A Novel. New York: Third Press/Joseph Okpaku, 1975.

The Waiting Years: Essays on American Negro Literature. Baton Rouge: Louisiana State University Press, 1976.

Studies of Blyden Jackson

Bryant, Jerry H. Review of *Operation Burning Candle. Nation* 217 (November 1973): 501–503.

McKenna, Stephen. Review of *Operation Burning Candle. Library Journal* 98 (November 1973): 3285.

Review of *Totem: A Novel. Black World* (January 1976): 80–81.

Watkins, Mel. Review of *Operation Burning Candle. New York Times Book Review* (February 17, 1974): 31.

CHARLES JOHNSON
(1948–   )

Christian Moraru

BIOGRAPHY

Fiction author, critic, philosopher, political cartoonist, screenwriter, editor, and professor of creative writing, Charles Johnson is a remarkably complex artist and intellectual. His astoundingly protean creativity brings to mind, among other African American contemporary writers, the creativity of Ishmael Reed. Much like Reed, not only does Johnson stand out as one of the best living American writers, regardless of race, but he has also become what one could call a cultural institution and, as such, has responded in a variety of ways to some of the most urgent issues of multicultural America.

Born in Evanston, Illinois, a major region in his fictional geography, Johnson was educated at Southern Illinois University and SUNY-Stony Brook between 1971 and 1976. At Carbondale, he worked with John Gardner, whose example, advice, and critical work (*The Forms of Fiction*) helped him realize a fundamental fact that, again, Reed has also understood: "The modern short story or novel may assume the form of any of the above [realism or fantasy] or, if you push this a bit further, any other narrative form people have employed—diaries, slave narratives, hymns, sermons, interlocking business documents—to clarify their experiences" (*Being and Race* 50).

Under the influence of James Baldwin,* Johnson wrote six novels, which he later on disowned as belonging to his apprenticeship. This stage ended in 1974, when *Faith and the Good Thing* came out, followed by *Oxherding Tale* in 1982 and *The Sorcerer's Apprentice*, nominated for the PEN/Faulkner Award, PEN American Center, in 1987. In 1990, Johnson published his best novel to date, *Middle Passage*, a National Book Award winner. Two years before *Middle Passage*, Indiana University Press printed *Being and Race: Black Writing since 1970*. Finally, *Black*

Men Speaking, an anthology on African American maleness and its challenges, which Johnson edited with John McCluskey, Jr., came out in 1997. Other works include drawings, screenplays, articles, editorial projects such as *Callaloo*'s 1984 special issue on fiction, which Johnson guest edited, and teaching. For more than two decades, Johnson has taught at University of Washington, where he has been professor of English since 1982 and served as director of the University's Creative Writing Program.

MAJOR WORKS AND THEMES

Drawing on Maurice Merleau-Ponty's phenomenological view of language as a pathway to the "Other" (*The Prose of the World*), Johnson works out his own theory of writing in *Being and Race*. "To read," he argues, "is to inhabit the role and real place of others"; "to write," he adds, "is a stranger experience yet, for it involves a corresponding act of self-surrender such that my perceptions and experiences are allowed to coincide with those who came before me and despoiled words, shaped their sense and use" (39). It follows that insofar as it entails dealing with language, writing also presupposes confronting the "others." These have used and misused the linguistic material before and thereby left their marks— their values, meanings, and viewpoints—on words. As Johnson stresses, "like a palimpsest, the word is a tissue of interpretations, . . . the experience, the sight (broad or blind) of others formed into word" (39).

Such a decidedly "palimpsestic" view of language and cultural history in general shapes Johnson's entire work. Grounded in an intersubjective view of the literature, his novels and tales set up a vivid dialogue with literary history and forms, with those countless "dead artists" whose names are inscribed in the "graveyard" of the writer's own prose. Lifted from André Malraux's *The Voices of Silence* (*Being and Race* 52), this "spectral" trope of cultural continuity captures the essence of Johnson's "postmodern," programmatic intertextuality. Importantly, he sees literature as a ceaseless exchange, a steady reading and rereading of the past. New writing refashions this past, endowing it with novel meanings in an attempt, as literary as political, to write off, as it were, the negativity embedded in texts and in the words that constitute them. For, as Johnson contends, words are anything but innocent; many of them may be "male-chauvinist," "bigoted," or simply "blind" (39).

The struggle to displace the words' "blindness" and the spell it casts on people subtly lies at the core of Johnson's literary project. To prevent this project from slipping "toward dogma that ends the process of literary discovery, . . . toward Kitsch" (29), the "counteracting of cultural lies" likely to engender new images and allow people to control their own representations must take into consideration that no experience, the African American included, is "raw" (31), that is, "[un]*interpreted* by others" (4). This means that the writer cannot but address the historical mediation of this experience, unwrapping and recycling the various cultural packages in which the "facts" come. In Johnson's work, this involves the daring, both serious and playful, flaunting of a twofold conversation: first, with the African American tradition, with the folktale, the slave narrative, William Wells Brown's "pivotal book" (7), *Clotelle* (1853), as well as with great modernists like James Baldwin, Richard Wright, and Ralph Ellison*; second, but equally important to Johnson, the African American writer cannot avoid the dialogue with the white epic and philosophical tradition since "cross-cultural fertilization" is the one that "keeps the form alive" (*Being and Race* 47).

Faith and the Good Thing shows how instrumental cross-cultural exchange and intertextuality can be to Johnson's attempt to "clarify" (3) the African American experience. One could identify at least three cultural layers in the novel's structure. The first and probably the deepest contains black mythology and humor, witchcraft and necromantic practices, folktales and storytelling styles. The second, also interweaving African American materials, marks off an exclusively literary zone: Johnson's ironic dialogue with Wright and, more specifically, Ellison's *Invisible Man*. The third carries out the author's intervention in the picaro tradition, a genre informing the plot of virtually all of Johnson's narratives; it is also here that Johnson takes up, albeit in a roundabout way, literary figures such as Dreiser and Melville.

The protagonist of the novel is a black woman picaro, Faith. "Signifyin(g)," as Henry Louis Gates would put it, on Dreiser's Carrie and Wright's *The Outsider*, Faith moves from southern Georgia to Chicago after her mother's death, seeking a better life and the "Good Thing" lost since the mythic dawn of the world. Faith's faith is both representative and symbolic, her story foregrounding the traumas of the Great Migration as well as "the winter of the Age of Reason" (*Faith* 192). Blending the allegoric suggestiveness of the classical quest romance, early twentieth-century naturalism, and postmodern juggling of philosophical vocabularies, Johnson's novel sheds light on the excesses of rationality. Through its rampaging "curse of questioning" (30), the latter divests the world of its poetic depth. Faith's search "for absolute certainty" (93) ironically takes her through a series of urban ordeals, including a rape in a cockroach motel and a boring marriage to Maxwell, a petty bourgeois journalist who cares only about his career. Holmes, former lover and "post-realistic" painter, links her to the past she has tried to flee. Finally, Faith returns to Georgia, completing the narrative loop by putting on the Swamp Woman's "skin." Thus, she becomes the werewitch herself, after she "suffered several roles: the innocent, the whore, the housewife" (195). Paradoxically, one could argue that the novel's moral is pretty transparent, though the Swamp Woman, apparently Johnson's philosophical alter ego, rejects crystal-clear, univocal truths. There is no ultimate "Good Thing" "binding" us all and whose possession will bring us the solution to our problems, including the blacks' "bondage." Yet the quest for the "Good Thing" does matter as such a quest is bound to take narrative form. In doing so it becomes a story beautiful in its epic development and therefore meaningful. This tale is ultimately (the) *good* (Thing) as it gives unique shape to the possibility somebody's search for absolute truth takes.

Using as an epigraph the Kafkian hypothesis of "the existence of different subjects in the same human being," *Oxherding Tale* moves along similar philosophical lines. The picaresque structure also informs the plot, but the dominant genre is this time an autobiographic narrative combining mid-nineteenth-century African American sources (especially Frederick Douglass) and playfully fictionalized autobiography in the Lawrence Sterne tradition (Coleman 634). Like *Tristram Shandy*, the novel opens with the story of the narrating protagonist's conception. The narration of Andrew Hawkins' "origins" is characteristic of Johnson's cross-cultural strategy as the writer employs a prestigious intertext to play out miscegenation anxieties. Conceived through a trick as the son of a white woman and her slave, Hawkins is symbolically cross-fertilized by two cultural traditions: the picaro and the trickster. He lives under different names, goes places and appears able to embody strikingly diverse facets of "Being." He is successively a servant at Cripplegate, the South Carolina cotton plantation where Ezekiel tutors him in the liberal arts; "in the service of the senses," that is, Flo Hatfield's senses, at Leviathan; a runaway hunted by Soulcatcher; and a husband of Peggy Undercliff. His "identity" is dynamic, hard to pin down, as he is able to pass for a white man into whose "World" he works an "unmarked" passage (128). In fact, on one hand, his story mounts a radical challenge to "the belief in personal identity," as the Vet tells Hawkins (*Oxherding Tale* 58). The latter's counterargument sounds rather unconvincing—and we do glimpse here Johnson's long-standing critique of racial "essentialism." On the other hand, even though there are no " 'Negroes,' . . . [no] *essences*" (146), Hawkins' identity preserves its "difference," as Soulcatcher's relentlessness painfully proves. Johnson seems to imply, however, that, even though we remain inescapably different, we are deeply engaged in an unremitting "production" of our difference: we are different in terms of race, gender, or class, but we embody distinct possibilities within these categories as well.

At the "metafictional" level, the author is deeply concerned with earning, so to speak, such an "intracategorial" difference. He plays on Western (Schopenhauerian, Marxist, transcendentalist) and African American notions and rhetorical modes alike. Chapters 8 ("On the Nature of Slave Narratives") and 11 ("The Manumission of the First-Person Viewpoint") open up brief, yet dense, "intermissions" where Johnson theorizes the fundamental link between the bondage of slavery and the obedience to traditional literary forms. Once again, the Self comes out as "a palimpsest, interwoven with everything" (152). This postulates a postmodern mobility of the narrative viewpoint and lack of stylistic inhibition—in brief, a radical "liberation" (153) from the canonical model of the slave narrative, which, according to the author/narrator, ties in with the protagonist's impending emancipation.

Replacing autobiography, the diary, the logbook, and travel narrative mold the Johnsonian theme of the African American picaro in *Middle Passage*, another "anti-essentialist space in which the individual character is a shape-shifting construct" (Nielsen 167). Rutherford Calhoon, the first-person narrator and main hero, definitely follows in Andrew Hawkins' footsteps. A "petty thief" from Illinois, Calhoon is attracted to New Orleans' "exotic fringes of life" (2). He stows away, though, on a slave clipper, the *Republic*, on April 14, 1830, to evade Isadora Bailey, whom Philippe "Papa" Zeringue, the local "Ur-Type of Gangster" (13), has decided that Calhoon must join in holy matrimony. The stowaway's transatlantic exploits deftly rewrite Melville's *Moby-Dick* and *Benito Cereno*: the *Republic* recalls the *Pequod* (but also Poe's errant ships); Captain Ebezener Falcon comes across in his journals as "possessing a few of the solitary virtues and the entire twisted will of Puritanism" (51); his weird anatomy and drive of "Americanizing" the planet ironically recast Ahab's obsessions. Falcon's hunting the *black(s)*—not the *white*—rests, according to him, on the transcendental makeup of the human mind, that is, on the split between subject and object. On the way back from Africa, though, the "objects," Johnson's mysterious tribe, Allmuseri, take over the ship. But, like in *Benito Cereno*, the Africans are unable to "govern" it. The *Republic* is slowly falling apart and drifts off its course; cannibalistic acts testing the "limit of bein' human" (174) and similar ordeals follow suit until the ship goes down. If Ishmael survives on Queequeg's coffin, Calhoon stays afloat on a hammock until is taken aboard by the *Juno*. Here, deus ex machina, he bumps into "Papa," about to marry Isadora himself. Calhoon pulls out his logbook, which shows that Papa was among the *Republic*'s shareholders, stops the wedding, and regains his faithful Penelope.

Published in 1986, *The Sorcerer's Apprentice* gathers "tales and conjurations" that appeared between 1977 and 1983. The stories take up virtually all of the themes and techniques of Johnson's longer pieces: the enigmatic Allmuseri; the relations between the Other and the Self; the pedagogical narrative and its moral (Mingo turns into a replica of his teacher-master in "The Education of Mingo"); the technique of rewriting and allusion (involving Defoe's *Robinson Crusoe* and Mary Shelley's *Frankenstein*); tongue-in-cheek philosophical arguments ("Popper's Disease") and Italo Calvino-like science fictional parables of race; irony, pastiche, sorcery, and their limits ("The Sorcerer's Apprentice").

CRITICAL RECEPTION

Calling Johnson a "Voodoo Calvino," a *San Francisco Examiner* critic contends in a blurb on *The Sorcerer's Apprentice*'s back cover that *Middle Passage*'s author is "one of the best [writers] we've got, black or white." This opinion is definitely spreading: Johnson is emerging as a central figure of the contemporary canon, African American and American at large. *Oxherding Tale* and *Middle Passage* are widely taught, and his insightful essays are getting increasing attention, beginning to dispel critics' impression that he is still a disproportionately underread author. Aside from reviews, dictionary entries, and less accessible dissertations, a growing number of cogent and learned articles have appeared since the late 1980s showing a largely sympathetic approach to Johnson's work. Jonathan Little, also the author of an interview with Johnson, deals, for example, with *Oxherding Tale*'s main hero as a "palimpsest," but advancing the somewhat problematic hypothesis of Johnson's "relatively apolitical notions of individual identity" (10). Discussing the same text, Jennifer Hayward dwells on the construction of the feminine, arguing that the novel aims at "reconcil[ing] not only the white–black but also the male–female and master–slave splits" (702). Also with reference to *Oxherding Tale*, William Gleason analyzes in his turn Johnson's endeavors to move beyond black fiction's expected themes and style. One could call this effort Johnson's own "manumission" campaign, similar to the narrative emancipation advocated in *Oxherding Tale* and analyzed, among others, by Klaus Benesch. Ashraf H. A. Rushdy, S. X. Goudie, Aldon L. Nielsen, and critics like Coleman, Scott, and Walby, whose contributions make up the core of *African American Review*'s special topic issue on Johnson, focus on themes of identity, freedom, and textual reappropriation in the author's most-read texts. It is likely that the same works and the same subjects will keep attracting commentators' interest, giving rise to a fast expanding body of sophisticated criticism.

BIBLIOGRAPHY

Works by Charles Johnson

Fictional Works

Faith and the Good Thing. New York: Viking Press, 1974.
Oxherding Tale. Bloomington: Indiana University Press, 1982.
The Sorcerer's Apprentice. Tales and Conjurations. New York: Atheneum, 1986; 2d ed. New York: Penguin, 1994.
Middle Passage. New York: Atheneum, 1990.

Other Works

Black Humor. Drawings. Chicago: Johnson, 1970.
Charlie's Pad. Drawing program, PBS, 1971.
Half-Past Nation-Time. Drawings. Chicago: Johnson, 1972.
Charlie Smith and the Fritter Tree. Screenplay, PBS, 1978a.
"Philosophy and Black Fiction." *Obsidian: Black Literature in Review* 6.1–2 (Spring–Summer 1980): 55–61.
"Whole Sight: Notes on New Black Fiction." *Callaloo* 7.3 (Fall 1984): 1–6. Special issue: Fiction. Charles Johnson, guest ed.
Being and Race: Black Writing since 1970. Bloomington and Indianapolis: Indiana University Press, 1988.
And John Allman. *Booker.* Teleplay. Prod. Whitney Green and Avon Kirkland. Dir. Stan Lathan. New Images Productions, 1990.
"The Second Front: A Reflection on Milk Bottles, Male Elders, the Enemy Within, Bar Mitzvah, and Martin Luther King, Jr." Ed. Charles Johnson and John McCluskey, Jr. *Black Men Speaking.* Bloomington and Indianapolis: Indiana University Press, 1997. 177–188.

And John McCluskey, Jr., eds. Art by Jacob Lawrence. *Black Men Speaking*. Bloomington and Indianapolis: Indiana University Press, 1997.

Studies of Charles Johnson

Benesch, Klaus. "The Manumission of the First-Person Viewpoint: Identität und Autobiographie in Charles Johnson's *Oxherding Tale*." *Arbeiten aus Anglistik und Amerikanistik* 17.1 (1992): 3–22.

Coleman, James W. "Charles Johnson's Quest for Black Freedom in *Oxherding Tale*." *African American Review* 29.4 (Winter 1995): 631–644.

Gleason, William. "The Liberation of Perception: Charles Johnson's *Oxherding Tale*." *Black American Literature Forum* 25.4 (Winter 1991): 705–728.

Goudie, S. X. " 'Leavin' a Mark on the Wor(l)d': Marksmen and Marked Men in *Middle Passage*." *African American Review* 29.1 (Spring 1995): 109–122.

Hayward, Jennifer. "Something to Serve: Constructs of the Feminine in Charles Johnson's *Oxherding Tale*." *Black American Literature Forum* 25.4 (Winter 1991): 689–703.

Little, Jonathan. "Charles Johnson's Revolutionary *Oxherding Tale*." *Studies in American Fiction* 19.2 (Autumn 1991): 141–151.

———. "An Interview with Charles Johnson." *Contemporary Literature* 34.2 (Summer 1993): 159–181.

McCullough, Ken. "Reflections on Film, Philosophy, and Fiction: An Interview with Charles Johnson." *Callaloo* 1.4 (Oct. 1978b): 118–128.

Nielsen, Aldon L. *Writing between the Lines: Race and Intertextuality*. Athens and London: University of Georgia Press, 1994. 157–171.

Rushdy, Ashraf H. A. "The Phenomenology of the Allmuseri: Charles Johnson and the Subject of the Narrative of Slavery." *African American Review* 26.3 (Fall 1992): 373–394.

———. "The Properties of Desire: Forms of Slave Identity in Charles Johnson's *Middle Passage*." *Arizona Quarterly* 50.2 (Summer 1994): 73–108.

Scott, Daniel M., III. "Interrogating Identity: Appropriation and Transformation in *Middle Passage*." *African American Review* 29.4 (Winter 1995): 645–655.

Walby, Celestin. "The African Sacrificial Kinship Ritual and Johnson's *Middle Passage*." *African American Review* 29.4 (Winter 1995): 657–669.

GAYL JONES
(1949–   )

Kimberly N. Brown

BIOGRAPHY

Gayl Jones remains a literary enigma. Born in Lexington, Kentucky, on 23 November 1949, one can't help but wonder what influences prompt Jones to continuously delve into the fantastical and sometimes psychotic nether regions of her characters' minds. In an interview with Claudia Tate, Tate states that Jones "refuses to divulge additional biographical information [other than her birthplace and date and only slight information about her college career], contending that her work must live independently of its creator, that it must sustain its own character and artistic autonomy" (*Black American Literary Forum* 142). Consequently, her biography seems somewhat impersonal and reads like a curriculum vita, charting her scholarly and literary accomplishments.

We do know, however, that Jones attended segregated schools until the tenth grade. In an interview with African American poet and college mentor Michael Harper, Jones explains that the inferiority of Kentucky's segregated school system caused her "language/word foundations" to be oral rather than written. Jones states, "But I was also learning how to read and write at the same time I was listening to people talk. In the beginning, *all* of the richness came from people rather than from books because in those days you were reading some really unfortunate kinds of books in school" (Harper 352). Despite the inadequacies of her precollege education, Jones has been writing fiction since the second grade and credits her fifth grade teacher, Mrs. Hodges, who encouraged her to read by making students listen to music before writing.

Jones' decision to become a storyteller (a term she prefers because it implies a privileging of African oral traditions) could almost be seen as hereditary, something passed down from her matrilineal heritage, given that her grandmother,

Amanda Wilson, was a playwright and her mother, Lucille Jones, was a fiction writer whose work appeared frequently in *Obsidian*. Her mother would also read children stories she wrote specifically for both Jones and her brother, Franklin.

Kentucky, where Jones learned to write fiction by listening to the rhythms and cadences of "grown-folks" talk, serves as the site for much of her work. Jones didn't leave Kentucky until she entered Connecticut College, where she graduated with a B.A. in English in 1971. Jones obtained an M.A. and a D.A., both in creative writing, from Brown University in 1973 and 1974, respectively. Jones' literary career begins with her play *Chile Woman*; its attention to blues and the legacy of slavery sets the stage for her first book, *Corregidora*. *Corregidora* was published in 1975, when Jones was only twenty-six, with Toni Morrison* serving as her editor. Also in 1975 Jones became an assistant professor in the English Department at the University of Michigan. While at Michigan, Jones was a recipient of the Howard Foundation Award in 1975 and won a National Endowment for the Arts Grant in 1976. She was a member of the faculty at Michigan until February 1985, when she disappeared from the publishing arena and the public eye until she resurfaced in 1991 with the publishing of *Liberating Voices*, a scholarly work dealing with the oral tradition found in the works of several African American writers. Since *Liberating Voices*, Jones has contributed several reprinted stories and some new stories and essays to several anthologies like *Ancestral House* (1995) and journals like *Callaloo*.

MAJOR WORKS AND THEMES

With her play *Chile Woman*, Jones begins her exploration of slavery's legacy to twentieth-century African Americans and marks her growing interest in the blues. Both *Chile Woman* (1974) and *Corregidora* (1975) present characters who are blues singers and who must come to terms with their past. The desire to have her characters come to terms with their past, whether it be the legacy of slavery and/or a personal history of sexual abuse, are both recurring themes in Jones' work. In *Corregidora* specifically, Jones introduces us to Ursa Corregidora, a 1940s blues singer who must forever carry the name and story of her Portuguese great-grandfather, a slave owner who fathered both Ursa's grandmother and mother and who used her great-grandmother and grandmother as prostitutes. Ursa is charged with the mission to "make generations" so that the story of their abuse will always live on. However, when Ursa loses her womb after her husband, Mutt, pushes her down the steps, she is forced to reevaluate her position as the preserver of slavery's legacy. Through singing the blues, Ursa expresses the pain and brutality of love, interweaving both slavery's past with her love and final reconciliation with Mutt after twenty-two years.

The legacy of the blues is found not just in the occupations of Jones' characters but also in the structural form of her work. Jones structures her texts in what she calls an "improvisational" manner reminiscent of the blues to flesh out relationships between women and men from the specific viewpoint of the woman. Jones' use of the first-person narration in most of her works demonstrates her concern with the orality and "psychology" of language. Her use of the first person is also a variation of the naturalistic style in that Jones refuses to make any judgments of her characters save what they make themselves. Jones also states that she avoids "normal" characters, possibly because of her interest in abnormal psychology. *Eva's Man* (1976) is improvisational in a different manner from that of her earlier works. Although the reader is still subjected to the disjointed narration that was found in *Corregidora*, we are not supposed to trust Eva as a narrator. Placed in a psychiatric ward after Eva has bitten off the penis of her lover, who had kept her locked up in a one-room apartment to use for his sexual pleasure, Eva is definitely not a reliable narrator. The novel is told from Eva's point of view and signifies a shifting of time and space; Eva's memory of others and her interactions with them melt together in a deliberate and incomprehensible fashion. Jones has stated that constructing Eva's narrative in this manner was a way of granting Eva a sense of "autonomy": Eva gains strength by telling her story in the fashion she chooses. A bizarre character, to say the least, Eva fulfills what Jones sees as the purpose of fiction, to ask, rather than answer, questions. In an interview with Claudia Tate, Jones states, "The question that the listener would continually hear would be: How much of Eva's story is true and how much is deliberately not true; that is, how much of a game is she playing with her listeners/ psychiatrists/others? And finally how much of her story is her own fantasy of the past?" (143).

In her short story collection, *White Rat* (1977), Jones continues the blues and jazz motifs and the focus on the orality of language by having ten of the twelve stories told in the first person. Again we see the themes of madness in "The Return: A Fantasy," while "Jevata" deals with a dysfunctional male–female relationship.

Song for Anniho (1981) and *Xarque and Other Poems* (1985) both are book-length narrative poems that revisit the Brazilian history first mentioned in *Corregidora*. Set in the late seventeenth century on the Palmares maroon settlement, *Song for Anniho* tells the story through the voice of Almeyda, who sings about being reunited with her husband, Anniho. We learn that Almeyda was separated from him after a Portuguese slave master cuts off her breasts and throws her off a cliff. Again, the theme of not forgetting one's past resurfaces with Almeyda's grandmother's instructions not to forget her African heritage. *Xarque* continues the story of Almeyda by focusing on her granddaughter Euclida and examines what happens when unity among African people begins to disintegrate.

CRITICAL RECEPTION

To date, critical assessments of Gayl Jones' work focuses primarily on her novels *Corregidora* and *Eva's Man* and her collection of short stories, *White Rat*. Critical reviews of *Corregidora* were quite favorable; some critics, however, were disappointed in the lack of physical descriptions of her characters. Many critics believed the novel to be about sexual warfare; however, in her analysis, Tate differs by stating that the novel delivers a realistic and unromanticized portrayal of love and that it is about the "dialects of love." Tate also identifies *Corregidora*'s structure as containing three "concentrical circles" of memory that revolve around the personal histories, told in three parts, of Ursa's great-grandmother and grandmother, her mother, and, finally, Ursa herself.

Reactions to *Eva's Man* were not so flattering and are reminiscent of earlier reactions to Richard Wright's *Native Son*. This is perhaps because of Jones' almost naturalistic style in depicting a character who possesses unflinching candor about sexuality and sexual violence and, in part, because of the perceived negative images of the black characters. June Jordan, for example, is aggressive in express-ing her disappointment with *Eva's Man* and even likens Eva to Wright's "Bigger Thomas," "minus the enemy white world." Jordan states that *Eva's Man* is "the blues that lost control. This is the rhythmic, monotone lamentation of one woman, Eva Medina, who is nobody I have ever known" (37). Jordan feels that not only does the novel re-inscribe negative stereotype of the black woman as " 'crazy whore/castrating bitch,' " but it also misrepresents gender relations within African American communities. Darryl Pinckney also chides Jones for her neg-ative depictions of blacks, although he is mainly concerned with her depiction of black men. He states that "Gayl Jones's novels are, finally, indictments against black men" (27).

White Rat received mixed reviews; many found the characters weak and thought the short story format didn't leave enough room for growth. With the emergence of *Callaloo*'s special section on Jones, however, we see a resurgence of interest in her work, not to mention a reassessment of her novels and poetry. The *Callaloo* section features a new interview with Jones, conducted by Charles Rowell, as well as Trudier Harris' brilliant analysis of *Song for Anniho*.

BIBLIOGRAPHY

Works by Gayl Jones

Chile Woman. *Shubert Playbook Series* 2.5 (1974).
B.O.P. *(Blacks on Paper)*. Providence, RI: Brown University Press, 1975a.
Corregidora. Boston: Beacon Press, 1975b.
Eva's Man. Boston: Beacon Press, 1976.
White Rat: Short Stories. Boston: Northeastern University Press, 1977.
Song for Anniho. Detroit: Lotus Press, 1981.
The Hermit Woman: Poems. Detroit: Lotus Press, 1983.
Xarque and Other Poems. Detroit: Lotus Press, 1985.
Liberating Voices: Oral Tradition in African American Literature. Cambridge: Harvard Uni-
      versity Press, 1991.

Studies of Gayl Jones

Ash, Susan. " 'All the Fraught Politics': Race, Gender, and the Female Traveler." *SPAN: Journal of the South Pacific Association Commonwealth Literature and Language Studies* 36 (1993): 347–56.

Barksdale, Richard K. "Castration Symbolism in Recent Black American Fiction." *College Language Association Journal* 29.4 (1986): 400–413.

Bell, Roseann P. "Gayl Jones: A Voice in the Whirlwind." *Studia Africana* 1.1 (1977).

———. "Gayl Jones Takes a Look at *Corregidora*: An Interview." *Sturdy Black Bridges: Vision of Black Women in Literature.* Ed. Bettye J. Parker, Roseann P. Bell, and Beverly Guy-Sheftall. Garden City, NY: Doubleday (Anchor), 1979. 282–87.

Byerman, Keith. "Black Vortex: The Gothic Structure of *Eva's Man.*" *MELUS* 7.4 (1980): 93–101.

———. "Intense Behaviors: The Use of the Grotesque in *The Bluest Eye* and *Eva's Man.*" *College Language Association Journal* 25.4 (1982): 447–57.

Coser, Stelamaris. *Bridging the Americas: The Literature of Paule Marshall, Toni Morrison, and Gayl Jones.* Philadelphia: Temple University Press, 1995.

Davidson, Carol Margaret. " 'Love 'em and Lynch 'em': The Castration Motif in Gayl Jones's *Eva's Man.*" *African American Review (AAR)* 29.3 (1995): 393–410.

Dixon, Melvin. "Singing a Deep Song: Language as Evidence in the Novels of Gayl Jones." *Black Women Writers (1950–1980): A Critical Evaluation.* Ed. Mari Evans. Garden City, NY: Anchor-Doubleday, 1984. 236–48.

———. *Ride Out the Wilderness: Geography and Identity in African-American Literature.* Urbana: University of Chicago Press, 1987.

Draper, James P. ed. *Black Literary Criticism.* Vol. 2. Detroit: Gale Research, 1992.

Dubey, Maduh. "Gayl Jones and the Matrilineal Metaphor of Tradition." *Signs: Journal of Women in Culture and Society* 2.2 (1995): 245–67.

Gottfried, Amy S. "Angry Acts: Silence, Speech, and Song in Gayl Jones's *Corregidora.*" *African American Review (AAR)* 28.4 (1994): 559–70.

Harper, Michael S. "Gayl Jones: An Interview." *Massachusetts Review: A Quarterly of Literature, the Arts, and Public Affairs* 18 (1971): 692–715.

———. "Gayl Jones: In Interview." *Chant of Saints: A Gathering of African American Literature, Art, and Scholarship.* Ed. Michael S. Harper, Robert B. Stepto, and John Hope Franklin. Urbana: University of Illinois Press, 1979. 352–75.

Harris, Janice. "Gayl Jones's *Corregidora.*" *Frontiers: A Journal of Women Studies* 5.3 (1980): 1–5.

Harris, Trudier. "A Spiritual Journey: Gayl Jones's Song for Anninho." *Callaloo: A Journal of African-American and African Arts and Letters* 5.3 (1982): 105–11.

Hyman, Rebecca. "Women as Figures of Exchange in Gayl Jones's *Corregidora.*" *Xanadu: A Literary Journal* 14 (1991): 40–51.

Jordan, June. Rev. of *Eva's Man. The New York Times Book Review* (16 May 1976): 37.

Kester, Gunilla Theander. "The Forbidden Fruit and Female Disorderly Eating: Three Versions of Eve." *Disorderly Eaters: Texts in Self-Empowerment.* Ed. Lilian R. Furst and Peter W. Graham. University Park: Penn State University. 231–40.

Lee, Valerie Gray. "The Use of the Folktale in Novels by Black Women Writers." *College Language Association Journal* 23 (1980): 266–72.

Lionnet, Francoise. "Geographies of Pain: Captive Bodies and Violent Acts in the Fictions of Myriam Warner-Vieyra, Gayl Jones, and Bessie Head." *Callaloo: A Journal of African-American and African Arts and Letters* 16.1 (1993): 132–52.

———. *Postcolonial Representations: Women, Literature, Identity.* Ithaca, NY: Cornell University Press, 1995.

McKible, Adam. " 'These Are the Faces of the Darky's History': Thinking History and Reading Names in Four African American Texts." *African American Review (AAR)* 28.2 (1994): 223–35.

Pinckney, Darryl. *Review of Eva's Man. The New Republic* (19 June 1976): 27.

Pullin, Faith. "Landscapes of Reality: The Fiction of Contemporary Afro-American Women." In *Black Fiction: New Studies in the Afro-American Novel since 1945.* Ed. Robert A. Lee. New York: Barnes and Noble, 1980. 173–203.

Robinson, Sally. *Engendering the Subject: Gender and Self-Representation in Contemporary Women's Fiction.* Albany: State University of New York Press, 1991.

Rowell, Charles H. "An Interview with Gayl Jones." *Callaloo: A Journal of African-American and African Arts and Letters* 5.3 (1982): 32–53.

Simon, Bruce. "Traumatic Repetition: Gayl Jones's *Corregidora*." *Race Consciousness: African-American States for the New Century.* New York: New York University Press, 1997.

Smith, Valerie, ed. *African American Writers.* New York: Charles Scribner's Sons, 1991.

Tate, Claudia. "*Corregidora*: Ursa's Blues Medley" followed by "An Interview with Gayl Jones." *Black American Literature Forum* 13 (1979): 139–48.

———. "Gayl Jones." *Black Women Writers at Work.* Ed. Claudia Tate. New York: Continuum, 1983. 89–99.

Ward, Jerry W., Jr. "Escape from Trublem: The Fiction of Gayl Jones." *Callaloo: A Journal of African-American and African Arts and Letters* 5.3 (1982): 95–104.

Weixlmann, Joe. "A Gayl Jones Bibliography." *Callaloo: A Journal of African-American and African Arts and Letters* 7.1 (1984): 119–31.

Wilcox, Janelle. "The Reception and Reappraisal of Gayl Jones's Novels: An Annotated Bibliography of Reviews and Criticism." *Bulletin of Bibliography* 52.2 (1995): 113–20.

———. "Resistant Silence, Resistant Subject: (Re)Reading Gayl Jones's *Eva's Man*." *Bodies of Writing, Bodies in Performance.* Ed. Thomas Foster, Carol Siegel and Ellen E. Berry. New York: New York University Press, 1996. 72–96.

JUNE JORDAN
(1936–   )

Kimberly N. Brown

BIOGRAPHY

Born in Harlem on July 9, 1936, to Jamaican immigrants Mildred and Granville Jordan, June Jordan grew up in the Bedford-Stuyvesant section of Brooklyn and began writing poetry at the age of seven. Her father first introduced her to the "Word" through the Scriptures, Shakespeare, Edgar Allan Poe, and Paul Laurence Dunbar's southern dialect poetry. These men, most of whom were white, were to serve as Jordan's model of the poetic greatness to which she aspired. At an early age, Jordan was left to reconcile her desire to master the Word with the realities of being a black woman-child. Given few models that resembled her, Jordan found her own voice in the rhythms of neighborhood speech and in her favorite uncle's mastery of black English in his storytelling.

In 1953, Jordan graduated from Northfield School for Girls in Massachusetts after transferring there in her sophomore year. Upon graduation, Jordan returned to New York City to attend Barnard College, where she met Michael Meyer, a white Columbia University student whom she later married in 1955. In 1958, Jordan gave birth to Christopher David Meyer, their only son. Jordan and Meyer divorced in 1965, although they had already been separated because of Meyer's decision to attend graduate school at the University of Chicago. Throughout the 1960s, Jordan supported herself and her son by publishing stories and poems in various periodicals and also by becoming assistant to the producer of the film *The Cool World* (1963), set in Harlem and centered around the black youth of the neighborhood.

The year 1966 marked a turning point in Jordan's life: her mother committed suicide. The same year also marks the start of her academic career as a professor of English at the City University of New York, where she counted Toni Cade

Bambara,* Barbara Christian, Addison Gayle, Jr., David Henderson, Audre Lorde,* Ray Patterson, and Mina Shaughnessy among her intellectual colleagues. The publication of Jordan's third book of poetry, *New Days*, in 1974 was released the same year as her father's death and includes a dedication to his memory.

Since the publication of her first work, *Who Look at Me* (1969), Jordan has continued to demonstrate her versatility and brilliance in writing not only poetry but children's novels and essays. In 1969, Jordan won a Rockefeller grant for creative writing, and in 1971 *His Own Where*, a novel written for young adults entirely in black English, was hailed as one of the year's outstanding works by the *New York Times*. Currently, Jordan is a professor of African American and women's studies at the University of California, Berkeley.

MAJOR WORKS AND THEMES

In the foreword of the 1995 edition of her book of essays, *Civil Wars*, Jordan states, "Early on, the scriptural concept that 'in the beginning was the Word and the Word was with God and the Word was God'—the idea that the word could represent and then deliver into reality what the word symbolized—this possibility of language, of writing, seemed to me to be magical and basic and irresistible" (xii). Jordan's writing exhibits not only the "possibility of language" but also the power of the "word" to effect change. Jordan fuses art with politics by showing readers the "intimate face of universal struggle"—for writing to be effective, the author or poet must participate in a conscious exploration of her connection to the larger world.

The themes that arise from Jordan's poetry can also be found in her critical works, as well as in works written for children. Jordan is concerned with the themes of black subjectivity, the power of black love, violence against women, the diasporan link between African Americans and other Third World peoples, and the relevance of black English as an expression of an African American consciousness.

Jordan's novel *His Own Where* (1971) demonstrates the weighted emphasis she places on the relevancy of black English by electing to create an omniscient narrator who speaks in the urban black dialect of Jordan's own Bedford-Stuyvesant neighborhood. The effect is a poetic rendering of the story of a boy's struggling to find his place in the world and a safe place for loving in an often cruel city, "his own where."

The narrative centers around Buddy Rivers, a sixteen-year-old boy who must grow up quickly, having been abandoned by his mother at an early age and after his father, who raised him, has been critically injured after being hit by a car. While visiting his father in the hospital, Buddy meets Angela Figueroa, the overprotected daughter of his father's nurse.

As their romance blossoms, so do the suspicions of Mrs. Figueroa. When she tells Angela's father that she suspects that the two have become intimate, he beats Angela so severely that she escapes to Buddy's house, and he, in turn, takes her to the hospital. As a result, Angela is placed in a girls' shelter, and the rest of her siblings are scattered in foster homes around the city.

What is fascinating about *His Own Where* is that Jordan manages to capture the idealism of youth amid the grim realities of child abuse and city living. On a weekend visit, Angela decides to stay with Buddy after facing the cold shoulder of her own mother. Buddy now lives in the house he once shared with his father alone and has been in the process of modestly remodeling the house. Their relationship is finally consummated, and together they plan a future. The story ironically ends in the cemetery—the physical manifestation of Buddy's "Where." Buddy and Angela contemplate building a family and new life amid the dead. In *His Own Where*, the reader can become caught up in the optimism of Buddy and Angela and leave the novel thinking, like the characters, that anything is possible.

CRITICAL RECEPTION

Perhaps because *His Own Where* is a novel for young adults, critical assessments of the book have been limited to reviews written shortly after the novel's publication and to an in-depth biobibliographical work, *Afro-American Writers after 1955: Dramatists and Prose Writers*, in which Peter Erickson demonstrates the connection between Jordan's preoccupation with urban renewal, as evidenced by her collaboration on a project to redesign Harlem during the mid-1960s, and the "apt assimilation of Jordan's architectural impulse into the medium of fiction" (155), which Erickson believes can be found in Jordan's detailed descriptions of urban decay and in Buddy's desire to remodel his house and his attempts to build a new one in an abandoned shack in the cemetery. Erickson further demonstrates that Jordan's preoccupations with urban redesign and black English are "two crucial means by which environment is aesthetically shaped" (*Afro-American Writers* 155) and that, given these preoccupations, the novel itself calls for a reevaluation of " 'realism' from the perspective of poetic vision."

Margot Heatoff questions the book's attention to realism by calling the language of the text "idealized." Heatoff also links Jordan's novels with a genre of children's books that began in the 1960s and contained "a nightmare quality of a world in which adolescents live always at the edge of breakdown and isolation." Heatoff posits these texts against books of her own childhood that ignored the harsh realities of war and the depression and opted, instead, for fantasies of grandeur. Heatoff's point is that to shield children from the world is no more realistic than to exaggerate the world's evil for children's consumption. Heatoff also doesn't see any redemption in the novel's end and reads the ending as a metaphor of death rather than the mark of a new beginning.

Heatoff's reading is balanced by that of Sarah Webster Fabio, who believes that the language is realistic and "moves freely, violating syntax to get to deeper levels of meaning" (6). Heatoff's reading also stands in stark contrast to that of Rosalind K. Goddard, who states that "it's impossible to dismiss [Buddy] as an unreal or unbelievable character" (4190) because of how thoroughly Buddy is entrenched in inner-city life. Reviewer Sidney D. Long sees *His Own Where* as a realistic portrayal of an urban love affair in which the images "never seem melodramatic or contrived" (620). Both Long and Goddard highlight the "stream-of-consciousness" style as a strength of the text that "remove(s) the barrier between words and experiences" (Long 620) and that absorbs the reader wholly into the story and Buddy's determination to make his own where.

BIBLIOGRAPHY

Works by June Jordan

Poetry and Fiction

Who Look at Me. New York: Crowell, 1969.
Soulscript; Afro-American Poetry. Garden City, NY: Doubleday, 1970.
His Own Where. New York: Crowell, 1971.
Some Changes. New York: Dutton, 1971.
Dry Victories. New York: Avon, 1972.
New Life: New Room. New York: Crowell, 1973.
New Days: Poems of Exile and Return. New York: Emerson Hall, 1974.
Niagra Falls. Huntington, NY: A Poem of the Month Club, 1977a.
Things That I Do in the Dark: Selected Poetry. New York: Random House, 1977b.
Unemployment: Monologue. New York: Out and Out Books, 1978.
Passion: New Poems, 1977–1980. Boston: Beacon Press, 1980.
Living Room: New Poems. New York: Thunder's Mouth Press, 1985.
Lyrical Campaigns: Selected Poems. London: Virago, 1989a.
Moving towards Home: Political Essays. London: Virago, 1989b.
Naming Our Destiny: New and Selected Poems. New York and St. Paul, MN: Thunder's Mouth Press, 1989c.
Kimako's Story. Boston: Houghton Mifflin, 1991.
Haruko: Love Poems. London: Virago, 1993.
I Was Looking at the Ceiling and Then I Saw the Sky: Earthquake/Romance. New York: Scribner, 1995a.
June Jordan's Poetry from the People: A Revolutionary Blueprint. New York: Routledge, 1995b.
Kissing God Goodbye: Poems: 1991–1996. New York: Anchor, 1997.

Nonfiction

Ed. *Soulscript: Afro-American Poetry.* (Anthology). Garden City, NY: Zenith, 1970.
Fannie Lou Hammer. (Biography). New York: Crowell, 1972.
"Black English: The Politics of Translation." *Library Journal* 98 (1973): 1631–1634.
"Where Is the Love?" In *In the Memory and Spirit of Frances, Zora, and Lorraine: Essays and Interviews on Black Women and Writing.* Washington, DC: Institute for the Arts and Humanities, Howard University, 1979.
Civil Wars. Boston: Beacon Press, 1981.
On Call: Political Essays. Boston: South End Press, 1985.

"The Difficult Miracle of Black Poetry in America; Or, Something like a Sonnet for Phillis Wheatley." *Massachusetts Review: A Quarterly of Literature, the Arts, and Public Affairs* 27, no. 2 (Summer 1986): 252–262.

Technical Difficulties: African-American Notes on the State of the Union. New York: Vintage Books, 1994.

"Waiting for a Taxi." In *Names We Call Home: Autobiography on Racial Identity.* New York: Routledge, 1996.

Studies of June Jordan

Abowitz, Richard. "Revolution by Search Committee." *The New Criterion* 7, no. 8 (April 1989): 30–35.

Brogan, Jacqueline Vaught. "Planets on the Table: From Wallace Stephens and Elizabeth Bishop to Adrienne Rich and June Jordan." *The Wallace Stevens Journal: A Publication of the Wallace Stevens Society* 19, no. 2 (Fall 1995): 255–278.

Carroll, Rebecca, ed. *I Know What Red Clay Looks Like: The Voice and Vision of Black American Women Writers.* New York: Carol Southern Books, 1994.

Cliff, Michelle. "The Lover: June Jordan's Revolution." *Village Voice Literary Supplement* 126, (June 1994): 27–29.

Erickson, Peter. "After Identity: A Conversation with June Jordan." *Transition: An International Review* (1994): 132–149.

———. "June Jordan." *Afro-American Writers after 1955: Dramatists and Prose Writers.* Detroit: Bruccoli Clark, 1982: 146–162.

———. "The Love Poetry of June Jordan." *Callaloo: A Journal of African-American and African Arts and Letters* 9, no. 1 (Winter 1986): 221–234.

———. "Putting Her Life on the Line—The Poetry of June Jordan, 1990." *Hurricane Alice: A Feminist Quarterly* 7, nos. 1–2 (Winter–Spring 1990): 4–5.

———. "State of the Union." *Transition: An International Review* 59 (1993): 104–109.

Fabio, Sarah Webster. Review. *New York Times Book Review.* Pt. 2. (Nov. 7, 1971): 6.

Goddard, Rosalind K. Review. *Library Journal* 96 (Dec. 15, 1971): 4, 190.

Harjo, Joy. "An Interview with June Jordan." *High Plains Literary Review* 3, no. 2 (Fall 1988): 60–76.

Heatoff, Margot. Rev. of *His Own Where. New York Times Review of Books*, 20 April 1972: 18.

Long, Sidney D. Review. *Horn Book* 47 (Dec. 1971): 620.

Pollon, Zelie. "Naming Her Destiny: June Jordan Speaks on Bisexuality." *Deneuve* 4, no. 1 (Feb. 1994): 27–28, 47.

Splawn, P. Jane. "New World Consciousness in the Poetry of Ntozake Shange and June Jordan: Two African-American Women's Responses to Expansion in the Third World." *College Language Association Journal* 39, no. 4 (June 1996): 417–432.

WILLIAM MELVIN KELLEY
(1937–)

Anissa J. Wardi

BIOGRAPHY

William Melvin Kelley was born in New York City on 1 November 1937 to William Melvin Kelley, Sr., and Narcissa Agatha (Garcia) Kelley. He grew up in the North Bronx, a predominantly Italian American community, even though his father was the editor of a Harlem-based African American newspaper, *Amsterdam News*.

Kelley was educated in private schools: he graduated from Fieldston in 1957, where he excelled in academics, sports, and student affairs, and subsequently attended Harvard University. At Harvard, Kelley had originally planned to study law but found the arts more to his liking. He took writing courses with John Hawkes and Archibald MacLeish and, in 1960, won the Dana Reed Prize for creative writing. Soon thereafter, Kelley dropped out of Harvard. At that time Kelley's parents had passed away, and Kelley turned to his maternal grandmother, Mrs. Jessie Garcia, for guidance in his career choice. Mrs. Garcia articulated a connection between her own art of making dresses and her grandson's writing, giving him strength to pursue his dream. Kelley pays tribute to the love and wisdom of his grandmother by dedicating his collection of short stories, *Dancers on the Shore*, to her.

William Melvin Kelley has been a writer in residence at the State University of New York at Geneseo and has taught at the New School for Social Research. He has also been a freelance writer. He won fellowships to the New York Writers' Conference and the Bread Loaf Writers' Conference as well as receiving the John Hay Whitney Foundation Award and Rosenthal Foundation Award of the National Institute of Arts and Letters for his first novel, *A Different Drummer*. He currently teaches at Sarah Lawrence College.

MAJOR WORKS AND THEMES

Kelley's first novel, *A Different Drummer* (a title taken from Thoreau), is a richly complex text. Set in the fictional Willson City, it is the story of a mid-twentieth-century African American man, Tucker Caliban, and the legend of his great-grandfather (the "African"). By refusing to give a proper name to this character, Kelley draws from the notion that African Americans have a common ancestor and thus a common history of resistance. The legend of the African is a powerful one: after arriving in Willson City in chains, holding a baby, he temporarily breaks free from his bondage but is shot before he has a chance to perform a mercy killing of his offspring. As a result, the African's descendants face years of enslavement.

Tucker is a sharecropper working the same land upon which his ancestors were enslaved. Hearing the beat of his forefather's drum, Tucker is compelled to purchase the land and, despite this investment, sets it ablaze. This is portrayed as a cleansing ritual, as Tucker destroys the very soil on which he and his people had been exploited and victimized. This quiet act of resistance is followed by his migration north, which is the catalyst for the mass southern exodus of all African Americans from the Deep South. Here, Kelley's text exemplifies the role of the individual in defining the course of history. This communal departure is quite metaphorical yet illustrates the power in nonviolent resistance and communal spirit. Through his provocative narrative technique, Kelley portrays the South in transition: despite the progress inspired by Tucker's heroism, the intransigence of the Old South hauntingly echoes through the final pages of the novel.

The interrelated stories in Kelley's *Dancers on the Shore* focus on two separate families: the working-class Bedlows and the middle-class Dunfords. These sixteen stories once again explore larger cultural issues by examining how individual men and women achieve identity and human dignity in a hostile and often hypocritical world. While many of the stories in this collection chronicle the racism, loneliness, and despair that circumscribe the characters' lives, the final story best articulates Kelley's early philosophy. "Cry for Me" is a powerful conclusion to the volume and also extends the narrative concern of *A Different Drummer*. Carlyle Bedlow narrates the story of his Uncle Wallace's arrival in New York City. As part of Tucker Caliban's mass exodus, Bedlow travels north to stay with his brother. This is an example of how Kelley's books intertextually call and respond to one another. This technique allows him to intricately explore the ramifications of social and historical events from one book to the next.

Wallace begins playing the blues in New York City and eventually becomes a famous musician. The overarching trope of the blues signals the importance Kelley places on African American people's recognizing their southern roots on northern soil. Wallace brings not merely the pain of the blues but the music of survival to the North. The blues, as an authentic narrative of African American experiences, provides a countertext to the faux scripts of white mass media. Thus, the collection closes with Wallace's masterful performance to a diverse crowd at

Carnegie Hall. The emotion from the music provides a catharsis for the audience: "[A]ll the rich white folks was on their feet in the aisles and their wives was hugging strangers, black and white, and taking off their jewelry and tossing it in the air and all the poor people was ignoring the jewelry, was dancing instead, and you could see everybody laughing like crazy and having the best old time ever" (199). The end of the performance finds Wallace Bedlow dead on the stage. Sacrificing himself for the community, Bedlow, like the African, becomes a mythical hero whose individual actions bring peace, if only briefly, to the community.

In *A Drop of Patience*, Kelley explores the cultural history of African Americans through the individual life of another musician, Ludlow Washington, a blind jazz instrumentalist. Kelley uses the distinctly African American art form of jazz as both theme and symbol for his second novel. At the age of five, Washington's father leaves him at an institution without any forewarning, and abdicates all responsibilities for the child. After being "signed over" to the school, the young boy's displacement in these alien surroundings is manifest when another resident (a six-year-old boy) claims ownership over Ludlow: " 'I'm your master. That means I own you' " (18). Ludlow thus lives in an allegorical state of imprisonment until he is purchased to work for a bandleader. Ludlow is pleased to leave the home, but "is left wondering how much he had been worth" (27).

He later marries and has a child but soon abandons them for the chance to perform with an accomplished singer in the North. Ludlow's life in the North is portrayed as unfulfilling, despite his success as an innovative musician. In this way, Ludlow's northward move is a symbol of urban migration. His professional achievement causes him to lose contact with his cultural heritage, an event symbolized by his affair with Ragan, a racist Euro-American woman. Ragan is also a symbol of the personal and musical exploitation of Ludlow in New York. When this woman abandons him, he has an emotional breakdown, which is literalized in a minstrel show that he performs onstage, signaling the end of his musical career and the beginning of many years in and out of mental institutions. At the end of the novel, Ludlow enjoys renewed cultural status as a jazz great, yet he refuses to capitalize on his fame by reentering the New York City music scene. Kelley's ending, while not overtly positive, does provide hope. Ludlow's return to a rural church in the South suggests a reintegration into African American folk culture, which seemingly will provide the necessary element in Ludlow's journey to wholeness. In fact, grounding his art in the culture from which it sprang removes the commercial aspect of Ludlow's success and allows his art to have a functional quality, by providing music to accompany the voices of his heritage.

Kelley's final novels, *dem* and *Dunfords Travels Everywheres*, mark a diversion from his earlier fiction. Less concerned with depicting cultural communion, these later novels nonetheless provide powerful social critiques. *dem*, a surrealistic text, explores the power of misleading narratives. Mitchell Pierce, a white advertising writer, is the central character. The cultural myths he creates in his profession symbolically mirror the racist narratives disseminated by his forefathers. The psychological damage inflicted by these stereotypes are made manifest in the vivid depiction of Mitchell's coworker, John Godwin, an ex-marine trained to kill seventy different ways with his bare hands. Turning his savagery on his own family, Godwin murders his wife and children after a seemingly benign domestic argument. Godwin and Mitchell are not merely individual characters in this text but embody the history of Euro-American domination, exploitation, and violence. Kelley indicts American society and suggests, through the life of Mitchell Pierce, that the only way to remedy this cultural inequity is for individuals to assume responsibility for their personal and collective history.

Kelley's final and most experimental novel, *Dunfords Travels Everywheres*, is a parody of James Joyce's *Finnegans Wake*. The novel begins with one of the protagonists, the Harvard-educated Chig Dunford, asleep. This symbolizes the character's lack of critical consciousness. Carlyle Bedlow, the other protagonist, is a counterpoint to this European expatriate and notably resides in Harlem.

Experimenting with unorthodox dream language and style, Kelley explores the role that language has assumed in the lives of African Americans. Kelley's overarching concern here is to catalog the history of African Americans in a language that bespeaks its diasporic complexity. In fact, the characters must abandon standard English and the values that are implicit in it in order to arrive at truths about their lives. Narrative style signals theme in this novel, as Kelley attempts to create a discourse capable of undermining the misleading texts of history and uncovering the societal truths that connect the Ivy League Chig to the streetwise Carlyle.

CRITICAL RECEPTION

Critical reaction to Kelley's work has been generally favorable. Specifically, reviews of *A Different Drummer* praise both subject and stylistics, and many state that it is the work of a promising young writer. His second work of fiction, *Dancers on the Shore*, was met with mixed reviews. Some reviewers claim that Kelley is in command of his material and is a powerful storyteller, while another, Louis Rubin, finds the collection "underdeveloped with the author having worked only at the surface of his material" (11). Similarly, while some critics claim to have been drawn into Ludlow Washington's world in *A Drop of Patience*, David Boroff, who first praises the novel as "a moving, painful and stinging experience," tempers his review in typical fashion of the time with a critique of Kelley's politics. Boroff claims that "a novel (the truism cannot be repeated too often) is not a civil rights rally" (41). Many sources, including *The New York Times Book Review*, conclude that Kelley's third novel, *dem*, raises provocative issues regarding the history of race relations in the country, and critic Houston Baker applauds Kelley's writing, stating that "*dem* is a biting, well conceived, and well executed satire" (12). Critical responses to *Dunfords Travels Everywheres* are generally in accordance. Most draw attention to the innovative language of Kelley's final novel, finding it an admirable undertaking but nevertheless difficult to understand. In this vein, Christopher Lehmann-Haupt writes that Kelley "has produced a novel as fascinating (and frustrating) as three-dimensional chess" (15).

BIBLIOGRAPHY

Works by William Melvin Kelley

A Different Drummer. 1962. New York: Doubleday, 1989.
Dancers on the Shore. 1964. Chatham, MA: Chatham Bookseller, 1973.
A Drop of Patience. 1965. Hopewell, PA: Ecco, 1995.
dem. Garden City, NY: Doubleday, 1967.
Dunfords Travels Everywheres. Garden City, NY: Doubleday, 1970.

Studies of William Melvin Kelley

Baker, Houston A., Jr. "A View of William Melvin Kelley's *dem.*" *Obsidian* 3.2 (1977): 12–16.
Boroff, David. "Ludlow Made His Own Music." Rev. of *A Drop of Patience*. *New York Times Book Review* (2 May 1965): 40–41.
Eckley, Grace. "The Awakening of Mr. Afrinnegan: Kelley's *Dunfords Travels Everywheres* and Joyce's *Finnegans Wake*." *Obsidian* 1.2 (1975): 27–41.
Faulkner, Howard J. "The Uses of Tradition: William Melvin Kelley's *A Different Drummer*." *Modern Fiction Studies* 21 (1975): 535–42.
Giles, James R. "Revolution and Myth: Kelley's *A Different Drummer* and Gaines' *The Autobiography of Miss Jane Pittman*." *Minority Voices* 1.2 (1977): 39–48.
Ingrasci, Hugh J. "Strategic Withdrawal or Retreat: Deliverance from Racial Oppression in Kelley's *A Different Drummer* and Faullkner's *Go Down, Moses*." *Studies in Black Fiction* 6.3 (1975): 1–6.
Klotman, Phyllis R. "An Examination of the Black Confidence Man in Two Black Novels: *The Man Who Cried I Am* and *dem*." *American Literature* 44 (1973): 596–611.
Lehmann-Haupt, Christopher. "Africans' Dream." Rev. of *Dunfords Travels Everywheres*. *New York Times*, 7 Sept. 1970: 15.
Rubin, Louis, Jr. "Picking Up the Beat." Rev. of *Dancers on the Shore*. *Book Week—New York Herald Tribune* (22 Mar. 1964): 11.
Thomas, H. Nigel "The Bad Nigger Figure in Selected Works of Richard Wright, William Melvin Kelley, and Ernest Gaines." *CLA Journal* 39.2 (1995): 143–64.
Weyant, Jill. "The Kelley Saga: Violence in America." *CLA Journal* 19 (1975): 210–20.
Weyl, Donald M. "The Vision of Man in the Novels of William Melvin Kelley." *Critique: Studies in Modern Fiction* 15.3 (1973): 15–33.

RANDALL KENAN
(1963–)

Chris Roark

BIOGRAPHY

Randall Kenan was born March 12, 1963, in Brooklyn and raised in Chinquapin, North Carolina. He is the author of three books, the first a novel entitled *A Visitation of Spirits* (1989), the second a collection of short stories entitled *Let the Dead Bury Their Dead* (1992), and the third a biography of James Baldwin (1994), as well as short stories published in anthologies and a few nonfiction essays.

Chinquapin is a small town in southeastern North Carolina that Kenan describes as "rural to a fault, with farms and tractors and hogs and chickens and fields of corn and tobacco. The church still occupied a place of omnipresence and order in the lives of the country folk" (Kenan, *Speak My Name* 62). Nearly all of Kenan's works are set in, or refer to, Tims Creek, North Carolina, in some respects a fictional transformation of Chinquapin. His characters draw their identity from a tightly knit community and yet also wage private battles against a place where difference is often unacceptable, especially homosexuality. Much like Zora Neale Hurston's fictional rendering of Eatonville, Kenan's work both critiques the limits of a cohesive community where older generations can inordinately dominate the younger, and religious fundamentalism is common and yet also appreciates the history and struggles of those who have lived in the fictional Tims Creek, especially as such things are embodied in, and handed down, by older characters. Kenan himself was raised primarily by older relatives, as are the two main characters of *A Visitation of Spirits*, Horace Green, a young homosexual man, and James Malachi Greene, a cousin who is now pastor of the Tims Creek Baptist Church (Kenan, *Speak My Name* 62–63).

Kenan's life as a gay African American, as he himself comments, informs the struggles of Horace (Hunt 416). Similar to James Baldwin,* Kenan, one could argue, sees the rejection of homosexuality as related to America's "greater overall fear of sex in general, as revealed in a debased notion of the relationship between the sexes and a corresponding unwillingness to accept the complexity of human behavior and possibilities" (Kenan, *Baldwin* 78). Kenan was educated at the University of North Carolina, first in physics and later in English, where he worked his way through the honors writing program and graduated with a B.A. in 1984. His works sometimes present what are ostensibly scientific perspectives toward the environment, for example, the disquisition about persimmons in the final story of *Let the Dead Bury Their Dead* or the specifics of slaughtering a hog or of a gunshot wound to the head, and yet such descriptions are also metaphors that embody a range of different attitudes, emotions, and conflicts.

Much of Kenan's writing depends on manipulating the sharp contrasts between literary and other influences. Faulkner, the Japanese writer Yukio Mishima, Garcia Marquez, Flannery O'Connor, and postmodern studies both merge with, and diverge from, the personal and the social influences of being raised in a small town primarily by women. This often gives Kenan's fiction and narrative style a unique edge. Experiments with narrative voice, chronology, and the supernatural are mixed with an ear for oral storytelling and a hard-headed, commonsense view of human relationships that comes from living in a farm community. Following work in the publishing industry in New York City after graduating from North Carolina, Kenan became a guest lecturer at Sarah Lawrence College in 1989.

MAJOR WORKS AND THEMES

A Visitation of Spirits takes place primarily during three days, April 29 and 30, 1984, and December 8, 1985, though the complex narrative frequently describes previous events. The narrative perspective asks readers to accept abrupt changes in time and place, even shifts to dialogue written in a dramatic format with stage directions. While such narrative experiments are part of much recent fiction, often the changing perspectives in *A Visitation of Spirits* are related to the oral culture Kenan sets out to depict. That is, similar to the work of John Wideman* and Toni Morrison,* Kenan's writing shows how the vernacular African American tradition of storytelling, particularly in his native region, uses changes in voice in a manner that intersects with what are considered postmodern techniques.

Another effective device in *A Visitation of Spirits* is the relationship between chronological time and dream time, which operate as complementary structures to reveal different aspects of the characters' community, family, and interior lives. In addition, a "confessional" voice reveals the characters' most profound conflicts, the private lives unable to be made public because of guilt, shame, and confusion. The heart of Kenan's fiction is manipulating different perspectives and techniques to make public in fiction what cannot be spoken, accepted, or understood in our social lives. In this sense, his work has a deep ethical thrust.

In *A Visitation of Spirits* we are brought slowly into the conflict between Horace's homosexuality and his family, church, and community, groups that see him as a potential leader while remaining unaware of his interior life and struggles. If Horace's soul is finally compelled to rebel against the community, James (usually referred to as "Jimmy") has capitulated almost entirely to the wishes of his grandmother, returning to Tims Creek to serve as an elementary school principal and pastor. Yet both are tortured by relationships that provide momentary fulfillment but also inevitable pain and confusion. Horace consummates his first love with Gideon after they are unexpectedly thrown together to complete a science project, but eventually he cannot bear the conflict between his desire and the strict moral code of the church. With his wife, Jimmy both has ideal sexual moments and is also unable to know her, and thus both remain ultimately alone. These relationships are rendered in the context of a family and community history that gives the characters strong identities while also pointing them inevitably toward tragedy. Thomas Cross, great-grandfather to Horace and Jimmy, like Shakespeare's King Lear, splits his lands between three children. Fathers and sons, mothers and daughters, sisters and brothers endure mutual betrayals that result from powerful personalities seeking to live and love fully.

The most pressing and vexing interpretive questions in Kenan's work concern his use of what has been termed magic realism. In *Let the Dead Bury Their Dead*, Kenan quotes Bakhtin:

[T]he fantastic in folklore is a *realistic* fantastic; in no way does it exceed the limit of the real, here and now material world, and it does not stitch together rents in that world with anything that is idealistic or other-worldly; it works with the ordinary expanses of time and space, and experiences these expanses and utilizes them in great breadth and depth. Such a fantastic relies on the real-life possibilities of human development. (275–276)

Horace's discrete and complex psychological realities are best rendered with dreams, illusions, and perhaps even real spirits that show sharply his all-too-real pain. On one level, he overtly embraces demonology and pagan ritual to free himself from the guilt he suffers as a result of living in, and drawing his identity from, a Christian community where homosexuality is a sin. His initial desire to transform himself into a bird, in part, refers to the traditional slave folklore of such a change leading to freedom. But, Faustus-like, Horace summons demons that dog his literal flight from himself and direct him to the chief places of conflict, the church in which he finds "the effluvium of souls that surround men daily," where community is "not a word but being," and the playhouse that was an important locus for his homosexual desire (73). In the playhouse, it seems, he confronts a form of himself but cannot embrace or love himself. Kenan's use of fantastic and dream elements demands more interpretive subtlety than can be rendered here. Yet such techniques effectively raise questions about identity, the importance of our imaginative lives, and, on a metafictional level, our ability to resolve problems and understand ourselves through creative acts, that is, through fiction and art.

Besides the short story genre, a significant difference between A *Visitation of Spirits* and *Let the Dead Bury Their Dead* is the greater use of comic elements, though often combined with the tragic, in the later work. The opening story, "Clarence *and* the Dead," begins with a brief description of Wilma Jones' claim that her hog Francis can talk, while "no one else had ever heard the swine utter word the first" (1). Throughout this story, Kenan uses humor to explore relationships that refuse to end with death, an idea pursued extensively in the first three and last three stories. The aims of the comic elements in these stories are aptly described in "Mr. Brown and the Sweet Science," an essay about a childhood role model: "Humor to him was a balm and a salve, a way to teach and transform the world, a way to gain distance and immediacy. Humor was weapon and medicine—with it he could do almost anything" (Kenan, *Speak My Name* 63).

Like A *Visitation of Spirits*, often the stories depict the consistent need for humans to connect with others sexually, emotionally, and, most of all, in terms of that elusive and significant rhythm and understanding that sexual and emotional connections can signify. Kenan shows both idealized moments of contact between characters, which usually take place in private and can cross racial, economic, and generational boundaries, but also the hatred, racism, and fear that complicate and crush such connections. Racial conflict figures significantly in four of the stories, in each case explored from a different point of view, the first that of an older and independent African American man, the next a fictional view of Booker T. Washington's perspective on his own life, the third an impoverished, gay, white man's perspective, and finally the view of an older, wealthy, white matron. Simply put, these diverse and sharply rendered perspectives regarding racial and sexual issues distinguish Kenan's work. Additionally, as in A *Visitation of Spirits*, the self-destructive shame Horace cannot escape is again examined here, now in stories about incest and infidelity.

A central motif of *Let the Dead Bury Their Dead* is the visitation from a spirit that transforms, for better or worse, a person or an entire community. In one sense, the spirits reiterate a repeated motif in Kenan's fiction, first luring the reader in with characters and moments we know all too well but then piercing our sense of "reality" with events that cut through the surface waste of everyday life. The final and title story of the collection is Kenan at his best: it juxtaposes play with an academic or scientific view of events (emphasizing the attempt at historical accuracy through both mock and real footnotes) with a vernacular storytelling style whose essence is paradoxical, that is, the forceful truths that come from telling the biggest lies.

Kenan's biography of James Baldwin was published in a series entitled "Lives of Notable Gays and Lesbians." Not surprisingly, the purpose of the series is to help gay and lesbian teenagers accept and validate their difference from mainstream culture through learning about the gay and lesbian past, a project that clearly relates to Kenan's fiction. Baldwin's notion of character and artistic credo is perhaps close to Kenan's own perspective. Quoting Baldwin, Kenan writes that a character is "something resolutely indefinable, unpredictable. In overlooking, denying, evading his complexity—which is nothing more than the disquieting complexity of ourselves—we are diminished and we perish; only within the web of ambiguity, paradox, this hunger, danger, darkness can we find at once ourselves and the power that will free us from ourselves" (Kenan, *Baldwin* 64).

CRITICAL RECEPTION

To date there have been few critical studies of Kenan's work. Trudier Harris offers a close reading of "Clarence *and* the Dead," describing the many implications of Kenan's use of traditional storytelling techniques. She cogently argues that the story is less about Clarence and, much like some of Zora Neale Hurston's stories, more about the narrator and the act of defining and creating a community through storytelling, especially as it relates to events where the world beyond death intrudes on everyday life and where taboo subjects like homosexuality threaten the community. Harris writes:

Under the guise of humor . . . the narrator is able to explore the small-town mentality that would be so hostile to same-sex relations, or even to rumors of it. In this context, it is worthy to note that southern African American writers considered treatments of homosexuality taboo. . . . For the narrator to use humor to express the town's attitudes toward homosexuality is a way to "normalize" responses to it, to slip it in, so to speak, in the least bothersome way to potential reader/hearers. (127)

Harris also writes, "In a modern manifestation of the Chaucerian urge to disclaim telling in the process of telling, southern narrators frequently confirm what they devote hours of talk or reams of paper denying" (135). We could elaborate and say that Kenan's work examines the irony of how those who strain to deny change or difference in their lives usually confirm the necessity of such things.

Robert McRuer examines Kenan's *A Visitation of Spirits* in the context of black queer theory. His aim is to expand our understanding of black gay cultural production beyond its primarily urban focus and to examine "how region plays a role in the construction of centers and margins" (221). McRuer states, "*A Visitation of Spirits* is a veritable treatise on the unstable opposition between sameness and difference" (227). He writes of the book's conclusion:

Horace's suicide is detailed in stark, scientific terms (and hence, "real") prose, and is juxtaposed to the "fantastic" events in this postmodern, magic realist text. The "realness" of the suicide moves the theoretical opposition "Is it Real?" / "Is it Fantasy?" to a more urgent level, and this violent conclusion to Horace's confusing circulation around categories of sameness and difference should emphasize the irreducibility of "difference" for black queer theory, and indeed, for queer theory in general. (229)

Again, we can make a similar point for Kenan's fiction, as it stands so far, as a whole. The mix of scientific precision with magic realism, of postmodern narrative devices with an oral tradition, of gay perspectives in settings highly resistant to difference, and of racial and political themes with good storytelling forges a unique tool that can clarify aspects of our relationships with others through rendering carefully complex, painful, and pleasurable experiences. The uniqueness of Kenan's approach, in some respects, is called for because his primary topic is difference.

BIBLIOGRAPHY

Works by Randall Kenan

Fiction

A Visitation of Spirits. New York: Grove Press, 1989.
Let the Dead Bury Their Dead. New York: Harcourt, Brace, 1992a.
"The Virtue Called Vanity." In The Rough Road Home: Stories by North Carolina Writers. Robert Gingher, ed. Chapel Hill: University of North Carolina Press, 1992b: 131–150.
"Hobbits and Hobgoblins." In Writers Harvest. William Shore, ed. New York: Harcourt, Brace, 1994: 13–23.
"Wash Me." In Shade: An Anthology of Fiction by Gay Men of African Descent. New York: Avon Books, 1996: 260–272.

Nonfiction

James Baldwin. New York: Chelsea House, 1994.
"Mr. Brown and the Sweet Science." In Speak My Name: Black Men on Masculinity and the American Dream. Don Belton, ed. Boston: Beacon Press, 1995.
"That Eternal Burning." In A Time Not Here. Photographs by Norman Mauskopf; essay by Randall Kenan. Santa Fe: Twin Palms, 1996.

Sound Recording

Soundings: New Southerners. Randall Kenan, Brent Wade. Research Triangle Park, NC: National Humanities Research Center, 1995.

Studies of Randall Kenan

Harris, Trudier. The Power of the Porch: The Storyteller's Craft in Zora Neale Hurston, Gloria Naylor, and Randall Kenan. Athens: University of Georgia Press, 1996.
Hunt, V. "A Conversation with Randall Kenan." African American Review 29:3 (1995): 411–420.
McRuer, Robert. "Randall Kenan." In Contemporary Gay American Novelists: A Bio-Bibliographical Critical Sourcebook. Emmanuel S. Nelson, ed. Westport, CT: Greenwood, 1993a.

————. "A Visitation of Difference: Randall Kenan and Black Queer Theory." In *Critical Essays: Gay and Lesbian Writers of Color*. Emmanuel S. Nelson, ed. New York: Haworth Press, 1993b: 221–232.
————. *The Queer Renaissance*. New York: New York University Press, 1997.

JOHN OLIVER KILLENS
(1916–1987)

Harish Chander

BIOGRAPHY

John Oliver Killens was born to Willie Lee Killens (née Coleman) and Charles Miles Killens of Virgin Street in Macon, Georgia, on 14 January 1916. He was the second of their three sons. Not only did his parents instill in him pride in his black heritage, but they sparked his interest in reading in general and African American literature in particular. While his mother, who was president of the Dunbar Literary Club, introduced him to African American literature, his father, who was a manager at a restaurant, encouraged him to read Langston Hughes' weekly column in the *Chicago Defender*. His paternal great-grandmother told him stories of African Americans' fortitude during slavery. In his autobiographical essay, "The Half Ain't Never Been Told," Killens singles out his great-grandmother as the main influence in his decision to become a writer. Puffing on her pipe, she would entertain the young Killens with memorable stories, often ending a tale with the remark: "Aaah Lord, Honey, THE HALF AIN'T EVER BEEN TOLD!" She would then challenge her grandson to attempt to tell the rest of that untold story (279). When Killens decided to become a writer, his great-grandmother's advice to tell the whole story, coupled with his early famil-iarity with African American history, folklore, and literature, stood him in good stead. Granny's advice gave Killens his purpose and mission as a writer, and the black experience and culture gave him the working material.

In the essay "The Myth of Non-Violence" in his book *Black Man's Burden*, Killens describes the racism he encountered growing up in Macon. He tells of a fight between a group of black children and a group of white children on their way home from their respective schools, both sides going home with cut lips and bloody noses. The police responded the next day by jailing students of the black school. Meanwhile, not a single white child was punished (103–5). In the essay "The Black Mystique" in the same book, Killens writes that he was frequently accused by white men of casting lascivious glances at their female companions when he worked one summer as a bellhop at a hotel (142–44). He also reveals that his maternal great-grandmother was raped at the age of twelve by her master's son, with the result that she gave birth to his grandfather (130). In the essay "Downsouth-Upsouth" in this book, Killens recalls his experience of being accosted by two white men in a black Packard. One of them said, "Hey, boy, you know where we can get a colored gal?" Killens shouted, "Go get your dear old mother like you been doing!" and ran (64).

Notwithstanding these ugly incidents, Killens has nostalgic sentiments about his life in his southern hometown. In "Downsouth-Upsouth," he remembers Christmas mornings when black children went from house to house delivering gifts and Easter mornings when black people gathered on the hill and sang of Jesus' resurrection (83–87). He attended a segregated public elementary school and, from the eighth grade onward, a private missionary school.

After high school, Killens attended black colleges in the South—first, Edward Walters College in Jacksonville, Florida (1934–1935), and then Morris Brown College in Atlanta, Georgia (1935–1936). While at Morris Brown, he participated in forums on Atlanta college campuses where black and white students met to discuss the "Negro problem." In "Downsouth-Upsouth," he remembers that at one of these meetings, a white student suggested a final solution: "The way to get rid of the nigrah problem is to collect all the nigrahs together and take them to the river and dump them in" (81). Killens moved to Washington, D.C., and began working for the National Labor Relations Board. In "Downsouth-Upsouth," he remembers his first day on the job, when he wandered around looking for the drinking fountain for colored people, puzzled when he didn't find any (67). While working, he obtained his baccalaureate degree through evening classes at Howard University. In 1939, he began his law studies at the Robert Terrel Law School but in 1942 abandoned his studies to join the army. He served in the U.S. Amphibian Forces in the South Pacific. By now, Killens had decided that he would not return to law school but would become a writer instead.

In 1946, after completing his military service, Killens rejoined the National Labor Relations Board, this time in New York. Brooklyn was then home to him, his wife, Grace Ward, and their two children, Jon Charles and Barbara Ellen. For the next two years, like Robby Youngblood, the hero of his first novel, *Youngblood*, he tried in vain to organize black and white workers for the Congress of Industrial Organizations. He failed largely because of the prejudices of a white working class that refused to join forces with blacks.

In 1948, Killens moved to New York and took writing courses at Columbia University and New York University to prepare himself for a career as a writer. In the late 1940s, he joined with John Henrik Clarke, Rosa Guy, and Walter Christmas to form the Harlem Writers Guild. At an early meeting of this organization Killens read, his voice trembling, the first chapter of *Youngblood*. Over time, the guild would serve as a forum for many African American writers, including Maya Angelou, Alice Childress,* Ossie Davis, and Paule Marshall.*

In 1955, Killens went to Alabama to research a screenplay on the Montgomery bus boycott and met with Dr. Martin Luther King, Jr. In "The Myth of Non-Violence," he says that Dr. King "loses me and many other Negroes when he calls upon us to love our abusers" (112). He found himself more in tune with Malcolm X's philosophy of retaliating against the perpetrators of violence, and with him he founded the Organization for Afro-American Unity in 1964. Earlier in the 1960s, as he writes in "The Half Ain't Never Been Told," he had visited a number of African countries as a researcher for a BBC documentary film crew (298).

From 1965 to 1987, Killens held numerous positions as a writer in residence at Fisk University, Columbia University, Howard University, Bronx Community College, and Medgar Evers College of the City University of New York. In 1969, he was elected vice president of the Black Academy of Arts and Letters. To research the life of the Russian poet Alexander Sergeievich Pushkin, he visited Russia in 1968 and 1970 and completed his biographical novel *Great Black Russian* before he died of cancer on October 27, 1987. His works have been translated into more than a dozen languages.

MAJOR WORKS AND THEMES

John Oliver Killens is, to borrow Eudora Welty's phrase, a crusader-novelist. He puts his art in the service of the war against racism. In his essay "The Writer and Black Liberation," Killens states: "Black writers, here and now, are warriors, almost one and all, because we have a world to win. . . . We have declared war to the death against white racism, which is the enemy of humankind" (270–71). He does not believe in art for art's sake, asserting unequivocally that "any literature worth the designation is social, has social significance, is engaged on one side or the other, for humanity or against" (266). In the essay "The Black Writer Vis-a-Vis His Country" in *Black Man's Burden*, Killens accuses the Western world for making "black the symbol of all that was evil and ugly" and forcibly taking "a great people from a great continent" and changing them into "niggers" (41). "To deniggerize the earth"—to reclaim the black man's greatness—is the black artist's greatest challenge, Killens proclaims in the essay that bears the same title as the book *Black Man's Burden* (176). True to this mission, Killens exposes in his fiction not only the evils of white racism but also the dangers of black classism. At the same time, Killens' fiction celebrates black culture and black brotherhood, as well as affirms black manhood.

Youngblood (1954), Killens' first book, set in the Georgia of the 1920s and 1930s, describes one black family's response to the question, "How do you live in a white man's world? Do you live on your knees . . . Or do you live like a man is supposed to live—with your head straight up?" (61). Joe and Laurie Lee Youngblood, their two children, and their friends cope with destructive pressures from whites. Sometimes they give in, as when Laurie Lee is compelled to whip her son Robby to save him from being sent to a reformatory. At other times, they stand up for their rights. When Robby is accused of raping a white girl, Laurie Lee refuses to accept the "compromise" offer of the reformatory made by the girl's mother. Joe Youngblood refuses to allow Mack Turner to continue to cheat him of a part of his weekly wages. Richard Myles, the teacher from New York, shows great courage in celebrating Jubilee Day by giving the history and meaning of Negro spirituals, to the chagrin of the town authorities. Robby Youngblood's recurring dream in which two armies—one white and the other black—face each other in an open space starkly presents the racial tension depicted in the novel.

In *Youngblood*, Killens employs folktales for thematic purposes, using their acerbic wit to show black resistance to racism. The white man in one tale says to the tall black man: "Hey, *boy*, where you going?" And the black man responds: "Mr. White folks, will you tell me something please, sir? How big do *mens* grow where you came from?" (emphasis added; 239). In another tale a black man goes to a Washington restaurant, and the waiter tells him, "We don't serve no niggers here." The black man responds, "Man, I don't want no niggers for breakfast. Just give me some stew beef" (109).

In *And Then We Heard the Thunder* (1962), Killens, drawing upon his own experiences, describes the humiliations and indignities suffered by black soldiers in World War II. As the comically named Buck Rogers remarks about the black soldier's experience: "You ain't even a second-class citizen any more. You're a second-class soldier" (97). The irony, of course, is that while these black soldiers are fighting a war to defeat fascism and racist ideology, they face discrimination during training in Georgia and during their operations in the South Pacific. As long as there are white soldiers to get on a bus, the novel's protagonist, Corporal Solly Saunders, has to wait, humiliated, in the colored line. Each bus pulling up and leaving with white soldiers takes with it some of his humanity and manhood. Fannie Mae Branton, the female protagonist, says to Solly Saunders: "Manhood is more important than money or promotions. . . . The one thing [most southern whites] will not stand for is for a black man to be a man" (185).

The novel's idealistic hero joins the army as an antifascist, believing in the "Double V"—victory over enemy abroad and the enemy at home, but he gradually becomes disillusioned. He is beaten by white police in Georgia and thrown out of a whites-only Australian Red Cross Club in Bainbridge, Australia. He joins the black cause and enthusiastically participates in the Battle of Bainbridge fought between the white and black Americans. He becomes the so-called race man, "proud of the specialness of black me" (418). When his white Australian mistress Celia complains about the unfairness of his rejection of her love, he shouts: "Fairness is a thing no white man has a right to ask of colored. . . . 'Fairness' is a word that should choke in the white man's throat" (413).

In *'Sippi* (1967), Killens develops the theme of the black struggle for voting rights and the broader black struggle for manhood. Set in the aftermath of the

Supreme Court decisions in *Brown v. Board of Education*, the novel revolves around the interaction between two Mississippi families, the Chaneys, who are black, and the Wakefields, who are white. Charles Wakefield claims to be a progressive Mississippian. Charles explains to Chuck Chaney that he can accept integration, but he cannot accept the ideology of black power because that amounts to rocking the boat. Chuck exclaims, "Our job is to capsize the boat—and build another one with accommodations for everybody" (399). Charles Wakefield retorts that "if it comes to that, I'll have to join up with the peckerwoods [poor whites] and shoot down Negroes on the streets of Wakefield City" (399).

The novel continues Killens' theme of the struggle for black manhood, positing Malcolm X and Paul Robeson as the embodiments of black manhood. Jesse Chaney says to his son: "Be a man, son Chuckie. Walk like a man. Live like a man. And die like one when the time comes" (13). Jesse Chaney explains to Chuck that he may see his father bowing before whites just to avoid trouble, but he draws the line at white abuse of black women. The black men in the novel face constant assaults on their manhood, as when Uncle Bish Carson is sexually degraded by five white men. Sherry Kingsley, the female protagonist, laments the death of Malcolm X: "He was the last hope that black folk could achieve manhood" (235). The title of the novel is derived from a folktale in which the black hero breaks southern custom by entering the front door of a white home and then asserts his manhood by shouting that he will no longer include "mister" or "miss" when addressing white people.

Killens' next important novel, *The Cotillion, or One Good Bull Is Half the Herd* (1971), exposes the evil of classism among blacks and the folly of the black bourgeoise in aping white customs and manners. The novel revolves around the staging of the Grand Cotillion at the Waldorf by the Femme Fatales, a fancy colored women's club from Crowning Heights, Brooklyn. The club decides to admit five "culturally deprived" (76) girls, including Yoruba Lovejoy, from the poor community of Harlem to the elite ranks of Crowning Heights debutantes. The Femme Fatales then give the debutantes elaborate instructions in ladyship, including lessons in dancing and cosmetology. Killens contrasts the sterility of the Crowning Heights community, characterized by ladies in wigs and plastic-covered furniture, with the cultural richness of the Harlem community, characterized by ladies in natural hairdos and lack of pretension. One of the characters, Ben Ali Lumumba, clearly giving voice to Killens' own feelings, ridicules the participants in the Cotillion for seeking to become white: "Monkey see, monkey do, aping white folks, them laughing at us. . . . We are never going to be liberated as long as we mimic the white boy's juju and his cultural symbols" (152). As the Cotillion approaches, Yoruba and others join a cleaning crew at a white debutante ball in Long Island. There they experience disenchantment with white people's "screwing privately and openly" (210), which makes Yoruba's mother, Lady Daphne, realize that white people may not deserve to be placed on a pedestal as the ideal. For Yoruba herself, it "was her grand debut into the maturation of her Blackness" (227), as she is imbued with pride in her own black beauty. Toward the end of the novel, her father, Matt Lovejoy, exhorts: "Black brothers and sisters, come out of the cotton patch, all you Toms and Aunt Jemimas! Follow us to liberation!" (255). He ends his call with "Up the Black Nation!" (255). Finally, Lady Daphne, Big Matt, Yoruba, and Lumumba unite to boycott the Cotillion.

In *Great Gittin' Up Morning: A Biography of Denmark Vesey* (1972) and *A Man Ain't Nothin' but a Man: The Adventures of John Henry* (1975), written for young adults, Killens provides two black profiles in courage. He portrays Vesey as a heroic figure who, after years of playing the lottery, gets lucky and uses the winnings to purchase his freedom and then plans the 1822 uprising in Charleston, South Carolina, to free slaves. However, betrayed by a slave-turned-informer, Vesey is arrested and swiftly put to death, thus becoming a martyr in the cause of black liberation. Killens points out that Vesey believed that "blood would have to flow before Black men would be liberated" and then adds, "History has not proven them mistaken" (134). In *A Man Ain't Nothin' but a Man*, Killens portrays the steel-driving black folk hero, "born with a hammer" in his hand (106). John Henry, who is "proud of being Black" (111), makes all black people proud when he wins a steel-driving contest with Robin Flannigan, the white champion. Then, at the cost of his own life, he wins a competition against the steam drill to save his fellow workers' jobs, thus promoting the cause of solidarity among workers.

Great Black Russian: A Novel on the Life and Times of Pushkin (1989) is Killens' last novel, completed shortly before his death. In describing the life of the great Russian poet Alexander Sergeievich Pushkin, Killens establishes another black hero and role model, one who takes pride in his African ancestry. Inspired by Grandma Hannibal's stories about his great-grandfather, Ibrahim Petrovich Hannibal, Pushkin learns to love himself, despite his own mother's hatred of him because of his Africanoid physiognomy. Ibrahim Hannibal had been an Ethiopian prince before he was captured by Turks and was acquired by Peter the Great, who valued his services and promoted him to the rank of a general in his army. Pushkin takes pride in his dual heritage: "Whatever I am today, whatever I have given the Russian people, I owe it to Africa and to Russia" (153). Pushkin had himself started to write a novel about his great-grandfather, *The Negro of Peter the Great*, but died in a duel before finishing it. Killens writes that Africa was an omnipresent influence in Pushkin's work: "Sometimes he'd cock his ears and think he heard African drums his grandfather had once listened to, and that the rhythm of his poetry was African-influenced. . . . He heard African violins playing in his poetry" (143–44).

Pushkin shares some of Killens' political beliefs. Like Killens, Pushkin, the visionary, wishes to solve the problems of the world, especially the problems of the laboring class. He constantly thinks about how to "create a world of beauty in lieu of poverty, ignorance and ugliness" (311). He believes that "men and women must fight against an intransigent Fate" and change their "destiny to the ultimate of their abilities" (311). Furthermore, Pushkin, in his poem "The Dagger," like Killens, upholds "violence as a legitimate weapon in the revolutionary struggle against tyranny" (188). Also, like Killens, who learned of his general subject of black American life by living it, Pushkin lives the serf's life: "[Pushkin] worked and sweated with them, went with them to their homes, their miserable huts, . . . and broke bread with them. . . . he danced with them in the village square" (84).

CRITICAL RECEPTION

Critical appraisals of John Oliver Killens' fictional works that focus on his ideology and substance of his message have generally been positive, whereas those that focus on form and structure have generally been negative. Mainstream critics fault Killens for not transcending the racial protest theme to write about universal human concerns. In "The Black Writer Vis-a-Vis His Country," Killens responds to these critics: "A creative writer is not a statesman. He must tell as much of the truth as he knows the painful truth to be, and let the flak fall where it may" (31). In an interview published in *The New York Times* of 2 March 1969, Killens denies the validity of criticism of black literature by whites: "White critics are totally—and I mean totally—incapable of criticizing the black writer. . . . They don't understand Afro-Americanese" (49).

Killens' first novel elicited favorable reviews. To Granville Hicks, *Youngblood* impresses as "a record of petty, mean-spirited, wanton discrimination" but one that is "often tiring" because of its "vernacular style" (24). Henry F. Winslow acclaims *Youngblood* for its "graphic portrait of people" and authenticity in characterization, especially in creation of "the tragic cracker [poor white man]" in Oscar Jefferson (511–12). Critics responded even more favorably to the message of Killens' second novel, *And Then We Heard the Thunder*, nominating it for the Pulitzer Prize. John Howard Griffin says that Killens' novel has "the depth and complexity of lived experience," and its battle scenes have "hallucinatory power" (46). However, P. A. Doyle, in a somewhat prudish review of *And Then We Heard the Thunder*, complains about the novel's "overdone" love scenes and "unusual frankness of language" but adds that "one tends to forgive most of these weaknesses because of the importance and validity of Mr. Killens' message" (407).

Killens' third novel, *'Sippi*, received mixed reviews. Penny Kaganoff calls it an "impressive testament to the civil rights movement," in which the author depicts the "brutal repressiveness of a backwater, bigoted Southern county in the 1950s and '60s" (103). In his article "The Structure and Dynamics of Folklore in the Novel Form: The Case of John O. Killens," William H. Wiggins, Jr., applauds Killens' dexterous weaving of folktales into the plot (102–6). However, Ronald Williams summarily dismisses *'Sippi* as a "classically bad novel with plodding events which lead nowhere" (85). Killens himself in "The Half Ain't Never Been Told" admits that *'Sippi* is "a critical bust" (296). *The Cotillion*, which was also nominated for the Pulitzer Prize, also received mixed reviews. Phoebe Adams comments: "If characters and author were white, this social comedy about the debutante racket would be trite as a Doris Day movie. Since the characters are black and the author is a wily blend of clown and porcupine, the moribund plot bounces merrily back to life" (129). J. R. Frakes observes that the book thrives on the use of exaggerations that "everything in this book is triple life-size, every character, every gesture, every emotion, every action," and affirms the black cultural heritage—"the Black nation, Afro-natural hairdos, dashikis, and Negritude." The novel exposes falsehood of black stereotypes believed in by whites as well as the silliness of "caste snobbery" among blacks (4+). Leonard Fleischer commends *The Cotillion* for "prose often buoyantly evocative and musical," employed to caricature "some of the more egregious foibles of black and white society" (36). Although Frakes would rather call *The Cotillion* "sui generis" rather than a novel, Addison Gayle, Jr. calls it "a satiric novel" and points out that its satire is effective because Killens' "wit and humor are directed at conditions, not at people" (332–33). Of *Great Gittin' Up Morning: A Biography of Denmark Vesey*, Eric Foner and Naomi Foner write: "The language of the book . . . reflects the politics of the 1960s as much as the history of the 1820s" (39).

Killens' last novel, *The Great Black Russian: A Novel on the Life and Times of Alexander Pushkin*, has received mixed critical reception. Sybil Steinberg writes that "the author's last work is a rather strident polemic, and suffers accordingly" (108). In the same vein, D. H. Stewart says that Killens' novel has "the racist emphasis on Pushkin's fractional blackness" and his Pushkin "approximates a proto-black-activist." However, Zofia Smardz sees the book quite differently: "*Great Black Russian* admirably avoids any polemics about race, dealing with the firebrand poet as the complex, puzzling character. Here is Pushkin the man, the writer, the African, the Russian, the aristocrat, the revolutionary, the womanizer and the husband" (20).

BIBLIOGRAPHY

Works by John Oliver Killens

Novels

Youngblood. New York: Dial, 1954.
And Then We Heard the Thunder. New York: Knopf, 1962.
'Sippi. New York: Trident, 1967.
The Cotillion, or One Good Bull Is Half the Herd. New York: Trident, 1971.
Great Gittin' Up Morning: A Biography of Denmark Vesey. New York: Doubleday, 1972.
A Man Ain't Nothing but a Man: The Adventures of John Henry. Boston: Little, Brown, 1975.
The Great Black Russian: A Novel on the Life and Times of Alexander Pushkin. Detroit: Wayne State University Press, 1989.

Short Stories

"God Bless America." *Black Literature in America*. Ed. Houston A. Baker, Jr. New York: McGraw-Hill, 1971. 339–43.
"The Stick Up." *The Best Short Stories by Negro Writers: An Anthology from 1899 to the Present*. Ed. Langston Hughes. Boston: Little, Brown, 1967. 188–91.

Screenplays

With Nelson Gidding. *Odds against Tomorrow*. Belafonte Productions/United Artists, 1959.
With Herbert J. Bieberman and Alida Sherman. *Slaves*. Theatre Guild-Walter Reade, 1969.

Essays

Black Man's Burden. New York: Trident, 1965.
"The Writer and Black Liberation." *In Black America: 1968—The Year of Awakening*. Ed. Patricia W. Romero. Washington, DC: United, 1969. 265–71.
"Black Panelists Link Arts to Politics." *New York Times* 29 May 1972: sec. L:15.
"The Half Ain't Never Been Told." *Contemporary Authors Autobiography Series*. Vol. 2. Gale: Detroit, 1985. 279–306.

Studies of John Oliver Killens

Adams, Phoebe. Rev. of *The Cotillion*. *Atlantic Monthly* (15 Feb. 1971): 129.
Doyle, P. A. Rev. of *And Then We Heard the Thunder*. *Best Sellers* (1 Feb. 1963): 407.
Fleischer, Leonard. Rev. of *The Cotillion*. *Saturday Review* (Mar. 1971): 36.
Foner, Eric, and Naomi Foner. Rev. of *Great Gittin' Up Morning*. *New York Review of Books* (20 Apr. 1972): 39.
Frakes, J. R. Rev. of *The Cotillion*. *New York Times Book Review* (17 Jan. 1971): 4+.
Gayle, Addison, Jr. *The Way of the New World: The Black Novel in America*. Garden City, NY: Anchor Press/Doubleday, 1976.
Goddard, Rosalind K. Rev. of *Great Gittin' Up Morning*. *The New York Times Book Review* (30 Apr. 1972): 8.
Griffin, J. H. Rev. of *And Then We Heard the Thunder*. *Saturday Review* (26 Jan. 1963): 46.
Hicks, Granville. Rev. of *Youngblood*. *New York Times*, (6 June 1954) sec. 7:24.
Interview. *New York Times* 2 Mar. 1969: 49.
Kaganoff, Penny. Rev. of *'Sippi*. *Publishers Weekly* (6 May 1988): 103.
Llorens, David. "Writers Converge at Fisk University." *Negro Digest* (June 1966): 54–58.
Metzger, Linda, et al. "John Oliver Killens." *Black Writers: A Selection of Sketches from Contemporary Authors*. Detroit: Gale, 1989. 324–26.
Smardz, Zofia. Rev. of *Great Black Russian*. *New York Times Book Review* (18 Feb. 1990), sec. 7:20.
Steinberg, Sybil. Rev. of *Great Black Russian*. *Publishers Weekly* (15 Sept. 1989): 108.
Stewart, D. H. Rev. of *Great Black Russian*. *Choice* (Mar. 1990): 1134.
Wiggins, William H., Jr. "John Oliver Killens." *Dictionary of Literary Biography* Vol. 33: *Afro-American Fiction Writers after 1955*. Detroit: Gale, 1984. 144–52.

———. "The Structure and Dynamics of Folklore in the Novel Form: The Case of John O. Killens." *Keystone Folklore Quarterly* 17 (1972): 92–118.

Williams, Ronald. Rev. of *'Sippi*. *Negro Digest* (Nov. 1967): 85.

Winslow, Henry F. Rev. of *Youngblood*. *The Crisis* (Oct. 1954): 511–12+.

JAMAICA KINCAID
(1949–   )

Ymitri Jayasundera

BIOGRAPHY

Jamaica Kincaid was born Elaine Potter Richardson in 1949 on the Caribbean island of St. Johns, Antigua, to a Carib Indian/African mother from Dominica and Antiguan Roderick Potter, who was nonexistent in her life. Kincaid considered her stepfather David Drew, a carpenter, her father, and he is the model for the father figures in her novels. Leaving Antigua in 1965 at the age of sixteen for economic reasons, to help her family, Kincaid worked as an au pair first in Westchester County, New York, then in New York City's Upper East Side. Although intending to study nursing, Kincaid studied photography and at various small colleges. In 1973 *Ingenue* magazine accepted her idea of interviewing celebrities for a series of interviews called "When I Was 17," and her first article was on Gloria Steinem. During the same year she changed her name to Jamaica Kincaid to ensure anonymity in case she failed as a writer and to be able to write what she wanted. She chose Jamaica for its resonance to the Caribbean and Kincaid because "it just seemed to go with it" (Cudjoe 220).

A year later Kincaid met William Shawn, editor of the *New Yorker*, through a publishing friend of hers, William S. Trow, "Talk of the Town" columnist of the *New Yorker* who frequently quoted her in his columns. She became a staff writer at the *New Yorker*, writing for the same column. Kincaid's first piece of fiction, "Girl," was published in the *New Yorker* in 1978, and it later became part of a short story collection, *At the Bottom of the River*. Most of her fiction was originally published in the *New Yorker* as short stories and later gathered into novels, but her series of nonfiction essays titled *A Small Place*, examining the hegemony of neocolonialism in Antigua, was rejected by the *New Yorker*'s new editor, Robert Gottlieb, as too angry. She did not return to Antigua to see her family until 1985; at this time she was informally banned from entering Antigua due to her criticism of the current administration; the ban was lifted in 1992. In 1992, Kincaid began a series of new columns for the *New Yorker* on gardening in which she used the metaphor of gardening to focus on the consequences of colonialism.

In 1979 Kincaid married composer Allen Shawn, son of William Shawn, editor of the *New Yorker*, and currently a professor at Bennington College. They have two children, daughter Annie, born in 1985 and named after Kincaid's mother, and son Harold, born in 1988. The family lives in Bennington, Vermont.

At the Bottom of the River is a series of lyrically experimental vignettes on the growing consciousness of a young girl in the Caribbean. It received the Morton Darwen Zabel Award of the American Academy and Institute of Arts and Letters and was nominated for PEN/Faulkner award. This was followed by the fictional autobiographical novel *Annie John*, which centers on a young girl's coming-of-age in the Caribbean and ends with her poised to leave Antigua to begin her education in England. It was a finalist for the prestigious international Ritz Paris Hemingway Award. *Lucy*, published in 1990, begins with a young woman arriving not in England, but like Kincaid, in New York to work as an au pair to a wealthy white family and to study to become a nurse.

Between these two novels, Kincaid published *Annie, Gwen, Lily, Pam and Tulip*, which is still relatively unknown and originally intended to be part of *At the Bottom of the River*. The very short text accompanying Eric Fischel's lithographs is composed of the dialogues of five female characters in the dreamlike imagistic style of *At the Bottom of the River*. *A Small Place*, the polemical and political essay, became controversial upon publication in 1988. Her circular and psychologically dense narrative is evident in *Autobiography of My Mother*, in which the female protagonist mourns her mother dead at her birth and tries to imaginatively reconstruct her. Tragedy struck Kincaid in 1995 when her youngest brother, Devon Drew, died of AIDS in Antigua. *My Brother*, published in 1997, chronicles her relationship with her brother during his illness and their frequently tense relationship with their mother.

MAJOR WORKS AND THEMES

Kincaid's major works, consisting of seven very slim volumes of fiction and prose, explore the domestic in terms of the mother–daughter dyad and the public through the metaphoric use of the authoritative biological mother as the omnipotent mother-colonizer and the frustrated daughter as the powerless child-colonized. Colonialism and its impact on the people of Antigua become more foregrounded in the later work, but all three novels focus on how colonialism has negated the female child's existence. The imperial powers besiege the questioning, self-aware young girl, demanding obedience and awe and punishing her for her rage and rebellion at having England upheld as an ideal to which she can never aspire. All the novels probe the rupture between mother and daughter, the daughter's attempt to reconcile herself to the loss of an adoring mother at childhood, the daughter's becoming, inexplicably upon her reaching adolescence, distant, critical, and judgmental, and finally her ambivalence and violent rejection of her mother. In *Annie John*, for example, the mother–daughter relationship begins in a prelapsian mode with both the center of each other's existence, but when Annie reaches adolescence, the violent conflict within her and with her mother is necessary for her to carve her separate identity. This psychodrama is paralleled by the daughter's increasing rebellion against the colonialism inscribed upon her and her people from imperial England.

Since the narratives of emerging consciousness focus on identity and self as it intersects issues of gender, race, and colonialism, both Annie John and Lucy, the title characters of the respective novels, violently reject the education that tries to teach them submission and acquiescence to the empire (Tapping 52). Alison Donnell suggests Annie John's and Lucy's vehement hatred of their mother is intimately bound to their rejection of the colonial motherland ("When Daughters Defy" 22) and the cultural reinscribing of the colonial domination. But in *Lucy* even the physical distance of living in New York cannot overthrow the profound loss and despair that Lucy feels in losing her mother's unconditional love and her rage as she observes the complacent liberalism of upper-class whites who unthinkingly maintain and project onto her imperialist policies that she, as a self-exiled colonial subject, had been subjected to. The implicit presence of imperial England in the daily lives of the people of Antigua and the education system glorifying England destroys the colonized's sense of self that Kincaid confirms by stating that it resulted in "my erasure—not my physical erasure, but my erasure all the same" ("On Seeing England" 14).

These ideologies are inscribed and internalized by mothers who favor sons' accomplishments rather than daughters', as within any colonial context, a son's rise is encouraged and favored, as Kincaid suggests in her own life—her mother seemingly arbitrarily removed her from school at the age of fifteen, even though she was a brilliant student. In *My Brother*, Kincaid's subtext is ultimately of the loss of her mother's unconditional love in childhood and the adult daughter's current tense relationship with her, which is repeated in her brothers, who may also go through periods of not speaking to her. This family psychodrama critiques the hopelessness of former colonies riddled in corruption and too poor to afford expensive Western medications and services of doctors who emigrate to the West for a better life. In Antigua an AIDS patient goes to the hospital to die because treatment is almost nonexistent.

A Small Place, which begins with the now famous address to the would-be white, privileged, Western tourist, "If you go to Antigua as a tourist, this is what you will see," is an antitravel narrative indicting neocolonialism in the newly independent Antigua. The Western tourists propagate the cultural and economic domination begun by the British, in which the tourist economy maintains the master–slave (servant) relationship by not granting Antiguans their subjectivity. The tourists blindly enjoy their holiday without acknowledging their responsibility in maintaining the poverty and corruption of the Third World. The essay also ironically reverses expectations by voicing the Antiguans' anger and resentment at the implicit imperialism of tourism.

At the Bottom of the River, Kincaid's first collection of short stories, exemplifies her evocative use of language and the convoluted technique of magical realism influenced, she says, from her coming from "a magical place"—Antigua. The first story, "Girl," which is probably the most important piece in the collection, is a series of hypnotic and incantatory admonitions by the mother to the daughter: "Wash the clothes on Monday and put them on the stone heap; wash the color clothes on Tuesday and put them on the clothesline to dry; don't walk barehead in the sun . . . soak salt fish overnight before you cook it . . . is it true that you sing benna in Sunday school? . . . on Sundays try to walk like a lady and not like the slut you are so bent on becoming" (3). The story evokes how culture is transmitted and women's internalization of the patriarchal politics of oppression. In the collection as a whole "the mesmerizing repetitions have the effect of putting the reader into the world of Kincaid's psyche, a world in which one reality constantly slides into another under cover of the ordinary rhythms of life" (Simmons 47). The almost dreamlike vignettes are deceptive since the book is constructed psychologically rather than chronologically, reflecting the growing awareness and selfhood of a young girl. Kincaid's later novels are not as obscure and include the magical realism techniques within a more straightforward chronological narrative.

CRITICAL RECEPTION

According to Frank Birbalsingh, Kincaid is "probably the most important West Indian woman writing today" (128), and two full-length studies, many interviews, and articles in books and journals attest to the importance placed on her, especially by feminist and postcolonial critics. With the explosion of Kincaid criticism since 1990, the scholarship rests mainly on her two novels, *Annie John* and *Lucy*, and her short story collection, *At the Bottom of the River*, with growing interest in her nonfiction work *A Small Place*. Upon publication it received mixed reviews of the work as being too angry, with charges of the author losing control of the material, or it was praised for being controlled and unsparing in its criticism (Simmons 19). Kincaid admits that she "liked it even more when a lot of reviews said it's so angry . . . [because] the first step in claiming yourself is anger" (Perry 133). *A Small Place* foregrounds Kincaid's anticolonial views that she had earlier been criticized for not focusing on in her fiction. Although *At the Bottom of the River* and the largely ignored *Annie, Gwen, Lily, Pam and Tulip* do include the theme of imperialism, it is largely secondary and implicit in the books. Moira Ferguson suggests that *At the Bottom of the River*, *Annie John*, and *A Small Place* form "an uneven and discontinuous trilogy about Jamaica Kincaid's life over four decades . . . in an ongoing bildungsroman" (*Jamaica Kincaid* 78), but Kincaid's later work also adds layers to the continuing coming-of-age saga. Postcolonial critics now focus on *A Small Place*'s sophisticated rhetorical strategies, its searingly honest examination of imperialism/postimperialism, and its relationship to the novels and to Kincaid's own life.

Kincaid appears to follow the Caribbean tradition of writing of her childhood or the bildungsroman with all her fiction on the coming-of-age of a young girl living in or from the Caribbean. Kincaid herself has become a major critic of her own work through her numerous interviews, which most critics use in citing her artistic, philosophical, and political views as part of their explication of her work, so that the criticism, to some extent, is also biocritical. Although refusing to categorize herself as a female or African American or Caribbean writer, she admits that her work is largely autobiographical and that she writes ultimately for herself and that she writes "great audience is this one-half Carib Indian woman [her mother] living in Antigua" (Bonetti 141).

Most Kincaid scholarship focuses on the mother–daughter conflict as it intersects issues of female subjectivity and imperialism, with *Annie John* and *Lucy* the center of critical explication. *Autobiography of My Mother*, occasionally mentioned in passing, is still largely ignored. Most critics use postcolonial and feminist theory as their basis with an element of psychoanalysis on the sometimes harshly rendered, tense mother–daughter conflict, which may be somewhat unsettling to the reader. Moira Ferguson and Diane Simmons, who have each simultaneously published a full-length study of Kincaid's work, offer detailed analysis of Kincaid's work. Simmons' book also include analysis of Kincaid's short uncollected pieces that may be helpful to a beginning reader. Ferguson and Alison Donnell, in her many articles on Kincaid, examine Kincaid's major themes of gender, but they also offer detailed analysis of specific aspects of Kincaid's novels. Both, for example, explore the intertexuality of daffodils in *Lucy* in relation to Wordsworth. The current scholarship on Kincaid seem to indicate her importance not only as a major Caribbean female writer but also as an American writer.

BIBLIOGRAPHY

Works by Jamaica Kincaid

Novels

Annie John. New York: New American Library, 1983.
Lucy. New York: Farrar, Straus, and Giroux, 1990.
Autobiography of My Mother. New York: Farrar, Straus, and Giroux, 1994.

Short Stories

"Antigua Crossing." *Rolling Stone* (29 June, 1978a): 48–50.
At the Bottom of the River. New York: Farrar, Straus, and Giroux, 1978b.
And Eric Fischel. *Annie, Gwen, Lily, Pam and Tulip*. New York: Whitney Museum of American Art, 1986; Alfred A. Knopf in association with the Whitney Museum, 1989.

"Ovando." *Conjunctions* 14 (1989):75–83.
"Song of Roland." *New Yorker* (12 April 1993): 94–98.

Autobiography

My Brother. New York: Farrar, Straus, and Giroux, 1997.

Nonfiction

A Small Place. New York: Farrar, Straus, and Giroux, 1988.
"On Seeing England for the First Time." *Transition* 51 (1991): 32–40; rptd. in *Harper's* (August 1991): 13–17.

Studies of Jamaica Kincaid

Caton, Louis F. "The Romantic Struggles: The Bildungsroman and Mother–Daughter Bonding in Jamaica Kincaid's *Annie John*." *Melus* 21 (1996): 125–42.
Chick, Nancy. "The Broken Clock: Time, Identity, and Autobiography in Jamaica Kincaid's *Lucy*." *College Language Association Journal* 40 (1996): 90–103.
Covi, Giovanna. "Jamaica Kincaid's Prismatic Self and the Decolonialisation of Language and Thought." *Framing the Word: Gender and Genre in Caribbean Women's Writing*. Ed. Joan Anim Addo. London: Whiting and Birch, 1996: 37–67.
Donnell, Alison. "Dreaming of Daffodils: Cultural Resistance in the Narratives of Theory." *Kunapipi* 14 (1992): 45–52.
———. "She Ties Her Tongue: The Problems of Cultural Paralysis in Postcolonial Criticism." *Ariel* 26 (1995): 101–15.
———. "When Daughters Defy: Jamaica Kincaid's Fiction." *Women: A Cultural Review* 4 (1993): 10–26.
———. "Writing for Resistance: Nationalism and Narratives of Liberation." *Framing the Word: Gender and Genre in Caribbean Women's Writing*. Ed. Joan Anim Addo. London: Whiting and Birch, 1996: 28–36.
Ferguson, Moira. *Jamaica Kincaid: Where the Land Meets the Body*. Charlottesville: University Press of Virginia, 1994.
———. "Lucy and the Mark of the Colonizer." *Modern Fiction Studies* 39 (1993): 237–59.
Frias, Maria. "Rites of Passage in Jamaica Kincaid's *Lucy*: Leaving the Sunny Island." *Contemporary Literature in the African Diaspora*. Ed. Olga Barrios and Bernard W. Bell. Salamanca, Spain: Universidad de Salamanca, 1997: 101–7.
Ismond, Patricia. "Jamaica Kincaid: 'First They Must Be Children.'" *World Literature Written in English* 28 (1988): 116–38.
Ledent, Benedicte. "Voyages into Otherness: *Cambridge* and *Lucy*." *Kunapipi* 14 (1992): 53–63.
Murdoch, H. Adlai. "Severing the (M)other Connection: The Representation of Cultural Identity in Jamaica Kincaid's *Annie John*." *Callaloo* 13 (1990): 325–40.
Nagel, James. "Desperate Hopes, Desperate Lives: Depression and Self-Realization in Jamaica Kincaid's *Annie John* and *Lucy*." *Traditions, Voices and Dreams: The American Novel since the 1960's*. Ed. Melvin J. Friedman and Ben Siegel. Newark: University of Delaware Press, 1995: 237–53.

Oczkowicz, Edyte. "Jamaica Kincaid's *Lucy*: Cultural 'Translation' as a Case of Creative Explorations of the Past." *Melus* 21 (1996): 143–57.

Perry, Donna. "Initiation in Jamaica Kincaid's *Annie John*." *Caribbean Women Writers: Essays from the First International Conference*. Ed. Selwyn R. Cudjoe. Wellesley, MA: Calaloux, 1990: 245–53.

Simmons, Diane. *Jamaica Kincaid*. New York: Twayne, 1994.

Tapping, Craig. "Children and History in the Caribbean Novel." *Kunapipi* 11.2 (1989): 51–59.

Tiffin, Helen. "Cold Hearts and (Foreign) Tongues: Recitation and the Reclamation of the Female Body in the Works of Erna Brodber and Jamaica Kincaid." *Callaloo* 16 (1993): 909–21.

Timothy, Helen Pyne. "Adolescent Rebellion and Gender Relations in *At the Bottom of the River* and *Annie John*." *Caribbean Women Writers: Essays from the First International Conference*. Ed. Selwyn R. Cudjoe. Wellesley, MA: Calaloux, 1990: 233–42.

Interviews

Birbalsingh, Frank. "Jamaica Kincaid: From Antigua to America." *Frontiers of Caribbean Literatures in English*. Ed. Frank Birbalsingh. New York: St. Martin's Press, 1996: 138–51.

Bonetti, Kay. "An Interview with Jamaica Kincaid." *Missouri Review* 15 (1993): 325–40.

Cudjoe, Selwyn. "Jamaica Kincaid and the Modernist Project: An Interview." *Caribbean Women Writers: Essays from the First International Conference*. Ed. Selwyn Cudjoe. Wellesley, MA: Calaloux, 1990: 215–32.

Ferguson, Moira. "A Lot of Memory: An Interview with Jamaica Kincaid." *The Kenyon Review* 16 (1994): 163–88.

Muirhead, Pamela Buchanan. "An Interview with Jamaica Kincaid." *Clockwatch Review* 9 (1994–95): 39–48.

Perry, Donna. "Jamaica Kincaid." *Backtalk: Women Writers Speak Out*. Ed. Donna Perry. New Brunswick, NJ: Rutgers University Press, 1993: 127–41.

Vorda, Allan. "An Interview with Jamaica Kincaid." *Mississippi Review* 20 (1991): 7–26; rptd. in *Face to Face: Interviews with Contemporary Novelists*. Ed. Allan Vorda and Daniel Stern. Houston: Rice University Press, 1993: 77–105.

ANDREA LEE
(1953–   )

Sarala Krishnamurthy

BIOGRAPHY

Andrea Lee was born in an educated, upper-middle-class family in Philadelphia. She grew up during the turbulent years of the Civil Rights movement. Educated in the best schools, Lee finished her master's degree in English from Harvard. At Harvard, she met and married Tom, who was specializing in Russian history. Subsequently, she accompanied Tom, who was awarded a fellowship to study in Russia, where she lived for ten months. Her experiences in Russia were recorded in a journal. After a year's stay, both Andrea and Tom returned to the United States, where Andrea took up a job and worked for several years as a staff reporter with the *New Yorker*. Now she lives with her husband in Paris.

Lee is renowned for the two books that she has written: *Russian Journal*, a nonfictional work culled from the entries in her diary that she maintained in Russia, and *Sarah Phillips*, a semiautobiographical novel for which she won the Jean Stein Award in 1984 from the American Academy and Institute of Arts and Letters. She has published several articles and short stories in periodicals like *New Yorker*, *New York Times*, *Vogue*, and others.

MAJOR WORKS AND THEMES

Russian Journal, which is Lee's first work, is a compilation of her experiences in Russia in the form of a series of vignettes. Being a student, she has access to the subculture and the dark underside of Russian life, which officially does not exist. A smattering of Russian helps her to maintain contact with the local people. In her book, Lee has depicted Russian life as it exists, shorn of hypocrisy, in the face of stringent oppression, and from the point of view of an unbiased narrator. She meets up with people from a variety of backgrounds such as students, politicians, farmers, aristocrats, musicians, and others.

She depicts the triumph of the individual spirit, which manifests itself in various ways. Some die-hard communists walk into the park at night to listen to a nightingale by moonlight. B. B. King's music moves the inhibited, but emotional, Russians, who weep in abandon while listening to him. The collections of music cassettes are proudly displayed to Lee and her husband.

The repression of individual consciousness and curtailment of freedom have created a clear demarcation between the rich party members who, because of their ideological affiliations, have access to riches beyond the imagination of Westerners like Tom and Lee and the larger majority of the oppressed class, who have to stand in ever-lengthening queues in order to scrounge for the basic necessities of life such as bread and cheese. *Russian Journal* captures these moments with rare candor and utmost sensitivity.

While in Russia, Lee does not seem to face any discrimination because of her color. In fact, *Russian Journal* does not reveal the racial origins of its writer. There is an oblique reference to her being an African American when she meets an Ethiopian called Ibrahim in Moscow. Ibrahim does not evince any interest in Lee's antecedents, embroiled as he is in the maelstrom of Ethiopian and Russian politics.

If *Russian Journal* encapsulates life in Russia, *Sarah Phillips* the novel depicts life in the United States in the 1960s.

Sarah Phillips encapsulates the heroine's quest for identity and selfhood. Generally, a quest for the self is a journey from innocence to experience, from potential fulfillment to actual accomplishment. But, in Sarah's case, this quest is not successful and leaves her tottering on the edge of an abyss that signifies the loss of self. This is because Sarah's journey through life is a journey away from her historical past and the mode of existence familiar to her parents. However hard she tries to ferret out a mode of perception for an intense, lived-in, subjective experience, she is never able to escape the existential truth of her own historicity. Throughout the novel, Sarah encounters people who could make her aware of the possibilities of her own existence. But these encounters never get transmuted into epiphanies.

Sarah is born into an upper-middle-class African American family. Her father, a preacher gifted with a ringing voice and a touching sense of humor, is actively involved in the Civil Rights movement. Her mother, a teacher, is engaged in community service. Sarah and her brother grow up in this environment. Sarah herself is a smart, sassy, intelligent, and rebellious young girl whose main goal in life is to seek the disapproval of her parents.

The novel opens with Sarah's sojourn in Paris in order to escape the debilitating influence of the upper-middle-class values that have been instilled into her. Her rite de passage in Paris involves interracial relationships with three men, easy nudity, disdain for career, and a total rejection of her past. Her moment of disillusionment with this bohemian life comes when she is called the offspring of "a mongrel Irish woman raped by a jazz musician as big and black as King-Kong" (42). Disconcerted, she returns to the United States.

The rest of the novel is taken up with scenes from Sarah's childhood carefully delineating the family and her life. Her first act of rebellion is her refusal to be baptized in the face of emotional pressure from her aunts. Her total rejection of the meaningless rituals that form the warp and woof of the social fabric of her father's life surprises him. For the first time he realizes that his daughter has a will of her own.

Not only is Mr. Phillips a popular and stentorian preacher, but he is also one of the leaders of the Civil Rights movement. His involvement in this political movement leaves his daughter untouched. When he is arrested for participating in a rally, and this feature is telecast over the national network, Sarah is embarrassed and slightly ashamed, as if somehow she has become tainted. At no point does she identify herself with her father, his beliefs and the Civil Rights movement, and the black cause.

Soon they move into a posh neighborhood, and Sarah is sent to Prescott, an all-white school. She finds herself initially to be an object of curiosity and later on is ignored by everybody. In a school where students and teachers are white, and the servants are black, Sarah becomes a misfit. She feels a sense of alienation because, being black, she is not accepted by her peers, and, because she belongs to a different social class, she cannot share a sense of camaraderie with the black servants. She develops a friendship with a girl called Gretchen, who is also marginalized in this setup. Together they explore the precincts of the school, and Sarah is surprised at the bleakness and squalor in which the black servants live. When the friendly black cook waves out to her, she is unable to respond. Later, she stares at him curiously, sensing that he has something to teach her, but she never learns. Her racial origins are brought home to her when she auditions for a play in school and is given the role of a black maid.

Having dissociated herself from her father and all that he represents and never having acquired a sense of self, Sarah leads a fragmented and alienated existence and is on the lookout for a new thrill every day.

Along with her schoolmates, she camps with a group of black boys from downtown called the Thunderbirds. This is her first brush with blacks who are poor, but tough and street-smart. These kids have an amazing sense of self-sufficiency and grit. However, she maintains a cool distance from them. Their joie de vivre strikes a chord in her, but she does not step across the wide gulf that divides them.

At the age of twelve, Sarah meets Mrs. Jeller, an old lady who is visited by her mother as a part of her social service program. Mrs. Jeller narrates her own dismal past when she was raped, became pregnant, got married, lost her baby, and was separated by the time she was fourteen. Mrs. Jeller's story forces Sarah to acknowledge the harsher realities of life. Her relationship with her mother undergoes a subtle change after this incident.

One day she meets some gypsies who, despite being relegated to the fringes of the white society, express a form of snobbery upon seeing black people living in a posh, but insular, neighborhood like Franklin Place. Sarah realizes that Franklin Place is a part of a larger social construct, but she is unaware of its possibilities.

As she grows up, Sarah defies her parents and breaks the codes they live by. The rigid social stratification of her own family disappoints her when her parents voice their disapproval of her brother Mathew's Jewish girlfriend, but she does not express her feelings. She rebels against her parents by indulging in interracial sex at Harvard, where she goes to pursue her education.

In Harvard, she meets Curry Daniels, whom she likes, but they decide not to get married to each other because their match would have pleased their parents. Both Sarah and Curry try to carve a future for themselves that has not been envisaged for them by their parents.

Her father's death is the turning point in Sarah's life. Even the loss of her beloved parent leaves her cold. She comes to Franklin Place to attend his funeral, but she is more conscious of how beautifully tragic she looks in her attire than her grief.

Sarah Phillips flits from moment to moment in her pursuit of selfhood. Since she never acknowledges the continuity of her historical and racial past, she never acquires a sense of self.

CRITICAL RECEPTION

There have been several reviews of both *Russian Journal* and *Sarah Phillips*. Most reviews have praised Andrea Lee for being a consummate technician and a keen observer. Her authority as a writer has been recognized because of her unstinting honesty and style, which has been described as "at once simple and luminous" (Shreve 13). By and large, the reviews have been favorable.

The importance of a novel like *Sarah Phillips* has been noted by several reviewers. While some critics have praised the novel for not having a flag-waving agenda, other commentators have pointed out that this, precisely, is the weakness of the novel. Obolensky has misgivings about Lee's style in *Sarah Phillips*. She states that the novel seems to be made up of several short stories. Further, Obolensky opines, Lee never really dramatizes the dilemma in the novel, which is the conflict between the moral and emotional worlds of her heroine, and rejects the novel as the work of an "elitist snob" (42). Williams argues that Sarah Phillips renounces the oral culture of the black people and holds up to mockery the outworn rituals of the community. Further, she adds, the novel does not alter the image of the black bourgeoisie.

Smith's analysis of Lee's *Sarah Phillips* provides a fresh perspective on the novel. *Sarah Phillips* is, according to Smith, about a heroine who is both privileged and marginal. The episodes in the novel enact the tension between "the narrative of the community of privilege, posited as ahistorical, and a destabilizing eruption, posited as inescapably historical" (51). The heroine of the novel locates herself within the bourgeois community. But the presence of the "other" disrupts and destabilizes her. Smith believes that in the very act of conceptualizing the self as insider, Sarah Phillips fetishizes the "other." Focusing on the gypsy episode in the novel, Smith elaborates that the presence of the gypsies reminds the residents of Franklin Place of their privileged position. The heroine, therefore, is not a rebel but an insider to this exclusionary community, and *Sarah Phillips* thematizes the relationship between those "who occupy privileged discursive spaces and the 'other' " (57).

Gibson comments that the book is far more complicated than it first appears because the author is aware of the tensions produced by "the intersections of race, class and color" (166). Extending the argument further, Hogue says that, though Sarah rejects her own historical past and the old-fashioned bourgeois values, she is never able to transcend them. In short, he states, that "neither Sarah Phillips nor Andrea Lee is able to visualize a new social model outside the conventions of the black middle class" (90). This causes a severe limitation in the novel, because of which it cannot realize its full potential.

BIBLIOGRAPHY

Works by Andrea Lee

Russian Journal (nonfiction). New York: Random House, 1981.
Sarah Phillips (fiction). New York: Random House, 1984.

Studies of Andrea Lee

Gibson, Donald B. "Sarah Phillips." Review of *Sarah Phillips*. *African American Review* 29.1 (Spring 1995): 164–66.
Goskowski, Francis. "Sarah Phillips." Review of *Sarah Phillips*. *Best Sellers* 44.11 (February 1985): 408.
Hogue, W. Lawrence. "The Limits of Modernity: Andrea Lee's *Sarah Phillips*." *MELUS* 19.4 (Winter 1994): 75–90.
Kapp, Isa. "The First Time Around." Review of *Sarah Phillips*. *The New Leader* 67.22 (December 10, 1984): 5–8.
Lehmann-Haupt, Christopher. "Sarah Phillips." Review of *Sarah Phillips*. *New York Times* (December 6, 1984): C 22.
Obolensky, Laura. "Scenes from a Girlhood." Review of *Sarah Phillips*. *The New Republic* 191:21 (November 19, 1984): 41–42.
Shreve, Susan Richards. "Unsentimental Journey." Review of *Sarah Phillips*. *The New York Times Book Review* (November 18, 1984): 13.
Smith, Valerie. "Black Feminist Theory and the Representation of the "Other." *Changing Our Own Words: Essays on Criticism, Theory and Writing*. Ed. Cheryl A. Wall. New Brunswick, NJ: Rutgers University Press, 1989: 38–57.
Taylor, Linda. "The Weapon of Laughter." Review of *Sarah Phillips* and *Merle* by Paule Marshall. *TLS* (April 5, 1985): 8.

Vigderman, Patricia. "Sarah Phillips." Review of *Sarah Phillips*. *Boston Review* (February 1985): 23–24.

Williams, Sherley Anne. "Roots of Privilege." Review of *Sarah Phillips*. *Ms.* 13 (June 1985): 69–72.

Wyngarden, Bruce Van. "Pieces of the Past." Review of *Sarah Phillips*. *Saturday Review* 11.1 (February 1985): 74.

AUDREY LEE
(1930?–?)

Charles Tita

BIOGRAPHY

Audrey Lee was born in Philadelphia, but details relating to her birth are very elusive. She attended Temple University and later attended a creative writing class at Columbia University. Although she has authored several short stories, Lee is known mostly for her two novels, *The Clarion People* (1968) and *The Workers* (1969). Few other biographical details are available. At the beginning of *The Clarion People*, the protagonist gives us a portrait of herself—one characterized by a certain "distancing"—that perhaps sheds light on Lee's biographical enigma:

Call me a romantic. But I have sought to gain an edge on life by keeping my distance. Lillian Peoples is my name. Presently of the rest home. Formerly a tenant of a white brick apartment house five blocks from the main street of the city. And if I persist upon your ear, it is because my trouble is your trouble; my concern, your concern.

MAJOR WORKS AND THEMES

The Clarion People—Lee's first novel—tells, with considerable linguistic and structural inventiveness, the story of its young protagonist, Lillian Peoples, who is pitted against the vagaries of city life. Because Lillian Peoples was born and raised in a rural setting, her innocence becomes the backdrop against which the various depressing statistics of city living are defamiliarized. From the outset, everything about the city shocks Lillian as she notes that "something is always happening in the city. People and movement" (7).

The theme of growth is very evident in *The Clarion People*, which reads as a bildungsroman. The growth and maturation of the protagonist are a major project in *Clarion People*. Prior to her arrival in the city to become a hospital worker, Lillian Peoples is portrayed as a virtuous young woman in a pure and natural environment. However, her innocence is based on guarded virtue and ignorance; it is infantile virtue that has not faced the test of experience. As the novel unfolds, Lillian Peoples has the opportunity to undergo the full development of a Blakeian progression: innocence→experience→higher innocence. At twenty-one, Lillian leaves her tranquil country home for the city, where she loses her virginity, her belief in God, and her sanity. In spite of her total immersion in an amorphous cauldron of city experiences, Lillian Peoples comes to the self-realization that she can still recapture her innocence. Thus, as she recovers from a nervous breakdown in a rest home, she meditates on her life and finally recaptures, psychologically, a tangible state of innocence. Like the rest home, which is located in the middle of the city but still provides resting and healing, Lillian Peoples comes to the understanding that virtue can be extracted from vice and that tested innocence (higher innocence) is impossible in the absence of experience.

Lillian Peoples "loses" her virginity (85) in order to gain a new sense of self; thus, it is not a loss but a process of forging a new self: "Virginity. And the loss of it. Why is the one called pure? Does purity pass with the passing of virginity?" (109). This theme of growth is captured more tangibly via an epiphanic moment in which Lillian Peoples sees the ironic verity of change: "Once I saw a man stop his car at a traffic light and jump out of the car with a shovel. He scooped a shovelful of horse manure, as pleased as a man who had recovered a lost treasure. Fertilizer. Waste that can be used to aid growth" (50–51). Like horse dung that fosters plant growth, knowledge of vice (experience) leads to a resilient and tested innocence.

The narrative of *The Clarion People* is punctuated with discourses of morbidity and naturalistic realism. Bitter over the death of a neighbor who leads a troubled life and who finally dies a miserable death and is "wrapped in a sack" and "denied the dignity of riding in a hearse" (83), Lillian Peoples questions "what God could deal such an injustice?" (83). The narrative addresses death as an indifferent leveler: "You are born to suffer and die. What you do between birth and death does not matter. The end result is the same for everyone" (83). Lillian Peoples then meditates on the value of proper burials and wonderful eulogies. Do these homages really matter to the dead? "It is a play in itself. Reading and praying over, and eulogizing a corpse. To hell with the corpse. What about the man? Did they eulogize the man? Did they respect the man and feel sorry for the man?" (93). These are existentialist perspectives that raise questions about the human condition.

In spite of the seeming meaninglessness of life as depicted in the novel, the narrative seeks to convey to us that meaning and satisfaction are achievable goals. The narrator points out that the significance of living relies in the realization that one could lose life: "When you come so near to death, that is when you see the value of life. The true value. You want to drain it of all its potentiality for you. You swell within it. . . . I said I hadn't any aspirations before then" (115).

The Clarion People also evokes some of the grim ironies of modernity. Cities, for example, are a product of human civilization, but in the novel the city is portrayed as savage, chaotic, and unsavory. *The Clarion People* is, indeed, a depiction of the madness of uncivilized happenings transacted by "civilized" people whom the narrator describes as "haggard, depraved, vegetating" (17). As Lillian Peoples notes, we are all involved in the travesty of civilized living—no one is free from this ironic twist: "Clarion voices penetrate my apartment. Idlers pound the pavement night and day. Profusion of profanity. And yet I cannot see beyond the mote in my own eye that reflects upon itself, lest I forget" (109).

In a short epistolary note entitled "In Our Times," the narrative synthesizes the futile quest for satisfaction in our times—the times we call "civilized":

In our times, more than in any time past, there is a desperate search for meaning. . . . We sense a great void in our lives. A great leak in all our efforts toward self-fulfillment. We earn money and purchase all kinds of material goods with it. We marry and we have children. Still there is some lack we cannot explain. . . . More frustrations. So we change husbands and wives. Have more children. Earn more money and purchase more material goods. Still no satisfaction. So we attack our neighbors and our friends. And then we die of exhaustion, never knowing what it was we lacked. A simple word like "meaning," like "faith," like "God." (90)

The Clarion People is also a commentary on the creative process. Through her insightful comments, the narrator leads us to see the deeper levels of narrative expression that foreground the art of writing. Herbert, Lillian's confidant, tells her of how the death of his mother turned his world upside down and how he managed to regain perspective. In spite of all the confusions around us, Herbert asserts that "there is an internal order, even in seeming chaos" (36). The central discourse of *The Clarion People* affirms this paradox of beauty in chaos. The creative process as depicted in this novel mimics the primal act of creation in which God's spoken word spun a beautiful world out of chaotic emptiness. It is the same formula that the narrator here is following as she attempts to reconcile existentialist contradictions by simply appealing to the power of the word.

Audrey Lee's second novel, *The Workers* (1969), is a more straightforward narrative in which she reveals her extraordinary powers of character analysis. In this novel, Lee's philosophical capacity to delve into complex existentialist questions is at once comparable to Fyodor Dostoyevsky's. Because *The Workers* raises various dialectics of economic determinism as a pervasive historical reality of the twentieth century, it readily lends itself to Marxist explorations—explorations that might link all major themes in this novel.

The death of sensibility is a major theme in *The Workers*. The high premium that the eighteenth century placed on "sensibility" was a reaction to the "stoicism" of the seventeenth century. Athough the term "sensibility" is used in a totally different sense in the twentieth century, it is used in *The Workers* in much the same way as "sensibility" was used in the eighteenth century. The twentieth century is a complex industrial age in which monstrous economic rationales seek to supplant, in the beggar's words to Harvie (the protagonist), the human "touch": "What you need is touch, Harvie. You are out of touch. You've been working with machines too long, Harvie" (7).

Although the Industrial Revolution was brought about by people's quest to improve the quality of life, this rationale is held up to ridicule in *The Workers*. There is no doubt that machines have improved the the quality of life, but in so doing, they also turned our hearts and brains into machines that lack human touch. Harvie is a noted employee whose "human" dexterity has brought him great recognition, but he is fired by his employer, Mr. Davidson, when he is unable to keep up with the changing pace of the machine age. The narratorial commentary points out the irony of the industrial age: "see how the faithful are rewarded? Realizing that he [Harvie] was just another tool for the job, the other part of the machine. Had the machine reacted to Harvie, Mr. Davidson would have decided the machine needed repairing. But then, Harvie reacted to the machine, and Mr. Davidson decided that Harvie needed replacing" (21).

The Workers is an allegory in which a person is reduced to a tool or a spare part to be used and discarded by the monstrous machine called "industrialism." Who is in charge of this machinery? Is it a mechanism in which a person is exploiting a person? These are fundamental questions that the novel raises. Although human greed is at the base of the capitalist project, the monstrous spirit itself, not a person, is shown to be in charge. Harvie is an "everyman" through whose consciousness the value of work and of the worker is reassessed in the large context of the machine age. The coat hanger metaphor is used, also, to capture the pervasive spirit of individualism that permeates the industrial age. People seem to be chasing the same goods and services, and there is a painful indifference when one person falls in the course of the chase. When David, a factory hand, dies in the hospital, his colleagues seem to be more worried about who will replace him permanently. Why all this struggle? Anne, another factory hand, tells Harvie that "you can have everything if you don't want too much" (51).

Trapped in an exhausting machine age that is continually demanding of him and that is less rewarding to his inner demands, Harvie contemplates suicide: "He'd often thought of dying just before his bills were due so that he could escape having to pay them. He had imagined a holocaust that would destroy all records of his indebtedness" (127). Harvie comes to the conclusion that, although work is ennobling for many people, for others it is simply a humdrum ordeal that leads to nowhere. Seeing Gertrude Swank, a restaurant employee, do her menial job is an epiphanic moment in which Harvie sees his own entrapment in the clutches of work. So he kills her, as he puts it, because "she kept mocking me" (142). He visualizes the futility of work that lacks human touch and kills Gertrude—in his justification—to save her and himself.

CRITICAL RECEPTION

In spite of her creative ingenuity, Audrey Lee is still largely unknown to the literary world. Immediately following publication of *The Clarion People* and *The Workers*, a few reviews of the two novels appeared in such renowned periodicals as *Negro Digest* and *New York Times Book Review*. Martin Levin noted that *The Clarion People* is a novel in which its protagonist "records her impressions of slum life with a mixture of alertness and wisdom. Both frightened and fascinated, she has a clear eye for the street scenes outside her window. The best interludes in Audrey Lee's appealing book are these sidewalk vignettes" (37). In the same review, Levin goes on to say that Lee "is less successful at describing what goes on within a heroine almost submerged in urban corruption" (37). This is an important review because its analysis of Lee's style enables the reader to see *The Clarion People* as a novel of incident—like Daniel Defoe's *Robinson Crusoe*—in which incidents, rather than character, are foregrounded. Lee must have paid attention to such reviews, because in *The Workers* character is foregrounded.

It is, indeed, surprising that during the last twenty-five years there has hardly been any critical writing on Audrey Lee's work, nor has there been inclusion of her work in any major anthology of American/African American literature.

BIBLIOGRAPHY

Works by Audrey Lee

Novels

The Clarion People. New York: McGraw, 1968.
The Workers. New York: McGraw, 1969.

Short Fiction and Essays

"A Man Is a Man." *Essence* 1 (February 1969a): 40–41, 68, 70.
"Moma; Story." *Negro Digest* 18 (February 1969b): 53–65.
"I'm Going to Move Out of This Emotional Ghetto." *Negro Digest* 19 (December 1969): 63–68.
"The Ride." *Essence* 1 (June 1970): 60–61.
"The Block." *Black World* 19 (October 1970): 65–72.
"Alienation." *Black World* 21 (November 1971): 64–66.
"Antonio Is a Man." *Essence* 2 (January 1972): 44–45.
"Eulogy for a Public Servant." *Black World* 25 (January 1976): 54–57.

Studies of Audrey Lee

Casey, G. Rev. of *The Clarion People*. *Best Sellers* 15 (May 1968): 89.
Giovanni, N. Rev. of *The Clarion People*. *Negro Digest* 17 (September/October 1968): 14.
Levin, M. Rev. of *The Clarion People*. *New York Times Book Review* 19 (May 1968): 37.

Morse, J. M. Rev. of *The Clarion People*. *Hudson Review* 21 (Autumn 1968): 522.

Rev. of *The Clarion People*. *Publishers Weekly* 12 (February 1968): 71.

Rev. of *The Clarion People*. *Kirkus* 15 (March 1968): 357.

Rev. of *The Clarion People*. *Library Journal* 15 (June 1968): 2521.

Rev. of *The Workers*. *Publishers Weekly* 30 (June 1969): 62.

Rev. of *The Workers*. *Kirkus* 1 (July 1969a): 694.

Rev. of *The Workers*. *Library Journal* 94 (July 1969b): 2640.

PHILIP LEWIS
(?–)

Jeffrey B. Dunham

BIOGRAPHY

Born in Atlanta, Philip Lewis attended Howard University in Washington, D.C., a major research center for African and African American studies. Currently, Lewis resides in Adelphi, Maryland. Further details of his life are currently unavailable.

MAJOR WORKS AND THEMES

Life of Death is an explosive novel that seethes with anger and rage. The similarity between the name of the novel's protagonist, Louis Phillips, and Philip Lewis suggests that the story may be at least semiautobiographical. Chapter 1 of the novel is reminiscent of the Prologue in Ralph Ellison's* *Invisible Man*, as the narrator directly addresses the audience and gives some insight into his motivation in the story: "What I really wanted deep down was to pay back the impossible for all those long years and months and weeks and days and nights of pure insanity, chaos, hopelessness and despair" (10). From the beginning, Lewis tries to influence the reader's expectations by providing a Prologue that presents a reflective narrator assessing the manner in which he will be received. As the invisible man predicts that the audience will find him "a horrible, irresponsible bastard" (14) in Ellison's *Invisible Man*, Phillips assumes his audience will find his story "an object of the utmost evil, an outright pack of lies, some sickly piece of insanity thrown together by some psycho nigger" (9). Phillips is of mixed racial heritage, his father being African American and his mother Portuguese. His mother stifles his early desire to be an artist, contributing to his rejection of what he considers to be their bourgeois lifestyle, and increasingly he adopts a rebellious, nihilistic view of life. What follows is an emotional, rambling diatribe against his parents, his job, his position in society, and society in general.

At his mother's insistence, Phillips enrolls in college to study business and soon begins to despise Coon State University, which he considers to be "that old bastion of Negro education where we all go to get as white as cream, and just as cold, too" (17). Determined that he was not going to be "assimilated," Phillips experiences an epiphany of sorts, drops out of college, and dreams of expatriation by escaping to Istanbul or Amsterdam. Desperate for money to finance his trip abroad, Phillips obtains a job at a restaurant chain called the Dummheit Cafe, which employs minorities and pays low wages. He is treated abusively by his employers and observes egregiously violent behavior in his fellow employees yet is unable to leave his job in spite of the horrible working conditions. Phillips feels trapped by his circumstances, as his parents' behavior mirrors that of his coworkers, causing him to be equally unable to assert himself against them as well as his employers. Phillips's coworkers engage in a series of increasingly violent sexual acts, in some of which he participates. He is eventually driven to steal money from the restaurant safe and escape to Istanbul. Phillips generalizes the atmosphere at the Dummheit Cafe to life in America in general: "It wasn't just the Dummheit because the Dummheit was a reflection of what was going on all over the country" (225).

Thematically, Lewis writes in opposition to the traditional treatment of the theme of community and individual identity in African American literature. African American literature usually privileges the individual's journey back to the community. However, in *Life of Death*, we have a protagonist who is in opposition to his community. Louis Phillips' emerging consciousness and identity have no place in American society, but we never really get the sense that Istanbul or Amsterdam will provide him with the acceptance he seeks. He desires only to escape the madness and insanity that he has experienced. Every time that he has tried to define himself on his own terms, he has been stifled and repressed. For example, his desire to be an artist is vehemently discouraged by his mother, who insists that he go into some form of business as an occupation. He is unhappy about the unethical treatment that he receives at the Dummheit Cafe but feels that his need to save money for his escape has left him no choice but to endure even the most humiliating treatment.

As Phillips becomes more aware of his emerging identity, he becomes curiously sensitive to the paradox of death existing within life. In response to his experiences at the Dummheit Cafe, Phillips considers that "if I ever took it into my head to write a book, it would unquestionably be about the inner private life I dwelled in and not this death life of plexiglass and daily body counts" (70). A dichotomy obviously exists between Phillips' own perception of life and the reality represented by the Dummheit Cafe. It is reconciling himself with, or coming to terms with, this external reality that his character fails to do. Phillips' sexual identity informs and encompasses his entire existence: "For at bottom, everything is sex in this life of death, everything leads to sex, and nothing else . . . really has any more value" (83–84). Indeed, the novel depicts one sexual experience after another, often in the violent context of rape. Lewis presents sex as a pervasive element of life that is often the basis of much of the violence perpetrated on the disfranchised and exploited. Also, the reference to the title in the previous passage is no accident. Lewis is aware of the connection between sex and death and that sexual tensions are often at the core of racial tensions. Phillips constantly ponders the hopelessness of his situation but demonstrates an almost Hamlet-like inability to extricate himself from it. He feels as if he is "walking in a damn sleeping bag, a death womb. No one deserves to live or feel this way, no matter what anyone says" (126). For Louis Phillips, the death he is experiencing in life refers to the false values, insincerity, hypocrisy, and violence of society.

Phillips is ostensibly using his experience at the Dummheit Cafe to embark on a journey of his own. He hopes that this journey will lead to the self-discovery that he cannot obtain in America. However, he is unable to separate himself completely from the environment in which he is maturing. In spite of the fact that he openly reviles the behavior of his employers and coworkers, he cannot resist participating in some of their repulsive acts. While Phillips may be able to escape the physical reality of the world represented by the Dummheit Cafe, he will not be able to transcend his participation in that world. At the end of the novel, Phillips has finally escaped to Istanbul but continues to receive news of the often tragic fate of his coworkers in America. Ironically, the cycle of exploitation begins again. Phillips' naive female Egyptian companion, eager for work and the promise of prosperity in America, excitedly reads the same advertisement for employment at the Dummheit Cafe that began his own journey.

CRITICAL RECEPTION

Philip Lewis has received little scholarly or critical attention, with the exception of three reviews of *Life of Death*, two of which appeared immediately after the release of the book in 1993 and the other in 1996. The reviews were generally positive in terms of Lewis' graphic portrayal of the life of the food service worker but were critical of his unwillingness to present any of his characters as redeemable amid the chaos and satire. On the jacket of the novel, John A. Williams compares *Life of Death* to Dante's *Inferno*. Indeed, Louis Phillips' descent into the madness and insanity of life at the Dummheit Cafe parallels a descent into hell, giving the novel a mythical dimension. Lewis' narrative structure gives the impression of a descent into madness from which there is no escape. Sentences gradually run on and ramble hysterically, giving the impression of a stream of consciousness gone insane.

James Hannaham commented at length on Lewis' use of satire. According to Hannaham, Lewis writes "with a narrative so abrasive, outrageous, and violent that it can only have been meant satirically. Unfortunately, it isn't very funny, even as Black black humor" (58). Hannaham points to one weakness of the novel as being the fact that the characters are presented as one-dimensional caricatures lacking a full range of human qualities. He also notes that Phillips has some complicity with his coworkers' actions and is not an innocent victim of circumstance. In fact, Hannaham asserts that "he's just as unredeemable as his coworkers," as he eavesdrops on a violent rape scene without making a move to intervene (58). The numerous rape scenes in the novel often function as satire, which Hannaham criticizes. By having Phillips participate in the degrading acts that characterize the depths of his despair, Lewis misses the opportunity to engage the reader with his message. However, he does point out that the realistic depiction of the dreadful working conditions and the relations between employers and employees demonstrates an understanding of the lack of empowerment experienced by many black Americans.

In a favorable review Kwaku O. Kushindana suggests that "the Dummheit Cafe becomes an operational theater to illustrate that the pathology afoot in this society is not confined to any single patient. Indeed, the madness has reached pandemic proportions" (44). Kushindana points out the pervasive sense of hysteria in the novel, noting the acceptability of such violent acts as rape. The actions of the characters in the novel become so outrageous that criminal acts of sex and violence become normal. Kushindana proposes that the Dummheit Cafe is a metaphor for life in America, showcasing the various ethnic and socioeconomic differences in American society and how these differences interact. Kushindana praises Lewis as a nonconformist and compliments him for his skill in exposing "how the downtrodden and disenfranchised . . . are used as scapegoats for the ills of society" (44).

In a more recent review Jerome Klinkowitz focuses on Lewis' ability to use language to transcend the disturbing and horrifying scenes in the novel. He suggests that "Lewis is able to use such material transformatively, offering a picture of life that is inventively instructive rather than ironically surreal" (149). Lewis keeps the unbelievably exaggerated characters in the novel alive by focusing on language, creating a linguistic structure in which these caricatures can realistically exist. Klinkowitz notes that "it is [Lewis'] eminently postmodern understanding of language's role in the construction of reality that makes this fixture possible" (149). Klinkowitz also finds Lewis' social commentary to be significant and valid. The outrageous actions of the characters and the situations in which they find themselves do not supersede another of Lewis' goals, which is to expose the plight of the food service worker in corporate America.

Perhaps because he has written only one novel, no further critical attention has been given to Philip Lewis other than these relatively brief reviews. This is unfortunate, considering the power of his language and the favorable response elicited from reviewers. If Lewis were to generate a larger body of work, he would almost certainly attract the attention of literary critics.

BIBLIOGRAPHY

Works by Philip Lewis

Novel

Life of Death. Normal: Fiction Collective Two, 1993.

Review

Rev. of *Iron House: Stories from the Yard* by Jerome Washington. *African American Review* 30 (1996): 497–99.

Studies of Philip Lewis

Hannaham, James. "Rapes of Wrath." Rev. of *Life of Death. Village Voice* (30 Nov. 1993): 58.
Klinkowitz, Jerome. Rev. of *Life of Death. African American Review* 30 (1996): 148–49.
Kushindana, Kwaku O. Rev. of *Life of Death. Small Press* 12 (1993): 44.

AUDRE LORDE
(1934–1992)

AnnLouise Keating

BIOGRAPHY

The daughter of West Indian immigrant parents, Audre Lorde was born and raised in New York City. This self-described "Black Woman Warrior Poet" developed an emotional relationship to poetry early in her life: she did not begin speaking until she was four years old and for many years expressed herself primarily by quoting from the poetry she read. She left home shortly after graduating from high school and entered into a series of relationships with women and men. During this time, she worked to put herself through Hunter College and Columbia University School of Library Science. After a brief interracial marriage resulting in two children, Lorde adopted a highly political lesbian identity. She supported her writing by teaching English at several New York colleges.

For Lorde, there was no separation between writing and life. Throughout her career, she extended her personal experiences outward and combined activism with art, creating poetry, prose, and fiction that defy preestablished categories of meaning. Drawing on her long-term relationship with a white-identified woman, her experiences as a lesbian mother of two children, including one son, and her life as a black woman in twentieth-century U.S. society, she challenged multiple issues simultaneously, including racism and sexism in lesbian/feminist communities, sexism in the Black Power movement, and ethnocentrism and classism in U.S. feminism. Diagnosed with cancer in 1978, Lorde underwent a radical mastectomy. She describes this experience in *The Cancer Journals*, where she underscores the importance of speaking out. Six years later she learned that she had liver cancer, metastasized from the breast cancer. She charts her painful battle with this cancer in *A Burst of Light* and many of the poems posthumously published in *The Marvelous Arithmatics of Distance*. During the last eight years of her

life she spent much time in Germany, where she sought alternative cancer treatments. Despite her declining health, she remained actively involved in local and
international political issues.

Author of ten books of poetry and four of prose, Lorde received numerous
awards and acquired international recognition as a cultural worker and visionary
artist of change. In addition to lecturing throughout the United States and in
Europe, Australia, and New Zealand, she played founding roles in many national
and international groups, including Kitchen of Table Press and SISA (Sisterhood
in Support of Sisters in South Africa). In 1991 she became the first woman
appointed poet laureate of New York state. Lorde died of cancer in 1992 in St.
Croix. Shortly before her death, Lorde changed her name to Gamda Adisa—
"Warrior—She Who Makes Her Meaning Known."

MAJOR WORKS AND THEMES

Zami: A New Spelling of My Name defies easy classification. Variously labeled
a novel, an autobiography, or a prose poem, Lorde herself provides the most
useful description, naming it "biomythography." As the term implies, she synthesizes autobiography, biography, fiction, cultural history, and myth into a hybrid literary form. Lorde utilizes an episodic structure and employs highly poetic,
often ritualized language bordering at times on invocation to celebrate the mythic
and historic women in her life. By entitling her book "*Zami*"—which she trans-
lates as "*women who work together as friends and lovers*" (255)—she underscores
the vital role women played in her self-naming process. She implies that through
language and silence the women in her life—her mother, Gennie, Ginger, Eudora, Muriel, and Kitty/Afrekete—shaped her; by so doing, they enabled her to
redefine herself, creating "a new spelling of [her] name." This "new spelling"
represents an innovative departure in U.S. literature: it is the first full-length
representation of African American lesbian identity.

Throughout the early sections of *Zami* Lorde retraces her complex relationship
with her light-skinned West Indian mother. Although her mother provided her
with a vital image of feminine power, her silence concerning the realities of
racism in everyday life had a less positive effect on her daughter's self-worth. In
order to deny the prejudice that threatened her family, Audre's mother would
not openly acknowledge her own "blackness," nor would she discuss the differences in skin tone between herself, her husband, and her three daughters. This
maternal silence concerning racism and colorism restricted Audre's ability to
define herself and prevented her from understanding how her skin color positioned her in the racialized structure of twentieth-century U.S. social systems.
Because she "had no words for racism," she could not understand its impact in
her life. Instead, assuming she was somehow personally flawed, young Audre
became silent and withdrawn.

Lorde charts her transition from silence to language and the concurrent growth
in self-knowledge and self-acceptance as she describes her relationships with

women. As she writes in the "Epigraph," "Every woman I have ever loved has left her print upon me, where I loved some invaluable piece of myself apart from me—so different that I had to stretch and grow in order to recognize her. And in that growing, we came to separation, that place where work begins. Another meeting" (255). These negotiations between difference and commonality, between meeting, growth, and departure structure Lorde's biomythography. Each relationship teaches Audre important lessons about herself and important lessons about loving women. With Gennie, her "first true friend" (87), Audre learns the value of intimacy. With Ginger, her first female lover, Audre learns to trust her body's erotic power. This episode illustrates the performative, transformational nature of Lorde's self-naming process: only when Ginger names her an experienced lover of women can Audre act on her unacknowledged, unspoken desires for women. With Eudora, Audre learns to transform her experience into language; because Eudora taught her "how to love and live to tell the story, and with flair" (209), she can acknowledge and openly express her emotions. With Muriel, Audre learns the importance of articulating differences among women. This episode illustrates another component of Lorde's self-naming process, as well as a recurring pattern in her work, where the erasure of differences—even when motivated by the desire to establish bonds among differently situated subjects—inadvertently creates further divisions. With Kitty/Afrekete, Audre learns to celebrate her own body in new ways.

This final, highly erotic episode underscores the central role revisionist mythmaking plays in Lorde's construction of individual and collective black lesbian identities. Drawing analogies between Kitty/Afrekete and Yoruban/Fon myth, she associates her lesbianism with precolonial West African communal traditions and connects her erotic love for women with her mother's Caribbean homeland.

By depicting her complex relationships with women from a variety of economic classes, sexualities, and colors, Lorde demonstrates that no matter how concise the identity markers might seem to be, they do not automatically unite women into self-affirming communities. Throughout *Zami*, she draws on the numerous forms of alienation she experienced to complicate simplistic notions of commonality based on ethnic, gender, or sexual identities: "*Being women together was not enough. We were different. Being gay-girls together was not enough. We were different. Being Black together was not enough. We were different. Being Black women together was not enough. We were different. Being Black dykes together was not enough. We were different*" (226). Significantly, this acknowledgment does not compel Lorde to adopt a separatist stance. Instead, she maintains that the recognition of differences generates new forms of bonding.

CRITICAL RECEPTION

Although *Zami*'s importance has been recognized by feminist scholars of all colors, its openly political, lesbian dimensions have prevented mainstream U.S. and African American scholars from acknowledging its place in twentieth-century canons. Generally, critical reception focuses on Lorde's revolutionary construction of a black U.S. lesbian identity and its impact on African and European American female literary traditions.

Early essays by Barbara Christian, Barbara Smith, and others read *Zami* in the context of contemporary African American women's writings, emphasizing the text's groundbreaking nature. Smith, for instance, argues that—unlike previous writings, which generally ignore lesbian experience—Lorde attains new levels of "verisimilitude and authenticity" (696). Later essays expand this focus by locating *Zami* within intersecting traditions. Anna Wilson, for example, argues that *Zami* draws on, and revises, both Euro-American lesbian and African American heterosexual literature. Katie King uses Lorde's biomythography—especially the descriptions of 1950s lesbian bars—to analyze racialized relations of power in lesbian and gay histories. Bonnie Zimmerman reads *Zami* in the context of contemporary U.S. lesbian literature, arguing that Lorde and other ethnic/racialized lesbian writers "undertake a more complex search for the source and meaning of identity" than do "lesbian writers of the dominant culture" (199); in so doing, they "unsettle the static and conventional notions of self and community created by the dominant mythology of white lesbian feminists" (205). Focusing on the lesbian body, Cheryl Kader positions *Zami* at the intersections of contemporary lesbian and feminist writings to demonstrate that Lorde's text "invok[es] the possibility of a new discursive and historical subject" (183). Similarly, Erin Carlston argues that Lorde's construction of an " 'impure' and nonstatic" racialized, gendered, sexual identity challenges simplistic notions of feminist identity politics (233).

Others examine Lorde's revisionist mythmaking and maternal imagery. Chinosole, for example, argues that Lorde draws on her mother's mythic, cultural roots to create a "matrilineal diaspora" (386) and an ethnic-specific identity. Similarly, Claudine Raynaud claims that Lorde uses her mother's poetic language and West African myth to invent "the black woman of the future" (238). In " 'making our shattered faces whole' " AnnLouise Keating extends these interpretations and argues that Lorde's revisionary myth utilizes yet goes beyond culturally specific traditions to create a multiethnic, gender-specific collective identity. In *Women Reading Women Writing* Keating explores the roles maternal silence and Yoruban/Fon myth play in Lorde's construction of racialized "black" and "white" identities. She argues that Lorde uses revisionist myth to develop an interactional model of identity formation and a nondual epistemology capable of transforming her readers as well as herself.

BIBLIOGRAPHY

Works by Audre Lorde

The Cancer Journals. San Francisco: Spinsters/Aunt Lute, 1980.
Zami: A New Spelling of My Name. Freedom, CA: Crossing Press, 1982.

A Burst of Light. Ithaca, NY: Firebrand, 1988.
The Marvelous Arithmatics of Distance. New York: Norton, 1993.

Studies of Audre Lorde

Carlston, Erin. "*Zami* and the Politics of Plural Identity." *Sexual Practice, Textual Theory: Lesbian Cultural Criticism.* Ed. Susan J. Wolfe and Julia Penelope. Cambridge: Blackwell, 1993. 237–50.

Chinosole. "Audre Lorde and Matrilineal Diaspora: 'Moving History beyond Nightmare into Structures for the Future.'" *Wild Women in the Whirlwind: Afra-American Culture and the Contemporary Literary Renaissance.* Ed. Joanne M. Braxton and Andrée Nicola McLaughin. New Brunswick, NJ: Rutgers University Press, 1990. 379–94.

Christian, Barbara. "No More Buried Lives: The Theme of Lesbianism in Audre Lorde's *Zami*, Gloria Naylor's *The Women of Brewster Place*, Ntozake Shange's *Sassafras, Cypress and Indigo*, and Alice Walker's *The Color Purple*. *Black Feminist Criticism: Perspectives on Black Women Writers.* New York: Pergamon Press, 1985.

Kader, Cheryl. "'The Very House of Difference': *Zami*, Audre Lorde's Lesbian-Centered Text." *Critical Essays: Gay and Lesbian Writers of Color.* Ed. Emmanuel S. Nelson. New York: Haworth Press, 1993. 181–94.

Keating, AnnLouise. *Women Reading Women Writing: Self-Invention in Paula Gunn Allen, Gloria Anzaldúa, and Audre Lorde.* Philadelphia: Temple University Press, 1996.

Keating, AnnLouise. "Making 'Our Shattered Faces Whole': The Black Goddess and Audre Lorde's Revision of Patriarchal Myth." *Frontiers: A Journal of Women Studies* 13 (1992): 20–33.

King, Katie. "Audre Lorde's Lacquered Layerings: The Lesbian Bar as a Site of Literary Production." *Lesbian Criticism: Literary and Cultural Readings.* Ed. Sally Munt. New York: Columbia University Press, 1992. 51–74.

Raynaud, Claudine. "'A Nutmeg Nestled inside Its Covering of Mace': Audre Lorde's *Zami*." *Life/Lines: Theorizing Women's Autobiography.* Ed. Bella Brodzki and Celeste Schenck. Ithaca, NY: Cornell University Press, 1988. 221–42.

Smith, Barbara. "The Truth That Never Hurts: Black Lesbians in Fiction in the 1980s." *Wild Women in the Whirlwind: Afra-American Culture and the Contemporary Literary Renaissance.* Ed. Joanne M. Braxton and Andrée Nicola McLaughlin. New Brunswick, NJ: Rutgers University Press, 1990.

Wilson, Anna. "Audre Lorde and the African-American Tradition: When the Family Is Not Enough." *Lesbian Criticism: Literary and Cultural Readings.* Ed. Sally Munt. New York: Columbia University Press, 1992. 75–94.

Zimmerman, Bonnie. *The Safe Sea of Women: Lesbian Fiction 1969–1989.* Boston: Beacon, 1990.

CLARENCE MAJOR
(1936–   )

Tracie Church Guzzio

BIOGRAPHY

Clarence Major was born December 31, 1936, in Atlanta, Georgia. At age ten, Major's parents divorced, and he moved to Chicago with his mother. At the Art Institute of Chicago, Major discovered the works of Vincent van Gogh and Paul Cezanne, which he has described as "catalysts" for his painting and writing. At seventeen, Major received a fellowship to the Art Institute of Chicago and began to explore his own work. Frustrated with his attempts, Major remained at the institute for less than a year. The urgency and experimental spirit of modern art and Major's own work as an artist, however, would be important influences on his writing. In the same year he left the institute, Major published a small pamphlet of poems.

Following two years in the air force (1955–1957), Major published his first story, "Ulysses, Who Slept Across from Me." He also became the editor of the *Coercion Review* (1958–1961). After moving to New York in 1966, Major became the associate editor of the *Journal of Black Poetry*, a position he held for three years. While there, Major wrote the essay "A Black Criteria," which espoused aesthetics like those of the Black Arts movement. He would later argue that any agenda that forces a writer to conform to political or artistic beliefs is "repulsive," adding that "we have to get away from this rigid notion that there are certain topics and methods reserved for black writers" (O'Brien 127). In 1969, Major's first novel, *All-Night Visitors*, was published.

During these years, Major taught literature and creative writing at Brooklyn College and Sarah Lawrence. He would later teach at Howard, University of Washington, and University of Colorado after earning his Ph.D. In the early 1970s, Major, along with Ronald Sukenick and Raymond Federman, established the Fiction Collective, whose goal was to publish experimental work that would otherwise be overlooked by mainstream presses. During these years, Major wrote the popular column "Open Letters" for *American Poetry Review*. Written as letters to artists and cultural figures (real and fictional), the column discussed art, politics, and African American issues. Major also contributed reviews to *The New York Times Book Review*, *The Kenyon Review*, *The Review of Contemporary Fiction*, and others.

Both Major's poetry and fiction have brought him critical attention. *Swallow the Lake* (one of Major's twelve collections of poetry) received the National Council of the Arts Award (1970). *My Amputations* won the Western States Book Award (1986); *Such Was the Season*, the *New York Times Book Review* "Summer Reading" Citation (1988); and *Painted Turtle: Woman with Guitar*, the *New York Times Book Review* "Notable Book of the Year" Citation (1988). Major was granted a Fulbright in 1981 and received two Pushcart Prizes (1976, 1990). He is currently a professor of African American literature and creative writing at the University of California, Davis.

MAJOR WORKS AND THEMES

Clarence Major's fiction has often been characterized as "experimental" or "new" realism. Many of Major's novels reflect his belief that the novel is "*totally independent of the reality of things in everyday life. . . . It's certainly not the kind of reflection that's suggested by the metaphor of the mirror*" (O'Brien 130). Major's characters search for identities in a world where other people's words and perceptions have sought to define them. This struggle for identity connects Major's work to the slave narratives and African American quest stories. Unable to reconcile the pictures of themselves drawn by others and the self that they are seeking to find, these characters' voices and, consequently, the structure of the novels are fragmented. Major's work does, in a sense, mirror the "reality" of postmodern society; it is often unresolved, disruptive, and violently confusing. Fiction alone cannot capture the complexity of life in this society. This is especially true of those characters and people who are already suffering from "double-consciousness." The structure of Major's early work, while not traditionally mimetic, reflects the double-consciousness of African Americans and illustrates that "blacks, and members of other historically oppressed groups, must develop their own definitions of truth" (Weixlmann, "Culture" 31).

All-Night Visitors follows Eli Bolton in search of his identity. Unlike the typical quest story, this novel proceeds backward. The "discovery" of Bolton's identity lies in the painful past, including a tour of Vietnam and life on the streets of Chicago, which has already shaped him. Major parodies the stereotype of the sexually aggressive African American male through Bolton. In order to survive, Bolton will have to redefine himself. Sexual identity in the novel is at once the source of the destructive African American male stereotype and a site for regeneration. Bolton revises the stereotype when he sacrifices his own home for a pregnant woman and her children. This act empowers his voice and frees him from society's definitions of African American manhood.

Major's second novel, *NO*, further investigates the problems of achieving identity as an African American male. The main character, Moses Westby, is the lone survivor of a family tragedy. In the beginning of the novel it is difficult to determine if we are seeing the "boy" or his father, also called Moses Westby. The boy is also referred to by various nicknames. These names make the boy seem less like an individual and more like a representative of all young, African American men. It is unclear if events in the novel are "real" or illusory, especially in the last section of the novel, where Westby makes physical contact with a bull during a bullfight. Westby's desire to touch the bull reflects his need to rewrite the image of himself that others have given him. The bull symbolizes the power of both a masculine self and resurrection (Byerman 266). Westby states here that for the first time he no longer feels "like a victim." He has broken free at last from the definitions of others.

Major's next two novels further his concern with form and language. *Reflex and Bone Structure* revises the detective novel and discusses the nature of writing and epistemological knowledge. It is one of the few African American metafictions (Weixlmann, "Culture" 30). We are told that there has been a murder, and the narrator is determined to solve the crime. Several different versions of how and where the victims died are simultaneously revealed. Every possible version of the crime, and thus the story, is introduced, as if a jazz chord is being "played over and over again, from all possible angles, in all possible combinations" (Klinkowitz, "Notes" 47). Eventually, the narrator admits that he has manufactured some of the clues. He also admits to being jealous of the murdered Cora and her lover, Dale, and, finally, admits to the murder itself. He is, after all, "the author." The objective private "eye" of the genre is replaced with a subjective "I."

The narrator/author is also a character in the novel *Emergency Exit*. The story revolves around the "threshold laws" of a small Connecticut town. Major, through his form and technique, violates the "threshold" between fact and fiction, between poetry and prose, much as he does in *Reflex and Bone Structure*. *Emergency Exit* is a montage composed of telephone numbers, dictionary definitions, paintings and photographs by Major, and news stories. Spliced between are scenes of the Ingram family. The narrative jump-cuts between these texts like a silent movie camera. The threshold of the narrative is dissolved when at the end the narrator reveals that one of the characters is now his lover.

My Amputations also questions the position of the author in the text. The main character, Mason Ellis, believes that he has had his identity stolen by a famous author with the initials C. M. Ellis kidnaps the author and takes his place on a book tour. Ellis tells us that he is in "the process of inventing" himself and that we should think of him "as a character in a book." Unable to determine reality from illusion, Ellis cannot establish his identity. His tour takes him to Africa, where he is given a note that says, "*Keep* this nigger . . . [boy running!]"

(204). The note signifies on the African American quest story, particularly *Invisible Man*, but Ellis fails to find his identity in Africa; he is disconnected from his American present and his African past.

Major experiments with different points of view in *Such Was the Season* and *Painted Turtle: Woman with Guitar*. *Such Was the Season* is told in the folk voice of a southern, elderly, African American woman. While the structure of the text is more linear than we have previously seen from Major, the novel still struggles with issues of identity and double-consciousness. Junebug, the narrator's nephew, is a successful doctor who can't reconcile his new life with his southern childhood. Despite her appearance and voice, the narrator's words of advice come not from an African American past but from soap operas.

Painted Turtle: Woman with Guitar is told through the voice of "Baldy," a Native American man, who describes the life and feelings of his lover, Painted Turtle. This limited point of view reflects the way that we often judge others by our perceptions of them rather than by their "real" selves. The narrator controls this story and thus controls the life of Painted Turtle, much as others in her family and community have done because she does not fit their vision of a traditional Native American woman. Like other Major characters, her identity has been defined by others to the point that we have little sense of who she really is.

Major's most recent novel, *Dirty Bird Blues*, also deals with the struggle of reconciling different identities. The narrator, Manfred Banks, a twenty-five-year-old blues musician, is caught between his responsibilities as father and husband and the life of a blues musician, a possibly dangerous stereotype that he is beginning to embrace. Despite the more traditional form of these last novels, Major argues that his purpose has not changed. He is interested in exploring identity in the most creative manner, and the new works are an "evolution" of his art (McCaffery and Kutnik 125).

CRITICAL RECEPTION

Major's work has been well received by critics, and the *African-American Review* and the *Black American Literature Forum* have both devoted an issue to the study of his work.

Most critics have focused on Major's postmodern techniques and projects. Joe Weixlmann suggests that Major's most significant contribution to the postmodern African American novel is his work's indeterminacy and questioning of reality ("African" 67). Keith Byerman and Bernard Bell draw specific attention to Major's first four novels. These works, Bell argues, "extend the experimental tradition of the Afro-American novel by their subordination of race to a phenomenological exploration of sex and language as a ritualistic rebirth and affirmation of self" ("Afro-American" 320). Many critics discuss Major's revision of the detective novel, suggesting that Major is the "anti-detective" refusing to integrate the clues, or fragments, into a unified whole or fictionalization of self

(McCaffery and Gregory 40). Charles Johnson believes that Major's work is about the "failure of fiction" to reveal truth and that his technique projects this failure into form (60).

Like most critics, Jerome Klinkowitz's work primarily focuses on *Reflex and Bone Structure* and *Emergency Exit*. Klinkowitz credits Major with the invention of "pure writing," which stands "apart from any conventional narrative function; . . . words and sentences and even scenes are free from the burden to tell some kind of story" ("Notes" 48). While Klinkowitz observes the poet in the novelist, Lisa Roney and Stuart Klawans analyze Major's training as an artist and its appearance in his novels. Wherever critics decide to focus their attention, there is still a consensus that Major has been an important contributor to the postmodern and African American novel.

BIBLIOGRAPHY

Works by Clarence Major

Novels

All-Night Visitors. New York: Olympia, 1969.
NO. New York: Emerson Hall, 1973.
Reflex and Bone Structure. New York: Fiction Collective, 1975.
Emergency Exit. New York: Fiction Collective, 1979.
My Amputations. New York: Fiction Collective, 1986.
Such Was the Season. San Francisco: Mercury House, 1987.
Painted Turtle: Woman with Guitar. Los Angeles: Sun and Moon, 1988.
Dirty Bird Blues. San Francisco: Mercury House, 1996.

Collection

Fun and Games: Short Fictions. Duluth: Holy Cow! 1990.

Nonfiction

"A Black Criteria." *Journal of Black Poetry* 1 (Spring 1967): 15.
The Dark and the Feeling: Black American Writers and Their Work. New York: Third Press, 1974.
Juba to Jive: A Dictionary of African-American Slang. New York: Viking Penguin, 1994a.
"Necessary Distance: Afterthoughts on Becoming a Writer." *African-American Review* 28.1 (1994b): 37–47.

Anthologies (as editor)

The New Black Poetry. With an Introduction. New York: International, 1969.
Calling the Wind: Twentieth-Century African-American Short Stories. With an Introduction. New York: HarperCollins, 1993.
The Garden Thrives: Twentieth-Century African-American Poetry. With an Introduction. New York: HarperCollins, 1996.

Studies of Clarence Major

Bell, Bernard. *The Afro-American Novel and Its Tradition.* Amherst: University of Massachusetts Press, 1987.

———. "Clarence Major's Homecoming Voice in *Such Was the Season.*" *African-American Review* 28.1 (1994a): 89–94.

———. "Introduction: Clarence Major's Double Consciousness as a Black Postmodernist Artist." *African-American Review* 28.1 (1994b): 5–9.

Bolling, Doug. "A Reading of Clarence Major's Short Fiction." *Black American Literature Forum* 13.2 (1979): 51–56.

Bradfield, Larry. "Beyond Mimetic Exhaustion: The *Reflex and Bone Structure* Experiment." *Black American Literature Forum* 17.3 (1983): 120–123.

Byerman, Keith. *Fingering the Jagged Grain: Tradition and Form in Recent Black Fiction.* Athens: University of Georgia Press, 1985.

Cagidemetrio, Alide. "The Real Thing." *Critical Angles: European Views on Contemporary American Literature.* Ed. Marc Chènetier. Carbondale: Southern Illinois University Press, 1986. 3–14.

Coleman, James. "Clarence Major's *All-Night Visitors*: Calabanic Discourse and Black Male Expression." *African-American Review* 28.1 (1994): 95–108.

Hayward, Steve. "Against Commodification: Zuni Culture in Clarence Major's Native American Texts." *African-American Review* 28.1 (1994): 109–119.

Johnson, Charles. *Being and Race: Black Writing since 1970.* Terre Haute: Indiana University Press, 1988.

Klawans, Stuart. " 'I Was a Weird Example of Art': My *Amputations* as Cubist Confession." *African-American Review* 28.1 (1994): 77–87.

Klinkowitz, Jerome. "Clarence Major: An Interview with a Post-Contemporary Author." *Black American Literature Forum* 12.1 (1978): 32–37.

———. "Clarence Major's Innovation Fiction." *African-American Review* 28.1 (1994): 57–63.

———. *The Life of Fiction.* Champaign: University of Illinois Press, 1977.

———. "Notes on a Novel-in-Progress: Clarence Major's *Emergency Exit.*" *Black American Literature Forum* 13.2 (1979): 46–50.

———. "The Self-Apparent Word: Clarence Major's Innovative Fiction." *Studies in Black American Literature.* Vol. 1: *Black American Prose Theory.* Ed. Joe Weixlmann and Chester Fontenot. Greenwood, FL: Penkeville, 1984. 199–214.

McCaffery, Larry, and Jerry Kutnik. " 'I Follow My Eyes': An Interview with Clarence Major." *African-American Review* 28.1 (1994): 121–138.

McCaffery, Larry, and Sinda Gregory. "Major's *Reflex and Bone Structure* and the Anti-Detective Tradition." *Black American Literature Forum* 13.2 (1979): 39–45.

O'Brien, John. *Interviews with Black Writers.* New York: Liveright, 1973.

Quartermain, Peter. "Trusting the Reader." *Chicago Review* 32.2 (1980): 65–74.

Roney, Lisa. "The Double Vision of Clarence Major, Painter and Writer." *African-American Review* 28.1 (1994): 65–75.

Weixlmann, Joe. "African-American Deconstruction of the Novel in the Works of Ishmael Reed and Clarence Major." *MELUS* 17.4 (Winter 1991–1992): 57–79.

———. "Culture Clash, Survival, and Trans-Formation: A Study of Some Innovative Afro-American Novels of Detection." *Mississippi Quarterly* 38.1 (Winter 1984–1985): 21–31.

PAULE MARSHALL
(1929–   )

Shanna D. Greene

BIOGRAPHY

Paule Marshall was born on 9 April 1929 in Stuyvesant Heights, New York (now Bedford-Stuyvesant), to Barbadian immigrant parents Ada and Samuel Burke. Marshall's links to American and West Indian culture emerge in her writing as tensions whose resolutions lie in the reclamation of one's African roots. The origins of Marshall's dual-pronged approach to literary creation began when she was a young girl. The group of women she has since called the "kitchen poets" were seminal in Marshall's ability to accurately transfer oral speech to written texts. After spending the day "cleaning house," Marshall's mother and her friends would sit around the kitchen table and talk. This kitchen talk introduced Marshall to Caribbean images, gestures, and rituals—all of which have become key aspects of her writing.

The polyphonic voice that emerges in Marshall's literature was not influenced by the "kitchen poets" alone. Thomas Mann, Charles Dickens, and, subsequently, Paul Lawrence Dunbar aided in the development of Marshall's literary voice. Likewise, Ralph Ellison's* collection of essays *Shadow and Act* helped Marshall to develop an approach to writing that expressed the complexity of black American life and simultaneously insisted upon the presence of a culture that must be reclaimed and celebrated.

In 1953 she graduated cum laude from Brooklyn College and later served as a librarian for the New York Public Library. Between 1955 and 1956 she worked for an African American magazine called *Our World* in the fashion and food section. In 1957, she married Kenneth Marshall. Their marriage produced her only son, Evan-Keith. Then, in 1959, Marshall completed her first novel, *Brown Girl, Brownstones*, which marked the beginning of a series of novels by Marshall whose fundamental purpose was to investigate the interior consciousness of black female protagonists. One year later, in 1960, Marshall received a Guggenheim Fellowship.

Marshall's next work, *Soul Clap Hands and Sing*, a book of four short stories first published in 1961, deviated from this theme and, instead, focused on the lives of four elderly men and the way in which they attempt to confront the effects of cold materialism by enriching the warmth of the soul. For this work, the National Institute of Arts and Letters awarded Marshall the Rosenthal Award. From 1964 to 1965 she worked under the auspices of a Ford Foundation Grant. Then, in 1969, Marshall published *The Chosen Place, the Timeless People*.

In 1970, Marshall married Nourry Menard. Not until thirteen years after her marriage, however, did Marshall publish again. In 1983 she produced *Praisesong for the Widow*, a novel, and a collection of short stories entitled *Reena and Other Stories*. *Praisesong* garnered Marshall the Before Columbus Foundation American Book Award in 1984. Unbeknownst to Marshall, *Reena* contained what was to be her most anthologized piece of work: "To Da-duh in Memoriam." In 1991, Marshall published her most recent work to date, *Daughters*. One year later, in 1992, she received the MacArthur Prize for lifetime achievement.

MAJOR WORKS AND THEMES

Strains of Marshall's upbringing in New York's Barbadian community as well as the influence of her self-proclaimed multiracial literary ancestry direct the major themes in her work. Instead of adhering to any strict, dichotomous methodology in her literary approach, Marshall's work expresses a personal desire to make sense of her own bicultural tensions. These tensions are expressed through themes that include an interest in the African American's relationship to the African diaspora, identity formation, materialism in the "new world," and the relationship of the individual to her ancestors and progeny. Furthermore, Marshall complicates the nature of binaries by illuminating their inadequacy and simultaneously highlighting their usefulness in bringing individuals to terms with their demons. Those characters who adopt too stringently a particular ideology suffer. On the other hand, those who travel the path of identity formation and make use of a range of divergent energies experience a joy of self-discovery previously unknown.

Marshall's first novel, *Brown Girl, Brownstones*, is important for, among others, two reasons: first, it explored a *black girl's* psychological development, a theme that had hitherto been neglected. Second, it established Marshall, along with Gwendolyn Brooks* for *Maud Martha* and Zora Neale Hurston for *Their Eyes Were Watching God*, as a black woman writing in the tradition of the bildungsroman. While *Brown Girl, Brownstones* was praised in numerous reviews upon its publication, it did not garner significant critical attention until the 1980s, when scholars finally recognized it for its complex and accurate portrayal of a black woman's coming-of-age.

Slightly autobiographical in content, *Brown Girl, Brownstones* tells the story of Selina Boyce—a girl born in New York to Barbadian parents—and her journey toward a full and complete knowledge of self. A major conflict in the novel involves Selina's mother, Silla, who wants to stay in New York and buy a home while her husband, Deighton, dreams of returning to Barbados. When he inherits land in Barbados, Deighton believes that his dreams are finally coming true. A series of tenuous moments of deception, betrayed trust, and misfortune lead Deighton to the cult of Father Peace. In accordance with the rules of the cult, Deighton abandons his family and relinquishes his material wealth. Outraged, Silla reports Deighton's illegal immigrant status, and, as a result, he is deported. Just before his boat reaches the shores of Barbados, Deighton hurls himself overboard and commits suicide.

After this episode, Selina goes on a quest to piece together her fragmented life. She encounters persons like Suggie and Miss Thompson, both of whom have different lessons to teach and spaces in their lives that Selina can fill. When she meets the first love of her life, Clive Springer, Selina begins to understand racist attitudes and ways to combat them. Notwithstanding Suggie, Miss Thompson, and Clive's support, Selina's journey is one that she must travel alone. By the end of the novel, the pained relationship between mother and daughter becomes reconciled when Selina realizes that her mother's strength has given her the courage to travel to the West Indies and gain a true understanding of her self by reconnecting with her roots.

The action of the novel brings to the fore Marshall's own concern with themes of alienation, the tenuousness of bicultural allegiances, and the power of reclaiming "African roots through Caribbean experiences" (Byerman 135). Deighton Boyce, who possesses an acute awareness of racism within the public sphere, wants to return to Barbados because he envisions America as the white man's land. His wife, Silla, on the other hand, has no nostalgic memories of Barbados. She seeks the material wealth of New York and rejects the sentimentality of her husband's view.

Instead of offering readers a panacea for Selina's bicultural tensions, Marshall uses Selina's decision to travel to the West Indies as a window of opportunity through which she can achieve psychic healing. Finally, Selina understands just what her mother has meant to her development. While Selina spends the majority of the text relating most intimately with her father's sweet-tempered nature, by the end of the novel she is forced to understand the impact of Silla's fortitude and work ethic upon her development. In *Brown Girl, Brownstones*, the law of the mother and a rootedness by way of the maternal prevail.

While Selina's development in *Brown Girl, Brownstones* represents the importance of possessing a personality that, instead of reflecting extremes, reflects moderation, *Soul Clap Hands and Sing* explores the pitfalls of relying too heavily upon one philosophy in living life and finding love. This text, compiled of four novellas entitled *Barbados*, *British Guiana*, *Brooklyn*, and *Brazil*, looks intimately into the lives of four elderly men who have lived their lives in pursuit of material gain. Despite the focus of each novel on capitalism, commercialism, and materialism,

Marshall also expertly weaves in a network of issues that include race, gender, and national allegiance. The text supports Marshall's interest in the ways that black Americans come to know themselves and realize the full measure of their humanity through their relationships with others.

Barbados tells the story of Mr. Watford, a man who, after acquiring great wealth in the United States, has returned home where he, because of his money, condescends to the locals. For Watford, money has always stood as proxy for love in his life. Not until he turns to his young servant girl for love and is rejected, does he understand just what his life is for. Max Berman in *Brooklyn* experiences a similar fate when he tries to seduce one of his students. A Jewish teacher of French, Berman becomes enthralled with a black female student of his. Their relationship not only affects Berman but also helps the fair black woman he is interested in come to terms with her blackness. In *British Guiana*, the main character, Gerald Motley, faces issues of identity politics enacted by his Hindu, Chinese, and black ancestry. His problems involving identity and his unsuccessful business decisions become compounded by the return of his ex-girlfriend Sybil. The final novella, *Brazil*, highlights the life of a nightclub entertainer who goes by the name "O Grand Caliban." After spending a significant part of his life masquerading, he eventually recognizes the extent to which he has bought into the mask and can no longer reach his true self. Not only does Caliban forfeit the ability to reclaim his lost identity, but his interaction with partner Miranda also emphasizes the impact of colonial ideology upon his fabricated facade. Together, these texts depict Marshall's ever-developing sense of the individual's relationship to place as well as the ways in which we learn about ourselves through others.

Marshall follows in a similar vein in *The Chosen Place, the Timeless People*, where she juxtaposes several characters of opposing viewpoints to make a political statement. An epigraph at the beginning of the novel, taken from the Tiv of West Africa, summarizes the tension that guides the course of the text: "Once a great wrong has been done, it never dies." This sentiment is important in understanding Marshall's development from her previous projects, *Brown Girl, Brownstones* and *Soul Clap Hands and Sing*. Where these first two works investigate the impact of a certain ideology on a particular person, *The Chosen Place, the Timeless People* illustrates how, "[a]s Marshall herself mature[d], her emphasis move[d] from the way a world affects an individual psyche to how our many psyches create a world" (Collier 135).

The novel is divided into four sections: "Heirs and Descendants," "Bournehills," "Carnival," and "Whitsun." Marshall uses the first two books as exposition and relies on the last two to explore the relationship between the characters and how their relationships tell a political story. For Merle Kinbona, material wealth cannot squelch the psychological trauma that burns within. She returns to Bourne Island after living in London, where she experienced a nervous breakdown at the hands of a failed relationship. She represents "the voice of Bournehills" that maintains Africa's role in the healing process.

The characters of *The Chosen Place, the Timeless People* work together and against each other to make a statement about the relationship between the individual and her world. Harriet Amron's issues around identity are not unlike Selina's in *Brown Girl, Brownstones*. Troubled by her mother's seemingly useless life, Harriet spends hers trying to prove that she is nothing like her mother. To feel useful, Harriet must find someone who will rely on her. When such a relationship never materializes, Harriet commits suicide. Saul Amron experiences a similar dilemma as he spends his life trying to put the image of his dying wife out of his mind by immersing himself in work. Unlike Harriet, Saul finds a way to reconcile the past and present by creating a new life. Lyle Hutson, who was born on Bourne Island, is an extremely bright young man who earns an education at Oxford, the London School of Economics, and the Inns of Count. Supposedly a liberal, he is nothing more than a sellout. These characters serve as a contrast to other major characters in the novel, some of whom include the white colonizing force of Sir John Stokes and the poverty-stricken Ferguson and Stinger. In relation to one another, these characters represent the most basic nature of a mirror's image: the presentation of the exact opposite.

These opposing forces combine to reveal Marshall's own political views about the nature of "selling out," the role of technology in a given culture, and the ways in which healing can occur. In *The Chosen Place, the Timeless People*, as in her previous works, identity formation plays a major role in the development of each character. Unlike her previous works, however, their individual selves become linked together in a "web of relationships" through which none can escape the other.

In *Praisesong for the Widow*, Marshall uses the life of Avatara "Avey" Johnson to demonstrate the importance of this "web" in African Americans' physical and psychological health. This text differs from Marshall's previous three works because it focuses on the inner psychology of an individual instead of a variety of characters who, via relationships, come to realize their fundamental lack of self-knowledge. While the themes of materialism, identity formation, and the African diaspora remain important, *Praisesong for the Widow* posits the need for relationships with the present, past, and future as an essential element in African Americans' mental well-being.

The novel begins with Avey Johnson on her third cruise to the Caribbean. En route, Avey gets several signs that something is not quite right, the most powerful of which is a dream about her Aunt Cuney. In this dream, Cuney drags Avey, laced in high heels and a mink stole, to the Ibo Landing in Tatem. This dream is so powerful that Avey leaves the boat the next morning at Grenada so that she can board the next flight to New York. While at a hotel in Grenada, Avey dreams about her dead husband, Jay Johnson, who chastises her for wasting $1,500 by leaving the cruise early. This dream reminds Avey of the early playful years of their marriage, before Jay began his quest to obtain material wealth, move to the suburbs, and adopt a "white" way of life. Grenada becomes the site where Avey begins to reconcile the ghosts of her past.

In a coincidental trip to Lebert Joseph's rum shop, Avey tells her dreams to the old man, who, besides selling rum, is a seer. They travel together on the Carriacou Excursion, where he determines that Avey is of the sort "who can't call their nation." Through a series of rites and rituals, Avey comes to understand who she is and whence she came. As a result of her transformation, Avey sells her home in White Plains and moves to South Carolina to make sure that future generations know the stories of their past.

Within the context of Marshall's major themes, *Praisesong for the Widow* uses Avey to show that a comfortable home, a middle-class lifestyle, and significant income are no protection against the inner need to feel whole. A scene at the end of the novel marks the point where Avey finally begins to understand her connectedness with her ancestors and future generations alike. The image of the web acts as a metaphor for Avey's development. Her spiritual connection becomes tangible when, "for the first time since she was a girl, she felt the threads, that myriad of shiny, silken, brightly colored threads . . . which were thin to the point of invisibility yet as strong as the ropes at Coney Island. . . . she felt the threads streaming out from the old people around her in Lebert Joseph's yard" (158). The "web of relationships" prefigured in *Soul Clap Hands and Sing* finally becomes realized in *Praisesong for the Widow*, where Avey Johnson reclaims her ancestry and acknowledges her responsibility to generations to come.

Marshall's themes of identity, ancestry, politics, and African diasporic relations come together in *Daughters*—a novel that, in its form and content, presents a spinning vortex of energies that engage the individual's relationship to the political state. The novel travels along two related story lines: the life of Ursa Mackenzie and the political career of her father, Primus.

Ursa's story traces her attempts to form a relationship with her self amid troubled relationships with her career, Lowell Carruthers, and her parents. Her life seems to be spinning without direction. Despite academic success, Ursa cannot decide upon an appropriate career path. The relationship between Ursa and Lowell, her longtime lover, has regressed to rote episodes of knee-jerk expressions of affection—most of which are dictated by a calendar instead of emotional impulse. Finally, Ursa must deal with the misguided politics of her father—a man who risks selling out the island to wealthy Westerners who plan to turn the island into a resort. Despite her love for her father, Ursa knows that his plan will do nothing to improve the conditions for persons living on the island. So, along with her mother, Ursa undermines her father's election campaign. Their efforts represent Marshall's desire to place value in people and places instead of individual material gain.

Marshall's narrative strategies in *Daughters* complement the complicated story line. Not only does Marshall use dreams and flashbacks to enrich our understanding of the characters' lives and motivations, but she uses letters to supplement the text. Overall, *Daughters* represents a culmination of themes and narrative devices that Marshall had previously employed. The issue of identity and materialism, begun in *Brown Girl, Brownstones*, is continued in, and expanded upon, in *Soul Clap Hands and Sing*, where relationships teach lessons. *The Chosen Place, the Timeless People* marks Marshall's coming to terms with the connection between individual actions and the world they create. Then, in *Praisesong for the Widow*, Marshall takes an introspective look at the ways in which issues of identity, ancestry, and materialism affect the psychology of African Americans. Finally, in *Daughters*, these issues crash together in a narrative that, through its lack of chronology and its fragmented narrative structure, illustrates the pieces that make up a person as well as the difficulty in reconciling them.

CRITICAL RECEPTION

While Paule Marshall's work has garnered increasing critical attention in recent years, her texts received spotty consideration in the early days of her publishing career. The first significant piece emerged in 1978 from L. Lee Talbert, who analyzes Marshall's major techniques and motifs. In 1978, Gloria T. Hull's work proved important because it reclaimed and reintroduced Marshall's 1962 story into the African American literary canon.

Not until 1983, however, did Marshall's work receive the sweeping critical attention it deserved. The editor of *Callaloo*, Charles H. Rowell, published a special issue in tribute to Marshall's indispensable essay "From Poets in the Kitchen." In this edition, Dorothy L. Dennison, Marilyn Nelson Waniek, Trudier Harris, Sandra Y. Govan, Joseph T. Skerrett, Jr., and Barbara T. Christian contributed studies that established a foundation for later studies of Marshall's work. Thanks to the work of these scholars, when Marshall published *Praisesong for the Widow*, critics were able to trace the development of her work. Eugenia Collier's "The Closing of the Circle," and John McCluskey, Jr.'s "And Called Every Generation Blessed: Theme, Setting, and Ritual in the Works of Paule Marshall" were two important projects in which Marshall's maturation was key.

Since then, while Marshall's work has acquired a steady stream of critical attention, the publication of Dorothy Hamer Dennison's *The Fiction of Paule Marshall: Reconstructions of History, Culture, and Gender* and Joyce Pettis' *Toward Wholeness in Paule Marshall's Fiction* granted Marshall's work the extensive critical analysis that was long overdue—proving that the voice that articulated the dilemma of a dual cultural heritage and the healing power of Africa was finally heard.

BIBLIOGRAPHY

Works by Paule Marshall

Novels

Brown Girl, Brownstones. Old Westbury, NY: Feminist Press, [1981] 1959.
The Chosen Place, the Timeless People. New York: Vintage Books, [1984] 1969.

Praisesong for the Widow. New York: New American Library, 1983.
Daughters. New York: Plume, 1991.

Short Stories and Essays

Reena and Other Stories. Old Westbury, NY: Feminist Press, 1983.
Soul Clap Hands and Sing. Washington, DC: Howard University Press, [1988] 1961.
Merle: A Novella and Other Stories. London: Virago Press, 1985.
"From Poets in the Kitchen." *Callaloo* 18 (Spring/Summer 1983): 23–30.
"To Da-duh in Memoriam." *New World Quarterly* 3 (1966–67): 97–101.

Studies of Paule Marshall

Brathwaite, Edward. "Rehabilitations." *Critical Quarterly* 13 (Summer 1971): 175–183.
Busia, Abena P. "What Is Your Nation? Reconnecting Africa and Her Diaspora through Paule Marshall's Praisesong for the Widow." *Changing Our Own Words: Essays on Criticism, Theory, and Writing by Black Women.* Ed. Cheryl Wall. New Brunswick, NJ: Rutgers University Press, 1989. 196–211.
Byerman, Keith E. "Gender, Culture, and Identity in Paule Marshall's *Brown Girl, Brownstones.*" *Redefining Autobiography in Twentieth-Century Women's Fiction: An Essay Collection.* Ed. Janice Morgan, Colette T. Hall, et al. New York: Garland, 1991. 135–147.
Christian, Barbara. "Paule Marshall." *Afro-American Fiction Writers after 1955.* Ed. Thadious M. Davis and Trudier Harris. Vol. 33 of *Dictionary of Literary Biography.* Detroit: Bruccoli Clark, 1984.
Collier, Eugenia. "The Closing of the Circle: Movement from Division to Wholeness in Paule Marshall's Fiction." *Black Women Writers (1950–1980): A Critical Evaluation.* Ed. Mari Evans. Garden City, NY: Anchor-Doubleday, 1984. 295–315.
Coser, Stelamaris. *Bridging the Americas: the Literature of Paule Marshall, Toni Morrison, and Gayl Jones.* Philadelphia: Temple University Press, 1995.
Dennison, Dorothy Hamer. *The Fiction of Paule Marshall: Reconstruction of History, Culture, and Gender.* Knoxville: University of Tennessee Press, c.1995.
Graulich, Melody, and Lisa Sisco. "Meditations on Language and the Self: A Conversation with *Paule Marshall.*" *NWSA Journal* 4.3 (Fall 1992): 282–302.
Hull, Gloria T. " 'To Be a Black Woman in America': A Reading of Paule Marshall's 'Reena.' " *Obsidian* 4.3 (1978): 5–15.
Kapai, Leela. "Dominant Themes and Technique in Paule Marshall's Fiction." *College Language Association Journal* 16 (1972): 49–59.
Kulkarni, Harihar. "Paule Marshall: A Bibliography." *Callaloo* 16.1 (Winter 1993): 245–267.
McCluskey, Jr., John. "And Called Every Generation Blessed: Theme, Setting, and Ritual in the Works of Paule Marshall." *Black Women Writers (1950–1980): A Critical Evaluation.* Ed. Mari Evans. Garden City, NY: Anchor-Doubleday, 1984. 316–334.
Pettis, Joyce. "A MELUS Interview: *Paule Marshall.*" *MELUS* 19.4 (Winter 1994): 117–129.
———. *Towards Wholeness in Paule Marshall's Fiction.* Charlottesville: University Press of Virginia, 1995.
Spillers, Hortense. "Chosen Place, Timeless People: Some Figurations on the New

World." *Conjuring: Black Women, Fiction, and Literary Tradition.* Ed. Marjorie Pryse. Bloomington: Indiana University Press, 1985. 151–175.

Waniek, Marilyn Nelson. "Paltry Things: Immigrants and Marginal Men in Paule Marshall's Short Fiction." *Callaloo* 6.2 (Spring–Summer 1983): 46–56.

Werner, Craig H. "Paule Marshall." *Black American Women Novelists.* Pasadena, CA: Salem Press, 1989. 162–174.

SHARON BELL MATHIS
(1937–   )

Gwendolyn S. Jones

BIOGRAPHY

Sharon Bell Mathis, a writer for children and young adults, has earned honors and awards for her prose (fiction and nonfiction) and poetry. Her various career choices reflect her love of reading and her considerable talents in writing. In addition to receiving awards for her books, she is an honored classroom teacher, librarian, library media specialist, and interviewer.

Mathis was born in Atlantic City, New Jersey, but moved with her family to Brooklyn, New York, in 1940. Her interest in reading and writing was nurtured at an early age by her parents, especially her mother, who was an avid reader, a writer, and an artist. During her early years, Mathis wrote poems and short stories at the same times that her mother wrote poems and sketched. She had opportunities to view theatrical productions with her parents. In addition to being a frequent visitor to public libraries, she also had access to her mother's considerable collection of books. High school teachers encouraged her by inviting her to read original compositions in class.

Sharon Bell Mathis earned a bachelor's degree in sociology from Morgan State College in 1958 and a master's degree in library science from Catholic University of America in 1975. Her professional positions ranged from interviewer, to fifth grade teacher, to special education teacher, to librarian, to library media specialist. Although she had been writing since she was a child, becoming a published writer became a goal early in her professional career.

Her early attempts at publication resulted in two stories in a confessions-type magazine in 1969. Yet, the appearance of "The Fire Escape," her first story for children, in a *Scholastic Weekly* magazine (also in 1969) "launched her career as a writer." Because of her success as a writer, she was appointed director of the

Children's Literature Division of the Black Writer's Workshop, was a writer in residence at Howard University, and was a fellow at the Breadloaf Writer's Conference.

In addition to honors and awards for her books, Sharon Bell Mathis earned several personal awards because of competent, efficient professional activities: a tribute from the District of Columbia public schools; an award from the District of Columbia Association of School Librarians; the Arts and Humanities Award from the archdiocese of Washington; the "Arts and Humanities" Award from Club Twenty in celebration of International Women's Year; the Wallace Johnson Memorial Award for Outstanding Contributions to the Literary Arts; the Boys and Girls Clubs of Greater Washington Arts and Letters Award; the Delta Sigma Theta Arts and Letters Award; Writing to Read Program's Outstanding Writer Award.

She retired from the school system in 1995 but is available for substitute teaching, mainly to "stay in touch with children." Mathis is currently working on a young adult novel with the working title *Wooden Biscuit*.

MAJOR WORKS AND THEMES

Sharon Bell Mathis has published nine books for children and young adults. Of these, five have won awards: four books of fiction and one of nonfiction. *Ray Charles*, a biography for juveniles, was awarded the Coretta Scott King Book Award in 1974. *Red Dog, Blue Fly: Football Poems* was published in 1991; *Running Girl: The Diary of Ebonee Rose* was published in 1997. Mathis' works also include articles, columns, and short fiction.

The novels written by Sharon Mathis attract the attention of classroom teachers not only for their literary merit but also because they help children develop skills related to academic achievement and personal growth. Because of their high interest levels, the novels are used to encourage the development of skill in reading; passages from some books are used to teach concepts in mathematics; *The Hundred Penny Box*, for example, is used to teach persuasive speaking and writing and was also selected to help children develop critical thinking skills while reading fiction.

In Mathis' prizewinning books, African American children and young adults are the focal points. She recognized early in her career as a writer that her "characterizations of children were superior to her depiction of adults." In her stories, no matter how depressing, sad, or unpleasant the situations are, there are always hope, a way to manage, and the will to succeed by the young protagonists. Through the very real, everyday situations, the protagonists exhibit love, concern for others, and determination. The situations include the effects on a family with a problem such as aging, death, drug abuse, alcoholism, or eviction. Well-developed, dynamic, believable people work through the problems. Language, dialogue, and tone are descriptive and appropriate.

The unpublished manuscript for *Sidewalk Story* received an award from the

Council on Interracial Books for Children in 1970 and was published by Viking Press in 1971. This book was also listed by the Child Study Association of America's Children's Book of the Year. In *Sidewalk Story*, nine-year-old Lilly Etta Allen tries to prevent her best friend's family from being evicted, even if it means disobeying her mother. While the idea of eviction may be depressing for children to read about, they see that concern for others and persistence help solve problems.

In *Teacup Full of Roses* (1972), the topic is drug addiction. In a family that can be described as dysfunctional, Joe Brooks, a seventeen-year-old, struggles to hold his family together. This family consists of a talented artist/heroin-addicted older brother; an athlete/honor student younger brother; a mother absorbed in the problems of the son who is addicted to drugs; an unemployed, ill father; and an eccentric aunt. Although he tries, Joe's love for his family is not enough to hold them together. *Teacup Full of Roses* won the American Library Association's Notable Book Award; the Child Study Association of America's Children's Books of the Year Award: was included in the New York Times Best Books of the Year list; and was a runner-up for the Coretta Scott King award.

Listen for the Fig Tree (1974) is an American Library Association Notable Book for Children and Young Adults; won the Children's Literature Association Phoenix Award; and is a Caldecott Honor Book. The protagonist here, sixteen-year-old Muffin Johnson, who happens to be blind, is faced with her father's murder; her mother's increasing drunkenness as the anniversary of her husband's death approaches; her own attempted rape; and her relationship with a young man. Muffin loves her mother and believes that it is her responsibility to look after her. She approaches the problems with the support of a neighbor and her boyfriend.

The Hundred Penny Box is a Newbery Honor Book, an American Library Association Notable Children's Book, and a Boston Globe-Horn Book Honor Book. It tells the story of Michael's love for his great-great-aunt who has come to live with his family. Michael's mother wants to get rid of an old box, which holds 100 pennies, and replace it with a new one. For Aunt Dew's sake, Michael must convince his mother to keep the old box.

Brooklyn Story, her first published children's book, is about conflicts that arise when the mother of a teenaged son and daughter returns home for a visit. In *Cartwheels*, Zettie, a twelve-year-old, is determined to win the fifty dollar first prize in a neighborhood gymnastics contest. Zettie has to contend with Fawn, a teenager who lives with her family, and three neighborhood girls.

CRITICAL RECEPTION

Reviewers and critics of Mathis' works agree on several elements of her writing. The most obvious is her concern for children and young adults. That her works are for and about African American children and young adults is evident in the way she develops characters. Her characters portray her sensitivity and pride for her readers and her characters. They are caring individuals, and they are everyday people with everyday concerns. She presents these multifaceted, honest people and the events in which they are involved realistically.

Roginski points out that Mathis places the reader "into the immediate action of the story" (844). His comments and those of other critics regarding plot development, character analysis, themes, and approach are positive.

If there are negative aspects of Mathis' work, it is the concern by a few reviewers that her themes—drug addiction, alcoholism, aging, senility, and death—are sad and depressing. They fear the reactions of children to these depictions. On the other hand, Matthews sees that these sad stories are treated sympathetically and that resolutions are realistic (21). Readers see that problems are approached from a base of hope and are resolved with pride and love. Because these sad situations are facts of life for many readers, these stories will reach them. At the same time, the stories are entertaining and they provide direction. They allow readers see that there are solutions and that the healing power of love works.

In her review of *Teacup Full of Roses*, Greenfield notes that her comments for this book apply as well to *Brooklyn Story* and to *Sidewalk Story*. "Black children and teenagers face and attempt to cope with the very same situations our youth defy daily. . . . every young person trying to grow up and survive physically, emotionally, mentally and spiritually will recognize them as truth" (87). Mathis wrote these novels more than twenty years ago; Greenfield wrote her critique more than twenty years ago. The relevance of the themes of the novels *and* the critiques by Greenfield and others has not diminished.

BIBLIOGRAPHY

Works by Sharon Bell Mathis

Fiction

Brooklyn Story. New York: Hill and Wang, 1970.
Sidewalk Story. New York: Viking, 1971.
Teacup Full of Roses. New York: Viking, 1972.
Listen for the Fig Tree. New York: Viking, 1974.
The Hundred Penny Box. New York: Viking, 1975.
Cartwheels. New York: Scholastic, 1977.

Nonfiction

Ray Charles. New York: Crowell, 1973.

Poetry

Red Dog, Blue Fly: Football Poems. New York: Viking, 1991.
Running Girl: The Diary of Ebonee Rose. New York: Harcourt, Brace, 1997.

Studies of Sharon Bell Mathis

Foster, Frances Smith. "Sharon Bell Mathis." *Dictionary of Literary Biography: Afro-American Fiction Writers after 1955*. Detroit: Gale Research, 1984.

Greenfield, Eloise. Review of *Teacup Full of Roses* by Sharon Bell Mathis. *Black World* (August 1973): 86–87.

Kutenplon, Deborah, and Ellen Olmstead. "Mathis, Sharon Bell." *Young Adult Fiction by African American Writers. 1968–1994: A Critical and Annotated Guide*. New York: Garland, 1996.

Liggins, Sandra. "Mathis, Sharon Bell." *Oxford Companion to African American Literature*. New York: Oxford University Press, 1997.

Matthews, Avis D. "The Books of Sharon Bell Mathis." *Book Links: Connecting Books, Libraries and Classrooms* 3 (January 1994).

Metzger, Linda, ed. "Mathis, Sharon Bell." *Black Writers: A Selection of Sketches from Contemporary Authors*. Detroit: Gale Research, 1989.

Roginski, James W. "Mathis, Sharon Bell." *Twentieth Century Children's Writers*. New York: St. Martin's Press, 1978.

Valade, Roger M., III, ed. "Sharon Bell Mathis." *The Schomburg Center Guide to Black Literature: From the Eighteenth Century to the Present*. New York: Gale Research, 1995.

JOHN A. McCLUSKEY, JR.
(1944–   )

Frank E. Dobson, Jr.

BIOGRAPHY

John A. McCluskey, Jr., was born to John A. and Helen Harris McCluskey in Middletown, Ohio. His father was a truck driver in Middletown, an industrial town in southwestern Ohio, approximately thirty miles north of Cincinnati. A fine student and athlete in high school, McCluskey was active in scholastic sports, excelling in both football and track. Upon graduating from high school, he was awarded a scholarship to Harvard University, where he also played football. He studied social relations at Harvard, receiving a B.A. cum laude in 1966; at Harvard he also took his first courses in creative writing. Following his years at Harvard, McCluskey attended Stanford University and studied creative writing, earning his M.A. in 1972. While at Stanford, McCluskey began his first novel, which was completed years later. McCluskey has taught at a number of colleges and universities, including Miles College in Birmingham, Alabama, and Valparaiso University in Valparaiso, Indiana. From 1969 to 1977, he taught Afro-American and American Studies at Case Western Reserve University. Since June 1977, he has been an associate professor of African American Studies at Indiana University in Bloomington, Indiana.

McCluskey is the author of two novels, *Look What They Done to My Song* (1974) and *Mr. America's Last Season Blues* (1983). McCluskey has also served as the editor of several works: *Blacks in History* (1975); *Blacks in Ohio History* (1976); and *The City of Refuge: The Collected Stories of Rudolph Fisher* (1987). His fiction and essays have appeared in a number of journals and anthologies. In 1997, he coedited, along with Charles Johnson, *Black Men Speaking*, a collection of stories, essays, and poems by a diverse cross-section of African American males. McCluskey is currently working on a novel entitled, *The River People*.

MAJOR WORKS AND THEMES

McCluskey's first novel, *Look What They Done to My Song* (1974), is a highly episodic, first-person narrative told by Mack, the protagonist, a twenty-six-year-old itinerant saxophone player. The central themes of the novel are the vitality of the oral tradition, the search for commitment and a sense of place, and the importance of positive African American rituals that help build community. The plot of the novel is simple. It begins with Mack's messianic calling and details his migration to the East Coast; there, we follow his adventures in New Bedford, Boston, and neighboring communities. The novel ends in a triumphantly joyous scene in Crumbly Rock Baptist Church.

When we first encounter Mack, he is leaning upon his horn in Santa Fe, New Mexico, contemplating the death of Malcolm X. While in Santa Fe, Mack is seemingly aimless, yet the rituals of the oral tradition are still with him. He sits in parks and slaps out "hambone" on his thighs and perfects his dozens repertoire. Mack is an itinerant in search of a calling and a home. His mother has told him that he will return home a minister, and he senses within himself a messianic call of sorts. However, Mack wants nothing to do with being a messianic leader or any kind of leader, apart from music: "After all, the horn is the only voice I want to move folks with. To say I'm like a leader in any other way is to place a heavy weight on me" (12–13).

Mack feels a messianic call but is unsure of how to fulfill that call. While on his pilgrimage east, he sojourns through several places. Eventually, however, he makes it east by hitchhiking, and once there he is taken in by an elderly black couple named the Sledges who live in Cape Cod: "An elderly couple took me to their home where they fed me and asked me to stay on for a few days. That was a month ago. A month and the Sledges are paying their dues" (10). The Sledges immediately take to the personable Mack, and they subsequently "adopt" him as their son. It is not coincidental, either, that the Sledges are from Bessemer, Alabama; their heritage serves by extension to connect the wandering Mack to black southern culture and traditions.

In addition to the Sledges, several other characters contribute to the color and flavor of the novel and also heavily influence Mack as he searches for an identity. One such character is Ubangi Jones, a colorful character from Calypso, North Carolina, who soon becomes Mack's best friend. Novella Turner, Mack's girlfriend, is a single parent and also a transplanted southerner from Charlotte, North Carolina; she provides a linkage to the black church that allows Mack to finally realize his messianic calling. Antar, or Andrew Dolphy, is a young militant whose changed name, ownership of an African gift shop, and earlier "adoption" by the Sledges stimulate his friendship with Mack. Wendell Keyes is a gay Shakespearean actor who disavows his blackness until he is beaten by the police in a case of mistaken identity. Reverend C. E. Fuller is the streetwise, yet spiritual, pastor of Crumbly Rock Baptist, Novella's church.

In *Look What They Done*, the climax occurs at the novel's end, in a scene in which Mack finally realizes his messianic calling by musically "preaching" to the congregation of Crumbly Rock Baptist. Mack preaches at Crumbly Rock because the Reverend C. E. Fuller is ready to relinquish the pastorate to someone younger. Fuller notes that the church does not need "one of them old-time whoopers"; rather, it needs "a modern man," one "who cares about what he's doing" and "has something to say" (207–208). As they converse, Mack notes his reluctance to go along with Fuller: "What you need is a magician." Mack's "preaching" actually fulfills all of the preceding conditions: he becomes a magician who fulfills spiritual needs through music. Mack desires to preach openness and acceptance through his music, which he now calls "unity music." Mack, as picaro, travels here and there, living by his wits and carrying two "burdens," a sax and a messianic calling, and they finally come together in the end. His numerous encounters with others seemingly affect him little until the climax, when he symbolically synthesizes all he's encountered and felt through "unity music." By the novel's end, one sees that Mack's search has been a cyclical process that reaches back to the generations and black rituals represented by the Sledges and Rev. Fuller and forward through "unity music." Mack's wanderings evidence his search, both through music and to music, the culmination of which lies in the reaching of others. His sax sermon is a synthesis of the sacred and secular styles. Mack, because he is an itinerant, a black picaro, should be seen as a hybrid, a transplanted black who has not lost touch with his roots but who is also representative of, as Reverend Fuller says, "modern man." The Reverend C. E. Fuller's last message appropriately ushers in Mack's first message. Fuller's sermon contains many of the conventions of black church sermons. It begins with a spiritual that is blueslike in its message and is filled with ritualistic language, the theme of which is deliverance from bondage, the quintessential message for the black preacher and for the black person. Within the unfettered context of the black church, Mack is finally able to realize the promise of his messianic calling.

McCluskey's second novel, *Mr. America's Last Season Blues*, is a work again heavily influenced by black music, this time the music of the blues. It is, however, a fuller, more complex treatment of many of the problems facing black men, families, and communities. As a blues novel, it is organized musically and tells the story of Roscoe Americus, Jr., its protagonist, a former All America offensive tackle for Ohio State and star rookie with the Cleveland Browns. However, a knee injury during his rookie season cuts short Roscoe's professional career.

The blues of Roscoe Americus, Jr., is the music of unfulfilled dreams and unrealized potential. As the middle-aged Roscoe attempts a comeback with the local black semipro team in Union City, Ohio, he also struggles to revive his failed marriage and to reunite his siblings, a family that which has not functioned as such since the deaths of their parents. Roscoe Americus, Jr., is haunted by the circumstances of his life; and within this poignant novel, in which he converses with the ghost of his deceased father, Roscoe attempts unsuccessfully to save the son of his lover, who is unjustly charged with murdering a white youth. Roscoe's efforts to gather evidence that would free the young man are thwarted not only by the racism of the all-white jury but by the complacency and silence of those within the African American community whose testimony could lead to the youth's acquittal. As Roscoe attempts to save the youth, it is clear that Roscoe's blues is a sad tune that confronts the entire Union City black community, a blues of low expectations and contentment with mediocrity. By the novel's end, Roscoe, "a man of many lives" (238), has begun to successfully confront the demons of his past life, and he is beginning to assume responsibility for his life in the present. As with McCluskey's first novel, this work contains a journey motif; by the novel's end, Roscoe embarks on a new journey, to find his lost brother, after having begun to find himself, an endeavor that, McCluskey's novel indicates, is a continual process.

In addition to his two novels, McCluskey has published a number of short stories, poems, and articles. As in his novels, McCluskey's themes in the stories center around the search of the individual (usually a black male) for wholeness and community, involving either a physical or spiritual journey or both.

CRITICAL RECEPTION

Although the work of McCluskey has not received the attention it deserves, it has been fairly well received. Reviews of his novels have generally praised the works for their utilization of the oral tradition and elements of African American culture. Frank Moorer, in speaking of both novels, applauds McCluskey's "strong awareness of history" (181). John Lang compares McCluskey's work to that of Ralph Ellison* regarding his ability to deal with social and political issues without becoming polemical (487). James Kilgore terms *Look What They Done* a "novel about the eternal quests: survival, freedom, and love" (51). Norman Harris, in the most extensive critical treatment of a work by the author to date, examines the way in which *Look What They Done* treats the decade of the 1960s. Particularly, Harris discusses the way in which Mack, the protagonist, develops into seeing himself as "a central force in infusing African and Afro-American history into . . . the black church" (120).

BIBLIOGRAPHY

Works by John A. McCluskey, Jr.

Fiction

Look What They Done to My Song. New York: Random House, 1974.
Mr. America's Last Season Blues. Baton Rouge: Louisiana State University Press, 1983.

Nonfiction

Ed. *Blacks in History*. Vol. 2. Cleveland: New Day Press, 1975.
Ed. *Blacks in Ohio History*. Cleveland: New Day Press, 1976.

Ed., with an Introduction. *The City of Refuge: The Collected Stories of Rudolph Fisher*. Columbia: University of Missouri Press, 1987.

Coed. with Charles Johnson. *Black Men Speaking*. Bloomington: Indiana University Press, 1997.

Studies of John A. McCluskey, Jr.

Blunden, Janet Boyarin. Review of *Mr. America's Last Season Blues*. *Library Journal* 108 (August 1983): 1503.

El-Kati, Mahmoud. Review of *Look What They Done to My Song*. *Black Scholar* 7 (March 1976): 49–50.

Harris, Norman. *Connecting Times: The Sixties in Afro-American Fiction*. Jackson: University Press of Mississippi, 1988.

Kent, George. Review of *Look What They Done to My Song*. *Phylon* 36 (June 1975): 189–190.

Kilgore, James C. Review of *Look What They Done to My Song*. *Black World* 24 (July 1975): 51–52.

Lang, John. "John A. McCluskey, Jr." *The Oxford Companion to African American Literature*. Ed. William L. Andrews, Francis Foster, and Trudier Harris. New York: Oxford, 1997. 487–488.

Levin, Martin. Review of *Look What They Done to My Song*. *New York Times Book Review* (17 November 1974): 52.

Moorer, Frank E. "John A. McCluskey, Jr." In *Dictionary of Literary Biography*. Vol. 33, *Afro-American Fiction Writers after 1955*. Ed. Thadious M. Davis and Trudier Harris, 1984. 179–181.

Thompson, Jean A. Review of *Look What They Done to My Song*. *Library Journal* (15 April 1975): 49.

REGINALD McKNIGHT
(1956–   )

Laurie Champion

BIOGRAPHY

Reginald McKnight was born on 26 February 1956, in Fürstenfeldbrück, Germany, the son of Frank McKnight and Pearl M. (Anderson) McKnight. Because his father was in the air force, his family relocated frequently. From childhood through early adulthood, he lived in New York, California, Colorado, Texas, Alabama, Louisiana, and other states; but in a 1994 interview he said, "I had most of my major rites of passage in Colorado, so I call it home" (Walsh 28).

After serving in the Marine Corps, McKnight attended Pikes Peak Community College until 1978. He earned a B.A. from Colorado College in 1981, followed by an M.A. from the University of Denver in 1987. Between 1982 and 1989, he taught English at several Colorado colleges and universities, including Arapahoe Community College and Metropolitan State University. In 1989, he moved to Pittsburgh and taught at the University of Pittsburgh. He left the University of Pittsburgh when a friend who had attended a university-related party where racist jokes were told informed McKnight that some of his colleagues often expressed racist attitudes when McKnight was not present. After leaving the University of Pittsburgh, McKnight taught for a short while at Carnegie-Mellon University.

Between 1981 and 1982, McKnight taught English as a foreign language at the American Cultural Center in Dakar, Senegal. In 1985, he received a Thomas J. Watson Foundation Fellowship that allowed him to spend a year in Africa. These opportunities offered him valuable personal experiences for writing *I Get on the Bus* and his stories set in Africa.

In 1985, McKnight married Michele Davis, and he currently lives with his wife and daughter, Rachael, in College Park, where he teaches at the University of Maryland. He is the fiction editor for *African American Review* and serves on the editorial board for *Callaloo*.

MAJOR WORKS AND THEMES

Although he has published one novel, McKnight is distinguished more as a short story writer than as a novelist. Many subjects and themes emerge throughout his works, but they all capture the African American experience. McKnight defines the scope of his works: "Very generally my work deals with the deracinated African-Americans who came of age after the civil rights struggle. These are people who are at the front lines of the current struggle for *human* rights" (*Contemporary Authors* 297). Prominent themes in McKnight's works concern the search for cultural and individual identity. Much of McKnight's fiction is set in West Africa, where his characters have traveled in search of knowledge about their cultural heritage. In many of his other works, adolescent males struggle for a sense of belonging as well as for a sense of individuality. Other subjects that emerge throughout McKnight's fiction are betrayal and loneliness that are exacerbated by race-related conflicts. Frequently, in his depiction of racial conflicts, McKnight demonstrates forms of racism such as racial jokes and racial slurs.

Many of McKnight's short stories characterize adolescent experiences that specifically relate to African American males. Adolescents struggle for identity amid a social atmosphere that seeks to degrade them because they are black. Because they are surrounded mostly by white peers, they have few friends and almost no one in whom they can confide. For example, in one of his best known stories, "The Kind of Light That Shines on Texas," set in 1966, only three black children attend a Texas school. The teacher tells racist jokes, never chooses the black children to perform class honors, and accuses the black children when something is stolen. The story is told from the adult Clint's perspective, wherein he recalls having attended the school. Years later, Clint is still haunted because he betrayed one of the other black students. He has since realized the value of true friendship and of fighting for one's convictions. He recalls his own behavior toward the teacher and realizes he acted like an Uncle Tom and was not proud of his African American heritage.

"The More I Like Flies" is also told from the point of view of a mature narrator who recalls an adolescent experience. When a fly lands on the narrator's hand, he recalls a time in high school when his friend, Dianna, accused him of stealing her wallet and left a poem in his locker that said, " 'Only two things in this world that I despise / One of them's niggers / The other one's flies / Only one thing to say about each of these guys / The more I see niggers / The more I like flies' " (*White Boys* 58). The narrator realizes that even now, seven years since the incident, he cannot think of words to hurt Dianna in the way she had hurt and betrayed him.

Derrick Oates, the adolescent protagonist of "White Boys," has recently moved from Texas to Louisiana, where he lives next door to the racist Sergeant Hooker and befriends his son Garret. The story ends with Garret's brothers' discussion of Sergeant Hooker's plans to take Derrick on a fishing trip and pretend he will lynch him. Although he is unaware of the details of his father's scheme, Garret knows the fishing trip is some sort of setup for Derrick. Garret calls Derrick a stream of racial slurs so he will not go fishing. Ironically, he uses racist tactics and what appears as betrayal to prevent Derrick from becoming the victim of Sergeant Hooker's racism and to prevent an even greater betrayal. "Getting to Be like the Studs" is almost the reversal of "White Boys." Here, a white adolescent has recently moved from Texas to Louisiana and befriends Lenny, who is black. The story is told from the white boy's point of view and shows how he uses racial slurs to end his friendship with Lenny in order to gain acceptance from the other white boys. He tries to rationalize his betrayal of Lenny by concluding, "Since I cussed out ol black Lenny, I'm gettin to be a hell of a lot more like the studs every day" (*Moustapha's Eclipse* 61).

Like "White Boys" and "Getting to Be like Studs," "The Honey Boys" involves adolescent interracial friendship. The narrator, Spider, plays straight man to Camel, who tells racist jokes. Spider becomes Jewish because his only friend at a previous school was Jewish, and he noticed that neither his friend nor the God he served was racist. Camel tells a joke that offends Jews, Spider hits him, and the friendship ends. Spider's epiphany occurs when he realizes that he and Camel will never resume their friendship because of complex differences that are unexplainable.

If collected in a single volume, McKnight's stories "Mali Is Very Dangerous," "Uncle Moustapha's Eclipse," "How I Met Ida at the Bassi Dakaru Restaurant," "He Sleeps," and "Palm Wine" could constitute a short story cycle, or "novita," a term McKnight coined to define "full-sized books compiled from short stories published together in a collection of short stories" (Carlin E5). The stories are all set in West Africa, where a young African American anthropologist has traveled on a research grant. As part of their struggles for cultural identity, the narrators observe African rituals and customs and learn African proverbs. In "Mali Is Very Dangerous," an African peddler tells a parable to the narrator to persuade him to purchase a "juju" belt that will protect him from physical and spiritual harm. "Uncle Moustapha's Eclipse" and "How I Met Ida" consist of a framed narrative, wherein Ida, a native African tour guide, tells the anthropologist a tale that involves African folklore. In "He Sleeps," Bertrand begins for the first time to dream when a young African couple moves in with him. The story is told in eleven parts, each reflecting various aspects of cultural concepts Bertrand seeks to understand. In "Palm Wine," Bertrand goes to Dakar to buy palm wine. Here, he encounters Doudou, the mythiclike character who is offended that Bertrand, an anthropologist/outsider, judges African culture. The story ends with a surrealistic mythical journey, wherein Bertrand encounters figures such as headless men.

Also set in West Africa, McKnight's novel, *I Get on the Bus*, is told from the point of view of Evan Norris, an African American Peace Corps volunteer. The novel is told in the present tense, first person, with chapters that describe actions such as "I Quit," "I Order Fish and Rice," and "I Steal a Kiss." Whether in his malaria-and-headache-driven hallucinations or in reality, Evan continuously moves around West Africa and frequently is described as either getting on or off a bus. The novel defies plot summary, as it portrays Senegalese culture through Evan's psychological journey that involves his search for identity. Ironically, Evan's denial of his American heritage, his obsessive search for personal identity, and his reluctance to claim one cultural heritage exclusively prevent him from discovering personal or cultural identity.

McKnight's characters search both for cultural identity and for individuality. His works offer insights about African culture; and with his portrayals of both Americans in Africa and Africans in America, he demonstrates the inherently dual nature of being an African American. McKnight has an incredible ability to establish strong plots, wherein his characters are placed in complicated conflicts. Many of their struggles, especially those that involve adolescent experiences, are relevant to all people; however their dilemmas are intensified by the social and personal consequences of racism. McKnight offers readers insights about these important issues from all points of view, thus demonstrating various ways people confront personal and social barriers to their needs for individuality.

CRITICAL RECEPTION

Although few critical studies of McKnight's works have appeared, his works generally have received favorable reviews and have earned him many prestigious awards. Assessments of *Moustapha's Eclipse* include John Roux's reference to McKnight's "rare insight and imagination" (36) and Greg Johnson's assertion that, although some of the characterizations are stereotyped, "the notably quirky, original stories display McKnight's impressive skill with language and narrative structure" (414). Reviewing *I Get on the Bus*, Karen Brailsford noted Evan's struggle "to balance his American and African selves" (22), while the *New Yorker* reviewer compared McKnight with Ralph Ellison.* In her review of *The Kind of Light That Shines on Texas*, Joyce Reiser Kornblatt noted McKnight's dazzling voice, his strong wit, and his ability to develop unexpected but believable plots.

In 1985, McKnight received the Bernice M. Slote Award from *Prairie Schooner* for "Uncle Moustapha's Eclipse." His master's thesis, *Moustapha's Eclipse*, won the 1988 Drue Heinz Literature Prize from University of Pittsburgh Press and the 1989 Ernest Hemingway Foundation Award from PEN American Center. "The Kind of Light That Shines on Texas" received both the *Kenyon Review* New Fiction Prize and an O. Henry Award, and "The More I Like Flies" received a 1996 Pushcart Prize. In 1991, McKnight received a grant from the National Endowment of the Arts.

In one of the few critical analyses of McKnight's works, Carolyn E. Megan focuses on ways rhythm, meter, and sound create textual meaning in McKnight's fiction, particularly the short story "Into Night." McKnight's works deserve more critical attention, especially studies that take a broad approach and examine the important social and cultural issues addressed throughout his fiction.

BIBLIOGRAPHY

Works by Reginald McKnight

Novel

I Get on the Bus. Boston: Little, Brown, 1990.

Short Stories

Moustapha's Eclipse. Pittsburgh: University of Pittsburgh Press, 1988.
The Kind of Light That Shines on Texas. Boston: Little, Brown, 1992.
White Boys: Stories. New York: Henry Holt, 1998.

Reference Book

African-American Wisdom. San Rafael, CA: New World Library, 1994.

Studies of Reginald McKnight

Brailsford, Karen. "Fiction." Rev. of *I Get on the Bus. New York Times Book Review* (16 Sept. 1990): 22.
"Briefly Noted Fiction." Rev. of *I Get on the Bus. New Yorker* (16 July 1990): 85–86.
Carlin, Margaret. "Mental Gymnastics: Author Reginald McKnight Writes Lies, Truthfully Told." *Denver Rocky Mountain News,* 31 Jan. 1993. *Newsbank: Literature,* fiche 21, grids E5–6.
Giddins, Paula. "Reginald McKnight." *Essence* 21 (Mar. 1991): 40.
Johnson, Greg. "Wonderful Geographies." Rev. of *Moustapha's Eclipse. Georgia Review* 43 (1989): 412–14.
Kornblatt, Joyce Reiser. "One Up on the Other Guy." Rev. of *The Kind of Light That Shines on Texas. New York Times Book Review* (8 Mar. 1992): 8–9.
Larson, Charles R. "Cultures in Collision." Rev. of *I Get on the Bus. Washington Post Book World* (17 June 1990): 1, 11.
Lesser, Ellen. "Telling Tales: In Search of the New Short Story." Rev. of *Moustapha's Eclipse. New England Review and Bread Loaf Quarterly* 12 (1989): 106–8.
Megan, Carolyn E. "New Perceptions on Rhythm in Reginald McKnight's Fiction." *Kenyon Review* 16 (1994): 56–62.
O'Brien, George. "I Get on the Bus." *Masterplots II.* African American Literature Ser., Vol. 2. Ed. Frank N. Magill. Pasadena, CA: Salem Press, 1994. 563–68.
"Reginald McKnight." *Contemporary Authors.* Vol. 129. Ed. Susan M. Trosley. Detroit: Gale, 1990. 297.
Roux, John. "Fiction." Rev. of *Moustapha's Eclipse. New York Times Book Review* (16 Oct. 1988): 36.
Walsh, William. "We Are, in Fact, a Civilization: An Interview with Reginald McKnight." *Kenyon Review* 16 (1994): 27–42.

TERRY McMILLAN
(1951–   )

Rita B. Dandridge

BIOGRAPHY

Terry McMillan was the oldest of five children born in Port Huron, Michigan, to working-class parents. Her mother primarily supported the family and was frequently abused by McMillan's alcholic father, Edward Lewis McMillan, now deceased. The Midwest setting and some family circumstances are echoed in McMillan's first novel *Mama* (1987), in which the protagonist, Mildred Peacock, a mother of five, resides in Point Haven, Michigan, is married to an abusive, alcoholic sanitation worker, and is herself temporarily employed as a factory worker. To her mother, Madeline Tillman, McMillan dedicates *Mama*.

At sixteen years old, McMillan worked as a page in the Port Huron city library, making $1.25 per hour. Her discovery there of James Baldwin's* works raised her consciousness about black writers and black pride. The following year, 1968, she left Port Huron to seek a new life in Los Angeles, where she later enrolled in a black literary classics course at Los Angeles City College. Her early interest in black writers is hinted at in *Mama*'s Freda, Mildred's oldest daughter.

In 1973, McMillan transferred to the University of California at Berkeley, where her study of journalism increased her interest in writing. While there, she met Ishmael Reed,* a popular novelist and founder of Before Columbus Foundation, which helps ethnic writers to circulate their works. In 1976, Reed published McMillan's "The End," a short story detailing a stressful day in the life of Pobre Blackstone, an assembly worker at Detroit's Ford Motor Company.

After receiving her bachelor's degree from University of California at Berkeley, McMillan moved to New York and enrolled in the master's program at Columbia University to study film. She received her M.F.A. in 1979, worked as a word processor, and participated in a Harlem Writers Guild workshop, where she found her voice as a fiction writer. During a two-week stay at the MacDowell colony in 1983, McMillan completed the first draft of *Mama*. Refusing to rely solely on conventional marketing techniques, she promoted *Mama* by sending out thousands of letters primarily to African American organizations and offering to read sections of her book. The result was that all copies of the first printing of *Mama* were sold before publication date.

Following the publication of *Mama*, not only did McMillan secure an instructorship at the University of Wyoming at Laramie (1987–1990), but her persistent marketing techniques also proved advantageous for her second novel, *Disappearing Acts* (1989), which became a national best-seller. It sold more than 100,000 paperback copies. Its publication provoked a $5 million lawsuit from Leonard Welch, the father of McMillan's son, Solomon, born in 1984. Welch claimed that the abusive Franklin Swift, in *Disappearing Acts*, portrayed and defamed him. Welch lost his case, and his appeal was denied.

In 1990, McMillan moved to Tucson, Arizona, where she began to teach at the University of Arizona. The same year saw the publication of *Breaking Ice: An Anthology of Contemporary African-American Fiction*, in which is included McMillan's short story "Ma 'Dear," a first-person narrative about a feisty seventy-two-year-old food stamp recipient. Two years later, McMillan published her third novel, *Waiting to Exhale* (1992), which she dedicated to her father. It is a stimulating narrative about four classy African American women and their inability to find eligible mates. Its commercial success has been astounding. During its first eleven weeks, the novel made the *New York Times* best-seller list, and it sold more than 700,000 hardcover copies the same year (Skow 77). In 1996, it became one of the top motion pictures.

The success of *Waiting to Exhale* earned McMillan a $6 million advance for her fourth novel, *How Stella Got Her Groove Back* (1996), which details the romantic relationship between Stella Payne and Winston Shakespeare during Stella's one-week vacation in Jamaica. McMillan dedicates this novel to Jonathan P., a young Jamaican named Jonathan Plummer, whom she met in 1995 while on her vacation in Jamaica. Written in one month, the novel had a first printing of 1 million copies.

McMillan resides in Danville, California, with her son Solomon. She is currently engaged in writing the screenplay for a film based on *Disappearing Acts*.

MAJOR WORKS AND THEMES

Mama is a sensitive and realistic tale of a poor, black, urban mother who at one point celebrates her ability to have children but, as time progresses, becomes disillusioned with her maternal status in the face of insurmountable financial odds. The novel's major theme is the destructive influence of the motherhood myth on an indigent black woman. Rooted in Eurocentric Christian thought, the motherhood myth emphasizes motherhood as woman's sacred calling and celebrates her Christian duty to have many children. McMillan deflates the myth by pointing to the assumptions associated with it that are inapplicable to Mildred as a poor, black, inner-city dweller. Mildred's circumstances differ significantly from the traditional assumptions that motherhood occurs within a traditional family, that males and females have rigid sex roles, and that mothers are financially dependent on their husbands. She divorces her husband, functions as mother and father to her children, and works at odd jobs before prostituting herself.

Mama reads as a contemporary revision of a racialized Christian history that tied the black woman's value to her reproductive assets. Set in Point Haven, the story actually unfolds in the South Park, an isolated urban ghetto in Michigan reminiscent of an insular slave plantation. Here Mildred, an infrequent church-goer, gives birth to five unplanned-for children, who are supported by the welfare system when her husband deserts them.

The speciousness of motherhood manifests itself in various tropes, most noticeably in Mildred's blond wig, representing a gilded halo. While Mildred herself is less than the exalted mother traditionally expected to wear a halo, she is, nevertheless, a good mother. Contradictory though she is, she is also authentic.

McMillan's second novel, *Disappearing Acts* (1989), turns to romance. Its central theme is that love often overlooks incompatibilities that can make a difference. Structured into thirty-four, alternating first-person monologues, the novel centers on Zora Banks, high school music teacher, and Franklin Swift, her live-in seasonal construction worker. Zora falls head over heels in love with Franklin when she first sees him, but his marital separation, nonsupport of his children, dope-smoking, and abuse make him an unattractive lover. Their love begets hatred, not marriage. The child they have together rarely sees his father.

Disappearing Acts centers on the thematic myth that a woman must have a man to validate her existence. The assumption is that a woman is not a whole person without one. McMillan deflates the myth by revealing that Zora's wholeness as a woman precedes Franklin's arrival and resumes after his departure. A single, educated, employed woman with money saved, Zora realizes that she is better off without him. However, Franklin impregnates Zora while he is married to another, delays his career, wants her money for his friends, and has difficulty holding a job.

In her third novel, *Waiting to Exhale*, McMillan entertains as her major theme the beauty myth and its harmful effects on African American women. Eurocentric in origin, the myth assigns beauty to those who possess youth, virginity, white skin, Caucasian features, and low body weight. The myth also emphasizes competition, materialism, individualism, and independence, all qualities embodied in the survival of the fittest ideology. In this novel, McMillan exposes four assumptions of the myth: that good looks automatically attract a good (as opposed to a bad) man; that acceptance of the myth increases (rather than limits) African American women's chances for happiness; that women are at harmony (instead of at war) with their bodies; and that competitive beauty creates closeness (instead of animosity) among women (see Dandridge's analysis of McMillan's use of the myth 121–133).

Through a ritual of victimization and purgation, each of McMillan's women eventually embraces an Afrocentric aesthetic that encodes cooperation, spirituality, collectivism, and interdependence. Savannah, Bernadine, Gloria, and Robin redefine their reality by seeking emotionally responsive relationships and by embracing black popular art such as black music, art, African-derived names, soul food, beauty salons, and self-help groups. These elements serve as counterforces against the corporeal glamour that capitalistic America mass-markets.

The four women reside in Phoenix, Arizona, the city whose name is reminiscent of the beautiful bird that sacrifices itself on a pyre to be reborn. Like the bird that has endured centuries of victimization, Savannah, Bernadine, Gloria, and Robin have lived with the damaging effects of a Eurocentric beauty myth before purging themselves of the myth's falsehoods and restoring themselves with an Afrocentric aesthetic.

McMillan in her fourth novel, *How Stella Got Her Groove Back* (1996), once again turns to romance. Revealing the author's feminist consciousness, the novel treats the theme of an older woman's love for a younger man and society's disdain for such a union: "Men have been dating younger women for . . . centuries," McMillan's Stella observes angrily, "and does anybody say anything to them?" (225).

Essentially, the novel is a parody of the older man/younger woman myth, which celebrates the rejuvenation of a subsiding male. Even though McMillan reverses the socially acceptable older man/younger woman affair and addresses the still socially unacceptable older woman/younger man union, she points to certain realities in the myth. A primary reality is that the older partner self-imposes obsessive concern about the age difference to the extent of self-doubt. Another reality is that the younger partner often becomes less aggressive after the relationship begins. These truths plague the relationship between Stella and Winston and actually slow the pace of the narrative.

Always the social observer, McMillan reveals race, gender, and class consciousness in her four novels. Witty, urbane, and down-to-earth, she never fails to point to those outmoded myths awaiting the unsuspecting. Her works embrace universal myths and themes, but African American women primarily buy her books. They line up by the hundreds for her autograph on her book tours.

CRITICAL RECEPTION

Critical assessments of McMillan's novels have been confined largely to reviews. Some of these have been trivial and personal, such as Richard Bernstein's comparing *How Stella Got Her Groove Back* to "a backyard barbecue" (C17) and John Skow's observing about the same novel that this "silly wish-fulfillment fantasy . . . isn't fantasy after all" because McMillan flew to Jamaica on vacation and fell in love with . . . 20-ish resort hotel employee Jonathan Plummer" (77). Other reviews are more substantive and judicious. David Nicholson praises Mc-Millan for creating in *Disappearing Acts* "a whole new literary category—the post-feminist black urban romance novel" (67), and Michael Awkward links McMillan's first novel, *Mama*, to Alice Walker's* *The Color Purple* and Paule Marshall's* *Praisesong for the Widow* (650).

Mama mostly garnered attention for its saucy portrayal of Mildred Peacock, a fierce survivor and poverty-stricken mother of five who changes jobs frequently and lies to bill collectors to make ends meet. Critics, however, differ in their responses to Mildred. Elizabeth Alexander regards the protagonist as a compelling character and relates her embellishment to McMillan's use of such literary devices as similes and vernacular humor found in Zora Neale Hurston's fiction (46). Kamili Anderson sees no literary quality in the novel at all and has no compassion for Mildred and her children, "who come across as pitiable nobodies going nowhere fast" (9). Deborah Robertson notes the "sociological commentary" contained in *Mama* (684), but, like other critics, she fails to connect this commentary meaningfully to Mildred's struggles as a poor urban mother.

In reviewing *Disappearing Acts*, critics congratulate McMillan on her warm telling of a love affair, yet they cite unevenness in her portrayal of Zora Banks and Franklin Swift. While Zora's "shallow voice" (Sayers 8) and "maddeningly passive character" (Nicholson 6) are considered as flaws, others cite as positives Franklin's authentic voice (Bernikow 42) and "sexual bravado" (Barbieri 64).

In addition, several critics compare McMillan to Zora Neale Hurston. After all, McMillan names her heroine Zora Banks and pays homage to this literary foremother by having Zora place a photograph of her dead mother next to Hurston's *Their Eyes Were Watching God*. Despite McMillan's allusions, however, critics see little resemblance between McMillan's Zora and Hurston. Zora's voice "is way too flat," says Valerie Sayers, when compared to Hurston, who "knew how to make imagery streak and crackle" (8). Elsewhere, Jeffrey Richards comments that in this updated rendition of Hurston's *Their Eyes Were Watching God*, McMillan "pours out all the backwater lilt and country dirt of the 1937 original" and fills her story "with hot talk and urban ash." The difference between the two authors, continues Richards, is that Hurston "knew enough to stop at [page] 286" (D5).

By far, McMillan has received the most critical attention for her best-seller *Waiting to Exhale*, which critics label "popular fiction" (Max 20), a "romance of allegiance and gripe" (Dodd 11), and a chronicler of black life in the 1990s (Hubbard 93). Audrey Edwards compares reading the novel to "greasing down on a Big Mac" because it is "sinfully delicious" (78). John Boudreau comments on the readability of the novel because its text is "men's fear of commitment and women's fear of growing old" (E1). Its "vibrant street talk" and realistic "sexual issues" garnered praise from Frances Stead Sellers, who otherwise regards the novel's literary merits as "modest" (20).

Although considerably different from the novel, the film version of *Waiting to*

Exhale met with tremendous success. It proved to be as popular as the screen rendition of Alice Walker's *The Color Purple*. Like *The Color Purple*, it received positive and negative reviews. Audrey B. Chapman welcomes the "discourse about the silent war that continues to divide African-American men and women," but she believes the film presents a "one-sided view of the issue" (118). Michael Eric Dyson notes that the film affirms woman bonding but that it also "calls attention to the silly mistakes some women make in their quest for meaningful companionship" (118). Beverly Guy-Sheftall acknowledges the popularity of the film but quickly points out, and rightly so, the marked difference between the film and the novel. She notes the film's failure to give the women "racial consciousness or ties to the community," its insistence on "the only love that a Black man openly expresses is for a White woman," and its portrayal of "skin-color politics" (122).

McMillan's fourth novel, *How Stella Got Her Groove Back*, also received mixed reviews. Sarah Ferguson says the novel is a "guilty-pleasure sex-and-shopping fantasy" but that it proves that if older men can "rev their engines" with "young trophy wives," then "middle-aged women" can have their "dreamy, dishy boy toys" (21). James Wolcott comments on the " 'You go, girl' slapstick" and the excessively long sentences with punctuation to convey the protagonist's quick pace (102). Corrine O. Nelson finds Winston Shakespeare boring and the descriptions of Jamaica, the vacation resort, weak; she believes this novel is not "a worthy follow-up" to *Waiting to Exhale* (84).

Understandably, critics vary in their assessment of McMillan's novels, and McMillan has her own responses to these critics. She has expressed disappointment in the lack of enthusiastic reception she has received from black female critics, especially from Thulani Davis, who says McMillan's works are "miscegenating" (29). Davis' remark insulted McMillan, who quipped that "black critics [are] our worst enemies" (Trescott D4). McMillan also resents the view of some critics that she is a confessional writer and insists that her novels are not biographies.

BIBLIOGRAPHY

Works by Terry McMillan

"The End." *Yardbird Reader* V. Berkeley, CA: Yardbird, 1976. 384–392.
Mama. New York: Houghton Mifflin, 1987.
Disappearing Acts. New York: Viking, 1989.
"Ma 'Dear." *Breaking Ice: An Anthology of Contemporary African-American Fiction.* Ed. Terry McMillan. New York: Viking, 1990. 457–465.
Waiting to Exhale. New York: Viking, 1992.
How Stella Got Her Groove Back. New York: Viking, 1996.
"Swept Away." *People* (29 Apr. 1996): 115–119.

Studies of Terry McMillan

Alexander, Elizabeth. "Hot 'Mama.' " Review of *Mama. Village Voice* (24 Mar. 1987): 46.

Anderson, Kamili. Review of *Mama. Belles Lettres: A Review of Books by Women* 3 (Sept.–Oct. 1987): 9.

Awkward, Michael. "Chronicling Everyday Travails and Triumphs." *Callaloo* 11 (Summer 1988): 649–650.

Barbieri, Richard. "Speaking from a New Tradition." Review of *Disappearing Acts. Independent School* 50 (Fall 1990): 64–69.

Bernikow, Louise. Review of *Disappearing Acts. Cosmopolitan* (Aug. 1989): 42.

Bernstein, Richard. "Black, Affluent, and Looking for More." Review of *How Stella Got Her Groove Back. New York Times*, 15 May 1996: C17.

Boudreau, John. "Looking for Mr. Right." Review of *Waiting to Exhale. Los Angeles Times*, 19 June 1992: E1.

Chapman, Audrey B. "Was the Movie Fair to Black Men and Black Women?" Review of *Waiting to Exhale. Ebony* (Apr. 1996): 116+.

Dandridge, Rita B. "Debunking the Beauty Myth with Black Pop Culture in Terry McMillan's *Waiting to Exhale.*" *Language, Rhythm, and Sound.* Ed. Joseph K. Adjaye and Adrianne R. Andrews. Pittsburgh: University of Pittsburgh Press, 1997. 121–133.

Davis, Thulani. "Don't Worry, Be Buppie." *Village Voice Literary Supplement* (May 1990): 26–29.

Dodd, Susan. "Women, Sisters, and Friends." Review of *Waiting to Exhale. Washington Post*, 24 May 1992: Book World Sec. 11.

Dyson, Michael Eric. "Was the Movie Fair to Black Men and Black Women?" Review of *Waiting to Exhale. Ebony.* (Apr. 1996): 118–120.

Edwards, Audrey. Review of *Waiting to Exhale. Essence* (Oct. 1992): 77+.

Ferguson, Sarah. Review of *How Stella Got Her Groove Back. New York Times Book Review* (2 June 1996): 21.

Guy-Sheftall, Beverly. "Was the Movie Fair to Black Men and Black Women?" Review of *Waiting to Exhale. Ebony* (Apr. 1996): 120–122.

Hubbard, Kim. "A Good Man Is Hard to Find." Review of *Waiting to Exhale. People* (20 July 1992): 93–94.

Max, Daniel. "McMillan's Millions." Review of *Waiting to Exhale. New York Times Magazine* (9 Aug. 1992): 20+.

Nelson, Corrine O. Review of *How Stella Got Her Groove Back. Library Journal* (15 May 1996): 84.

Nicholson, David. "Love's Old Sweet Song." Review of *Disappearing Acts. Washington Post*, 27 Aug. 1989, sec. Book World: 6.

Porter, Evette. "My Novel, My Self." Review of *How Stella Got Her Groove Back. Village Voice* (21 May 1996): 11.

Richards, Jeffrey. Review of *Disappearing Acts.* (Raleigh, NC) *News and Observer*, 15 Oct. 1989: D5.

Robertson, Deborah G. Review of *Mama. Booklist* (1 Jan. 1987): 684.

Sayers, Valerie. "Someone to Walk over Me." Review of *Disappearing Acts. New York Times Book Review* (6 Aug. 1989): 8.

Sellers, Frances Stead. Review of *Waiting to Exhale*. *Times Literary Supplement* (6 Nov. 1992): 20.

Skow, John. "Some Groove with Her New Book, Money and Man: Is Terry McMillan Going All Happy on Us?" Review of *How Stella Got Her Groove Back*. *Time* (6 May 1996): 77+.

Trescott, Jacqueline. "The Urban Author, Straight to the Point." *Washington Post*, 17 Nov. 1990: D1+.

Wolcott, James. "Showcase: Terry McMillan." Review of *How Stella Got Her Groove Back*. *The New Yorker* (29 Apr. 1996): 102–103.

LOUISE MERIWETHER
(1923–)

Kathy White

BIOGRAPHY

Louise Meriwether was born in Haverstraw, New York, the only daughter of Julia and Marion Lloyd Jenkins, who moved his family from South Carolina to New York in search of a better life. Meriwether's father, a bricklayer in Haverstraw, moved his family of five children to Brooklyn during the Depression, where he became a number runner to augment the income the family received from welfare programs. Meriwether attended P.S. 81 in Harlem and graduated from Central Commercial High School in Manhattan and went on to receive a B.A. in English from New York University.

Meriwether married a graduate student at Columbia, Angelo Meriwether, with whom she moved to Los Angeles in the 1950s. This first marriage ended in divorce, as did her second marriage to Earl Howe. She held several interesting jobs in Los Angeles that moved her toward her goal of being a writer. She worked as a legal secretary, a real estate salesperson, a reporter for the *Los Angeles Sentinel*, and the first black story analyst for Universal studios. Finally, in 1965, she received a master's degree in journalism from the University of California at Los Angeles, where she documented her early concern with the mistreatment of blacks in America.

In the early 1960s, Meriwether published book reviews and articles on black Americans primarily in black journals, articles about blacks who overcame great odds to achieve success: Matthew Hensen, Leontyne Price, Grace Bumbry, and Audrey Boswell. In the late 1960s, she began writing fiction.

MAJOR WORKS AND THEMES

Daddy Was a Number Runner, Meriwether's first novel and the first novel to come out of the Watts Writers Workshop, was published in 1970 after five years of work. Although this is a work of fiction, the life of the heroine, twelve-year-old Francie Coffin, bears much resemblance to that of the adolescent Meriwether. Francie is the only daughter of a family struggling to survive on a welfare pittance in Harlem during the depression. As she struggles with approaching womanhood, she is forced into a bleak and hopeless mind-set as she watches her family fall apart under the stress of surviving.

Her father, James, finally abandons the family to live with a neighborhood widow who hosts gambling and drinking parties continuously while her mother, Henrietta, is forced in Francie's presence to repeatedly relinquish her self-respect to beg the welfare authorities to give her enough money to feed her children. Francie's brothers, driven away from the home by the hardness of their lives and their father, find what she considers to be equally tragic occupations: James, Jr., becomes a pimp, while Sterling, the accomplished scholar and symbol of hope for the family, drops out of school and becomes a menial laborer. Lacking the inspiring models of her nonfiction, this work ends with a dejected, angry Francie cursing her own options in a world that would not allow her family the smallest success. She could become a prostitute like her friend's sister, work herself into an early grave like her mother, have babies for welfare money, or run gambling games, no options at all for a young black woman.

Meriwether's most recent novel, *Fragments of the Ark*, is based on the life of military hero Robert Smalls. The novel foregrounds the involvement of slaves in the Civil War, telling the story of gunboat pilot Peter Mango, who steals the *Swanee*, a confederate military vessel, and turns it over to the Union.

At the start of the war, Peter Mango is loaned to the Confederate cause and forced to fight against the Union soldiers, who are ironically fighting for his freedom. Inspired by the story of Denmark Vesey, Mango bides his time until an opportunity for successful rebellion presents itself. Finally, when Charleston is overrun by the Union Army, necessity requires that he learn to pilot the *Swanee* and to hatch a potentially deadly plan to defect. Mango expertly guides the boat through the ring of Confederate sentries who surround the harbor and makes his way to the Union strongholds in the Sea Islands of South Carolina, where his wife, Rain, his children, and his mother, Lily, struggle to make a life for themselves while Mango aids in the capture of Confederate territory.

At the end of the war, Mango retires from the Union Navy in which he had served with high distinction and demonstrated uncommon heroism. However, like many other African American soldiers who fought in the Civil War, he faces an uncertain future in a turbulent and defeated South.

Fragments of the Ark is a historical novel. It reveals Meriwether's passionate interest in African American history and her commitment to reimagining that history and reinscribing its forgotten heroes. In its revisionist intent, *Fragments of the Ark* resembles other African American works of fiction that are loosely based on significant moments or figures in history, such as Toni Morrison's *Beloved* and Sherley Anne Williams' *Dessa Rose*.

CRITICAL RECEPTION

Meriwether's novels have generally received mixed reviews. James Baldwin,* who wrote the foreword to *Daddy Was a Number Runner*, eloquently praises Meriwether's ability to tell a tragic story in an intentionally minor key. E. M. Guiney, while conceding that the novel does have some minor flaws, argues that "it is superior to much current fiction" (685). Others, however, see sociological value but little literary merit in the work. Meriwether's most recent novel also has elicited mixed assessments. For example, Valerie Smith writes of *Fragments of the Ark*: "The novel is not flawless . . . some secondary characters are insufficiently developed . . . Meriwether leaves too many unanswered questions about the motivations of Mango's wife and mother." However, she goes on:

Such limitations do not interfere with the book's impact. Given its scope and acuity, this long-awaited work is certain to compel and enlighten future generations of readers about the varied ways that African-Americans contributed to the struggle for their own emancipation. (2)

Meriwether's significance is indisputable. She is the voice of suppressed history, a voice this country desperately needs.

BIBLIOGRAPHY

Works By Louise Meriwether

Daddy Was a Number Runner. Englewood Cliffs, NJ: Prentice-Hall, 1970.
The Freedom Ship of Robert Smalls. Englewood Cliffs, NJ: Prentice-Hall, 1971.
The Heart Man: Dr. Daniel Hale Williams. Englewood Cliffs, NJ: Prentice-Hall, 1972.
Don't Ride the Bus on Monday: The Rosa Parks Story. Englewood Cliffs, NJ: Prentice-Hall, 1973.
Fragments of the Ark. New York: Simon and Schuster, 1994.

Studies of Louise Meriwether

Bourne, Kay. "Two Fresh Voices Sound." *Bay State Banner* (May 1994). Ethnic NewsWatch Available at http://www3/elibrary.com/s/edumark/getdoc
Braun, Patricia. Rev. of *Fragments of the Ark*. *Booklist* 90 (1994): 1068.
Burns, Ann. Rev. of *Fragments of the Ark*. *Library Journal* 118 (1993): 120.
Crayton, Pearl. *Quarterly Black Review of Books* (February 1994). Ethnic NewsWatch Available at http://www3/elibrary.com/s/edumark/getdoc
Dandridge, Rita B. "From Economic Insecurity to Disintegration: A Study of Character in Louise Meriwether's *Daddy Was a Number Runner*." *Negro American Literature Forum* 9 (1975): 82–85.
Guiney, E. M. Rev. of *Daddy Was a Number Runner*. *Library Journal* 95 (1970): 685.

————. Rev. of *Fragments of the Ark*. *African American Review* 30 (1996): 494–97.
Keymer, David. Rev. of *Fragments of the Ark*. *Library Journal* 119 (1994): 163.
Schraufnagel, Noel. *From Apology to Protest: The Black American Novel*. DeLand, FL: Everett/Edwards, 1973.
Smith, Valerie. " 'Fragments' Pulls Together Lives Split by the Civil War." *Emerge*. (4 Dec. 1993). Ethnic NewsWatch Available at http://www3/elibrary.com/s/edumark/getdoc
Steinberg, Sybil S. Rev. of *Fragments of the Ark*. *Publishers Weekly* 240 (1993): 49.

TONI MORRISON
(1931–)

Eberhard Alsen

BIOGRAPHY

Toni Morrison was born Chloe Ardellia Wofford on 18 February 1931. She was the second oldest of four children. Her parents, George and Ramah Wofford, were the descendants of sharecroppers from Alabama and Georgia. Morrison grew up in the small steel-mill town of Lorain, Ohio, located on Lake Erie, twenty-five miles west of Cleveland. The population of Lorain consisted largely of European immigrants, and schools were not segregated. In fact, when Morrison started grade school, she was the only black child in her class and the only one who could already read.

Despite the fact that her school was integrated and that she was the best student in her class, Morrison experienced the effects of racism early, for even the children of newly arrived immigrants who could not speak English were immediately taught that they and their families were not at the bottom of American society but that blacks were below them. Moreover, Morrison also experienced racist attitudes at home. She admits that she grew up "in a basically racist household with more than a child's share of contempt for white people." She imbibed this contempt from her father, who had witnessed whites committing atrocities against blacks in the South and had therefore come to the conviction that white people "were in some way fundamentally, genetically corrupt" ("Slow Walk" 152).

In addition to passing on to his daughter a feeling of moral superiority over whites, Morrison's father also bequeathed her his perfectionism as a craftsman, for he was a master shipyard welder who "loved excellence." But she might also have inherited her perfectionism from her maternal grandfather, Solomon Willis, who was not only an artist—he had taught himself to play the violin—but also a first-rate carpenter.

From both her father, George Wofford, and her grandmother, Ardellia Willis, Toni Morrison inherited a love of storytelling, especially ghost stories. In several interviews, Morrison reports that one of her family's evening pastimes was to take turns telling stories and that the children were invited to contribute. Because of these stories, so Morrison says, she became "intimate with the supernatural" from an early age. To this day, Morrison believes in spirits. For instance, when an interviewer's tape recorder broke down while Morrison was talking about her dead father, she said: "I know why. I told you something I wasn't supposed to tell you. So my father took care of it. I'm not surprised. He's done that before" (Strouse 57).

During high school, Morrison developed a love for literature, studied Latin for four years, and formed the decision to become a teacher. After graduating from high school with honors, Morrison enrolled as an English major at Howard University in Washington, D.C. She minored in the classics, performed on the stage with the Howard University Players, and changed her first name from Chloe to Toni. Having received her B.A. degree from Howard in 1953, she entered the graduate program in English at Cornell University in Ithaca, New York. There she studied under David Daiches and wrote a master's thesis entitled "Virginia Woolf's and William Faulkner's Treatment of the Alienated."

After receiving her M.A. degree from Cornell in 1955, Morrison taught for two years at Texas Southern University, in Houston, before she joined the faculty at her alma mater, Howard University. While teaching at Howard, she married the Jamaican architect Harold Morrison and gave birth to two sons, Harold Ford and Slade Kevin. Her marriage ended around 1964, the year that she was denied tenure at Howard University because she did not have a Ph.D. degree.

The mid-1960s were the most depressing years of Morrison's life. After living with her parents in Lorain, Ohio, for a while, she moved to Syracuse, New York, where she worked as a textbook editor for L. W. Singer, a subsidiary of Random House. To overcome her depression, Morrison decided to rework a short story she had written at Howard University and to turn it into a novel. That novel became *The Bluest Eye*. Morrison had a hard time getting it published. Several publishers turned it down before Holt, Rinehart, and Winston finally printed it in 1970.

In the meantime, Morrison had moved to New York because Random House had promoted her to senior editor in charge of black literature. In that capacity, she advanced the careers of several black women writers, including Toni Cade Bambara* and Gayl Jones.* She also edited an important book on African American history, *The Black Book* (1974), and she occasionally wrote for *The New York Times Book Review*.

In the 1970s, Morrison's career suddenly took flight. When she published *Sula* (1973) and *Song of Solomon* (1977), she became recognized as one of the most important new voices in American fiction. The success of *Sula* earned Morrison an appointment as lecturer at Yale University, and *Song of Solomon* won her the National Book Critics' Circle Award. In 1980, President Jimmy Carter appointed her to the National Council of the Arts, and in 1981, she was inducted into the American Academy of Arts and Letters.

Also in 1981, Morrison published her fourth novel, *Tar Baby*. Although the novel drew mixed reviews, *Newsweek* put Morrison's picture on its cover and published a long interview article on her life and work. Three years later, in 1984, Morrison left Random House to devote herself exclusively to her writing and to teaching, her first career choice. All along, she had been teaching in various places on the side, including Bard College and the State University of New York at Purchase.

In 1984, Morrison was appointed to the Albert Schweitzer Professorship of the Humanities at the State University of New York in Albany. While she was at Albany, she wrote and directed the performance of a play, *Dreaming Emmett* (1986). But more importantly, she also wrote and published *Beloved* (1987), the novel for which she received the Pulitzer Prize.

Since 1989, Morrison has been Robert F. Goheen Professor in the Humanities at Princeton University. She has also lectured at many universities, among them Harvard; and in 1992, she published three of her Harvard lectures under the title, *Playing in the Dark: Whiteness and the Literary Imagination*. That same year, she also published her sixth novel, *Jazz*, which was greeted with moderate praise.

Morrison's lasting fame was secured in 1993, when she was awarded the Nobel Prize in literature. She was the first black person and only the eighth woman to receive that recognition. In explaining the choice of Morrison, Sture Ahlen, the secretary of the academy that bestows the award, said about her: "She delves into the language itself, a language she wants to liberate from the letters of race. And she addresses us with the luster of poetry" (Darnton C17). Language was also the focus of Morrison's address to the Nobel Prize Committee. Morrison said: "Language can never 'pin down' slavery, genocide, war. Nor should it yearn for the arrogance to do so. Its force, its felicity, is in its reach toward the ineffable" (Nobel Speech 21).

MAJOR WORKS AND THEMES

Recurring themes in Toni Morrison's fiction are the failure of love; the quest for an authentic identity, or, conversely the failure to achieve such an identity; and the clash between material and spiritual values, between the belief that the physical world is all there is and the belief that beyond the physical world there exists a spiritual world. Moreover, on some level Morrison always deals with the role of women in African American society.

In Morrison's first novel, *The Bluest Eye* (1970), the two most important themes are the failure of love and the reasons some African Americans repudiate their racial identity by adopting the values of white society. The novel begins with a parody of a first grade reader for middle-class white children:

Here is the house. It is green and white. It has a red door. It is very pretty. Here is the family. Mother, Father, Dick, and Jane live in the green-and-white house. They are very happy. . . . See Father. He is big and strong. Father, will you play with Jane? Father is smiling. Smile, Father, smile. (7)

This text is shown to be ironic when Morrison uses parts of it as chapter headings. For instance, the chapter that begins with "[H]ere is the house. . . . It is very pretty," shows that the apartment in which the eleven-year-old Pecola Breedlove lives is everything but pretty; in fact, it is dirty and run-down and has its toilet in the kitchen. The chapter that begins with "Here is the family. . . . They are very happy" shows that the family is everything but happy; in fact, the father often comes home drunk and beats the mother. Finally, the chapter that begins with "See the Father. He is big and strong. . . . Father is smiling" shows the father to be anything but strong and smiling; in fact, in this chapter the father rapes his eleven-year-old daughter and gets her pregnant. At the end of the novel, Pecola's baby comes too early and dies, and Pecola withdraws into insanity.

The novel is a tour de force intended to show us that it is not the rape and the miscarriage that drive Pecola insane but the inability or unwillingness of those around Pecola, from her mother to her neighbors and her schoolmates, to show Pecola any love. Pecola desperately needs that love because she not only is very black and has very ugly features, but, more importantly, she is also aware of how starkly her life contrasts with that of the white girl Jane in the grade school textbook. Unlike the novel's black, middle-class narrator, Claudia McTeer, Pecola does not understand how oppressive the values of that grade school textbook are. Claudia McTeer dismembers the blond, blue-eyed, white dolls she gets for Christmas, but Pecola Breedlove buys into what Morrison has called "the Master Narrative" (Moyers), the value system of the white culture. While Claudia hates Shirley Temple and wishes she could strangle her, Pecola prays to God to give her the same kind of blue eyes that Shirley Temple has.

If she could only have blue eyes, so Pecola feels, she would be loved by her parents, her neighbors, and her schoolmates. This desire for blue eyes gets more intense as the squalor of her life increases. When she is several months pregnant by her own father, she decides to see a local charlatan named Soaphead Church, a light-skinned West Indian, who slicks his hair down with soap and who claims to be able to make people's dreams come true. When she asks to be granted blue eyes, Soaphead gives her a piece of meat to feed to a dog and to watch the dog closely. If the dog acts strangely, then his behavior will be a sign from God that her wish has been granted. What Soaphead doesn't tell Pecola is that he has poisoned the meat. When the dog goes into convulsions and dies, Pecola believes that she now has blue eyes. In the last chapter of the novel, in a section that begins with the heading "Here comes a friend," Pecola turns schizophrenic and talks to a nonexistent friend about the miracle that has given her blue eyes.

At the end of the novel, Morrison has her narrator, Claudia McTeer, meditate on the fate of Pecola Breedlove. Claudia claims that it is not Pecola's father,

Cholly Breedlove, or Soaphead Church that destroyed Pecola but she, Claudia, together with Pecola's other schoolmates. She says: "All of us—all who knew her—felt so wholesome after we cleaned ourselves on her. We were so beautiful when we stood astride her ugliness" (159). By contrast, so Claudia asserts, "Cholly loved her. I'm sure he did. He, at any rate, was the one who loved her enough to touch her, envelop her, give something of himself to her. But this touch was fatal, and the something he gave her filled the matrix of her agony with death" (159).

In its form, Morrison's first novel shows none of the organic structure or any of the oral quality of the African American storytelling that she grew up with. Instead, its contrived structure and its overly poetic style show the influence of the time she spent analyzing the fiction of Virginia Woolf and William Faulkner. Moreover, she may also have been influenced by the then fashionable, disjunctive fiction of John Barth (*Lost in the Funhouse* 1967), Donald Barthelme's (*City Life* 1968), and Robert Coover (*Pricksongs and Descants* 1969).

Morrison's second novel, *Sula* (1973), has a less contrived structure, and its style comes closer to that of folk narrative. The central concern in *Sula* is the quest for personal identity, but this quest is taken to an egocentric extreme. Thus, a related theme is the evil that inevitably grows when we are so absorbed with ourselves that we become unable to love others. Morrison has explained that the protagonist, Sula Peace, and her best friend, Nellie Wright, are symbolic of good and evil people. While Nel represents those who "carry the weight of the world," Sula is an extreme example of a person who "didn't care for nobody" but her own instincts (Parker 253–254).

Four incidents illustrate why even Sula's best friend, Nel, comes to think of her as evil. When Sula is twelve years old, she grabs a five-year-old boy named Chicken Little, swings him around and around by his hands, and then lets him sail into the river. The boy drowns without Sula making any attempt to rescue him. Later she remembers "the good feeling she had when Chicken's hands slipped" (146). When Sula is eighteen years old, her mother accidentally sets her own clothes on fire, and Sula does not try to put out the fire. Instead, so she later says: "I stood there watching her burn and was thrilled. I wanted her to keep on jerking like that, to keep on dancing" (127). Even though her mother dies from those burns, Sula never feels any remorse. When Sula is twenty-seven years old, she has her grandmother declared mentally incompetent and has her put in an old folks home so she can take possession of her grandmother's house and collect her monthly pension checks. That same year, Sula sleeps with the husband of her best friend, Nel, with the result that he abandons Nel and her three children. Nel later asks her, "I was good to you, Sula, why don't that matter. . . . And you didn't love me enough to leave him alone. To let him love me. You had to take him away." Sula doesn't understand why Nel is angry at her and asks: "What do you mean take him away? I didn't kill him. I just fucked him. If we were such good friends why couldn't you get over it?" (124–125).

For Sula the only thing that matters is the freedom to do whatever she wants to—a freedom that whites deny black males and that white and black males deny to black females. As a result, she becomes a pariah in her own community. When she dies, the only ones who mourn her passing are Nel Green and the town's idiot, Shadrack, who had a crush on Sula. Thus, Sula comes across as a character whose life is a cautionary tale, and the novel affirms the values that are the opposite of Sula's.

Sula is the first novel in which Morrison makes explicit her belief that there is a spiritual world beyond the physical one. This happens in the novel's last lines, which describe Sula's thoughts after she has died. The narrator tells us that Sula "was not breathing because she didn't have to. Her body did not need oxygen. She was dead." Then we are told that the dead Sula feels that her face is smiling: "Well, I'll be damned," she thought, "it didn't even hurt. Wait'll I tell Nel" (128).

We get even more supernatural elements in Morrison's next novel, *Song of Solomon* (1977). For this reason, a case can be made that *Song of Solomon* isn't a novel at all but a romance. As the nineteenth-century novelist Nathaniel Hawthorne said in the "Custom House" Preface to *The Scarlet Letter* (1851), the mark of the romance is that it creates "a neutral territory, somewhere between the real world and fairy-land, where the Actual and the Imaginary may meet and each imbue itself with the nature of the other" (105). The actual in the case of *Song of Solomon* is the realistic settings, and the imaginary is the extraordinary characters and the unusual and supernatural events.

The major themes in *Song of Solomon* are the search for identity and the clash between materialist and idealist values. These themes are developed in a plot that describes the spiritual coming-of-age of Milkman Dead. The events of the plot combine the actual and the imaginary, the natural and the supernatural.

Throughout his life, Milkman is exposed to two different influences, that of his materialist father, Macon, and that of his spiritual aunt, Pilate. His father tries to instill his materialism in Milkman when the boy is twelve years old. At that time, Macon says to Milkman:

Pilate can't teach you a thing you can use in this world. Maybe the next, but not this one. Let me tell you right now the one important thing you'll ever need to know: Own things. And let the things you own own other things. Then you'll own yourself and other people too. Starting Monday, I'm going to teach you how. (55)

For many years, Macon is successful in shaping his son's attitudes. Even when Milkman is thirty-one years old, his decisions are still being shaped by his father. For instance, Macon tells Milkman about some gold that his Aunt Pilate is supposedly keeping in a mysterious green canvas sack that is hanging from the ceiling of her living room. Macon convinces Milkman and his friend Guitar to break into Pilate's house and steal the sack, but it turns out that the sack contains only rocks and bones. Macon therefore believes that Pilate must have left the gold in a cave in Pennsylvania, and he sends Milkman to go and look for it.

On this trip Milkman's spiritual change occurs. Unable to find the gold in the cave in Pennsylvania, he continues on to a place in Virginia where Pilate had lived before coming to Pennsylvania. There he finds something more valuable than gold, a legend involving his great-grandfather, a slave by the name of Solomon who was able to fly. When Solomon was no longer able to bear the yoke of slavery, so the legend goes, he went to the top of a hill that is still called Solomon's Leap, spun around, and flew off to Africa. Solomon left behind twenty-one children, and to this day, almost everyone in the area has the surname Solomon, and even the little village where they live is a corruption of that name, Shalimar. But above all, the children in the area keep alive the memory of their ancestor by singing a song that begins with the statement, "Jake the only son of Solomon . . . Whirled about and touched the sun." The song ends with these words: "Solomon done fly, Solomon done gone/Solomon cut across the sky, Solomon gone home" (306–307). Because Milkman knows that his grandfather's name was Jake and because the song includes a line about Solomon's trying to take along his son Jake but dropping him, Milkman suspects that Solomon is his great-grandfather. Milkman is able to confirm his hunch by tracking down distant relatives. He also finds out that the bones that his aunt Pilate had been keeping in her mysterious green sack were those of her murdered father and that she had therefore been visited regularly by her father's spirit.

These events lead to Milkman's acceptance of the supernatural and of his Aunt Pilate's vision of life, according to which the ultimate reality is not matter but spirit. At the end of the novel, Milkman and Pilate return to Shalimar to bury Jake Solomon's bones on Solomon's Leap. As he is digging the hole, Milkman is shot at by his friend Guitar because Milkman had promised to share the gold with him, and now it seems to Guitar that Milkman is trying to bury the gold to keep it for himself. Guitar misses Milkman and hits Pilate. As Pilate dies in Milkman's arms, the narrator says: "Now he knew why he loved her so. Without ever leaving the ground, she could fly" (340). Then Milkman turns to face Guitar, who is looking up at him from a lower outcropping of rock. And this is how the novel ends:

Without wiping away the tears, taking a deep breath, or even bending his knees—he leaped. As fleet and bright as a lodestar he wheeled toward Guitar and it did not matter which one of them would give up his ghost in the killing arms of his brother. For now he knew what Shalimar knew: If you surrendered to the air, you could *ride* it. (341)

What Milkman has come to know is that it doesn't matter whether Guitar kills him or not; his spirit will continue to soar. Thus, the ending of the novel is an assertion of the supremacy of spirit over matter, an expression of an idealist vision of life.

In her next novel, *Tar Baby* (1981), Morrison gives a new twist to the familiar themes of the repudiation of racial identity and that of the conflict between material and spiritual values. For one thing, most of the action takes place not in the United States but on an imaginary French Caribbean island named Isle des Chevaliers. For another, for most of the novel, the milieu is not that of an African American community but that of the island mansion of a white million-aire, Valerian Street. However, the novel again asserts the existence of a spiritual world beyond the material one because once again the living are visited by ghosts of the dead. Also Nature—the island and its fauna and flora—is described as an all-encompassing, sentient being.

The protagonist of *Tar Baby* is a young black woman, Jadine Childs, who is the niece of the millionaire's black servants Sidney and Ondine. She was edu-cated at the Sorbonne University in Paris and later became a top fashion model. When the novel begins, Jadine has come to spend Christmas on the island to decide what do with the rest of her life. The Streets are also expecting their son Michael for the holidays, but Michael doesn't show up. Instead, a sailor who jumped ship is discovered hiding in the mansion. He is very black, wears dread-locks, and calls himself Son, but his real name is William Green. Instead of turning Son over to the police as an intruder, Valerian Street treats him as a houseguest.

In a series of long conversations with the Streets, with their two black servants, and with Jadine, Son points out the inauthenticity of all of their lives and the unacknowledged racism that shapes all of their attitudes. In her first conversation with Son, Jadine warns him that she'll have him thrown to the alligators if he tries to rape her. Son's response is: "Why you white girls always think somebody's trying to rape you?" Jadine is outraged at having been called a white girl, but Son tells her: "Then why'nt you settle down and stop acting like it" (121).

Despite this early sparring between the two, Jadine and Son become lovers and leave the island, first to go to New York City and then to visit Son's home-town of Eloe, in rural northern Florida. While they are in the small town of Eloe, Jadine realizes that she doesn't fit into a black community, that she is, in fact, more white than black. As a result of this realization, she breaks off her rela-tionship with Son and returns to Paris to marry her French lover.

Son returns to the Isle des Chevaliers to earn his living as a simple fisherman and to live with a visionary native woman named Thérèse, who had warned him against Jadine as being an unnatural creature. At the novel's ending, a symbolic mist lifts from Son's eyes "to make the way easier for a certain type of man" (306). That type of man is someone who is attuned to the spiritual world and to nature, as was Pilate in *Song of Solomon*.

Six years after *Tar Baby*, Morrison published *Beloved*, which is based on a historical incident. In 1856, in Cincinnati, a fugitive slave by the name of Mar-garet Warner tried to kill her four children when slave catchers came to take them back to the Kentucky plantation from which she and her children had escaped. *Beloved* explores this incident from two angles, a historical and a moral one. Thus, a major theme in the novel is the history of the treatment that black female slaves have received from whites ever since they were packed onto the slave ships that brought them to America. But the central theme is a moral one, because the most clearly developed pattern in the novel's structure is the protagonist Sethe's trying to answer the question whether it was morally right for her to kill her child in order to preserve the child from a life that she, Sethe, considered not worth living. The structural red thread that runs through the novel is Sethe's gradual change, her psychological deterioration as she feels more and more guilty and tries to atone for the murder.

The title, *Beloved*, refers to the child whom Sethe killed and who, twenty years later, returns to her mother not only as her dead baby grown up but also as a person able to remember several previous incarnations all the way back to the Middle Passage and beyond that to Africa. In an interview, Morrison said about the title character: "She is a spirit on one hand, literally she is what Sethe thinks she is, her child returned to her from the dead. . . . She is also another kind of dead which is not spiritual but flesh, which is, a survivor from the true, factual slave ship" (Darling 247). Some of the most harrowing passages in the novel are those in which Beloved recalls what it was like to be jammed in between the dead and the dying in the hold of a ship.

At the beginning of the novel, the ghost of Beloved terrorizes Sethe's house in Cincinnati until she is driven out by Paul D., a former slave on the plantation from which Sethe escaped. When Paul shows up at Sethe's house one day, he not only shares Sethe's bed but also shares her long-suppressed memories of the horrors they both experienced on the Kentucky plantation named "Sweet Home." Right after Paul's arrival, the ghost of the baby is particularly active, almost as if jealous of Paul. One evening, when the ghost is rocking the house in order to keep Sethe and Paul from making love, Paul decides to fight back, and he is so determined that he manages to drive the ghost away.

Just when Sethe and Paul are beginning to enjoy the comforts of family life, their peace is disturbed by the arrival of a mysterious young woman who has suffered some kind of trauma that she refuses to speak about. Sethe takes the girl in without realizing who she is, even though the girl calls herself Beloved, and Beloved is the only word that Sethe could afford to put on the tombstone of the baby she killed. The girl immediately develops an intensive attachment to Sethe. At first Sethe, Paul, and Sethe's daughter, Denver, take this attachment to be a sign of her gratitude to Sethe for allowing her to stay at her home. But gradually, both Denver and Paul begin to notice that the girl is jealous of them. Beloved even seduces Paul into having sex with her in order to break up his relationship with Sethe.

But when Paul's and Sethe's relationship breaks up, it is not because Paul had sex with Beloved; it is because he and Sethe disagree over Sethe's killing of her baby. Paul tells her, "What you did was wrong, Sethe." When Sethe explains that she killed Beloved out of love because she didn't want her to grow up in slavery, Paul responds, "You got two feet, Sethe, not four." At this point, so the narrator tells us, "a forest sprang up between them; trackless and quiet" (164–165). After this argument, Paul moves out. With Paul out of the way, Beloved has to share Sethe with only her sister, Denver.

Next, Beloved shuts out Denver by revealing to Sethe that she is the baby Sethe had killed twenty years ago. Because of this revelation Sethe is no longer sure that she really did the right thing in killing Beloved. To make amends, Sethe plans to "tend to her as no mother ever tended a child" (200). Sethe's guilt feelings increase with Beloved's demands. The narrator says about Beloved: "Anything she wanted she got, and when Sethe ran out of things to give her, Beloved invented desire . . . and the more she took, the more Sethe began to talk, explain" (240–241). Because of her profound guilt feelings, Sethe becomes incapable of leading a normal life. She loses her job as a cook at a restaurant because she is often late for work and because she is caught stealing choice pieces of food for Beloved. After she is fired, Sethe doesn't want to leave the house anymore because Beloved doesn't go out now that she is big with Paul's child. All along, Sethe is desperate to make Beloved understand why she killed her. Denver overhears a conversation in which Sethe is trying to explain to Beloved that she had killed her out of love so that she could not be hurt by the white masters: "The best thing she was, was her children. Whites might dirty *her* all right, but not her best thing, her beautiful, magical best thing, the part of her that was clean" (251).

Eventually, Denver realizes that the relationship between Sethe and Beloved is becoming pathological. As the narrator says: "It was as though Sethe didn't really want forgiveness given; she wanted it refused. And Beloved helped her out" (252). Denver decides that something must be done to break Beloved's influence over Sethe, and she begs her white employer, the philanthropist Edward Bodwin, to interfere. At the same time that Mr. Bodwin comes to talk to Sethe, thirty neighborhood women decide to do the same thing.

The spell is broken when Mr. Bodwin and the thirty black women arrive at Sethe's house at the same time. Seeing a white man with a hat and a whip stopping his buggy in front of her house, Sethe believes he is the same white man who once came to take her and her children back to the plantation in Kentucky. She takes an ice pick and attacks Mr. Bodwin, but before she can stab him, one of her female neighbors punches Sethe in the jaw, and then Denver and the other women pile on Sethe to hold her down. While Sethe is being subdued, Beloved disappears. Some people say she "exploded right before their eyes" (263), while a neighborhood boy claims that he saw "cutting through the woods, a naked women with fish for hair" (267).

After Beloved is gone, Sethe loses her will to live. When Paul hears that she doesn't eat and refuses to get out of bed, he returns to convince Sethe that life is worth living. As Paul sits down on her bed, Sethe breaks down and cries about Beloved's having left her. "She was my best thing," Sethe says. Paul disagrees, but he breaks his disagreement to Sethe in a very gentle, loving way: "You your best thing, Sethe. You are." Incredulous, Sethe asks, "Me? Me?" (273). The way that Sethe has been treated throughout her life makes it difficult for her to believe that anyone should think she has value as a person, that she is her own best thing. If anyone can convince her, it is Paul, who has shared so much of her life, both in slavery and in freedom: "Sethe," he says, "me and you, we got more yesterday than anybody. We need some kind of tomorrow" (273).

Because Sethe seems to accept Paul's opinion that she herself is her best thing and not her children, the novel's ending resolves the moral argument in Paul's favor without condemning Sethe. Morrison said in a television interview that what Sethe did was, on one hand, very noble and, on the other hand, quite wrong: "Someone gave me the line for it at one time which I have found useful: 'It was the right thing to do but she had no right to do it' " (Moyers Part II).

Morrison got her idea for her sixth novel, *Jazz* (1992), from a book of photographs of dead Harlem residents entitled *The Harlem Book of the Dead*, for which she wrote the Introduction. One of the pictures shows a young girl who had been shot at a dance in 1925. Morrison invented a name for the girl, Dorcas Manfred. Then she invented the events leading up to, and following, her death. These events form one of the two major strands of the novel's narrative. The other strand has to do with the ancestry of the girl, of the girl's married lover, Joe Trace, and of his wife, Violet. The events of this second strand of narrative go back to the Reconstruction period in the late nineteenth century. What the two parts of the novel's plot have in common is the theme of the failure of love.

The plot of the primary narrative is that in October 1925, the fifty-two-year old Joe Trace begins an affair with the eighteen-year-old high school girl Dorcas Manfred. In January 1926, Dorcas takes a younger lover and tells Joe she is tired of him. Joe finds Dorcas at a dance and shoots her in the shoulder. Dorcas not only refuses to reveal who shot her, but she also refuses medical attention. As a result, she bleeds to death. Joe's wife, Violet, attends Dorcas' funeral and tries to slash the dead girl's face with a knife. But she succeeds only in making a small nick in the throat of the corpse before ushers pull her away from the coffin. While Joe grieves for Dorcas for three months, Violet befriends Dorcas' aunt to find out what it was about the girl that her husband loved. Finally, Dorcas' best friend, Felice, comes to see the Traces to find out the whereabouts of a valuable opal ring that she allowed Dorcas to wear on the night she was killed. By revealing to Joe and Violet what a superficial and materialistic person Dorcas was, Felice heals Joe's and Violet's marriage.

As the narrative unfolds, the narrator, a female neighbor of the Traces, keeps commenting on the difficulties she has in telling the story. At one point, she admits that her storytelling is "unreliable" (160), and at another she realizes that she is missing the most important things that are going on in her characters' lives because, so she says, "It never occurred to me that they were thinking other thoughts, feeling other feelings, putting their lives together in ways I never dreamed of" (221).

To stop the characters from running away with the story, the narrator delves into their past and the lives of their ancestors. These stories include accounts of Violet's grandmother, True Belle, taking care of a rich white lady and her mulatto son, Golden Gray; of Golden Gray's saving the life of Joe Trace's mother when she was a young girl; of Joe's trying to find his mother, who is called "Wild" because she lives in the forest like an animal; and of Dorcas' parents' getting killed in the St. Louis race riots.

In addition, the narrator adds meditations on the influence of jazz—particularly, sexually explicit jazz lyrics—on the attitudes of people during the time between 1919 and 1929. She also adds descriptions of the ambience of New York at different times of the year, with a heavy emphasis on the changing of the seasons.

While the book's narrative development is hard to follow, *Jazz* spells out Morrison's philosophical idealism more clearly than her previous novels. In the middle of the novel, Joe Trace goes to track down his mother, whom he has never seen and who supposedly lives alone in a cave deep in the woods. He finds the cave, but the person living there has apparently just left. As Joe comes out of the cave, he senses that someone is hiding in the underbrush nearby. He calls out:

"Is it you? Just say it. Say anything." . . . "Give me a sign, then. You don't have to say nothing. Let me see your hand. Just stick it out someplace and I'll go; I promise. A sign." He begged, pleaded. . . . "You my mother?" Yes. No. Both. Either. But not this nothing. (178)

But not this nothing. This passage reflects Morrison's rejection of the nihilism that is still fashionable among many contemporary writers and critics. Unwilling to accept nothingness, Morrison keeps looking for signs of transcendence.

Morrison's seventh novel, *Paradise* (1998), breaks new ground because it doesn't focus on a single protagonist but develops a conflict between two opposed groups of people, because its central theme is that of bigotry among African Americans, and because its vision of life has strong religious undertones.

The action of the novel takes place in 1974 and 1975 in and near the fictional town of Ruby, Oklahoma, whose population of 360 souls is 100 percent African American. The central event in the novel is an armed attack by nine leading citizens of the town on a group of women who live at the Convent, a decaying mansion seventeen miles north of town. During that assault two of the women, one white and one black, are shot to death, but the remaining three black women—one of them clutching a newborn baby—manage to escape.

To explain the reasons for the raid on the Convent, Morrison not only gives us the life stories of the five women and of their antagonists but also develops the history of the town. The townspeople trace their lineage back to a group of 158 blue-black freedmen who migrated north from Mississippi and Louisiana during Reconstruction. On their way north, these freedmen had a defining experience that they later called the "Disallowing." Because of their extremely black skin, they were not allowed to stay for longer than a night's rest at any of the African American communities they encountered on their trek. As the narrator says: "The sign of racial purity they had taken for granted had become a stain" (194). But they refused to accept their extreme blackness as a stigma, and when they set up their own community, which became Haven, Oklahoma, they resolved to keep out anyone whose skin wasn't as dark as theirs. However, after World War II, a number of black families moved away and sold their property to whites. Unwilling to accept racial impurity, fifteen families, descendants of the original settlers, left Haven and founded the new community of Ruby. Because of their very dark skin, these fifteen original families of Ruby called themselves "8-rock," after a deep level in the coal mines.

Twenty-five years later, citizens of Ruby still consider their town to be a paradise because there is no crime and no police, no motel or bar, no television or movie theater. However, the male residents of this paradise feel their peace threatened by the women of the Convent. Not only are these women lighter-skinned than the citizens of Ruby, but they accept a white woman into their commune, they don't go to church, they drink, they provide a haven for women who are mistreated by their husbands, and some of them have affairs with men from the town. As the banker Deacon Morgan says: "They don't need men and they don't need God. . . . They meddle. Drawing folks out there like flies to shit and everybody who goes near them is maimed somehow and the mess is seeping back into *our* homes, *our* families" (276). Deacon should know; after all, he had an affair with one of the women from the Convent; and Deacon's wife, Soane, went there for an abortion.

However, the real reason for the attack on the Convent is not moral outrage but bigotry. This bigotry has two sides; one of them concerns skin color, and the other gender. The Reverend Richard Misner realizes that one-half of the "8-rock's" bigotry is "born out of an old hatred, one that began when one kind of black man scorned another kind and that kind took the hatred to a new level" (306). Billie Delia, a woman who had been treated kindly by the women at the Convent, realizes what the other half of the town fathers' bigotry is all about when she says that they "had seen in lively, free, unarmed females the mutiny of the mares and so got rid of them" (308).

What underlies the bigotry of the leading citizens of Ruby is not only hatred but also fear. This is why the Reverend Richard Misner—who seems to be Morrison's mouthpiece—keeps preaching against the town's motto, inscribed on the communal baking oven: "Beware the Furrow of His Brow." Misner does not want the community to be guided by the fear of God's wrath because to Misner God is immanent in humans, especially in "the way humans loved one another" (147). In one of his sermons, Misner says: "God being intelligence itself, generosity itself, He has given us Mind to know His subtlety. To know His Elegance. His Purity" (308). This abstract and almost transcendentalist conception of God is something new in Morrison's fiction, perhaps a harbinger of more religious fiction to come from her pen.

CRITICAL RECEPTION

After Toni Morrison had published her first two novels, many critics spoke of her as a writer of great promise. These early supporters were more than vindicated when she was awarded the Nobel Prize in literature. It is therefore not surprising to find that the majority of all printed reviews of Morrison's work are favorable. However, there have always been critics whose stylistic or political sensibilities have been offended by Morrison's fiction. Moreover, Morrison's assertive personality has rubbed some critics the wrong way and made them read her work with jaundiced eyes. Thus, even her two masterpieces, *Song of Solomon* and *Beloved*, have received some unfavorable reviews.

One of the first reviewers to recognize Morrison's talent was Haskel Frankel, who reviewed *The Bluest Eye* (1970) for the *New York Times Book Review*. In his balanced review essay, Frankel called Morrison "a writer of considerable power and tenderness" because she "can cast back to the living, bleeding heart of childhood and capture it on paper." However, Frankel also found the structure of the novel unconvincing, and he pointed out some far-fetched imagery such as the opening line of the "Autumn" section, "Nuns go by quiet as lust," and the sentence, "He will not unrazor his lips until spring." Still and all, Frankel concluded that Morrison is "a writer to seek out and to encourage" (47).

After the publication of *Sula* (1973), Morrison began to reap the first of the unqualified praise that marks much of the critical reception of her work. The reviewer for *Newsweek* called *Sula* "one of [the] brightest ornaments" among the novels that came out in 1973, "an exemplary fable, its brevity belied by its surprising scope and depth." Then he went on to say: "Toni Morrsion's narrative contains symbolical and fabulous elements and is laid out in small set pieces, snapshots arranged in a pattern that cannot be anticipated until the author is done with her surprises" (Prescott 63). Just as complimentary was the review of literary critic Jerry Bryant, who was struck by the novel's unusual characters and themes. Bryant noted that "something new is happening in black fiction," and that is a preoccupation with fierce characters who defy moral conventions (23). Bryant therefore found *Sula* to be just as innovative in its own way as John Barth's *Chimera* (1972) or Thomas Pynchon's *Gravity's Rainbow* (1973). According to Bryant, *Sula* represents "the thrust of some powerful new force, loosening the foundations of the old stereotypes and conventional manners." He concluded that the novel's "prophecy is that all our old assumptions about morality are disintegrating before a peculiarly black assault against them" (24).

Song of Solomon (1977) received even more praise than *Sula*; moreover, it was also awarded the National Book Critics' Circle Award as the best novel of 1977. The reviews were overwhelmingly positive. *Harper's Magazine* rated Morrison as "one of our best novelists" (Talifaro 94). The *Saturday Review of Literature* called the novel the "vision of an original, eccentric inventive imagination" (Kuehl 41). The *New York Times Review of Books* called *Song of Solomon* "better than good," concluding with these words: "Toni Morrison has earned attention and praise. Few Americans know, and can say, more than she has in this wise and spacious novel" (Price 48). One of the few sour notes was struck by the reviewer for *Newsweek*, who found the novel "less striking and less original" than Morrison's previous work (95A) and deplored a "structural conflict" between the novel's "assorted subplots" (Jefferson 96).

One of the three novels of Morrison's that received what are called "mixed reviews," that is, an equal number of positive and negative evaluations, is *Tar Baby* (1981). On one hand, fellow novelist John Irving called *Tar Baby* Morrison's "most ambitious book" (1) and noted that "the precision of Miss Morrison's minor characters and scenes reveals her craftsmanship" (30). However, "Morrison's greatest achievement," so Irving concluded, "is that she has raised her novel above the social realism that too many black novels and women's novels are trapped in. She has succeeded in writing about race and women symbolically" (31). On the other hand, Susan Lardner expressed the opinion that *Tar Baby* suffers from "an absence of shape and purpose" and that the style occasionally "topples into dreadful pits of bombast." To support that statement, she quoted one passage in which Morrison compares the fruits of an avocado tree to "the tight-to-breaking breasts of a pubescent girl three months pregnant" and another in which Morrison says that on Christmas Eve, "the whole island was vomiting up color like a drunk" (Lardner 150–151).

Morrison's stylistic boldness was received more favorably when she published *Beloved* (1987). In fact, Keith Mano began his piece in the *National Review* with these words: "Toni Morrison's language is thick as menstrual flow. Rich as clotted milk on the shirtfront of a nursing mother" (54). Mano gives Morrison credit for being "an extremely sophisticated writer" and finds her style appropriate to her subject. He concludes his review by saying: "*Beloved* has proven that slave experience is legitimate and fruitful artistic material. And, in so doing, it presents an intelligent, complex position that black people can take toward their own history" (55). Also extremely laudatory was the piece that Canadian novelist Margaret Atwood wrote. Atwood called *Beloved* "another triumph" and said that "Ms. Morrison's versatility and technical and emotional range appear to know no bounds" (1). Commenting on the novel's style, Atwood said that it is "written in an antiminimalist prose that is by turns rich, graceful, eccentric, rough, sinuous, colloquial and very much to the point" (50). The most notable voice raised against *Beloved* was that of black critic Stanley Crouch, who called *Beloved* a "blackface holocaust novel" and accused Morrison of sentimentalizing the subject of slavery. Moreover, he misread the novel, claiming that *Beloved* "explains black behavior in terms of social conditioning, as if listing atrocities solves the mystery of human motive and behavior" (40).

Morrison's sixth novel, *Jazz* (1992), was greeted by both positive and negative reviews, but even the laudatory reviews noted some flaws in the novel. For instance, Jane Mendelsohn praised the novel as a "supple, sophisticated love story which explores the possibilities of romance as both a natural phenomenon and a literary form" (25). Although Mendelsohn said that *Jazz* "can be at times almost painfully exciting to read," she remarked that the novel "can also be disjointed, unconvincing, even irritatingly repetitive." However, Mendelsohn concluded that "afterwards the poetry of the book stays in the mind" (26). Similarly ambivalent was Edna O'Brien, who gave Morrison credit for conjuring up the world of jazz-age New York "with complete authority." She also lauded Morrison's "robust language," which makes us see "the sidewalks, the curbstones, Egyptian beads, Kansas fried chicken, doors ajar to speakeasies, an invitation to the low-down hellfire induction to music and sex" (29). However, when O'Brien compared *Jazz* with great works of world literature such as William Faulkner's *Light in August*, James Joyce's *Ulysses*, and Leo Tolstoy's *Anna Karenina*, she found that Morrison's novel falls short. O'Brien speculated that Morrison might have been so "bedazzled by her own virtuosity" that what she created were "the bold arresting strokes of a poster and not the cold astonishment of a painting" (30).

Like *Jazz*, Morrison's seventh novel, *Paradise* (1998), received both enthusiastic praise and harsh criticism. Again, even the enthusiastic reviews mentioned some of the novel's shortcomings. The two reviews that the *New York Times* printed five days apart are representative of the mixed reception that the novel received. In the first review, Michiko Kakutani called *Paradise* "a clunky, leaden novel" because "it's a heavy-handed, schematic piece of writing, thoroughly lacking in the novelistic magic Ms. Morrison has wielded so effortlessly in the past." According to Kakutani, "nearly every one of the characters is a two dimensional cliché," and to make matters worse, "Ms. Morrison is constantly having her characters spell out the meaning of her story" (E8). In the second *New York Times* review, Brooke Allen called Morrison's *Paradise* "possibly her best work to date" because "with 'Paradise,' Morrison has put it all together, the poetry, the emotion, the broad symbolic plan." But Allen admitted that the novel "is not an easy read—dense, repetitive and obscure, it requires close scrutiny and concentration" (7).

Seen in retrospect, the critical reception that Morrison's work received from academe was at first tepid. Although some literary scholars supported Morrison from the very start, the literary establishment as a whole was slow to warm up to her work. This hesitancy was due not only to race and gender prejudice but also to ideology. During the 1970s and 1980s, some of the most influential critics were followers of the French nihilist philosopher Jacques Derrida, who advocates an aesthetics of disjunction and denies the existence of any "transcendental signified" (1,118). The establishment celebrated writers whose fiction was nihilistic and disjunctive, and they marginalized writers such as Toni Morrison, whose work was marked by a concern for unity and a belief in transcendence. For instance, according to the 1990 *Columbia History of the American Novel*, the mainstream of contemporary fiction consists of the work of such writers as Kathy Acker, Donald Bartheleme, Robert Coover, and Ishmael Reed.* Toni Morrison is mentioned only as a representative of African American literature.

After the publication of *Beloved* (1987), many fair-minded people felt that the white literary establishment was not giving Toni Morrison her due. Therefore, forty-eight black writers and critics published a statement in the *New York Times Book Review*, deploring the fact that "despite the international stature of Toni Morrison, she has yet to receive the national recognition that her five major works of fiction entirely deserve. She has yet to receive the keystone honors of the National Book Award or the Pulitzer Prize" ("Black Writers" 36). This statement created an uproar that shamed the Pulitzer Prize Committee into giving the award to *Beloved* belatedly, one year after its publication.

Since 1993, when Morrison received the Nobel Prize, more dissertations, articles, and books on her work are being written every year. By the spring of 1998, the on-line bibliography of the Modern Language Association (MLA) on the Internet listed over 600 items. Of these, 26 are book-length studies (three of them in German, one in Italian), 7 are collections of critical articles, and 2 are collections of interviews with Toni Morrison. In the following bibliography, I list only what seem to me the most important contributions to Morrison scholarship.

BIBLIOGRAPHY

Works by Toni Morrison

Fiction

The Bluest Eye (1970). New York: Pocket Books, 1972.
Sula (1973). New York: Penguin, 1982a.
Tar Baby (1981). New York: New American Library, 1982b.
Beloved. New York: Knopf, 1987a.
Song of Solomon (1977). New York: Penguin, 1987b.
Jazz. New York: Knopf, 1992.
Paradise. New York: Knopf, 1998.

Selected Nonfiction

"Virginia Woolf's and William Faulkner's Treatment of the Alienated." M.A. thesis, Cornell University, 1955.
"Slow Walk of Trees . . ." *New York Times Magazine* (4 July 1976): 104, 151+.
"Rootedness: The Ancestor as Foundation." In *Black Women Writers (1950–1980)*. Ed. Mari Evans. New York: Doubleday, 1984.
"Unspeakable Things Unspoken: The Afro-American Presence in American Literature." *Michigan Quarterly Review* 28 (Winter 1989): 1–34.
Playing in the Dark: Whiteness and the Literary Imagination. Cambridge: Harvard University Press, 1992.
Lecture and Speech of Acceptance upon the Award of the Nobel Prize in Literature. New York: Knopf, 1994.
Ed. with Claudia Brodsky. *Birth of a Nation'hood: Gaze, Script, and Spectacle in the O. J. Simpson Case*. New York: Pantheon, 1997.

Studies of Toni Morrison

Allen, Brooke. "The Promised Land" [Rev. of *Paradise*]. *New York Times Review of Books* (11 Jan. 1998): 6–7.
Atwood, Margaret. "Haunted by Nightmares" [Rev. of *Beloved*]. *New York Times Book Review* (13 Sept. 1987): 1, 49–50.

"Black Writers in Praise of Toni Morrison." *New York Times Book Review* (24 Jan. 1988): 36.

Bloom, Harold, ed. *Toni Morrison: Modern Critical Views*. New York: Chelsea House, 1990.

Bryant, Jerry H. "Something Ominous Here" [Rev. of *Sula*]. *The Nation* (6 July 1974): 23–24.

Crouch, Stanley. "Aunt Medea" [Rev. of *Beloved*]. *New Republic* (19 Oct. 1987): 38–43.

Darling, Marsha. "In the Realm of Responsibility: A Conversation with Toni Morrison." In *Conversations with Toni Morrison*. Ed. Danille Taylor-Guthrie. Jackson: University of Mississippi Press, 1994: 246–254.

Darnton, John. "In Sweden, Proof of the Power of Words." *New York Times*, 8 Dec. 1993: C17/C20.

Derrida, Jacques. "Structure Sign and Play in the Discourse of the Human Sciences." In *Critical Theory since Plato*. Ed. Hazard Adams. Rev. ed. New York: Harcourt, Brace, 1992: 1,116–1,126.

Frankel, Haskel. "The Bluest Eye" [Rev.]. *New York Times Book Review* (1 Nov. 1970): 46–47.

Gates, Henry L., and K. A. Appiah, eds. *Toni Morrison: Critical Perspectives Past and Present*. New York: Amistad, 1993.

Harris, Trudier. *Fiction and Folklore: The Novels of Toni Morrison*. Knoxville: University of Tennessee Press, 1991.

Hawthorne, Nathaniel. "The Custom House." In *The Complete Novels and Selected Tales*. Ed. Norman Holmes Pearson. New York: New Library, 1965.

Heinze, Denise. *The Dilemma of "Double Consciousness": Toni Morrison's Novels*. Athens: University of Georgia Press, 1993.

Hite, Molly. "Postmodern Fiction." In *The Columbia History of the American Novel*. Ed. Elliott Emory. New York: Columbia University Press, 1990.

Holloway, Karla, and Stephanie Dematrakopoulos. *New Dimensions of Spirituality: A Bi-Racial and Bi-Cultural Reading of Toni Morrison*. New York: Greenwood, 1987.

Irving, John. "Morrison's Black Fable" [Rev. of *Tar Baby*]. *New York Times Book Review* (29 Mar. 1981): 1, 30–31.

Jefferson, Margo. "Black Gold" [Rev. of *Song of Solomon*]. *Newsweek* (12 Sept. 1977): 93+.

Kakutani, Michiko. "Worthy Women, Unredeemable Men" [Rev. of *Paradise*]. *New York Times*, 6 Jan. 1998: E8.

Kuehl, Linda. "*Song of Solomon* by Toni Morrison." *Saturday Review of Literature* (17 Sept. 1977): 41.

Lardner, Susan. "Unastonished Eye" [Rev. of *Tar Baby*]. *New Yorker* (15 June 1981): 147–151.

Mano, Keith D. "Poignant Instant, Stubborn Evil" [Rev. of *Beloved*]. *National Review* (4 Dec. 1987): 54–55.

Mendelsohn, Jane. "Harlem on Her Mind: Toni Morrison's Language of Love" [Rev. of *Jazz*]. [*Village*] *Voice Literary Supplement* 105 (May 1992): 25–26.

Middleton, David, ed. *Morrison's Fiction: Contemporary Criticism*. New York: Garland, 1997.

Moyers, Bill. *A World of Ideas: Toni Morrison*. [Two-Part Interview]. New York: Public Affairs TV, 1989.

O'Brien, Edna. "The Clearest Eye" [Rev. of *Jazz*]. *New York Times Book Review* (5 Apr. 1992): 1, 29–30.

Parker, Bettye J. "Complexity: Toni Morrison's Women—An Interview Essay." In *Sturdy Black Bridges: Visions of Black Women in Literature*. Ed. Roseanne P. Bell et al. Garden City, NY: Anchor Books, 1979: 251–257.

Prescott, Peter S. "Dangerous Witness" [Rev. of *Sula*]. *Newsweek* (7 Jan. 1974): 63–64.

Price, Reynolds. "Black Family Chronicle" [Rev. of *Song of Solomon*]. *New York Times Book Review* (11 Sept. 1977): 1, 48, 50.

Strouse, Jean. "Toni Morrison's Black Magic" [Interview Essay]. *Newsweek* (30 Mar. 1981): 52–57.

Talifaro, Francis. "Books in Brief" [Rev. of *Song of Solomon*]. *Harper's Magazine* (Jan. 1978): 94.

Van der Zee, James, et al. Foreword. *The Harlem Book of the Dead*. Dobbs Ferry, NY: Morgan, 1978.

WALTER MOSLEY
(1952–)

Kristina L. Knotts

BIOGRAPHY

Walter Mosley was born in 1952 in south-central Los Angeles and lived there for the first twelve years of his life. After spending his formative years in Los Angeles, he moved east to attend Goddard College in Vermont before later receiving his B.A. from Johnson State University in 1975. In 1981, Mosley moved to New York City, where he has lived since (Wilkinson 1863).

Prior to writing fiction, Mosley worked as a computer programmer in New York City (Whetstone 110). During his early thirties, when he began to write, Mosley enrolled in the writing program at the City College of New York and was befriended by novelist Frederick Tuten, who later showed the *Devil in a Blue Dress* manuscript to his agent without notifying Mosley. *Devil in a Blue Dress* was soon published by Norton, as were most of his subsequent novels (McCullough 67).

MAJOR WORKS AND THEMES

A critical and popular success, Walter Mosley stands as one of the foremost writers of detective fiction in the United States today. His Easy Rawlins novels— *Devil in a Blue Dress, A Red Death, White Butterfly, Black Betty, A Little Yellow Dog,* and *Gone Fishin': A Novel*—recount the adventures of Mosley's gumshoe in Los Angeles and Texas. *R. L.'s Dream*, a "blues" novel, depicts the last days of Soupspoon Wise, a dying bluesman who once played with the famed Robert Johnson and who is haunted by that experience throughout the novel. *R. L.'s Dream* features the unlikely friendship between an elderly African American bluesman and a young, white, southern woman in New York City and, added to Mosley's detective oeuvre, reveals his multifaceted artistic range.

Mosley writes, he says, for the African American men of his father's generation who migrated from the South to Los Angeles to escape racism and to search for economic opportunity. While Mosley has lived in New York for much of his adult life and has stated that Los Angeles is "not my city," clearly Los Angeles has left an indelible influence on him; five of his seven novels are set there (Bruckner C13). The image of Los Angeles as a promised land for migrating southern African Americans figures prominently in his fiction. In *Devil in a Blue Dress*, Easy Rawlins, the main character, observes that

California was like heaven for the southern Negro. People told stories of how you could eat fruit right off the trees and get enough work to retire in one day. The stories were true for the most part but the truth wasn't like the dream. Life was still hard in L.A. and if you worked every day you still found yourself on the bottom. (34)

California, Los Angeles in particular, works well as "the ambiguous center of the American Dream for African Americans" in Mosley's novels (Muller 300).

By Mosley's own admission, the Easy Rawlins series, which begins in the mid-1940s after Easy returns from military service in World War II, will stretch until the 1970s or 1980s (Bruckner C16). The first novel in the cycle, *Devil in a Blue Dress*, is set just after the end of World War II in 1948 and folllows Easy's search for the elusive Daphne Monet. His second novel, *A Red Death*, is placed during the McCarthy era and pits Easy against the Internal Revenue Service (IRS). *White Butterfly*, set just a few years later in 1956, traces Easy's search for an alleged serial killer. *Black Betty* is set in 1961 and follows Easy on his search for Elizabeth Eady, a femme fatale from his past who turns up missing. *A Little Yellow Dog* depicts Easy in 1963 and in search of a missing schoolteacher, her dead husband, and his brother-in-law. *Gone Fishin'*, although published most recently, was actually written in the 1980s and portrays the early friendship and misadventures of Easy and his friend Raymond "Mouse" Alexander, tracing their connection back to their days in south Texas.

Mosley's purpose in writing, besides honoring the stories and struggles of his father's generation, is to write about the lives of working-class black men and women. As such, Mosley sees himself in a tradition with other black writers such as Langston Hughes and Zora Neale Hurston: "I've tried to write about Black people as Black people. Not as black people in relation to white people, not as victims of whatever, but Black people living their lives" (Hogness 112).

Not only is Mosley's fiction influenced by African American writers like Hughes and Hurston, but he also confesses the influence of existentialist writer Albert Camus' *The Stranger* on his detective fiction. Works like Camus', he says, are what draw him to consider ethical questions in his own writing:

Mysteries, stories about crime, about detectives, are the ones that really ask the existentialist questions . . . such as "How do I act in an imperfect world when I want to be perfect?" . . . I like the moral questions. (Bruckner C13)

Within each Easy Rawlins mystery, Easy must confront the ambiguous boundaries between right and wrong; often, he finds himself mired in murky ethical dilemmas. In *A Red Death*, a suspicious Easy agrees to help the Federal Bureau of Investigation (FBI) and spy on a former Polish resistance fighter; in return, they will ignore his unpaid back taxes.

In addition to being influenced by Camus, Mosley's fiction shares similarities with prior detective writers, Raymond Chandler and Chester Himes* being the most obvious influences. Like Chandler's mysteries, Mosley's novels reveal the "dark underside of the California dream" (Frieberger 101). Also like Chandler, Mosley has created a character in Easy Rawlins as memorable as Chandler's Phillip Marlowe. But while his fiction shares some commonalities with Raymond Chandler's, Mosley is not an African American Raymond Chandler; his fiction is, indeed, unique. Although Mosley has certainly borrowed from the genre of crime fiction, he has reworked some of its premises. Stephen Soitos, author of *The Blues Detective: A Story of African American Detective Fiction*, describes the way in which African American writers of detective fiction have taken conventions of the detective genre and reshaped them to comment on American society:

Through the use of black detective personas, double-consciousness detection, black vernaculars, and hoodoo creations, African American detective writers signify on elements of the detective genre to their own ends. (3)

Mosley's own work incorporates these elements to an extent, especially the use of double-consciousness and the play between standard English and black vernacular, both of which are evident in the persona of Easy Rawlins.

Even though Easy embodies many of the qualities of the basic hard-boiled detective, he also constantly changes in each novel; he is always dynamic. As Mosley has said of his creation,

In most detective series the main characters don't change. But I want mine to change. It gives me a chance to explore a lot of things, including how things changed for blacks from the 50s on. (Bruckner C13)

Although Easy is streetwise, he most cherishes his home and his two children, both of whom he adopts at various points in the series. In *Devil in a Blue Dress*, Easy speaks lovingly of his house: "I loved going home. Maybe it was that I was raised on a sharecropper's farm or that I never owned anything until I bought that house, but I loved my little home" (19). Yet, throughout many of the novels, Easy's fierce protectiveness of his property—his own stake in the American Dream—instigates his involvement in private detective work; he often accepts detective work in order to make mortgage payments. He usually stays on a case, though, in order to answer the moral dilemmas to which he becomes privy. Often, he has uneasy feelings about the violence he encounters, violence in which he is often complicit. In *Black Betty*, for example, the novel begins as Easy awakens from a troubled nightmare about witnessing a murder committed by his friend and gleefully homicidal sidekick, Mouse; the memory of the murder haunts him for years. Easy's multifaceted and dynamic personality also extends to his desire for intellectual improvement; Easy is self-educated. In each novel, he usually apprises the reader of his current reading habits, which range from Mark Twain, to Zola, to Marcus Aurelius. Above all, Easy is a very American character: self-educated and self-made.

Although Mosley states his intention is not to write about African Americans as victims of a dominant white society, his novels certainly interrogate the problem of racism in America. His novels, while always critiquing racial politics in America, reveal how relentlessly intertwined race and class politics are. Most of Mosley's Easy Rawlins detective novels contain a color in the title, just as Easy must negotiate the problem of race in each novel. R. W. B. Lewis observes that Easy "has to confront the matter of race at every turn. It affects every negotiation, limits or distorts every exchange—especially police officers, who are always arresting him" (18). Mosley's presentation of racism in Los Angeles is not monolithic, however. Easy always points out those white characters who have helped him, such as Alamo, the sociopathic, but fair, white man whose aid Easy enlists in *Black Betty*. Mosley's blues novel, *R. L.'s Dream*, shows the difficulties inherent in black–white friendships but also the possibilities.

Walter Mosley's contribution to the American literary scene is his reinvigoration of the usually conservative detective genre with a heightened political and social consciousness. Whether writing about Easy's adventures on the mean streets of postwar L.A. or about an aging bluesman's last days in contemporary New York, Walter Mosley has exhibited an undeniable talent for giving a voice to segments of African American history that have often gone unheard.

CRITICAL RECEPTION

Mosley's works have been warmly received by critics. Thus far, the majority of Mosley's press has come from book reviews and interviews, although his work has stimulated several articles as well. His novels have also garnered positive endorsements from several outstanding critics and authors, among them R. W. B. Lewis, who calls Mosley "a literary artist as well as a master of mystery" (18), and Ernest Gaines, who lauds Mosley's "tremendous ear for diaglogue" (3).

The popularity of Mosley's novels has been fueled, in part, by the 1992 presidential election, when candidate Bill Clinton endorsed Mosley as his favorite mystery writer (Whetstone 110). Mosley's novels have also been nominated for several awards, including the Gold Dagger and the Edgar Awards, and a film version of *Devil in a Blue Dress*, directed by Carl Franklin and starring Denzel Washington, was released in 1995.

BIBLIOGRAPHY

Works by Walter Mosley

Devil in a Blue Dress. New York: Norton, 1990.
A Red Death. New York: Norton, 1991.
White Butterfly. New York: Norton, 1992.
Black Betty. New York: Norton, 1994.
R. L.'s Dream. New York: Norton, 1995.
A Little Yellow Dog. New York: Norton, 1996.
Gone Fishin': A Novel. Baltimore: Black Classic Press, 1997.

Studies of Walter Mosley

Bruckner, D. J. R. "Mystery Stories Are Novelist's Route to Moral Questions." *New York Times* 4 Sept. 1990: C13+.
Frieberger, William. "James Ellroy, Walter Mosley, and the Politics of the Los Angeles Crime Novel." *Clues: A Journal of Detection* 17.2 (1996): 87–104.
Gaines, Ernest. "Easy Rawlins, Just a Little Older." *Los Angeles Times Book Review* 5 June 1994: 3, 12.
Hogness, Peter. "How Walter Mosley Discovered His Audience—And the Voice of His Fiction." *Writer's Digest* 76 (1996): 8–9.
Lewis, R. W. B. "It's Not Easy Being Easy." Rev. of *A Little Yellow Dog*. *New York Times Book Review* 16 June 1996: 18.
McCullough, Bob. "Walter Mosley with Bob McCullough." *Publishers Weekly* 241.21 (1994): 67–68.
Muller, Gilbert. "Double Agent: The Los Angeles Crime Cycle of Walter Mosley." *Los Angeles in Fiction: A Collection of Essays.* Ed. David Fine. Albuquerque: University of New Mexico Press, 1995. 287–301.
Soitos, Stephen. *The Blues Detective: A Study of African American Detective Fiction.* Amherst: University of Massachusetts Press, 1996.
Whetstone, Muriel. "The Mystery of Walter Mosley: Hollywood Discovers Best-Selling Author." *Ebony* Dec. 1995: 106.
Wilkinson, Pamela. "Walter Mosley." *Encyclopedia of African-American Culture and History.* 5 vols. Ed. Jack Salzman, David Lionel Smith, and Cornel West. New York: Macmillan, 1996.

ALBERT MURRAY
(1916–)

Roy Kay

BIOGRAPHY

Albert Murray's life, like the life of his fictional hero Scooter (aka Schoolboy, Jack the Rabbit, Jack the Bear, and many other nicknames), is a life born and bred in the briar-patch of a world in which he has been engaged in a heroic struggle to articulate a theory of modernity, human experience, and language through an investigation of the blues.

Born in Nokomis, Alabama, but raised in Magazine Point, Murray's own beginnings have a storybook quality. The biological son of John Young and Sudie Graham, Murray was named and raised by Hugh and Hattie Murray. Graham and Young were part of the black middle class. Single and fearing public embarrassment, Graham gave the Murrays, who were childless and of a lower social and economic status than Young and Graham, Albert when he was only minutes old. Having two sets of parents of different backgrounds not only has mythological resonances for Murray and his work on the hero but also plays an important role in his understanding of the self as an unstable, changing semiotic construction.

Murray emerged on the American literary scene with the publication of *The Omni-Americans* in 1970. He has since published eight other books, but before he became a writer, he had a distinguished career as a U.S. Air Force major (1943–62). Prior to his air force career Murray obtained a B.S. in education from Tuskegee Institute in Alabama (1939). (At Tuskegee Murray met Ralph Ellison*). After the Second World War Murray moved to New York City, where he currently lives, and received his M.A. in English at New York University (1948). A teacher since his early twenties, Murray taught at Tuskegee in the early 1940s, and since the late 1960s he has taught as either a lecturer, a writer in residence, or a visiting professor at numerous colleges and universities in the United States such as Columbia, Colgate, Massachusetts, Missouri, Emory, and Barnard. The vast majority of Murray's career as a teacher has been intertwined with his career as a writer.

As evident by his most recent work, *The Blue Devils of Nada* (1996), Murray continues to work on articulating a theory of the blues idiom in American music, literature, language, and modernity in general.

MAJOR WORKS AND THEMES

Albert Murray's trilogy, *Train Whistle Guitar* (1974), *The Spyglass Tree* (1991), and *The Seven League Boots* (1995), constitutes one of the few attempts in African American fiction to investigate the nature of experience and its relationship to language. Murray's central thesis of his life and his work is that "the fundamental condition of human life" is the "ceaseless struggle for form against chaos, of sense against nonsense" (*The Hero and the Blues*, 16). For Murray, experience—in other words, tradition, art, and personal stylization—is the tool that creates order out of disorder and meaning out of meaninglessness.

The thematic dominance of the blues in Murray's work indicates not only his central preoccupation but also the elusive nature of the blues itself. As Murray explains in his nonfictional prose *The Hero and the Blues* (1973), *Stomping the Blues* (1976), and *The Blue Devils of Nada*, "the blues" is a living phrase that belongs to many referential fields. The popular meaning of the blues is known largely by its metaphors that signify an emotional or psychological state of existing—being depressed, down, melancholy, or having low spirits. Murray calls this type of blues "the blues as such" and personifies it as blue devils. These antagonistic, invisible, insubstantial, numerous, capricious entities are the incessant forces of chaos and meaninglessness that bedevil and upset life and, in doing so, produce the blues in their human hosts. Murray argues that the counterphrase to these inhuman entities of adversity and discontinuity is "the blues as music." Designed to drive the malevolent blue demons away, even if it is only momentary, "the blues as music" is a musical—and, more importantly, a dance—form that constitutes an engagement and a response to "the blues as such." The blues idiom also constitutes a rhetorical approach to living in the world and with other human beings. As the blues musician does during her performance to the blue devils, the blues hero stomps "the blues as such" through his riposte to them in life.

Murray's blues hero, Scooter, lives a life in the midst of the blue devils, persevering and counterphrasing their capricious and chaotic forces. Beginning with Scooter's adolescence in the 1920s and following him into adulthood in the 1930s as Schoolboy, Murray's trilogy has the thematic appearance of belonging to the subgenre of the bildungsroman (novels of formation), the *künstlerroman* (artist novel, or the novel of the self-realization of the protagonist as an artist); however, this is not the case. Murray's novels lack both plots and telos. Each novel takes place within a specific space and time. *Train Whistle Guitar* occurs in the 1920s in Gasoline Point, Alabama, *The Spyglass Tree* takes place in the early 1930s at a black university in Alabama reminiscent of Tuskegee, and *The Seven League Boots* is set in the mid- to late 1930s, during which Schoolboy is living the life of an itinerant professional jazz musician romantically involved with an older woman.

Murray's trilogy is Scooter's and Schoolboy's autobiographies. It is clear in reading these autobiographies that the narrators' selves are not something that they have to find or something always already there but something that they continually rewrite. Scooter and Schoolboy are masters of the rhetorical figure of *prosopopeia*, or the giving of a face, a persona, to the faceless. Living in a world without inherent form or meaning, Scooter and Schoolboy must read the events and the signs of this world and make counterphrases in response. (They rewrite themselves in light of their reading.) This rewriting constitutes a facial makeover in which the blues hero is never identical to himself because the self is in process of semiosis, predicated on continual reading, inscription, and rewriting. The self of the blues hero in Murray's work is always in the process of rewriting itself because he always finds himself in situations that need to be read, requiring a response to the forces of chaos and meaninglessness.

In Murray's prosaic world there are no ready-made individuals or selves. Contrary to the naturalization of race in American literature, Scooter and Schoolboy undergo continual inscriptions that are of a nonracial character. Scooter and Schoolboy live their lives with people who are racially defined as black in America. However, the relationship between race and self is never treated as homologous. In other words, in Murray's world one's phenotype does not determine one's existence and, more importantly, one's possibilities. In *The Seven League Boots* Schoolboy is introduced to a grandfatherly tap dancer known as Royal Highness, who reminds him of the down-home teachings about the relationship of race and existence:

Don't you ever let nobody tell you that you were put here on God's earth to spend your life worrying and bellyaching about some old jaspers. Excuse my language, but fuck that shit, young soldier. . . .
I ain't never bellyached to no jaspers in my life. Because the notion I was brought up on down home was that you just go out there and show the somitches. Do whatever the hell you do and let them get to that. Some of them are always going to be looking for ways to deny you your talent. Hell, that's the game of life, young soldier. (47f)

The advice given by Royal Highness to Schoolboy is a dominant refrain of Scooter and Schoolboy's narrations, which they call "the ancestral imperative." It is down-home knowledge, which is to say, ancestral knowledge, of how someone becomes somebody. From Scooter's childhood to Schoolboy's life as a musician, they have been encouraged "*to do something and become something and be somebody*" (*The Spyglass Tree* 23) in a world that will try to deny them these possibilities. The adults who shaped Scooter's life, such as Luzana Cholly and Stagolee Dupas (*Train Whistle Guitar*), did not bellyache about any jaspers and did not allow social and political definitions of race to define their possibilities. Scooter and Schoolboy adhere to the imperative to write and rewrite themselves into existence regardless of life's obstacles.

CRITICAL RECEPTION

In *Thirteen Ways of Looking at a Black Man* (1997) Henry Louis Gates concludes his chapter on Murray by writing that "this is Albert Murray's century; we just live in it" (46). A statement of this magnitude by a scholar of Gates' stature is an indication of the importance and significance of Murray's work. Even though journal essays and dissertations are beginning to appear, to date Murray has not received the critical attention his work deserves. His work constitutes an untimely constellation that will prove fruitful for a future generation of scholars and thinkers. What Wright and Ellison were to African American literature and literary criticism after World War II, Chester Himes* and Murray will be to these fields in the twenty-first century.

In numerous review essays Murray's work has been well received. Some critics such as Gene Seymour and Alexander Star see Murray's fiction as didactic, if not dogmatic, in his articulation of the blues idiom. Nevertheless, Murray's fiction is praised for its musical and vernacular resonances, in addition to its indebtedness and improvisation upon the works of Mann, Joyce, and Faulkner. The critical assessments by Elizabeth Schultz, Robert O'Meally, and John Wideman demonstrate a complex engagement with Murray's work that goes to the heart of his fiction, the dominance, joy, and playfulness of language. For example, in the foreword to the 1989 edition of *Train Whistle Guitar*, O'Meally emphasizes the importance of naming, listening, and language in Scooter's autobiography: "The initiate, Scooter, learns that by listening and reading, by confronting and improvising, by counter stating and 'leapfrogging' the world awaits him" (xviii).

BIBLIOGRAPHY

Works by Albert Murray

The Omni-Americans. 1970. New York: Vintage, 1983.
South to a Very Old Place. New York: McGraw, 1972.
The Hero and the Blues. 1973. New York: Vintage, 1995.
Train Whistle Guitar (novel). 1974. Boston: Northeastern University Press, 1989.
Stomping the Blues. 1976. New York: Vintage, 1982.
Good Morning Blues: The Autobiography of Count Basie (as told to Albert Murray). New York: Primus, 1985.
The Spyglass Tree (novel). 1991. New York: Vintage, 1992.

The Blue Devils of Nada. 1996. New York: Vintage, 1997a.
The Seven League Boots: A Novel. 1995. New York: Vintage, 1997b.

Studies of Albert Murray

Carson, Warren. "Albert Murray: Literary Reconstruction of the Vernacular Community." *African American Review* 27.2 (1993): 287–95.

Gates, Henry Louis, Jr. "King of Cats." In *Thirteen Ways of Looking at a Black Man.* New York: Random, 1997. 21–46.

Karrer, Wolfgang. "The Novel as Blues: Albert Murray's *Train Whistle Guitar* (1974)." In *The Afro-American Novel since 1960.* Ed. Peter Bruck and Wolfgang Karrer. Amsterdam: B. R. Grüner, 1982. 237–62.

O'Meally, Robert G. "Foreword." *Train Whistle Guitar.* Boston: Northeastern University Press, 1989. vii–xix.

Schultz, Elizabeth. "Albert L. Murray." *The Dictionary of Literary Biography: Afro-American Writers since 1955: Dramatists and Prose Writers.* Vol. 38. Ed. Trudier Harris and Thadious M. Davis. Gale, 1985. 214–23.

Seymour, Gene. "Albert Murray at 80." *The Nation* (March 25, 1996): 25–28.

Star, Alexander. "Blues and the Concrete Truth." Review of *The Spyglass Tree. New Republic* (February 3, 1992): 39–41.

Wideman, John. "Luzana Cholly and the Citizens of Gasoline Point, Ala." Review of *Train Whistle Guitar. New York Times Book Review* (May 12, 1974): 7.

———. Review of *Stomping the Blues. American Poetry Review* (July/August 1978): 42–45.

WALTER DEAN MYERS
(1937–)

Terry Novak

BIOGRAPHY

Walter Dean Myers was born Walter Milton Myers on August 12, 1937, in Martinsburg, West Virginia. His mother died in childbirth when Myers was three, whereupon he was given by his overburdened father to the Dean family as a foster child. Myers honored his foster parents by using their name with his given one on his writings. The Dean family moved to Harlem with Myers; ironically, his birth family eventually also relocated to Harlem and moved just around the corner from the Dean family, although this fact was not known to either family at the time.

Myers himself reports his childhood as having been a good and warm experience. He always enjoyed reading and could read before entering school. He did, however, suffer from a speech impediment during his childhood years. Myers discovered while in high school that his foster parents would be unable to send him to college. Disappointed by this knowledge, he dropped out of school and joined the army, an experience that he later used to some extent in his writings, especially *Fallen Angels*.

Myers worked at the post office for a few years after being discharged from the army, then went on to hold a series of personally unsatisfying jobs. In 1960 he married his first wife, Joyce. They had two children together before the marriage ended in divorce.

At the age of thirty-two Myers turned to writing, using the typewriter his foster father, despite being barely able to read and write and possessing little understanding of the intellectual life, had purchased for him. He entered the children's story *Where Does the Day Go?* in a contest sponsored by the Council on Interracial Books for Children. He won the contest with the picture book. Shortly thereafter, in 1970, Myers became an acquisitions editor at Bobbs-Merrill Company. The first book he acquired for the company was Nikki Giovanni's *Gemini*. While at the publishing company, Myers produced several more books, beginning to use the name Walter Dean Myers at that time. He also married his second and current wife, Constance Brendel, in 1973. This marriage produced a third child for Myers. In 1977 Myers left the publishing house and began writing full-time. He has been a successful and prolific writer ever since.

MAJOR WORKS AND THEMES

Walter Dean Myers has had a full writing career to this point, beginning with his first work, the children's picture book *Where Does the Day Go?* Published in 1969, it is the charming story of a black father out with his son and his son's friends. The father asks the children what happens to the day when night falls and receives various answers from them. Particularly interesting about this book is the fact that the children represent various races and cultures—black, Asian, and Puerto Rican. This fact is treated nonchalantly by the author, which adds to its effectiveness. The tale also places distinct emphasis on the importance of a strong father figure in a child's life, a theme to which Myers returns often, although in most works he makes this fact clear in a negative way.

Though Myers has written several other children's picture books, he is best known for his young adult novels, which range from historical adventures to harsh realism. Most often Myers focuses on the realities of modern black urban life in his novels. Many personal influences can be seen in the works of Myers. Most important to his works seems to be his commitment to reaching out to modern youth on their own terms. In *Fast Sam, Cool Clyde, and Stuff*, first published in 1975, Myers presents thirteen stories told from the memory of Francis, better known as Stuff, about growing up in the city on 116th Street. While the book deals with everyday issues of growing up that can be related to by any group of young people, it also deals with race-specific issues such as the societal assumption that a group of young blacks must be troublemakers, though they are, indeed, innocent of any wrongdoing. There are humorous as well as heart-wrenching stories included in the book. The group of friends form a club called the 116th Street Good People, which serves as a support group of sorts and as a definite bonding element for the group.

Myers continues along with his theme of the angst of youth with the 1984 novel *Motown and Didi*. This novel tells the story of seventeen-year-old Motown, who grew up in foster homes after his parents were killed in a fire. At seventeen he has evolved into a loner. His friendship with "the Professor," an older man who serves as a father figure to Motown, helps to give him direction in life. The Professor lends Motown books and also teaches him about racial pride and the importance of identifying with, and working with, what he terms "the tribe." Motown meets Didi when he saves her from an attempted attack by her brother's drug partners. The love element enters the story at this point. Motown finds himself nearly getting trapped into a violent revenge mode, at Didi's urging, but is saved at the last minute by the Professor.

Another novel critical to Myers' canon is *Fallen Angels*, a Vietnam story published in 1988. It relates the story of seventeen-year-old Richard Perry, who joins the army without seriously thinking through the consequences of such an action. Perry has a bad knee and is mistakenly confident that this will be discovered by army officials and will keep him out of combat. Instead, he is thrust into the world of war, where he quickly learns both terror and grief. Myers carries the reader through Perry's emotional distance—achieved by the second time he is forced to kill a person face-to-face—and through Perry's bonding with fellow soldiers, especially Pewee Gates, another black soldier. Perry becomes a hero, earning two Purple Hearts. He also learns to survive largely by keeping his younger brother in mind. Perry is a father figure to his brother, as the boys' father abandoned them some time ago, and as their mother struggles with alcoholism, thereby making her a poor substitute for paternal guidance. Perry takes his responsibility to his brother quite seriously, as do most father figures in Myers' novels. Myers followed *Fallen Angels* with the 1993 publication of *A Place Called Heartbreak: A Story of Vietnam*, which tells the story of Major Fred Cherry, who was a prisoner of war in Hanoi for seven and a half years.

Besides his realism novels, Myers has also written several adventure tales. Four books in the Arrow Adventure Series—*Adventure in Granada*, *The Hidden Shrine*, *Duel in the Desert*, and *Ambush in the Amazon*—utilize white teenagers Chris and Ken Arrow as protagonists. Another adventure tale, *The Legend of Tarik*, combines fantasy with adventure to spin the tale of a black West African knight seeking revenge for the murder of his people.

Myers has also written a historical novel titled *The Glory Field*. This 1994 novel tells the story of an African American family from its beginnings with the enslavement of an African boy in the 1750s through 250 years into modern times. The 1991 nonfiction history *Now Is Your Time! The African-American Struggle for Freedom* acts as a companion piece of sorts to the novel, presenting to children the history of African Americans from 1619 to the present.

Myers' fiction canon is rounded out with several short stories for an adult audience. He remains, however, best known as a writer of young adult novels.

CRITICAL RECEPTION

One of the best measures of critical esteem for Myers lies in the awards with which he has been honored throughout his career. Among these awards are the 1994 Margaret A. Edwards Award for *Hoops*, *Motown and Didi*, *Fallen Angels*, and *Scorpions*, Newberry Honor Medals in 1989 and 1992, four Coretta Scott King Awards, and the Caldecott Medal Honor for *Harlem*, a 1997 work of poetry. Many critics have paid special attention to Myers' thematic use of the importance of a father figure in a young man's life. Rudine Sims Bishop points out that father–son relationships in Myers' novels are crucial; when such a relationship is lacking, the results are evidently damaging to the young heroes. Speaking of novels such as *Motown and Didi*, Bishop states, "It is significant that the young people in these novels . . . are fatherless, or virtually so. . . . The odds against the survival of the young people in these novels are made worse by the absence of a strong, two-parent family" (67).

Along these same lines, Dennis Vellucci remarks, "Mothers, particularly in *Hoops* and *Scorpions*, but to a lesser degree in *Fallen Angels* as well, may be self-sacrificing and well-intentioned, but they are ultimately ineffectual as they attempt to instill values or to keep their family together" (198). Vellucci gives high praise to Myers' portrayal of young black males as, despite the odds, "able to maintain a significant measure of personal and moral integrity in environments that are relentlessly inimical to such integrity" (194).

On the other hand, Frances Smith Foster finds some redeeming value in Myers' portrayals of women, although not from the standpoint of portrayals of mothers. She writes that "Myers tends to focus upon male relationships but his female protagonists are neither stereotypical nor predictable" (522). The protagonists she speaks specifically of are the title female characters in *Crystal* and *Motown and Didi*.

Critical attention has also been given to Myers' distinct and artistic use of black English in his novels. Bishop writes, "He uses the grammar, the semantics, and the rhetorical styles of Black English vernacular to full advantage, both as part of the dialogue and as part of the narration" (36).

BIBLIOGRAPHY

Works by Walter Dean Myers

Young Adult Novels

Fast Sam, Cool Clyde, and Stuff. New York: Viking, 1975.
Brainstorm. New York: Franklin Watts, 1977a.
Mojo and the Russians. New York: Viking, 1977b.
It Ain't All for Nothin'. New York: Viking, 1978.
The Young Landlords. New York: Viking, 1979.
Hoops. New York: Delacorte, 1981a.
The Legend of Tarik. New York: Viking, 1981b.
Won't Know Till I Get There. New York: Viking, 1982.
The Nicholas Factor. New York: Viking, 1983a.
Tales of a Dead King. New York: Morrow, 1983b.
Motown and Didi. New York: Viking, 1984a.
The Outside Shot. New York: Delacorte, 1984b.
Adventure in Granada. New York: Viking Puffin, 1985a.
The Hidden Shrine. New York: Viking Puffin, 1985b.
Ambush in the Amazon. New York: Viking Puffin, 1986a.
Duel in the Desert. New York: Viking Puffin, 1986b.
Sweet Illusions. New York: Teachers and Writers Collaborative, 1986c.

Crystal. New York: Viking, 1987.
Fallen Angels. New York: Scholastic, 1988a.
Me, Mop, and the Moondance Kid. New York: Delacorte, 1988b.
Scorpions. New York: Harper, 1988c.
The Mouse Rap. New York: Harper and Row, 1990.
Somewhere in the Darkness. New York: Scholastic, 1992.
The Glory Field. New York: Scholastic, 1994.

Children's Books

The Dancers. New York: Parents Magazine Press, 1969a.
Where Does the Day Go? New York: Parents Magazine Press, 1969b.
The Dragon Takes a Wife. Indianapolis: Bobbs-Merrill, 1972.
Fly, Jimmy, Fly. New York: Putnam, 1974.
The Black Pearl and the Ghost; or, One Mystery after Another. New York: Viking, 1980a.
The Golden Serpent. New York: Viking, 1980b.
Mr. Monkey and the Gotcha Bird. New York: Delacorte Press, 1984.
How Mr. Monkey Saw the Whole World. New York: Doubleday, 1996.
Harlem. New York: Scholastic, 1997.

Short Stories

"How Long Is Forever?" *Negro Digest.* June 1969. 52–57.
"Dark Side of the Moon." *Black Creation.* Fall 1971a. 26–29.
"The Fare to Crown Point." In *What We Must See: Young Black Storytellers.* Ed. Orde
    Coombs. New York: Dodd, Mead, 1971b. 113–117.
"The Going On." *Black World.* March 1971c. 61–67.
"Juby." *Black Creation.* April 1971d. 26–27.
"Bubba." *Essence.* November 1972. 56, 74, 76.
"Gums." In *We Be Word Sorcerers.* Ed. Sonia Sanchez. New York: Bantam, 1973. 181–
    188.
"The Vision of Felipe." *The Black Scholar.* November–December 1978. 2–9.

Nonfiction Books

The World of Work: A Guide to Choosing a Career. Indianapolis: Bobbs-Merrill, 1975.
Social Welfare. New York: Franklin Watts, 1976.
Now Is Your Time! The African-American Struggle for Freedom. New York: HarperCollins,
    1991.
Malcolm X: By Any Means Necessary. New York: Scholastic, 1993.
A Place Called Heartbreak: A Story of Vietnam. Austin, TX: Raintree, 1993.
One More River to Cross: An African-American Photographic Album. New York: Harcourt,
    Brace, 1995.
Toussaint L'Ouverture: The Fight for Haiti's Freedom. New York: Simon and Schuster, 1996.

Studies of Walter Dean Myers

Bishop, Rudine Sims. *Presenting Walter Dean Myers.* Boston: Twayne, 1990.
Chance, Rosemary, et al. "And the Winner Is . . . A Teleconference with Walter Dean
    Myers." *Journal of Reading.* November 1994. 246–249.

Foster, Frances Smith. "Walter Dean Myers." *The Oxford Companion to African American Literature*. New York: Oxford University Press, 1997.

Smith, Amanda. "Walter Dean Myers." *Publishers Weekly*. July 20, 1992. 217–218.

Subryan, Carmen. "Walter Dean Myers." *Dictionary of Literary Biography*. Vol. 33: *Afro-American Fiction Writers after 1955*. Ed. Thadious M. Davis and Trudier Harris. Detroit: Gale, 1984. 199–202.

Vellucci, Dennis. "Man to Man: Portraits of the Male Adolescent in the Novels of Walter Dean Myers." In *African-American Voices in Young Adult Literature: Tradition, Transition, Transformation*. Ed. Karen Patricia Smith. Metuchen, NJ: Scarecrow Press, 1994. 193–223.

GLORIA NAYLOR
(1950–)

Sarah Wheliss and Emmanuel S. Nelson

BIOGRAPHY

In her four novels to date, Gloria Naylor creates distinct literary landscapes, replete with complex characters reflecting both the glaring inequalities of America's multiracial society as well as the more subtle shadings of modern African American life. Common thematic threads course through Naylor's works—the burdensome plight of present-day African Americans, faced with overwhelming odds against success, both personal and professional, the strength derived from matrilineal ancestral presence within the African American community, and the corrosive effect of white materialism for blacks in this country. Within her novels, Naylor remodels classical writers through, for example, her appropriation of either Shakespeare's *The Tempest* or Dante's *Inferno*. Her extensive knowledge of the formal history of the African American literary tradition has, as Henry Louis Gates, Jr., notes, earned Naylor citizenship within "the republic of literature in the broadest and most cosmopolitan sense" (Gates and Appiah ix). More specifically, Naylor's extensive knowledge of specific works of other African American female writers has provided her with the strength and guidance of a matrilineal African American literary community, placing her within the ranks of such noted authors as Zora Neale Hurston, Toni Morrison,* or Ntozake Shange.* Such authors serve as primary influences on Naylor's work. In fact, Naylor has claimed that, even though the writers she "had been taught to love were either white or male," her first encounter with Toni Morrison's *The Bluest Eye* provided "the authority . . . to enter this forbidden terrain" ("Conversation" 567). Naylor recalls, "It said to a young poet, struggling to break into prose that the barriers were flexible. . . . And it said to a young black woman, struggling to find a mirror of her worth in this society, not only is your story worth telling but it can be told in words so painstakingly eloquent that it becomes a song" ("Conversation" 567). In her four novels—*The Women of Brewster Place, Linden Hills, Mama Day,* and *Bailey's Cafe*—Gloria Naylor renders her own song detailing the experiences of black men and women struggling to survive and succeed in America against, as Naylor would argue, the odds. Through appropriating the textual forms of patriarchal white literary tradition and through revisioning these forms using distinctly African American literary models, Naylor creates her own unique vision of modern African American society.

While Gloria Naylor's novels reflect two separate, but complementary, literary heritages, so, too, her own life reflects two distinctive American landscapes— the American South, her ancestral heritage, and the North, her residence for most of her life. Her mother, Alberta McAlpin, and her father, Roosevelt Naylor, were each one of eight siblings in neighboring sharecropping families in Robinsonville, Mississippi. Both families worked twelve hours a day in the field "from can't see to can't see" (Naylor "Reflections" 68). Large families were an asset on such farms because, as the author acknowledges, "the additional child meant that in less than ten years there would be an extra pair of hands to add to the collective earnings" ("Reflections" 68).

Alberta, Naylor's mother, sought deliverance from this exhausting world through books and reading. Even though her family was too poor to purchase books, and she was, as a black child in Mississippi, unable to use the public library, Alberta hired herself out on Saturdays to earn extra money. Naylor recollects that her mother "got a sum total of fifty cents a day for doing that. At the end of the month, though, she had two dollars. And she could take that two dollars and she would send away to book clubs, and that's how she was able to feed her love of learning" (Bellinelli). Alberta, who married her neighbor Roosevelt Naylor in June 1949, wanted her children to have the freedom to learn, and she thus vowed to marry only a man who would grant her an escape from the oppressive South. As promised with their betrothal, a pregnant Alberta and Roosevelt boarded a train for the North, and Gloria, their first child, was born 25 January 1950, in New York City.

The Naylor home in the Bronx was, ironically, a "southern home, with southern food, southern language, southern values, southern codes of behavior" (Fowler 4). Her mother also transplanted her interest in religion to the Naylors' northern household. Alberta's subsequent conversion to the faith of the Jehovah's Witnesses led Naylor back to the South and eventually into writing. After graduating from high school, Naylor decided against attending Hunter College and instead became a Jehovah's Witness, following in her mother's footsteps. For most of her seven years as a Witness, Naylor continued to live in her parents' home. In her final year with the Jehovah's Witnesses, Naylor became a "pioneer," or full-time preacher, living first in Dunn, North Carolina, and then Jacksonville, Florida. In 1975, Naylor abandoned her witnessing and returned to New York City, where she enrolled at Medgar Evers College to study nursing. When Naylor found herself spending far more time on her English classes, she transferred to

Brooklyn College, where she discovered the writings of such African American authors as Toni Morrison, Ntozake Shange, and Nikki Giovanni, writers and feminists she credits with establishing her own foundation as a black female writer. While Morrison provided Naylor with authority, authors such as Shange and Giovanni were "black feminist voices . . . that helped me just with establishing a separate entity in my mind as the black woman" (Fowler 149).

While working full-time as a nighttime hotel switchboard operator, Naylor pursued both her studies and her own writing. When Naylor received a marriage proposal at this time, she accepted because, "marrying somebody—anybody— was very traveled terrain, because I grew up feeling somehow that that was how you made your definition" ("Conversation" 570). Instead of finding companionship with her husband, Naylor found that her marriage to, and with, her writing offered the personal definition she was seeking. In 1981, the divorced Naylor not only received a B.A. in English from Brooklyn College but also completed *The Women of Brewster Place*, her first novel, in the same month. Two years later, Naylor earned a master's degree in Afro-American studies from Yale University, and *The Women of Brewster Place* won an American Book Award for first fiction.

In the years since, Naylor has published three additional novels (*Linden Hills* in 1985, *Mama Day* in 1988, and *Bailey's Cafe* in 1992); she has taught at universities such as George Washington University, New York University, the University of Pennsylvania, and Princeton University; she has won numerous awards and honors; she has established her own multimedia production company, One Way Productions, in order to promote both her own works and the works of other African Americans; and she has, most definitely, defined herself through these achievements. Naylor has stated, "I want to present positive images of the black community to as many people in America and the world as possible. That's the goal" (Fowler 153). Through her four novels to date, Gloria Naylor has apparently reached this goal.

MAJOR WORKS AND THEMES

Naylor, in her first novel, *The Women of Brewster Place: A Novel in Seven Stories*, creates a dead-end street in an unnamed northern city as her first literary landscape for exploration of African American female experiences. Brewster Place offers little physical comfort to its residents—the buildings are dilapidated, the curbs are littered, the street itself is separated from the bustling city by a brick wall at one end. Brewster Place, by all accounts, is a dying neighborhood. What thrives in this decaying environment, however, is a community of women, each rising from the dismal atmosphere like "an ebony phoenix, each in her own time" (*Brewster Place* 5). Naylor's novel details the lives of seven of these resident females, with a chapter of the novel dedicated to each of their stories.

The Women of Brewster Place is a gritty, powerful work in which Naylor outlines many of the concerns facing the African American female community. Mattie Michael, the first character introduced in the novel, is the figurative matriarch of this community of women. Mattie, an elderly, robust, and unmarried woman, cares for her friend Ciel, a young, married woman, when Ciel's daughter dies in a household accident. Both heart- and spirit-broken, Ciel appears on the verge of death herself until Mattie envelops her within her own arms and her own strength, nursing and protecting Ciel back into life. Mattie also provides a sanctuary of sorts for her closest friend, Etta Mae Johnson, an attractive woman whose self-esteem rises and falls solely based on her relationships with men. Mattie's friendship, guidance, and unconditional acceptance offer Etta Mae strength and companionship that no man can provide.

But while Mattie protects, nurses, and guards the lives of other women, she also fails to provide any sense of manhood or personal responsibility for her spoiled son Basil. When Basil is arrested for killing a man, Mattie puts her own home up for collateral, a move that ultimately causes her move to Brewster Place after the flight of her son, who, trained by years of overprotectiveness and smothering attention from his single mother, knows exactly how to manipulate Mattie. Naylor states of this recurring theme of single mothers, "I'm not saying that single mothers are responsible for crime in the streets. But I do believe this: that they are responsible for how their sons perceive women. And perceive of themselves as men. Mattie, I held her accountable for the monster that she had created" (Fowler 153–154).

Naylor's examination, both positive and critical, of the role of matriarchy in the African American community is further evidenced in other characters on Brewster Street. Ciel, after reluctantly aborting her second child, devotes herself solely to protecting and caring for Serena, her first child. While Ciel and her husband, Eugene, argue, Serena, chasing a roach in the dilapidated building, pokes a fork into an electrical outlet and is electrocuted. Ciel wills herself to die, believing she has failed as a mother, until Mattie mothers the grieving Ciel back into life. Cora Lee, a young, unmarried high school dropout, is a proverbial child herself. When she is forced to give up her dolls at the age of thirteen, Cora Lee begins instead having children of her own, "dolls" for her to cuddle and hold. She craves the "shadows" that visit her in the night and provide her with the seed for another "doll" to add to her countless brood. Naylor explains, "I *do* think that mothers, either single or married, are part of the reason why women are not thought of better by young men, I really do. And I'm not going to back off from that" (Fowler 154).

In her second novel, *Linden Hills*, Naylor uses the model of Dante's *Inferno* to mold her own modern allegory on the horrors of materialism. Her literary landscape is the northern neighborhood of Linden Hills, a place where wealthy African Americans battle each other to live closer in proximity to Luther Nedeed, the proprietor and evil manipulator of both the land and the families who reside there. Nedeed (de-Eden spelled backward) lives and rules from the bottom of a valley, and the ironical quest for the residents of Linden Hills is to move down in the world to be closer to the Nedeed home.

As in *The Women of Brewster Place*, Naylor continues, in this second novel, to pursue controversial themes. Many residents of Linden Hills abandon any true sense of self in order to achieve material status, often through negating their past or even masking their skin color. The homosexual Winston Alcott, for example, marries a woman he does not love, because marriage is expected and encouraged among the residents of Linden Hills. In this neighborhood, after all, appearance is, literally, everything. Although he betrays his true lover, who ironically serves as best man at his wedding, Winston is presented with the deed to a piece of prime real estate closer to Luther Nedeed's home, representing his further descent into "success" or, to return to Dante's model, hell. Maxwell Smyth, a successful young executive with General Motors, strives for complete control of his body as well as his environment. He sleeps only three hours a night; he eats and drinks only the purest of foods; he manipulates humidifiers and thermostats in order to perfectly control the air he breathes. He is, in essence, purging himself of any evidence of his human existence, trying to become invisible in every realm but corporate success. As Naylor writes in the novel, "He would have found the comments that he was trying to be white totally bizarre. Being white was the furthest thing from his mind, since he spent every waking moment trying to be no color at all" (106).

Within this world where most of the residents of Linden Hills have relinquished any and all sense of self in their descent into materialism, the two characters of Willie and Willa reflect the only sliver of hope for retribution in the hellish world of Linden Hills. These two characters refuse to fall into the abyss of white materialism surrounding and enveloping Linden Hills, Willie resisting by choice and Willa by force. Willie Mason, a young, romantic poet who lives in the neighboring slums, believes that only through engaging himself with an existence outside predominantly white-created institutions (such as public education) can he fully lay claim to his African American voice. Through a progression of odd jobs in the Linden Hills neighborhood, Willie recognizes the validity of his deeply held beliefs. He sees the hypocrisy of Winston's wedding; he recognizes the ultimate price paid by Mr. Olson, who works himself to death in two jobs to keep his family in the prestigious neighborhood; he discovers that the Reverend Hollis, the only voice of God in this neighborhood, is himself an alcoholic and a liar. Disturbed and affected by his descent into the Linden Hills neighborhood, Willie vows to leave and pledges never to return.

Willa Prescott Nedeed, Luther's wife, differs from the wives of generations of Nedeed men preceding her. While the previous wives have all been pale-skinned, Willa is dark; while the previous wives have all been faceless and helpless in the face of the Nedeed evil, Willa battles her way into selfhood by the novel's conclusion. Viewed by Luther as simply a breeder, Willa unfortunately produces for him a pale son. Luther fails to recognize his son as such and locks both his son and Willa in the basement, where the son dies. Willa's examination of the material and written remnants of the other Nedeed wives that she finds hidden in a trunk in the basement leads her to realize her own strength and will to live. By the novel's end she leaves the basement to fight her way into existence; her physical battle with Luther at the novel's conclusion leads to the Nedeed home's being engulfed with flames and evidences Willa's own divine retribution in the name of all other faceless Nedeed wives.

Mama Day, Naylor's third novel, presents a drastically different and also perhaps her most appealing literary landscape, that of Willow Springs, a fictional island located off the coast of South Carolina and Georgia and solely inhabited by African Americans. In this novel, Naylor returns to a thematic examination of matrilineal heritage, but a decided tone of magical realism invades this new literary locale, far different from the naturalistic settings of her earlier two novels. Separated from the mainland by an ancient wooden bridge, Willow Springs is a mystical island where voices of old souls course through the overhanging branches of ancient trees; the wind delivers the soothing presence of spirits as well as a cool breeze; and the cresting waves of the ocean speak volumes of history with the sound of rippling water.

The novel's opening pages detail the story of Sapphira Wade, "a true conjure woman: satin black, biscuit cream, red as Georgia clay: depending on which of us takes a mind to her" (3). Sapphira, a former slave of Bascombe Wade's, not only gave birth to seven sons but also gave figurative birth to the island itself, since she "persuaded Bascombe Wade in a thousand days to deed all his slaves every inch of land in Willow Springs" (3). The novel's namesake, Miranda (Mama) Day is a direct descendant of Sapphira Wade's and acts as the island's matriarch. Whether in spirit through her communication with deceased souls or in deed through her midwifery, Mama Day is just that—Mama for the modern-day residents of Willow Springs.

The novel's action centers around the love story between Cocoa (real name Ophelia), the grandniece of Mama Day, and George, an orphaned African American from the North whose scientific and rational mind prevents his acceptance of the spiritual and metaphysical side of the island. During the couple's visit to Willow Springs, Cocoa's life is jeopardized through the folkloric spell of a jealous woman. George attempts to find a scientific answer to his plight through action (in his attempts to return to the mainland for help) instead of through, as Mama Day counsels him, belief in the strength of his own spirit, especially in union with the matriarchal lineage of the island. Although Cocoa's life is ultimately saved, George himself dies due to his inability to heed, to even hear the voices of the island itself.

As in *Mama Day*, Naylor addresses similar themes and concerns in her latest novel, *Bailey's Cafe*, published in 1992. In this novel, Naylor's literary landscape is that of a magical, mystical café, where Naylor uses the café and the sensuality of food and eating to address female sexuality. Naylor states, "The core of the work is indeed the way in which the word *whore* has been used against women or to manipulate feminine sexual identity" (Fowler 150). While addressing the issue of female sexuality, Naylor at times neglects plot development; however, this is well within her purpose since she conversely develops some of her more three-dimensional male characters. The café's proprietor, Bailey, for example, demonstrates a complexity of character that has to date not appeared in Naylor's fiction, and his empathy with African American females shows Naylor's own authorial growth. While this latest novel, structured as a series of monologues, may not be as complex as *Linden Hills* or as thematically magical as *Mama Day*, *Bailey's Cafe* does offer compelling characters and evidence of a developing aesthetic. Naylor states, "My last book is a more mature work; I have learned to evoke emotion quietly" (Fowler 150).

While Naylor has learned quiet strength in her writing, she has also, as evidenced by the complex themes and ambitious goals threading through her works, demonstrated her aptitude for luxurious literary landscapes, fertile ground for her exploration of modern African American society.

CRITICAL RECEPTION

The four novels that Gloria Naylor has published so far have generated considerable, often very favorable, critical response. *The Women of Brewster Place* elicited enthusiastic reviews and subsequently was made into a miniseries for television by Oprah Winfrey's production company. Many reviewers of the novel point to the exceptional elegance with which Naylor handles the English language, her ability to develop her characters, and her capacity to tell a compelling story. Naylor's effortless command of various narrative techniques receives close attention in Michael Awkward's *Inspiriting Influences: Tradition, Revision, and Afro-American Novels*; he also situates Naylor in the company of Alice Walker,* Toni Morrison, and Zora Neale Hurston and engagingly comments on the intertextual links among their works.

Though *Linden Hills* received slightly less enthusiastic reception than Naylor's first novel, it has become recently the subject of many substantial scholarly articles. Catherine C. Ward, for example, offers a fine analysis of Naylor's intensely moral vision and highlights Naylor's appropriation of the Dantesque view of hell to launch a devastating attack on the spiritual barrenness and political vacuity that Naylor sees at the core of the African American upper-class life. Mel Watkins calls *Linden Hills* "a provocative, iconoclastic novel" (11), while Sherley Anne Williams considers it a testament to the fact that Naylor "is a mature literary talent of formidable skill" (70).

Naylor's third novel, *Mama Day*, was reviewed widely and praised extravagantly. Her most recent novel, *Bailey's Cafe*, too, has met with a similar reception both in the popular press and in academic circles. Gay Wilentz calls *Bailey's Cafe* "Naylor's finest novel to date," which establishes "a context for the mutilations women have suffered and a space for curing their (our) souls" (15). Some reviewers comment on Naylor's expert use of the blues and jazz in *Bailey's Cafe* as structural as well as thematic devices. Maxine L. Montgomery considers *Bailey's Cafe* "a hauntingly lyrical text steeped in biblical allusions" (27) and a novel that is a "culmination" (33) of many of Naylor's concerns.

Naylor's novels have earned her a secure place in contemporary American writing. Along with many other gifted African American women writers of her generation, she has helped redefine the directions of American literature in the final two decades of the twentieth century. There is more than some delicious irony in this impressive phenomenon: that the voices of African American women, once ignored and repressed, should emerge with such vengeful eloquence on the international literary scene during the last twenty years or so. Naylor's voice strikes a singularly graceful note in that sweet chorus.

BIBLIOGRAPHY

Works by Gloria Naylor

Novels

The Women of Brewster Place: A Novel in Seven Stories. New York: Viking, 1982; New York: Penguin, 1983.
Linden Hills. New York: Ticknor and Fields, 1985; New York: Penguin, 1986.
Mama Day. New York: Ticknor and Fields, 1988; New York: Vintage, 1989.
Bailey's Cafe. New York: Harcourt, Brace, Jovanovich, 1992; New York: Vintage/Random House, 1993.

Essays

"A Conversation between Gloria Naylor and Toni Morrison." *The Southern Review* 21.3 (Summer 1985): 567–593.
"Love and Sex in the Afro-American Novel." *The Yale Review* 78.1 (Autumn 1989): 19–31.
"Reflections." *Centennial.* Ed. Michael Rosenthal. New York: Pindar Books, 1986. 68–71.

Studies of Gloria Naylor

Andrews, Larry. "Black Sisterhood in Gloria Naylor's Novels." *CLA Journal* 33 (1989): 1–25.
Awkward, Michael. *Inspiriting Influences: Tradition, Revision and Afro-American Women's Novels.* New York: Columbia University Press, 1989.
Bellinelli, Mateo, dir. *A Conversation with Gloria Naylor* (videotape). Produced by RTSJ-Swiss Television. California Newsreel, 1992.
Bouvier, Luke. "Reading in Black and White: Space and Race in *Linden Hills.*" In Gates and Appiah, 140–151.
Branzburg, Judith V. "Seven Women and a Wall." *Callaloo* 7 (Spring/Summer 1984): 116–119.
Brown, Amy Benson. "Writing Home: The Bible and Gloria Naylor's *Bailey's Cafe.*" *Homemaking: Women Writers and the Politics and Poetics of Home.* Ed. Catherine Wiley and Fiona R. Barnes. New York: Garland, 1996. 23–42.
Christian, Barbara. "Naylor's Geography: Community, Class and Patriarchy in *The Women of Brewster Place* and *Linden Hills.*" *Reading Black/Reading Feminist.* Ed. Henry Louis Gates, Jr. 1986. 348–373. Rpt. in Gates and Appiah, 106–125.

———. *Black Feminist Criticism*. New York: Pergamon Press, 1985.

Collins, Grace E. "Narrative Structure in *Linden Hills*." *CLA Journal* 34 (1991): 290–300.

Eckard, Paula Gallant. "The Prismatic Past in *Oral History* and *Mama Day*." *MELUS: The Journal of the Society for the Study of Multi-Ethnic Literature* 20.3 (Fall 1995): 121–135.

Eko, Ebele. "Beyond the Myth of Confrontation: A Comparative Study of African and African-American Female Protagonists." *Ariel* 17 (October 1986): 139–152.

Eriskon, Peter. [Review of *Bailey's Cafe*]. *Kenyon Review* 15 (Summer 1993). Rpt. in Gates and Appiah, 32–34.

———. " 'Shakespeare's Black?' The Role of Shakespeare in Naylor's Novels." In his *Rewriting Shakespeare, Rewriting Ourselves*. Berkeley: University of California Press, 1991. Rpt. in Gates and Appiah, 231–248.

———. "Shakespeare's Naylor, Naylor's Shakespeare: Shakespearean Allusion as Appropriation in Gloria Naylor's Quartet." *Literary Influence and African-American Writers*. Ed. Tracy Mishkin. New York: Garland, 1996. 325–357.

Fenton, Sharon, and Michelle C. Loris. *The Critical Response to Gloria Naylor*. Westport, CT: Greenwood Press, 1997.

Fils-Aime, Holly W. "The Sweet Scent of Ginger: Understanding the Roots of *Song of Solomon* and *Mama Day*." *Griot: Official Journal of the Southern Conference on Afro-American Studies* 15.1 (Spring 1996): 27–33.

Fowler, Virginia C. *Gloria Naylor: In Charge of Sanctuary*. New York: Twayne/Simon and Schuster, 1996.

Fraser, Celeste. "Stealing B(l)ack Voices: The Myth of the Matriarchy and *The Women of Brewster Place*." *Critical Matrix* 5 (Fall/Winter 1989): 65–68. Rpt. in Gates and Appiah, 90–105.

Gates, Henry Louis, Jr. "Significant Others." *Contemporary Literature* 29 (1988): 606–623.

Gates, Henry Louis, Jr., and K. A. Appiah, eds. *Gloria Naylor: Critical Perspectives Past and Present*. New York: Amistad, 1993.

Goddu, Teresa. "Reconstructing History in *Linden Hills*." In Gates and Appiah, 215–230.

Harris, Trudier, and Thadious M. Davis. *The Power of the Porch: The Storyteller's Craft in Zora Neale Hurston, Gloria Naylor and Randall Kenan*. Athens: University of Georgia Press, 1996.

Haralson, Eric L. "Gloria Naylor." *African American Writers: Profiles of Their Lives and Works*. Ed. Valerie Smith, Lea Baechler, and A. Walton Litz. New York: Macmillan/Collier, 1991. 267–278.

Holloway, Karla F. *Moorings and Metaphors: Figures of Culture and Gender in Black Women's Literature*. New Brunswick, NJ: Rutgers University Press, 1992.

Homans, Margaret. "The Woman in the Cave: Recent Feminist Fictions and the Classical Underworld." *Contemporary Literature* 29 (1988): 369–402. Rpt. in Gates and Appiah, 152–181.

Juhasz, Suzanne. *Reading from the Heart: Women, Literature and the Search for True Love*. New York: Viking/Penguin, 1994.

Kelley, Margot Anne. "Sisters' Choices: Quilting Aesthetics in Contemporary African-American Women's Fictions." *Quilt Culture: Tracing the Pattern*. Ed. Cheryl B. Torsney and Judith Elsley. Columbia: University of Missouri Press, 1994. 49–67.

Kelly, Lori Duin. "The Dream Sequence in *The Women of Brewster Place*." *Notes on Contemporary Literature* 21 (September 1991): 8–10.

Kubitschek, Missy Dehn. "Toward a New Order: Shakespeare, Morrison, and Gloria Naylor's *Mama Day."* *MELUS: The Journal of the Society for the Study of Multi-Ethnic Literature of the United States* 19.3 (Fall 1994): 75–90.

Levy, Helen Fiddyment. *Fiction of the Home Place: Jewett, Cather, Glasgow, Porter, Welty and Naylor.* Jackson: University of Mississippi Press, 1992.

Matus, Jill L. "Dream, Deferral, and Closure in *The Women of Brewster Place." Black American Literature Forum* 24 (1990): 49–64. Rpt. in Gates and Appiah, 126–139.

Meisenhelder, Susan. " 'Eating Cane' in Gloria Naylor's *The Women of Brewster Place* and Zora Neale Hurston's 'Sweat.' " *Notes on Contemporary Literature* 23.2 (March 1993): 5–7.

———. " 'The Whole Picture' in Gloria Naylor's *Mama Day." African American Review* 27 (1993): 405–419.

Montgomery, Maxine L. "Authority, Multivocality, and the New World Order in Gloria Naylor's *Bailey's Cafe." African American Review* 29.1 (Spring 1995): 27–33.

———. "The Fathomless Dream: Gloria Naylor's Use of the Descent Motif in *The Women of Brewster Place." CLA Journal* 36 (1992): 1–11.

Novy, Marianne. *Engaging with Shakespeare: Responses of George Eliot and Other Women Novelists.* Athens: University of Georgia Press, 1994.

Page, Philip. "Living with the Abyss in Gloria Naylor's *Bailey's Cafe." CLA Journal* 40.1 (September 1996): 21–45.

Palumbo, Kathryn. "The Uses of Female Imagery in Naylor's *The Women of Brewster Place." Notes on Contemporary Literature* 15 (May 1985): 6–7.

Pearlman, Mickey. "An Interview with Gloria Naylor." *High Plains Literary Review* 5.1 (Spring 1990): 98–107.

Reckley, Ralph, Sr. "Science, Faith and Religion in Gloria Naylor's *Mama Day." Twentieth-Century Black American Women in Print: Essays by Ralph Reckley, Sr.* Ed. Lola E. Jones. Acton, MA: Copley, 1991. 87–95.

Russell, Sandi. *Render Me My Song: African-American Women Writers from Slavery to the Present.* New York: St. Martin's Press, 1990.

Sandiford, Keith. "Gothic and Intertextual Constructions in *Linden Hills." Arizona Quarterly* 47 (1991): 117–139. Rpt. in Gates and Appiah, 249–262.

Saunders, James Robert. "The Ornamentation of Old Ideas: Gloria Naylor's First Three Novels." *Hollins Critic* 27.2 (April 1990): 1–11. Rpt. in Gates and Appiah, 249–262.

Showalter, Elaine. *Sister's Choice: Tradition and Change in American Women's Writing.* New York: Clarendon/Oxford, 1991.

Smith, Barbara. "The Truth That Never Hurts: Lesbians in Fiction in the 1980s." *Wild Women in the Whirlwind: Afro-American Culture and the Contemporary Literary Renaissance.* Ed. Joanne M. Braxton and Andree Nicola McLaughlin. New Brunswick, NJ: Rutgers University Press, 1990. 213–245.

Storhoff, Gary. " 'The Only Voice Is Your Own': Gloria Naylor's Revision of *The Tempest." African American Review* 29.1 (Spring 1995): 35–45.

Tanner, Laura E. "Reading Rape: *Sanctuary* and *The Women of Brewster Place." American Literature* 62 (1990): 559–582. Rpt. in Gates and Appiah, 71–89.

Toombs, Charles P. "The Confluence of Food and Identity in Gloria Naylor's *Linden Hills:* 'What We Eat Is Who We Is.' " *CLA Journal* 37 (1993): 1–18.

Tucker, Lindsey. "Recovering the Conjure Woman: Texts and Contexts in Gloria Naylor's *Mama Day." African American Review* 28 (Summer 1994): 173–188.

Wagner-Martin, Linda. "Quilting in Gloria Naylor's *Mama Day*." *Notes on Contemporary Literature* 18 (May 1988): 6–7.

Ward, Catherine C. "Gloria Naylor's *Linden Hills*: A Modern Inferno." *Contemporary Literature* 28 (1987): 67–81. Rpt. in Gates and Appiah, 182–194.

Watkins, Mel. Rev. of *Linden Hills*. *New York Times Book Review* (3 March 1995): 11.

Wilentz, Gay. Rev. of *Linden Hills*. *Women's Review of Books* 10 (February 1993): 15.

Williams, Sherley Anne. "Roots of Privilege: New Black Fiction." *Ms.* 13.12 (June 1985): 69–72.

Winsbro, Bonnie. *Supernatural Forces: Belief, Difference, and Power in Contemporary Works by Ethnic Women*. Amherst: University of Massachusetts Press, 1993.

ANN PETRY
(1908–1997)

Marlene D. Allen

BIOGRAPHY

Ann Lane Petry was born on October 12, 1908, in Old Saybrook, Connecticut, the youngest of three children of Peter C. and Bertha James Lane. Her family was able to provide a comfortable and stable family life for Petry and her older sister (the oldest Petry child having died at age two), and the family had a persistent interest in the sciences. Her father, aunt, and grandfather were pharmacists who operated drugstores in Old Saybrook and Old Lyme, Connecticut, and her mother was a licensed chiropodist (podiatrist). Petry's family was one of the only two black families living in Old Saybrook, and the conflicts stemming from her life growing up in a predominantly white New England community, coupled with her firsthand experiences while living in all-black Harlem, would surface often as themes in her writing.

In 1925, Petry graduated from Old Saybrook High School, the only African American in her class, and she subsequently went on to study at the Connecticut College of Pharmacy (now the University of Connecticut School of Pharmacy). After receiving her Ph.G. degree in 1931 (once again she was the only African American in her graduating class), Petry worked as a pharmacist in her family's drugstores in Old Saybrook and Old Lyme for seven years. On February 22, 1938, she married George D. Petry of New Iberia, Louisiana, and the couple moved to New York City. After this move, Petry decided to try her hand at writing full-time. Her work was first published in 1939, when she was paid $5 by the *Afro-American*, a Baltimore newspaper, for her short story "Marie of the Cabin Club." From 1938 to 1941, she worked as a salesperson and journalist for New York's *Amsterdam News*, and from 1941 to 1944, she edited the women's pages and wrote news for Adam Clayton Powell's weekly, *People's Voice*. During this period in her life Petry encountered the realities of Harlem life for African Americans, an experience that she would relate in great detail in *The Street* and her short stories. From 1942 to 1944 she enrolled in a creative writing workshop at Columbia University, and in 1943 she sold a second story, "On Saturday the Siren Sounds at Noon," to the National Association for the Advancement of Colored People's (NAACP) *Crisis* magazine. She received a literary fellowship and stipend of $2,400 in 1945 from Houghton Mifflin Publishing Company after submitting five chapters from her first novel, *The Street*, to the company at the invitation of one of its editors. She also published two other stories in *Crisis* in 1945, "Olaf and His Girl Friend" and "Like a Winding Sheet," a story that brought her national acclaim. The story was later published in Martha Foley's *Best American Stories of 1946*.

In 1946 Petry's *The Street* was published. The book became the first novel by an African American woman to sell over 1 million copies. Considered by many critics to be her finest work, the book relates the struggles of a young, attractive black woman, Lutie Johnson, to achieve the American dream but who is unable to do so because of the dual trappings of race and gender. Petry's second novel, *Country Place*, was published in 1947.

In 1948, Petry and her husband returned to Old Saybrook, where she would live for the rest of her life. Her only child, Elizabeth Ann Petry, was born there in 1949. After the move back to Connecticut, Petry went on to publish several more books, many of them for children. They include *The Drugstore Cat* (1949), *The Narrows* (1953), *Harriet Tubman. Conductor on the Underground Railroad* (1955), *Tituba of Salem Village* (1964), and *Legends of the Saints* (1970). In addition, Petry is the author of a collection of short stories, *Miss Muriel and Other Stories*, which includes many of her earlier published stories in addition to new ones. She received honorary doctorates from Suffolk University (1983), the University of Connecticut (1988), and Mount Holyoke College (1989) and served as visiting professor of English at the University of Hawaii in 1974. In 1992 she received the Connecticut Arts Award from the Connecticut Commission on the Arts in Stamford. Petry died early in 1997.

MAJOR WORKS AND THEMES

The Street, Petry's most widely acclaimed work, is a powerful and complex work of art. The novel incorporates many of the themes Petry includes in her other works, such as the effects of racism on young African Americans. *The Street* details the struggles of the young protagonist, Lutie Johnson, an attractive and extremely ambitious black woman, and her quest to achieve the American Dream in face of overwhelming odds. Lutie finds the achievement of this dream, easily attained by her hero, Benjamin Franklin, elusive to her as a black woman caught in a world where both her race and her sex are devalued.

One of the major themes of the text that surfaces in *The Street* is community;

community in the book denotes both geographical space and identification with those from similar backgrounds. Lutie's Harlem community, however, proves not to be a space where she can feel completely safe, despite her dwelling among fellow African Americans. Petry depicts 116th Street in Harlem, where Lutie takes an apartment, almost as a character in itself; the street becomes a symbol for the oppression that blacks face from the outside white world. As Lutie is walking down the street at the beginning of the novel, a "cold November wind" is blowing down the street, obstructing her and the other walkers' progress:

> It did everything it could to discourage the people walking along the street. It found all the dirt and dust and grime on the sidewalk and lifted it up so that the dirt got into their noses, making it difficult to breathe; the dust got into their eyes and blinded them; and the grit stung their skins. It wrapped newspaper around their feet entangling them until the people cursed deep in their throats, stamped their feet, kicked at the paper. . . . The wind lifted Lutie Johnson's hair away from the back of her neck so that she felt suddenly naked and bald, for her hair had been resting softly and warmly against her skin. (*The Street* 2)

This initial description of the street becomes a metaphor for the strangulation and confinement suffered by the black inhabitants of Harlem, who are cut off from mainstream American society by whites who relegate them to this place. In addition to her metaphorical presentation of 116th Street, Petry depicts the street in realistic detail; it is a place where prostitutes, pimps, and other criminals live and where her young son, Bub, is in constant danger when left alone. Indeed, Petry's depiction of the Harlem community where Lutie lives has caused critics to classify her as a naturalistic or realistic novelist in the vein of Stephen Crane, Theodore Dreiser, and fellow African American writers Richard Wright and Chester Himes.*

At the beginning of the text, Lutie conceives of this Harlem community as a refuge from her troubled relationships with her father and husband. She also sees it as an escape from her position as maid in the fractured, all-white world of the Chandlers, whose friends continually insinuate that the beautiful Lutie may attempt to seduce the drunken Mr. Chandler, despite her disgust at the idea. The whites' conception of Lutie as seductress foreshadows her experiences in Harlem; even there Lutie is seen by the men she encounters (the white businessman Junto, Boots Smith, and the Super) as primarily a sexual being because she is a beautiful black woman. Thus, Lutie soon discovers that, from white America, there is no escape for blacks and for black women; Harlem is not even free of white influence. The whites even control the influx of basic commodities to the community, with those who live in Harlem being relegated to "the leavings, sweepings, the impossible, unsalable merchandise, the dregs and dross that were especially reserved to Harlem" (158). Hilary Holladay notes, "For every glimpse of cohesiveness, Petry includes a reminder of the community's unhappy subordination to the surrounding white society. . . . While Lutie and her fellow Harlem residents may feel larger and more relaxed in their own community, they cannot altogether stop being 'small' just because they are home" (25). After she is forced to murder Boots when he attempts to rape her, Lutie loses her optimistic faith in the American Dream and her vision of herself as the modern-day equivalent to Benjamin Franklin because she now sees that this avenue has never been open to her as a black woman in America.

Petry's second novel, *Country Place* (1947), focuses upon many similar themes as *The Street*. However, unlike her first novel, *Country Place*'s major characters are white, and the story takes place in a rural small town, Lennox, Connecticut. The novel, unsurprisingly, draws upon many elements from Petry's own life; the main character, George Fraser, is a druggist, like her father, grandfather, and Petry herself, and the story relates the occurrences in a small New England town, though it centers mostly upon the town's white inhabitants. As in *The Street*, *Country Place* attempts to debunk the American myth of the cohesive small American town. Instead, Petry portrays Lennox, Connecticut, as a place where all is not as it may seem on the surface. As literary critic Bernard Bell expresses, "In contrast to traditional stories and images of the beneficence, continuity, integrity, and homogeneity of values in small, rural communities, [*Country Place*] reveals the hypocrisy, violence, prejudice, and stagnation of a small, post World War II, New England town" ("Ann Petry's" 110). The white characters of the text are trapped by their antiblack, anti-Catholic, and anti-Semitic stance, and Petry uses the story to express "the inevitability of change and of the tragic disillusionment that those who refuse to adjust to it must suffer" (Alexander 144).

Her third novel, *The Narrows*, published in 1953, also deals with a claustrophobic New England community and the way the characters who live in the town are affected by it. Set in the black neighborhood of Monmouth, Connecticut, the story details the relationship between Link Williams, a black orphan and graduate of Dartmouth College, and Camilo Treadway, a white heiress who at first conceals her true identity from Link. In what Bernard Bell characterizes as her best novel, Petry introduces a new thematic focus—miscegenation. She uses the relationship between Link and Camilo to show that interracial relationships are doomed to catastrophic ends in America. When Link is murdered by Camilo's mother and husband for daring to embark upon a relationship with a white woman, Petry illustrates that "the weight of their [Link and Camilo's] personal histories and the history of American racism and New England hypocrisy are too heavy a burden for Link and Camilo's love to survive" (Bell, "Ann Petry's" 112). Thus, in this novel history once again becomes the burden that crushes one of Petry's black characters.

Petry also wrote several books for juveniles, stemming from her displeasure at the lack of literature for black youth. In *Harriet Tubman, Conductor on the Underground Railroad*, she provides a portrait of the famous abolitionist, a portrait "made real by her sympathetic presentation of the fears and internal struggles that the Underground Railroad conductor must have suffered in her precarious, self-imposed occupation" (Alexander 146). *Tituba of Salem Village* tells the story of the Salem witch trials from the perspective of the black slave woman who was branded a witch in seventeenth-century Massachusetts. Both books reveal Petry's attempts to represent history from the black, female viewpoint. Her last published book, *Miss Muriel and Other Stories*, reprints several previously published stories in addition to presenting new work. Many of the stories in the collection, such as "The New Mirror," and the title piece, "Miss Muriel," center upon similar issues of race, sex, and community with which her novels deal.

CRITICAL RECEPTION

Much of the existing criticism of Petry's work centers on her most critically acclaimed and popular novel, *The Street*, which received generally good reviews by her contemporary commentators. Although a few denounced the novel because they felt it dwelled upon the sordid and tragic aspects of black life and did not show a more balanced community, most praised the novel's strongly naturalistic portrait of Harlem. She was placed by many in the realistic camp along with Richard Wright; indeed, some critics see *The Street* as a rewriting of Wright's *Native Son*, with Lutie as Petry's female counterpart to Wright's Bigger Thomas. However, Barbara Christian sees the novel as more than a mere revision of Wright's text: "One of the major differences between Wright's novel and Petry's is her voluminous use of external detail. Wright's novel is more about Bigger Thomas's psychological state, his reaction to his condition, than the presentation of the external condition itself. . . . While Wright endows his material with psychological overtones, Petry employs the tone of the commonplace. She is particularly effective in selecting the many details and seemingly trivial struggles that poor women can seldom avoid" (64).

Furthermore, the work drew praise for Petry's use of dramatic irony in the text to underscore the discrepancy between the myth of the American Dream and the realities of life in the United States for African Americans and for women, in particular for how she shows the irony between Lutie's conception of herself as a contemporary, black female equivalent to Benjamin Franklin and the racial and sexual exploitation of which she becomes a victim after moving to the street. Other critics have noted Petry's influence upon later African American women writers. Hilary Holladay relates that one can see the recurrence of Petry's preoccupation with community and communal relationships among African Americans in such recent works as Gloria Naylor's* *The Women of Brewster Place*, Toni Morrison's* *Song of Solomon*, and Alice Walker's* *The Color Purple*.

BIBLIOGRAPHY

Works by Ann Petry

The Street. Boston: Houghton Mifflin, 1946.
Country Place. Boston: Houghton Mifflin, 1947.

The Drugstore Cat. New York: Crowell, 1949.
The Narrows. Boston: Houghton Mifflin, 1953.
Harriet Tubman, Conductor on the Underground Railroad. New York: Crowell, 1955.
Tituba of Salem Village. New York: Crowell, 1964.
Legends of the Saints. New York: Crowell, 1970.
Miss Muriel and Other Stories. Boston: Houghton Mifflin, 1971.

Nonfiction

"The Novel as Social Criticism." *The Writer's Book.* Ed. Helen Hull. New York: Harper and Brothers, 1950. 32–39.

Studies of Ann Petry

Alexander, Sandra Carlton. "Ann Petry." *Dictionary of Literary Biography: Afro-American Writers 1940–1955.* Vol. 6. Ed. Trudier Harris. Detroit: Gale Research, 1988.
Andrews, Larry R. "The Sensory Assault of the City in Ann Petry's *The Street*." *The City in African American Literature.* Madison, NJ: Fairleigh Dickinson University Press, 1995.
Bell, Bernard W. *The Afro-American Novel and Its Tradition.* Amherst: University of Massachusetts Press, 1987.
———. "Ann Petry's Demythologizing of American Culture and Afro-American Character." *Conjuring: Black Women, Fiction, and Literary Tradition.* Ed. Marjorie Pryse and Hortense J. Spillers. Bloomington: Indiana University Press, 1985.
Christian, Barbara. *Black Women Novelists: The Development of a Tradition, 1892–1976.* Westport, CT: Greenwood Press, 1980.
Clark, Keith. "A Distaff Dream Deferred? Ann Petry and the Art of Subversion." *African American Review* 26.3 (1992): 495–505.
Davis, Arthur P. *From the Dark Tower: Afro-American Writers 1900 to 1960.* Washington, DC: Howard University Press, 1974.
Dempsey, David. "Uncle Tom's Ghost and the Literary Abolitionists." *Antioch Review* 6 (1946): 442–48.
Ervin, Hazel Arnett. *Ann Petry: A Bio-Bibliography.* New York: G. K. Hall, 1993.
Gayle, Addison, Jr. *The Way of the New World: The Black Novel in America.* Garden City, NY: Anchor/Doubleday, 1975.
Gross, Theodore L. "Ann Petry: The Novelist as Social Critic." *Black Fiction: New Studies in the Afro-American Novel since 1945.* Ed. Robert A. Lee. New York: Barnes and Noble, 1980.
Harris, Trudier. "On Southern and Northern Maids: Geography, Mammies, and Militants." *From Mammies to Militants: Domestics in Black American Literature.* Philadelphia: Temple University Press, 1982.
Holladay, Hilary. *Ann Petry.* New York: Twayne, 1996.
Hughes, Carl Milton. *The Negro Novelist: A Discussion of the Writings of American Negro Novelists, 1940–1950.* New York: Citadel Press, 1953. Reprint 1970.
Joyce, Joyce Ann. "Ann Petry." *Nethula* 2 (1982): 16–20.
McDowell, Margaret. "*The Narrows*: A Fuller View of Ann Petry." *Black American Literature Forum* 14.4 (1980): 135–41.
McKay, Nellie Y. "Ann Petry's *The Street* and *The Narrows*: A Study of the Influence of

Class, Race, and Gender on Afro-American Women's Lives." *Women and War: The Changing Status of American Women from the 1930s to the 1950s.* Ed. Maria Diedrich and Dorothea Fischer-Hornung. New York: Berg, 1990. 127–40.

———. Introduction. *The Narrows.* Boston: Beacon Press, 1988.

Pryse, Marjorie. " 'Pattern against the Sky': Deism and Motherhood in Ann Petry's *The Street.*" *Conjuring: Black Women, Fiction, and Literary Tradition.* Ed. Marjorie Pryse and Hortense J. Spillers. Bloomington: Indiana University Press, 1985.

Shinn, Thelma J. "Women in the Novels of Ann Petry." *Critique* 16.1 (1974): 110–20.

Washington, Gladys J. "A World Made Cunningly: A Closer Look at Ann Petry's Short Fiction." *CLA Journal* 30.1 (Sept. 1986): 14–29.

Washington, Mary Helen. *Invented Lives: Narratives of Black Women, 1860–1960.* New York: Doubleday, 1987.

Weir, Sybil. "*The Narrows:* A Black New England Novel." *Studies in American Fiction* 15.1 (1987): 80–93.

CARLENE HATCHER POLITE
(1932–   )

Frank E. Dobson, Jr.

BIOGRAPHY

Carlene Hatcher (Polite) was born in Detroit, Michigan, on 28 August 1932 to John and Lillian (Cook) Hatcher, international representatives of the United Automobile Workers–Congress of Industrial Organizations (UAW-CIO). Novelist, essayist, dancer, activist, and educator, Polite is the author of two novels, *The Flagellants* (1966) and *Sister X and the Victims of Foul Play* (1975). In these works, Polite crafted a prose style that has earned her comparison to such contemporary African American writers as Ishmael Reed,* Charles Wright, and William Melvin Kelley.* Polite attended Detroit public schools prior to matriculating at Sarah Lawrence College in New York, which she attended briefly before entering the Martha Graham School of Contemporary Dance. From 1955 to 1963, she pursued a career as a professional dancer. Polite performed onstage with the Concert Dance Theater of New York City (1955–1959) and the Detroit Equity Theater and Vanguard Playhouse (1960–1962). Polite appeared as a specialty dancer in *The King and I, The Boy Friend,* and *Dark of the Moon.* She taught modern dance in the Martha Graham technique at the Detroit Young Women's Christian Association (YWCA) (1960–1962), the Detroit Young Men's Christian Association (YMCA) (1962–1963), and Wayne State University.

In the early 1960s, Polite was active in political organizing and civil rights issues. In 1962 she was elected to the Michigan State Central Committee of the Democratic Party. She coordinated the Detroit Council for Human Rights and participated in the June 1963 Walk for Freedom and the November 1963 Freedom Now Rally to protest the Birmingham, Alabama, church bombings. In 1963, Polite organized the Northern Negro Leadership Conference. In 1964, following the closing of the Detroit Council for Human Rights, Polite moved to Paris, where she lived until 1971. The influential French editor Dominique de Roux encouraged Polite's writing, and in 1966 *The Flagellants* was published in French by Christian Bourgois Editeur, a new publishing house, which chose the novel as its first book. Farrar, Straus, and Giroux published the novel in English the following year. Polite received a National Foundation of the Arts and Humanities Fellowship in 1967 and a Rockefeller Foundation Fellowship in 1968. In 1971, Polite began teaching literature and creative writing as an associate professor of English at the State University of New York at Buffalo. *Sister X and the Victims of Foul Play* was published in 1975. The mother of two daughters, Glynda and Lila, Polite is currently a full professor of English; she continues work on two other novels.

MAJOR WORKS AND THEMES

Carlene Hatcher Polite's first novel, *The Flagellants*, is a tour de force, a dazzling work heavily influenced by black music and dance. A dancer by training, her artistic mission in the work seems to be to make words dance. In her second novel, *Sister X and the Victims of Foul Play*, Polite poses the following question through Abyssinia, the novel's main character: "When will we begin giving our lives to the cause of living?" (75). Within both of her novels, Polite probes not only the *when* of that question but also the *how*, which is complicated by such factors as classism, racism, and sexism.

Polite's first novel addresses the problems caused by traditional gender roles in relationships between African American women and men. Through a series of interior monologues and exchanges between Ideal, the protagonist of the work, and Jimson, her lover, Polite also explores existential questions of identity. Ideal, a young African American female and dancer raised in the rural South, and Jimson, a young African American male and aspiring poet, meet in Greenwich Village during the 1960s and fall in love. The couple then attempts to sustain their love in the face of limiting, stereotypical gender roles and the psychological effects of racism. The novel consists of a series of interior monologues and exchanges between the couple. Once Ideal reveals her innermost thoughts, a passage follows presenting Jimson's thoughts as rebuttal. Throughout their exchanges, each character flagellates the other as they struggle with their respective pasts and insecurities.

The novel's Prologue introduces Ideal as a child living in "the Bottom," a black, racially segregated community in the South. During this initial sequence, Ideal is poised on a brass bed and then compelled to dance to the music of a blues guitar. Led away from this scene by her great-grandmother, a former slave, Ideal receives the following advice: "Always walk tall. Never bow down to anything or anyone, unless, of course you feel like bowing" (5). Her great-grandmother's act of passing down an admonition of black survival and pride reminds one of similar acts in works such as Hurston's *Their Eyes Were Watching God* and Petry's* *The Street*. Ironically, in the text, the male protagonist, Jimson, is raised by a father with a similar philosophy. Of Jimson's upbringing, his father confesses to Ideal,

I wanted the best for my boy. I knew what it was like to be poor and hungry, walking miles down red clay road to school, living in a clapboard shack, hearing mamma and poppa praying to the Lord to relieve them and give them the strength to move on. I know what it is to live behind the sun . . . I swore that no child of mine would ever know that life or hold his hat in his hand before a living soul; and that he would be better off than everyone I knew, and able to match wits with all that I did not know. (69)

Ideal attempts to incorporate her great-grandmother's message into her relationship with Jimson; however, burdened with the stereotype of the black matriarch, especially in the eyes of her lover, she struggles to live up to her forebear's words and to love Jimson in the process. Despite their constant quarreling, Ideal asserts her determination regarding their relationship: "In order that I am able to refute the warnings of my blasé company, and believe that I have not wasted time, energy, violated my flesh, not appeared the utter ass, I must make this love" (37). Additional tension between the pair stems from financial pressures; Ideal is depressed by their poverty, which necessitates that she work at a secretarial job, supporting them both. She resents Jimson's prideful irresponsibility, which will not allow him to take a job he considers beneath him. In Ideal's eyes, he sees himself as a black messianic hero, the "Giver of Light" (54).

Jimson desires submission on the part of Ideal; however, incapacitated by fears of losing his manhood and becoming like his ancestors, particularly Papa Boo, who lived the role of Uncle Tom, "he fought for the rights of those who beat him into dust and upheld his sense of worth only in the company of his brothers" (56). Plagued by the legacy bequeathed him by Papa Boo and, at times, luxuriating in that legacy while using it as a crutch, Jimson's ongoing war with Ideal is, in reality, a war within himself, against seeing himself as "the Prince of Darkness, a shame before God, the ugliest child in the world" (58). As a result of this self-image and his arrogance, Jimson moves through a variety of jobs, including one where a white librarian attempts to seduce him. Jimson rejects her advances and leaves the job, but subsequently he becomes suicidal and hostile to Ideal's attempts to help him. When he finally secures a job with the Bureaucratique, an agency similar to the United Nations, dealing in social services and peace activism, he urges Ideal to become a homemaker, a role for which she is unsuited. Jimson is excited by the opportunity to work at a meaningful position that he believes is requisite to his talents; however, he is soon disappointed to learn from his supervisor that he need do nothing besides look busy and discreetly avail himself of as many job perks as possible. The Bureaucratique is, as its name suggests, a sham; Jimson writes poetry while on the job.

As the novel builds to its dramatic conclusion, the couple engage in a violent dispute. Jimson strikes Ideal. Later, Ideal is set up by Jimson with a date with a coworker from the Bureaucratique. This coworker attempts to rape Ideal and, once resisted, divulges Jimson's infidelity to Ideal. She chastises Jimson for his betrayal, but he defends himself by claiming that, although he does, indeed, love her, she forced him to be unfaithful. He contends that her demands are over-bearing, like those of all black women, who seem to need to reduce the stature of their men in order to maintain their own status as strong matriarchs. The novel ends with Jimson's telling Ideal that now that she has suffered as much as he has, he wants to remain with her. Ideal's final words are: "[G]o out there and find . . . your giant, kill him, become his spirit" (214).

The characters' names imply their symbolic significance. Ideal's name suggests that she is the perfect model of black womanhood, the epitome of the self-sacrificing black matriarch. Ironically, Jimson wishes for her to become Aunt Jemima, relegated to the kitchen. Jimson's boyish name hints that he represents the emasculated black "son" who is subservient, like Papa Boo, to the white master and who is supported and "mothered" by the black woman. Moreover, Ideal's willingness to abandon her artistic goals as a dancer in order to support the couple suggests the sacrifice of the stereotypical black matriarch, whose func-tion as caretaker of others comes at the expense of her own fulfillment. Jimson, in contrast, refuses to relinquish his dreams regarding writing poetry.

As the novel's title suggests, flagellation, the act of whipping oneself for public penance or for sexual arousal, is a central theme. This idea of public penance also implies that Ideal and Jimson, who scourge each other both verbally and physically, are acting in response to societal forces that have historically menaced black women and men and that seem to ultimately spell doom for these two lovers.

Polite's second novel, *Sister X and the Victims of Foul Play*, relates the story of a dead African American dancer in Paris who was a victim of foul play. As with *The Flagellants*, this novel develops characters and themes by means of extended monologues and speeches, and the language used is the language of the black street and musical lexicon, music as jazz riff. The account of the life of the dead Sister X, Arista Prolo, is told by the novel's protagonist, Abyssinia, Sister X's former costume designer, and Willis B. Black (Black Will), her former lover. All three of the characters are expatriates from the United States living in Paris. Abyssinia and Black Will discuss over a breakfast of grits Arista's mysterious death in Abyssinia's apartment.

The mystery surrounding Sister X's death lies in a dispute over its cause; while the attending physician terms it cancer, Abyssinia disagrees and relates to Will the real cause of Arista's death. As Abyssinia recounts the story to Black Will, it is clear that Sister X overcame many of the obstacles that African Americans have traditionally faced, such as racism and a negative self-image:

> "What do you want to be when you grow up, little girl?"
> "An opera singer."
> "A what?"
> Arista's mother . . . turned to her daughter, and asked her (in dead seriousness) if she

didn't know better than that. "That" meaning: "Don't you know 'that' Black Girls cannot grow up to become opera singers?' " (49)

Despite this background of limited expectations, Arista Prolo becomes an artist, not an opera diva, but a diva of dance. And dance she does, throughout the world. While Abyssinia weaves the tale for Black Will, she also launches a verbal assault on Western society that is both preachy and satirical, biting and comic. For example, she believes that "Black Folk die from CCC," national "diseases" beginning with the letter C, such as cotton fields, chain gangs, colonial correctional facilities, and Crow, Jim (43). However, as Abyssinia continues her tirade, her focus is larger than simply black oppression; she believes that all humanity is trapped in a "Dead World," and her indictment stretches beyond the color line: "It is evident historically that this is the kind of 'merchandise and spectacle' society in which we have been and are being daily taught to live. In this, our 'civilized' society, our entire psychological makeup is founded on violence, death, hoggish self-fulfillment, ambition, exploitation, combative chauvinism, competition, binding contracts, promises, hatred" (74).

Within her rambling speech, Abyssinia tells the story of Sister X's life and death to Black Will, laying out for him seven of the costumes she designed for Arista, costumes that enabled the dancer to assume various identities while onstage, from the Scottish Glynda, Girl of the Glen, to an Egyptian, Chloe de Cleopatre. Throughout their travels, these two black women from Detroit lived in the picaresque tradition, surviving by pluck and determination. During Abyssinia's telling of the tale, Black Will is a listener, speaking mainly to lead Abyssinia back to the Sister X story or to ask for clarification regarding one of her philosophical tangents that are often embedded in black history: "I wonder sometimes if our ancestors buried in those cotton and sugar cane fields still fertilize those crops out there" (104).

The second chapter of the novel, entitled "Gettin' a Witness," provides just that, a great many witnesses, a roll call of famous black dancers, from Bill Bojangles Robinson, Florence Mills, and Josephine Baker, to Alvin Ailey, Arthur Mitchell, and Judith Jamieson. This listing of dancers occurs at that point in the narrative when Abyssinia is explaining the conflict between Sister X and the last club she danced for, the club where she meets her death. An artist in the tradition of Josephine Baker, Arista refuses the management's demand that she dance naked, and she is thus dismissed. After her dismissal, Sister X returns to the club to receive her final pay. Once there, she makes the rounds of the dressing rooms and becomes involved in a shoving match taking place onstage, where she has an altercation with her replacement. Her replacement, Miss Ann White of Birmingham, Alabama, is a young white woman masquerading as black through the application of makeup. After Sister X mysteriously falls from the stage, she is taken to a hospital, where she dies. There are several questions surrounding her death. Did Miss Ann White push her? What was the cause of her death? As stated earlier, a French physician reports the cause of her death as cancer, a cause disputed by Abyssinia. As Abyssinia's story indicates, the causes of death for "Black Folk" are numerous; at an early point in the narrative she rants about the "jive death certificate" and tells the questioning Black Will, "Death killed her" (4). The French physician's diagnosis of the cause of death is ironically correct; Sister X died at the hands of a cancerous society that victimizes individuals and groups, particularly black folk, assailing their dreams and aspirations. The overall theme of this novel is that the "Dead World," a racist, sexist society, is the real cause of Arita's death. This "Dead World," a world of the past, of outmoded ideologies and creeds, must be negotiated, like the picaro, but also confronted, as does the tragic, yet also heroic, Sister X.

CRITICAL RECEPTION

Polite's work has not received the critical attention that it merits. Aside from a few reviews and even fewer critical discussions, her novels have been virtually ignored by literary scholars. Responses to *The Flagellants*, Polite's first novel, have been mixed. Some reviewers hailed Polite as an innovator especially forceful in her examination of gender roles. In his review of the work, Gross calls Polite an original and stylistically gifted writer, comparing her with other contemporary African American authors such as Reed and Gaines. Howe discusses the thematic importance of *The Flagellants* but condemns what he considers its excessive use of hyperbolic language. Herbert Lottman praised the novel as "The Theater of Cruelty in book form" (20), while Roger Ebert called it "a book which makes one wish the author had not told so truthfully of a hopeless human agony" (682). Hemmett Worthington-Smith suggests that the novel helped usher in an "era in which Afro-American fiction moved beyond the convention of realism," while also citing its "bleak" conclusion and "unrelenting" (217) vision. Penelope Pellizon suggests that the novel be viewed in comparison to other works that focus on individual relationships and gender stereotypes rather than on larger political issues. In perhaps the most sensitive discussion of the novel to date, Claudia Tate places it in the context of a flowering of black fiction that occurred during the late 1960s and early 1970s. Comparing the novel to Jones' *Corregidora*, Morrison's* *The Bluest Eye*, and Walker's* *The Third Life of Grange Copeland*, Tate contends that "it was one of the first novels to probe questions of freedom that lie outside the perimeter of civil liberties" (xxxvi). Tate also cites the influence of French existentialist writers like Camus on the work. She suggests that any reading of the novel must acknowledge the presence of a set of rules or a code for reading the novel.

Less widely reviewed than *The Flagellants, Sister X and the Victims of Foul Play* received praise from critics who acknowledged its inventiveness and force but criticized its plastic characters and political abstraction. Frederick Busch noted his admiration for Polite's talent as a writer while also labeling her "grim rhetoric" (24) as repetitive and tiring. Hemmett Worthington-Smith suggests that this novel, like Polite's first, reflects the author's diverse background in "tough, hard-edged, poetic prose" (218).

BIBLIOGRAPHY

Works by Carlene Hatcher Polite

Les Flagellents. Trans. Pierre Alien. Paris: Christian Bourgois Editeur, 1966; republished as *The Flagellants*. New York: Farrar, Straus, and Giroux, 1967; rpt., Boston: Beacon, 1987.
Sister X and the Victims of Foul Play. New York: Farrar, Straus, and Giroux, 1975.

Studies of Carlene Hatcher Polite

Busch, Frederick. *"Sister X and the Victims of Foul Play." Times Book Review* (23 November 1975): 24.
Ebert, Roger. "First Novels by Young Negroes." *American Scholar* (Autumn 1967): 682–686.
Gross, Robert A. "The Black Novelists: 'Our Turn.' " *Newsweek* 73 (16 June 1969): 94.
Howe, Irving. "New Black Writers." *Harper* 239 (December 1969): 130–131.
Johnson, Ronna C. "Carlene Hatcher Polite." *The Oxford Companion to African American Literature*. Ed. William L. Andrew, Frances Smith Foster, and Trudier Harris. New York: Oxford, 1997. 595.
Lottman, Herbert R. "Authors and Editors." *Publishers Weekly* (12 June 1967): 20–21.
Pellizon, Penelope V. *"The Flagellants." Masterplots II: African American Literature Series*. Ed. Frank N. Magill. Pasadena, CA: Salem, 1994. 455–459.
Tate, Claudia. Introduction to *The Flagellants*, 1967; rpt. 1987, Boston: Beacon. vii–xxxi.
Worthington-Smith, Hemmett. "Carlene Hatcher Polite." In *Dictionary of Literary Biography*, vol. 33, *Afro-American Fiction Writers after 1955*. Ed. Thadious M. Davis and Trudier Harris. 215–218. Detroit: Gale, 1984.

ISHMAEL REED
(1938–)

Pierre-Damien Mvuyekure

BIOGRAPHY

Ishmael Reed was born in Chattanooga, Tennessee, and grew up in Buffalo, New York, where he attended Buffalo Technical High School, Millard Fillmore College, and the University of Buffalo. In 1995, the State University of New York at Buffalo awarded him an honorary doctorate in letters. When he was fourteen years old, he wrote his own jazz column in *Empire State Weekly*, an African American newspaper in Buffalo. Later on, jazz would have a great influence on his writing style, just as his first novel contains jazz critic characters. During the same period, he wrote a rhymed poem about Christmas and was commissioned by his mother to write a birthday poem for a coworker. In 1982 and 1989, he wrote two Christmas novels, *The Terrible Twos* and *The Terrible Threes*.

According to *Conversations with Ishmael Reed* (Dick and Singh), between 1955 and 1960, Reed wrote "Something Pure," a short story that got the attention of an English teacher, who recommended him to the University of Buffalo. During this time, Reed performed in *Mooney's Kid Don't Cry* and Jean Anouilh's *Antigone*, "opposite poet Lucille Clifton." At the University of Buffalo, Reed studied Yeats, Pound, and Blake, who were later to influence his first poems. But around 1960, he dropped out of the university, claiming that he did not want to be anybody's reading list's slave, and moved to New York City, where he joined *Umbra* magazine and attended *Umbra* workshops. These workshops shaped and launched his literary career, for some of his first poems were written under the influence of the Umbra workshops, especially the collage of "images and symbols from the cultures of Europe and Africa and Afro-America" (*Conjure* vii). This has been developed into Neo-HooDooism or Neo-HooDoo Aesthetic, the hallmark of all Reed's novels, plays, and poems.

Reed is a multifaceted writer: novelist, poet, songwriter, saxophone player, television producer, editor, publisher, playwright, founder of the Before Columbus Foundation and There City Cinema, literary critic, and essayist. He has taught at Yale, Harvard, Dartmouth, the State University of New York at Buffalo, Calhoun College, Sitka Community Association, the University of Arkansas at Fayetteville, the University of Washington (Seattle), and the University of California at Santa Barbara. For more than twenty years, he has been teaching at the University of California at Berkeley; he lives in Oakland, California.

MAJOR WORKS AND THEMES

To date Reed has published more than twenty books, including nine novels, five collections of poetry, four essay books, five plays, and several anthologies. He is now writing *The Terrible Fours* and an O. J. Simpson novel. Thematically, it would be a disservice to pinpoint a single theme in these novels, for Reed combines several nonrelated cultural, historical, political, folkloric elements and literary allusions as metaphors for multiculturalism and multiethnicity. Granted, the starting point in Reed's novels tends to be the conflict between European-based hegemonic beliefs/attitudes and African American traditions, but the ultimate concerns are not solely the plight of African American culture or African Americans but also that of Native Americans, Puerto Ricans, Chinese Americans, Japanese Americans, Jews, and people from developing countries. Thus, a thoroughgoing analysis of Reed's novels must start by recognizing their underlying multicultural poetics. Indeed, reading Reed's fiction is like being involved in an ethnographer's fieldwork, except that Reed's novels record several cultures at once. In other words, reading Reed is like savoring and devouring *Gombo Févi* or Gumbo à la Creole.

Although people have been taught to be careful whenever writers describe their own work, they must listen to what Reed says about his own aesthetic, lest they misread or misinterpret his work. In effect, he has so much blurred the division between prose, fiction, and poetry that several passages from his essays are repeated verbatim in his novels and vice versa, just as in his poems and essays he elaborates theories that undergird the fictional worlds of his novels. Thus, to understand Reed's fiction, one must read his poetry and essays either before or after reading the novels, because therein Reed adumbrates his Neo-HooDooism or Neo-HooDoo Aesthetic, an African-based aesthetic.

Without doubt, the dominant traits and informing ideas of voodoo religion and Reed's Neo-HooDooism are diversity, creativity, artistic freedom, and cultural democracy, issues that permeate Reed's books. For Reed, voodoo is "the perfect metaphor for the multiculture," because "[v]oodoo comes out of the fact that all these different tribes and cultures were brought from Africa to Haiti" with all "of their mythologies, knowledges, and herbal medicines, their folklores, jelled" (*Shrovetide* 232–233). In other words, the very syncretic and synchronistic nature of voodoo and hoodoo and their polytheistic systems and values, which are built into the genealogical makeup of all people, are the crux of Neo-HooDooism. That is, each of the nine novels combines multifarious elements in its plot and puts different elements from different time periods into one time frame. As Reed has explained in an essay from his *Writin' Is Fightin'*, this multicultural aspect of voodoo aesthetic attracted him to voodoo. Because "there seems to be no room" for "intellectual meanness" in African and African American religious systems, the latter "could mix with other cultures with no thought of 'contamination,' or 'corruption,' but usefulness. In this light, Catholic saints could perform the functions of African gods, just as in Guadeloupe "the gods of the immigrant Indians were added to the neo-African pantheon, and a curry dish, with Indian origins, has become the national dish of this Caribbean country" (141).

In "The Neo-HooDoo Aesthetic," "Neo-HooDoo Manifesto," and "Catechism of d Neoamerican Hoodoo Church," three poems from *catechism of d neoamerican hoodoo church* (1970) and *Conjure* (1972), Reed elaborates his theory of Neo-HooDooism. In "The Neo-HooDoo Aesthetic," a poem about how to make *Gombo Févi* and *Gombo Filé*, the poet explores the relation between food and art and makes it clear that *Gombo Févi* is a metaphor for art and syncretic writing. In the concluding lines, he explains that he calls it Neo-HooDoo Aesthetic because the amount of ingredients to make *Gombo Févi* or *Gumbo Filé* is entirely incumbent on the cook (*New and Collected Poems* 26)—the gumbo metaphor underlies the text of *The Last Days of Louisiana Red*. Loop Garoo Kid echoes these aesthetic views in the HooDoo western novel *Yellow Back Radio Broke-Down* when he argues that no one says that a novel has to be one thing. "It can be anything it wants to be, a vaudeville show, the six o'clock news, the mumblings of wild men saddled by demons" (136).

The freedom to determine the amount of ingredients for the cook/artist also emerges from the poem "Catechism of d Neoamerican Church," a poem that solemnly declares that writers, unlike computers, are not programmable and that their pens are free. In "Neo-HooDoo Manifesto," it is announced that Neo-HooDoo originates from Haitian voodoo, elates to dance and music, and traces its origins back to Africa. In effect, the poem enumerates musicians from James Brown, Louis Jordan Ma Rainey, Aretha Franklin, and many more singers and groups of artists as Neo-HooDooists. *Mumbo Jumbo* heavily explores these ideas about the intricate relationships between dance, drum, music, and voodoo religion—dance and music are used to conjure up deities and ancestral spirits.

An understanding of Neo-HooDooism helps one to discover that Reed's novels are multivoiced novels in which the cultures of the world crisscross and that, like gumbo, they are exquisite and delicious combinations of political, cultural, religious, literary, cinematic, and folkloric forms. Besides, they testify to the fact that Reed is influenced by many traditions—African, African American, American, Asian, European, and Native American. What is more, the signifyin(g) revisions and parodic intertexts allow him to tackle the issues concerning gender, race, and ethnicity, involving poignant historical events such as the lynchings of Emmett Till and Leo Frank in *Reckless Eyeballing*, the bombing of Hiroshima and Nagasaki, the murder of Patrice Lumumba, the murder of Attica prisoners in *The Terrible Twos* and *The Terrible Threes*, the three "Yellow" wars, Japan bashing, and the plight of ethnic studies on American campuses in *Japanese by Spring*.

The Free-Lance Pallbearers is a collage of parodies of the toasts of the urban ghetto traditions, the German voodoo film *The Cabinet of Dr. Caligari*, Kafka's *Metamorphosis*, Nathaniel West's *The Dream Life of Balso Snell*, Reed's unpublished works *Ethan Booker* and "Something Pure," the legend of Booker T. Washington, and the American Dream. Bukka Doopeyduck, the protagonist and narrator of the novel based on Daffy Duck, is characterized as an alienated "Negro" who leaves college to learn the Nazarene manual whereby he hopes to become one of the Nazarene bishops and big man for HARRY SAM, the name of both a dictator and a country. The first sentence in the novel calls HARRY SAM a "big not-to-be-believed out-of-sight, sometimes referred to as O-BOP-SHE-BANG or KLANG-A-LANG-A-DING-DONG" (1). This sentence is just one example of the language of bebop and the experimental aspect of *The Free-Lance Pallbearers*. Just as in bebop, an innovative form of jazz introduced by Charlie Parker—Reed has been called the Charlie Parker of fiction—innovation and improvisation are instrumental, and there is an open-endedness of melody and harmony, so do *The Free-Lance Pallbearers* and the other eight novels improvise in plots.

Bukka Doopeyduck is so alienated from his black cultural values that he is even afraid of using dialect, lest the assistant dean of arts and sciences and the students from the University of Buffalo circulate a petition about the "ADULTERATION OF HER TONGUE" (100). Moreover, he refuses an invitation to discuss the contemporary black writer's role in society, especially whether he should "glare at Charlie [Parker]" or "kinda stick out his lower lip and look mean," or "snag at Charlie's pants legs until his mouth is full of ankles and calves" (106)—jazz and Charlie are some of the main themes of *Mumbo Jumbo*. In sharp contrast, Elijah Raven, "the heretic Nazarene apprentice" who leads the opposition against the dictator, always uses dialect and warns Bukka Doopeyduck that he is being used by Cipher X.

Bukka Doopeyduck's alienation from black vernacular is also seen when Bukka Doopeyduck is hoodooed—though the name "Bukka" Doopeyduck relates to his mother's second cousin, who used hoodoo gloves on a social worker—by his mother-in-law for having broken up with her daughter. He refuses to believe that hoodoo is real until U2 Polyglot, his former teacher—Polyglot has been pushing a ball of shit the world over as an experiment for his paper, " 'The Egyptian Dung Beetle in Kafka's 'Metamorphosis' "—convinces him that he needs an antidote and sells it to him. The point to be made here is that although hoodoo appears as negative force—Bukka Doopeyduck is good for nothing anyway—voodoo and hoodoo aesthetics are the cornerstone of the next novels.

In *Yellow Back Radio Broke-Down* (1969), Ishmael Reed revises the western genre and transforms Bukka Doopeyduck into Loop Garoo Kid, a black voodoo and hoodoo cowboy who challenges the monoculturalism of the American Wild West and Catholicism. Initially, it is hoodoo spiritual forces against the guns of Drag Gibson, but soon the personal and political conflict becomes a cultural one as Drag Gibson loses ground and calls on Pope Innocent VIII to help him eliminate the hoodoo cowboy. To Drag Gibson's disappointment, not only does the pontiff acknowledge that Christianity has been trying to wipe out African-based religions such as juju and voodoo, an African religion from Dahomey and Angola brought by slaves, but he also leads to the discovery that Loop Garoo Kid is an apocryphal of Christ. For this reason, the pope refuses to kill the black cowboy and actually pleads with the latter to follow him. In addition, the novel comments upon American history in the nineteenth century, science fiction, African American and Native American folklore, and Pope Innocent VIII.

Mumbo Jumbo is probably one of the most influential novels in American letters, because it inspired Henry Louis Gates, Jr., to write his seminal work *The Signifying Monkey: A Theory of African-American Literary Criticism*. If in *Yellow Back Radio Broke-Down*, Loop Garoo Kid indicts Judeo-Christianity for trying to wipe out African-based religions and cultures, the hoodoo detective and therapist PaPa LaBas of *Mumbo Jumbo* really takes time to demonstrate how Greek civilization, the basis for European civilization, is Egyptian-derived. The subtexts and paratexts of *Mumbo Jumbo* are endless, for they include a 104-title partial bibliography, photographs, drawings, headlines, newspaper clippings, ads, the Harlem Renaissance, the African origin of African American culture via Haiti, Egyptian mythology, and European myths, *The Conjure-Man Dies*, *De Mayor of Harlem*, and African American tradition of mysteries. Besides these subtexts, which should be interpreted as elements of multiculturalism, the novel contains an international and multiethnic group of "art-nappers" called the M'utafikah, whose role is to steal art and religious objects from Western museums and repatriate them back to their countries of origin. More importantly, Jes Grew, the point of the conflict in *Mumbo Jumbo*, is a metaphor for multiculturalism; although its detractors like the Atonists call it a plague, it becomes clear that Jes Grew is a form of possession related to voodoo through dances and songs.

The same PaPa LaBas reappears in *The Last Days of Louisiana Red* as a detective to solve the murder of Ed Yellings, a hoodoo therapist who is murdered because he was trying to get rid of Louisiana Red, a neo-slave mentality that led African Americans to kill one another like crabs in a barrel. The novel revises the detective story, Cab Calloway's song "Minnie the Moocher," Sophocles' and Anouihl's *Antigone*, Richard Wright's *Native Son*, *Amos 'n' Andy Show*, and the Congolese history in the 1960s. Clearly, the prefatory gumbo recipe from *The Picayune Creole Cook Book* is suggestive of all these intertexts and bears on the meaning of the novel as a whole, because Ed Yellings is in the Gumbo Business— "Business" and "Work" are coded names for voodoo hoodoo to avoid detection. In this saga, an analysis suggests that Ed Yellings' children are shaped after Sophocles' *Antigone*: Minnie the Moocher is Antigone, Wolf is Eteocles, Street is Polynices, Sister is Ismene, and PaPa LaBas is Creon, while Ed Yellings parallels Oedipus. But Reed makes it clear that there is also an Egyptian version of Antigone, and his judgment is against Antigone.

It is worth noting that with *The Last Days of Louisiana Red* hoodoo goes underground in Reed's fiction; that is, the Neo-HooDooism is still there, but there is no longer in-your-face theory about it. In *Flight to Canada*, the implicit Neo-HooDooism allows Reed to incorporate variegated allusions from different traditions and cultures and in so doing closes the gap between the past of the times of slavery and the Civil War, and the present of the bicentennial year, as well as the future. Structurally, the novel is presented as a text about Harriet Beecher Stowe in the first part, "Naughty Harriet," and Abraham Lincoln in the second part, "Lincoln the Player." Furthermore, not only does the novel revise the slave narrative and the historical novel, but it also parodies Harriet Beecher Stowe's *Uncle Tom's Cabin*, just as the Native American myth of the raven and E. A. Poe's poem "The Raven" and African voodoo are part of the aesthetic of *Flight to Canada*.

While on the surface *Flight to Canada* is the story of Raven Quickskill, an escaped slave who flies to Canada but eventually comes back to the plantation to free other slaves and write Uncle Robin's biography, it is a comment upon the present plight of African Americans, Native Americans, and other minorities in America. More importantly, the quest for literacy and freedom is so poignant that *Flight to Canada* moves from an oral tradition of voodoo and hoodoo to a literary tradition. Indeed, Raven Quickskill sees his writing as "his HooDoo. Others had their way of HooDoo, but his was his writing; his typewriter was his drum he danced to" (88).

With *The Terrible Twos* and *The Terrible Threes*, fictional allegories on the Reagan and Bush administrations, Reed adds Rastafarianism and calypso, aesthetics used by several Caribbean writers, to Neo-HooDooism to make a social commentary on Christmas, especially the way Christmas has been monopolized by big corporations for the rich. While the two novels take their structure and some of their characters from Charles Dickens' *A Christmas Carol*, there are other intertexts, such as the Bible, Ben Wattenberg's *Birth Dearths*, John A. Williams' *The Man Who Cried I Am*, Dante's *The Divine Comedy*, and the myths of Santa Claus, St. Nicholas, and Black Peter.

Using Rastafarian theology, Black Peter, a descendant of the ventriloquist Pompey in *Flight to Canada*, joins the Nicolaites and substitutes Haile Selassie, former emperor of Ethiopia and patron of Rastafarians, for St. Nicholas. His argument is that since both figures ride horses, as suggested in Revelations and in the legends of St. Nicholas, then there is no harm in adopting Haile Selassie as a gesture to developing countries that the Nicolaites are not a racist group. Additionally, not only is Santa Claus replaced by a zombie—actually, Snow Man's revived corpse—but also the song "Santa Claus Is Coming to Town" is given a reggae twist to bring things "into modern times." Just as Rastafarianism and calypso are used to make social commentaries, so does Black Peter charge America and its politicians with behaving like Scrooge and the two-year-olds. Although St. Nicholas takes Dean Clift, the American president, to the American Hell to see the atrocities committed by Dwight Eisenhower, Harry Truman, and Nelson Rockefeller, the endings of *The Terrible Twos* and *The Terrible Threes* suggest that the present and future for minorities and the poor in America are still bleak. In effect, not only is the changed Dean Clift kidnapped twice and prevented from getting rid of the Terrible Twos, but the person who is running the country, Reverend Johnes, has connived with Satan to eliminate St. Nicholas.

Reckless Eyeballing is the most misunderstood and misinterpreted of Reed's novels because of the way it handles multiculturalism in regard to anti-Semitism, feminism, race, and gender issues. By failing to investigate the parodic intertexts such as Scott Joplin's *Treemonisha*, the film version of Alice Walker's* *The Color Purple,* and the lynchings of Emmett Till and Leo Frank, critics have wrongly charged both *Reckless Eyeballing* and its author with misogyny. But a closer analysis of the intertexts as underpinnings of multiculturalism suggests that the novel moves from binary oppositions to multicultural spectrums. The novel seems to suggest that it is detrimental to polarize the world of women and men, for doing so disallows the multiplicity of diverse ethnicities among women and men. Moreover, because multiculturalism is inclusive, not polarizing, the bipolar world of us and them, women and men, blacks and Jews, and black male writers and black female writers denies the difference that cultures make. More importantly, Tremonisha Smarts comes out of the novel in better shape than Ian Ball, the Bugs Bunny sexist playwright, does.

Reed's poetics of multiculturalism reaches a higher level in *Japanese by Spring*, a novel written in three languages, English, Japanese, and Yoruba. Through the linguistic code-switching, Reed both reconnects his writing to Yoruba oral traditions and Japanese culture and moves the center from English to Japanese, Yoruba, and other linguistic centers. Equally interesting is the fact that *Japanese by Spring* explicitly discusses the issues of multiculturalism by opposing the Miltonists/monoculturalists to a group called Glossos, clearly a version of the M'utafikah. Just as Dean Clift converts to world literature in *The Terrible Threes*, so does Professor Crabtree, a former Miltonist, learn and teach Yoruba. This is the ultimate message that Reed conveys in his novels: monoculturalism and cultural bigotry can be overcome by learning about other cultures.

CRITICAL RECEPTION

Critic Joyce A. Joyce has abhorred the fact that the literary establishment supports the writings "of less than a handful of Black women writers and downplays the importance of a writer like Ishmael Reed, who has come quite close to publishing more novels and essays than Toni Morrison,* Alice Walker and Terry McMillan* put together" (244). Although Reed has written more than twenty books, and his literary career spans more than three decades, there are several articles and chapters in books but not enough book-length critical works. The problem seems to be that critics have been complaining about the fact that Ishmael Reed's novels are difficult to read because of their numerous subtexts, "lack of plot," and "stock characters." The truth is that Reed always has many things going on at the same time, while his readers and critics tend to follow a straight line or one thing at a time in their reading. On the other hand, Reed has been complaining that both readers and critics have failed to investigate the allusions used in his work, which has led to negative and scathing reviews, misreadings, and misinterpretations.

To be fair, critics like Henry Louis Gates, Robert Elliot Fox, Joyce A. Joyce, James De Jong, Peter Nazareth, and several others have written chapters in books and published excellent articles on Reed, primarily focusing on Neo-HooDoo aesthetic as the blackness of blackness. But other critics like Jerry Klinkowitz, Jeffrey Melnick, and Sämi Ludwig have attempted to interpret Reed's fiction from a multicultural perspective. Recently, Bruce Dick and Amritjit Singh have edited a collection of Ishmael Reed's interviews, which is a big step into Reed study, and Patric McGee published a book-length study of Reed. In other words, there is great need for more book-length studies of this global writer. It is worth noting that, despite the scarcity of critics' works, Reed's books are still in print and are being increasingly anthologized.

BIBLIOGRAPHY

Works by Ishmael Reed

Novels

The Free-Lance Pallbearers. New York: Atheneum, 1967.
Yellow Back Radio Broke-Down. New York: Atheneum, 1969.
Mumbo Jumbo. New York: Atheneum, 1972.
The Last Days of Louisiana Red. New York: Atheneum, 1974.
Flight to Canada. New York: Atheneum, 1976.
The Terrible Twos. New York: Atheneum, 1982.
Reckless Eyeballing. New York: Atheneum, 1986.
The Terrible Threes. New York: Atheneum, 1989.
Japanese by Spring. New York: Atheneum, 1993.

Essays

Shrovetide in Old New Orleans. New York: Atheneum, 1978.
God Made Alaska for the Indians: Selected Essays. New York: Garland, 1982.
Writin' Is Fightin': Thirty-Seven Years of Boxing on Paper. New York: Atheneum, 1988.
Airing Dirty Laundry. New York: Addison-Wesley, 1993.

Poetry

catechism of d neoamerican hoodoo church. London: Paul Breman, 1970.
Conjure: Selected Poems, 1963–1970. Amherst: University of Massachusetts Press, 1972.

Chattanooga. New York: Random House, 1973.
A Secretary to the Spirits. New York: NOK, 1978.
New and Collected Poems. New York: Atheneum, 1989.

Anthologies

19 Necromancers from Now. New York: Doubleday, 1970.
The Before Columbus Foundation Poetry Anthology. New York: W. W. Norton, 1992.
The Before Columbus Foundation Fiction Anthology. New York: W. W. Norton, 1992.
The Harper Collins Literary Mosaic Series. New York: HarperCollins, 1995.
MultiAmerica: Essays on Cultural Wars and Cultural Peace. New York: Viking, 1997.

Studies of Ishmael Reed

Boyer, Jay. *Ishmael Reed*. Boise, ID: Boise State University Press, 1993.
Dick, Bruce, and Amritjit Singh, eds. *Conversations with Ishmael Reed*. Jackson: University Press of Mississippi, 1995.
Fabre, Michel. "Ishmael Reed's *Free-Lance Pallbearers* or the Dialectics of Shit." *Obsidian* 3.3 (Winter 1977): 5–19.
Fox, Robert Elliot. *Conscientious Sorcerers: The Black Postmodernist Fiction of LeRoi Jones/ Amiri Baraka, Ishmael Reed, and Samuel R. Delany*. New York: Greenwood Press, 1987.
———. "Blacking the Zero: Toward a Semiotics of Neo-Hoodoo." *Masters of the Drum: Black Lit/oratures across the Continuum*. New York: Greenwood Press, 1995: 49–62.
Hardack, Richard. "Swing to the White, Back to the Black: Writing and 'Sourcery' in Ishmael Reed's *Mumbo Jumbo*." *Literary Influence and African-American Writers: Collected Essays*. Ed. Tracy Mishkin. New York: Garland, 1996: 271–300.
Harris, Norman. "The Last Days of Louisiana Red: The HooDoo Solution." *Connecting Times: The Sixties in Afro-American Fiction*. Jackson: University Press of Mississippi, 1988: 166–188.
Joyce, Joyce A. "Falling through the Minefields of Black Feminist Criticism: Ishmael Reed, a Case in Point." *Warriors, Conjurers, and Priests: Defining African-Centered Literary Criticism*. Chicago: Third World Press, 1994: 243–272.
Klinkowitz, Jerome. "Ishmael Reed's Multicultural Aesthetic." *Literary Subversions: New American Fiction and the Practice of Criticism*. Carbondale: Southern Illinois University Press, 1985: 18–33.
Lindroth, James. "Images of Subversions: Ishmael Reed and the Hoodoo Trickster." *African American Review* 30.2 (Summer 1996): 185–196.
Ludwig, Sämi. "Dialogic Possession in Ishmael Reed's *Mumbo Jumbo*: Bakhtin, Voodoo, and the Materiality of Multicultural Discourse." *The Black Columbiad: Defining Moments in African American Literature and Culture*. Ed. Werner Sollors. Cambridge, MA: Harvard University Press, 1994: 325–336.
Martin, Reginald. *Ishmael Reed and the New Black Aesthetic Critics*. New York: St. Martin's Press, 1988.
Mason, Theodore O., Jr. "Performance, History, and Myth: The Problem of Ishmael Reed's *Mumbo Jumbo*." *Modern Fiction Studies* 34.1 (Spring 1988): 97–109.
McConnell, Frank. "Ishmael Reed's Fiction: Da Hoodoo Is Put on America." *Black Fiction:*

New Studies in the Afro-American Novel since 1945. Ed. Robert Lee. New York: Barnes and Noble, 1980: 136–148.

McGee, Patric. *Ishmael Reed and the Ends of Race*. New York: St. Martin's Press, 1997.

Melnick, Jeffrey. " 'What You Lookin' At': Ishmael Reed's *Reckless Eyeballing*." *The Black Columbiad: Defining Moments in African American Literature and Culture*. Ed. Werner Sollors. Cambridge, MA: Harvard University Press, 1994: 298–311.

Nazareth, Peter. *In the Trickster Tradition: The Novels of Andrew Salkey, Francis Ebejar, and Ishmael Reed*. London: Bogle-L'Ouverture Press, 1994.

Wallace, Michele. "Ishmael Reed's Female Troubles." *Invisibility Blues: From Pop to Theory*. New York: Verso, 1990: 146–154.

Weixlmann, Joe. "African American Deconstruction of the Novel in the Work of Ishmael Reed and Clarence Major." *MELUS* 17.4 (Winter 1991–1992): 57–79.

JEWELL PARKER RHODES
(1954–)

Pierre-Damien Mvuyekure

BIOGRAPHY

Jewell Parker Rhodes was born in Pittsburgh, where she lived until she was in the third grade and then moved to California. When she was fifteen, she went back to Pittsburgh to live with her grandmother. But Rhodes very much grew up alone, because her mother left home when she was very young. This is reflected in *Voodoo Dreams: A Novel of Marie Laveau*, her first novel. In an interview with Barbara C. Rhodes, Jewell Parker Rhodes points out that when she started writing the novel about Marie Laveau, "it dawned on me that I was writing about my own relationship to my grandmother and to my mother" (598).

Because Rhodes was hooked on television when she was growing up, her dream was to become an actress. Then, when she attended Carnegie-Mellon Hall University, she majored in theater with emphasis on creative writing; she holds a doctorate of arts degree in creative writing from there. Although she was always writing stories, she did not know that she would become a writer. But everything changed when she discovered Gayl Jones'* novel *Corregidora*, a book that inspired her to become a writer—John's incestuous relations with three Maries in *Voodoo Dreams* are shaped after Corregidora's relations to Ursa Corregidora's Great-Grandma, Grandma, and Ma.

Other literary influences of Rhodes' include Zora Neale Hurston, who, besides Ishmael Reed,* has probably done more research on, and embraced, voodoo than anybody else in North America, and Toni Morrison,* whose work Rhodes is so fond of that her next novel is to revise Cholly Breedlove of *The Bluest Eye* into a more positive black male. In Barbara Rhodes' interview, Jewell Parker Rhodes adds that if she "could one day do one sliver of what she [Toni Morrison] accomplished in *Beloved*, [she] would be very happy" (602). In addition, Rhodes has acknowledged that her being "plot-oriented" and having the "sensibility of just telling and having a convoluted plot—perhaps too convoluted" comes from Charles Dickens (602).

More important perhaps is the fact that Rhodes writes from the African American traditions, especially the traditions of voodoo and African-based metaphysics, which noninformed critics have called "magic realism." This is clearly demonstrated in her use of voodoo gods and goddesses from the African pantheon, as well as the Voodoo Queen of New Orleans in *Voodoo Dreams*, while in *Magic City* she uses necromancy, a technique whereby the living communicate with the dead. The confluence of these African-based metaphysical concepts, coupled with African dance aesthetic, the Negro spirituals and blues, allows Rhodes to deconstruct the conventional format of the historical novel.

MAJOR WORKS AND THEMES

As the title suggests, *Voodoo Dreams: A Novel of Marie Laveau* is a historical novel that celebrates Marie Laveau, the famous New Orleans mambo or voodoo priestess, whose life has been woven in myths and legends. In the author's note, Rhodes posits that she wove into Marie Laveau's story "a matrilineal line of knowledge and power" and that Marie's quest for self-re/discovery becomes "a metaphor for a larger process of rediscovery of lost [African] traditions and lost vision" (436). While this is true to a certain extent, *Voodoo Dreams* deals with several other themes, including sexuality and power, voodoo and Catholicism, black and white, South and North, and three generations of Marie versus John. All these themes spiral outward from the center, Marie and her African pantheon, via voodoo possessions.

An analysis of the structure of *Voodoo Dreams* is instrumental in order to understand not only the character of Marie and her relations to other characters but also how each theme relates to other themes in the novel. First, the text of *Voodoo Dreams* contains italicized newspaper articles and journal entries from Louis DeLavier, whose purpose is to provide objectivity to the novel and thereby sharply contrast with the italicized passages about dreams, ancestral visits, and voodoo possessions. Second, *Voodoo Dreams* unexpectedly starts and ends with the same section called "The Middle, 1822"—both sections showcase how Marie Laveau lets the python strangle John—which spirals from this center to two sections called "The Beginning, 1812" and "Another Beginning, 1819." The opening italicized passage, excerpted from Louis DeLavier's journal, explains that *Voodoo Dreams* starts by the middle because "the middle is the beginning": *"Everything spirals outward from the center. Lies, pain, and loss haunt the future as well as the past"* (3). Also in the Epilogue section, one of Marie Laveau's last statements to Louis DeLavier is that *"Life is a spiral. Everything starts over, spiraling, outward from the center"* (431). In the light of the spiral metaphor, each of the four sections is accompanied by the drawing of a spiral encapsulated inside a square, with the spiral spiraling outward from the center.

That a spiral is linked to the concept of time is significant insofar as in African philosophy and voodoo religion, time past is time present and future, which allows one to move freely from one time to another. This explains how in *Voodoo Dreams* Marie interacts with her dead mother and African deities. Moreover, the spiral reminds one of a snake that recoils from its head to the tail; this is no trivial matter, because the only voodoo god that possesses Marie Laveau the most throughout the novel is Damballah, the African deity of fecundity and creativity, represented by a snake—John has given Marie a python to use during the possessions by Damballah. Equally interesting is the fact that voodoo possessions are at the center of *Voodoo Dreams*; when people are possessed or ridden by spirits in voodoo, the possession moves from inside to outside. That is, what people consider to be the signs of possession, like dancing and doing "strange things," are an outward manifestation of the interaction between the possessed and the spirit inside the body.

Marie is a dynamic character who moves from Marie in Teché, "bayou of snakes," to Marie Laveau, the Voodooienne of New Orleans. Although the journey from Teché to New Orleans is intended to find a husband for Marie, the latter has something else in mind. When Marie accepts to marry Jacques, she simply wants the "dark man" to come on the wedding day and tell her who she is by telling her about Maman, voodoo, and "the voices" in her dreams. Clearly, the true quest for self-discovery begins when Marie leaves Jacques, her husband, for John, "the dark man," thus unleashing a long power struggle that ends in John's deserved death.

Just as he had done with Grandmère and Maman before, so does John see Marie as an object whereby to gain sexual power through rape and brutal lovemaking, as well as financial power through voodoo possessions, charms, and magic potions. Not only does he order her to cover herself so that Ribaud, the drummer, does not covet "what is his," but also throughout the novel he uses lovemaking to both hurt Marie and express his power. After one of the ceremonies of Marie's possession by Damballah, John is so jealous and angry that his gentle lovemaking turns into slamming Marie's head against the headboard screaming, " 'Tricks. Tricks.' He bit her nipples, then thrust himself inside her. 'Remember—I am the King' " (158). Despite the abuse and bruises, Marie stays with John because she knows that Damballah is teaching her the knowledge of power.

The balance of power shifts, however, thanks to the possessions by Damballah and Marie's discovery of African religion. That is, the more Marie learns about African voodoo gods and goddesses such as Ogun, Legba, Ezili, Agué, and several other deities, the more spiritually powerful she becomes. Through these possessions she earns the name of Marie Laveau, the Voodooienne, thus completing the connection to Maman and Grandmère. The quest for self, power, and Damballah climaxes when Marie plunges into the water and then walks "*on the surface of water as if it were earth.*" The novel makes it clear that in the water Marie and Damballah have become one, for in the water, Damballah has "shown her how to reconnect herself to both a past and a future. Time spirals outward from the center, and the center was Damballah, who could make spirits—and the spirit in her—whole" (307). Additionally, it is reported that Marie feels "a new light of being" and "a light inside her, guiding her, if she let it, to peace and safety" (307).

Consequently, whereas Marie starts focusing on her exuberant followers and ignoring John, the latter attempts his last control by lashing at whoever is "near his imaginary line of safety for Marie" (307). Walking on water is also a very important event in *Voodoo Dreams*, not simply because it makes Marie Laveau a Christ figure—there are several other instances—but also because it is part of the mythmaking about Marie Laveau. Because John has abused three generations of voodoo women and is threatening to molest Marie Laveau's daughter, Marie Laveau's quest for self-discovery and African lost traditions comes to a denouement when Marie Laveau lets the python suffocate John, thus ending the tragedy of three Maries and ensuring that the power (of voodoo) is "*passed down through the generations*" (436).

In *Magic City*, Rhodes' latest novel, Rhodes unearths one of the most hidden and suppressed events in American history: the 1920 Tulsa riot during which the National Guard bombed Greenwood, a thriving black neighborhood, from the air. Although *Magic City* is a fictional account of the bombing of Greenwood, and Rhodes disclaims that Joseph David Samuels and Mary Keane bear any resemblance to Dick Rowland and Sarah Page—Dick Rowland was accused of allegedly molesting Sarah Page in an elevator—it nevertheless goes to the heart of the questions that incited the Tulsa riot, such as why and how blacks migrated to Oklahoma and why whites allowed a black community to establish itself but disallowed its economic success and empowerment.

These underlying themes are woven into more apparent themes of magic, dream, escape, and survival, as clearly announced in two epigraphs from Dunn's *Western Travel Guide* and the Negro spirituals. An excerpt from Dunn's work refers to Tulsa as the "magic city" and a "dream land" where oil spews from the ground. As for the Negro spiritual, it asks Moses to tell Pharaoh in Egyptland to let the enslaved people go. Not only does *Magic City* contain two characters, Joe Samuels and Mary Keane, who daydream and receive visions from the dead, but it also explores the common fate of blacks and Jews as they face the Ku Klux Klan (KKK)—throughout the novel, Joe Samuels is identified with David Reubens, a Jew who was lynched because he was fighting for the workers' rights. Furthermore, because of oil Douglass Abraham Samuels stole the land from his father, sold it to Ambrose, and became the first black banker in Tulsa—Joe learns about this dark story through the conversation with his dead brother, Henry Samuels.

Joe Samuels has preferred to shine shoes in Ambrose Building over working in his father's bank. During one of their verbal fights he storms out of the house and heads to Ambrose's building, where he meets Mary Keane in the elevator—Mary Keane operates the elevator, and the washroom for blacks is on the fourteenth floor. When Mary screams in the elevator, everybody immediately concludes that Joe Samuels has raped her. Ironically, only few hours before the elevator incident Mary Keane was raped by a white man, Dell, who hoped to force her into marriage.

Clearly, magic, escape, and survival are so essential to the text that the first two sentences of *Magic City* point out that Joe Samuels has decided not only to stop dreaming but also "to stop dreaming about leaving Tulsa, of discovering new horizons streaked with magic" (1). Thus, the opening sentences foreshadow the events in the last chapter, in which Joe Samuels, despite the threat of the KKK, leaves the train and the protection of Sheriff Clay and decides to stay in Tulsa to rebuild Deep Greenwood from the ashes. This parallels the actual Greenwood in the sense that the latter has, like the phoenix, risen from its own ashes. Also, when Joe Samuels is reluctant to believe that Houdini's ghost is talking to him in the cell, Houdini responds, " '*Magic is survival, escape. Moses' magic turned a rod into a snake, transformed the Nile into blood, and freed the Israelites. The magic of all time, Joe*' " (152–153).

Also, the concept of magic and escape finds its true meaning in several images of the train and its associated imagery. In the aesthetic of the blues, the train is a powerful metaphor for journey and possibilities. *Magic City* contains a blues musician, Lying Man, who plays the black folk song "Run, Nigger, Run," a leitmotif throughout the novel, a song that constantly echoes a slave's escape from slave patrols—in the novel there are references to "patterrollers."

CRITICAL RECEPTION

Rhodes is a new writer, and therefore the critical body of her work has not yet built up. All reviewers agree that Rhodes is an excellent writer who has an excellent command of form and knows how to combine oral traditions, storytelling, and history. In his review of *Voodoo Dreams*, Houston Baker posits not only that the novel displays "a splendid and deft narrative style" but also that Rhodes "ably demonstrates that she possesses as much conjuring literary ability as some of the most outstanding (and more frequently reviewed) writers in the United States" (158).

Barbara C. Rhodes has praised Rhodes' craft, which "emerges most visibly in the structure and format of the novel" (501), but has faulted Rhodes for not only demonizing the historical Dr. John but also ignoring the "rich mix of dialects and speech patterns of the indigenous people of the bayou" (503).

BIBLIOGRAPHY

Works by Jewell Parker Rhodes

Novels

Voodoo Dreams: A Novel of Marie Laveau. New York: Picador USA, 1993.
Magic City. New York: HarperCollins, 1997.

Short Stories

"Long Distances." *Peregrine* 7 (Summer 1989): 27–54.

"Marie Laveau, Voodoo Queen." *Feminist Studies* 16.2 (Summer 1990): 331–344.

"Enough Rides." *Callaloo* 14.1 (1991): 12–19.

"Caroline Seeds." *The Raven Chronicles* 2 (Summer 1992): 15–20.

"Block Party." *All Together, Heath Middle Literature*. Washington, DC: Heath, 1995a: 96–101.

"Mirror, Mirror." *Bakumin* 5.2 (Winter 1995b): 75–93.

Studies of Jewell Parker Rhodes

Baker, Houston A., Jr. Rev. of *Voodoo Dreams: A Novel of Marie Laveau*. *African American Review* 29.1 (Spring 1995): 157–160.

Handman, Fran. Rev. of *Voodoo Dreams: A Novel of Marie Laveau*. *The New York Review of Books* (1994): 24.

Rhodes, Barbara. Rev. of *Voodoo Dreams: A Novel of Marie Laveau*. *CLA Journal* 39.4 (1996): 498–503.

Rhodes, Barbara, and Allen Ramsey. "An Interview with Jewell Parker Rhodes." *African American Review* 29.4 (Winter 1995): 593–603.

DORI SANDERS
(1934–   )

Nicholyn Hutchinson

BIOGRAPHY

Discovering biographical information about Dori Sanders is a difficult task because Sanders refuses to talk about herself in any formulated manner. Her refusal is not a conscious one borne out of a need for privacy but is a consequence of her lapsing into a rhapsodic tale, which often may or may not be related to herself. Ignited by the spark of a word, her memories become stories themselves, and one consequently forgets that the conversation has turned. However, if one asks Sanders about farming, then there is a wealth of information to be had. The daughter of a high school teacher and a farmer, Dori Sanders was born on her father's farm in York County, South Carolina, and still lives and works there today.

Unlike many of her siblings, Sanders has spent the majority of her life on the farm, instead of leaving the familial nest for college. While she did work temporarily as a banquet manager and often found herself scribbling lines for stories on dinner napkins until a coworker suggested she write with a more serious purpose, she decided to return to the family farm. Having bought the land in 1915, Sanders' father became one of the county's first black landowning farmers, and Dori Sanders continues this tradition of firsts by being the first published novelist who also runs a farm stand alongside a Carolina highway. For Sanders, farming and selling the fruits and vegetables she grows on the farm are as important to her as her writing, if not more so. The two of them are inexorably connected. Referring to the relationship of farming to her literary career, Sanders has said, "I don't think I could write without it. It's the wellspring for my writing" (Walters 14).

MAJOR WORKS AND THEMES

Because farming is the "wellspring" for Dori Sanders' writing, it is unsurprising that the majority of her fictional work to date is also related to rural life in the South. Sanders' first novel, *Clover*, is set in a small African American southern community named Round Hill, South Carolina. The novel's heroine, Clover, is a ten-year-old black child who is forced to live with her new stepmother, Sara Kate, when her father (Gaten Hill) is killed in a car accident hours after his marriage to her. While Clover and Sara Kate have to struggle to come to terms with their new family situation, it is complicated by Sara Kate's ethnicity: she is white. Because of her "foreignness," the Round Hill community and Gaten's family are distrustful of Sara Kate and worry about her ability to properly raise Clover. Although the two initially have problems adjusting to each other culturally, Clover and Sara Kate find themselves forming an unlikely alliance. As Clover grows to love her stepmother, she finds herself torn between the family, where everyone tells her she belongs (her father's family), and the one in which she is beginning to feel the love shared between a mother and a daughter. Eventually, after a crisis causes Clover's family to reassess their opinion of Sara Kate, the Hill family accepts her and learns the lesson that Clover has already learned about the underlying bond of humanity that transcends race.

While Dori Sanders often observes that it is not her intention to write about racial matters, ironically, the subject of race pervades *Clover*. For example, at the novel's beginning, Clover finds herself faced with the problem of whether to wear black or white to her father's funeral. Consequently, Sanders metaphorically sets up the conflict that structurally becomes the novel's center. Throughout the novel there are other examples of this black–white cultural conflict. Sara Kate is culturally disadvantaged in the predominantly black Round Hill and, because she buys her food instead of growing it, she is considered snobbish. Thus, these minor differences illustrate *Clover*'s major theme, as simplistic as it may seem, which is racial tolerance and understanding in the face of racial conflict. While the author was a product of the segregated Old South, Clover is the daughter of the integrated New South, which is symbolized in the novel by the interracial marriage. When Sara Kate and Clover struggle to adjust themselves to their new situation and emerge triumphant, their reconciliation becomes symbolic of Sanders' own hope for the future of the South.

In her second and most recently published novel, *Her Own Place*, Sanders tells the story of a woman spanning over fifty years of her life. Set in Rising Ridge, South Carolina, the novel follows the trials and tribulations of Mae Lee Barnes as she tries to make sense of the changing world around her. At the beginning of the novel, Mae Lee is a young, recently wed war bride who has bought her own farm and land through a lot of hard work and hope. When her husband returns from the war as a changed man, her life course is changed forever. He abruptly leaves her, and Mae Lee is forced to fend for herself and their five children. For the rest of the novel, Mae Lee overcomes numerous obstacles as the passage of time is marked by brief references to such historical moments as John F. Kennedy's death and the Vietnam War. Just as Mae Lee struggles to cultivate the farm so that the money earned from the yielded crops will feed her family, she also struggles to ensure that her children have everything they need to become successful and productive members of society. Throughout *Her Own Place*, Mae Lee measures her success in terms of the success of her children. She is as proud of their accomplishments as if they were hers. Like the vegetables on her farm, Mae Lee's children are her winning crop. When her children grow up and leave home to attend college and eventually raise families of their own, Mae Lee moves from the farm to the outskirts of a newly built suburb. Trading in her farm for a small garden beside her new home, she embarks on a new passage in her life when she begins working for a local hospital. At the novel's conclusion, there is the intimation of a blooming romance with her boarder, Mr. Owens.

In *Her Own Place*, Sanders presents a portrait of a black matriarch that seldom is seen in African American fiction. Instead of the domineering black mother, Sanders' Mae Lee is so nurturing and supportive of her family that she almost seems passive, even in the way she allows change to happen to her instead of vice versa. However, precisely in this seeming passivity lies the strength of Mae Lee and the novel. Like *Clover, Her Own Place* is, as its title implies, a story about adjustment, which is one of Sanders' major themes. By placing her down-home characters in the position of dealing with the fickle hand of fate, she effectively creates unlikely heroines. While *Her Own Place* lacks any dramatic action, it is interesting to follow Mae Lee's journey through life as she, like the author, dots her life's happenings with clever witticisms and memorable anecdotes. However, their shared love of anecdotes is not the only similarity between Mae Lee and Sanders. Sanders also uses the novel as a forum to discuss her favorite interests—farming and the farming community. One cannot help but draw a connection between how Mae Lee leads her life and how she runs her farm. Life on the farm becomes a metaphoric reminder for how we do not always reap what we sow in life and how, because of this fact, we must be stronger. Through her powerful narrative voice, Sanders not only draws memorable characters and portraits of southern life but also teaches her readers a valuable lesson.

CRITICAL RECEPTION

Currently, critical analysis of Dori Sanders' work is lacking, and the only major discussions of her work have been book reviews. Many of the reviews of both her literary endeavors discuss the warmth of her novels and her storytelling ability. Sanders is often credited for her realistic use of vernacular, her eye for the physical landscape of the South, and colorful characters. While the majority of the reviews on Sanders' work appear to discuss mostly her narrative style, one of major criticisms of her work revolves around the simplicity of her plots. Addressing what she sees as the predictability and the lack of excitement in *Her Own Place*, one reviewer observes, "Perhaps someone is willing to pay . . . for the privilege of reading something that feels good and leads nowhere" (Smith 48).

Related to this idea of simplicity, another criticism of Sanders' work is what some reviewers have characterized as her lack of character development. One of the primary points in this argument is that, although Sanders allows her characters to evolve on some level, she neglects to give either the characters or her readers any real insight into how experiences really affect them. Of *Clover*, Ursula Hegi observes how "Sanders' major characters lack . . . richness. They seem vague. Their experiences affect them, but only on superficial levels" (2). Hegi feels that ultimately the characters' lack of insight prevents the novel from being a successful one. However, despite such criticism, readers find Sanders' novels, as Patricia Smith puts it in her review of *Her Own Place*, "so warm, so comforting, so principled, homey and morally upright that it would be a shame not to love [them]" (48).

BIBLIOGRAPHY

Works by Dori Sanders

Clover. Chapel Hill, NC: Algonquin Books, 1990.
Her Own Place. Chapel Hill, NC: Algonquin Books, 1993.

Studies of Dori Sanders

Egerton, Judith. Review of *Clover*. *Gannet News Service*. 14 May 1990.
Hegi, Ursula. Review of *Clover*. *Los Angeles Times*. 15 April 1990: 2.
Smith, Patricia. Review of *Her Own Place*. *Boston Globe*. 28 May 1993: 48.
Stabiner, Karen. Review of *Her Own Place*. *Los Angeles Times*. 6 June 1993: 6.
Sullivan, Jack. Review of *Clover*. *New York Times*. 20 May 1990: 30.
Walters, Louise Shaper. Review of *Her Own Place*. *The Christian Science Monitor*. 24 June 1993: 14.
White, Evelyn C. Review of *Clover*. *The San Francisco Chronicle*. 18 April 1990: E4.

SAPPHIRE
(1950–)

Tracey Walters

BIOGRAPHY

Poet, performance artist, and novelist, Sapphire was born on August 4, 1950, and grew up on military bases with her army-enlisted parents and three siblings. Sapphire experienced a tumultuous early life. At the age of approximately three or four Sapphire was sexually abused by her father—a fact that she blocked from memory until her early thirties. When Sapphire was thirteen, her mother abandoned her family, and shortly thereafter, Sapphire dropped out of school. At twenty-one Sapphire moved to San Francisco. Intrigued by the New Age movement, Sapphire changed her name from Ramona to Sapphire. She also took premed classes at San Francisco City College and studied dance. While in San Francisco, Sapphire became acquainted with the poetry of Don L. Lee, Ntozake Shange,* Sonia Sanchez, and Jayne Cortez, writers who would greatly influence Sapphire's poetry.

Before long Sapphire left California and went to New York to follow a professional dancing career. Unfortunately, like many aspiring dancers, Sapphire made ends meet by using her dancing talents as a stripper, an experience that is later described in her poetry. In 1983, Sapphire graduated with a bachelor's degree from the City University of New York and later earned her M.F.A. from Brooklyn College. While at Brooklyn College Sapphire worked under the tutelage of poet Allen Ginsberg. Ginsberg's influence on Sapphire is most noted in Sapphire's poems, which use abrasive language and controversial themes. Prior to the publication of her poetry, Sapphire performed her poems on the stage and in poetry clubs. In 1987, she published her first book of poetry, *Meditations on the Rainbow*, and in 1994, her second book, *American Dreams*. Sapphire also published her poetry in texts such as *Common Lives/Lesbian Lives: A Lesbian*

Quarterly, Sinister Wisdom, War after War, and *The New Fuck You: Adventures in Lesbian Reading.*

For several years Sapphire taught reading and writing to teens and adults in Harlem and the Bronx. As a teacher Sapphire listened to firsthand accounts of students who had been sexually abused by their parents and pregnant before they reached their teens. Sapphire's novel *PUSH* is a composite of the women Sapphire encountered in her classroom and in her neighborhood. *PUSH* is attributed to propelling Sapphire to national acclaim. The novel's provocative themes and experimental, artistic style made Sapphire a target for reviewers, who both praised and condemned the novel.

Sapphire currently resides in Brooklyn, where she continues to write and perform her poetry and prose.

MAJOR WORKS AND THEMES

Meditations on the Rainbow (1987) captures the spirit of Sapphire's fiery diatribes. As a black, lesbian, feminist, and survivor of abuse, Sapphire's early poems reflect her passionate anger against a society that tolerates racism, homophobia, sexism, classism, global warfare, and capitalism—all themes Sapphire returns to. *Meditations* comprises seven "colorful" poems: "yellow," "red," "black," "lavender," "wite," "green," and "blue." Each poem deals with the poet's perception of color and how these colors relate to the world around her. In poems like "green," "lavender," and "blue" Sapphire indicts capitalism and imperialism, celebrates lesbianism, and heralds the blues. Hence, "green" describes the imperialistic notions of white Americans who strip others of their land and then kill the land with nuclear warfare. Sapphire says we must save the land from destruction; "I want the world to live" (54), she writes.

On the other end of the spectrum, "lavender" describes the trials of lesbians and homosexuals who are ostracized by a society that would like them to hide their homosexuality. The poem "blue" is a melancholy, bittersweet blues that reflects the black American nightmare of rape, racism, stolen music, and stolen dreams. Like the blues, this poem takes readers on a roller coaster of emotions that both please and anger us. Essentially, *Meditations* reflects Sapphire's ability to couple poetic imagery with social commentary.

American Dreams (1994) is an ironically titled collection of poetry and prose that reflect American dreams deferred. The title poem, "American Dreams," asserts that America is not the happy-go-lucky world depicted in 1970s television shows like *Donna Reed.* Sapphire contends that as long as there is intraracism, murder, and global warfare, the American Dream will never come to fruition.

Other poems in *American Dreams* highlight the nightmares of young children who are physically and sexually abused by their parents. Often colored with profanity and graphic, violent images, these poems seek to evoke images of pain, suffering, and horror. Short prose narratives such as "Reflections from Glass Breaking" and poems "Are You Ready to Rock?," "in my father's house," and "boys love baseball (or a quarter buys a lot in 1952)" use a child's voice to describe how young girls and boys are victims of incestuous rape. "Mickey Mouse Was a Scorpio" (which also appears in Queer Press Collective, ed., *Loving in Fear: An Anthology of Lesbian and Gay Survivors of Childhood Sexual Abuse* [Toronto: Queer Press, 1991] under the title "Crooked Man") illustrates, by using images of childhood toys and nursery rhymes hardened into images of perversion and confusion, how sexually abused children are stripped of their childhood innocence and psychologically damaged forever.

Other poems in this collection provide social commentary about the sexual exploitation and abuse of young women. For example, "poem for jennifer, marla, tawana & me" retells the stories of several women who, during the late 1980s, suffered violent crimes at the hands of men. Sapphire describes how in each case women were blamed for their assaults. She asserts that "a woman must be a good girl, virgin, myth of a thing in order to be raped. any other kind of woman brought it on herself, did it to herself, it was her own fault, her own fault" (111). Many of the poems in *American Dreams* have also appeared in other anthologies, including *Women on Women: An Anthology of American Lesbian Short Fiction, High Risk 2: Writings on Sex, Death & Subversion*, and *Critical Condition: Women on the Edge of Violence*. While the poems in *American Dreams* reflect subjects that are important for analysis and discussion, Sapphire's often brutal depictions of sex and violence might discourage sensitive readers.

Sapphire's first novel, *PUSH* (1996), tells the story of Claireece Precious Jones, a sixteen-year-old HIV-positive Harlem mother of two who struggles to find her place in a society that continuously fails her. But there is hope. Despite the fact that Precious' father impregnates her first at twelve and again at sixteen, Precious is a fighter who overcomes the forces that nearly destroy her. In order for us to view the world through Precious' eyes, Sapphire uses an authentic urban dialect to capture Precious' voice.

While Precious' story is horrific, it is not new to the African American literary canon. Both Toni Morrison's* *The Bluest Eye* and Alice Walker's* *The Color Purple* deal with issues of sexual abuse and fathers impregnating their daughters. There are obvious similarities between *PUSH, The Bluest Eye*, and *The Color Purple*. For example, like Morrison's character Pecola, Precious believes blond hair and blue eyes signify beauty. At one point, Precious thinks her mother allows her father to abuse her because she is dark-skinned, overweight, and unattractive. Precious thinks, "She ain' come in here and say . . . Git off Precious like that! Can't you see Precious is a beautiful chile like white chile in magazines or on toilet paper wrapper. Precious is a blue-eye skinny chile whose hair is long braids" (64).

Similarities between Precious and Walker's character Celie are evident when Precious goes to school and begins to write in a dialogue journal. Like Celie, Precious learns that through writing one can love her self and be free of psychological oppression. Ironically, Precious' teacher instructs her class to read *The Color Purple*, a text, for obvious reasons, to which Precious relates. When Sapphire goes to school, she changes her life. With the support and encouragement of her teacher Ms. Rain and her other classmates, Precious realizes that knowledge is power, at one point asserting, "School gonna help me get out dis house" (35).

When Precious discovers she has AIDS, she starts having difficulty thinking and writing clearly, and her story drops into short passages of stream of consciousness. Fortunately, the love and support of Precious' teacher and friends prompt her to accept her HIV status and work toward her dreams of becoming a poet, rapper, or artist. The novel concludes with a series of poems by Precious and three short life stories of Precious' classmates who were also raped and molested. Sapphire presents the classmates' stories to reinforce the fact that Precious' story is one of many. However, these stories are underdeveloped and may have served better within the body of the story or in a separate text altogether.

CRITICAL RECEPTION

As a relatively new artist, Sapphire has yet to receive much critical assessment. To date, her work has received attention mostly in book reviews, few of which are useful for serious analysis of the texts. Until the appearance of Terri L. Jewell's entry, *Meditations* was virtually ignored by reviewers and critics alike. Jewell provides insightful analysis of the text. Jewell remarks, "*Meditations on the Rainbow* reads like one long stream-of-consciousness poem that is broken up into sections of color. . . . Sapphire uses clear, vivid language that impact the reader line by line" (504).

Fortunately, *American Dreams* has earned more critical attention than *Meditations*. Reviewers have noted Sapphire's cynical view of American society and abundant use of violent images. As such, Sapphire's poetry is often compared to the poetry of Allen Ginsberg. For example, Whitney Scott contends, "These harsh but sometimes beautiful pieces may be seen as barbaric yawp howled Ginsberg-like into the wind, but their words and the images they evoke are hard to miss" (895).

PUSH has also elicited a fair number of reviews. Some critics have observed the comparative similarities to Morrison's *The Bluest Eye* and Walker's *The Color Purple*. For example, Judith Lewis writes: "Precious is a lot like Celie the battered wife of Alice Walker's *The Color Purple*. . . . [I]t's as if Sapphire ripped Celie out of a Southern fairy tale and made her face up to real life in Harlem" (42). Other critics of the novel discuss Sapphire's use of dialect and ineffective narrative strategies. For example, William Powers states that "at one point . . . the narration mysteriously switches from Precious's yeasty vernacular to a sophisticated third-person voice, and then back again, to no good effect" (B1). Jewelle Gomez comments on Sapphire's failure to maintain a consistent narrative structure: "Unfortunately, the impact of the story is short-circuited by real editing failures. . . . The narrative voice slips from first person to third, then back to first person. If there is a stylistic reason, it's not apparent" (60). Gomez also comments on the text's contrived ending: "Poems and journal entries written for Blue Rain's class by Precious and other students seem extraneous; they don't amplify the story and are not integrated into the novel in a way that fills out the characters" (60).

Writing about Sapphire's experimentation with dialect, Rosemary Mahoney describes Sapphire's dialect as "halting dialect, a hobbled, minimal English that defies the convention of spelling and usage and dispenses with all verbal decorum" (9). Moreover, Mahoney argues that "Precious' persona swiftly overrides whatever irritation the reader may feel at having to puzzle through her not always convincingly misshapen words" (9). Similarly, Gomez applauds Sapphire's play with dialect: "Sapphire's carefully reproduced dialect draws the reader into the relentless, claustrophobic sorrow Precious inhabits. If readers will float with the dialect, even begin by reading it aloud, the rhythm of Sapphire's work will quickly sweep them up" (60).

BIBLIOGRAPHY

Works by Sapphire

Meditations on the Rainbow. New York: Crystal Bananas Press, 1987.
American Dreams. New York: High Risk Books/Serpent's Tail, 1994; New York: Vintage Books, 1996a.
PUSH. New York: Alfred A. Knopf, 1996b.

Studies of Sapphire

DeLombard, Jeannine. Review of *American Dreams. The New York Times Book Review* (Feb. 27, 1994): 26.
Gomez, Jewelle. Review of *PUSH. The Advocate* (June 11, 1996): 59–60.
Ingraham, Janet. Review of *PUSH. Library Journal* 121.10 (June 1, 1996): 152.
Jewell, Terri L. "Sapphire." *Contemporary Lesbian Writers of the United States. A Bio-Bibliographical Critical Sourcebook.* Ed. Sandra Pollack and Denise D. Knight. Westport, CT: Greenwood Press, 1993. 503–6.
Lewis, Judith. "Hard Times in Harlem." Review of *PUSH. LA Weekly* (July 19–25, 1996): 42.
Mahoney, Rosemary. "Don't Nobody Want Me. Don't Nobody Need Me." Review of *PUSH. The New York Times Book Review* (July 7, 1996): 9.
Marvel, Mark. "Sapphire's Big Push." Review of *PUSH. Interview* 26.6 (June 1996): 28+.
Powers, William. "Sapphire's Raw Gem." Review of *PUSH. Washington Post* (Aug. 6, 1996): B1.
Scott, Whitney. Review of *American Dreams. Booklist* 90.10 (Jan. 15, 1994): 894–95.

GIL SCOTT-HERON
(1949–   )

Suzanne Hotte Massa

BIOGRAPHY

Gil Scott-Heron was born on 1 April 1949, in Chicago but spent his early childhood with his grandmother in Jackson, Tennessee. He later moved to the Bronx
in New York City to live with his mother, where he attended high school at the
prestigious Fieldstone School. He did not meet his father, a professional soccer
player and librarian, until Scott-Heron was an adult. As a young child he began
to exhibit his interest in music and writing. Not only was he playing the piano,
but he was writing detective stories as well.

After high school he attended Lincoln University in southeastern Pennsylvania. The small, private, rural, black college served as the model for Sutton
University in his novel *The Nigger Factory*. Scott-Heron, who had long been a
fan of Langston Hughes, received the Lincoln University Langston Hughes Creative Writing Award in 1968. During his interim at Lincoln University, Scott-
Heron met some of the people who greatly influenced his writing and musical
career. Gylan Kain, a poet, and Steve Cannon, a novelist, were on the faculty.
Writers Ishmael Reed* and Larry Neal visited the campus as lecturers. Brian
Jackson, who later collaborated with Scott-Heron on musical ventures, was a
fellow student at Lincoln.

At the age of twenty, Scott-Heron published a collection of poems, *Small Talk
at 125th & Lenox*, and his first novel, *The Vulture*. He used his poems from *Small
Talk at 125th & Lenox* for the lyrics of his first album, which was released that
year as well. Scott-Heron's early work was a commentary on the social injustice
that permeates American life, particularly for African Americans. As he matured,
so did the breadth of his ideas, stretching to include not only the plight of

oppressed peoples worldwide but some of the manifestations of those oppressions, such as drug abuse and alcoholism.

Following his early success in publishing, Scott-Heron attended Johns Hopkins University, where he earned his master's degree in creative writing. From 1972 until 1976 he was a creative writing teacher at Federal City College in Washington, D.C. Scott-Heron continued to work on blending his poetry with music. During the late 1960s, in a climate of rampant social and political activism, Scott-Heron's searing lyrics and hard-driving jazz-funk melodies won him both recognition and popularity as a musician. Determined to express his ideas, he found his niche in the ancient communication medium of the oral tradition.

MAJOR WORKS AND THEMES

Gil Scott-Heron's first book, *The Vulture*, is an exposé of the drug culture in Chelsea—an African American and Puerto Rican neighborhood in New York City. The book opens with the apparent murder of John Lee, a notorious drug pusher, and unfolds by acquainting us with four characters whose lives are connected in some way to John Lee's. During the twelve months prior to Lee's death, we learn a little bit about the ideas and actions of each of the young men. Spade, at the ripe age of eighteen, is becoming a collector of profits from the pushers on the street. Seventeen-year-old Junior Jones aspires to be someone just like Spade. Afro, on the other hand, is a college educated man who is trying to improve the world of his black brothers and sisters through appropriate and effective education. As a member of BAMBU (Black American Men for Black Unity), Afro attempts to introduce a culture-specific curriculum in black schools, but unwittingly gets involved in the ongoing war staged by the drug bosses. Finally, there is Ivan Quinn (IQ), who is renowned for his ability to quote lines from classic literature in spite of his pot-smoking habit. All four are under the age of twenty-one. Although each of the four characters possesses the motive to kill Lee, the novel's surprise denouement exonerates them all.

In Scott-Heron's untethered, radical voice, he boldly dramatizes the desperate lives of people in the ghetto: "We all used each other. The women used us for sex, and we used them the same way. A double cross with no winner, because all the participants were aware of the swindle" (36). By introducing a wide range of characters, Scott-Heron exposes the diversity within the Chelsea community and, ostensibly, other neighborhoods like it. Ironically, the diversity within this community is a microcosm for America at large. The novel's strongest asset lies in its ability to eradicate ghetto stereotypes. Spade, Junior, Afro, and IQ, while members of the same community, are drastically different human beings. Spade has compromised his morality for the financial security guaranteed by his connection with the drug dealers. Junior glorifies that lifestyle, so does not comprehend its inherent evil. Afro, a young idealist who is committed to improving the quality of life in Chelsea, promotes education for and by African Americans. He proudly wears a dashiki as a sign of cultural self-assertion: " 'It's called a dashiki, brother. I think they're better than the white man's shirts' " (143). As a staunch supporter of black nationalism, he ultimately takes a job in the dashiki store. IQ, whose voice is remarkably similar to Scott-Heron's sarcastic and biting revolutionary musical voice, is an intellectual. His mind is in constant overdrive, assessing and reassessing the meaning of every encounter.

The murder mystery depicts people whose lives are shaped by the stress of oppression. In short, it is a coming-of-age story from the perspective of underprivileged Americans. In the Chelsea culture money is a very attractive lure; it is so attractive that the method of acquisition is often unimportant. For African Americans and Puerto Ricans with little chance of satisfactory employment, a career in almost any branch of drug peddling is lucrative. Like a vulture, the boss of all the dealers preys upon all of the many victims who perform the menial tasks of delivering drugs and collecting payment. The vulture is concerned only with his profit and not the wasting of the countless lives that are negatively affected by drug use and abuse. Spade is fully aware of his role in the business, recognizing that his cog, like every other cog in the wheel, is guilty of the exploitation of his people:

The sad thing was that I was not much better off. I never touched the skag that the junkies were ridin' on, but I touched the money that they got together by mugging and stealing and selling their women's bodies . . . I was just another link in the chain that was wrapped around the body of so many slaves. (54)

Spade is participating in his own demise while perpetuating the subjugation of his peers, family members, and future generations in the ghetto. *The Vulture* shines a spotlight on the futility of life for Americans trapped in ghettos.

Scott-Heron's second novel, *The Nigger Factory*, is another mystery narrative. This time he blends adventure with the racial and political disturbances that were characteristic of the late 1960s. Scott-Heron's maturity as a writer makes this novel an improvement over his first attempt at fiction and therefore more compelling.

The Nigger Factory confronts the issue of conventional education and its validity for African Americans. It takes place on the campus of Sutton University, an all-black liberal arts college. A conflict arises when the radical group MJUMBE (Swahili for messenger) steals a list of requests from the office of Earl Thomas, the student government president. MJUMBE presents the list to the school president, Ogden Calhoun, in the form of demands. The preposterous ultimatum that Calhoun should respond positively to all issues by noon the next day ensures MJUMBE's failure. Realizing that the avenue for negotiation is closed, Calhoun decides to close the college and requires all of the students to leave the campus. However, the members of MJUMBE stage a protest. They decide to stay on campus to demonstrate their opposition to Calhoun. Calhoun calls in the National Guard, which prompts one of MJUMBE's overzealous and angry members to build and detonate some bombs, thereby causing extensive destruction. Unfortunately, all of the members of MJUMBE are blamed for bringing a violent and completely unsatisfactory end to the conflict.

This novel expands on the ideas of BAMBU introduced in *The Vulture*. MJUMBE's primary concern is to provide education that is relevant to African Americans. In their haste to achieve their goals, however, the students forgo the diplomacy that would be necessary to effect change. Here Scott-Heron effectively captures the straightforward idealism of energetic youths and the general aura of dissatisfaction in the 1960s.

The plan failed more because of the militant method MJUMBE members chose to use than because their requests were unreasonable. Calhoun was infuriated by their immaturity: " 'We're trying to teach the boys and girls at Sutton how to be men and women and cope with their lives outside. You can't take a note to your boss saying to do this and that by tomorrow noon or else. . . . Channels have been established!' " (79). Only Earl, however, was aware of the proper channels. Knowing that the requests would never even be considered, Earl admonished the members of MJUMBE for their rash behavior: " 'Each and every one of these things coulda been worked out in time' " (98). Nonetheless, Earl Thomas supported the members of MJUMBE in order to present a unified group to Calhoun.

The members of MJUMBE fell victim to their own haste, rendering their attempted revolution futile. In *The Nigger Factory*, Scott-Heron represents militant activism as self-defeating, thus intimating that negotiation and compromise are the more effective methods of reaching mutually satisfactory goals.

An aggressive critique of American society of the 1960s permeates Scott-Heron's work. In the author's note from *The Nigger Factory*, Scott-Heron writes, "Fantasies about the American Dream are now recognized by the Black people as hoaxes" (ix). Each of his novels reveals some plausible manifestations of those hoaxes and provides a realistic appraisal of that era.

CRITICAL RECEPTION

Reviews of both novels vary and are diametrically opposed, from glowing to scathing. His uncompromisingly honest language and volatile themes inspired passionate responses.

Eric Moon calls *The Vulture* "ultimately disappointing" (2520) but admits that Scott-Heron "knows the milieu of the city streets well and writes about it with realism and accuracy" (2520). On a positive note, Liz Grant finds *The Vulture* to be a refreshing change in the genre of African American novels, which, she argues, have "come perilously close to falling into a rut: over-emphasis on the autobiographical. This tendency is not new. It can be traced back to the slave narratives where the telling of our life story served to help us gather friends in the struggle for our freedom" (97).

An anonymous critic from *Choice* finds no redeeming qualities in *The Nigger Factory*: "Scott-Heron's style is neither readable, convincing, nor artistic. . . . It is hard to take, and that is unfortunate because of the vitality of the subject matter" (817). But A. L. Fessler acknowledges the superior artistic quality of Scott-Heron's second novel: "This novel proceeds by means of short scenes, like small fires started here and there, which grow and coalesce into one large, fearsome conflagration—swift, all-consuming, and irresistible" (517).

In a climate of multicultural awareness, Scott-Heron's subject matter is no longer innovative but is nonetheless relevant. His fiction provides an accurate glimpse into the unrest that characterized America in the late 1960s. Due to Gil Scott-Heron's increasing popularity as a musician, his literary work is being more favorably received in retrospect.

BIBLIOGRAPHY

Works by Gil Scott-Heron

Small Talk at 125th & Lenox. New York: World, 1970a. (Poetry)
The Vulture. New York: World, 1970b.
The Nigger Factory. New York: Dial Press, 1972.

Studies of Gil Scott-Heron

Davis, L. J. Review of *The Nigger Factory. Book World* 12 March 1972: 11.
Fessler, A. L. Review of *The Nigger Factory. Library Journal* 1 February 1972: 517.
Gant, Liz. Review of *The Vulture. Black World* July 1971: 96–98.
Moon, Eric. Review of *The Vulture. Library Journal* July 1970: 2520.
Review of *The Nigger Factory. Kirkus Review* 15 January 1972: 95.
Review of *The Nigger Factory. Publishers Weekly* 17 January 1972: 57.
Review of *The Nigger Factory. The New Yorker* 20 May 1972: 139.
Review of *The Nigger Factory. Choice* September 1972: 817.
Review of *The Vulture. Kirkus Review* 1 May 1970: 528.
Review of *The Vulture. Publishers Weekly* 11 May 1970: 40.
Woodson, Jon. "Gil Scott-Heron." *Dictionary of Literary Biography.* Vol. 41. Detroit: Gale, 1985: 307–311.

NTOZAKE SHANGE
(1948–   )

Sarah Wheliss and Emmanuel S. Nelson

BIOGRAPHY

Although she is perhaps best known as an award-winning, revolutionary play-wright and poet, Ntozake Shange's novels also merit critical attention. The au-thor of three novels to date, *Sassafrass, Cypress & Indigo, Betsey Brown*, and *Liliane*, Shange's work documents the struggle of the modern African American woman to obtain and retain autonomy while immersed in human relationships, particularly with men, but also in community with other women. While growing up in a distinctly affluent household, Shange's childhood provided the future poet, playwright, and novelist with wide exposure to the arts. Born Paulette Williams on October 18, 1948, to surgeon Paul T. Williams and psychiatric social worker Eloise Owens Williams, Shange's New Jersey household reverberated with music, literature readings, and weekly family drama productions. Her parents, successful professionals who traveled widely, frequently entertained, with names such as musicians Dizzy Gillespie and Miles Davis or authors such as W. E. B. Du Bois appearing on the guest lists. The family also held ritual Sunday afternoon variety shows where different art forms were encouraged and explored. Shange attributes much of her fascination with the literary arts to this early exposure within her own home. She states in her book *nappy edges*:

my mama wd read from dunbar, shakespeare, countee cullen, t. s. eliot. my dad wd play congas & do magic tricks. my two sisters & my brother & i wd doa soft-shoe & then pick up the instruments for a quartet of some sort: a violin, a cello, flute & saxophone. we all read constantly. anything. anywhere. we also tore the prints outta art books to carry around with us. sounds/images, any explorations of personal visions was the focus of my world. (19)

When Shange was eight, however, the family moved from the security of a black community into the white community of St. Louis, Missouri. In her novel *Betsey Brown*, Shange details her experiences with this foreign environment, where she was one of the first integrated children in the school system. After five years in Missouri, Shange's family returned to New Jersey, and the thirteen-year-old wrote short stories and poems, only to be discouraged while in high school from pursuing such avocations and criticized for the exclusively black voice permeating her works.

Shange attended Barnard College in 1966, but after her separation from her first husband at the age of nineteen, she entered a downward spiral of frustration and depression. Despite four suicide attempts during her college years, Shange obtained her degree with honors in American studies. A graduate degree from the University of Southern California followed, and in California the author associated with dancers, writers, and musicians.

During her residence in California, first in Los Angeles and then in San Francisco, Shange rapidly discovered the cathartic effect of both writing and performing and rapidly redefined herself as a woman determined to declare and promulgate the power of the black woman. She assumed her African name, Ntozake, which means "she who comes with her own things," and Shange, which means she "who walks like a lion." She immersed herself in a community of female authors and artists, participated in frequent poetry readings, and dedicated herself to exploring the role of dance for self-expression. The result of her experiences in California was the award-winning *for colored girls who have considered suicide/when the rainbow is enuf: A choreopoem*, which appeared to rave reviews and numerous awards in the mid-1970s. For the past twenty years, pen in hand, Shange has pledged herself to examining and exposing the state of the African American female in our modern society in plays, poetry, prose, and novels.

MAJOR WORKS AND THEMES

When Ntozake Shange crafted her play *for colored girls who have considered suicide/when the rainbow is enuf*, she introduced many of the concerns and themes that infuse not only her plays and poetry but also each of her three novels to date. The choreopoem, a curious and original blend of poetry, music, dance, and drama, first appeared off-Broadway in November 1975 to remarkable critical acclaim. In the work, seven women attempt to restore the life of a black girl who has long been silenced. Through song, dance, and drama, the seven women ultimately find strength and resolve within themselves and within their community, declaring in one voice at the play's conclusion that they have "found god" (63) within themselves.

In Shange's three full-length novels, as in *for colored girls*, characters constantly seek the "god" within themselves, searching for redemption and for potency as black women in modern American society. Shange's first full-length novel, *Sassafrass, Cypress & Indigo*, opens with the sentence "where there is a woman there is magic" (3), and through the characters of Sassafrass the weaver, Cypress the dancer, and Indigo the midwife/healer, Shange weaves a tightly knit tapestry picturing the role of relationships, the focus on family, and the importance of individuality for the modern African American female. These women leave both the comfort and security of their Charleston, South Carolina, home as well as the protective embrace of their mother, Hilda Effania, to develop their own identities—Sassafrass in Los Angeles, Cypress in New York City, and Indigo in Difuskie, farther south from Charleston. Through effortlessly weaving together the three daughters' stories in this 1982 work, Shange introduces her own distinct rhetorical style with a narrative crafted through a combination of recipes, poems, songs, and journal entries testifying to the richly textured experience of the African American female. Whether through her exploration of Cypress' bisexuality, through her graphic depiction of Sassafrass' abusive relationship with Mitch, or through her magical and mystical examination of the spiritual forces informing Indigo in this youngest daughter's quest to preserve and protect her African American heritage, Shange demonstrates her dedication to declaring and defending the strength of the African American female. Each of these three characters achieves selfhood and independence, but not without personal cost. Cypress must mute her own artistic voice to marry a musician; a pregnant Sassafrass finally leaves the abusive Mitch but must face single parenthood; and Indigo finally recognizes that her powers may always be misunderstood by those she loves the most, for while her mother "knew Indigo had an interest in folklore" (224), she "had no idea that Indigo was the folks" (224). Hilda Effania, like many other African Americans whom Indigo encounters, does not grasp her spiritual and mystical ties to ancestral African American souls. The novel's conclusion finds all three daughters back in Charleston for the occasion of the birth of Sassafrass' child, clear testament to the importance of matriarchal themes, as well as feminine concerns, for Ntozake Shange.

In *Betsey Brown: A Novel* (1985) Shange further pursues the societal status of the African American female with her second novel, detailing a thirteen-year-old, middle-class, black girl's difficult and frequently painful journey to adulthood. This bildungsroman of sorts occurs in the newly integrated St. Louis of the late 1950s, reflecting Shange's own struggles growing up in an affluent black household. Contradictions in Betsey's world reflect the precarious place of African Americans during the early stages of integration—while Betsey attends a white school, her father, Greer, a physician at the segregated hospital, dedicates himself to instilling black pride within his household; while she learns about the African American's oppressive "invisibility" through her classmates' and her teachers' refusal to acknowledge her presence, Betsey learns at home about the great accomplishments of the African American people, through constant exposure to culturally specific jazz, rhythm and blues, dancing, and poetry in her home; while battling overt racism within the white community at school, Betsey also finds herself surrounded by intraracial racism at home in her grandmother Vida, who believes Betsey's mother has married beneath herself by choosing a dark-skinned black man as opposed to a man of lighter hue. Throughout the novel, Betsey battles to find her own place within both family and community and to place herself solidly on the color spectrum of American society.

In Shange's third novel, *Liliane: Resurrection of the Daughter*, published in 1994, the author merges the rhetorical style first presented in *Sassafrass, Cypress & Indigo* and the themes and concerns facing African American daughters in this society as further explored in *Betsey Brown* with her own preoccupation with the role of art in the lives of African American females. The title character is Liliane Lincoln, an artist who searches for more self-awareness and security through revelatory conversations with her friends, her lovers, and her psychoanalyst. Though able to express herself through artworks filled with sexual and feminine images, she is unable at the novel's inception to understand a society where men are abusive and can't "stand to hear the music" (8) in the African American female artist. The array of voices present within this novel sings a song of survival for this African American female; the novel itself reads as an improvisational jazz tune with nonlinear narrative, dream sequences, and multiple voices circulating throughout the text. Though less complexly rendered than the intricate textual tapestry of *Sassafrass, Cypress & Indigo* or the autobiographical and historically compelling *Betsey Brown*, Shange's third novel clearly relishes African American art forms and adds yet another instrument to the author's symphonic exploration of the varied lives of modern African American females.

In all three novels, Shange clearly relishes the power of the written word, since language is, for this author, the African American female's most powerful tool:

It's very scary to me as a woman that we're denied and defiled in language. . . . So, for me, the challenge was to kill off these things and to trip [language] and to trick it and use it in ways "they're" not expecting but in ways that people speaking the language I speak would receive and feel a sense of joy in. Language is a liberator. (Neal, "Ntozake" 221)

Using language in original and powerful novels, Shange sings a song of liberation for the African American female.

CRITICAL RECEPTION

While Shange's poetry and plays have won her considerable acclaim, her novels have received mostly mixed reviews and elicited only limited scholarly attention. Arlene Elder's work remains the only major critical article that has been published on Shange's fiction so far. Elder compares the novel to the slave narratives of the nineteenth century and explores Shange's use of the blues idiom. Just as useful is Elder's focus on the novel's feminist stance; she calls it a "Black woman's bildungsroman" (100) that offers a "Black and female semiotic and signifying commentaries on the Western conventions of dialogue, characterization, and linear narrative" (99).

Shange's second novel, *Betsey Brown*, was reviewed more widely. Nancy Willard, in her largely enthusiastic review, calls Shange "a superb storyteller . . . with an extraordinary ear for the spoken word" (12). She adds that the "characters are so finely drawn that they can be recognized by their speech alone" (12). But it is precisely the use of language that Sherley Anne Williams finds unconvincing. Williams calls the novel "disappointing" (72) and asserts that it disingenuously elides the class distinctions among the various characters. Susan Schindehette, on the other hand, points to a narrative flaw. While she finds the characters, the dialogue, and Shange's exquisite prose alluring, she notes that "there is no glue to bind those elements into a flowing whole" (74). She concludes that *Betsey Brown* is not a novel at all but a play that is "masquerading as a novel" (74).

Similar reception has greeted Shange's most recent novel as well. Donna Seaman's comment is quite typical: she calls *Liliane: Resurrection of the Daughter* a "novel with personality" (3) but insists that "Shange is still a more potent poet and playwright than novelist" (3). Janet Ingraham compares the novel favorably with the works of Paule Marshall* and Toni Morrison.* Valerie Sayers, while acknowledging some reservations about the dizzying pace of the novel, nonetheless concludes that it is a pleasure "to hear Ntozake Shange singing in so many different tempos" and that the novel is "a dense, ambitious, worthy song" (6).

BIBLIOGRAPHY

Works by Ntozake Shange

Novels

Sassafrass (novella). San Lorenzo, CA: Shameless Hussy Press, 1976.
Sassafrass, Cypress & Indigo: A Novel. New York: St. Martin's, 1982.
Betsey Brown: A Novel. New York: St. Martin's, 1985.
Liliane. New York: St. Martin's, 1994.

Selected Plays, Poems, and Prose

for colored girls who have considered suicide/when the rainbow is enuf: A choreopoem. New York: Macmillan, 1976.
nappy edges. New York: St. Martin's, 1978.
three pieces: Spell #7; A Photograph: Lovers in Motion; Boogie Woogie Landscapes. New York: St. Martin's, 1981.
A Daughter's Geography. New York: St. Martin's, 1983.
From Okra to Greens: Poems. New York: Coffee House Press, 1984a.
See No Evil: Prefaces, Essays and Accounts, 1976–1983. San Francisco: Momo's Press, 1984b.
Ridin' the Moon in Texas: Word Paintings. New York: St. Martin's, 1987.
The Love Space Demands: A Continuing Saga. New York: St. Martin's, 1991.

Studies of Ntozake Shange

Elder, Arlene. "*Sassafrass, Cypress & Indigo*: Ntozake Shange's Neo-Slave/Blues Narrative." *African-American Review* 26.1 (Fall 1992): 99–106.

Griffin, Gabriele. " 'Writing the Body': Reading Joan Riley, Grace Nichols and Ntozake Shange." *Black Women's Writing*. Ed. Gina Wisker. New York: St. Martin's, 1993. 19–42.

Holloway, Karla F. C. *Moorings and Metaphors: Figures of Culture and Gender in Black Women's Literature*. New Brunswick, NJ: Rutgers University Press, 1992.

Ingraham, Janet. Rev. of *Liliane: Resurrection of the Daughter*. *Library Journal* 119 (October 15, 1994): 88.

Kent, Assunta. "The Rich Multiplicity of *Betsey Brown*." *Journal of Dramatic Theory and Criticism* 7.1 (Fall 1992): 151–161.

Neal, Lester A. "Ntozake Shange." *Speaking on Stage: Interviews with Contemporary American Playwrights*. Ed. Philip C. Kolin and Colby H. Kullman. Tuscaloosa: University of Alabama Press, 1996. 216–229.

———. *Ntozake Shange: A Critical Study of the Plays*. New York: Garland, 1995.

Qureshi, Amber. "Where the Womanisms Grow: Ritual and Romanticism in *for colored girls who have considered suicide*." *Notes on Contemporary Literature* 26.4 (September 1996): 6–8.

Sayers, Valerie. Rev. of *Liliane: Resurrection of the Daughter*. *New York Times Book Review*. (January 1, 1995): 6.

Saldiver, Jose David. "The Real and the Marvelous in Charleston, South Carolina: Ntozake Shange's *Sassafrass, Cypress and Indigo*." *Genealogy and Literature*. Ed. Lee Quinby. Minneapolis: University of Minnesota Press, 1995. 175–192.

Schindehette, Susan. Rev. of *Liliane: Resurrection of the Daughter*. *Saturday Review* 11.14 (May–June 1985): 74.

Seaman, Donna. Rev. of *Liliane: Resurrection of the Daughter*. *Booklist* 91 (September 1, 1994): 3.

Steinitz, Hilary J. "Shaping Interior Spaces: Ntozake Shange's Construction of the 'Room' for Art." *West Virginia University Philological Papers* 38 (1992): 280–287.

Thompson-Cager, Chezia. "Superstition, Magic and the Occult in Two Versions of Ntozake Shange's Chorepoem *for colored girls* and Novel *Sassafrass, Cypress and Indigo*." *MAWA Review* 4.2 (December 1989): 37–41.

Washington, Mary Helen. "Ntozake Shange." *The Playwright's Art: Conversations with Contemporary American Dramatists*. Ed. Jackson R. Bryer. New Brunswick, NJ: Rutgers University Press, 1995. 205–220.

Waxman, Barbara Frey. "Dancing out of Form, Dancing into Self: Genre and Metaphor in Marshall, Shange and Walker." *MELUS: The Journal of the Society for the Study of the Multi-Ethnic Literature of the United States* 19.3 (Fall 1994): 91–106.

Willard, Nancy. Rev. of *Betsey Brown*. *New York Times Book Review* (May 12, 1985): 12.

Williams, Sherley Anne. "Roots of Privilege: New Black Fiction." *Ms.* 13.12 (June 1985): 69–72.

CHARLOTTE WATSON SHERMAN
(1958–)

Bindu Malieckal

BIOGRAPHY

Charlotte Watson Sherman was born in Seattle on 14 October 1958. Like Rayna, the protagonist of her novel *Touch*, Sherman studied at Seattle University and graduated with a B.A. in social sciences in 1980. While in college, Sherman wrote poetry. Later, as her poems started getting longer, she decided to write fiction, which she began in 1988. Her first short stories snared several awards. The Seattle Arts Commission, for example, granted her the Individual Artist Award for fiction in 1989, and, in the same year, she received the Fiction Publication Award from the Kings County Arts Commission.

Sherman's first collection of short stories, *Killing Color*, was published in 1992. The stories from the collection have been anthologized in various volumes. *Killing Color* received critical acclaim and earned the Great Lakes Colleges Association Fiction Award and the Governor's Writers Award, both in 1993. In the same year, the Washington State Arts Commission offered her a literary fellowship. Also, in 1993, Sherman's first novel, *One Dark Body*, was published. Her second novel, *Touch*, appeared in 1995. *Granta* named Sherman to its "Fabulous 52" list in 1995, establishing Sherman as one of the more talented African American authors of contemporary times.

In addition to short stories and novels, Sherman writes nonfiction and juvenile literature. She edited an anthology, titled *Sisterfire: Black Womanist Fiction and Poetry* (1994). Sherman has written two children's books: *Nia and the Golden Stool* (1988) and *Eli and the Swamp Man* (1995). Presently, Sherman is completing a work of nonfiction—*The Blues Ain't Nothing but a Good Woman Feeling Bad*—on black women and depression.

MAJOR WORKS AND THEMES

In the Introduction to *Sisterfire: Black Womanist Fiction and Poetry*, Sherman explains the importance of black women writers: "The words of these griots-historians-shamans-seers-wise women encompass the Black female experience from a womanist perspective. They speak to the lives of contemporary black women, raise our voices, and help make us visible" (xviii). While Sherman is specifically referring to the contributors to the anthology, she also elucidates the womanist bent of her own fiction, or, as she records in an autobiographical essay, "The way I try to intertwine that duality [of "African-Americanness" and "femaleness"] in my own writing is to reverse the negativity around darkness" (Carroll 221). According to Sherman, writing can heal the psychological and emotional "wounds" of African American history, the tragic residues of which are still being experienced (Carroll 223). The subject matter of her fiction is clear; she specifies, "I write out of my fascination with the supernatural—spirits, visions, healing dreams, ancestral memories" ("To Divine the Hidden" 85). Magic realism is Sherman's preferred stylistic device. She identifies Toni Morrison,* August Wilson, Latin American, Native American, and African writers as her influences (Carroll 217–218). Seattle is the setting for most of Sherman's fiction because she was raised in Seattle and still lives there. As she explains, "The mythical landscape of the Northwest touches me in the deep places of my dreams" ("To Divine the Hidden" 90).

The short stories of *Killing Color* are set in Mississippi and Seattle and are told by women narrators in black dialect. Sherman evokes the supernatural, the mystical, and the magical in these stories about black women's dreams, desires, fears, and expectations, from menstruation to space exploration. The most memorable stories of the collection are "Killing Color," "Swimming Lesson," and "Emerald City: Third and Pike," all of which elucidate the theme of women and possibility. In "Killing Color," Mavis, whose eyes flicker with the yellow fire of revenge, punishes the Klansmen who murdered her husband. In "Swimming Lesson," the child narrator watches with awe and dread as a lame playmate miraculously walks on water. In "Emerald City," a homeless woman named "Oya" tells a young Seattle-ite how she murdered her boss, a white woman, for being a "dreamkiller," in other words, for crushing Oya's dream of becoming an astronaut.

While *Killing Color* provides glimpses of Sherman's interest in themes relating the past and present, *One Dark Body* fully explores relationships between descendants and ancestors in the context of lost connections to African rituals. The title of the novel suggests that the focus will be on one specific person or "one dark body," such as the "wanga man" Blue's father's corpse, floating in the lake, but since Sherman's focus concerns reacquainting descendants and ancestors, souls and bodies, any "one dark body" represents the essential twoness of black folk or, as the opening quotation from W.E.B. Du Bois explains, "One ever feels his twoness—an American, a negro; two souls, two thoughts, two unreconciled strivings; two warring ideals in one dark body." While the immediate conflicts of the novel concern the tenuous affiliation between Nola Barnett and her daughter Raisin and between Blue and the fatherless Sin-Sin, these relationships mirror the other estrangements of the novel, such as those between Nola and her mother, Ouida, as well as the whole lack of parent–sibling connections between Miss Marius' foster children—MC, Wilhelmina, Douglas—and their absent parents. The parent–sibling disaffections are part of a larger problem: the estrangement of forebears and offsprings, ancient traditions and present practices, memory and existence, and the soul and the body. Ultimately, in the novel, physical and spiritual healing for all the characters comes about when severed ties are relinked.

Nature plays a key role in *One Dark Body*. All the characters enjoy visiting or living in the forest, the stability and longevity of which provide solace and vitality. A host of myths circulate about the disembodied inhabitants of the forest: the snakelike, yellow-eyed "Night People" who live in the trees and the "Old Ones" or ancestors whose spirits speak from the forest floor. The forest is a symbol of the ancient African homeland and is the setting for both Sin-Sin's initiation rites and Raisin's ascension to womanhood. It is also the antithesis of the daily grind, of the deep, dark death of mining, the industry surrounding the forest. Also, while the trees of Pearl constantly remind of lynchings—as evidenced by the image of the snakelike tree people—all the characters retool the image to make the trees instruments of healing, not malevolence. Thus, Blue and his mentor, Mr. Goodnight, live in the forest, and Nola and Raisin eventually do the same.

In terms of style, Sherman's writing masterfully captures the sense of loss and longing in Raisin and Sin-Sin, but the magical realism of *One Dark Body*, with its accompanying metaphors and images, is the novel's strongest feature. Sherman endows inanimate objects and concepts with volatility and mass. For example, consider the following quotations, written in the style of Zora Neale Hurston: "She [Nola] hadn't seen El in a week, and something inside the ground of herself shifted" (33); "But hard as she [Nola] tried to forget Pearl, Pearl had planted its roots into the fertile soil of her life" (45); "And inside my mind I [Raisin] say, Mama? You my mama? But I can't let it slip out into the air where she might hear and catch and turn the words into something pointy that stings" (87).

Touch, Sherman's latest novel, explores the consequences and emotions, physical, sexual, mental, and social, of being HIV-positive and of being a black woman who is HIV-positive. The novel's protagonist is Rayna Sargent, a thirty-five-year-old artist-cum-crisis counselor who learns that she carries the AIDS virus. *Touch* boldly and knowledgeably illustrates a topic that is the subject of fiction only marginally, since literary taboos often mirror social taboos, or, as one of Rayna's friends, Novel Lewis, demonstrates, "I don't even want to think about AIDS. One time I sat down and tried to list all the people I'd been with and I got depressed" (6). Interestingly, the novel does not dwell on how Rayna contracted the virus; rather, *Touch* concentrates on living with HIV. *Touch* is divided into two sections: the first deals with Rayna's life before HIV, testing HIV-positive, and her anguish; in the second part of the novel, Rayna tells her parents, friends, and lover that she is HIV-positive. The second half also provides information on medication, therapy, support groups, and sex after an HIV diagnosis.

The title of the novel refers to the simple, human contact that people who have AIDS or HIV are often deprived of. After learning that she is HIV-positive, Rayna regrets that she can never be sexually active: "And to think that no one will ever want to touch me again makes me want to beat my head against the wall" (113). Theodore Massey, Rayna's sensitive lover, disproves her conclusions. According to Theodore, "We don't have to be afraid of loving, he said. This is not the time to be without touch, he said. Now is when we need it more than ever. And I'm not talking about sex, I'm talking about touch, he said" (172). He sends her a card with a picture of a boy and a girl holding hands, the caption of which reads, "The spirit is in the touch" (68). Theodore teaches Rayna that they can have safe sex. The ability to be sexually active again allows Rayna to continue the business of living, to feel alive. In turn, Rayna touches, mothers, loves, and revitalizes Anika, a ten-year-old child who has full-blown AIDS. Like Rayna, whose own mother was mentally ill and unable to care for her, Anika's mother was a drug addict and neglectful of her child. Rayna sees herself, as a child and a woman, in Anika, but, through Anika's courage, Rayna also learns to thrive despite HIV.

CRITICAL RECEPTION

Despite her many awards for fiction, Sherman's writing has yet to receive a great deal of critical attention, though, undoubtedly, it will. In one particularly detailed study, Madelyn Jablon analyzes Sherman's use of various voices, including those of the dead and living, in *One Dark Body*. Jablon shows how the multiple narratives blend to form "communal narration" (120), which has a dual purpose: to express black dialect, African American oral tradition, and the trends of African American literature and to evoke a paradigm for remedying emotional injuries. As Jablon clarifies, "Sherman mines the vernacular tradition to uncover the voice of experience" (112). Thus, Jablon believes that *One Dark Body* exemplifies a new literature: "It is metanarrative that disrupts the foundations on which definitions of fiction rest: static, distinct identities, individuality, difference" (122).

Unlike critical analyses, reviews of Sherman's books are plentiful. Reviews unequivocally commend the magical stories of *Killing Color*. Maxine Clair heralds Sherman's "originality" in the use of metaphors, dreams, mystery, and myth (3). Paula Marie Parker gushes, "Her writing is poetry and song and imagery" (4). While Dawn Michelle Baude admits that "Sherman is definitely at her best writing Black English" (20), she criticizes the poor editing of the volume and believes that the stories "Big Water" and "A Season," which are constrained by "academic prose style," should not have been included in the volume (20).

In general, reviewers hail *One Dark Body* as a promising debut novel and admire Sherman's lyrical prose, but most criticize the form and scope of the novel. Tina McElroy Ansa, for example, writes, "*One Dark Body* is too much of a story, too wide-ranging and mystical a story to fit into the author's 209 pages" (11). While Saba Bahar appreciates the plot and purpose of the novel, she notes that it is "[not] tightly constructed" and rebukes the form: "[t]he rites of passage read more like poetic anthropology and less like a novel" (105). Anne duCille complains that the book contains "too many issues, causes, and calamities . . . too many disparate beings" and goes so far to call it "cacophony" (23). In her review, Kamili Anderson observes that *One Dark Body* has too many similarities to Toni Morrison's *Beloved*, and she implies that Sherman should seek a clearer separation from Morrison's magical realism (19).

Reviews of *Touch* are more positive, though reviewers still have concerns with Sherman's style. Sybil Steinberg admits that *Touch* is "moving," but she also declares it "preachy" (70). Jill Petty compliments Sherman on writing "a thinking woman's *Waiting to Exhale*," and she adds, "Sherman has a gift for rendering the peculiar inner dialogues that personal crises can force" (78). On the other hand, while Patricia Elam Ruff finds the subject of AIDS in *Touch* timely and relevant, she finds the dialogue problematic, or, as she writes, "[The dialogue] reads like it was lifted straight from a health pamphlet" (88).

BIBLIOGRAPHY

Works by Charlotte Watson Sherman

Short Story

Killing Color. Corvallis, OR: Calyx Books, 1992.

Novels

One Dark Body. New York: HarperCollins, 1993.
Touch. New York: HarperPerennial, 1995.

Children's Literature

Nia and the Golden Stool. Nashville: Winston-Derek, 1988.
Eli and the Swamp Man. New York: HarperCollins, 1995.

Editorial Work

Sisterfire: Black Womanist Fiction and Poetry. New York: HarperPerennial, 1994.

Nonfiction

"To Divine the Hidden." *Edge Walking on the Western Rim: New Works by Twelve Northwest Writers*. Ed. Mayumi Tsutakawa. Seattle: Sasquatch Books, 1994. 84–93.

Studies of Charlotte Watson Sherman

Anderson, Kamili. "Dreamstory." Rev of *One Dark Body*. *Belles Lettres* (Summer 1993): 19.

Ansa, Tina McElroy. "Broken Children, Broken Lives." Rev. of *One Dark Body. Los Angeles Times*, 27 June 1993: 11.

Bahar, Saba. Rev. of *One Dark Body. Race and Class* 36.1 (1994): 104–105.

Baude, Dawn Michelle. "Technical Talent." Rev. of *Killing Color. The American Book Review* 15.3 (Aug. 1993): 20.

Carroll, Rebecca. *I Know What the Red Clay Looks Like: The Vision of Black Women Writers.* New York: Crowne Trade, 1994.

Clair, Maxine. "Sleight of Voice." Rev. of *Killing Color. Belles Lettres* (Summer 1992): 3.

duCille, Anne. "Haunts of History." Rev. of *One Dark Body. Women's Review of Books* 10.10–11 (July 1993): 23.

Jablon, Madelyn. *Black Metafiction: Self-Consciousness in African American Literature.* Iowa City: University of Iowa Press, 1997.

Parker, Paula Marie. "Women of Mystery, Women of Strength." Rev. of *Killing Color. San Francisco Chronicle*, 10 May 1992: 4.

Petty, Jill. "The Human Touch." Rev. of *Touch. Ms.* 6.2 (Sept. 1995): 78–79.

Ruff, Patricia Elam. "The Healing Hands of Family, Friends." Rev. of *Touch. Emerge* 7.2 (Nov. 1995): 88, 90.

Steinberg, Sybil. Rev. of *Touch. Publishers Weekly* (14 Aug. 1995): 70.

ANN ALLEN SHOCKLEY
(1927–   )

Adenike Marie Davidson

BIOGRAPHY

Ann Allen Shockley was born on 21 June 1927 in Louisville, Kentucky, to Bessie Lucas and Henry Allen, both social workers. She found literature a pleasant escape and was encouraged to read and write creatively at an early age. Her eighth grade teacher, Harriet La Forrest, had a tremendous influence on Shockley, recognizing her imaginative talents and pushing her to put her ideas in print. Shockley began thinking of the short story form after reading Richard Wright's collection *Uncle Tom's Children*.

Shockley edited her junior high school newspaper and continued such pursuits as an undergraduate, becoming a columnist and fiction editor for the *Fisk University Herald*, as well as a staff writer for the *Louisville Defender*, which she continued for eighteen years. After graduating from Fisk in 1948, she married William Shockley, a teacher, and bore two children, William Leslie, Jr., and Tamara Ann. In 1949 she began a weekly column called "Ebony Topics"—news pertaining to the African American community—for Maryland's *Federal Times*, a white-owned newspaper. In 1950, she began a similar column for the *Bridgeville News* in Delaware, where she lived with her family. These accomplishments were even more important because Shockley was the first African American to write for both papers. She also published articles in Baltimore's *Afro-American* and the *Pittsburgh Courier*. She returned to education and graduated from Case Western in 1960 with a master's degree in library science. In 1959, Shockley wrote the first of several works on librarianship with an emphasis on African American collections. In 1969, she began another career at Fisk University as librarian in the Special Negro Collection.

Along with her library science work, Shockley is a prolific short story writer, novelist, and feminist. She states, "Writing is like a compulsion to me. It is something I *have* to do. I am always working on something; I never let up" (Houston 233). Her nonfiction books have been "firsts" of their kind, and her fiction has also broken many barriers. Her awards include the American Association of University Women (AAUW) Short Story Award (1962), the Hatshepsut Award for Literature (1981), the MLK, Jr., Black Author Award (1982), the Susan Koppelman Award (1988), and the Outlook Award for Outstanding Pioneering Contribution to Lesbian and Gay Writing (1990). She has made contributions in a wide range of fields and yet remains virtually unknown to the majority of mainstream America.

MAJOR WORKS AND THEMES

Shockley's nonfiction has aided in the research and retention of black history; her fiction nonetheless continues in the same realm, filling in the gaps of subject matter not before presented. She explores the themes of racism, sexism, homophobia, interracial relationships, and, of course, the everyday struggles of being an African American. She concentrates the exploration of her themes within an African American community because "this threat of being identified as gay, queer, funny, or a bulldagger in Black linguistics is embedded deeply within the overall homophobic attitude of the Black community, a phenomenon stemming from social, religious, and 'biological' convictions" ("The Black Lesbian in American Literature" 84). Such themes are consistent with the times in which she writes: the Civil Rights movement, the feminist movement, and the gay and lesbian movements are the political and social struggles of the 1960s and 1970s. Yet Shockley's writing seems to always attempt to break new ground.

Before publishing a full-length work of fiction, Shockley had published more than thirty short stories in newspapers and periodicals. *Loving Her*, Shockley's first novel, is the first African American novel with an African American lesbian as the main character and the first such novel to deal with interracial lesbian love. Such a character was never validated in fiction before Shockley, and we see this novel as a precursor paving the way for such novels following as *Sula* by Toni Morrison* and *The Color Purple* by Alice Walker.* Shockley provides the reader with an exploration of the difficulties of being African American, female, and lesbian in twentieth-century America. Renay, an African American singer and the central character, leaves a bad marriage with physical and emotional abuse and pursues a relationship with a wealthy white woman writer, Terry. Through this triangle of husband-wife-lover, Shockley addresses Renay's developing awareness of her own sexuality as well as societal attitudes toward both lesbians and interracial relationships. Shockley attacks the Prince Charming myth as an attempt to explain the lesbian lifestyle Renay chooses, a possible alternative for women who have been disappointed by heterosexuality. She presents the reader with a diverse society—some are repulsed by the idea of lesbian sex, and others by the mixing of races, and still others have also grappled with their own sexuality and, although arriving at the same conclusion as Renay, have chosen to remain covert. In the end, Renay accepts her true sexuality, her self. With Renay's daughter, Denise, Shockley must also explore the issue of parenting when one is a lesbian. Those represented as tolerant are other homosexuals and older women. The African American community generally is presented as intolerant and homophobic.

Shockley's collection of short stories, *The Black and White of It*, nominated for the American Library Association Task Force 1980 Book Award, explores lesbians living within, and battling against, the constraints of the racist and homophobic society of America. The majority of the characters are professional women who either still suffer because of, or still feel compelled to deny, their sexuality. In "Play It but Don't Say It," Congresswoman Mattie Beatrice Brown claims, "They may *think* it, but they don't *know*" (37). In "Holly Craft Isn't Gay," a successful singer decides to get pregnant because "straight people [are] hung up on women having babies" (77). In "Home to Meet the Folks," the parent says, "I wish you hadn't told me—!" (59). Generally the attitude of the African American community is presented as negative and intolerant. Yet the collection is not merely about struggle. Shockley manages to disperse some strong and loving lesbian relationships throughout, women who are emotionally healthy and self-accepting.

Say Jesus and Come to Me, Shockley's second novel, continues to explore the issue of homophobia but moves the critique to the African American church. Rev. Myrtle Black, a charismatic African American female evangelist, uses her power as pulpit leader to seduce a young female singer, Travis Lee. Rev. Black, having accepted her sexuality, uses her position, as do the heterosexual male counterparts, to pursue intimate relationships. Yet Rev. Black deconstructs patriarchal Christianity in order to survive and thrive, while her male counterpart preserves it for the same reasons. Travis Lee, on the other hand, is still coming to know herself and in the end accepts her lesbianism. Shockley explores the issues of homophobia in the church, as well as the conservatism of southern African American and white women, especially regarding sexism and feminism.

CRITICAL RECEPTION

Although vastly published for three decades, Shockley is relatively unknown. One reason may be the obscurity and loss of archival records of the journals and newspapers to which she contributed early in her career. Shockley's fiction has not attained the popularity of her nonfiction. She attributes the lack of acceptance to the subject matter and the immediate wants of mainstream publishers: "This unique Black woman, analogous to Ralph Ellison's* 'invisible man,' was seen but not seen because of what the eyes did not wish to behold" ("The Black Lesbian in American Literature" 83). *Loving Her* received mixed reviews, mostly criticizing Shockley's writing style, which was characterized for its excessive propaganda, faulty plot structure, and disregard for time relevance. Critical response of *The Black and White of It*, although mixed, has generally been favorable, recognizing Shockley's candid look at social myths and heralding the work as an important contribution in lesbian fiction. *Say Jesus and Come to Me* was recognized as a work with an iconoclastic character never before represented so intensely in African American fiction. Her works, especially her collection of short stories, have been criticized as portraying futility in the possibility of satisfying and loving lesbian relationships. Although her works may seem bleak at times, she certainly validates lesbian love despite overwhelming social oppression. Her fiction is generally overlooked by critics, especially African Americans, except for a few feminists such as Alice Walker, Rita Dandridge, and Nellie McKay. She explains that "the Black female heterosexual reviewers who *could* be sensitive to these works are usually . . . frightened of being tagged a closet lesbian, or a traitor to the Black male" ("The Black Lesbian in American Literature" 92). Moreover, although her themes have attempted to stretch beyond contemporary mainstream, her female characters, despite great oppression, have not gone insane, attempted suicide, or died; such a feisty presentation does more than suggest that lesbian life is not as tragic as one may think. Shockley's exposure of lesbian experience in African American literature leaves the reader with a great richness.

BIBLIOGRAPHY

Works by Ann Allen Shockley

Nonfiction

A History of Public Library Services to Negroes in the South, 1900–1955. (monograph) Dover: Delaware State College, 1960.
"Does the Negro College Library Need a Special Negro Collection?" *Library Journal* 86 (1 June 1961): 2049–2050.
A Handbook for the Administration of Special Black Collections. Nashville: Fisk University Library, 1970a.
"Tell It Like It Is: A Criterion for Children's Books in Black and White." *Southeastern Libraries* 30 (Spring 1970b): 30–33.
"Pauline Elizabeth Hopkins: A Biographical Excursion into Obscurity." *Phylon* 33 (Spring 1972): 22–26.
Comp. with Sue P. Chandler. *Living Black American Authors: A Biographical Directory*. New York: Bowker, 1973.
"American Anti-Slavery Literature: An Overview—1693–1859." *Negro History Bulletin* 37 (April/May 1974a): 232–235.
"The New Black Feminists." *Northwest Journal of African and Black American Studies* 2 (Winter 1974b): 1–5.
"Black Publishers and Black Librarians: A Necessary Union." *Black World* 26 (March 1975): 38–44.
Comp. and ed. with E. J. Josey. *A Handbook of Black Librarianship*. Littleton, CO: Libraries Unlimited, 1977.

"The Black Lesbian in American Literature." *Conditions: Five* 11 (Autumn 1979): 133–142. Rpt. in *Home Girls: A Black Feminist Anthology*. Ed. Barbara Smith. New York: Kitchen Table, Women of Color Press, 1983. 83–93.

"Black Lesbian Biography: Lifting the Veil." *Other Black Woman* 1 (1982): 5–9.

"On Lesbian/Feminist Book Reviewing." *Sojourner: The Women's Forum* 9 (April 1984): 18.

Afro-American Women Writers, 1746–1933: An Anthology and Critical Guide. Boston: G. K. Hall, 1988.

Fiction

"Abraham and the Spirit." *Negro Digest* 8 (July 1950a): 85–91.

Not to Be Alone. Unpublished novel, 1950b.

A World of Lonely Strangers. Unpublished novel, 1960.

"The Picture Prize." *Negro Digest* 11 (October 1962): 53–60.

"A Far Off Sound." *Umbra* 2 (December 1963): 11–17.

"The Funeral." *Phylon* 28 (Spring 1967): 95–101.

"The President." *Freedomways* 10 (4th quarter 1970): 343–349.

"Crying for Her Man." *Liberator* 11 (January–February 1971a): 14–17.

"Is She Relevant?" *Black World* 20 (January 1971b): 58–65.

"Her Own Thing." *Black America* 2 (August 1972): 58–61.

"Ah: The Young Black Poet." *New Letters* 41 (Winter 1974a): 45–60.

Loving Her. Indianapolis: Bobbs-Merrill, 1974b.

"The More Things Change." *Essence* 8 (October 1977): 78+.

"A Case of Telemania." *Azalea* 1 (Fall 1978): 1–5.

The Black and White of It. Weatherby Lake, MO: Naiad Press, 1980.

Say Jesus and Come to Me. New York: Avon, 1982.

"The World of Rosie Polk." (1987) *The African American Short Story, 1970–1990*. Ed. Barbara Puschmann-Nalenz. Trier: Wissenschaftlicher Verlag, 1993. 181–192.

Studies of Ann Allen Shockley

Bogus, SDiane. "Themes and Portraiture in the Fiction of Ann Allen Shockley." Diss., Miami University, 1988.

Dandridge, Rita B. *Ann Allen Shockley: An Annotated Primary and Secondary Bibliography*. New York: Greenwood Press, 1987.

Houston, Helen R. "Ann Allen Shockley." *Dictionary of Literary Biography: Afro-American Writers after 1955*. Ed. Thadious Davis and Trudier Harris. Detroit: Gale, 1984.

Krantz, Carrie. "The Political Power in Reverend Black's Sermons." *MAWA Review* 4.2 (December 1989): 42–44.

White, Evelyn C. "Comprehensive Oppression: Lesbians and Race in the Work of Ann Allen Shockley." *Backbone* 3 (1979): 38–40.

APRIL SINCLAIR
(1954–)

Jacqueline C. Jones

BIOGRAPHY

Born in 1954, April Sinclair was raised on the south side of Chicago. She began writing poetry at the age of ten. After graduating from Western Illinois University, Sinclair lived in San Francisco for one year before moving to Oakland. She was the director of the Emergency Food Coalition and also worked as a teacher at the Read-a-Lot Program in Oakland. She sometimes wrote for small womanist and feminist publications. Sinclair took graduate courses in film at San Francisco State University, where she was discouraged from pursuing her goal of making films. Advised that it was easier to have a novel adapted to a screenplay, Sinclair began work on her first novel. Wildly successful readings from her novel in progress at San Francisco Bay Area bookstores led to a book contract. Her first novel, *Coffee Will Make You Black*, was published in 1994 and received an enthusiastic reception.

Ain't Gonna Be the Same Fool Twice, April Sinclair's second novel, was published in 1996. She also wrote an article on the perception of smiling in the African American community for *Allure*. She is currently at work on her third novel, which centers on a forty-one-year-old woman who is "seeking her other half and discovers her own wholeness." April Sinclair resides in the San Francisco Bay Area.

MAJOR WORKS AND THEMES

Sinclair's two published novels examine the theme of identity through the experiences of a young African American woman, Jean Eloise Stevenson

("Steve"). Set in Chicago, Sinclair's novels promote pride in self, in race, and in identity. Sinclair adds a historical perspective by probing generational attitudes toward skin color, hair, class, nationalism, homosexuality, and interracial friendships. Sinclair's novels are often thought to be autobiographical, an issue Sinclair addressed in an interview: "No, it is not autobiographical, says Sinclair. I really think that when people ask that, it's a polite way of asking my business. There are incidents that actually happened. You do draw from your own experiences, but it's a mixture, it's fiction" (Reed 24). Both *Coffee Will Make You Black* and *Ain't Gonna Be the Same Fool Twice* combine African American vernacular speech, humor, and a breathtaking array of historical references to create a sense of time and place.

Coffee Will Make You Black is a female bildungsroman or coming-of-age novel that follows Stevie's development as she matures from age eleven to sixteen. The title of the novel is indicative of Sinclair's critique of colorism in the African American community. The emphasis on light skin and straight hair, along with the rise of the Black Power movement, leads Stevie to define for herself what constitutes beauty. She questions a childhood game in which girls compare their arms to see who has the lightest skin. She rejects the bleaching creams that her mother offers her. Stevie instinctively knows the fallacy of equating the color black with negativity. The generational conflict in the novel allows Sinclair to show how destructive colorism and elitism can be. One of the turning points in *Coffee* is when Stevie's mother begins to accept blackness in terms of hair texture and skin color.

Stevie questions all forms of her identity, including her sexuality. This aspect of Stevie's exploration makes Sinclair's novels controversial to some readers. Sexual initiation is a key element of *Coffee*. During the course of the novel, Stevie experiences her first kiss and a physical attraction to a woman. Peer pressure leads Stevie to examine her friendship with the white school nurse, Diane Horn. Her attraction to Nurse Horn frightens her because of Nurse Horn's race and gender. Sinclair says that she "can relate to Stevie's dilemma—liking someone who's white, and having feelings of rage and anger about racism" (Rubin E10). Stevie's desire to be "normal" almost leads her to have sex before she is truly ready. Initially accepting of her community's views toward homosexuality, Stevie eventually learns to evaluate people for their individual qualities. Stevie's poem ("What good is life, if you can't be free? / And what good am I, if I can't be me?" [168]) is an announcement of her self-acceptance.

Ain't Gonna Be the Same Fool Twice continues Stevie's journey of self-exploration. She moves to San Francisco after graduating from college and begins a romantic relationship with a woman. Life in California is full of challenges for Stevie, and she is forced to make difficult choices about her personal life. Stevie vacillates between the values that she was raised with and living in a culture that is very different from what she has known. She learns that only her sense of herself is what matters. *Ain't Gonna Be the Same Fool Twice* covers just four years of Stevie's life, but its fast pace leaves the reader breathless. From drugs to lesbianism to black power, *Ain't Gonna Be the Same Fool Twice* presents a portrait of life in the San Francisco Bay Area during the 1970s.

Sinclair's novels offer a refreshing look at budding black womanhood. She challenges assumptions about gender, race, and sexuality and explores what some consider to be taboo subjects with charm and humor. Sinclair sends a liberatory message to young women who are learning to define themselves.

CRITICAL RECEPTION

There has been virtually no scholarly attention paid to Sinclair's fiction. Both of her novels were widely reviewed in magazines and newspapers. *Coffee* was generally well received. Reviewers praised Sinclair's ability to capture the spirit and confusion of adolescence. Joan Philpott, like many reviewers, praised Sinclair's "keen ear for speech and idiom [that] keeps her dialogue crackling all the way from touching to downright hilarious" (73). Donna Seaman cites the historical context of the novel as one of its highlights. "Sinclair parallels Stevie's personal growth from child to woman with the evolution of African Americans' self-image from the teasing yet self-effacing attitude of the book's title to the proud declaration, 'Black is Beautiful' " (738).

Many critics, such as Veronica Chambers, point to Sinclair's use of humor as one of the most pleasing qualities of *Coffee*. "Whether she's dealing with a subject as monumental as the civil rights movement or as intimate as Stevie's first sexual encounters, Sinclair never fails to make you laugh and never sacrifices the narrative to make a point" (E12). The reviewer for *The New Yorker* found that "[m]uch of the charm of this first novel comes from its matter-of-fact initiation into Chicago's African American culture and a virtual glossary of sixties expressions and values" (109). Paschal Fowlkes offers what is possibly the most insightful reading of *Coffee*. Fowlkes found that "Sinclair creates a poignant nexus between the politics of the civil rights movement and the sexual revolution and the inner struggle of adolescence" (14).

Ain't Gonna Be the Same Fool Twice has received a mixed response from reviewers. A combination of high expectations based on *Coffee* and resistance to the novel's exploration of lesbianism and bisexuality led to many negative reviews. Autumn Stephens calls the novel "disappointing." "Too often, *Ain't Gonna Be the Same Fool Twice* reads more like the script for a documentary film about the 1970s, right down to 'A Woman Needs a Man Like a Fish Needs a Bicycle' posters" (3). Teresa Moore offers a fairly typical review in that she considers Sinclair's second novel in light of her first. "*Coffee Will Make You Black* was funny and engaging in its thoughtful creation of a young girl's emotional evolution. But throughout much of *Ain't Gonna Be the Same Fool Twice*, Stevie displays a bemused but game air that doesn't seem to suit her" (C2).

BIBLIOGRAPHY

Works by April Sinclair

Novels

Coffee Will Make You Black. New York: Hyperion Press, 1994.
Ain't Gonna Be the Same Fool Twice. New York: Hyperion Press, 1996.

Article

"Showing Some Teeth." *Allure* June 1996: 76–79.

Studies of April Sinclair

Beauregard, Sue-Ellen. Rev. of *Ain't Gonna Be the Same Fool Twice. Booklist,* 15 Dec. 1995: 693.

Blinkhorn, Lois. "2nd Time's Not Quite the Charm." Rev. of *Ain't Gonna Be the Same Fool Twice. Milwaukee Journal Sentinel,* 25 Feb. 1996, Cue 14, All: 14.

Booker, Jackie R. " 'Fool' Explores Taboo of Black Homosexuality." Rev. of *Ain't Gonna Be the Same Fool Twice. Virginian-Pilot and The Ledger-Star,* 25 Feb. 1996, final: J3.

Brown, Malaika. "Growing Up Was Never This Fun." Rev. of *Coffee Will Make You Black. Los Angeles Sentinel,* 16 Feb. 1995: C4.

Burns, Ann. Rev. of *Coffee Will Make You Black. Library Journal,* 1 Nov. 1993: 120.

Chambers, Veronica. "The Path to Womanhood Cuts across 2 Color Lines." Rev. of *Coffee Will Make You Black. Los Angeles Times,* 4 Feb. 1994: E12.

Christiansen, Richard. "Coming of Age." Rev. of *Coffee Will Make You Black. Chicago Tribune,* 31 May 1996: 5,2: 4.

Cliff, Michelle. " 'Coffee' Steeped in Stereotypes." Rev. of *Coffee Will Make You Black. Washington Post,* 6 Jan. 1994: C2.

" 'Coffee' Is the Real Deal." Rev. of *Coffee Will Make You Black. Chicago Defender,* 8 Feb. 1994: C13.

Dagnal-Myron, Cynthia. "2nd Novel a Disappointment." Rev. of *Ain't Gonna Be the Same Fool Twice. Arizona Daily Star,* 14 Apr. 1996: 7F.

Dawsey, Kierna Mayo. "A Sister's Journey of Self-Discovery." Rev. of *Ain't Gonna Be the Same Fool Twice. Emerge,* Mar. 1996: 58–59.

Fowlkes, Paschal. "Revolution's Voice." Rev. of *Coffee Will Make You Black. San Francisco Review of Books* (Feb./Mar. 1994): 14.

Gilbert, Katherine. "Summer Reading." Rev. of *Coffee Will Make You Black. Christian Century,* 31 July–7 Aug. 1996: 740.

Graham, Renee. "A Child Born Negro, Growing Up Black." Rev. of *Coffee Will Make You Black. Boston Globe,* 1 Apr. 1994: 52.

Greggs, LaTicia D. "Nobody's Fool." Rev. of *Ain't Gonna Be the Same Fool Twice. Chicago Defender,* 6 Feb. 1996: 13.

Hawkins-Bond, Portia. "Nouveau Novels." Rev. of *Coffee Will Make You Black. Essence,* Feb. 1994: 56.

Kaplan, Paul. "Awakenings in the Sixties." Rev. of *Coffee Will Make You Black*. *Library Journal*, 1 May 1994: 164.

Kilpatrick, Thomas L. "Tales of the Windy City." Rev. of *Coffee Will Make You Black*. *Library Journal*, 1 June 1995: S22.

Lewis, Lillian. Rev. of *Ain't Gonna Be the Same Fool Twice*. *Booklist*, 15 Dec. 1995: 687.

Lodge, Sally. Rev. of *Coffee Will Make You Black*. *Publishers Weekly*, 30 Aug. 1993: 66.

Moore, Teresa. "After Hot 'Coffee,' a Weak Refill." Rev. of *Ain't Gonna Be the Same Fool Twice*. *Washington Post*, 22 Feb. 1996: C2.

Nelson, Sara. "The Next Chapter." Rev. of *Coffee Will Make You Black*. *Glamour*, Jan. 1994: 100.

Peters, Ida. Rev. of *Coffee Will Make You Black*. *Washington Afro-American*, 14 May 1994: B8.

———. "April Sinclair's Explosive 'Ain't Gonna Be the Same Fool Twice.' " Rev. of *Ain't Gonna Be the Same Fool Twice*. *Washington Afro-American*, 20 Jan. 1996: B6.

Phillips, Julie. Rev. of *Coffee Will Make You Black*. *Village Voice Literary Supplement*, Mar. 1994: 5.

Philpott, Joan. "Recollections of Two Turbulent Childhoods." Rev. of *Coffee Will Make You Black*. *Ms.*, Jan. 1994: 73.

Reed, Lori. "Sinclair's Stevie: Book Two in the Life of an Irrepressible Heroine." Rev. of *Ain't Gonna Be the Same Fool Twice*. *St. Louis Post-Dispatch*, 1 Feb. 1996: 24.

Rev. of *Coffee Will Make You Black*. *Lambda Book Report*, Mar. 1994: 41.

Rev. of *Coffee Will Make You Black*. *New Yorker*, 2 May 1994: 109.

Rev. of *Coffee Will Make You Black*. *Lambda Book Report*, Mar. 1995: 41, 42.

Rev. of *Coffee Will Make You Black*. *Booklist*, 1 Apr. 1995: 1404.

Rev. of *Coffee Will Make You Black*. *New Yorker*, 5 Feb. 1996: 74.

Ross, Shenise. Rev. of *Ain't Gonna Be the Same Fool Twice*. *Library Journal*, Dec. 1995: 160.

Rubin, Sylvia. "A Novel Way to Sell a Book." *San Francisco Chronicle*, 4 Feb. 1994: E10.

Seaman, Donna. "Steps toward Adulthood." Rev. of *Coffee Will Make You Black*. *Booklist*, 15 Dec. 1993: 738.

Steinberg, Sybil S. Rev. of *Coffee Will Make You Black*. *Publishers Weekly*, 22 Nov. 1993: 50.

———. Rev. of *Ain't Gonna Be the Same Fool Twice*. *Publishers Weekly*, 20 Nov. 1995: 66–67.

Stephens, Autumn. "An African American 'Tales of the City.' " Rev. of *Ain't Gonna Be the Same Fool Twice*. *San Francisco Chronicle Book Review*, 28 Jan. 1996: 3.

Turner, Paige. "April Sinclair Brings Character 'Stevie' Back to Life in Second Novel, 'Ain't Gonna Be the Same Fool Twice.' " Rev. of *Ain't Gonna Be the Same Fool Twice*. *Call and Post*, 28 Dec. 1995: 4.

Whitehouse, Anne. "On the South Side: April Sinclair's Tale of a Girl's Journey toward Self-Discovery." Rev. of *Coffee Will Make You Black*. *Chicago Tribune*, 13 Feb. 1994: C9.

Wren, Andrea M. "Long, Hard Journey to Self-Awareness." Rev. of *Coffee Will Make You Black*. *St. Louis Post-Dispatch*, 6 Feb. 1994: C5.

Wynn, Judith. "Fool for Love." Rev. of *Ain't Gonna Be the Same Fool Twice*. *Boston Herald*, 3 Mar. 1996, Books: 01.

ELLEASE SOUTHERLAND
(1943–)

Cherron A. Barnwell

BIOGRAPHY

A native New Yorker, born in Brooklyn, Ellease Southerland is an African American poet and (auto)biographical novelist, critic, and teacher of African and African American literatures whose writings and teachings reflect strong spirituality, close ties to black southern life, and pride in her African heritage. In Southerland's writings, there is no escaping what she calls in her most recent autobiographical article "I Got a Horn, You Got a Horn" (1987) "the presence of the South in her girlhood years" (175). As for her African heritage, Southerland makes a concentrated effort to show that Africa is undeniably linked to African American life. From writing poetry that exalts Africa, as in the poems "Nigeria" and "Ibo Man," and even in the self-defining poem "Ellease," to employing African symbolism, as in the poem "Seconds" (1974) or as in "Retelling" (1972), to writing the article "Seventeen Days in Nigeria: A Diary," Southerland often insists that she is as much a part of Africa as it is a part of her. During a two-week trip to Egypt, Southerland learned that her family upbringing contained manifestations of African traditions: She realized that her father's sense of morality reflected aspects of ancient Egyptian spirituality.

In the classroom as well, Southerland displays her spiritual bond to African lore, culture, and history. As a professor, Southerland teaches and thus instills pride in the "Africanness" of African American culture. At the Borough of Manhattan Community College, where she taught Afro-American literature, Southerland stressed to her (predominantly black) students the importance of thinking freely in a society that directs our thoughts. Showing how stories such as fairy tales and biblical proverbs have their genesis in the Egyptian language, Southerland induced her students to embrace, with pride, African culture.

Southerland's writing about her own pride in her African ancestry counters nicely the not-so-nice recollections of southern racism that she also writes about—like the indignities her father had to endure as a young man. Keeping her focus on family, Southerland's writing maintains an affirmative attitude in tradition. Southerland grew up in a large family; she is the first daughter, the third child, of fifteen children born to Ellease Dozier and Monroe Penrose Southerland. Named after her mother, Southerland and her mother had a very loving relationship—one, she says, that made her feel more like a co-mother rather than a daughter. Her mother was amazingly encouraging, says Southerland, and had no doubt that she would complete her first novel. In fact, her mother attempted to create the cover design for the novel.

In the nurturing mother–co-mother relationship, Southerland witnessed closely and learned her mother's commitment to love, marriage, and family. Unfortunately, Southerland had to use these lessons when she had to assume the role of mother of her younger siblings after her mother's early death from cancer. The impact of her mother's death is a pronounced theme in Southerland's writing.

In a family where reading and writing were regular pastimes, Southerland could not resist a love for literature; she could not resist a career in writing. Having witnessed at ten years her uncle recite his own poetry in her father's church during the Sunday poetry sessions that she often conducted, Southerland was immediately impressed and decided that she would write poetry. The poem Southerland wrote in the fifth grade—a poem that revealed a quick wit and precociousness—foreshadowed the perspicuity, brevity, and impressionistic style that would become Southerland's writing style.

One year before completing her undergraduate degree at Queens College of the City University of New York (CUNY), Southerland wrote the John Golden Award-winning novella *White Shadow* (1964). Southerland received her B.A. from Queens College, CUNY, in 1965; she received her M.F.A. from Columbia University in 1974. From 1973 to 1976, Southerland taught English at Columbia University, Community Educational Exchange Program, New York City. During her tenure at Columbia, Southerland published her first book, *The Magic Sun Spins* (1975). In 1979, Southerland wrote her first semiautobiographical and critically acclaimed novel, *Let the Lion Eat Straw*. Currently, Southerland teaches African and African American literature at the Borough of Manhattan Community College, CUNY; she is an adjunct professor/lecturer and poet in residence at Pace University, New York. Still, Southerland writes. Her latest published work is an excerpt from the forthcoming novel *A Feast of Fools* appearing in Terry McMillan's anthology *Breaking Ice*. The excerpt seizes upon her 1966–1972 experience as a caseworker for the Department of Social Services, New York City. Southerland appears in the 1996/1997 edition of *Who's Who among African Americans*.

MAJOR WORKS AND THEMES

Southerland entered the African American literary milieu with the publication of poetry. Her earliest published poetry appeared in several journals such as *Journal of Black Poetry*, *Poet Lore*, and *Présence Africaine*. Between the years of 1971 and 1975, Southerland regularly submitted poetry to journal *Black World*. Southerland's poetry gained immediate acclaim, especially for "Warlock," which earned her the Gwendolyn Brooks* Award in 1971. Receiving this award was, for Southerland, a great honor; she considers Gwendolyn Brooks her "literary mother." Southerland shows a reverence for Brooks in her adaptation of some of Brooks' blueslike rhythms in her verse.

"Warlock" and other previously published poems eventually appeared in her major compilation of poetry, *The Magic Sun Spins*, published in 1975. The book's title actually signifies on the first line of the prideful poem, "Black Is," which was first published in the May 1972 issue of *Black World* and which also appears in this compilation. Touching on themes about the Vietnam War, self-determination, family, pride, and tradition, *The Magic Sun Spins* captures Southerland's magical vision of life's experiences, both inherited and lived.

Many of the poems in *The Magic Sun Spins* reflect Southerland's writing versatility. "Recitation" shows in its alliteration and rhythmic verse Southerland's blueslike style. The musical orientation that she received from her parents suffuses her poetry. Southerland's brevity captures the joy in simple action that makes up the simpleness of life. The poems "Two fishing villages" and "Vallejo" condemn the destruction of life that people justify in war. The poem titled "That love survives" speaks of the pain of her mother's death and the comforting memories of her mother's love. "Nigerian rain" and "Blue clay" are poems in this compilation that celebrate African culture.

In *Let the Lion Eat Straw* published in 1979, Southerland makes her most critically acclaimed contribution to the African American literary milieu. *Let the Lion Eat Straw* captures the love, admiration, and reverence Southerland has for her mother. It took Southerland five years to complete the novel, which presents snapshots of her mother's life from childhood, at the age of six, to an early death from cancer.

The language of *Let the Lion Eat Straw* rings of conversational black dialect. In a griotlike tone that more than likely gave Southerland the distance she needed to convey the personal events just as they were, Southerland illustrates the tribulations and the wonders of being a large black family that together overcame the harsh realities of racism in America. It received the award of the "Best Book for Young Adults 1979" by the Young Adult Services Division of the American Library Association.

Like her poetry, the prose in *Let the Lion Eat Straw* not only is terse but also contains blueslike rhythms. When Southerland interpolates a song into the text, she reveals that writing and music are inseparable. Southerland writes a scene where the young Abeba, who portrays Southerland's real mother, and Abeba's midwife/mother Mother Habblesham stroll down a New York City street and pass a circle of boys singing "Hey-bob-a-ree-bob/She's my baby./Hey-bob-a-ree-bob/Don't mean maybe" (16–17). This musical pattern echoes the significant orientation of music in the story, in her mother's life, and in her own personal life.

Because *Let the Lion Eat Straw* centers on Abeba, the character who portrays Southerland's mother, it captures her mother's triumphs as a black woman committed to her husband, his ministry, and a family of thirteen children. *Let the Lion Eat Straw* illustrates a daughter (Abeba) who abandoned a potential career as a concert pianist to pursue the love between her and Daniel Torch, a Baptist minister from St. Augustine. Despite her mother's disappointment that manifested itself in spiteful, verbally abusive attacks, Abeba remained committed to loving her family, her husband, and her God. Abeba would remain dignified in her decision until the moment of her death.

In 1987, Southerland would write again about herself and her family in the article "I Got a Horn, You Got a Horn." Southerland's paternal grandmother "visit[ed] many times, traveling more than a thousand miles, bringing the sun with her" (176), writes Southerland. Southerland also writes about her family's trials. The most important feature is her family's solidarity, which is sustained by the strength of her mother's love and commitment to family despite its large size. The family's size, its solidarity, kept them motivated in their interests, especially their musical interests. Obviously, the title of the article, "I Got a Horn, You Got a Horn," reflects this aspect. "I Got a Horn, You Got a Horn" is an autobiographical article based on how "through the years her family trio had grown" and became "a full chorus and brass band" (199).

CRITICAL RECEPTION

Already included in four biobibliographies prior to this one, discussions about Southerland's work stay focused on the personal intimacy that permeates her writings. Acclaimed for its succinctness, its conversational tone, and impressionism, Southerland's prose is said to reflect her inherent talent as poet. Mary Hughes Brookhart asserts that "what Southerland has written is meticulously distilled. Although it may seem as accessible as conversation and as immediate as a sense impression, her poetry and fiction are also dense with motifs, allusions, and symbols" (240).

Assessment of Southerland's work remains mainly in the form of book reviews. From the period 1979–1980, book reviews focused mostly upon Southerland's major (auto)biographical novel *Let the Lion Eat Straw*. Recognizing Southerland's literary reputation as a poet, book reviews concentrated on the poetic style that infuses her prose. *Bestsellers* stated, "The absence of a plot *per se* allows Southerland to weave a story line around the poetic, clinging images of her characters" (162). *The New York Review of Books* focused more on the "sensory impact of language as it proceeds in short bursts—word by word, line by line—than with the creation of broad and rapid effects" (44). *Commonweal* observes that Southerland "writes in the cadence of black English speech without use of dialect" (114). The *Washington Post* compares Southerland to Toni Morrison* and James McPherson, thereby making her akin to African American authors "who do not shun violence or social stands." The *Washington Post* also notes that Maya Angelou praises Southerland as "a seer of the interior human landscape" (B1). Southerland expresses her appreciation for Maya Angelou's praise in an interview in the *Contemporary Authors*: "The first response I got in a very dramatic way was from Maya Angelou, and that meant a great deal because she and I share the same world of imagery. It's pretty much an African tradition that the senior member welcome in some ceremonious way the junior member, so I felt that an African ceremony was completed when she gave me that welcome" ("Southerland," 1983, 481). Lastly, Hoyt Fuller notes that despite "the small incentives by the institutions of black writing," Southerland has maintained a determination to publish her novel: "We should have known. The strength was always there, as much inherent in the vision as in the talent. Ellease Southerland, still only a name to us, has triumphed. This past spring, Scribner's brought out her first novel, *Let the Lion Eat Straw*, and all the beauty is there" (52). Southerland's *Let the Lion Eat Straw* went through several republications, the latest in 1986. Although *Let the Lion Eat Straw* is currently out of print, an "author-search" on the Internet will list the many library holdings of the novel.

BIBLIOGRAPHY

Works by Ellease Southerland

White Shadow. Unpublished. (Novella)
The Magic Sun Spins. London: Paul Breman, 1975. (Poetry)
Let the Lion Eat Straw. New York: Scribner, 1979. (Fiction)
"I Got a Horn, You Got a Horn." *A World Unsuspected: Portraits of Southern Childhood*. Chapel Hill: University of North Carolina Press, 1987. (Nonfiction)
    Other works consist of short stories, critical essays, diary, poetry published in journals, and an excerpt from the still forthcoming novel *A Feast of Fools*, in *Breaking Ice: An Anthology of Contemporary African-American Fiction*. Ed. Terry McMillan. New York: Penguin Books, 1990.

Studies of Ellease Southerland

Bernays, Anne. "Black Track." Rev. of *Let the Lion Eat Straw*. *The Christian Science Monitor*, 11 July 1979: 19.
Bikman, Minda. "Southern Grit." Rev. of *Let the Lion Eat Straw*. *Chicago Tribune Book World*, 13 May 1979: sec. 7: 3+.
Brookhart, Mary Hughes. "Ellease Southerland." *Dictionary of Literary Biography: Afro-American Fiction Writers after 1955*. Vol. 33. Detroit: Gale, 1984. 239–44.

Daniels, Mark. "Southerland, Ellease." Rev. of *Let the Lion Eat Straw*. *Bestsellers*, 5 Aug. 1979: 162.

"Ellease Southerland." *Black Writers: A Selection of Sketches from "Contemporary Authors."* Ed. Linda Metzger. Detroit: Gale, 1989. 210–13.

Fuller, Hoyt, et al. "Two Views: *Let the Lion Eat Straw*." *First World* 2.3 (1979): 49–52.

Kilgore, James C., Angela Jackson, and Hoyt W. Fuller. "Two Views: *Let the Lion Eat Straw*." Rev. of *Let the Lion Eat Straw*. *First World* 2, no. 3 (1979): 49–52.

Leonard, John. "Book of the Times." Rev. of *Let the Lion Eat Straw*. *New York Times*, 10 May 1979: 102D.

Mitchell, Carolyn. "Southerland, Ellease." *Black Women in America: An Historical Encyclopedia*. Vol. 2. New York: Carlson, 1993. 1090–91.

Rev. of *Let the Lion Eat Straw*. *Commonweal*, 29 Feb. 1980.

"Southerland, Ellease." *Contemporary Authors*. Vol. 107. Detroit: Gale Research Co., 1983. 480–82

"Southerland, Ellease." Rev. of *The Magic Sun Spins*. *Choice*, Oct. 1976: 974.

"Southerland, Ellease." *Who's Who among African Americans*. Ed. Shirelle Phelps. Detroit: Gale, 1997. 1403.

Swan, Annalyn. "Love Story." Rev. of *Let the Lion Eat Straw*. *Time*, 18 June 1979: 85–86.

Towers, Robert. Rev. of *Let the Lion Eat Straw*. *New York Review of Books*, 11 Oct. 1979: 43–44.

Trescott, Jacqueline. "*Let the Lion Eat Straw*. Let the Author Win Glory." *Washington Post*, 6 Aug. 1979: B1, B11.

Watkins, Mel. "The Woman Surviving." Rev. of *Let the Lion Eat Straw*. *New York Times Book Review*, 3 June 1979: 14, 43.

JOYCE CAROL THOMAS
(1938–   )

Amy E. Earhart

BIOGRAPHY

Joyce Carol Thomas was born in Ponca, Oklahoma, on May 25, 1938. Thomas has returned to her birthplace and the experiences that occurred there throughout her career, using the town as a setting for her novels *Marked by Fire*, *Bright Shadow*, and *The Golden Pasture*. Her experiences working in the Oklahoma cotton fields, which delayed her entry to school each year, find their way into her work. In addition, Thomas learned much about language and storytelling from her family, friends, and community. She remembers the "porch sitters" in her hometown, the elders of the community who told and retold stories. Her experiences at church resound in the imagery, language, and rhythms of her writing. In fact, much of her work with language attempts to re-create the sounds of singing remembered from her childhood church experiences.

At ten, Thomas' family moved to Tracy, California, a rural town in the San Joaquin Valley. She fondly remembers the language of those who worked with her during the summers that she spent picking crops, including the language of Spanish-speaking migrant workers. Thomas comments, "I found foreign languages, the language of the church, and that of the Ponca and Tracy people to be a fitting foundation for writing." She continues, "The music of the word is what I want to create in my writing of books" ("Joyce," *Authors and Artists* 208).

Thomas completed a B.A. in Spanish and French at San Jose State University in 1966 and an M.A. in education at Stanford University in 1967. As she was working on her doctorate in education at Berkeley, she recognized that she had a talent for creative writing. Thomas has held various positions in education and English departments, including a full professorship in the Department of English at the University of Tennessee. She has recently returned to Berkeley, California, and continues to write.

MAJOR WORKS AND THEMES

Thomas' work spans genres from young adult novels, to poetry, to plays. She states, "When I began to write novels, I still continued to write poems" ("Joyce," *Authors and Artists* 209). Her novels explore young adults' search to understand and come to terms with the joys and pains of life, as well as their desire to understand community, family, and identity. The novels utilize lyrical language, merge realism with the mystical, the natural with urban, and lovingly explore the life of the black community and church.

Her first novel, *Marked by Fire*, was highly acclaimed and brought comparisons to contemporary author Maya Angelou. The story begins a now-three-novel examination of Abyssinia Jackson, her family, and her community of Ponca City, Oklahoma, Thomas' hometown. Thomas creates sequential, dated, poetic vignettes to tell the story of Abyssinia, born in a cotton field and marked by an ember for a life of joy and pain. The novel follows Abyssinia's childhood joys experienced through music, community, and love, which are ruptured by her rape at age ten, forcing her violent entry into a confusing and painful adult life. Abyssinia retreats into muteness, and only through the strength of the community of Ponca City women does she fight the terrors, symbolized by the mad torture of Trembling Sally.

The sequel to *Marked by Fire* is *Bright Shadow*, which follows Abyssinia to college. Much like *Marked by Fire*, *Bright Shadow* emphasizes the need for Abyssinia to cope with the horrors of life through faith, hope, and love. After a dream of impending doom, Abyssinia discovers that her Aunt Serena has been brutally murdered and skinned alive by her mad husband, the Reverend Rufus Jordan. The loss of Aunt Serena, her best-loved aunt, leaves her devastated. After this brutal crime, she must also cope with the loss of Carl Lee Jefferson, her boyfriend, during the time in which Carl Lee leaves his abusive, alcoholic father and searches for his lost mother. Abyssinia learns, through these experiences, that with unspeakable joy comes unspeakable evil. The text emphasizes life's hope with nature's unusual signs: violets bloom in January, a cat leaves blooming flowers in its paw prints, and birds protect a young kitten. In addition, the text deals frankly with domestic violence, through both Aunt Serena's horrific marriage and the women's quilting gossip regarding an abused neighbor.

Water Girl expands Thomas' focus from Abyssinia to her extended family, as the main character, Amber Westbrook, discovers an old letter that exposes her cousin Abyssinia to be her mother. Amber embarks on a spiritual quest in the wilderness to understand the revelation. Through a vision and help from animals and music, she is able to reorganize her life. A strong female character, Amber is a tomboy who is an excellent hunter and outdoorswoman. Through Amber's character, Thomas is also able to explore issues of colonization, prejudice, and genocide.

Thomas returns to Carl Lee Jefferson's story in *The Golden Pasture*, which chronicles the young Carl Lee's journey to an understanding of his father, Samuel Jefferson. Through a rescue of an injured Appaloosa horse and his rodeo grandfather's wisdom, Carl Lee moves from childhood to emerging manhood. Thomas fuses tall tales and folklore with magical events to produce a fanciful ending. Unlike her other novels, which focus on women's interaction, this is her only novel that focuses on men's communities; *The Golden Pasture* was written as a response to Thomas' son's request for a novel about boys.

Journey focuses on Meggie, blessed at birth by a tarantula, who finds herself at the center of a horrifying mystery. When Meggie stumbles upon one of the several teenagers killed in the Eucalyptus Forest, she embarks on an adventure that leads her to the center of a strange organ-harvesting plot. Meggie is a self-reliant, unafraid female character who bravely forces the resolution of the murders, remembering her Reverend's admonition to "[k]eep a light in your heart" (148). Thomas merges lyrical passages laden with refrains from religion and folklore with mystical spiders and protective animals to create a story that explores the life cycle. In addition, the story's subtext examines ingrained prejudices, intercultural violence, and the effect of both on children and adults.

When the Nightingale Sings, Thomas' most recent novel, follows the fantastic journey of a young girl, Marigold, and three adult sisters, who move from disjunction over an old love affair to a family reunion. Focusing on the search for a new Queen Mother Rhythm, the healing and blessing head gospel singer of the Rose of Sharon Baptist Church, Thomas merges descriptive written passages with extended gospel songs. Her characters, Marigold, the orphaned child, Anthony, Minister of Music, and River Rainbow and Sparrow Sunrise, Royal Runners, merge into the swamp in which the action occurs. The beautiful descriptions of the swamp and the blending of the birds with human characters, such as the nightingale with Marigold during her search for her singing voice and her position as the new Queen Mother Rhythm, help to aptly describe a young woman's coming-of-age. *When the Nightingale Sings* was also rewritten and performed as a musical play.

CRITICAL RECEPTION

Joyce Carol Thomas' work has garnered generally positive critical responses and a variety of awards, including the American Book Award (now National Book Award) for *Marked by Fire* and the Coretta Scott King Award fom the American Library Association for *Bright Shadow*. In addition, both *Marked by Fire* and *Bright Shadow* have become standard texts in many public schools. Critical discussions of Thomas' work have been limited to reviews of her texts and reference articles. Of her young adult fiction, *Marked by Fire* and *The Golden Pasture* have received the most enthusiastic responses, with writers Maya Angelou, James Baldwin,* and Alice Childress,* among others, praising the novels. Reviews of her other novels have been mixed.

Critics consistently comment on Thomas' use of lyrical language. Carolyn Caywood, in a review of *Bright Shadow*, notes Thomas' "sensuously descriptive passages celebrating the physical beauty of the black characters" (90). Other critics praise Thomas' "delicate hand with language" (Davis 50) and her novel's "lyrical style grounded in black experience" (*Kirkus Reviews* 1410) and call her a "weaver of words" (*Publishers Weekly* 191).

Critics seem less comfortable with Thomas' mixture of reality and fantasy. Alice Childress, in a review of *Marked by Fire*, praises Thomas' ability to find "a marvelous fairy tale quality in everyday happenings" (38). But critics were less comfortable with the use of fantasy in *Journey*; for example, LaTronica notes, "This discordant mixture of fantasy and mystery is composed of too many elements that never blend successfully" (165).

Positive were responses to Thomas' treatment of black youths. *Kirkus Reviews* states that "Thomas has neatly integrated into it [the plot] a celebration of black youth" (1410). *Booklist* calls *Marked by Fire* a "lyrical celebration of black womanhood" that also "evoke[s] a vital sense of a rural black community as well as individuals within it" (754).

BIBLIOGRAPHY

Works by Joyce Carol Thomas

Bittersweet. Berkeley, CA: Firesign, 1973. (Poetry)
Crystal Breezes. Berkeley, CA: Firesign, 1974. (Poetry)
Blessing. Berkeley, CA: Jocato, 1975. (Poetry)
Look! What a Wonder! Berkeley Community Theatre, Berkeley, CA. 1976a. (Play)
A Song in the Sky. Montgomery Theater, San Francisco. 1976b. (Play)
Magnolia. Old San Francisco Opera House, San Francisco. 1977. (Play)
Ambrosia. Little Fox Theatre, San Francisco. 1978. (Play)
Black Child. New York: Zamani, 1981. (Poetry)
Inside the Rainbow. Palo Alto, CA: Zikawuna, 1982a. (Poetry)
Marked by Fire. New York: Avon, 1982b. (Novel)
Bright Shadow. New York: Avon, 1983. (Novel)
The Golden Pasture. New York: Scholastic, 1986a. (Novel)
The Water Girl. New York: Avon, 1986b. (Novel)
Journey. New York: Scholastic, 1988. (Novel)
Gospel Roots. California State University, Carson City. 1989a. (Play)
I Have Heard of a Land. Classen Theatre, Oklahoma City. 1989b. (Play)
Ed. "Young Reverend Zelma Lee Moses." *A Gathering of Flowers: Stories about Being Young in America.* New York: HarperCollins, 1990. 99–134. (Short Story and Anthology Editor)
When the Nightingale Sings. Clarence Brown Theatre, University of Tennessee, Knoxville. 1991. (Play)

When the Nightingale Sings. New York: HarperCollins, 1992. (Novel)
Brown Honey in Broomwheat Tea. New York: HarperCollins, 1993. (Poetry)
Gingerbread Days. New York: HarperCollins, 1995. (Poetry)

Studies of Joyce Carol Thomas

Caywood, Carolyn. Rev. of *Bright Shadow. School Library Journal* 30.5 (1984): 89–90.
Childress, Alice. Rev. of *Marked by Fire. New York Times Book Review* (18 April 1982): 38.
Davis, Thulani. Rev. of *Bright Shadow. Essence* 14.12 (1984): 50.
Estes, Sally. *Booklist* 82.12 (1986): 861–62.
"Joyce Carol Thomas." *Authors and Artists for Young Adults.* Ed. Kevin S. Hill. Vol. 12. Detroit: Gale, 1994. 205–13.
"Joyce Carol Thomas." *Black Writers.* Ed. Sharon Malinowski. 2d ed. Detroit: Gale, 1994. 614–16.
"Joyce Carol Thomas." *Contemporary Authors: New Revision Series.* Ed. Pamela S. Dear. Vol. 48. Detroit: Gale, 1995. 439–43.
"Joyce Carol Thomas." *Contemporary Literary Criticism.* Ed. Daniel G. Marowski. Vol. 35. Detroit: Gale, 1985. 405–7.
"Joyce Carol Thomas." *Inter/View: Talks with America's Writing Women.* Ed. Mickey Pearlman and Katherine Henderson. Louisville: University of Kentucky Press, 1990. 125–31.
"Joyce Carol Thomas." *Literary Criticism Series: Children's Literature Review.* Ed. Gerard J. Senick. Vol. 19. Detroit: Gale, 1990. 219–23.
"Joyce Carol Thomas." *Meet the Authors.* Ed. Debbie Kovacs. New York: Scholastic Professional Books, 1995. 92–95.
"Joyce Carol Thomas." *Something about the Author.* Ed. Joyce Nakamura. Vol. 40. Detroit: Gale, 1986. 208–9.
"Joyce Carol Thomas." *Women Writers of the West Coast.* Ed. Marilyn Yalom. Santa Barbara, CA: Capra, 1983. 31–39.
LaTronica, Starr. Rev. of *Journey. School Library Journal* 35.2 (1988): 165.
Raburn, Josephine. "Bright Shadow." *Masterpieces of African-American Literature.* Ed. Frank N. Magill. New York: HarperCollins, 1992. 79–82.
———. "Marked by Fire." *Masterpieces of African-American Literature.* Ed. Frank N. Magill. New York: HarperCollins, 1992. 285–88.
Rev. of *The Golden Pasture. Publishers Weekly* 230.4 (1996): 191.
Rev. of *Journey. Kirkus Reviews* 56.18 (1988): 1410.
Rev. of *Marked by Fire. Booklist* 78.12 (1982): 754.
Toombs, Charles P. "Joyce Carol Thomas." *Dictionary of Literary Biography: Afro-American Fiction Writers after 1955.* Ed. Thadious M. Davis and Trudier Harris. Vol. 33. Detroit: Gale, 1984. 245–50.

DAWN TURNER TRICE
(1965–)

Lean'tin Bracks

BIOGRAPHY

Dawn Turner Trice, a young African American writer and upcoming author in the world of literary fiction, understands well the struggle as a newcomer in having her stories heard. Trice received numerous rejections while attempting to publish her novel in the early stages of her authorship. She has described this experience and her ultimate success through the words of the old Negro Spiritual, which says," He may not come when you want, but He's right on time." Whether we interpret this as "right" or "write," it still serves to convey this author's experiences.

Although *Only Twice I've Wished for Heaven* is Trice's first publication, the art of weaving a good tale is not new to her. The Turner family, which consisted of Dawn's parents and one younger sister by three years, would often vie for the opportunity to share stories around the family table. This gathering was important for Dawn and her family, as well as friends and relatives, while she was growing up in Chicago. Her joy of reading was also fueled in her early years by her parents, who went so far as to allow a delay in chores if one was engrossed in a good book. Dawn fondly remembers her use of this option to delay housework, but reading and the wonders of stories and storytelling had already become a pleasurable part of her life. Those childhood experiences supported the rich development of her love of reading and weaving a good tale.

Dawn began her college years at the University of Illinois in Champaign with an interest in premed, but she soon realized that the art of telling a good story was a part of her life that needed to be shared. She recognized the early rejections of her novel as technical and not spiritual. While reconfirming her commitment to telling a good story and thus redoing the book, she was deeply wounded by the loss of her only sister from a heart attack. As she dealt with the emotional terms of both of these situations, her life perspectives and subsequently her novel took on deeper dimensions.

Dawn Turner Trice, an editor at the *Chicago Tribune* for over ten years, is now working on her second novel. She continues to strive toward telling a good story that shares a moral or a moment of challenge for her reader, while being blessed with the love and companionship of her husband, David, and her daughter, Hannah. Although she has stated that her first novel is about "[s]aving children and the responsibility of adults to shepherd children along their path," she eagerly seeks to continue to grow as an artist and explore new themes.

MAJOR WORKS AND THEMES

Only Twice I've Wished for Heaven offers a contemporary perspective on segregation and class division as it affects the African American community. Trice's novel unfolds through the primary narratives of an eleven-year-old girl, Tempestt Rosa Saville, and her urban guide and protector, Miss Jonetta Goode. The narrative technique of the young girl, Tempestt, invokes the experiences of coming-of-age and the loss of innocence, while Miss Jonetta shares experiences of sadness, secrets, and death that transcend time.

The story takes place in 1975, when Tempestt and her family are chosen through a lottery, entered by her father, to move into an elite black neighborhood in Chicago called Lakeland. Lakeland is inhabited by blacks who, "once removed from salt pork, fatback, and biscuits, now dine on caviar and escargot" (120). There, amid upwardly mobile blacks who have mentally and physically shut themselves away from the economic and moral turmoil of urban black America, Tempestt's father must rediscover the true meaning of community. Outside Lakeland on Thirty-fifth Street, the urban black community struggles against the cycles of destruction from which Lakeland offers a safe haven. These two worlds are separated by a "wrought-iron" fence covered with ivy that is meant to impose a naturalness to this unnatural separation.

Tempestt, in her youthful curiosity, is drawn beyond the boundaries of Lakeland and crawls under the fence and into the world of Thirty-fifth Street. She moves throughout the story between her family in Lakeland and her acquired family on Thirty-fifth Street, who are the constant patrons of Miss Jonetta's liquor store and O'Cala's Food and Drug. This family consists of Fat Daddy, Mr. Chitty, and Hump, who have traveled through those urban streets, caught in the unrelenting mud that attaches itself to all who pass through. Miss Jonetta, whose life reflects the destructive cycle of Thirty-fifth Street, knows the dangers of this place. "I remember . . . bowing my head and wishing for heaven. Wishing hard that there was such a place I could hang my hat. Wishing the way you do when you ain't got nothing else to reach for and you find yourself sinking into a hole so deep and dark and cold" (120). In the eyes of the street preacher Alfred Mayes Tempestt first discovers Thirty-fifth Street. Mayes was a connoisseur of "fine young things" and was "God-like in stature and form. He was an explosion, all-consuming and equally devastating" (35). Miss Jonetta understands that even as she warns Tempestt, whom she calls Child, Child will return to the excitement and to the terror of Thirty-fifth Street. It thus becomes Miss Jonetta's mission to protect Child as best she can.

In Lakeland, Tempestt's father and mother try to cope with this new culturally correct environment as Miss Lily the maid brings news of the truths and the lies that seem indistinguishable in this selective environment. The story continues to move back and forth between the communities and the lives of Tempestt and Miss Jonetta as they share experiences that eventually culminate in the tragic life of Valerie Nicholae, Tempestt's friend from Lakeland. Valerie's life, which teeters between going to Lakeland school in the day and spending evenings with her mother on Thirty-fifth street, eventually brings a confrontation between the two communities. Valerie's life reveals the destruction of community that exists on Thirty-fifth Street as well as in Lakeland. Valerie's freedom through death also causes Tempestt's father to see past the illusion of material happiness, and this realization eventually sets "all" free from their constructed lives of assumed safety and continual suffering.

This story is filled with love, rage, and the complexity of living that exist in a world where the spiritual and moral quality of life is sacrificed for material gain and social acceptance. The children bear the burden of this destruction, instead of being nurtured in the love that makes us all whole and healthy. Ultimately, the future of the children and thus the community stands out as Trice's most poignant theme.

CRITICAL RECEPTION

Trice's first novel has been acknowledged as a promising beginning, for it brings to the reading public a perspective that is fresh and stirring. As critic Amy Begg says, "This novel will stay with the reader long after the final chapter has been finished" (98). Critics such as Joanne Wilkinson also comment that "Trice's effort to blend metaphor and social realism is striking and inventive" (573). Reviews of Trice's novel center around coming-of-age and the issues of class that separate the privileged and the disfranchised in the African American community. Valerie Smith notes in her review how Trice falls prey to the trap of presenting the middle class as dull and superficial, while working-class people are romanticized and much more connected to the reality of the world they live in. Characters such as Tempestt and her father go through major changes in their lives, yet many questions go unanswered. As for Lakeland professionals, Jabari Asim comments that Trice used "too broad a brush and too heavy a hammer" (D4). In spite of the concern regarding the presentation of characters and the twists and turns that the plot takes, what permeates all the reviews is the welcoming of a style that is touching, melodic, and insightful and that adds a new perspective to the urban African American experience and the experiences of communities as a whole.

BIBLIOGRAPHY

Work by Dawn Turner Trice

Only Twice I've Wished for Heaven. New York: Random House, 1996.

Studies of Dawn Turner Trice

Asim, Jabari. "Looping around Chicago: An African American Girl's Class Trip." Rev. of *Only Twice I've Wished for Heaven. The Washington Post Book World* (April 14, 1997): D4.

Begg, Amy. Rev. of *Only Twice I've Wished for Heaven. Library Journal* 121 (September 15, 1996): 98.

Coughlin, Ruth. Rev. of *Only Twice I've Wished for Heaven. The New York Times Book Review* 146 (February 23, 1997): 16.

Smith, Valerie. "Adult Aspirations, Childhood Dreams." Rev of *Only Twice I've Wished for Heaven. Emerge* (March 1997): 16.

Steinberg, Sybil. Rev. of *Only Twice I've Wished for Heaven. Publishers Weekly* 243.45 (November 4, 1996): 62.

Wilkinson, Joanne. Rev. of *Only Twice I've Wished for Heaven. Booklist* 93 (November 15, 1996): 573.

ALICE WALKER
(1944–)

Molly Roden

BIOGRAPHY

The author of the Pulitzer Prize-winning novel *The Color Purple* (1982), Alice Walker rose from relative obscurity to celebrity status within a short time period. *The Color Purple* is far from being Walker's only literary accomplishment. As a poet, short story writer, essayist, critic, editor, and author of children's books, Alice Walker has proven her mastery of a multitude of genres time and again. Many of Walker's works have been heavily influenced by her own experience as a southerner, as an African American, and as a woman.

Alice Malsenior Walker was born on 9 February 1944, in Eatonton, Georgia. She was the last child of eight in a sharecropping family. The circumstances of her upbringing and her family would play a major role in many of Walker's later writings. *The Third Life of Grange Copeland* (1970), Walker's first novel, is set in an impoverished area of Georgia similar to Walker's own birthplace and deals with the economic oppression and resultant desperation of three generations of a black sharecropping family. In that novel, the character of Mem is partly based upon Minnie Tallulah Grant Walker, Alice's mother: "Like Mem . . . , my mother adorned with flowers whatever house we were forced to live in" (*In Search of Our Mothers' Gardens* 241). The idea of female creativity as a means of overcoming oppression and the transcendence that may occur through such artistic expression as was demonstrated by her mother are further explored throughout Walker's fiction.

The event in Walker's childhood that first sparked her literary life was a BB gun accident that blinded eight-year-old Alice in one eye. It took six years for the scar tissue on her eye to be removed, during which time Alice's eye was severely disfigured. Paradoxically perhaps, Walker's blindness deepened her ability to "see": "I believe . . . that it was from this period—from my solitary, lonely position of an outcast—that I began really to see people and things. . . . I retreated into solitude, and read stories and began to write poems" (*In Search of Our Mothers' Gardens* 244–245). In 1961, Walker graduated from high school as valedictorian. The tragic loss of her eye again yielded positive results when she was awarded a rehabilitation scholarship that enabled her to go to college. When Walker left Eatonton to attend Spelman College in Atlanta, she was given a seventy-five-dollar contribution from her neighbors as well as three significant presents from her mother: a suitcase with which to depart from her poor, rural surroundings; a typewriter with which to write; and a sewing machine, which afforded her the economic freedom to create her own clothing as Celie does with her pants-making enterprise in *The Color Purple*.

Walker attended Spelman College for two and a half years before transferring to Sarah Lawrence College in New York. Her college years served to shape Walker in a number of ways. As an all-black southern school, Spelman was affected by the Civil Rights movement, and Walker's understanding of civil rights issues grew during her time in Atlanta. At Sarah Lawrence, Walker was one of few African American students, making her own search for identity even more pronounced. Walker also began to question the Christian religious tradition that had pervaded her childhood: "As a college student I came to reject the Christianity of my parents, and it took me years to realize that though they had been force-fed a white man's palliative, in the form of religion, they had made it into something at once simple and noble" (*In Search of Our Mothers' Gardens* 17–18). This ambivalence toward Christianity recurs throughout Walker's works.

Walker's last year of college was one of intense emotion and volatile experiences. Walker had gone on a trip to Africa and Europe the previous summer, a journey that yielded many of the poems for *Once*, her first book of poetry published three years later in 1968. Images of, and journeys to, Africa figure prominently in many of Walker's novels, including *The Color Purple, The Temple of My Familiar* (1989), and *Possessing the Secret of Joy* (1992). However, in addition to returning to the United States with a vibrant excitement about her travels, Walker also returned from her trip to Africa pregnant. The African poems in *Once* are thus interspersed with poems that reveal the depression and contemplation of suicide that Walker endured during this period. With the help of several friends, Walker was able to get an abortion, and she poured all the emotion of her ordeal into her poetry. Had she not overcome this experience through her writing, Walker says, "I firmly believe I would never have survived to be a writer. I know I would not have survived at all" (*In Search of Our Mothers' Gardens* 249).

Walker graduated from Sarah Lawrence in 1965 and began working for the welfare department in New York City. She left that job in order to increase her involvement with the Civil Rights movement, first in Georgia and then in Mississippi, mostly working on voter registration projects. Her experiences at Spelman coupled with her time as a civil rights worker in the deep South laid the foundation for her second novel, *Meridian*. Also during this period, Walker married Melvyn Roseman Leventhal, a Jewish civil rights lawyer. Walker continued to write, and her first novel, *The Third Life of Grange Copeland*, was completed three days before the birth of their daughter, Rebecca Grant, in 1969. During the next several years, Walker taught at various colleges, including Jackson State in Mississippi, Tougalou College, Wellesley College, and the University of Massachusetts. Her writing continued to gain recognition as well. In 1973, Walker's third book of poetry, *Revolutionary Petunias*, was nominated for the National Book Award. *In Love and Trouble*, her first collection of short stories, was published in 1973 and took the Rosenthal Award of the National Institute of Arts and Letters.

In 1975, Walker became a contributing editor to the feminist magazine Ms. In 1976, Walker and Leventhal divorced, and in the same year, Walker's second novel, *Meridian*, was published. While Walker received a Guggenheim Fellowship in 1977 and a teaching appointment at Yale, her highest honors have been in connection with her third novel, *The Color Purple*, for which she won the American Book Award and the Pulitzer Prize in 1983 and which was transformed into a major motion picture under Steven Spielberg's direction in 1985. *The Color Purple* speaks to many experiences in Walker's personal life and family history, including its setting in the Deep South, its relationship to the rape of Walker's great-grandmother at the age of twelve, its inclusion of images of Africa, and its focus on African American women, for to Walker, "black women are the most fascinating creatures in the world" (*In Search of Our Mothers' Gardens* 251).

The Color Purple, in some ways, laid the foundation for Walker's "womanist" philosophy, which she fully explores in her 1983 collection of prose entitled *In Search of Our Mothers' Gardens*. "Womanist," Walker explains in the opening pages of her collection, can be defined in the following ways:

Womanist 1. From *womanish*. (Opp. of "girlish," i.e., frivolous, irresponsible, not serious.) A black feminist or feminist of color. From the black folk expression of mothers to female children, "You acting womanish," i.e., like a woman. Usually referring to outrageous, audacious, courageous or *willful* behavior. Wanting to know more and in greater depth than is considered "good" for one. Interested in grown-up doings. Acting grown up. Being grown up. Interchangeable with another black folk expression: "You trying to be grown." Responsible. In charge. *Serious*.

Another definition reads:

3. Loves music. Loves dance. Loves the moon. *Loves* the Spirit. Loves love and food and roundness. Loves struggle. *Loves* the Folk. Loves herself. *Regardless*.

Walker continued to develop her womanist ideology through her subsequent two novels, *The Temple of My Familiar* and *Possessing the Secret of Joy*, both of which include several of the characters first introduced in *The Color Purple*.

Additional publications include an edited anthology of Zora Neale Hurston's work, a writer of the Harlem Renaissance who greatly impacted Walker; two books of poetry, *Good Night, Willie Lee, I'll See You in the Morning* (1979) and *Horses Make the Landscape More Beautiful* (1984); *You Can't Keep a Good Woman Down* (1981), a collection of short stories; two children's books, *To Hell with Dying* (1987) and *Finding the Green Stone* (1991); a volume of essays, *Living by the Word* (1988); and a compilation of poetry entitled, *Her Blue Body Everything We Know: Earthling Poems 1965–1990* (1991). Walker lives in northern California.

MAJOR WORKS AND THEMES

Alice Walker's novels deal with the human experience in general, but especially the human experience from the perspective of the suffering and the downtrodden, the hurt and the oppressed. The characters of *The Third Life of Grange Copeland* are all victims of racial and economic oppression as they attempt to live a meaningful and dignified life amid the degrading circumstances of a sharecropping life. In *The Color Purple*, Celie suffers severe emotional and physical abuse at the hands of her husband, Mr. _____. The title character of *Meridian* comes from an impoverished background, is maltreated by whites and men in her life, and ultimately sacrifices herself in the name of fighting injustices, such as those she herself has endured, for all. Evelyn/Tashi in *Possessing the Secret of Joy* is genitally mutilated in order to uphold misogynistic African traditions and is driven to the point of madness by her realization that her suffering was based upon the cruel and evil lies of her people.

Walker's characters, however, particularly her women, do not lie down and play dead in the face of such immense oppression. Rather, they manage to transcend their desperate and painful circumstances in order to affirm Life. *The Third Life of Grange Copeland* is somewhat unusual in that it features a man as its newly enlightened protagonist. Grange Copeland evolves from a victim of abuse by his white "boss" to a perpetrator of abuse against his own wife and son and finally, in his "third life," into the protector and guardian of his beloved granddaughter, Ruth. Thus, although a great deal of suffering is involved along the way, Grange is able to rise above his own meanness and degradation through his pure and true love for Ruth.

Love also plays a role in Celie's ability to transcend her bitter life with Mr. _____. Celie and Shug's love for one another, her love of God, and her love for her sister, Nettie, and her children all propel Celie to stand up to Mr. _____ and to make a joyous and meaningful life for herself. Mr. _____, meanwhile, ends his days pathetically, unable to love and thus unable to transcend the difficult circumstances of his life.

Love of her people similarly allows Meridian to overcome the pain in her life. Although she is sickly and considered strange by the people whom she helps, Meridian takes on a magical quality as the years progress. Through the work that she does, Meridian's life transcends itself and becomes representative of an empowered life of action, of the ability to *do* rather than to have things done *to* one. This is clear to Truman as, at the end of the novel, he prepares to take over for Meridian where she has left off.

Aside from love, another common thread running through each of these transcendent characters is best articulated, perhaps, in *Possessing the Secret of Joy*. The secret of joy, realizes Tashi at the novel's close, is *resistance*. Indeed, in Tashi's act of murdering the woman who mutilated her body, she expresses her resistance to the cultural practice that killed her sister and ruined the lives of so many innocent girls and women, including herself.

While love and resistance serve to empower many of Walker's characters, another source of power is found through connecting oneself to one's ancestral past. This idea is most thoroughly and ambitiously explored in Walker's *The Temple of My Familiar*, a novel that spans time from prehistoric days to the present. The characters in this novel learn to merge their past, present, and future in order to create meaning in their lives. The woman who has most completely mastered this lesson is Miss Lissie, who can remember each of her previous lives, in which she existed as everything from a pygmy, to a white man, to a lion. Miss Lissie is able to integrate the history of her ancient selves with her present life in order to create a healthy whole.

Understanding one's cultural history is equally important in understanding one's present. For example, it is vital to know the history of myth and the ways in which those myths have been revised, for mythological constructs shape our daily lives. In *The Temple of My Familiar*, patriarchal myths are traced back to their roots in ancient goddess worship and a society in which women were revered rather than oppressed. Knowledge of such myths is vital for a woman's knowledge of herself. The experience of Tashi in *Possessing the Secret of Joy* also points out the need for an understanding of one's past and one's cultural history in order to understand one's present. Tashi must mentally revisit the moments in her past when she heard the screams of her sister during a mutilation ceremony and when she listened to a group of old men recount a creation myth that supports the practice of "female circumcision." The two events are linked in time as well as in significance; the ancient cultural myth is largely responsible for the horror of the present practice.

Meridian also understands the healing power of the past for present society. She thus appoints herself, in a manner of speaking, as the keeper of her people's ancestral past, as the keeper of "the song of the people": "For it is the song of the people, transformed by the experiences of each generation, that holds them together, and if any part of it is lost the people suffer and are without soul. If I can only do that, my role will not have been a useless one after all" (*Meridian* 201).

In keeping with Walker's interest in the ancestral past of her people, and as was alluded to in the biographical sketch offered earlier, Walker felt a marked ambivalence toward Christianity and shows in her novels a curiosity about pagan religions of ancient days as well as modern alternatives to the Christian paradigm. In *Meridian*, Meridian's mother creates prayer pillows out of her need to fill the emptiness in her life. These pillows, however, are symbolic of the failings of the Christian religion to ease or even to make sense out of the suffering of human life, for "they were too small for kneeling. They would only fit one knee, which Meridian's mother never seemed to notice" (*Meridian* 30).

The characters of *The Color Purple*, particularly Celie, undergo a complex and significant change in terms of their understanding of God and Christianity. There is a shift from the beginning to the end in the epistolary form of the novel itself as Celie stops writing her self-reflective letters to God and begins to write them to her sister, Nettie. The fact that the Christian God is fashioned as a white male becomes completely disagreeable to Celie, as it already has to her friend and lover, Shug. He is the God of the "white folks," not of the African American woman. Nettie, who is doing missionary work in Africa, also begins to question the relevance of Christianity for black people. As she begins to hang pictures of Christ, Mary, and the Apostles in a fabric-covered African dwelling, she confesses that the pictures "made me feel very small and unhappy, so I took them down. Even the picture of Christ which generally looks good anywhere looks peculiar here" (*The Color Purple* 165). The title of the novel also highlights the spiritual quest that permeates the story. As Celie and Shug discuss who God is and how He may be characterized, they decide upon the following: "I think it pisses God off if you walk by the color purple in a field somewhere and don't notice it" (*The Color Purple* 203). Thus, all that is beautiful is imbued with the spiritual; Christianity is therefore an unnecessary mediator for the soul.

Both *The Temple of My Familiar* and *Possessing the Secret of Joy* continue to explore questions of religion and spirituality. In *The Temple of My Familiar*, Christianity is dismissed as a fictive creation, while a deeper, established tradition of goddess worship is resurrected. Walker takes us back through the rewriting of cultural myths, unweaving the patriarchy of Christianity and laying bare the cloth of ancient pagan cultures. Walker writes of times when women were priests, and the female community was central; she recalls original spiritual myths and explains how they have been distorted through time; and Walker ties these ancient religious structures to the present through her female characters. Zede the Younger maintains her mother's tradition of the magical creation of capes. Miss Lissie is a self-professed "witch doctor" and "sorceress." Fanny uses crystals in her work as a masseuse in order to call upon greater healing powers.

However, while Christianity seems to be safely buried away by the end of *The Temple of My Familiar*, ambivalence again resurfaces in *Possessing the Secret of Joy*. Here pagan religion, though distorted to justify the quelling of female sexual power, perpetuates the genital mutilation of women. Christianity, by contrast, represents the Western mode of thought, which would do away with this barbaric procedure. As does any fine author, Walker again raises more questions than she answers.

CRITICAL RECEPTION

Walker's first two novels, *The Third Life of Grange Copeland* and *Meridian*, received little critical attention when they were first published. Her most recent novel, *Possessing the Secret of Joy*, was also largely overlooked. However, with her third novel, *The Color Purple*, Alice Walker was catapulted into the spotlight, both for good and for bad, and remained there for the reception of her fourth novel, *The Temple of My Familiar*.

As it received both the American Book Award and the Pulitzer Prize, *The Color Purple* obviously received much high commendation from the literary community. Gloria Steinem, for example, praised Walker not only for writing a feminist novel that "doesn't ignore any women because of race or class" (90) but also for her skillful use of "black folk English," her fluid storytelling style, and her handling of moral themes, both internal and external, throughout the novel.

However, while Steinem voiced the opinion of many, others voiced largely negative views about the novel. Criticism of *The Color Purple* seemed to center around two primary complaints: (1) that the novel perpetuates degrading racial stereotypes and (2) that the hugely successful reception of the novel untenably positions Walker as *the* voice for the female, black experience.

The use of language that Steinem so lauded received criticism from many "who attacked her use of black dialect as degrading to black people" (Bell 11). Many besides Steinem came to Walker's defense in this regard, and Walker herself responded to the attacks in one of the essays in *Living by the Word: Selected Writings 1973–1987*: "Language is an intrinsic part of who we are and what has, for good or evil, happened to us. And, amazingly, it has sustained us more securely than the arms of angels."

Another aspect of *The Color Purple* that several critics felt reinforced damaging stereotypes of blacks is the novel's images of violence of men toward women within the African American community. Trudier Harris wrote that the violence endured by Celie for years and years was "used too readily to affirm what the uninformed or the ill-informed believe is a general pattern of violence and abuse for black women" ("On *The Color Purple*" 156). Richard Wesley explained that "what angers black men as they read [*The Color Purple*] . . . is that *all* the black men are portrayed as fools; the women are portrayed as noble and long-suffering" (62). Wesley added, however, that Walker has every right to portray her characters however she sees fit: "No one in America—and black America, especially—should be telling writers what they may or may not say. Writers are the antennae of any society. They have to speak when others dare not" (90–91).

Trudier Harris countered this argument with her articulation of the second largest complaint against *The Color Purple*. Harris argued that while Walker's voice should, indeed, be heard, her voice has worked to silence the voices of others. The media hyped the novel to such a degree that "critics, especially black women critics, have seemingly been reluctant to offer detailed, carefully considered criticisms of it" ("On *The Color Purple*" 155). As *The Color Purple* came to be equated with the "authentic" black femininity, black females who disagreed with the ideas posed in the novel did not feel safe to express their opinions. This, Harris declared, is extremely dangerous.

After weathering the critical battle that settled on *The Color Purple*, Walker's next novel, *The Temple of My Familiar*, again met with mixed reviews. As a novel that spans generations and incorporates dozens of characters, most critics would agree that this was an ambitious project. Some felt that the project was a success. Wrote Ursula LeGuin, "The richness of Alice Walker's [*The Temple of My Familiar*] is amazing, overwhelming" (12). Christopher Zinn agreed: "In dazzling fashion, the novel moves along . . . various streams of conversation, storytelling and memory, recovering the various combinations of ancestry and incident that, pasted together, form the long foreground of these contemporary African-American lives" (90).

Other critics failed to see the novel as a coherent whole. James Wolcott put it extremely bluntly: "Cover to cover, Alice Walker's *The Temple of My Familiar* is the nuttiest novel I've ever read. . . . Helpful, talky, *The Temple of My Familiar* subordinates fictional interest—character, plot, atmosphere; stuff like that—in order to function as a workshop. It's many workshops in one" (28). J. M. Coetzee was also bothered by Walker's experimental approach: "*The Temple of My Familiar* is a novel only in a loose sense. Rather, it is a mixture of mythic fantasy, revisionary history, exemplary biography and sermon. It is short on narrative tension, long on inspirational message" (7). Paul Gray was disturbed more by the content of the novel than by its "loose" form. Gray wrote that the book is governed by Walker's own "sociopolitical agenda" and that, rather than being a "novel of ideas," it is a "novel of allegations" (69). Furthermore, the realistic and heartfelt voices of *The Color Purple*, many argued, were lost not only in *The Temple of My Familiar*—"Her characters are merely mouths at the workshop mikes" (Wolcott 29)—but also in *Possessing the Secret of Joy*, where "the alternation of narrators becomes somewhat muted by the similarity among the characters' voices" (Schiffman 654).

Despite varying responses to Walker's aesthetics and style, there is no denying the great impact that Alice Walker has had on contemporary African American feminist thought as well as on American literature in general. She has been a courageous spokesperson for many women's causes, from domestic violence to female circumcision. She has used her writing in a politically engaged and socially responsible manner. In short, she has been a pioneering literary figure, creating new voices and new visions of the role literature can play in shaping and critiquing society.

BIBLIOGRAPHY

Works by Alice Walker

Novels

The Third Life of Grange Copeland. San Diego: Harcourt Brace Jovanovich, 1970.
Meridian. New York: Washington Square Press, 1976.
The Color Purple. New York: Pocket Books, 1982.
The Temple of My Familiar. New York: Pocket Books, 1989.
Possessing the Secret of Joy. New York: Harcourt Brace Jovanovich, 1992.

Poetry

Once: Poems. New York: Harcourt Brace and World, 1968.
Five Poems. Detroit: Broadside Press, 1972.
Revolutionary Petunias and Other Poems. New York: Harcourt Brace Jovanovich, 1973.
Good Night, Willie Lee, I'll See You in the Morning. New York: Dial, 1979.
Horses Make a Landscape Look More Beautiful. San Diego: Harcourt Brace Jovanovich, 1984.
Her Blue Body Everything We Know. San Diego: Harcourt Brace Jovanovich, 1991.

Short Stories

In Love and Trouble: Stories of Black Women. New York: Harcourt Brace Jovanovich, 1973.
You Can't Keep a Good Woman Down: Stories. New York: Harcourt Brace Jovanovich, 1981.

Children's Literature

Langston Hughes, American Poet. New York: Harper and Row, 1974.
To Hell with Dying. San Diego: Harcourt Brace Jovanovich, 1987.
Finding the Green Stone. San Diego: Harcourt Brace Jovanovich, 1991.

Edited Anthology

I Love Myself When I Am Laughing . . . and Then Again When I Am Looking Mean and Impressive: A Zora Neale Hurston Reader. Old Westbury, NY: Feminist Press, 1979.

Essays

In Search of Our Mothers' Gardens: Womanist Prose. San Diego: Harcourt Brace Jovanovich, 1983.
Living by the Word. San Diego: Harcourt Brace Jovanovich, 1988.

Studies of Alice Walker

Abbandonato, Linda. "A View from 'Elsewhere': Subversive Sexuality and the Rewriting of the Heroine's Story in *The Color Purple*." *PMLA* 106.5 (Oct. 1991): 1106–1115.
Applegate, Nancy. "Feminine Sexuality in Alice Walker's *Possessing the Secret of Joy*." *Notes on Contemporary Literature* 24.4 (Sept. 1994): 11.

Bell, Derrick. "The Word from Alice Walker." Rev. of *Living by the Word. Los Angeles Times Book Review* (29 May 1988): 11.

Bobo, Jacqueline. "Sifting through the Controversy: Reading *The Color Purple.*" *Callaloo* 12.2 (Spring 1989): 332–342.

Brown, Joseph A. " 'All Saints Should Walk Away': The Mystical Pilgrimage of *Meridian.*" *Callaloo* 12.2 (Spring 1989): 310–320.

Buckman, Alyson R. "The Body as a Site of Colonization: Alice Walker's *Possessing the Secret of Joy.*" *Journal of American Culture* 18.2 (Summer 1995): 89–94.

Butler, Robert James. "Alice Walker's Vision of the South in *The Third Life of Grange Copeland.*" *African American Review* 27.2 (Summer 1993): 195–204.

Christian, Barbara. "Alice Walker: The Black Woman Artist as Wayward." In *Black Women Writers (1950–1980): A Critical Evaluation*, ed. Mari Evans. Garden City, NY: Anchor-Doubleday, 1984.

Coetzee, J. M. "The Beginnings of (Wo)man in Africa." Rev. of *The Temple of My Familiar. The New York Times Book Review* (Apr. 1989): 7.

Danielson, Susan. "Alice Walker's *Meridian*, Feminism, and the 'Movement.' " *Women's Studies: An Interdisciplinary Journal* 16.3–4 (1989): 317–330.

Davis, Thadious. "Alice Walker's Celebration of Self in Southern Generations." *The Southern Quarterly* 21.4 (Summer 1983): 39–53.

DeLancey, Frenzella Elaine. "Squaring the Afrocentric Circle: Womanism and Humanism in Alice Walker's *Meridian.*" *MAWA Review* 7.2 (Dec. 1992): 94–101.

Dieke, Ikenna. "Toward a Monastic Idealism: The Thematics of Alice Walker's *The Temple of My Familiar.*" *African American Review* 26.3 (Fall 1992): 507–514.

Fifer, Elizabeth. "Alice Walker: The Dialect and Letters of *The Color Purple.*" In *Contemporary American Women Writers: Narrative Strategies*, ed. Catherine Rainwater. Lexington: University Press of Kentucky, 1985.

Gaston, Karen C. "Women in the Lives of Grange Copeland." *College Language Association Journal* 24.3 (Mar. 1981): 276–286.

Gray, Paul. "A Myth to Be Taken on Faith." Rev. of *The Temple of My Familiar. Time* 133.18 (May 1989): 69.

Hall, Christine. "Art, Action and the Ancestors: Alice Walker's *Meridian* in Its Context." In *Black Women's Writing*, ed. Gina Wisker. New York: St. Martin's, 1993.

Harris, Trudier. "On *The Color Purple*, Stereotypes, and Silence." *Black American Literature Forum* 18.4 (Winter 1984): 155–161.

———. "From Victimization to Free Enterprise: Alice Walker's *The Color Purple.*" *Studies in American Fiction* 14.1 (Spring 1986): 1–17.

Howard, Lillie P., ed. *Alice Walker and Zora Neale Hurston: The Common Bond.* Westport, CT: Greenwood, 1993.

Jamison-Hall, Angelene. "She's Just Too Womanish for Them: Alice Walker and *The Color Purple.*" In *Censored Books: Critical Viewpoints*, ed. Nicholas J. Karolides. Metuchen, NJ: Scarecrow, 1993.

Juncker, Clara. "Black Magic: Woman(ist) as Artist in Alice Walker's *The Temple of My Familiar.*" *American Studies in Scandinavia* 24.1 (1992): 37–49.

Kelly, Lori Duin. "Theology and Androgyny: The Role of Religion in *The Color Purple.*" *Notes on Contemporary Literature* 18.2 (Mar. 1988): 7–8.

LeGuin, Ursula K. "All Those at the Banquet." Rev. of *The Temple of My Familiar. San Francisco Review of Books* (Summer 1989): 12–13.

Mason, Theodore O. "Alice Walker's *The Third Life of Grange Copeland*: The Dynamics of Enclosure." *Callaloo* 12.2 (Spring 1989): 297–309.

McDowell, Deborah E. "The Self in Bloom: Alice Walker's *Meridian*." *College Language Association Journal* 24.3 (Mar. 1981): 262–275.

McGowan, Martha J. "Atonement and Release in Alice Walker's *Meridian*." *Critique* 23.1 (1981): 25–36.

Powers, Peter Kerry. " 'Pa Is Not Our Pa': Sacred History and Political Imagination in *The Color Purple*." *South Atlantic Review* 60.2 (May 1995): 69–72.

Pramo, Cassie. "Lessons for Life in *Meridian* and *The Color Purple*." *North Carolina Humanities* (Spring 1993): 35–45.

Pratt, Louis H. "Alice Walker's Men: Profiles in the Quest for Love and Personal Values." *Studies in Popular Culture* 12.1 (1989): 42–57.

Proudfit, Charles L. "Celie's Search for Identity: A Psychoanalytic Developmental Reading of Alice Walker's *The Color Purple*." *Contemporary Literature* 32.1 (Spring 1991): 12–37.

Schiffman, Barbara Elman. Rev. of *Possessing the Secret of Joy*. *Magill's Literary Annual* (1993): 651–654.

Selzer, Linda. "Race and Domesticity in *The Color Purple*." *African American Review* 29.1 (Spring 1995): 67–82.

Smith, Felipe. "Alice Walker's Redemptive Art." *African American Review* 26.3 (Fall 1992): 437–451.

Steinem, Gloria. "Do You Know This Woman? She Knows You: A Profile of Alice Walker." *Ms.* 10.12 (June 1982): 35, 37, 89–94.

Thomas, H. Nigel. "Alice Walker's Grange Copeland as a Trickster Figure." *Obsidian II: Black Literature in Review* 6.1 (Spring 1991): 60–72.

Tucker, Lindsey. "Alice Walker's *The Color Purple*: Emergent Woman, Emergent Text." *Black American Literature Forum* 22.1 (Spring 1988): 81–95.

Wade-Gayles, Gloria. "Black, Southern, and Womanist: The Genius of Alice Walker." In *Southern Women Writers: The New Generation*, ed. Tonette Bond Inge. Tuscaloosa: University of Alabama Press, 1990.

Wesley, Richard. "*The Color Purple* Debate: Reading between the Lines." *Ms.* 15.3 (Sept. 1986): 62, 90–92.

Weston, Ruth D. "Inversion of Patriarchal Mantle Images in Alice Walker's *Meridian*." *The Southern Quarterly* 25.2 (Winter 1987): 102–107.

White, Evelyn C. "Alice Walker's Compassionate Crusade." *Sojourner: The Women's Forum* 19.7 (Mar. 1994): 1H–2H.

Wolcott, James. "Party of Animals." Rev. of *The Temple of My Familiar*. *The New Republic* 200.22 (May 1989): 28–30.

Zinn, Christopher. Rev. of *The Temple of My Familiar*. *America* 161.4 (Aug. 1989): 90–92.

MARGARET WALKER
(1915–   )

Annette Debo

BIOGRAPHY

Margaret Walker was born on July 7, 1915, in Birmingham, Alabama, and has lived most of her life in the South. Tellingly, she has called Mississippi her "epicenter." Her university-educated parents—a mother who taught music and a Methodist Episcopal minister father—had high expectations for Walker, which she repeatedly met. She began writing poetry at age twelve and, when only nineteen, published the poem "Daydreaming" in *The Crisis.* Shortly before her twentieth birthday in 1935, Walker completed her B.A. at Northwestern University, after which she worked in the WPA Writers' Project in Chicago. Her first book of poetry, *For My People,* the winner of the Yale Award for Younger Poets, was published in 1942, closely following the completion of her M.A. in 1940 at the University of Iowa. Also at Iowa, Walker completed her Ph.D. in 1965 with the dissertation project *Jubilee,* which was published the next year and which received the Houghton Mifflin Literary Fellowship. Over the many years of its development, her research for *Jubilee* was also supported by other awards: the Rosenwald Fellowship for Creative Writing in 1944 and a Ford Fellowship at Yale University in 1954. Walker began her teaching career at West Virginia State College and Livingstone College, but the bulk of her career (1949–1979) was spent at Jackson State University, where she also developed and directed the Institute for the Study of the History, Life, and Culture of Black People. In the midst of her many professional achievements, Walker married and raised four children, often struggling to balance her writing ambitions and supporting her family. Currently, Walker is retired from Jackson State, with many writing projects, including her autobiography and a sequel to *Jubilee,* under way.

Jubilee, Walker's only novel, is a culmination of thirty years of work, originating in the bedtime stories her maternal grandmother, Elvira Ware Dozier (who becomes Minna in the novel), told about Walker's great-grandmother, Margaret Duggans Ware Brown, upon whom the character Vyry is based. In her essay "How I Wrote Jubilee," Walker describes how whenever her grandmother was accused of stretching the truth and telling "tale tales," she would indignantly claim, " 'I'm not telling her tales; I'm telling her the naked truth' " (51). Walker realized the value of these stories even in her adolescence and collected details from her grandmother, in essence assembling oral narratives from the mouth of an ex-slave. The novel fulfills a promise she made to her grandmother that she would someday write her family's story of slavery and freedom. Her grandmother's story was corroborated by her grandmother's youngest sister, whom Walker located in 1953, as well as by her years of far-reaching research. For example, she found legal records substantiating that Randall Ware, her great-grandfather, indeed did sell his property, probably under duress, to white men during Reconstruction. Out of the amalgamation of oral family history and recorded national history comes *Jubilee*.

MAJOR WORKS AND THEMES

Using a tripartite structure, beginning in antebellum times, continuing through the Civil War, and ending during Reconstruction, *Jubilee* chronicles the life of Vyry, a slave on a southern plantation born to a mother who dies in the birth of her fifteenth child fathered by the plantation owner, John Dutton. *Jubilee* is foremost a historical novel working on four levels—national politics, plantation life, the African American community, and Vyry's personal life. National politics becomes the novel's background, and Walker shows how the institution of slavery functioned, the white southern hopes for the Civil War, the dissolution of the plantation during the war (symbolically, all the Duttons die from accident, war injury, and stroke except for the daughter, who loses her mind), the treatment of free blacks in the South before and after the war, and the continuing violence and racism during Reconstruction. On the plantation itself where Vyry's early life is lived, Walker documents plantation life from the overseer's duties, to the slaves' labor, to the owner's excesses. Next is the slave community, to which Walker gives the most attention, carefully detailing it. With the guidance of her elders, Vyry goes to church deep in the swamps, plays games in the slave quarters, picks the healing herbs in the swamp, learns to cook—all lessons of communal survival and spirit. These elements create the "folk novel" Walker set out to write, a story of the slaves themselves. Finally, Vyry's personal history anchors the novel, structuring it as firmly as the national politics is influencing her life. The plantation section ends with Vyry's being brutally whipped after trying to escape; the war section closes with Vyry's second marriage and journey into the unknown world; and the Reconstruction section finishes with Vyry's new home and successful farm, as well as the return of her first husband, who takes their son to attend school. Weaving the different historical strands, Walker offers a panoramic sweep of a tumultuous time.

Accompanying *Jubilee*'s immense historical scope are many related themes. First, Walker investigates how slavery broke family ties and affected the role of motherhood. The maternal line is strong here, as in the novels of Toni Morrison,* but disrupted. Vyry's biological mother dies when she is two, and her surrogate mother dies from the plague soon after. Then, after Vyry develops close ties with Aunt Sally, Sally, too, disappears from her life, sold away. Vyry finds her own maternal feelings so strong that she refuses to escape without her children, and in her one escape attempt, slowed down by them, she is captured and badly beaten.

Southern miscegenation is also an important theme. Because Vyry is biracial and, with her sandy hair and light skin, can pass for her white half sister's twin, she receives the brunt of Salina Dutton's anger about her husband's infidelities. In one instance, Salina tortures Vyry as a child, hanging her up by her thumbs when she breaks a china dish. Vyry's color remains an issue after the war, when she is often taken for a white woman and treated accordingly, amusing her dark husband and annoying her. The emphasis on skin color in race relations and on the mixing of the races challenges the South's seemingly rigid race lines.

Walker also explores class tensions. The plantation owners have poor white relatives to whom they give handouts and occasional jobs. They also foster hatred between the slaves and these poor whites, a class that includes their own overseer, so that the groups will not bond over their economic plight. In essence, the opulence of plantation multicourse dinners and society weddings is fueled by the labor and poverty of both these groups.

CRITICAL RECEPTION

Walker's novel has not generated as much critical attention as might be expected; however, its body of scholarship is increasing. Many critics praise *Jubilee* for its historical accuracy, considering it, in Bernard W. Bell's terminology, the "first major neoslave narrative" in a line of Ernest Gaines'* *The Autobiography of Miss Jane Pittman*, Sherley Ann Williams'* *Dessa Rose*, Toni Morrison's *Beloved*, and Octavia Butler's* *Kindred* (Bell 289). A few, like Bertie J. Powell and Delores S. Williams, see it as a portrait of authentic black experience. In the same vein, James E. Spears traces many of the folk elements in *Jubilee*, arguing that the novel demonstrates "insight into authentic folkways" (13). He discusses aspects such as the folk songs, the authenticity of dialect, religion, medicine, and folk sayings, supporting Walker's own statement that "I always intended *Jubilee* to be a folk novel based on folk material: folk sayings, folk belief, folkways" ("How I Wrote Jubilee" 62). Other critics, however, view it as revisionist history, inflected with the time period during which it was written. Barbara Christian includes *Jubilee* in her discussion of African American women's early historical novels. For her, the novel's achievement is "the establishment of an African-American culture which enabled the ordinary slave to survive" and the revision of the nineteenth-century mulatto figure into the realistic Vyry (335).

Phyllis Rauch Klotman argues that Walker is an important historian because her story is the black woman's. Moreover, she claims that *Jubilee*'s structure is reminiscent of the slave narrative tradition from which it comes: bondage, escape, and freedom are descriptions of the novel's three parts. Charlotte Goodman also emphasizes the importance of telling African American women's history in contrasting *Jubilee* with Stowe's *Uncle Tom's Cabin*. While maintaining the importance of Stowe's novel, Goodman points out that it does not accurately portray the lives of black women, as *Jubilee* does. Its folklore, which is passed on through the maternal line, includes black folk medicine, cooking, quilting, and the verbal texts, including "female lore about menstruation, cautionary tales about sexual matters, information about pregnancy and childbirth, folk sayings, songs, and passages from the Old Testament" (335). Altogether, it is "a compelling picture of the community of black women during the Civil War period" (Goodman 336).

On the other hand, Mary Condé positions *Jubilee* as "very much *Gone with the Wind* from a black point of view" (213). She contends that all fiction by African Americans about the Civil War period is, to some extent, a response to Mitchell's book because of its huge popularity. What she finds in the novels of Walker and others is a " 'tribal' response" to Mitchell's novel in which the African American women indulge in "wishful thinking" in their somewhat "utopian" visions (217). In Walker's work, she particularly cites the ending, Vyry's decision for conciliation between the races, as wishful and perhaps a response to 1960s militancy.

Similarly, Melissa Walker sees *Jubilee* as less a novel capturing a portrait of slavery than a Civil Rights novel inscribing 1960s goals and desires into slavery and Reconstruction. She claims that "events in this novel about slavery and its aftermath, and even the form of the novel, are directly related to the struggle for civil rights that peaked in the mid-1960's" (18). For example, at the end of the novel, Vyry and both her husbands speak their piece, parts that Melissa Walker reads as the "three conflicting positions dividing the black community" (22). Randall Ware becomes a separatist; Innis Brown argues for accommodation; and Vyry, as a biracial woman, "represents that integrated society dreamed of by Martin Luther King, Jr." (23), one of coalition.

Walker's characterization also receives critical attention. Bell claims that *Jubilee* creates "character types of general appeal," particularly in the case of Vyry, who is "one of the most memorable women in contemporary Afro-American fiction" (287). He is impressed with her Christian faith and her dignity, making her a symbol for nineteenth-century black women. He does agree, however, that some of the characters are "stock representatives" (288). In contrast, Christian claims that, because Walker covers such a huge historical expanse, her characters necessarily become "the means by which we learn about the culture of slaves and slave holders and the historical period" rather than psychologically complex characters (334). However, Joyce Pettis believes that while "the outlines of some stereotypes are visible" because of the novel's wide scope, Walker has successfully moved beyond the usual rendering of black characters to find "individualistic characters united by their desire for autonomy" ("Margaret Walker" 12). Importantly, Pettis believes Vyry to become the prototypical characterization for future portraits of slave women: "her characterization essentially balances that of other types of enslaved women and provides the fundamental model upon which they may be structured" ("Margaret Walker" 13).

In addition, Minrose C. Gwin focuses on Vyry's interactions with white people and her forgiving spirit. She argues that Vyry's forgiveness of "the perverse and vicious cruelty of the southern white woman" is not passive acceptance but "an assertion of ontological black self" (148). Thus, Walker's brand of black humanism, which "embodies, at once, the necessity to rebel and the willingness to reconcile," allows Vyry to forgive and offers an answer to racial conflicts in the United States.

Finally, Eleanor Traylor ties *Jubilee* to the blues, another product of slavery, claiming that "music is the leitmotif" of the novel (513). Working with the epigraphs—which come from sacred and secular songs and Walker's grandmother's own words—the slaves' songs, and the novel's rhythmic prose, Traylor traces how Walker uses songs to "articulate progressive stages in her life" and enlarges them much "like the strategy of the bluesman's song whose tale of woe controlled by form invites the world to dance, is the rhythmic motion, the consummation of the modal heroine of the blues" (513–514).

BIBLIOGRAPHY

Works by Margaret Walker

Fiction

Jubilee. Boston: Houghton Mifflin, 1966.

Poetry and Essays

For My People. New Haven, CT: Yale University Press, 1942.
Prophets for a New Day. Detroit: Broadside Press, 1970.
October Journey. Detroit: Broadside Press, 1973.
With Nikki Giovanni. *A Poetic Equation: Conversations between Nikki Giovanni and Margaret Walker*. Washington, DC: Howard University Press, 1974.
"On Being Female, Black, and Free." *The Writer and Her Work*. Ed. Janet Sternburg. New York: Norton, 1980. 95–106.
Richard Wright: Daemonic Genius. New York: Warner Books, 1988.
This Is My Century: New and Collected Poems. Athens: University of Georgia Press, 1989.
How I Wrote Jubilee and Other Essays on Life and Literature. Ed. Maryemma Graham. New York: Feminist Press, 1990.

Studies of Margaret Walker

Bell, Bernard W. *The Afro-American Novel and Its Tradition*. Amherst: University of Massachusetts Press, 1987.

Christian, Barbara. " 'Somebody Forgot to Tell Somebody Something': African-American Women's Historical Novels." *Wild Women in the Whirlwind*. Ed. Joanne M. Braxton and Andrée Nicola McLaughlin. New Brunswick, NJ: Rutgers University Press, 1990. 326–341.

Condé, Mary. "Some African-American Fictional Responses to *Gone with the Wind*." *Yearbook of English Studies* 26 (1996): 208–217.

Goodman, Charlotte. "From *Uncle Tom's Cabin* to Vyry's Kitchen: The Black Female Folk Tradition in Margaret Walker's *Jubilee*." *Tradition and the Talents of Women*. Ed. Florence Howe. Urbana: University of Illinois Press, 1991. 328–337.

Gwin, Minrose. *Black and White Women of the Old South*. Knoxville: University of Tennessee Press, 1985.

Klotman, Phyllis Rauch. " 'Oh Freedom'—Women and History in Margaret Walker's *Jubilee*." *Black American Literature Forum* 11 (1977): 139–145.

Pettis, Joyce. "The Black Historial Novel as Best Seller." *Kentucky Folklore Record* 25. 3 (1979): 51–59.

———. "Margaret Walker: Black Woman Writer of the South." *Southern Women Writers: The New Generation*. Ed. Tonette Bond Inge. Tuscaloosa: University of Alabama Press, 1990. 9–19.

Powell, Bertie J. "The Black Experience in Margaret Walker's *Jubilee* and Lorraine Hansberry's *The Drinking Gourd*." *College Language Association Journal* 21 (1977): 304–311.

Spears, James E. "Black Folk Elements in Margaret Walker's *Jubilee*." *Mississippi Folklore Register* 14.1 (1980): 13–19.

Traylor, Eleanor. "Music as Theme: The Blues Mode in the Works of Margaret Walker." *Black Women Writers (1950–1980)*. Ed. Mari Evans. New York: Doubleday, 1984. 511–525.

Walker, Melissa. *Down from the Mountaintop*. New Haven, CT: Yale University Press, 1991.

Williams, Delores S. "Black Women's Literature and the Task of Feminist Theology." *Immaculate and Powerful: The Female in Sacred Image and Social Reality*. Ed. Clarissa W. Atkinson, Constance H. Buchanan, and Margaret R. Miles. Boston: Beacon Press, 1985. 88–110.

DOROTHY WEST
(1907–1998)

A. Yemisi Jimoh

BIOGRAPHY

Dorothy West was born into the successful household of Isaac Christopher West and Rachel Pease Benson West in Boston. West was an only child whose extended family shared the Wests' large home in Boston. Virginia-born Isaac West owned a wholesale fruit business in the Boston Market. Rachel West was from Camden, South Carolina; she made a place for her family among Boston's small circle of successful, black, upper-middle-class families and provided her daughter with the fuel for an ironic literary approach to the issues of gender, race, class, and color consciousness, which inform much of Dorothy West's writing.

By the time West was seven, she knew that she wanted a literary career—after her father showed pride in her writing (McDowell 266–68). She attended the Girls' Latin School in Boston and, later, Boston University as well as the Columbia University School of Journalism. Dorothy West entered the second annual *Opportunity* magazine literary contest. Her entry, "The Typewriter," shared second prize with Zora Neale Hurston's story "Muttsy." This literary accomplishment drew West—who was just seventeen—to New York for the *Opportunity* magazine awards banquet, which exposed her to the burgeoning Harlem Renaissance circle of writers and artists.

Dorothy West lived a writer's life for more than seventy years. During this time she published some of her writing under the pseudonyms Mary Christopher and Jane Isaac (Dalsgard 42). West's literary life included membership in the 1920s in the Boston African American writers' group the Saturday Evening Quill Club—some of her stories were published in its magazine, *The Saturday Evening Quill*; she had a brief stint with the Works Progress Administration—Federal Writers' Project in the 1930s; as founder of the literary magazines *Challenge* and

New Challenge, West sought to nurture new, post-Renaissance literary talent, notably, Margaret Walker* and Ralph Ellison;* for more than two decades— 1940s–1960s—she wrote short stories for the *New York Daily News;* and she contributed intermittently to the *Vineyard Gazette* from the 1960s until early in the 1990s, including a weekly column on the social activities around Oak Bluffs.

Dorothy West's father was among the first African Americans to purchase a vacation home in Oak Bluffs on Martha's Vineyard. West returned to her family's vacation home in the 1940s and lived year-round on the island until her death. While living on Martha's Vineyard, she published two novels, *The Living Is Easy* (1948) and *The Wedding* (1995) as well as a collection of short stories, sketches, and memoirs titled *The Richer, the Poorer* (1995). With a grant from the Mary Roberts Rinehart foundation in the 1940s, West began writing *The Wedding.* She also wrote two other pieces of long fiction that were never published: "Where the Wild Grape Grows" (McDowell 277) and "The White Tribe of Indians" (281), which is about the web of denials concerning ancestry among some African Americans.

In the mid-1990s, she was hailed as the last living Harlem Renaissance writer, and there was an upsurge of interest in Dorothy West as a writer and as a participant in the Harlem Renaissance. Projects such as the PBS film *As I Remember It: A Portrait of Dorothy West* (Clark, "Rediscovering" 47) and a 1998 film (Steinberg 34) based on her last novel all attest to the growing interest in recovering the literary career of Dorothy West. Into her ninth decade of life, West continued to plan new writing projects. Her latest was a historical book on Oak Bluffs.

MAJOR WORKS AND THEMES

For Dorothy West, short stories "are the most perfect literary form" (McDowell 281). West's first published story was "Promise and Fulfillment" (Ferguson, *Dictionary* 188). In "The Typewriter," her story for the *Opportunity* contest, a janitor dictates fictional letters to his daughter. He feels important and successful during these contrived business sessions, so he creates a fictional persona and begins to live in a fantasy world in which he is a successful businessman. This world crashes for the janitor after he reads in the newspaper that J. P. Morgan— with whom the janitor has had his most intense fantasy correspondence—has gone bankrupt. This story, among others, demonstrates West's inclination toward irony in her writing.

Seventeen of Dorothy West's stories are collected in *The Richer, the Poorer.* In stories such as "The Five Dollar Bill," "Funeral," "The Bird like No Other," "The Penny," and others she convincingly presents a child's perspective. Frequently, West's stories, written from the perspective of innocence, are moralistic yet engaging. Through the eyes of a child, West returns to adults the contradictions that children learn from adult examples. In "The Five Dollar Bill," a little girl named Judy—a name that recurs in West's stories with intelligent girl characters—witnesses and is affected deeply by her mother's duplicity.

West frequently writes about middle-class characters, yet not all of her short stories are set in a middle-class environment. When West does write about the African American middle class, she often uses irony to present a critique of their "counterfeit bourgeois" (Rodgers 161) attitudes and their "color foolishness" (Dalsgard 32). In stories such as "Jack in the Pot," however, West situates poverty and its effects on one's character in the foreground. "Jack in the Pot" is the story of Mrs. Edmunds, a woman who wins money—jack—after she has suffered through hunger and while she is on welfare. She and her husband have lost their middle-class lifestyle because hard times caused her husband to close his business. West says that this story is her "statement on poverty" (Dalsgard 43). When West writes about poverty, she does not sentimentalize the poor. She, in fact, depicts the emotional and psychological impact of poverty. Most of West's characters, though, are successful or are from the struggling working class that made up much of the African American middle class in its nascent stages.

In a number of West's stories, especially those that she wrote for the *New York Daily News*, the author does not describe her characters in ways that would indicate whether they are black people. In other stories—"Odyssey of an Egg" and "About a Woman Named Nancy"—she pushes the boundaries of characterization and setting by eliminating references to skin color. Further, in "Jack in the Pot" West's references to color are so subtle as to be nearly incidental to the overall story. In West's story *The Richer, the Poorer*, she writes about two sisters who take opposite paths in life. Bess lives in the moment, while Lottie is cautious and industrious. In this story, West emphasizes the poverty of Lottie's miserly "life never lived" (56) and the wealth in Bess' active life, but little in this story indicates that the characters are modeled after black women West knew. During an interview with Katrine Dalsgard, West comments on the colorlessness in some of her writing. When she began to write two short stories monthly for the *Daily News*, there was a tacit agreement between West and the publishers: "For their sake, and for my sake because I had to eat, I never mentioned the word 'black' " (37). West's own personal survival and the racial politics of publishing explain her silence on color in *The Richer, the Poorer*, "The Maple Tree," and other stories. As a writer, West often has had to strike a delicate balance between the demands of publishing and her desire to write from her experiences.

In many of Dorothy West's short stories, she presents in condensed form several of the issues and themes that are found in her novels. West's literary corpus demonstrates that she actively engages vernacular qualities such as the black sermonic tradition and music, both of which have informed African American literature; more specifically, though, West is concerned with intragroup issues relating to class and color. These vernacular qualities as well as class and color concerns in her writing are clearly illustrated in "An Unimportant Man," "Mammy," "Prologue to a Life," and "Hannah Byde." A compelling issue in Dorothy West's writing, however, is gender. A persistent motif in her fiction centers on the repressed female who dreams of, or connives, a position of power for herself. This quite frequently is a Pyrrhic victory for West's female characters.

Cleo, the main character in *The Living Is Easy*, is just such a woman. West takes her title for this novel from the song "Summertime," which is from Du Bose Heyward's Broadway play *Porgy*. This novel is set in Boston from July 1914 through April 1919. Cleo Jericho Judson is southern and beautiful. At nineteen, Cleo marries a significantly older, hardworking businessman from the South named Bart Judson. West prepares readers for Cleo's manipulations of her husband and her sisters as well as for her resistance to proscribed gender roles through flashbacks to Cleo's Southern childhood. An independently minded child, Cleo fights and beats a little boy who taunts her; then she wonders, "What was there to being a boy? What was there to being a man? Men just worked. That was easier than what women did" (21). As a married woman, Cleo wants to create her own domain over which she can rule. In fact, "It had never occurred to her in the ten years of her marriage that she might be his helpmate. She thought that was the same thing as being a man's slave" (71). In the summer of 1914, Cleo brings her sisters and their children to her home in Boston for a visit, and she effectively manipulates and deceives them until they are living with her and are estranged from their husbands. The Jericho sisters all illustrate the variety of ways that gender and power operate. Lily accepts dependence; she wants to "please" Bart; she will stay quiet to keep his protection (233). Charity feels empty without her husband and substitutes food. Serena wants her own independence—even from her sister Cleo—as well as love. Cleo wants a female domain. Bart, Cleo's husband, is the means through which she reproduces herself as well as her source of financial support. Judy, Cleo's only child, observes her mother and resists her control. Judy realizes that Cleo "was the boss of nothing but the young, the weak, the frightened. She ruled a pygmy kingdom" (308). Through Cleo, West complicates two prevalent images of black women. The author revises established representations of black, middle-class, female characters by refusing to create tragic sympathy for her near-white characters. Dorothy West also transforms the concept of the black woman as the enduring, loving matriarch.

Cleo's world disintegrates after Bart's business fails, in the same way as other black-owned businesses in the novel that did not respond effectively to the forces of modernity. While West illustrates in *The Living Is Easy* the small space that black, middle-class women occupy, she also delineates the weakly derivative and obsessively color-conscious base on which her black middle-class characters rest. This small, exclusive group consists in the struggling descendants of tailors and stable owners who prefer light skin color and avoid acknowledging anything as ugly as lynching. Throughout *The Living Is Easy* West illustrates her ironic stance toward middle-class color consciousness and imitative behavior with poignant narrative commentary. When, for example, a black man "failed in business, and blew his brains out just like a white man, [e]verybody was a little proud of his suicide" (112).

Cleo Judson's actions in this novel are misguided, but her motive is to situate her vision of the lifestyle and cultural base of the African American South within the economic base of middle-class Boston and to define a space for female power. Cleo is defeated by the broader economic and gender issues of her time as well as by her own overreaching. Cleo wonders if her sisters—because they are man-less—are less like the image of their mother that Cleo remembers. She remembers the face of her mother when their father "was no where in her thinking" (284). Cleo's dream of a female utopia has become strangely dystopic without Bart's support. West's novel demonstrates the power of the dominant discourse on race and gender.

Forty-seven years after the publication of Dorothy West's first novel, she re-turns readers—in her second novel, *The Wedding*—to the complexities of a class- and color-conscious environment in an exclusive circle of African Americans. The immediate action of the novel occurs in 1953 on Martha's Vineyard in the Oval, a fictional neighborhood on the island of Oak Bluffs. West's narrator, however, supplies readers with more than 100 years of history through flashbacks. The new guard in the Oval has moved away from the entrenched cultural rules. Previously, marrying light-skinned—not white—and marrying well had been the rule. Between them, Shelby Coles and her sister Liz have broken all the rules. Liz's husband is a dark-skinned physician whose occupation saves him from com-plete déclassé status in the Oval. Liz and Clark Coles—the sisters' father—unlike their mother and neighbors, are concerned that Shelby is rejecting black men out of fear. Shelby, notwithstanding everyone's restrained distress, is planning to marry a white jazz musician. Meade, her fiancé, is not a light-skinned black man; he is not a member of the right socioeconomic class; and his career is unsuitable for a resident of the Oval. Clark is worried about Shelby's marriage to Meade, because "I've never seen you give your respect to a colored man and I can't help but think that maybe that's some warped extension of this family's social snob-bery" (201). The only member of the Coles family who has no reservations about Shelby's marriage is Gram, Shelby's white great-grandmother who dreams of regenerating the white branch of her family, which was cut off when her daughter Josephine married Hannibal, the son of a woman who was formerly enslaved at Xanadu, the family's plantation.

With this novel, Dorothy West again interrogates issues of class, color, and, to a lesser extent, gender. She demonstrates the complexities of these issues through a story that illuminates the social construction of desire and race. She further shows the numerous moral and psychological convolutions in behavior and thought that restrictive color/class practices engender.

CRITICAL RECEPTION

Dorothy West's novel *The Living Is Easy* was reviewed widely when it was first published. These reviews were, for the most part, favorable. Most of the reviewers locate West's strength in her ability to present unforgettable characters, especially Cleo. Too often, though, these early reviews were concerned with the ways in which Cleo's actions affected Bart's male identity. West occasionally has been critiqued—rightly—for her weak ending of this novel. This same, very right complaint has been leveled against West's second novel, *The Wedding*. Most agree, however, that Dorothy West's weak endings do not nullify the value of her novels.

To date, the bulk of scholarship on Dorothy West focuses on *The Living Is Easy*. In Philip Butcher's 1948 essay, he presents West as one of the then-current "raceless writers." For Butcher, "The trend toward raceless authorship seems a loss to the Negro and to American literature" (15). In 1982 the Feminist Press reissued *The Living Is Easy* with an afterword by Adelaide Cromwell. Cromwell discusses the ways in which West's novel transforms literary representations of black women as well as the literary image of the lives of black people in the United States. Edward Clark's 1985 essay "Boston Black and White" is concerned with Cleo's failed desire to "be both Southern and Bostonian" (85). Lawrence Rodgers presents one of the most intriguing readings of *The Living Is Easy*. He does not believe this novel is compromised by the dominant society's middle-class values. For him, West "mocks these values" (161). Rodgers reads Cleo as "a complex archetypal trickster whose resistance to the binary is rooted in the folk tradition" (165) of black people in the South.

Mary Helen Washington initiates scholarly focus on gender in this novel. West, according to Washington, writes a novel that is "in contradiction with itself" because there is a "sisterly community which has deposed the powerful mother" Cleo (350–51). Gloria Wade-Gayles (1984) argues that African American mother–daughter relationships in literature are different from their European American counterparts because the socialization process among black women is rooted in gender and racial struggles. Eva Rueschmann investigates the importance of sister bonds, which allow black women a mirror that reflects a model for "identity formation," which is lacking in the dominant society. For Rueschmann, West's *The Living Is Easy* "comment[s] ironically on women's pre-scripted fantasies about their own development and underline[s] how standards for white women have shaped black women's self-perceptions and expectations" (130). Cleo, then, tries to find in her sisters just such a mirror of their mother and herself.

BIBLIOGRAPHY

Works by Dorothy West

"Hannah Byde." *The Messenger* 8 (July 1926): 197–199.
"Prologue to a Life." 1928. *The Sleeper Wakes: Harlem Renaissance Stories by Women*. Ed. Marcy Knopf. New Brunswick, NJ: Rutgers University Press, 1993. 84–94.
The Living Is Easy. 1948. Old Westbury, NY: Feminist Press, 1982.
The Richer, the Poorer: Stories, Sketches, and Reminiscences. New York: Doubleday, 1995a.
The Wedding. New York: Doubleday, 1995b.

Studies of Dorothy West

Butcher, Philip. "Our Raceless Writers." *Opportunity* 26 (Summer 1948): 113–115.
Clark, Dorothy A. "Rediscovering Dorothy West." *American Visions* 8 (1993): 46–47.

Clark, Edward. "Boston Black and White: The Voice of Fiction." *Black American Literature Forum* 19 (1985): 83–89.

Cromwell, Adelaide. Afterword. *The Living Is Easy*. By Dorothy West. Old Westbury, NY: Feminist Press, 1982. 349–362.

Dalsgard, Katrine. "Alive and Well and Living on the Island of Martha's Vineyard: An Interview with Dorothy West, October 29, 1988." *The Langston Hughes Review* 12 (1993): 28–44.

Daniel, Walter C. "*Challenge Magazine*: An Experiment That Failed." *CLAJ* 26 (June 1976): 494–503.

Ferguson, Sally Ann. "Dorothy West and Helene Johnson in *Infants of the Spring*." *Langston Hughes Review* 2.2 (1983): 22–24.

———. "Dorothy West." *Dictionary of Literary Biography*. Vol. 76. Ed. Trudier Harris. Detroit: Gale, 1988. 187–195.

McDowell, Deborah E. "Conversation with Dorothy West." *The Harlem Renaissance Re-Examined*. Ed. Victor A. Kramer. New York: AMS Press, 1987. 265–282.

Rodgers, Lawrence R. "Dorothy West's *The Living Is Easy* and the Ideal of Southern Folk Community." *AAR* 26 (1992): 161–172.

Roses, Lorraine Elena. "Interviews with Black Women Writers: Dorothy West at Oak Bluffs, Massachusetts July, 1984." *Sage* 2.1 (1985): 47–49.

Rueschmann, Eva. "Sister Bonds: Intersections of Family and Race in Jessie Redmon Fauset's *Plum Bun* and Dorothy West's *The Living Is Easy*. *The Significance of Sibling Relationships in Literature*. Ed. JoAnna Stephens Mink and Janet Doubler Ward. Bowling Green, OH: Bowling Green State University Popular Press, 1993. 120–132.

Steinberg, Sybil. "Dorothy West: Her Own Renaissance." *Publishers Weekly* 242 (3 July 1995): 34–35.

Wade-Gayles, Gloria. "The Truths of Our Mothers' Lives: Mother–Daughter Relationships in Black Women's Fiction." *Sage* 1.2 (1984): 8–12.

Washington, Mary Helen. "I Sign My Mother's Name: Maternal Power in Dorothy West's Novel, *The Living Is Easy*." *Invented Lives: Narratives of Black Women 1860–1960*. Garden City, NY: Anchor Press, 1987. 344–353.

JOHN EDGAR WIDEMAN
(1941–   )

Robin Lucy

BIOGRAPHY

John Edgar Wideman was born in Washington, D.C., but shortly before his first birthday his family moved to Homewood, a predominantly African American neighborhood in Pittsburgh. Wideman's great-great-great-grandmother, a fugitive slave, had found freedom there in the 1850s, and much of Wideman's extended family still lived there. His relatives transmitted a rich storytelling tradition: "I had around me a kind of world, a creative world, an imaginative world, which I could draw from and which I very much wanted to participate in" (Rowell 47). When Wideman was twelve, his family moved to Shadyside, a largely white, upper-middle-class section of Pittsburgh. Wideman starred on the basketball team, was senior class president, and was named valedictorian at his integrated high school. However, his existence was racially compartmentalized; he associated with his white friends in the gym and classroom and his African American friends outside school.

In 1959, Wideman won a scholarship to the University of Pennsylvania, majoring first in psychology, then switching to English. He won all-Ivy League status as a forward on the basketball team, but in his senior year he traded his dream of becoming an National Basketball Association (NBA) star for that of becoming a writer. He graduated Phi Beta Kappa in 1963 and was awarded a Rhodes Scholarship. He was only the second African American to receive it. Alain Locke had been the first, fifty-five years earlier. Wideman studied the eighteenth-century novel at Oxford University. He received a bachelor of philosophy degree in 1966 and returned to the United States with his wife, Judith Ann Goldman, whom he had married in 1965. His university experience intensified his sense of racial compartmentalization. He would later struggle to bring together "the life of the black kid growing up in a predominantly black neighborhood in Pittsburgh, and the life of a middle-class academic in a white world" (Rowell 52).

From 1966 to 1967, Wideman was Kent Fellow at the University of Iowa's Creative Writing Workshop. In 1967, he accepted a position at the University of Pennsylvania, eventually becoming that university's first black tenured professor. In 1968, two of Wideman's undergraduate students asked him to teach a course in African American literature. He initially refused, as he was then unfamiliar with the black literary tradition. However, he soon made the decision to teach the course and began to read widely in the field. He went on to found the University of Pennsylvania's first African American studies program, which he chaired from 1971 to 1973. For Wideman, this initial exposure to African American writing was crucial to his development as a writer: "It awakened in me a different sense of self-image and the whole notion of a third world" (O'Brien 216). He began to "sabotage" his "classical-European" education (Rowell 51) and experiment with the development of a distinctly black literary language.

In 1975, Wideman's youngest brother, Robby, was involved in an armed robbery that left one man dead and was sentenced to life imprisonment without parole. Wideman narrates these events in *Brothers and Keepers*. In that same year, Wideman accepted a teaching position at the University of Wyoming at Laramie. The move west was motivated by the need "to escape the demons Robby personified" (Wideman, *Brothers* 11). He also wanted to reevaluate the role his education and his professorship at an Ivy League college had played in shaping him, particularly in light of his involvement with African American studies: "I wanted to stand back and measure what all that had meant, what that had cost me, what it meant in terms of this new consciousness of blackness" (Rowell 52). In 1986, his own son, Jacob, was sentenced to life imprisonment for the murder of a friend, an event that resulted in the writing of *Fatheralong* eight years later. In 1986, Wideman left the University of Wyoming. John Edgar Wideman presently teaches in the English Department of the University of Massachusetts at Amherst. In addition to his fiction, he continues to publish criticism, primarily on the work of African American writers, and articles on African American literary theory, particularly the use of the black storytelling and vernacular tradition in literature.

MAJOR WORKS AND THEMES

Wideman's early writing was influenced by the techniques of the Euro-American modernists. Wideman moved away from modernism and a focus on the racial-existential dilemmas of the lone, male hero as he rediscovered the African American oral tradition, his "very own mother's voice" (Rowell 55). He restructured his writing to include this voice and refocused his narratives on the articulation of the African American community as a whole. The narrative voice of his fiction evolved from the stream-of-consciousness monologue of the alienated male protagonist to the voices of a type of African American griot, the speaker of collective memory and myth. The African American oral tradition, as embodied in his later texts, became a "counter-version" of the very social conditions that made necessary an aesthetic tradition of resistance and collective affirmation, one that "keeps telling the truth which brought it into being—the necessity of remaining human . . . resisting those destructive definitions in the Master's tongue, attitudes and art" (Wideman, "Architectonics" 44). In Wideman's later work, the storyteller/writer probes the potential dissolution of African American community under the impact of external and internal violence. At the same time, myriad American voices and narratives surface in his work, articulating the possibilities of, and the tragic failure to create, a multiracial, multicultural American nation. The teller of tales is deeply implicated in the fate of this American community; he or she "traditionally, should arm, should enlighten, should tell you what's *happening*, tell you what you need to do, what your choices are" (Lustig 457).

Wideman has called his early novels "divided" texts: African American experience provided the subject matter, but he felt compelled to "legitimize that world by infusing echoes" of the modernists (Rowell 54–55). The division between the subject matter and the rhetorical strategies of the texts reproduces the situation of the protagonists themselves: inhabitants of a liminal space between histories, cultures, and languages. *A Glance Away* is the story of Eddie Lawson, a recovering drug addict. He returns to Homewood in hope of recovering the "lost part" of himself. His story intersects with that of Brother Small, an albino black man who maintains a sexual liaison with a white, homosexual college professor, Robert Thurley. Although Eddie and Robert know each other only through Brother, they are inverted racial doubles filled with their own versions of fear and hatred. In the end, Robert attempts to redeem Eddie and himself. The pairing or mirroring of characters is one of Wideman's most frequently used devices. The novel introduces one of the author's primary concerns: the role of memory and time in the construction of self and community. Eddie attempts to reintegrate himself into the community by compressing all of experience into a continuous narrative of memory, "as if time were never more than the space between a glance away and back" (105).

Hurry Home is the story of Cecil Brathwaite, the first person in his community to become a lawyer and a figure of the black intellectual estranged from his community, a central theme in all of Wideman's novels. Cecil leaves his wife and travels to Spain and Africa in search of an answer to the "mystery of my own past" (51). In Europe he meets a white man in search of the half-black son he fathered but has never seen; Cecil becomes the lost son's double. Cecil had conceived a child, a son, with his wife before their marriage, but he died at birth. The death of the infant introduces another of Wideman's themes: the legacy of slavery. The baby died because he could not live as a "contradiction" to history, to slavery's legacy, even in the present. Cecil laments, "I wanted you to be full, complete, not a living hunger or a word written in the sea" (150). Cecil, like Eddie, returns to his family because "there has been no story, no telling, and I must begin" (167). Whether he will be able to tell his tale or rejoin the community remains unresolved.

In *The Lynchers*, four black men plot to lynch a white policeman in Philadelphia, an act that, according to their leader Littleman, signifies African American nationhood. The novel's "Matter Prefatory" reproduces accounts of three centuries of violence against African Americans. The problem of structuring African American memory and community is submerged in the problem of history and African American strategies of resistance to, and subversion of, its real and rhetorical rituals, the major theme of Wideman's later works. To Littleman, history determines the life of the community; there is no choice but "to reverse or destroy" it (72). However, the conspirators' plot involves the killing of a black prostitute who pays protection to the policeman, a parodic inversion of the symbolic role white women traditionally played in lynchings. This subplot forces Tom Wilkerson, who will eventually abort the scheme, to ask whether her murder might not justify the slaughter of all who are "guilty" of submitting to external power. Wilkerson cannot accept "a rite totally consistent with the logic of history" (172). Wideman introduces a sustained black vernacular voice into the text for the first time; it signals the rudimentary beginnings of community, the collective voice of those who have always "written their history with their mouths" (167).

In 1981, Wideman published the first two books of the Homewood Trilogy, *Damballah* and *Hiding Place*. In these texts, the African American storytelling voice and the black vernacular are the dominant forms of expression. Storytelling, an act of memory and imagination, is a form of resistance, a way to wrest control of history by subjecting it to a process of ongoing collective revision. "Imagination," Wideman writes, "has evolved as discipline, defense, coping mechanism, counterweight to the galling facts of life. We've learned to confer upon ourselves the power of making up our lives, changing them as we go along" ("Architectonics" 43). In the trilogy, African American women assume a central role in the preservation and transmission of the community's stories, what Wideman has called the "mother lode" of human experience (Rowell 55).

Damballah is composed of twelve interconnected short stories about the French-Hollinger clan. While most of the stories take place between 1900 and 1970, Wideman links the family to Africa with the figure of Orion, whose story begins the text, and to its African American ancestor, Sybela Owens, who lived on the same plantation as Orion and whose story ends the text. The narrative takes the form of a spiral, turning and looping back on itself, containing the historical and imaginative experience of Homewood's generations. Sybela, who escapes to Homewood with the man who will become her husband, her master's son—whose descendants, like Wideman's texts, inherit two racial legacies—passes on the family's stories through the female line. To tell these stories is to ensure that "*nothing is lost*" (198–99). They are necessary if Sybela's descendants are "to know the truth" (202). *Damballah* concludes with the "truth" that Tommy Lawson's, aka Robby's, imprisonment is analogous to Sybela's enslavement. The urban environment that made Robby's "choice" of "crime" a form of escape, of freedom is equally a form of slavery. The narrator asks Robby "if anything had changed in the years between her crimes and yours" (200). Wideman elaborates on his theme of slavery's contemporary manifestations and constructs the American city as a metaphor for the state of the nation as a whole. Wideman continues Tommy's story in *Hiding Place*. However, Tommy is killed by the police at the ancestral homestead where he has taken refuge with his relative Bess. She must descend to Homewood to resume her storytelling and tell his truth.

Sent for You Yesterday, the trilogy's final book, won the P.E.N./Faulkner Award in 1984. It is the story of Carl French, his albino friend Brother Tate, and his lover, and Brother's sister, Lucy. Carl's nephew, John (Doot) Lawson, returns to Homewood to learn the family's stories. The narrative voice moves between the central characters; individual identities are permeable and malleable. This sharing of identities, dreams, and voices is the way in which Homewood was created. However, in the present, the community is threatened by violence. Many of Homewood's buildings have been destroyed or abandoned; the neighborhood is crime-ridden and dangerous. The visions and voices that sustained John's family and community are fading. Lucy articulates the reasons for this failure: the "middle people," John's immediate forebears, turned away from the work of building community: "[W]e gave it all up. . . . We got scared and gave up too easy and now it's gone" (198). This legacy, or antilegacy, is a central theme in Wideman's next cycle of novels.

Reuben revises Wideman's earlier themes, telling the story of a black intellectual who finds a vital role in Homewood. Wideman's next two novels, however, pick up where the Homewood Trilogy left off, exploring the problem of violence and resistance to violence in America's cities, specifically, Philadelphia. *Philadelphia Fire* was inspired by the police bombing of MOVE headquarters in 1985. Ordered by Philadelphia's black mayor, it started a blaze that killed six adults and five children and gutted a city block. Cudjoe, a failed writer who has lived abroad for a decade, returns to Philadelphia to write a book about the incident and to find the boy seen running from the blaze. In the first part of the novel, Cudjoe's failed marriage to a white woman and his deliberate severing of ties with his children are told in flashback. The runaway boy is the double of his own "lost" children and a figure of society's collective abandonment of its offspring, the abdication of its generational responsibilities. Timbo, a black assistant to the mayor, articulates the African American community's complicity in the problem: "We had the whole world in our hands and we blew it. . . . Tossed it back to Daddy and exited for goddamn parts unknown" (82). Cudjoe's generation, too, has given up on the possibility of sustaining or changing the world. In the novel's second part, the runaway boy is transformed into Wideman's own imprisoned son, and the author details his painful efforts to communicate with him. In the last section, Shakespeare's *The Tempest* becomes a paradigm for present-day racial betrayal. Caliban and his descendants betray the secret of Life, reveal the hiding places of their peers, and sustain the occupier; because humanity shares in this secret, Caliban's betrayal of his race amounts to a betrayal of all people, a parable and parody of the Fall (167). The voices of new characters, all of them fragments and fictions of Cudjoe, dominate this section. These are not the intersecting voices and dreams of a community but the fractured narrative of a society breaking apart.

The Cattle Killing is an account of the 1793 persecution of African Americans by white residents of Philadelphia. They blamed blacks for the yellow fever epidemic that swept the city and pressed them into service during the crisis, believing them immune to the disease. The novel shifts abruptly in time and place from the eighteenth century to the present, from Africa to England and America. The narrative voices include, among others, those of an itinerant preacher, an orphaned boy, and the wife of a white Philadelphia doctor and her maid. The text is, according to its narrator, *"Not quite stories. True and not true. . . . Not exactly a novel. Hybrid"* (8). Like Caliban's betrayal of his people, the African Xhosa tribe's killing of its cattle in the belief that this would liberate them from the European invaders is, as Austin Clarke writes, "a metaphor for ethnic miscalculation" (D14). Wideman links this suicidal act with the fever of black-on-black violence, violence largely determined by the nation's violent racial history, and the danger of mistaking the nightmare of despair for prophetic vision. In an earlier version of the story in *Fever*, the plague is the legacy of slavery, of the inability to recognize a common humanity: it was "planted there when one of us decided to sell one of us to another" (133). In *Killing*, the de facto slavery of African Americans during the epidemic is the result of the city's fear of "the contagion of freedom" (34). The novel is Wideman's most complex treatment of the themes of his fiction. The preacher tries to keep alive with his storytelling the mysterious black woman who materializes at various times and in various places, even though "language [is] coming apart in my hands" (205). This woman has, it seems, crossed over from the world of the ancestors and generations unborn, bringing Wideman's concerns with time, memory, and collective knowledge more clearly into the realm of the metaphysical. The orphan boy, consigned to a cellar in the orphanage, burns his prison to the ground. This and the slaughter of African Americans by fearful whites cause the preacher to lose his faith, to cease imagining that such horror can be rewritten or redeemed. Can stories overwrite history, define the world so that each story "is never quite erased by the next, each story saving the space, saving itself, saving us[?]" (208).

CRITICAL RECEPTION

Recent criticism has focused on two aspects of Wideman's writing: the development of a black literary language and the autobiographical elements of his work. Several studies have focused on Wideman's overall career. James Coleman views Wideman's narrative development as a movement from an "uncritical acceptance of the forms and themes of mainstream modernism as practiced by white literary masters to a black voicing of modernism and postmodernism" (*Blackness*

6). He links this change in narrative strategies to Wideman's personal and thematic progression from that of a black intellectual estranged from his community
to that of intellectual/storyteller engaged with the stories and myths of that community ("Going" 328). James Saunders, following the same critical path as Coleman, argues that Du Bois' metaphor of African American double-consciousness
is the central trope of Wideman's life and work. Doreatha Mbalia significantly
revises these approaches to Wideman's work, placing his texts on a narrative
continuum that moves from the Eurocentric to the recovery and expression of
"the African Personality."

Criticism of Wideman's work of midcareer has focused on the trilogy. However, Trudier Harris has written on *The Lynchers*. By beginning the novel with
the records of racial violence, Wideman "freely admits his debt to history in the
creation of his fiction . . . in setting the two up side by side" in a way that few
other black writers have done (130). The failure of the conspirators' plot, Harris
argues, demonstrates Wideman's unwillingness to create a mythology for the
African American community based on violence. Criticism of the trilogy tends
to focus on Wideman's narrative strategies. Jacqueline Berben's discussion of
Hiding Place diverges from the general critical consensus on Wideman's development of a black literary language. She views the novel as one in which language
is an unreliable, even deceitful, medium more aligned with the world of dreams
than reality. Ashraf Rushdy, drawing on theories of African American vernacular
expression, makes African American musical structures and traditions the basis
of his discussion of Wideman's poetics. The trilogy traces the development of
the narrator's "blues voice," which mediates between personal and collective
experience, memory and history and permits the individuation of self through
the recognition of one's kinship with others. John Bennion's discussion of *Sent
for You Yesterday* parallels the structure of the novel with the structuring of John's
memory through the Homewood stories. The storyteller, or writer, is responsible
for keeping the community's reality intact because "the true forms of perception
exist backward in time and memory" (147).

Jan Clausen's article on *Philadelphia Fire* adopts a feminist perspective on the
protagonist Cudjoe. The novel is "*his* story," focusing on his alienation, his failed
fatherhood and relationships with women. Although Clausen stops short of ac-
cusing Wideman of misogyny, she views Wideman's reluctance to depict autonomous females in much of his fiction and the atomization of the female body and
lack of a sustained female voice in *Fire* as evidence that "women present a problem" to Wideman himself (52). Despite Clausen's insistence on a direct correspondence between the writer's life and art and her reluctance to recognize the
essential role of the female storytelling voice in much of Wideman's work, she
does identify aspects of Wideman's writing that betray a masculinist bias.

Gene Seymour's review of *The Cattle Killing* compares the novel's structure and
themes to Toni Morrison's* *Beloved*. The novel depicts America's "imagination
sickness," its inability to recognize a collective fate (58). The merging of the
authorial consciousness with the black and white characters of the novel is a

literary vaccination against the *fear* of the contagion of freedom, "as if the act of dreaming their dreams would somehow inoculate his readers against cowardice and dread of each other" (59). Austin Clarke describes Wideman's novel as one in which "the relentlessness of Wideman's language" leaves the reader "bruised in mind and limb." The novel is a "journey of penance" across time and space, a journey undertaken so that the reader might recover the possibility of freedom. Clarke sees a "crystallization" of the styles of James Baldwin,* Richard Wright, Ralph Ellison,* and William Faulkner in the book and writes that "this kind of concentric writing, tells me that the concern in the United States about the future of the novel by black men might be assuaged by *The Cattle Killing*" (D14).

BIBLIOGRAPHY

Works by John Edgar Wideman

Fiction

A Glance Away. New York: Harcourt, Brace, and World, 1967.
Hurry Home. New York: Harcourt, Brace, and World, 1970.
The Lynchers. New York: Harcourt Brace Jovanovich, 1973.
Damballah. New York: Bard-Avon, 1981a.
Hiding Place. New York: Bard-Avon, 1981b.
Sent for You Yesterday. New York: Bard-Avon, 1983.
Reuben. New York: Henry Holt, 1987.
Fever: Twelve Stories. New York: Henry Holt, 1989.
Philadelphia Fire. New York: Henry Holt, 1990.
The Stories of John Edgar Wideman. New York: Pantheon, 1992.
The Cattle Killing. Boston: Houghton Mifflin, 1996.

Nonfiction

Brothers and Keepers. New York: Holt, Rinehart, and Winston, 1984. "The Architectonics of Fiction." *Callaloo* 13.1 (1990): 42–46.
Fatheralong: A Meditation on Fathers and Sons, Race and Society. New York: Pantheon, 1994.

Studies of John Edgar Wideman

Bennion, John. "The Shape of Memory in John Edgar Wideman's *Sent for You Yesterday*." *Black American Literature Forum* 20.1/2 (1986): 143–150.
Berben, Jacqueline. "Beyond Discourse: The Unspoken versus Words in the Fiction of John Edgar Wideman." *Callaloo* 8.3 (1985): 525–534.
Clarke, Austin. "Venturing into the Beehive of Race." Review of *The Cattle Killing*. *Globe and Mail* (March 1, 1997): D14.
Clausen, Jan. "Native Fathers." *The Kenyon Review* 14.2 (1992): 44–55.
Coleman, James W. "Going Back Home: The Literary Development of John Edgar Wideman." *College Language Association Journal* 28.3 (1985): 326–343.

———. *Blackness and Modernism: The Literary Career of John Edgar Wideman*. Jackson: University Press of Mississippi, 1989.

Harris, Trudier. *Exorcising Blackness: Historical and Literary Lynching and Burning Rituals*. Bloomington: Indiana University Press, 1984.

Lustig, Jessica. "Home: An Interview with John Edgar Wideman." *African American Review* 26.3 (1992): 453–457.

Mbalia, Doreatha Drummond. *John Edgar Wideman: Reclaiming the African Personality*. Selinsgrove, PA: Susquehanna University Press, 1995.

O'Brien, John, ed. *Interviews with Black Writers*. New York: Liveright, 1973.

Rowell, Charles H. "An Interview with John Edgar Wideman." *Callaloo* 13.1 (1990): 47–61.

Rushdy, Ashraf H. A. "Fraternal Blues: John Edgar Wideman's Homewood Trilogy." *Contemporary Literature* 32.3 (1991): 312–345.

Saunders, James Robert. "Exorcizing the Demons: John Edgar Wideman's Literary Response." *The Hollins Critic* 29.5 (1992): 1–10.

Seymour, Gene. "Dream Surgeon." Review of *The Cattle Killing*. *The Nation* 263.13 (1996): 58–60.

SHERLEY ANNE WILLIAMS
(1944–   )

Trela Anderson

BIOGRAPHY

Born in Bakersfield, California, Sherley Anne Williams grew up in a Fresno housing project and spent most of her adolescent years picking cotton in the fields of the San Joaquin Valley alongside her parents. Her father, Jesse Winson Williams, died of tuberculosis when she was seven, and her mother, Lelia Marie Siler, died when she was sixteen. Williams was raised by her older sister Ruise, whom she cites as a major influence on her life.

Although Williams did not begin to write seriously until after she received her B.A. degree in history from California State University, Fresno, she always wrote with the intention of being published. Her first published short story, "Tell Martha Not to Moan," appeared in *Massachusetts Review* in 1967. In 1972, she earned an M.A. degree from Brown University, where she was also teaching in the African American studies program. She did not pursue a Ph.D. at Brown because, while a graduate degree had been necessary for her career as a teacher of African American literature, she did not want to spend the rest of her life trying to explain the world through someone else's eyes. She wanted to meld the experiences of her contemporaries with those of her own.

Initially, Williams wanted specifically to write about lower-class black women, whom she saw as marginal in the literature she had read. She felt that they were important, that something could be learned from them. In her writings, she mentions Toni Morrison,* Alice Walker,* Langston Hughes, Amiri Baraka (Leroi Jones), Sterling Brown, and James Baldwin* as artists who attempt to carry on the legacies of their ancestors in their writing. She has consciously added her name to this list. Her personal goal is to refashion a new tradition built on the synthesis of black oral traditions and Western literary forms.

Sherley Anne Williams has been a Fulbright lecturer at the University of Ghana and an associate professor of English at the University of California, Fresno. She is currently teaching and writing at the University of California, San Diego.

MAJOR WORKS AND THEMES

Dessa Rose, Williams' most highly acclaimed work, is a fictional representation of two historical events: a pregnant black woman who led a slave revolt on a coffle (a group of slaves chained together and sold at market) in Kentucky in 1839 and a white woman who gave sanctuary to runaway slaves in North Carolina in 1836. She read of the first incident in Angela Davis' essay "Reflection on the Black Woman's Role in the Community of Slaves" and discovered the second incident in Herbert Aptheker's *American Negro Slave Revolts*. Thus, the novel's large theme may be regarded as a realistic depiction of slavery that highlights the sexual exploitation of black men and women.

Although Williams tells her story from the viewpoint of two women, Dessa, the pregnant, whip-scarred slave is the central character. Throughout the novel, she recollects her life on the plantation with her lover Kaine, who is killed by their master. When Dessa learns of his death, she, in turn, kills the master, escapes arrests, and awaits death after the birth of her son, whom the slave owners consider valuable property. Adam Nehemiah, a white author who hopes to publish an analysis of Dessa's crimes, asks why she kills white men, and Dessa replies, "Cause I can" (13).

The interweaving of Dessa's story with that of Ruth's is interestingly effective in that it not only connects two historically related events but serves as the basis of the novel's tension. At first, Dessa views Rufel as "Miz Ruint" (172); she doubts her intentions of helping the slaves and disapproves of her sexual relationship with Nathan. However, as the narrative progresses, the two women discover that they are not so different. By experimenting with the dynamics of race and class, Williams explores the way in which friendship transcends these barriers.

Like all good writers, Williams has a sensitive ear for dialogue. She maintains a consistent dialect throughout the novel and creates a voice that readers can both trust and appreciate.

CRITICAL RECEPTION

Overall, *Dessa Rose* has received positive reviews. Most critics agree that the novel is an authentic, yet innovative, portrayal of the American South prior to the Civil War and commend Williams for her imaginative depiction of antebellum society. Although he praises the novel for its "absorbing fusion [of] both elegant poetry and powerful fiction" (7), David Bradley criticizes Williams' underdramatization of some scenes and her errors in pacing. He goes on to compliment the novel for its construction of a relationship that allows two women to overcome the concepts of race and gender.

Katherine Bucknell also discusses Williams' exploration of the relationship between blacks and whites. However, she says that Williams "falls into the cliche that blacks have deeper emotions than whites, emotions which whites can neither understand nor share" (765). Thus, the novel undermines history in favor of romance.

Other commentators, Christopher Lehmann-Haupt, for instance, focus on the historical aspect of the novel and say that Williams confronts more issues than are dreamed of in most history books.

BIBLIOGRAPHY

Works by Sherley Anne Williams

Give Birth to Brightness: A Thematic Study in Neo-Black Literature. New York: Dial, 1972.
The Peacock Poems. Middletown, CT: Wesleyan University Press, 1975.
Some One Sweet Angel Chile. New York: Morrow, 1982.
Dessa Rose. New York: Morrow, 1986.
Working Cotton. San Diego: Harcourt, 1992.
"The Lion's History: The Ghetto Writes Back." *Soundings* 76 (1993): 245–59.

Studies of Sherley Anne Williams

Bradley, David. Rev. of *Dessa Rose. New York Times Book Review* 3 Aug. 1986.
Bucknell, Katherine. Rev. of *Dessa Rose. Times Literary Supplement* 17 July 1987.
Davies, Carole-Boyce. "Mother Right/Write Revisited: *Beloved* and *Dessa Rose* and the Construction of Motherhood in Black Women's Fiction." *Narrating Mothers: Theorizing Maternal Subjectives.* Ed. Brenda O. Daly and Maureen T. Reddy. Knoxville: University of Tennessee Press, 1991. 44–57.
Davis, Mary Kemp. "Everybody Knows Her Name: The Recovery of the Past in Sherley Anne Williams's *Dessa Rose.*" *Callaloo* 12 (1989): 554–58.
Delancey, Dale B. "The Self's Own Kind: Literary Resistance in Sherley Anne Williams's *Dessa Rose.*" *MAWA-Review* 5 (1990): 59–62.
Gable, Mona. Interview with Sherley Anne Williams. *Los Angeles Times Magazine* 7 Dec. 1986.
Goldman, Anne E. " 'I Made the Ink': (Literary) Production in *Dessa Rose* and *Beloved.*' " *Feminist Studies* 16 (1990): 313–30.
Howard, Lillie P. "Sherley Anne Williams." *Dictionary of Literary Biography: Afro-American Poets since 1955* 41 (1985): 343–50.
Kekeh, Andree Anne. "Sherley Anne Williams's *Dessa Rose*: History and the Disruptive Power of Memory." *History and Memory in African American Culture.* Ed. Genevieve Fabre and Robert O'Meally. New York: Oxford University Press, 1994. 219–27.
King, Nicole R. "Meditations and Mediations: Issues of History and Fiction in *Dessa Rose.*" *Soundings* 76 (1993): 351–68.

Lehmann-Haupt, Christopher. Review of *Dessa Rose. New York Times* 12 July 1986.

Maida, Patricia. "Kindred and *Dessa Rose*: Two Novels That Reinvent Slavery." *CEA-Magazine* 4 (1991): 43–52.

McDowell, Deborah E. "Negotiating between Tenses: Witnessing Slavery after Freedom—*Dessa Rose*." *Slavery and the Literary Imagination.* Ed. Deborah McDowell and Arnold Rampersad. Baltimore: Johns Hopkins University Press, 1989. 144–63.

McKible, Adam. "These Are the Facts of the Darky's History: Thinking History and Reading Names in Four African American Texts." *African American Review* 28 (1994): 223–35.

Porter, Nancy. "Women's Interracial Friendships and Visions of Community in Meridian, The Salt Eaters, Civil Wars, and *Dessa Rose*." *Tradition and Talents of Women.* Ed. Florence Howe. Urbana: University of Illinois Press, 1991. 251–67.

Rushdy, Ashraf H. "Reading Mammy: The Subject of Relation in Sherley Anne Williams's *Dessa Rose*." *African American Review* 27 (1993): 365–89.

Sanchez, Marta E. "The Estrangement Effect in Sherley Anne Williams's *Dessa Rose*." *Genders* 15 (1992): 21–36.

Sinclair, Marta E. Rev. of *Dessa Rose. Times (London)* 19 Mar. 1987.

Smith-Wright, Geraldine. "A Response to Williams." *Soundings* 76 (1993): 261–63.

Stone, Albert E. *The Return of Nat Turner: History, Literature, and Cultural Politics.* Athens: University of Georgia Press, 1992.

Trapasso, Anne E. "Returning to the Site of Violence: The Restructuring of Slavery's Legacy in Sherley Anne Williams's *Dessa Rose*." *Violence, Silence and Anger: Women's Writing as Transgression.* Ed. Deirdre Lashgari. Charlottesville: University of Virginia Press, 1995. 219–30.

JACQUELINE WOODSON
(1963–   )

Nicola Morris

BIOGRAPHY

Jacqueline Woodson was born in Columbus, Ohio, in 1963. While she was still an infant, her parents divorced, and she moved with her older brother and sister to Greenville, North Carolina, where they lived with their grandparents. By the time she was in first grade she was living in Brooklyn, New York, with her mother, and during her teenage years she moved back and forth between New York and North Carolina. Diane R. Paylor notes that "having spent her adolescence being shuttled between South Carolina and New York City, Woodson never quite felt a part of either place—a feeling intensified by being raised as a Jehovah's Witness" (77). Woodson says that being a Jehovah's Witness helped her not feel lost as she grew up as an African American lesbian, because it gave her a sense of community and an understanding of marginality. The Vietnam years also had a profound influence on her. Paylor quotes her as saying, "You'd see the neighborhood changing and everyone coming back and being addicted to heroin or having lost their minds or their arms or legs . . . but nobody was talking about it" (77), and Woodson herself writes, "the bitterness of Vietnam, the scandal of Watergate, poverty, inadequate housing and education—the list goes on—became our everyday experience" ("Sign" 711). This experience shows up in her first adult novel, *Autobiography of a Family Photo*, which describes the gradual dissolution of a family after the eldest son dies in Vietnam.

As Woodson traveled back and forth between North Carolina and Brooklyn, she was also traveling through different social classes, moving between her wealthy grandparents and her mother, who was struggling to bring up four children alone. Woodson says that these contrasting experiences made her aware of what it is to have and to have not and believes that people need to be conscious of their class privilege, a belief reflected in several of her novels.

Woodson has written about her frustration as a young reader. "So few books published in the 1970's reflected the existence of marginal people—and already, at nine, ten, eleven, I understood myself to be marginal" ("Sign" 712). The experience of not finding herself reflected in her reading as a child has profoundly influenced her writing. She says, "I write about black girls because this world would like to keep us invisible. I write about all girls because I know what happens to self-esteem when we turn twelve, and I hope to show readers the number of ways in which we are strong" (713).

In 1985 Woodson graduated with a B.A. in English from Adelphi University in Garden City, New York, where she was a member of the influential African American sorority Alpha Kappa Alpha (AKA). She is still active in AKA and says that she loves the sense of belonging that her membership gives her. "It's another community for me to belong to." A central theme of her novels is the tension between belonging and being an outsider, reflecting her experience in the sorority and as a member of the Jehovah's Witnesses.

In 1987 she decided to stop working full-time so she could write. During the next few years she supported herself by doing freelance word processing and did drama therapy with runaways and homeless kids in East Harlem. In 1990 she was awarded a fellowship at the MacDowell Colony in Peterborough, New Hampshire, and in 1991–1992 she was awarded a residency at the Fine Arts Work Center in Provincetown, Massachusetts, where she lived for three years before returning to live in Brooklyn. She taught in the Master of Fine Arts in Writing Program at Goddard College in Vermont for two years and currently teaches in the Vermont College Master of Fine Arts in Writing for Children Program. *Granta Magazine* recognized Woodson with a Fifty Best American Authors under 40 Award in 1996, and she has also won the Coretta Scott King Honor Book Award in both 1995 and 1996 and both the Lambda Literary Award for Best Lesbian Fiction and the Best Children's Fiction Award for 1996.

MAJOR WORKS AND THEMES

Jacqueline Woodson is first and foremost a writer of young adult fiction. The themes she takes up, sexual identity, racism, class conflict, the difficulties of developing friendships across racial and class barriers, have been explored in adult fiction but not extensively in young adult fiction. Jacqueline Woodson has consistently explored these issues in her fiction. As she said in an article recently, "I want to leave a sign of having been here. The rest of my life is committed to changing the way the world thinks, one reader at a time" ("Sign" 715).

Woodson's books show a wide range of characters and situations. She has a particular gift for getting into the minds of teenagers, for capturing the many nuances of their lives and voices.

Woodson's first book, *Last Summer with Maizon*, is the start of a trilogy about the friendship of two young girls, Margaret and Maizon, whose relationship changes when Margaret's father dies, and Maizon goes to a boarding school on a scholarship. In the course of the novel Margaret discovers her writing talent, and Maizon confronts racism and alienation at her almost all-white boarding school and chooses to return home. The book does an excellent job of demonstrating both subtle and not so subtle racism and gently points to the ways in which class differences affect relationships and friendships. Maizon's time in the boarding school is detailed in the second book of the trilogy, *Maizon at Blue Hill*. Maizon explains to her teachers why she is leaving the boarding school that was her grandmother's dream for her: "I'm going to try and find a place where I can fit in being both black and smart. There has to be a place somewhere, right?" (126). Indeed, one of the messages of Woodson's books for children is that there is a place in the world for each child to be who she or he is. *Between Madison and Palmetto* concludes the trilogy and deals with eating disorders as well as issues of friendship and integration.

While the trilogy deals primarily with family and friendship, Woodson's other books take on tougher issues. In *The Dear One*, Afeni, a middle-class African American girl, copes with the arrival in Afeni's suburban home of Rebecca, a pregnant teenager from Harlem. Class differences are central to this book. Rebecca is both defensive and wondrous when she arrives in this house, and when Afeni's mother explains to her that Rebecca's family doesn't have money, Afeni says, "Then they should get some money" (56), showing her lack of understanding of poor people.

I Hadn't Meant to Tell You This further develops the theme of class difference. Marie, an twelve-year-old living in a prosperous black suburb, makes friends with Lena, a poor white girl, and comes to understand the effects of poverty while also coping with the revelation that Lena is being sexually molested by her father. Unusual for a young adult novel, this book has an inconclusive ending that reflects the impossibility of closure with such a subject matter; Woodson's reluctance to force closure demonstrates her strength and confidence as a writer.

Woodson's first adult book, *Autobiography of a Family Photo*, is stylistically adventurous, written in a series of vignettes with vivid scenes and lyrical prose. The novel describes the gradual dissolution of a family and one girl's survival and discovery of her own power and strength during the Vietnam era. As critic Catherine Bush points out, this book revisits some of the same themes of her young adult books, themes of community, sexual abuse, sexual identity, loss, and family dysfunction, but this book yields "a bleaker, more turbulent landscape" (14). Woodson's writing in this novel has tremendous force and power.

She puts the issue of sexual identity center stage in the moving young adult book *From the Notebooks of Melanin Sun*, the story of a preadolescent African American boy, Melanin Sun, who collects stamps of endangered species. To his horror, his single-parent mother, to whom he is very close, falls in love with a woman, and not just a woman but a white woman. The novel lets us inside Melanin Sun's mind as he first resists, then comes to terms with, his mother's sexual identity and with her lover. In the process he has to deal with the homophobia of his community and find the strength of his own values and commitments. It is a powerful novel that captures the boy's voice accurately.

CRITICAL RECEPTION

In *From Romance to Realism*, one of the few full-length critical discussions of young adult literature, Michael Cart talks about the development of realist fiction for young people and places Woodson within that tradition. In his discussion of incest in young adult literature he says that Woodson's *I Hadn't Meant to Tell You This* is "beautiful in [its] passion and in [its] righteous anger at the horrors the world visits on young women" (206). Cart also praises Woodson's use of characters who happen to be lesbians (in *The Dear One* Afeni's closest friends are a lesbian couple), pointing out that Woodson is one of few young adult writers who depict gay people of color.

Woodson's books have been extensively and well reviewed. Catherine Bush's review of *Autobiography of a Family Photo* says that the novel "brims with complicated emotion and nuanced social observation; its prose percolates with rage and tenderness and lyricism" (14). While Bush wishes that "the narrator's self-awareness and longing could be defined less exclusively in sexual terms, that she might yearn for something else as well" (14), she says that "even in these restrictive terms, the novel is the best kind of survival guide: clear-eyed, gut true" (14). Whitney Scott says that *Autobiography of a Family Photo* "told with painful clarity and fervor, deserves its share of general readers" (738).

Lois Metzger, reviewing *From the Notebooks of Melanin Sun*, writes that "Ms. Woodson, in this moving, lovely book, shows you Melanin's strength" and notes that "Ms. Woodson gets Melanin's instant, enveloping, mind-splintering fear absolutely right" (27). Hazel Moore notes that "Woodson has addressed with care and skill the sensitive issues of homosexuality within the family" (227).

In an article discussing young adult novels written by new African American writers, Rudine Sims Bishop says that "my first impression on reading Woodson's *The Dear One* was that here was a 'black woman's novel.' Her characters are all convincingly familiar. Adolescents will find it engaging in its frank and straight forward approach" (564).

Lauren Adams, reviewing *I Hadn't Meant to Tell You This*, also appreciates Woodson's gifts for characterization. She writes, "Woodson's characters are deftly drawn whole individuals" (602) and comments that Woodson's "spare prose, crystal images and the staccato rhythm of the short chapters combine to create a haunting and beautifully poetic novel" (602).

BIBLIOGRAPHY

Works by Jacqueline Woodson

Last Summer with Maizon. New York: Delacorte, 1990.
The Dear One. New York: Delacorte, 1991.

Maizon at Blue Hill. New York: Delacorte, 1992.
Between Madison and Palmetto. New York: Delacorte, 1993a.
The Book Chase. New York: Delacorte, 1993b.
I Hadn't Meant to Tell You This. New York: Delacorte, 1994.
Autobiography of a Family Photo. New York, Dutton, 1995a.
From the Notebooks of Melanin Sun. New York: Scholastic, 1995b.
"A Sign of Having Been Here." *Horn Book Magazine* Nov./Dec. 1995c: 711–715.
A Way Out of Now Way. New York: Holt, 1996.
The House You Pass on the Way. New York: Delacorte, 1997a.
We Had a Picnic This Sunday Past. New York: Hyperion, 1997b.
Sweet, Sweet Memory. New York: Hyperion, 1998a.
That Summer. New York: Putnam, 1998b.
Visiting Day. New York: Scholastic, 1998c.

Studies of Jacqueline Woodson

Adams, Lauren. Review of *I Hadn't Meant to Tell You This*. *Horn Book Magazine*, Sept./Oct. 1994: 601–602.
Bishop, Rudine Sims. "Books from Parallel Cultures: New African American Voices." *Horn Book Magazine*, Sept./Oct. 1994: 562–566.
Bush, Catherine. "A World without Childhood." *New York Times Book Review*, 26 Feb. 1995: 14.
Cart, Michael. *From Romance to Realism: 50 Years of Growth and Change in Young Adult Literature.* New York: HarperCollins, 1996.
Metzger, Lois. Review of *From the Notebooks of Melanin Sun*. *New York Times Book Review*, 16 July 1995: 27.
Moore, Hazel. Review of *The Dear One*. *Voice of Youth Advocates* Oct. 1995: 227.
Paylor, Diane R. "Bold Type: Jacqueline Woodson's 'Girl Stories.' " *Ms.*, Nov. 1994: 77.
Saalfield, Catherine. "Jacqueline Woodson." *Contemporary Lesbian Writers of the United States.* Ed. Sandra Pollack and Denise D. Knight. Westport, CT: Greenwood Press, 1993. 583–586.
Scott, Whitney. Review of *Autobiography of a Family Photo*. *Booklist*, 15 Dec. 1994: 736–737.
Telephone interview with Jacqueline Woodson, 6 Aug. 1997.

SARAH ELIZABETH WRIGHT
(1928–   )

Linda M. White

BIOGRAPHY

Sarah Elizabeth Wright was born on December 9, 1928, the third of nine children. Her mother, Mary Amelia Moore, and father, Willis Charles Wright, raised their children in the small town of Wetipquin, Maryland. A man of many trades, including oysterman, barber, and farmer, Willis Wright provided his family with stability and character during some of the most turbulent times in black American history. This education began in their home and was continued through Wright's attendance at Wetipquin Elementary School from 1934 to 1945 and then Salisbury Colored High School. Because of the encouragement from her fourth grade teacher and inspiration later from her high school librarian and Latin teacher, Ms. Brown, Wright continued to develop poetry that would soon place her in the auspicious setting of Howard University and in the presence of the literary scholar Sterling Brown. In 1945, at sixteen years old, Wright entered Howard University, working her way through college as well as contributing editorial work at the *49er*, the *Hilltop*, and the *Stylus*. Her roles as editor and reporter brought her closer to understanding the relationship between the written word and the society it represented. She would later make numerous analogies of the effect of the media (both written and visual) on the development of the African American identity in the United States.

Wright was greatly influenced by literary giants Langston Hughes (who wrote a poem in her honor) and Sterling Brown (who taught her at Howard University). Her longtime affiliation with John Oliver Killens and the Harlem Writers Guild helped instill in Wright an appreciation for constant vigilance in writing style and form. These associations would eventually aid her in the all-too-familiar battle with self-identity, an aspect of living in the United States that every

African American must face. Wright found an outlet through her writing, producing poetry that sketched the presence of the African American tradition and the nascence of the African American psyche.

MAJOR WORKS AND THEMES

From her early experimentation with poetry in the third grade to her current literary status, Wright has developed a multilevel discourse, defining and redefining the "Black Experience," a feat she wishes to achieve in order to combat the conceptions and misconceptions fostered by the media. Along this vein, Wright has found it necessary to publish more articles on the plight of the African American writer than to fictionalize her views. Her recent nonfictional account of the life of Asa Philip Randolph in A. *Philip Randolph: Integration in the Workplace* continues Wright's dialogue with the past and present inheritors of a rich African American culture. Therefore, she not only hails as one of the many voices echoing from the renaissance of literature during the 1950s and 1960s but also as a contemporary commentator on the changing definitions of what is known as the "Black Experience." However, this does not diminish the potency of the message Wright communicates in her poetry and fiction or her role as a viable literary figure. She has published poems in such publications as *Freedomways*, *American Pen*, *The American Negro Writer and His Roots*, and *Beyond the Blues*. Additionally, Wright has published a collection of poems, along with Lucy Smith, titled *Give Me a Child*.

Though poetry was Wright's first love, she has gained considerable recognition for her novel titled *This Child's Gonna Live*. This novel is set in a small harbor town called Tangierneck, where destitution and poverty are permanent guests of the community. Within this setting lies the struggle of a nation of African Americans caught between making a future for themselves and their children and combating the detrimental attitudes of European Americans. The characters, especially Mariah, occasionally break out of their stupor of self-denial and self-loathing to emerge as strong, energetic people who finally find a possible compromise between their spiritual connection (that cannot be eliminated by years of oppression) to their ancestral continent and the spiritual connection with the religions of the people who once owned them. Mariah, in fact, begins the story, appealing to the spirits of God and Jesus to bless the day that she might provide for her family. She looks toward her African ancestors who acknowledged an all-powerful spirit along with a respect for the forces of nature. The combination of appealing to God and of blessing the day provides an excellent example of the fusion of the worlds of the African and the American. However, her imagination takes over, and she decides that if the day is good to her, and the harvest is plenty, she will not tolerate any injustice from the white man:

And when Bannie Upshire Dudley's hired man wrinkled his old pokey face in consternation from handing her "that many!" tokens for all those solid loaded baskets [of potatoes] she got such a shortness of the breath from lugging up to the field shanty, and when he snicker to her, "Mariah, ain't you done stole some baskets from Martha from on Back-of-the-Creek?" she was gonna sic her big bad word doggies on him. Gonna sound worse than a starved-out bloodhound baying at the teasing smell of fresh-killed meat, ten thousand times worse than the menfolks do when they're way from the whiteman bosses. (7)

All of her bravado turns out to be a fantasy, one that many African American readers can identify with immediately. When she awakes with startled realization, she curses, not just from the unnerving depiction of her parents but from the helplessness that she sees in her dream. She knows she will never tell off the white man, nor will she ever grow up in her parents' eyes. In her dream the dilemma for the story is voiced. Mariah must forge a path for herself as a woman, an African American, and a human being. She must deal with the drudgery of reality and find a way to accept her life, though it is riddled with dissension.

CRITICAL RECEPTION

Some of the most productive criticism comes from one of Wright's mentors, John O. Killens, in his "An Appreciation" to *This Child's Gonna Live*. Killens echoes the criticism of most reviewers of Wright's book that it is of monumental importance to the story of African American literary heritage. It is a heritage rich in antiquity and ancient African lore. He writes:

Sarah Wright's powerful novel . . . is an overwhelming metaphor of the Black experience in these United States of North America. This is all the more powerful and truthful for having a protagonist who is a Black woman of unparalleled heroism in this white, racist, capitalistic, male-supremacist society. . . . The Black Psyche is complex. Sarah Wright deftly demonstrates this time and time again. There are no easy answers to understanding the Black personality. Life is dialectic. Life is full of contradictions. (Killens 277, 282)

Phoebe Adams, in a somewhat superficial reading of Wright's novel, saw Mariah as only a "poor, ignorant, black and desperately ambitious heroine" (110). Irving Howe echoes Adams in his summation that Wright's "local color" story attempts to:

put its characters on display, as if to evoke a patronizing kindliness from the reader: a fondness for elaborating local, in this case black idiom, so that patches of authentic detail clash with the overall need for pacing the narrative; and a failure to establish a disciplined remove from her materials, which are still too close to Miss Wright as life, suffering, and memory to be available for art. (133)

Albert Johnston notes that "the language is idiomatic and the characters are alive, but the story is sometimes sentimental and the narration obscure" (1970, 62).

Henry Du Bois, however, notices that Wright is "deliberately obscure . . . failing to establish time orientation or clear character relationships. . . . Miss Wright's delineation of black speech and culture, particularly the comfort and the encumbrance of religions, is convincing and effective in this first novel" (2,004). Albert Johnston in another review of the novel also negotiates the despair of the story to note that, though "the mood is somber and the outcome grim, Wright possesses the ability to evoke a time and place beautifully in a perceptive examination of one black woman's hopeless assault on life" (63). Wright is careful to illustrate the different ways African Americans think and react to situations, attempting to capture the true voice of African Americans through dialect and idioms. John O. Killens finds this feat one of the more compelling aspects of her novel. He writes: "The novel is rich with Afro-American nuances and idiom, with a special essence from the Eastern Shore in Tangierneck. . . . Sarah Wright, the poet, always captures the rhythms of Southern Afro-American speech" (Killens 279).

Though Wright has written only three major works, her contribution to the formation of the African American literary tradition cannot be denied.

BIBLIOGRAPHY

Works by Sarah Elizabeth Wright

"I Have Known Death." *Tomorrow* 10 (November 3, 1950): 46.
Give Me a Child (with Lucy Smith). Philadelphia: Kraft, 1955.
"Roadblocks to the Development of the Negro Writer." In *The American Negro Writer and His Roots.* New York: American Society of African Culture, 1960.
"Until They Have Stopped." *Freedomways* 5.3 (1965): 378.
"The Negro Woman in American Literature." *Freedomways* 6 (Winter 1966): 8–10.
This Child's Gonna Live. New York: Delacorte, 1969.
"Urgency" and "Window Pictures." In *Beyond the Blues,* edited by Rosey E. Pool. Detroit: Broadside Press, 1971.
"Lament of a Harlem Mother." *American Pen* 4 (Spring 1972): 23–27.
"Black Writers' Views of America." *Freedomways* 19.3 (1979a): 161–162.
"*Lorraine Hansberry* on Film." *Freedomways* 19.4 (1979b): 283–284.
A. Philip Randolph: Integration in the Workplace. Englewood Cliffs, NJ: Silver Burdett Press, 1990.

Studies of Sarah Elizabeth Wright

Adams, Phoebe. Review of *This Child's Gonna Live. Atlantic Monthly* 224 (July 1969): 110.
Amini, Johari. Review of *This Child's Gonna Live. Negro Digest* 18 (August 1969): 51.
Colimore, Vincent J. Review of *This Child's Gonna Live. Best Sellers* 29 (August 1, 1969): 168.
Du Bois, Henry J. Review of *This Child's Gonna Live. Library Journal* 94 (May 15, 1969): 2004.

Guilford, Virginia B. "Sarah Elizabeth Wright." *Dictionary of Literary Biography*. Vol. 33 Ann Arbor, MI: Gale Research, 1984. 293–300.

Howe, Irving. Review of *This Child's Gonna Live*. *Harper's Magazine* 239 (December 1969): 130.

Johnston, Albert. Review of *This Child's Gonna Live*. *Publishers Weekly* 195 (April 21, 1969): 63.

———. Review of *This Child's Gonna Live*. *Publishers Weekly* 198 (September 7, 1970): 62.

Killens, John O. "An Appreciation." In *This Child's Gonna Live*. New York: Delacorte, 1969. 277–278, 282.

Long, Joanna R., ed. Review of *A. Philip Randolph: Integration in the Workplace*. *Jim Kobak's Kirkus Reviews* 58 (December 15, 1990): 1745.

Manthorne, Jane. Review of *A. Philip Randolph: Integration in the Workplace*. *Horn Book Guide to Children's and Young Adult Books* 2 (July 1990): 140.

O'Conner, Patricia. Review of *This Child's Gonna Live*. *New York Times Book Review* 92 (May 3, 1987): 41.

Review of *A. Philip Randolph: Integration in the Workplace*. *Library Talk* 4 (May 1991): 36.

Review of *This Child's Gonna Live*. *Times Literary Supplement* (October 16, 1969): 1177.

Rohrlick, Paula F. Review of *A. Philip Randolph: Integration in the Workplace*. *Kliatt: Young Adult Paperback Book Guide* 25 (January 1991): 33.

Stevens, Shane. Review of *This Child's Gonna Live*. *New York Times Book Review* (June 29, 1969): 4.

Wolff, Alice, ed. Review of *This Child's Gonna Live*. *Kirkus Reviews* 37 (April 15, 1969): 474.

Zellers, Jara D. Review of *A. Philip Randolph: Integration in the Workplace*. *Book Report* 10 (September 1991): 55.

FRANK GARVIN YERBY
(1916–1991)

Louis Hill Pratt

BIOGRAPHY

Frank Garvin Yerby was born in Augusta, Georgia, on September 5, 1916, to Rufus Garvin and Willie Smythe Yerby. By the time he was seventeen, several of Yerby's poems had been published in small magazines. He graduated from Haines Institute (1933) and Paine College (1937) in his native city, received the M.A. degree from Fisk University in Nashville (1938), and studied toward the doctorate at the University of Chicago (1939). He served on the faculties of Florida A and M University (1939–1940) and Southern University (1940–1941). After leaving academe, Yerby spent the next four years as a technician at Ford Motor Company, Dearborn, Michigan (1941–1944), and at Ranger (Fairchild) Aircraft, Jamaica, New York (1944–1945).

Yerby's first literary success came in 1944, when his short story "Health Card" earned him the O. Henry Memorial Award. Two years later, after a failed protest novel, Yerby abandoned overt social protest and found his niche as a writer of popular fiction. His signature novel, *The Foxes of Harrow* (1946), launched his phenomenal rise as "king of the costume novel," and he became the first black writer to produce a best-selling novel. *Foxes* also became the first novel written by a black author to be purchased by a Hollywood studio. Over the last forty years, Yerby's thirty-three novels, including twelve best-sellers, have been translated into fourteen languages and produced sales in excess of 55 million copies.

In 1976 Fisk University conferred the doctor of letters degree on Yerby, and in 1977 he was honored by Paine College with the doctor of humane letters. That same year, by governor's proclamation, Yerby was named an honorary citizen of the state of Tennessee. He died of congestive heart failure in Madrid, Spain, on November 29, 1991.

Frank Yerby's artistic philosophy of the costume novel begins with the assumption that literature has multilevels of meaning and that readers benefit uniquely from a work of art in direct proportion to their personal levels of experiential and maturational development. This concept of universality requires that the writer present vibrant, living characters in an absorbing story, a "deliberate distortion" of life designed to provide pleasure and entertainment for the reading audience. The characters must emerge through a "strong, exteriorized conflict" and transcend themselves and their circumstances to contribute "something ennobling to life" ("How and Why I Write the Costume Novel" 148).

Yerby contends that the province of literature appropriately includes the themes of man versus evil, man versus himself, man versus God, man versus woman, and man versus fate. Therefore, he focuses on the individual and the specific problems of the individual, and he cautions that teaching and preaching are well outside artistic considerations. For this reason, Yerby refuses to pursue the theme common to many of his contemporary writers: the racial discrimination, oppression, and victimization of minorities in our society and our world. Arguing for the legitimacy of escapist art with the "deliberate intention to amuse and entertain" ("How and Why" 150), he categorically rejects the use of literature as a catalyst for social change. (See "How and Why I Write the Costume Novel" and Hill 1995 for a detailed discussion of Yerby's artistic philosophy.)

MAJOR WORKS AND THEMES

During the first quarter century of his career as a novelist (1946–1971), Frank Yerby produced twenty-three novels described by critic Darwin T. Turner as formulaic, or "recipe" fiction featuring white protagonists at the center of the action, while black characters functioned as peripherals. Boosted by book club sales, these novels sold approximately 20 million copies in hardback alone, and nearly all were reprinted in paperback. Because of these achievements, Turner credits Yerby in 1972 with having written "more best-selling novels than any other Afro-American in history, more in fact than most writers, regardless of race or nationality" ("Frank Yerby: Golden Debunker" 5). Another quarter century has passed, and this record remains unsurpassed.

Seven years after the publication of his first novel, Frank Yerby had produced three novels that were purchased by Hollywood studios and made into cinematic productions. The first of these, *The Foxes of Harrow* (1946), sold more than 2 million copies and reached the best-sellers list. *Foxes* covers the historical period 1825–1865 and focuses on the Civil War conflict from the perspectives of both individual families and the nation as a whole.

Stephen Fox, the charming gambler/scoundrel and protagonist, has been censored for sleights of hand at the gaming tables aboard the *Prairie Belle*, and he is forced from the ship onto a sandbar in New Orleans. Assisted by friends, he reaches the city with a determination to build a financial empire. Stephen woos and marries the enchanting Odalie Arcenaux, who gives birth to a son, Etienne.

By this time, Fox has gained acceptance in society and acquired enough money to build a grand mansion, Harrow. Meanwhile, Stephen carries on a torrid affair with Desiree, a quadroon on the plantation, and one of his favorite slaves, Achilles, marries Princess Le Sauvage. She gives birth to a son, Inch. Years later when the Civil War breaks out, Stephen, Etienne, and Inch enlist. By the time the war ends, Stephen lives to see Inch rise as a respectable man, while Harrow lies in ruin and his progeny in disgrace.

The movie rights for *The Foxes of Harrow* were purchased in 1947 for $150,000, a record for black writers at the time. Rex Harrison and Maureen O'Hara were cast in the starring roles.

Three years later, Yerby had shifted from southern romances to adventure and published another best-seller, *The Golden Hawk* (1948). Here Yerby presents Christopher "Kit" Gerardo, son of a French mother and a Spanish nobleman, who sets out on the Caribbean high seas at the end of the seventeenth century. He is supported by a motley crew: Bianco and Don Luis, the Spanish men, and Rouge, the voluptuous, red-haired Englishwoman-turned-pirate. An expert seaman, swordsman, and lover, Kit travels through a series of adventures and manages to survive an attempted mutiny as well as three natural disasters—a hurricane, a tidal wave, and an earthquake—to become victorious in a battle at sea and discover that his mother has died at the hands of a Spanish grandee who is revealed to be his natural father. The novel is also filled with amorous conquests highlighted by the Kit-Rouge-Don Luis triangle, which is resolved in the end when Kit and Rouge unite.

In 1952, Yerby published his seventh novel, *The Saracen Blade*. Set in thirteenth-century Europe, when chivalry was in vogue, *The Saracen Blade* unravels the story of Pietro di Donati, son of a blacksmith, who is born the same day and hour in the same Sicilian town as Frederick II of Hohenstaufen, future emperor of the Roman empire. Pietro's nomadic life leads him through Italy, France, Germany, Jerusalem, and Egypt in his quest for acceptance as a knight and a gentleman. He is surrounded by powerful friends—Frederick, who makes him a baron in Italy; Isaac, the Jew who teaches him the wisdom of the East; and Iolanthe, daughter of an Italian baron who pledges her unswerving support and devotion. Through their influence and through his bravery, wit, cleverness, and keen intelligence, Pietro distinguishes himself in a variety of situations.

Pietro also finds himself conquering the women of exotic beauty who surround him. Iolanthe of the golden hair offers steadfast love; Elaine, daughter of his enemies, offers wild, thunderous passion; Zenobia, the fascinating Greek slave girl, offers her ultimate love and self-denial; and Lady Yvette, wife of the ancient warrior, gives of herself in great abundance. But in the end, Zenobia's undying love and utter selflessness lead to Pietro's consummate happiness.

This adventure tale appeared on the silver screen in 1954 with Ricardo Montalban as the star of the movie.

As early as 1966, Yerby announced in an interview with Hoyt W. Fuller that he planned to shift his emphasis from entertainment in order to focus on a significant theme: "the relationship of man to the quality of evil in the world" and write "the most ambitious novel of my career" (193). But when *Judas, My Brother* (1969) was published, critics joined Jeffrey Parker in dismissing the book as a continuation of the tradition of the costume novel.

However, the thematic break did come in 1969, when Yerby began to explore the use of strong, black protagonists in his works. Although *Speak Now* (1969) and *A Darkness at Ingraham's Crest* (1979) presented black characters in major roles, Yerby's detractors gave these novels restrained applause because the resemblance of the black characters to the whites in his earlier novels was much too striking. For most of the reviewers, however, *The Dahomean* was another matter. Hailed by some reviewers as a "masterpiece," it is, arguably, Yerby's most widely acclaimed novel.

Published in 1971 and set in nineteenth-century black Africa, *The Dahomean* recounts the story of Nyasanu, one of two sons born to Gbenu, a high-ranking village chief who serves under King Gezo. Shortly after his marriage, Nyasanu and Gbenu are forced to support Gezo in defending the land against the invading Maxi tribe. When Gbenu is killed in battle, Nyasanu emerges as hero, and he is chosen over his jealous elder brother, Gbochi, to succeed his father as village chief. Eventually, Nyasanu rises to become governor of the province. However, this political success contrasts sharply with the problems in his personal life. Nyasanu's first wife dies in childbirth, and after he remarries, King Gezo offers him the hand of his daughter, Princess Yekpewa. In spite of his misgivings, Nyasanu accepts Yekpewa out of deference to the king. As his fortunes decline, he finds himself isolated from the people. Finally, Yekpewa, Gbochi, and a half brother conspire to sell him into slavery in America.

Critics praised Yerby for an impeccably researched, thrilling novel that focuses on a single black hero in the presentation of the rich, complex culture and history of the Dahomean people. South African reviewers were ecstatic in their appraisals, and Yerby felt vindicated by the acclamations. James Hill explains the appeal of the novel by reminding us that in Yerby's costume novels, the protagonist is always in control of his fate, and he must rely on his innate cleverness, strength, and intelligence to accomplish his goals. On the other hand, the credibility of *The Dahomean* rests on "the belief that some unknown force, divine and all-powerful, controls the events in the lives of men. . . . The characters . . . do not determine what they do; therefore, the reader does not hold them responsible for their actions" (152). In spite of the satisfaction that Yerby received from "two hundred odd reviews" and the confirmation that his readers "are not necessarily all idiots," he never returned to explore other novels with black protagonists at the center of the action (Hill 1995: 237).

CRITICAL RECEPTION

For virtually his entire career, Yerby's critical reception has been clouded by controversy, in large part because of the literary/cultural posture that he maintained. From the outset, Yerby rejected the term "black writer," and he steadfastly refused to embrace the idea of literature as an agent for social change. Instead, he pursued the illusive objective of achieving artistic integrity and respectability by establishing a legitimate niche for escapist art in American letters.

In documenting Yerby's failure to win critical recognition for the costume novel, Darwin T. Turner wrote nearly thirty years ago that his writing "deserves at least cursory examination, if for no reason but that he is the first to prove that a Negro American can write fiction which consistently sells well" ("Frank Yerby as Debunker" 570). Nevertheless, in spite of (or perhaps because of) the undisputed popularity of his work, Yerby remains largely unacknowledged. In her recent essay, Gwendolyn Morgan demonstrates that Yerby's work is still being deliberately and systematically omitted from anthologies of African American literature, and she argues with Turner for setting aside our prejudices and conducting an honest reevaluation and reappraisal of the vast body of his writing (21–26).

Although there are no book-length studies of Yerby, several other critics have contributed significantly to the literary scholarship. In an early analysis, Hugh M. Gloster asserts that, although *The Foxes of Harrow* and *The Vixens* struck pleasant chords with his readers, these novels failed to establish his reputation as a writer of exceptional talent. However, he credits Yerby with the ability "to shake himself free of the shakles [*sic*] of race and to use the treasure-trove of American experience—rather than restrictively Negro experience—as his literary province" (13). Although Darwin Turner criticizes Yerby for his character stereotypes, intrusive essays, and reliance on the deus ex machina to construct the endings of his novels, he contends that Yerby often "debunks the historical myth of culture and gentility" associated with the American South: "The males reputedly were aristocratic, cultured, brave, and honorable. The females were gentle and chaste" ("Frank Yerby as Debunker" 572–573, 576). Turner also argues that these unyielding assaults may prove to be Yerby's "major contribution to American culture" ("Frank Yerby: Golden Debunker" 31).

One of the few critics to defend Yerby against the charge of writing escapist fiction almost exclusively, Jack Moore contends that many of Yerby's early "white" novels examine the race issue "sometimes in obvious and sometimes in disguised fashion" (747). He concludes, therefore, that Yerby never abandoned his early role as a writer of protest: "Yerby has constantly written about elements of the black experience . . . the African slave pens . . . the economic emasculation of blacks, the individual accomplishments . . . the broader ethnic achievements . . . the dangers of assimilation . . . the corruption of the white world" (755–756). Phyllis Klotman argues that the cinematic version of *The Foxes of Harrow* departs from the tradition of *Gone with the Wind* by presenting Belle as "a fiercely proud and beautiful black woman" and mother who has the courage to attack the dominant institution of slavery. When Belle drowns after she has attempted to free her son and herself, Klotman contends that she has achieved control over both her "husband" and her master and that "it is the first time that she, a black woman and a slave, exerts power; it was the first time that such a scene was acted out in American cinema" (215, 216). In a similar comparison, Carl M. Hughes finds that the major distinction is in characterization: "Yerby makes his [character] Inch a man of letters and his Negro slave a princess. The reverse is true in *Gone with the Wind*" (151).

James L. Hill emphasizes the sense of isolation that Yerby felt as a result of his racial views and his conscious choice to write popular fiction. This sense of alienation, according to Hill, gave rise to Yerby's "great theme," the existential analysis of the "anti-hero hero, the outcast who fights his way into an alien culture" (144). The treatment of women is raised as an issue in Jeffrey D. Parker's criticism, and he excoriates Yerby for portraying women as "superficial targets" who are seduced by dominant males: "There exists no female character who is wholly admirable or complete, or . . . who can stand outside of a submissive relationship with a male counterpart. Women are often subjected to sexual or physical abuse" (228). Though Nick Aaron Ford was one of the first scholars to criticize Yerby's identifiable formula and his creation of black characters who have no control over the forces in their environment, he argues that "no American novelist surpasses him in his ability to evoke in the reader genuine feelings of tenderness and romantic love" (37).

These provocative assessments further emphasize a need for the in-depth, comprehensive study suggested by Yerby critics so that his legacy can finally be fully understood apart from the enigmas and the perplexities that often cause us to confuse substance with shadow.

BIBLIOGRAPHY

Selected Works by Frank Garvin Yerby

Best-Selling Novels

The Foxes of Harrow. New York: Dial, 1946.
The Vixens. New York: Dial, 1947.
The Golden Hawk. New York: Dial, 1948.
Floodtide. New York: Dial, 1950.
A Woman Called Fancy. New York: Dial, 1951
Benton's Row. New York: Dial, 1954.
Captain Rebel. New York: Dial, 1956.
Fairoaks. New York: Dial, 1957.
The Serpent and the Staff. New York: Dial, 1958.
Jarrett's Jade. New York: Dial, 1959.
Gillian. New York: Dial, 1960.
The Garfield Honor. New York: Dial, 1961.

Essay

"How and Why I Write the Costume Novel." *Harper's* 219 (October 1959): 145–150.

Studies of Frank Garvin Yerby

Draper, James, ed. "Frank Yerby." *Black Literature Criticism*. Vol. 3. Detroit: Gale Research, 1992. 2,022–2,031.
Ford, Nick A. "Four Popular Negro Novelists." *Phylon* 25.1 (1954): 29–39.
Fuller, Hoyt A. "Famous Writer Faces a Challenge." *Ebony* 21 (June 1966): 188–194.
Gloster, Hugh M. "The Significance of Frank Yerby." *The Crisis* 55.1 (January 1948): 12–13.
Graham, Maryemma. "Frank Yerby, King of the Costume Novel." *Essence* 6.6 (1975): 70+.
Hill, James L. "The Anti-Heroic Hero in Frank Yerby's Historical Novels." *Perspectives of Black Popular Culture*. Ed. Harry B. Shaw. Bowling Green, OH: Popular, 1990. 144–154.
———. "An Interview with Frank Garvin Yerby." *Resources for American Literary Study* 21.2 (1995): 206–239.
Hughes, Carl M. *The Negro Novelist*. New York: Citadel, 1953.
Klotman, Phyllis R. "A Harrowing Experience: Frank Yerby's First Novel to Film." *College Language Association Journal* 31.2 (December 1987): 210–222.
Metzger, Linda, et al., eds. "Frank Yerby." *Black Writers: A Selection of Sketches from Contemporary Authors*. Detroit: Gale Research, 1989. 613–616.
Moore, Jack B. "The Guilt of the Victim: Racial Themes in Some Frank Yerby Novels." *Journal of Popular Culture* 8.4 (Spring 1975): 747–756.
Morgan, Gwendolyn D. "Challenging the Black Aesthetic: The Silencing of Frank Yerby." *Florida A and M University Research Bulletin* 35 (September 1993): 19–30.
Parker, Jeffrey D. "Frank Yerby." *Afro-American Writers, 1940–1955*. Ed. Trudier Harris and Thadious M. Davis. Vol. 76. Detroit: Gale Research, 1988. 222–231.
Pratt, Louis Hill. "Frank Yerby." *Critical Survey of Short Fiction*. Vol. 6. Ed. Frank N. Magill. Englewood Cliffs, NJ: Salem, 1981. 2,475–2,480.
Schraufnagel, Noel. *The Black American Novel: From Apology to Protest*. Deland, FL: Everett and Edwards, 1973.
Turner, Darwin T. "Frank Yerby as Debunker." *Massachusetts Review* 20 (Summer 1968): 569–577.
———. "Frank Yerby: Golden Debunker." *Black Books Bulletin* 1 (1972): 4–9+.
———. "The Negro Novelist and the South." *Southern Humanities Review* 1 (1967): 21–29.

SELECTED BIBLIOGRAPHY

Awkward, Michael. *Inspiriting Influences: Tradition, Revision, and Afro-American Women's Novels*. New York: Columbia University Press, 1989.

Bell, Bernard. *The Afro-American Novel and Its Tradition*. Amherst: University of Massachusetts Press, 1987.

Bruccoli, Mathew, and Judith Baughman. *Modern African American Writers*. New York: Facts on File, 1994.

Bruck, Peter, and Wolfgang Karrer. *The Afro-American Novel since 1960*. Amsterdam: Gruner, 1982.

Bryant, Jerry. *Victims and Heroes: Racial Violence in the African American Novel*. Amherst: University of Massachusetts Press, 1997.

Butler-Evans, Elliot. *Race, Gender, and Desire: Narrative Strategies in the Fiction of Toni Cade Bambara, Toni Morrison and Alice Walker*. Philadelphia: Temple University Press, 1989.

Byerman, Keith E. *Fingering the Jagged Grain: Tradition and Form in Recent Black Fiction*. Athens: University of Georgia Press, 1985.

Callahan, John F. *In the African-American Grain: The Pursuit of Voice in Twentieth Century Black Fiction*. Urbana: University of Illinois Press, 1988.

Campbell, Jane. *Mythic Black Fiction: The Transformation of History*. Knoxville: University of Tennessee Press, 1986.

Christian, Barbara. *Black Women Novelists: The Development of a Tradition, 1892–1976*. Westport, CT: Greenwood Press, 1980.

Coser, Stelamaris. *Bridging the Americas: The Literature of Paule Marshall, Toni Morrison, and Gayl Jones*. Philadelphia: Temple University Press, 1995.

DeWeever, Jacqueline. *Mythmaking and Metaphor in Black Women's Fiction*. New York: St. Martin's Press, 1992.

Dubey, Madhu. *Black Women Novelists and the National Aesthetic*. Bloomington: Indiana University Press, 1994.

Ducille, Ann. *The Coupling Convention: Sex, Text, and Tradition in Black Women's Fiction*. New York: Oxford University Press, 1993.

Gates, Henry, Louis, Jr., ed. *Black Literature and Literary Theory*. New York: Methuen, 1984.

Griffin, Farah Jasmine. *Who Set You Flowin'? The African American Migration Narrative*. New York: Oxford University Press, 1995.

Harris, Norman. *Connecting Times: The Sixties in Afro-American Fiction*. Jackson: University Press of Mississippi, 1988.

Harris, Trudier, and Thadious M. Davis, eds. *Afro-American Fiction Writers after 1955*. Detroit: Gale Research, 1984.

———. *The Power of the Porch: The Storyteller's Craft in Zora Neale Hurston, Gloria Naylor, and Randall Kenan*. Athens: University of Georgia Press, 1996.

Jablon, Madelyn. *Black Metafiction: Self-Consciousness in African American Literature*. Iowa City: University Press of Iowa, 1997.

Kubitschek, Missy Dehn. *Claiming the Heritage: African-American Women Novelists and History*. Jackson: University Press of Mississippi, 1991.

LeSuer, Gita. *Ten Is the Age of Darkness: The Black Bildungsroman*. Columbia: University of Missouri Press, 1995.

McDowell, Deborah. *The Changing Same: Black Women's Literature, Criticism, and Theory*. Bloomington: Indiana University Press, 1995.

Montgomery, Maxine Levon. *The Apocolypse in African-American Fiction*. Gainesville: University Press of Florida, 1996.

Nelson, Emmanuel S. *Critical Essays: Gay and Lesbian Writers of Color*. New York: Haworth Press, 1993.

Scruggs, Charles. *Invisible Cities in the Afro-American Novel*. Baltimore: Johns Hopkins University Press, 1993.

Smith, Valerie. *Self-Discovery and Authority in Afro-American Narrative*. Cambridge, MA: Harvard University Press, 1987.

Sundquist, Eric. *The Hammers of Creation: Folk Culture in Modern African-American Fiction*. Athens: University of Georgia Press, 1992.

Thomas, Nigel. *From Folklore to Fiction: A Study of Folk Heroes and Rituals in the Black American Novel*. Westport, CT: Greenwood Press, 1988.

Walker, Melissa. *Down from the Mountaintop: Black Women's Novels in the Wake of the Civil Rights Movement, 1966–1989*. New Haven, CT: Yale University Press, 1991.

Werner, Craig Hansen. *Black American Women Novelists*. Pasadenia, CA: Salem Press, 1989.

Willis, Susan. *Specifying: Black Women Writing the American Experience*. Madison: University of Wisconsin Press, 1987.

INDEX

ABOUT THE EDITOR AND CONTRIBUTORS

CORA AGATUCCI teaches African culture and literature as well as women's studies at Central Oregon Community College in Bend. She has published critical articles on African American literature and on the works of Doris Lessing.

MARLENE D. ALLEN is a doctoral candidate at the University of Georgia at Athens, with a concentration in African American women's literature.

EBERHARD ALSEN is Professor of English at the State University College of New York at Cortland. A widely published scholar, he is most recently the author of *Romantic Postmodernism in American Fiction*.

TRELA ANDERSON is a doctoral candidate in English and Creative Writing at the University of Southwestern Louisiana.

CHERRON A. BARNWELL is a doctoral candidate in English at Howard University.

LEAN'TIN BRACKS is an Assistant Professor of English at Fisk University and the author of *Black Women Writers of the Diaspora*.

KIMBERLY N. BROWN is an Assistant Professor of English at Texas A&M University.

MARILYN D. BUTTON is Associate Professor of English at Lincoln University. She has published several scholarly articles on British as well as American women writers.

LAURIE CHAMPION, Assistant Professor of English, serves as the coordinator of women's studies at Sul Ross State University in Alpine, Texas.

HARISH CHANDER is Professor of English at Shaw University.

JOYCE L. CHERRY is Associate Professor of English at Albany State University, where she coordinates the Freshman Writing Sequence and teaches courses in American literature.

PETER G. CHRISTENSEN teaches in the Department of French, Italian, and Comparative Literature and in the School of Library and Information Science at the University of Wisconsin-Milwaukee.

RITA B. DANDRIDGE is Professor of English at Norfolk State University. Her most recent book is *Black Women's Blues: A Literary Anthology, 1934–1988.*

ADENIKE MARIE DAVIDSON is an Assistant Professor of English at the University of Central Florida.

ANNETTE DEBO is a doctoral candidate in English at the University of Maryland, College Park, where she is completing her dissertation on American literary modernism.

FRANK E. DOBSON, JR., is Assistant Professor of English at Wright State University in Dayton, Ohio.

JEFFREY B. DUNHAM is a graduate student in English at SUNY-Cortland.

AMY E. EARHART is a doctoral candidate at Texas A & M University.

SAMUEL B. GARREN is Professor of English at North Carolina A & T State University in Greensboro; he has published scholarly articles on Jean Toomer, William Attaway, and other twentieth-century writers.

BRUCE A. GLASRUD is Dean of the School of Arts and Sciences and Professor of history at Sul Ross State University in Alpine, Texas.

SHANNA D. GREENE is a graduate student in English at the University of Wisconsin at Madison.

TRACIE CHURCH GUZZIO is a doctoral candidate in English at Ohio University, where she is completing a dissertation on John Edgar Wideman.

ANDRÉ HOYRD is a doctoral candidate at Howard University. His poetry has appeared in *James White Review*; in 1995 he was awarded a Ford Foundation Fellowship.

NICHOLYN HUTCHINSON is a doctoral candidate in English at the University of Georgia; she is completing a dissertation on African-American literature.

YMITRI JAYASUNDERA is a doctoral candidate in English at the University of Massachusetts at Amherst.

A. YEMISI JIMOH teaches American literature and literary theory at the University of Arkansas at Fayetteville. She is currently writing a book on music in African American fiction.

EVORA JONES holds a doctorate in English and teaches writing at Howard University.

GWENDOLYN S. JONES is Professor of English at Tuskegee University. She teaches composition, literature, and speech communication.

JACQUELINE C. JONES is Assistant Professor of English and African American literature at Washington College, Maryland.

LEELA KAPAI is Professor of English at Prince George's Community College in Maryland. She has published numerous articles on multicultural literature.

ROY KAY is Assistant Professor of English at Macalester College. He is currently writing a book titled *Rewriting the Self in Emergent Literatures*.

ANNLOUISE KEATING is Associate Professor of English at Eastern New Mexico University, where she also directs the Freshman Composition Program. Author of *Women Reading Women Writing: Self-Invention in Paula Gunn Allen, Gloria Anzaldùa, and Audre Lorde*, she has published numerous articles on American writers.

KRISTINA L. KNOTTS is a doctoral candidate in English at the University of Tennessee at Knoxville. Currently, she is an instructor at Westfield State University in Massachusetts.

SARALA KRISHNAMURTHY is a Reader in the Department of English at Bangalore University in India. She is a specialist in postcolonial literature.

JEFFREY T. LOEB, senior teacher at the Pembroke Hill School in Kansas City, has published extensively on the literature of the Vietnam War.

ROBIN LUCY is a doctoral student at McMaster University in Canada, where she is completing a dissertation on African-American literary response to World War I.

BINDU MALIECKAL is a doctoral candidate in English at Baylor University and an instructor at the University of South Carolina at Spartanburg.

SUZANNE HOTTE MASSA is a graduate student in English at SUNY-Cortland; she also teaches multicultural literature at a private high school in Ithaca, New York.

TERRENCE J. McGOVERN is a librarian at the SUNY campus at Cortland.

SARAH McKEE teaches English and reading at A-B Technical Community College in Asheville, North Carolina.

ADAM MEYER is Assistant Professor of English at Fisk University. Author of a book on Raymond Carver, he has published several articles on contemporary writers.

CHRISTIAN MORARU is an Assistant Professor of English at the University of North Carolina, Greensboro. He is the author of *The Poetics of Reflection* and has published scholarly articles in numerous journals.

NICOLA MORRIS is on the faculty of the Goddard College Fine Arts Writing Program. A poet and fiction writer, she is the author of several critical articles in various journals.

NANETTE MORTON is a doctoral candidate in English at McMaster University in Canada. She is completing a dissertation on the autobiographies of Frederick Douglass.

PIERRE-DAMIEN MVUYEKURE is Assistant Professor of English at the University of Northern Iowa. His teaching and research interests include American multicultural literature as well as postcolonial writing.

EMMANUEL S. NELSON is Professor of English at SUNY-Cortland. Author of over thirty articles on various international literatures in English, he has edited several volumes, including *Connections: Essays on Black Literatures* (1988), *Writers of the Indian Diaspora* (Greenwood, 1993), and *Contemporary Gay American Novelists* (Greenwood, 1993).

TERRY NOVAK is Instructor at the University of Nevada, Las Vegas.

DEBORAH G. PLANT is Associate Professor of Africana Studies at the University of South Florida. She is the author of *Every Tub Must Sit on Its Own Bottom: The Philosophy and Politics of Zora Neale Hurston.*

LOUIS HILL PRATT is Professor of English at Florida A & M University. Author of *James Baldwin* (1978), he has edited *Alice Malsenior Walker: An Annotated Bibliography* (1988) and *Conversations with James Baldwin* (1989).

PEGGY STEVENSON RATLIFF is Chairperson of the Humanities Division at Claflin College, South Carolina.

CHRIS ROARK is Associate Professor of English at John Carroll University. He has published articles on a variety of writers ranging from Shakespeare to Malcolm X.

MOLLY RODEN teaches at the Brooklyn Friends School in Brooklyn, New York.

JOYCE RUSSELL-ROBINSON teaches literature at Fayetteville State University in North Carolina.

GRACE SIKORSKI teaches English at the Pennsylvania State University and at Juniata College.

RENNIE SIMSON is Lecturer in the African-American Studies Department at Syracuse University. She has published numerous articles on African American women writers.

P. JANE SPLAWN is an Assistant Professor of English at Beaver College, Pennsylvania.

CHARLES TITA is the Chairperson of the Department of Humanities at Shaw University.

TRACEY WALTERS is a doctoral candidate at Howard University; her areas of concentration include African American and Afro-British literatures.

ANISSA J. WARDI teaches English at Chatham College, where she also coordinates the Cultural Studies and African-American Studies Program.

SARAH WHELISS is a doctoral candidate at the University of North Carolina at Greensboro. Her areas of interest include African American literature and film.

KATHY WHITE teaches at A-B Community College in Asheville, North Carolina.

LINDA M. WHITE is a doctoral candidate in African American literature at Howard University.

DANA A. WILLIAMS is a doctoral candidate at Howard University. Her book on contemporary African American playwrights is scheduled for publication by Greenwood Press.

LORETTA G. WOODARD is Associate Professor of English at Marygrove College in Detroit. She is a contributing editor to *Benet's Reader's Encyclopedia* (1996).

ISBN 0-313-30501-3

HARDCOVER BAR CODE